CAMBRIDGE

ENGLISH LITERATURE B

A / AS Level for AQA

Student Book

Carol Atherton, Andrew Green and Gary Snapper

Series editor: Marcello Giovanelli

CAMBRIDGE
UNIVERSITY PRESS

University Printing House, Cambridge CB2 8BS, United Kingdom

Cambridge University Press is part of the University of Cambridge.

It furthers the University's mission by disseminating knowledge in the pursuit of education, learning and research at the highest international levels of excellence.

www.cambridge.org
Information on this title: www.cambridge.org/9781107468023 (Paperback)
www.cambridge.org/9781107468030 (Cambridge Elevate-enhanced Edition)
www.cambridge.org/9781107467965 (Paperback + Cambridge Elevate-enhanced Edition)

First published 2015

Printed in the United Kingdom by Latimer Trend

A catalogue record for this publication is available from the British Library

ISBN 978-1-107-46802-3 Paperback
ISBN 978-1-107-46803-0 Cambridge Elevate-enhanced Edition
ISBN 978-1-107-46796-5 Paperback + Cambridge Elevate-enhanced Edition

Additional resources for this publication at www.cambridge.org/ukschools

Approval message from AQA

This textbook has been approved by AQA for use with our qualification. This means that we have checked that it broadly covers the specification and we are satisfied with the overall quality. Full details of our approval process can be found on our website.

We approve textbooks because we know how important it is for teachers and students to have the right resources to support their teaching and learning. However, the publisher is ultimately responsible for the editorial control and quality of this book.

Please note that when teaching the AS and A Level English Literature B (7716, 7717) course, you must refer to AQA's specification as your definitive source of information. While this book has been written to match the specification, it cannot provide complete coverage of every aspect of the course.

A wide range of other useful resources can be found on the relevant subject pages of our website: aqa.org.uk

Contents

Introduction

Welcome to this student book for your AQA A/AS Level English Literature course!

The AQA English Literature B AS/A Level specifications provide an approach to the study of English literature through the critical lens of genre. At AS Level the genres available for study are tragedy and comedy. At A Level the genres are tragedy, comedy, crime writing and political and social protest writing.

In each unit of this book, we introduce you to the key concepts by surveying the development of one of these genres and the central literary elements of the genre. We take examples and passages from a wide range of texts (including all the set texts) to illustrate these ideas and to put the set texts in illuminating contexts. The majority of the texts to which we refer are taken from British literature. Although we also refer to some key texts and developments in literature from beyond Britain, limitations of space prevent us from ranging more widely in this area.

You will be assessed in a number of ways, including passage-based and single text questions, multiple text questions, open- and closed-book approaches and unseen material. This student book supports the specifications, prepares you for these assessments and helps you to develop the different skills you will be assessed on - skills which will stand you in good stead beyond AS or A Level, whatever you go on to do.

Beginning unit

Developing unit

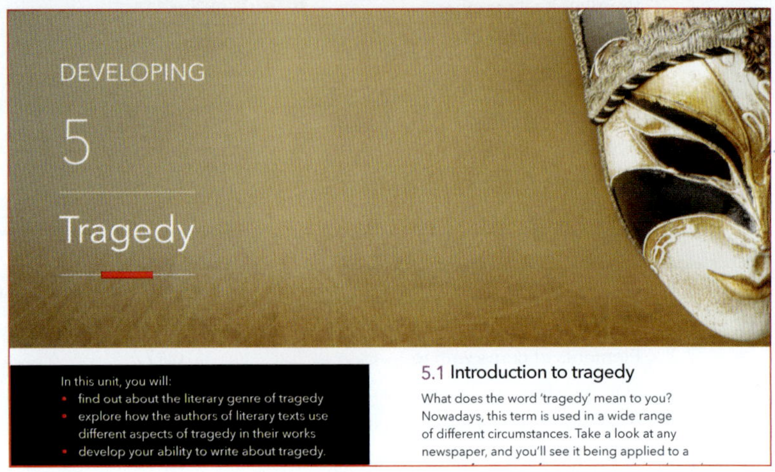

Enriching unit

Bringing it all together

6.5 Bringing it all together

6.5.1 How will your studies on Aspects of Comedy be assessed?

Aspects of Comedy is one of the two options for AS Level Papers 1 and 2, and for A Level Paper 1. Your knowledge will be tested by the exam.

Key terms box

Key terms

revenge tragedy: a form of tragedy particularly concerned with crime and vengeance

gothic fiction: a form of fiction that frequently deals with horror, the supernatural and socially unacceptable and criminal behaviour

canon: a core and established body of literary texts

Icons used in the book

- Cross reference
- Key Terms
- Glossary
- Critical Lens
- Check your responses
- Explore
- Set text focus
- Video

About the specifications

The AS Level specification has two components comprising an exploration of texts that are connected through a mainstream literary genre: either Aspects of Tragedy (Option A) or Aspects of Comedy (Option B).

<u>Paper 1: Literary genres: drama</u>
How it is assessed: 1½ hour closed-book exam worth 50% of your AS.

<u>Paper 2: Literary genres: prose and poetry</u>
How it is assessed: 1½ hour open-book exam worth 50% of your AS.

The A Level specification has three components comprising the study of texts within specific genres, writing about texts in different ways and engagement with a range of theoretical ideas.

<u>Paper 1: Literary genres</u>
What is assessed: Study of three texts: one Shakespeare text; a second drama text and one further text, of which one must be written pre-1900.
How it is assessed: 2½ hour closed-book exam worth 40% of your A Level.

<u>Paper 2: Texts and genres</u>
What is assessed: Study of three texts: one post-2000 prose text; one poetry and one further text, of which one must be written pre-1900.
How it is assessed: 3 hour open-book exam worth 40% of your A Level.

<u>Non-exam Assessment:Theory and independence</u>
What is assessed: Two essays of 1,250 – 1,500 words, one on a prose text and one on a poetry text, each responding to a different text and each will be linked to a different aspect of the Critical Anthology. One essay can be re-creative and the re-creative piece will be accompanied by a commentary.
How it is assessed: Two pieces of coursework worth 20% of your A Level.

There are more details about the specifications in the relevant Developing units, including the assessment objectives you will be measured against in the exam papers and – at A Level – in the non-exam assessment.

About this student book

This book follows an innovative three-part structure.

Part 1: Beginning units

These set out the key principles, issues and concepts that underpin the course and support you as you move from GCSE to AS and A Level work. Each Beginning unit contains activities to check understanding and progress, and provides a strong foundation from which to build upwards. The Beginning units can also be used as a stand-alone reference point to which you'll return when studying content in subsequent Developing units, and for revision purposes as you prepare for your exams.

Part 2: Developing units

These longer units are based around the main content in the AS and A Level specifications. They are designed to build on the ideas introduced in the Beginning units, extending knowledge and understanding where appropriate. These units follow the order of topics in the AQA specifications and contain a wider range of activities to develop skills and encourage independence. The start of each Developing unit tells you whether the content is suitable for AS, A Level or both.

Each Developing unit is built on the most up-to-date content and research, which is presented in an accessible and engaging way. Many of the activities in these units are enhanced by commentaries that will support your learning and help you to develop an analytical framework, with which you can consider topic areas more critically and broadly.

These units also contain a 'Bringing it all together' section, designed to support you in preparing for exam questions, and a 'How much do you know' section that allows you to review key learning for a particular topic and to plan your revision priorities. In addition, practice questions and discussion of the assessment objectives allow you to apply your learning and to think about the demands of individual sections within the exam papers.

Critical lens

Critical lens: feminist theory

In the extract from the *Newgate Calendar* in Text 7H, the perpetrator of the crime is a woman. Think about the way in which her crime is presented. Is there anything more terrible about her crime because she is a woman? What expectations does society have of women? How does the idea of crime relate to these views? How does the writer use language in relation to the female criminal?

Exploring a literary concept

Exploring theatre space

It may seem an obvious point to make, but remember that plays are generally performed in theatres. Look at images of different theatre spaces (many available online), such as:

- Shakespeare's Globe
- the Sam Wanamaker Playhouse
- the amphitheatre at Epidaurus
- the Minack Theatre in Cornwall
- a 19th-century proscenium arch theatre (for example, the Theatre Royal in York)
- a theatre-in-the-round (for example, the Royal Exchange Theatre in Manchester).

Think about the different kind of relationship with the audience that these particular kinds of stage may encourage, and then think about how differently the drama texts you're studying could be represented in each space.

Deconstructing exam questions

Text 11A

Focus on aspects of tragedy: in what ways are the poets writing in the tragic tradition?

'Explore the view that poets writing in the tragic tradition always convey a deep sense of sadness.'

Always? Is this true?

Where do the poets convey 'a deep sense of sadness'? What methods do they use to do this?

Tutorial Video available on Cambridge Elevate

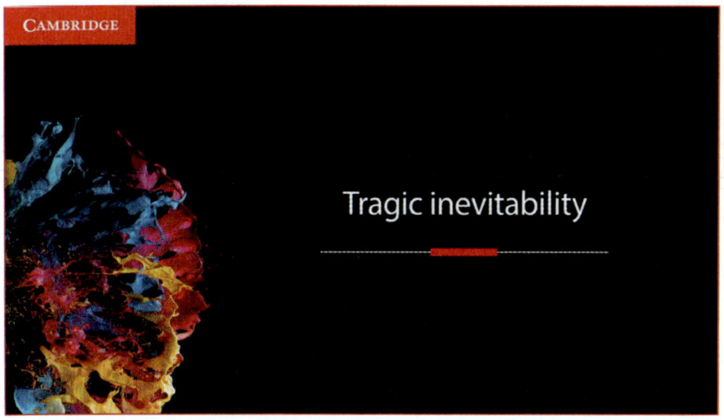

Enriching Interview Video available on Cambridge Elevate

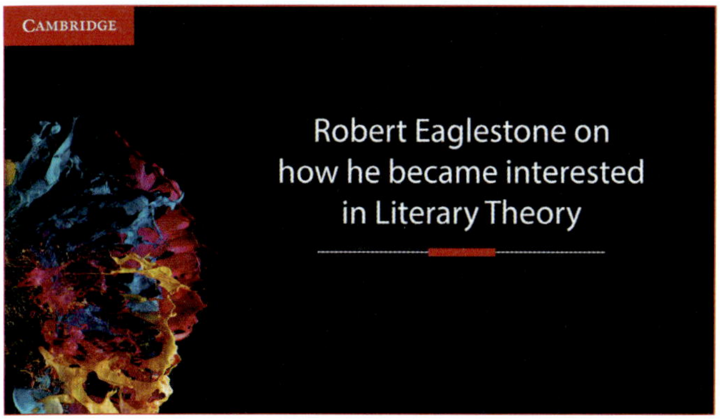

Links to video content on Cambridge Elevate

Watch tutorial video, Tragic Inevitability, via Cambridge Elevate

Watch Dan Rebellato, Professor of Drama and Theatre at Royal Holloway, University of London, talk about comedy on Cambridge Elevate

Part 3: Enriching units

Designed specifically for A Level students but with content that AS Level students will also find useful, these units support your work on the specification and extend your thinking beyond the topics covered in the Developing units in Part 2. These Enriching units contain extension activities on Developing unit topics, as well as ideas for extended independent study, details of wider reading that you will find useful and summaries of recent and relevant research from higher education.

The Enriching units also feature short articles exclusively written for this series by leading academics and professionals, with follow-up questions that offer an expert insight into certain aspects of the subject.

About Cambridge Elevate

Cambridge Elevate is the platform that hosts a digital version of this student book. If you have access to this digital version you can annotate different parts of the book, send and receive messages to and from your teacher and insert weblinks, among other things. You will also find video content on Cambridge Elevate, specifically:

- tutorial-style videos, designed to complement material covered in the Developing units and to refresh your knowledge while broadening your understanding of certain tricky concepts
- interviews with leading thinkers and researchers in their fields, which provide a unique resource for stimulating discussion.

I hope you enjoy your AS or A Level Literature course, as well as this book, and wish you well for the journey ahead.

Marcello Giovanelli
Series editor

BEGINNING

1 Key concepts for literary study

In this unit, you will:

- consider what is meant by the idea of genre
- explore some initial ideas about narrative
- think about the role of language in literature
- establish initial ideas about representation in literary texts.

1.1 Introduction: the elements of literary study

Your A Level English Literature course will bring you into contact with many of the well-known writers and great ideas of history and contemporary culture. It will enable you to expand your knowledge of literature and develop a set of critical reading, thinking, writing and discussion skills.

During the course, you will develop a detailed knowledge of a number of set literary texts. Through reading these, you will develop your knowledge about aspects of literature in general: the craft of the writer, the response of the reader and the contexts in which literature is written, read and interpreted.

1.1.1 The craft of the writer

You will develop your knowledge about the ways in which literary writers shape meanings, achieve powerful effects and convey messages - and at the same time, you will develop your own skills of written expression, becoming a versatile writer in a variety of forms.

1.1.2 The response of the reader and critic

You will develop your knowledge about the ways in which readers read, respond to and interpret literary texts, as well as about the particular purposes and methods of literary study and criticism. At the same time, you will develop your own skills of critical thinking and discussion.

1.1.3 The contexts of literature

You will develop your knowledge of the history of literature and the social and cultural contexts in which literary texts have been written, read and interpreted over the centuries. You will learn to make connections of many kinds between texts, developing your understanding of the ways in which writers work within, develop and break out of conventions of various kinds, and of the ways in which writers and readers respond to the cultures in which they live and work.

Of course, you already know a certain amount about these topics from your earlier studies of English. As you move into A Level, we hope that this book will help you to make the transition to the more specialised type of study you will encounter at A Level. We hope too that it will prepare you for whatever you go on to do after A Level, whether you go on to university or not, by helping you to attain knowledge and develop the skills to communicate effectively and think critically about the world around you.

1.2 Introducing key concepts for literary study

You will already have been introduced to a variety of ways of thinking about the study of literature. As you now start your A Level studies and develop your independent abilities to work with text, it is useful to think briefly about some key concepts that underpin the study of *any* literary text.

ACTIVITY 1

What do you think literary study is about?

Think back over your study of literature to date, particularly focusing on your most recent studies.

a What do you think is the purpose of studying literature?
b What approaches to studying literature have you experienced?
c What kinds of learning activity did you do?
d What are your preferred ways of studying literature?
e What do you think is the relationship between language and literature in studying English?
f How many texts did you study? What types of text were they?
g How much independence were you given? To what extent were you told what to do?
h How do you expect A Level to be different?

1.3 Genre

At its most basic, genre can be defined as a style or category of art, music, film or literature. Thus a musical composition may be designated as a symphony, a sonata, an overture, a concerto or a song. Each of these is seen as a distinct form of composition in its own right in that it shares certain properties in common with other compositions in the same form. Literature can be viewed in particular ways through genre, and the English Literature B Specification expects students to do this. Literary texts are often defined in the same way, and fall broadly into four categories:

- prose fiction (novels, **novellas**, short stories)
- poetry (both **lyric** and narrative)
- drama (mainly for the stage, but occasionally for the screen – both large and small)
- literary non-fiction (for example, some travel writing, biography, autobiography, memoirs, essays).

These are the main genres on which your study of literature will be based, and as such they are often seen as discrete entities. The picture is not quite as simple as this, however. Subcategories exist within all of these genres. Prose fiction, for instance, can be broken down into many subdivisions.

ACTIVITY 2

Subcategories of prose fiction

Think about the prose fiction you've read. It comes in many different shapes, sizes and forms. Jot down a list of these different types of fiction. Think about each type of fiction you identify. What characterises each type and makes it distinct as a category? In what ways do these categories cross over with each other?

You might recognise the types of fiction in Figure 1A, or be able to add others.

Figure 1A

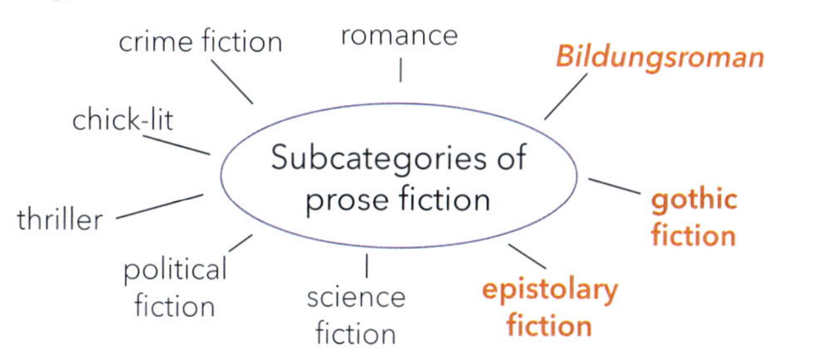

Key terms

novella: a work of prose fiction longer than a short story but shorter than a novel (for example, *Of Mice and Men* or *Animal Farm*)

lyric poetry: song-like poetry, usually with short regular **stanzas**, often expressing strong emotion or personal feelings

stanza: a group of lines in a poem divided from other lines by a blank line

***Bildungsroman*:** a novel dealing with a character's development from childhood into adulthood

gothic fiction: a form of fiction that frequently deals with horror, the supernatural and socially unacceptable and criminal behaviour

epistolary fiction: a work of prose fiction written mostly or completely in letter form (for example, Tobias Smollett's *The Expedition of Humphry Clinker*)

The various prose fiction categories could also cross over with each other. Both crime and romance, for example, could be epistolary; either could also be a *Bildungsroman*; chick-lit frequently deals with romance; a work of science fiction may also be a thriller.

Drama is also often sub-divided. The main forms are comedy and tragedy, but other sub-forms exist, as shown in Figure 1B.

Figure 1B

Key terms

melodrama: a sensational form of drama with exaggerated characters and exciting events

farce: a kind of energetic comedy that employs fast action and unlikely events

pastoral: dramatic works presenting the society of shepherds or other rural societies, free from the complexity and corruption of city life

kitchen sink drama: a form of drama from the 1950s and 1960s often depicting working- class domestic situations and exploring related social and political issues (for example, John Osborne's *Look Back in Anger* and Shelagh Delaney's *A Taste of Honey*)

Shakespeare – arguably the greatest dramatist of all time – recognises this proliferation humorously in *Hamlet* (Act 2, Scene 2) where Polonius makes the observation about the actors arrived at Elsinore, as shown in Text 1A.

Text 1A

The best actors in the world, either for tragedy, comedy, history, pastoral, pastoral-comical, historical-pastoral, tragical-historical, tragical-comical-historical-pastoral, scene individable, or poem unlimited.

Hamlet, Act 2, Scene 2

This list in Text 1A is obviously relevant to Elizabethan drama and sub genres but the range is wider today. While genre recognises formal and functional similarities that connect literary works – novels, for example, share certain common features – it is equally important to note that genre is not a fixed entity. There are significant examples of crossover between the main genres. *The Emperor's Babe* (Bernardine Evaristo), *The Marlowe Papers* (Ros Barber) and *Byrne* (Anthony Burgess), for example, are all novels in verse. *Hawksmoor* (a novel), *Dan Leno and the Limehouse Golem* (a novel) and *Dickens* (a biography) by Peter Ackroyd all include sections written in dramatic form – the former a pastiche of Restoration drama. *Soul Tourists*, also by Bernardine Evaristo, is a combination of prose fiction, poetry and screenplay. Why is this?

Consider the functions of certain types of text and note that there are substantial crossovers between them. Prose fiction, some literary non-fiction, most drama (for both the stage and the screen) and some poetry is narrative in function – the primary purpose is to tell us a story. It is not surprising, therefore, that while the *ways* in which stories are told and the *purposes* for which they are told may differ, there will also be significant shared elements between them. Lyric poetry often seeks to capture in highly figurative and imagistic terms the nature of a specific moment, place or mood, but this may also play a significant part at specific points in both prose fiction and drama.

1.3.1 Features of prose fiction, poetry, drama and literary non-fiction

It is important to recognise that literary works take different genre forms and you will certainly have encountered examples of all of the main literary genres in your studies so far.

ACTIVITY 3

Your understanding of genre so far

Look at Figure 1C and think about your existing knowledge of the main literary genres from your studies and personal reading.

Figure 1C

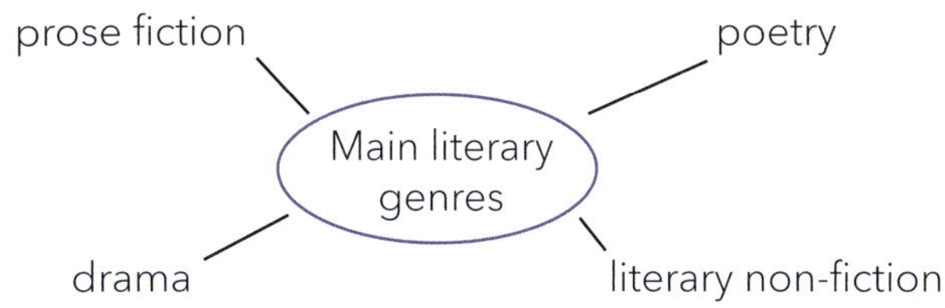

a What unique features can you identify relating to each of these genres?

b What sub-genres have you encountered in each genre?

c In what ways does each genre overlap with others?

d Are there some genres with which you're less familiar?

Developing your familiarity with genres

Everyone has areas of literature where they are less well read. Working with your teacher, set yourself some target reading to develop your familiarity with any genres with which you're less familiar.

1.3.2 Other ways of understanding genre

Genre can also be thought of in broader terms, as a body of work related to a particular theme, or a set of conventions in terms of places, characters, events, and so on. In fact, your A Level course is built around the idea of viewing texts through different features of genre:

- Aspects of tragedy
- Aspects of comedy
- Elements of crime writing
- Elements of political and social protest writing.

A Level studies

Those of you doing A Level will study either aspects of tragedy or aspects of comedy, AND either elements of crime writing or elements of political and social protest writing.

AS Level studies

Those of you doing AS Level will study only aspects of tragedy or aspects of comedy.

Instead of focusing on the fact that a text is a novel, a play or poetry, emphasis is shifted onto the outcomes of the writing (tragedy and comedy) or the focuses of the writing (crime and politics). You will be expected to consider the ways in which writers of prose fiction, poetry and drama have approached these issues, within and across genres. So, as well as studying *Othello* as a play, you'll study it as an example of tragedy; as well as thinking about 'The Rime of the Ancient Mariner' as a narrative poem, you'll explore it in relation to crime writing. Similarly, instead of looking at *Emma* primarily as a novel, you'll be expected to consider how it relates to aspects of comedy. This is not to say that the fact that *Othello* is a play, 'The Rime of the Ancient Mariner' is a poem and *Emma* is a novel doesn't matter. You will also be expected to know about how prose fiction, drama and poetry differ from one another, and there are detailed sections on each of these genres in this book.

As we saw earlier, genre boundaries are frequently blurred. Some of the texts you study may be conventional – *The Murder of Roger Ackroyd*, for instance, is a classic of the detective novel genre. Many of the texts you study, however, are not. To stay with the example of crime writing, *Hamlet*, while it deals with issues of crime is not a traditional crime text. Nor is *The Great Gatsby* generally considered as an example of tragedy. That is why the units you study are called 'aspects of' tragedy and comedy and 'elements of' crime or political writing. The texts you study in these units are not necessarily 'pure' examples of the genres, but they do all relate to a central set of ideas relating to tragedy, comedy, crime writing or political writing. Your job is to explore how writers work with these ideas, even if they deliberately undermine them.

So, as you study each unit you need to think carefully about central features of tragedy or comedy and crime or political writing.

- What key social, cultural and philosophical concepts typically underpin these works?
- What issues do they typically deal with?

- Which aspects or elements of these forms do authors engage with and which do they leave out? How does this affect your responses as a reader?
- How do the writers seek to represent the world?
- How and to what extent do the texts vary according to genre and the time at which texts were produced?
- How do we approach and receive these texts in the 21st century?

ACTIVITY 4

Getting started

a Think about each of the units for study:
- Aspects of tragedy
- Aspects of comedy
- Elements of crime writing
- Elements of political writing.

What texts have you read, either in your previous studies or for pleasure, that fit into each of these categories? Don't be surprised if you find that some texts fit into two or even three of the broad categories.

b Taking each unit in turn, see what you already know in relation to each of these areas of literature.

Check your responses in the Ideas section on Cambridge Elevate

1.3.3 Literary non-fiction

Although you might not encounter much literary non-fiction in your course, it's worth thinking briefly about this genre, which is often included in the study of literature. In contrast to the other main genres, literary non-fiction includes a variety of other literary forms that are more specifically 'factual' in nature, for example:

- investigative journalism (for example, Bernstein and Woodward's *All the President's Men* or Truman Capote's *In Cold Blood*)
- **reportage** (for example, Norman Mailer's *The Fight* which is based around Muhammad Ali's famous 'rumble in the jungle' boxing match; George Orwell's *Down and Out in Paris and London*)
- travel writing (for example, Jonathan Raban's *Old Glory* – an account of a trip down the length of the Mississippi River; the many popular works of Bill Bryson)
- biography (for example, Boswell's famous *The Life of Samuel Johnson* or Peter Ackroyd's sequence of biographies)
- essays (for example, Montaigne's Essays, but many literary writers have produced essays on a wide variety of subjects).

In addition, **literary criticism** and **literary theory** – writing about literature – are often regarded as types of literary non-fiction. You will encounter a range of literary criticism and theory during your course. They are important because they will:

- introduce you to a variety of ways of thinking about and reading literary texts
- provide you with excellent models for how to write about literature.

Narrative even has its own branch of literary criticism – narrative theory.

See 9.1 for more on literary theory

1.4 Narrative

Narrative is central to all the main genres. Prose fiction, narrative poetry, drama and many works of literary non-fiction are narratives, and even in poetry that does not actually tell a story, certain aspects of narrative such as **voice**, character and setting may be important.

Key terms

reportage: a factual, journalistic account presented in a book or other text

literary criticism: the art of making judgements about and commenting upon the qualities and character of literary works

literary theory: the study of the way in which we interpret literary texts

voice: the distinctive manner of expression of an author or narrator

See 9.4 for more on narrative theory

See 1.5.4 for more on voice

1.4.1 What is narrative?

At its simplest, narrative is the act of telling a story. The US media analyst Andrew Blau has commented that 'Human beings tell stories. It is how we learn and how we teach, how we preserve and transmit culture. It is how we understand ourselves and others. The instinct to tell stories and seek them out remains an essential part of being human' (2004: 1).

ACTIVITY 5

Narrative and you

a How do you respond to Blau's views about humans and narrative?

b How do you use story as a way of understanding yourself?

c How do you use story as a way of representing yourself to the world?

d How do those stories differ according to who you're telling them to and why you're telling them?

This simple view of narrative is, of course, only the starting point. Tzvetan Todorov (in David Lodge, *Nice Work,* 1988) says that thinking about narrative requires us to make a distinction between the content of a story (*fabula*) and the way it is ordered, organised and presented (*sjuzet*). It involves thinking about a variety of things.

- Who is telling the story?
- What kind of relationship is established between the narrator and the reader?
- How is the story told?
- What is explicitly told, what is implied and what is omitted?
- What values does the story convey?
- How does the teller feel about the story they are telling?

In other words, we need to ask why the story is being told in the way it is.

ACTIVITY 6

Fabula* and *sjuzet

a Think of a story that exists in several different versions – fairy tales are often very good for this.

b Are the details of the story (*fabula*) the same in each case?

c Now try to answer the questions in Activity 5 in relation to the way each version of the story is told (*sjuzet*).

1.4.2 How do narratives work?

Todorov goes on to set out a theory for narrative structure. He proposes a basic four-part model as shown in Figure 1D, which provides a very interesting way of thinking about stories in a variety of genres.

Figure 1D

Exposition – the narrative starts with a situation of balance

↓

Complication – disruption enters the narrative and destroys balance

↓

Climax – there is some form of confrontation/conflict that seeks to resolve matters

↓

Resolution – a return to a (transformed) balance

'Human beings tell stories. It is how we learn and how we teach…'

Andrew Blau

ACTIVITY 7

Todorov in action

a Think about a variety of different narratives that you're very familiar with – these could be novels, plays, poems, films, television dramas and so on.

b How far does Todorov's model apply to each?

c In what ways do different narratives diverge from the model?

d How do narratives differ according to genre? What methods of telling stories are available on screen, for example, that aren't available to a novelist?

1.4.3 Components of narrative

Narratives are made up of a range of different components and you should think about what each of these contributes to the development and representation of the story:

Component	The ways in which authors…
Characterisation	… build characters
Voice	… use narrative voices – sometimes more than one in the same text – to tell stories in particular ways
Perspective	… use differing points of view from which stories are told and read
Setting	… set the narrative in specific places and at specific times
Destination	… bring the narrative to an end that may suggest particular meanings

ACTIVITY 8

Unpicking aspects of narrative

Choose a narrative that you know particularly well or one that you're currently reading or studying. It could be a novel, a play, a narrative poem or a work of narrative non-fiction. You could also use a screen drama you know well or a video game. Think in detail about aspects of its narrative, as given in the lists of questions about setting, characterisation, voice, structure and destination in the box.

In order to explore differences between texts, you might want to do this activity for more than one text.

Narrative setting: scenes/places/locations

- When is it set? Where is it set? How many settings does it have?
- Are the settings real or imagined?
- What do the settings represent, suggest or symbolise?
- Are journeys between places important?
- What **imagery** is used to describe places?

Narrative characterisation

- Identify the characters. Which are major, which are minor?
- Are they realistic? Or are they **stereotypes** or symbolic?
- Are their names significant?
- How are the characters developed (for example, through description, dialogue, voice, employment, action)?
- Does the author use imagery to build character?

Narrative voice and perspective

- Who is the narrator(s)? Is the narrator the same as the writer?
- What 'voice' does the narrator(s) have?
- What do we know about the narrator?
- Whose point of view does the narrator represent?
- Do you trust the narrator?
- Who does the narrator address?
- What kinds of language does the narrator use?

Narrative structure

- What is the time and sequence of the narrative? (for example, how much time elapses? Is the narrative chronological? What is the pace of the narrative?)
- Is the narrative divided? If so, how (for example, stanzas, chapters, scenes)? What effect does this have on how the story is told and how you read it (for example, is it easier to take a break in reading if a book has lots of shorter chapters or fewer longer chapters)?
- How is tension created?
- What links, patterns or echoes are there between parts?
- How are beginnings and endings significant?

Narrative destination

- What might the overall meanings and/or messages of the narrative be?
- Is the title significant?
- How much ambiguity and room for interpretation is there in the narrative?

- How far are meanings dependent on a specific historical, cultural or social context?

By exploring these questions, you will have seen the extent to which writers deliberately shape their narratives and how language, form and structure can have an impact on how readers 'receive' and interpret stories. These aspects of narrative and the ways in which they apply to each of the main genres are all further explored throughout this book.

Key terms

imagery: the use of words to visually or figuratively suggest meaning

stereotype: a character embodying a set of limited, well-recognised features (for example, a nagging mother-in-law or a lazy, good-for-nothing husband)

See 1.5.6 for more on imagery

See 1.5.4 for more on voice

1.5 Language

In your previous study of literature, you will have learned to explore and analyse the ways in which authors express meaning and achieve effects through their use of language. Some students find this aspect of literary study challenging. Sometimes students ask whether authors actually mean to use language in particular ways – as if the imagery, rhyming patterns or narrative voices they find in literary texts all arrived there by accident. Usually writers select elements like these very carefully in order to affect their readers.

If you look at draft versions of writers' work, you can see that a lot of thought really does go into very precise choices.

ACTIVITY 9

Exploring early drafts

The poet Wilfred Owen (1893–1918) will always be associated with World War I. One of his most famous poems, 'Anthem for Doomed Youth', is a **sonnet** about the men who went to fight in the war and never returned. However, it wasn't always called 'Anthem for Doomed Youth'. The earliest surviving draft of the poem is titled 'Anthem for Dead Youth'. Why do you think Owen may have changed 'Dead' to 'Doomed'?

The first line of the poem, in Owen's first draft, reads as follows: 'What passing-bells for you who die in herds?' In the final draft, the line has been changed to: 'What passing-bells for these who die as cattle?'

What effect is created by changing 'herds' to 'cattle'? What effect is created by changing 'you' to 'these'?

Exploring Wilfred Owen's poetry

Images of the draft versions of Owen's poems can be found on the First World War Poetry Digital Archive

Visit the First world war poetry digital archive on Cambridge Elevate

Key terms

sonnet: a 14-line poem that can use a variety of rhyme schemes to usually make up the 14 lines

Often, people think of the writing process as something mysterious and inspired - as if the words suddenly appear from nowhere. It might help to imagine it as more of a craft that needs to be practised. Just as visual artists learn that watercolour produces very different results to charcoal, and just as musicians learn the effects of tempo and dynamics, writers learn that their choices of language will shape the meanings they communicate to their readers.

1.5.1 Form and structure

Form is a complex term to define as it has a number of related meanings. On a simple level, it can mean whether a piece of writing is in prose or verse.

Prose is the ordinary form of written language, organised into sentences and paragraphs. The easiest way to identify prose is to look at whether the lines go all the way to the right-hand side of the page or column (as they do, for instance, in this paragraph).

Verse is a poetic form of written language, organised into lines and stanzas. Poetry is written in verse, but we also find verse in drama (Shakespeare's plays, for instance, use verse and prose for a variety of reasons). Traditionally, verse has an identifiable metre, such as **iambic pentameter**, but much modern verse does not use metre.

Key terms

prose: the mode of language, mainly associated in literature with fiction, in which text is organised into paragraphs, as distinct from verse

verse: the mode of language, mainly associated in literature with poetry, in which text is organised into separate lines, as distinct from prose

iambic pentameter: a rhythm (metre) consisting of five iambic feet

See 2.3.2 for more on metre

Form can also refer to whether a piece of writing is a novel, poem or play - or, indeed, a short story or essay. Yet poems themselves can have different forms - such as the sonnet, **sestina** or **villanelle**.

Form can also be used to refer to the way an author has used a particular set of conventions related to the shape and layout of a piece of writing. The concept of form therefore overlaps with **structure**, which refers to the way in which a piece of writing is organised. For example, the play *form* is usually *structured* by being divided into acts. When we analyse a play, we consider how these divisions are used in the narrative (for example, how a particularly shocking revelation might be placed at the end of an act to create dramatic impact).

Key terms

sestina: a poem with six stanzas and a final triplet. Each stanza comprises six lines and ends with the same six words repeated in six different sequences

villanelle: a lyric poem with 19 lines, with only two rhymes throughout, and some repeated lines

structure: the way a piece of writing is organised within its form

Structure involves thinking about these points:

- how texts begin, unfold and end
- the use of time (chronological or non-chronological)
- the use of dual or multiple narrators
- the division of a text into acts and scenes, parts and chapters, stanzas or verse-paragraphs
- techniques such as **foreshadowing** and **flashbacks**.

Key terms

foreshadowing: a technique in which narrative refers to something that has not yet happened but will happen later

flashback: a technique in which narrative moves back in time to refer to something that has already happened

Here are three examples of the way in which texts are structured, each a different literary form: a novel, a play and a poem.

1 Andrea Levy's novel *Small Island* begins with a Prologue and is then divided into sections, titled '1948' and 'Before', that alternate between events in 1948 and events that took place before the outbreak of World War II. Each section is divided further into chapters named after their respective

narrators - Gilbert, Hortense, Queenie and Bernard. The use of different narrators and a non-chronological timescale allows Levy to explore a range of perspectives on the events that unfold.

2 Arthur Miller's play *A View from the Bridge* is divided into two acts. Each act begins with a short soliloquy spoken by Alfieri, who speaks directly to the audience to set the events that follow in context. Act One ends on a note of extreme tension, as the Italian immigrant, Marco, challenges the play's protagonist, Eddie, by threatening his position in his own household. The beginning of Act Two marks the passage of time and allows Miller to break the tension created at the end of the previous act.

3 U.A. Fanthorpe's poem 'Not My Best Side', which was inspired by Paolo Uccello's painting 'St George and the Dragon', is made up of three dramatic monologues - one spoken by the dragon in Uccello's painting, one by the princess who is being rescued, and one by St George himself. Each contains 19 lines and consists of the narrator's thoughts on the situation depicted in the painting.

1.5.2 Style

Style can be described as the overall manner in which a text is expressed. It could be simple and sparse or complex and dense; colloquial and accessible or sophisticated and difficult.

The examples in Texts 1B–1E are taken from a range of novels.

Text 1B

Can anything, my good Sir, be more painful to a friendly mind, than a necessity of communicating disagreeable intelligence? Indeed it is sometimes difficult to determine, whether the relator or the receiver of evil tidings is most to be pitied.

Frances Burney, *Evelina* (1778)

Text 1C

A Saturday afternoon in November was approaching the time of twilight, and the vast tract of unenclosed wild known as Egdon Heath embrowned itself moment by moment. Overhead the hollow stretch of whitish cloud shutting out the sky was as a tent which had the whole heath for its floor.

Thomas Hardy, *The Return of the Native* (1878)

Text 1D

You don't know about me without you have read a book by the name of The Adventures of Tom Sawyer; but that ain't no matter. That book was made by Mr. Mark Twain, and he told the truth, mainly. There was things which he stretched, but mainly he told the truth.

Mark Twain, *The Adventures of Huckleberry Finn* (1884)

Text 1E

The sky rained dismal. It rained humdrum. It rained the kind of rain that is so much wetter than normal rain, the kind of rain that comes down in big drops and splats, the kind of rain that is merely an upright sea with slots in it.

Terry Pratchett, *Truckers* (1989)

ACTIVITY 10

Thinking about style

How would you describe the different styles that these extracts represent? Write a brief paragraph about the style of each extract. Think, for example, about:

- the vocabulary
- the register of language
- how speech is represented
- how sentence structure is used to convey meaning.

1.5.3 Tone

Tone is best described as the attitude conveyed by a literary text, whether this is solemn or playful, serious or light-hearted, formal or informal, emotional or matter-of-fact, sincere or ironic. It is linked to the stance adopted by an author (or narrator) towards a particular topic, and, by extension, the stance that he or she wants the reader to adopt.

Key terms

tone: the attitude conveyed by a literary text

Tone can vary throughout a literary text. The narrator of Robert Browning's poem 'My Last Duchess', which is set in Renaissance Italy, is a nobleman who is negotiating his next marriage with a representative of his intended bride's family. His tone at the beginning of the poem, when he greets this representative and shows him a painting of his previous wife, is courteous as shown in Text 1F.

Text 1F

That's my last Duchess painted on the wall,
Looking as if she were alive. I call
That piece a wonder, now: **Frà Pandolf's** hands
Worked busily a day, and there she stands.
Will't please you sit and look at her?

Robert Browning, 'My Last Duchess'

Glossary

Frà Pandolf: the artist who painted the Last Duchess' portrait

Later in the poem, however, the narrator's tone becomes more chilling. It becomes apparent that his jealousy over his previous wife's behaviour became so intense that he ordered her death (Text 1G).

Text 1G

Oh sir, she smiled, no doubt,
Whene'er I passed her; but who passed without
Much the same smile? This grew; I gave commands;
Then all smiles stopped together.

Robert Browning, 'My Last Duchess'

1.5.4 Voice

Voice can be defined as the way in which a text is presented to the reader - the way in which a story is told. One of the most obvious things to consider when exploring voice is whether a text is narrated in the first person or the third person.

ACTIVITY 11

Thinking about voice

a Choose a text that you know well and think about the idea of 'voice'. Answer these questions about the 'voice' used:
- What kind of voice seems to be speaking to you?
- Is the voice involved in the story or not?
- How much does this voice seem to know?
- How much does this voice seem to be sharing with you?
- How reliable does this voice appear to be?
- Does this voice simply tell the story, or does it comment on what is happening as well?

b Now choose another text you know well in a different genre. How does this compare to the first text you chose with regard to voice?

c Consider how the narrative voices of these two texts differ.

1.5.5 Rhetoric

Rhetoric refers to the use of language to achieve certain effects. It is often associated with the use of particular devices:

- **rhetorical questions**
- exclamations
- repetition
- **tripartite patterning** (the 'rule of three')
- sound effects such as **alliteration**, **assonance**, **consonance**, rhyme and **onomatopoeia**
- particular sentence structures such as symmetrical or balanced sentences
- **enumeration**
- **allusion**.

The presence of such devices often gives language a heightened feel, drawing attention to what is being said.

See 2.3.2 for more on rhyme

Key terms

rhetoric: the use of language to achieve persuasive or impressive effects

rhetorical question: use of questions to which the answers are obvious, which do not require a response, or to which a response is not wanted ('What on earth do you think you're doing?')

tripartite patterning: when writers use a group of three to create effect ('the relentless, pounding, crushing impact of the waves')

alliteration: use of a repeated letter sound for effect ('In sooth I know not why I am so sad')

assonance: the use of repeated identical or similar vowel sounds in nearby words ('she needs cream for her feet')

consonance: repeated sounds produced by consonants at the beginning, middle or end of nearby words ('he chuckled as he kicked the bucket')

onomatopoeia: when words sound like what they mean (clap, bark, whistle)

enumeration: the listing of examples

allusion: an indirect reference to an object, person, place or idea ('he is playing the Romeo' as a way of referring to a young man in love)

ACTIVITY 12

Rhetoric

Read the passage in Text 1H, from the opening chapter of Charles Dickens' novel *Bleak House* (1853). What effects are created by the use of these devices?

- Repetition
- **Minor sentences**
- **Balanced sentence**
- Alliteration
- **Complex sentences** with multiple **clauses**

Key terms

minor sentence: a sentence that does not contain a main verb. For example, 'Fog everywhere.' If written in full, the sentence might read: 'There was fog everywhere.'

balanced sentence: sentences whose clauses are structured in the same way. For example, ' He walked, by way of routine, straight along the path. She walked, by way of superstition, around the ladder.'

complex sentence: a sentence consisting of at least one main clause and one subordinate clause. For example, 'Helen, who was an expert on the novels of Joseph Conrad, was invited to give a radio interview.' Note that the subordinate clause ('who was an expert on the novels of Joseph Conrad') cannot stand alone. It depends for its meaning on the surrounding main clause ('Helen… was invited to give a radio interview.'), which could stand on its own

clause: the smallest language unit capable of expressing a complete thought. In other words, a clause must contain at least a subject and a verb

Text 1H

Fog everywhere. Fog up the river, where it flows among green **aits** and meadows; fog down the river, where it rolls defiled among the tiers of shipping and the waterside pollutions of a great (and dirty) city. Fog on the Essex marshes, fog on the Kentish heights. Fog creeping into the **cabooses** of **collier-brigs**; fog lying out on the yards and hovering in the rigging of great ships; fog drooping on the **gunwales** of barges and small boats. Fog in the eyes and throats of ancient **Greenwich pensioners**, wheezing by the firesides of their **wards**; fog in the stem and bowl of the afternoon pipe of the wrathful skipper, down in his close cabin; fog cruelly pinching the toes and fingers of his shivering little **'prentice** boy on deck.

Charles Dickens, *Bleak House*

Glossary

ait: a small island in a river

caboose: kitchen on a ship's deck

collier-brig: a coal barge

gunwales: the upper edge of the side of a boat

Greenwich pensioners: ex-soldiers who are cared for by a charitable organisation

wards: shared rooms in which patients or the elderly are cared for

'prentice: apprentice

1.5.6 Imagery

Imagery is the use of words to visually or figuratively describe meaning. It includes techniques such as **metaphor** and **simile**, which make links between one concept or object and another thing that might be completely unrelated. It also encompasses the ways in which language can be used to appeal to the senses: we can talk about a text having vivid visual imagery, but we might also encounter a text with lots of auditory imagery (appealing to the sense of hearing) or tactile imagery (appealing to the sense of touch). John Keats' 'Ode to Autumn' ends by evoking the sounds the narrator can hear, using onomatopoeia ('whistles', 'twitter') and **sibilance** ('sing', 'soft', 'swallows') to create a richly detailed description (see Text 1I).

Text 1I

And full-grown lambs loud bleat from hilly **bourn**;
Hedge-crickets sing; and now with treble soft
The redbreast whistles from a garden-**croft**,
And gathering swallows twitter in the skies.

John Keats, 'Ode to Autumn'

Key terms

metaphor: when a word or phrase is applied to a thing that it is not literally applicable (for example, 'the men were trees in the mist') or when something is used to represent something else (for example, 'the flickering flame of a candle' could be a metaphor for the fragility of human life)

simile: comparison of one thing to another using 'like' or 'as' (for example, 'as cunning as a fox' or 'run like the wind')

sibilance: repeated use of the 's' sound created either by the letter 's' or the soft 'c'

Glossary

bourn: a stream

croft: land attached to a house used for growing crops

1.6 Representation, interpretation and criticism

Sometimes, when people think about literature, they imagine it as a mirror that is held up to the world, providing an accurate reflection that can be viewed in a straightforward manner. However, literary texts are not factual records of the world, and it is important for you to think about three related processes:

- representation – the ways in which authors represent particular versions of the world and of life
- interpretation – the ways in which different readers make sense of writers' representations of the world and life
- criticism – a critical process in which students of literature pursue a single informed view or evaluate differing interpretations against one another.

1.6.1 Representation

Writers do not necessarily seek to be factually accurate in the way they portray the world. A particular event, person or set of circumstances could be depicted in a variety of ways. Authors make choices about the manner in which they write, which might be conscious or unconscious: these choices might be a reflection of the author's individual philosophy, or of ideas and opinions that were common when the author was alive. Whatever their origin, these choices shape the ways in which authors represent the world. These representations are an important part of literary study.

Exploring representation

The writer Virginia Woolf (1882–1941) experimented with different forms of representation. One of her most famous experiments was with a technique known as **stream-of-consciousness**, which attempts to capture the movements of the mind and the way it filters different impressions and experiences. In an essay called 'Modern Fiction', written in 1919, Woolf stated that 'Life is not a series of gig lamps symmetrically arranged; life is a luminous halo, a semi-transparent envelope surrounding us from the beginning of consciousness to the end'. In saying this, Woolf was trying to draw attention to the fact that life does not have to be depicted in terms of straightforward, objective facts: it can be presented as something much more subjective and difficult to grasp.

Key terms

stream-of-consciousness: a writing technique that attempts to capture the movements of the mind and the way it filters different impressions and experiences

See 4.2.2, 9.3.2 and 9.5.3 for more on Virginia Woolf

As an example of the ways in which representations vary, think of the ways in which you and your friends might describe an event that you have all witnessed. These might include:

- telling the story chronologically, or beginning with some kind of explanation as to why this event was particularly important or striking
- emphasising descriptions, or re-creating dialogue
- using simple, colloquial language, or language that is more sophisticated and elaborate
- sympathising with one of the participants, or remaining impartial
- building sympathy, or trying to make listeners laugh.

These different re-tellings all offer different representations of the event, representing different perspectives and affecting listeners in different ways.

ACTIVITY 13

Experimenting with representations

a Write a short description of your English classroom. Make it as neutral and factual as possible.

b Now write another description of the same room. This time, try to make it sound as friendly and welcoming as possible.

c Finally, write a third description. This time, make the room sound sinister and threatening.

d What differences do you notice in the kind of language you use in each description?

Exploring literary representations often involves considering issues of power. The author is, effectively, controlling the way in which you, as the reader, perceive the events, issues and characters they are writing about. This is particularly significant when we think about the ways in which people are represented. Think of some of the texts you've read, and consider the ways in which they represent some of these groups:

- different social classes
- different genders
- different ethnic and cultural groups
- gay men and women
- people with disabilities
- orphans
- people who are adopted.

Of course, people from these groups might not feature in the texts you've read, but this in itself is something to think about. Are particular groups (such as powerful white men) over-represented in literary texts? Are other groups under-represented? How might you feel if you yourself belong to a group that is under-represented, or that tends to be represented in a certain way? Such representations are important because they can influence the ways in which people from particular social groups are perceived.

1.6.2 Interpretation

As we've just seen, there is no single, straightforward way of representing the world. Neither is there a single, straightforward way of interpreting literary texts. Studying literature is not like cracking a code or excavating buried treasure: the 'meaning' of a literary text is not something that sits inside it like an object in a safe, waiting to be unlocked with a magic key. Nor is studying literature a matter of trying to find out what the author of a text wants the text to mean. Instead, meanings are created by the ways in which we interpret a text. It's for this reason that people often say that in English Literature, 'there are no right or wrong answers'.

Your interpretations of literary texts can be shaped by a number of factors. Your age, gender, social class, political beliefs and past experiences might all play a part. Some people would argue that a text has as many potential interpretations as there are readers. Others would go further than this, and say that a text has as many potential interpretations as there are readings, since you might also interpret a text in different ways at different points in your life. For example, you might read George Orwell's novel *Animal Farm* (1945) as a child, and interpret it simply as a story about a group of animals who take over the farm on which they live. If you then reread it as a young adult, you will recognise that *Animal Farm* is much more complex – that it is an **allegory** about the Russian Revolution and the Stalinist era. You might, later, make links between the novel and events you have experienced or people you have encountered – such as an overbearing boss, or a colleague who is prepared to put their principles to one side in order to secure personal gain.

Key terms

allegory: a literary work or picture which contains a moral, political or religious meaning

Does this mean that a text can mean whatever you want it to mean? This is a trickier question than you might think. Nobody would argue that Shakespeare's play *Romeo and Juliet* is about football – but it's possible that you might find all manner of lines in *Romeo and Juliet* that touch on issues of loyalty and rivalry that are highly relevant to football. It is also possible to imagine a director setting a contemporary version of the play in the context of two rival groups of football fans. So while *Romeo and Juliet* is not *about* football, football might be used as a lens through which the play might be interpreted.

Nevertheless, it's fair to say that some interpretations are definitely more valid than others. Activity 14 will ask you to consider this issue in relation to Ted Hughes' poem 'Wind' (See Text 1J.)

Text 1J

Wind

This house has been far out at sea all night,
The woods crashing through darkness, the booming hills,
Winds stampeding the fields under the window
Floundering black astride and blinding wet

Till day rose; then under the orange sky
The hills had new places, and wind wielded
Blade-light, luminous black and emerald,
Flexing like the lens of a mad eye.

At noon I scaled along the house-side as far as
The coal-house door. Once I looked up –
Through the brunt wind that dented the balls of my eyes
The tent of the hills drummed and strained its guyrope,

The fields quivering, the skyline a grimace,
At any second to bang and vanish with a flap:
The wind flung a magpie away and a black-
Back gull bent like an iron bar slowly. The house

Rang like some fine green goblet in the note
That any second would shatter it. Now deep
In chairs, in front of the great fire, we grip
Our hearts and cannot entertain book, thought,

Or each other. We watch the fire blazing,
And feel the roots of the mouse move, but sit on,
Seeing the window tremble to come in,
Hearing the stones cry out under the horizons.

Ted Hughes

ACTIVITY 14

Considering interpretations

1 Statements A to J cover a number of interpretations of the poem 'Wind'. Read each interpretation and consider how valid you think it is.

- **A** This poem is about a boat at sea in a storm.
- **B** This poem is about a house in the countryside in a storm.
- **C** During the storm, trees are felled, animals stampede and there are landslides.
- **D** During the storm, the wind creates so much noise and movement that it seems to threaten the landscape.
- **E** The speaker of the poem goes climbing during the storm and receives an eye injury.
- **F** The speaker of the poem is a man.
- **G** Although on the surface the poem seems to be about a storm, it is actually about the tense relationships of the people in the house.
- **H** The main emphasis of the poem is on the violence of natural forces rather than on the lives of the people in the house.
- **I** The poem is a powerful description of the violent force of a storm.
- **J** A possible interpretation of the poem is that humans cannot dominate nature.

2 Think about how you made your decisions. How did you decide which interpretations were more valid than others?

3 What might your answer to the previous question suggest about the way we study literature?

Check your responses in the Ideas section on Cambridge Elevate

See 11.2.3, Expressing tentativeness for more on tentativeness

Texts can be interpreted, then, in a number of different ways - including ways that their authors might not have intended, and that they might never have imagined. The interpretations you put forward might not be 'right' or 'wrong', but they always have to be carefully argued, supported and evaluated. And remember, too, that you don't necessarily have to decide between different interpretations - you can hold them in your mind simultaneously. Indeed, many people would say that the potential to 'play around' with multiple interpretations of texts is one of the things that makes the study of English literature so fascinating.

1.6.3 Criticism

During your course, you will encounter critical ideas and theory in the form of literary criticism. Despite the name, literary criticism doesn't involve saying what is *wrong* with literary texts. What it *does* involve is literary analysis: writing (and talking) about literature, developing interpretations, looking at themes, language and imagery, exploring connections between texts and authors, and considering the ways in which texts are influenced by the contexts in which they're written. Figure 1E shows some of the different forms of literary criticism.

Figure 1E

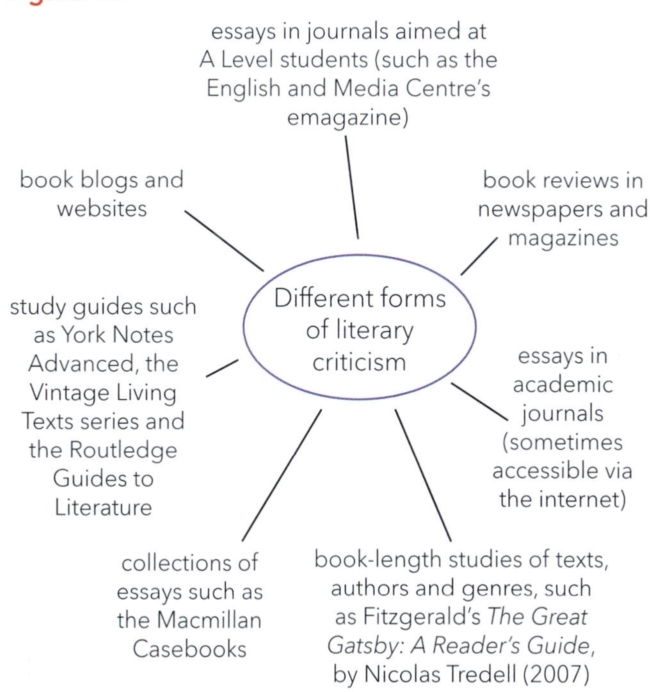

How do people get to be literary critics? Some literary critics are employed by universities, as lecturers and professors. They will almost always have done a degree in English, and will then have completed postgraduate qualifications such as a Master of Arts (MA) and Doctor of Philosophy (PhD). These qualifications act as a professional training route for people who want to teach English in a university. Literary critics who review books for the national press might also be English graduates, and they might have followed their English degrees with postgraduate training in journalism. But some literary critics - those who write book blogs and reviews on the internet - might not have any formal qualifications at all.

Some people, indeed, would argue that you do not need to study literature in any formal capacity in order to be able to respond to it: you just need to be a sensitive, thoughtful reader. Other people would say that studying literature alerts you to aspects of the text that you might not otherwise be aware of, such as the way its authors use methods to create meanings, the relationship between the text and its historical context, the way it draws on aspects of the literary tradition, and the different ways in which it can be interpreted. All of these, in fact, are the kinds of issues we address in this book.

One key point to remember about literary criticism is that it does not claim to offer the 'right answer' to questions about literary texts. Instead, it offers different answers - different ways of interpreting texts, influenced by critics' own beliefs and philosophies. You will learn more about these different ways of interpreting texts in Unit 9: Literary Theory.

1.7 Bringing it all together

1.7.1 How much do you know?

Questions 1-4 ask you to bring together the elements you have studied in this unit.

1 Jot down what you can recall about:
   - genre
   - the way genre is approached in your A Level course.

2 Identify the different aspects of narrative. What do you recall about each?

3 Identify three of the issues explored in relation to authorial method in literary texts.
   - Explain why you believe each is significant.
   - How do you think each contributes to your understanding of how writers seek to represent the world?

4 What do you see as your role as a reader in interpreting the meaning of literary texts?

1.7.2 Assessment objectives

- You have been introduced to a set of key concepts and terms that will apply to your study of all literary texts and you have begun to reflect on your role as a reader in developing informed, personal responses to literary texts (AO1).
- You have considered some key philosophical ideas underpinning the study of literature and how meanings are shaped in literary texts (AO2).
- You have begun to think about the contexts in which texts are produced and received (AO3).
- You have been given the opportunity to think about connections between literary texts (AO4).
- You have considered your own role in developing interpretations of literary texts and a variety of alternative perspectives (AO5).

Summary

In this unit, you have learned about:

- the main literary genres and the way that genre is approached in your course
- what characterisation, voice, perspective, setting and destination contribute to narrative
- the role of language, form and structure in literary texts
- how writers represent the world in literary texts
- how readers can interpret the meanings of literary texts.

BEGINNING

2

Poetry

In this unit, you will:

- explore the ways in which readers respond to and interpret poetry
- explore the ways in which poets craft their work and shape meaning
- explore the history of poetry and the way it has changed over time.

2.1 Introduction to poetry

In your A Level and AS Level courses you have to study poetry. At A Level you will have to read and write about poetry though the lens of Crime Writing or Political and Social Protest Writing and in the NEA where you will have to read poetry though the lens of critical ideas. You might also choose to study it for Paper 1 in your work on Tragedy or Comedy. At AS Level you will have to write about poetry though the lens of Tragedy or Comedy. This unit will enable you to do some preparatory work on poetry before you look at it though a specific optic.

Some students come to A Level as great poetry enthusiasts. For many, however, the main attraction is reading novels and plays. Whichever type of student you are, we hope that studying poetry at A Level will help you to build your appreciation of the power of poetry. As a first step, though, it's a good idea to explore some ideas about why and how poetry is seen differently from novels and plays, and why it plays such a central role in the study of literature.

2.1.1 Poetry in and out of the classroom

Many people today are enthusiastic readers of novels and stories, and consumers of drama and film – but are less likely to be voracious readers of poetry. Although poetry is thriving as a literary form, it's nevertheless true that we live more than ever in an age that is dominated by prose fiction and drama. To some extent, the very different pleasures of poetry have been pushed to the side of our literary culture.

For many people, poetry is mostly associated with school, and in particular with a certain kind of analysis. Poems tend to be quite short, and full of interesting ideas and ways of using language, which makes them ideal for studying literature; but the process of analysis can distract us to some extent from the

Figure 2A

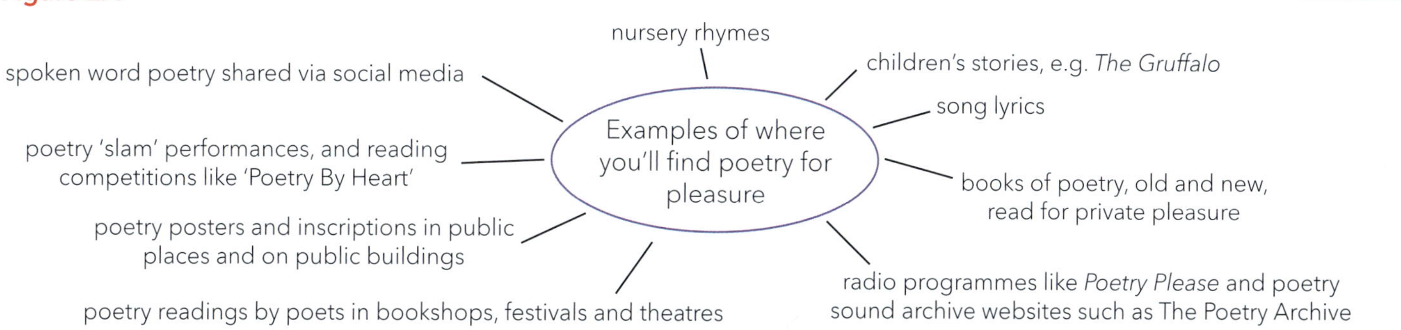

pleasure and *power* of poetry, and its independent life in the world *outside* school.

Arguably, the most important thing to remember about poems is that they are (and always have been) written to be read for pleasure, and not simply to be studied in school. Just as novels, plays and films are designed to give literary pleasure to *real* people in the *real* world, so poems are designed to be read for literary pleasure. As Figure 2A shows, poetry has its primary existence *outside* the classroom - where no kind of explicit analysis is required!

ACTIVITY 1

Experiences of poetry

a Think about your own experience of poetry in and out of school. How would you sum up your feelings about poetry? What kind of poetry have you enjoyed, or not? How are your experiences of poetry different in and out of school?

b Do the reasons given in the previous section for poetry's relative lack of popularity chime with your (or your classmates') experience? Can you suggest any other factors that might have an effect on the way people feel about poetry? What do you think might be done to help increase the popularity of poetry?

Exploring more poetry

Try to dip in and out of some really good anthologies of poetry such as *Poems for the Day* edited by Griff Rhys Jones, *The Nation's Favourite Poems* edited by Wendy Cope, or *Poems that Make Grown Men Cry* edited by Anthony Holden.

2.1.2 Studying poetry

If poetry is *not intended* to be read in school, then why is this? What is it about poetry that gives it such a central role in the teaching of English and literature?

First, of course, poetry has been a hugely significant part of culture - and literature in particular - for many centuries, and continues to have an important role. It therefore has an important place in a literature curriculum. Understanding the pleasure and power that people throughout history - both poets and readers - have found (and continue to find) in poetry is crucial in English.

Second, the study of English language or literature is about understanding how language works and how it can be used in powerful ways to communicate ideas and represent the world. It's also about empowering young people to learn how to use language for themselves. Poetry can be a particularly powerful way of playing with and shaping words in order to communicate ideas and learn about language.

We hope, therefore, that this unit will give you some fresh perspectives on poetry, encouraging you to think more broadly about the purposes and effects of poetry in our lives, and the ways that poets write and readers respond to poetry. We believe that to get to grips with poetry, you need to explore it as an art form and literary tradition, as well as analysing the individual poems you encounter in class.

ACTIVITY 2

Poetry for pleasure

a Which nursery rhymes or children's verses did you enjoy when you were a child? Why do you think children enjoy poetry like this so much? What poetic techniques do children's poems often use to make them enjoyable? Think of 'The Grand Old Duke of York', for example.

People often turn to poetry for special occasions - for instance, at birthdays, anniversaries, weddings and funerals, and for inscriptions on public buildings and monuments. One of the most-loved poems of recent

years is Text 2A, the poem 'Funeral Blues' by W.H. Auden, which was read at a funeral in the film *Four Weddings and a Funeral*.

b Why do you think people turn to poetry for special occasions like this? What is there in the language of this poem that makes so many people enjoy it so much?

Text 2A

Funeral Blues

Stop all the clocks, cut off the telephone,
Prevent the dog from barking with a juicy bone.
Silence the pianos and with muffled drum
Bring out the coffin, let the mourners come.

Let aeroplanes circle moaning overhead
Scribbling on the sky the message He is Dead,
Put crepe bows round the white necks of the public doves,
Let the traffic policemen wear black cotton gloves.

He was my North, my South, my East and West,
My working week and my Sunday rest,
My noon, my midnight, my talk, my song,
I thought that love would last forever: I was wrong.

The stars are not wanted now, put out every one;
Pack up the moon and dismantle the sun;
Pour away the ocean and sweep up the wood.
For nothing now can ever come to any good.

W.H. Auden

You may have discussed the use of rhyme, rhythm and repetition in poems such as this one: they are three of the most pleasurable aspects of poetry. This is partly because we don't use these features much in ordinary language, and partly because they make poems *sound* pleasurable, almost like music. Rhyme, rhythm and repetition in children's poetry also help children to learn to play with and enjoy language in their early years, but remain pleasurable for adults too.

See 2.3.2 for more on rhyme, rhythm and repetition

Perhaps you also noticed the use of unusual or even absurd ideas and images in these poems – another aspect of poetic language that sets it aside from much ordinary language.

Poetry presents language in a special way that does not follow the rules of ordinary language and so is often used for special occasions when a powerful experience is needed. It's no surprise that some of the techniques of poetry are also often used in other powerful kinds of language – such as speeches, advertising and newspaper headlines.

2.2 Poetry through history

Before the invention of writing and printing, communication was almost exclusively *oral,* and poetry's origins lie in this ancient oral culture, stretching back many thousands of years.

Exploring the difference between verse and prose

Over many centuries, two main modes of writing have been developed, which we call **verse** and **prose**.

- Verse is the mode that we associate mainly with poetry. Note, however, that verse is not only used in *poems*: until around 200 years ago, it was also the standard mode for writing *plays* as in, for instance, all of Shakespeare's plays.
  In verse, the lines of the text are separate and distinct from each other, with each line of text ending where the writer *chooses* to end. Traditionally, each line of verse begins with a capital letter (although many modern poets break this rule). Some poets choose to group lines together into **stanzas**. Verse also traditionally uses rhyme and metre, which helps to make it memorable and powerful when recited.
- Prose is the mode we associate mainly with more ordinary language and is similar to everyday spoken language. It is generally used in modern prose fiction – novels and stories – and drama, as well as a whole range of non-fiction.
  Prose is set out in paragraphs of varying sizes, rather than in lines and stanzas; each line of the text runs into the next line without a break. At the end of each paragraph, there is a break before the next paragraph begins. Rhyme and metre are not used in prose.
- It's important to note that both prose and verse can be *poetic*. The word 'poetic' refers to a particular quality of language – perhaps highly descriptive, passionate or original – which may be found in both verse and prose.

Key terms

verse: the mode of language, mainly associated in literature with poetry, in which text is organised into separate lines, as distinct from prose

prose: the mode of language, mainly associated in literature with fiction, in which text is organised into paragraphs, as distinct from verse

stanza: a group of lines in a poem divided from other lines by means of a blank line; traditionally, every stanza in a poem is the same length and shape; however, in modern poems the size and shape of stanzas can differ within the poem

2.2.1 Telling stories through verse

Until around 200 years ago, most narratives were told in verse. From Homer and Virgil's epic classical poems (the *Iliad*, the *Odyssey* and the *Aeneid*) and the great Greek tragedies, via the Anglo-Saxon epic *Beowulf*, Chaucer's *The Canterbury Tales* and Dante's *Inferno,* to all of Shakespeare´s plays, and Milton's *Paradise Lost* - and many other texts - **narrative poetry** and **verse drama** were the main ways in which writers told stories. Most of these long narratives used rhyming couplets or blank verse, with long metrical lines (for example, iambic pentameters) to achieve a story telling mood. In addition, there were the shorter, more accessible ballads which made up most ordinary people's experience of poetry.

See 2.3.2 for more on rhyming couplets, blank verse and iambic pentameters

See 2.3.2, 5.2.7 and 8.2.4 for more on ballads

It was only after the development of the novel form in the second half of the 18th century that prose narratives (novels and plays written in prose) became more common than verse, and poetry took on a mainly non-narrative character. Even after that, poets continued to tell stories, long and short, in various different verse forms, including such poems as Coleridge's 'The Rime of the Ancient Mariner', Crabbe's 'The Borough', Longfellow's 'The Song of Hiawatha', Yeats's 'The Death of Cuchulain', Belloc's *Cautionary Tales for Children*, and a range of narrative poetry by Burns, Keats, Browning, Rossetti, Tennyson, Hardy, Auden, Betjeman, Frost, and many others.

Although narrative verse is far less common today than in previous centuries, contemporary poets do still produce it, most often for children - and in modern versions or translations of older narratives such as Simon Armitage's recent re-telling of the great medieval poem 'Sir Gawain and the Green Knight'. Many recent poets, such as U.A. Fanthorpe, Liz Lochhead and Carol Ann Duffy, have written short narrative poems, for instance in the form of monologues.

2.2.2 Singing songs through verse

Verse has been associated with singing songs for as many thousands of years as it has been associated with storytelling - and even today poetry and song are closely connected. In Ancient Greece and Rome, **lyric poetry** was accompanied by a lyre or harp; later lyric verse lost its musical accompaniment, but retained its song-like form.

Unlike narrative poems, lyric poems tend to be short and reflective; they can usually be recognised by their regular stanzas, often (though not always) with relatively short lines, and often with strong repeating elements such as metre, rhyme or refrain.

Key terms

narrative poetry: stories told in verse

verse drama: plays written in verse

lyric poetry: song-like poetry, usually with short regular stanzas, often expressing strong emotion or personal feelings

See 2.3.2 for more on metre, rhyme, stanzas and refrain

Like narrative verse, lyric verse has thrived in English literature since the Anglo-Saxons. In the medieval era, much lyric verse was religious in nature, but it gradually became associated more with the idea of love poetry as, for instance, in the sonnets of Shakespeare and the metaphysical verse of Donne.

The Romantic and Victorian poets, as well as many 20th century poets, broadened the range of lyric verse beyond love poetry to discuss a range of personal feelings, emotions and views, as well as moral, philosophical and political ideas (from Blake's *Songs of Innocence and of Experience,* for instance, to the war poetry of Owen and Sassoon).

Many poets in the later 20th century and the current century have used lyric verse to describe or reflect on the realities of modern life, often using a less formal 'poetic' style of language than was traditionally associated with lyric verse (as, for instance, the poetry of Philip Larkin and Tony Harrison.)

Exploring the value of lyrics

The distinction between poetry and lyrics can be controversial. In 2008, English Literature exams at Cambridge University featured a question that asked students to compare the lyrics of love songs by Amy Winehouse, Bob Dylan and Billie Holiday with a love poem by the Elizabethan poet Sir Walter Raleigh. The inclusion of these in the exams caused a sensation in newspapers and television news that week.

Exploring the overlap between narrative and lyric verse

Although narrative and lyric verse are generally distinguished from each other, in fact there is some overlap between them, especially in the *ballad* form. The ballad is both lyric (song-like) and narrative (storytelling) verse. The ballad was a popular means of telling short stories in medieval times, and has continued to be popular in poetry and popular song to the present day.

See 2.3.2 for more on the ballad form

2.2.3 Exploring ideas through verse

Lyric and narrative have been two of the most important types of poetry throughout history. But there is also a third major category that is a little harder to define: extended **discursive poetry** exploring philosophical and political ideas in depth, in the form of a long poetic essay. Such works might, for instance, set out to explore ideas about meaning in life, or to make arguments about culture, society or history, or satirise current attitudes or events.

Poets used verse for this type of exploration partly to make what might otherwise seem quite dry subject matter into something that would inspire both reason and the imagination through the use of poetic language. Like narrative verse, such poetry tended to be written in long lines of continuous verse using rhyming couplets or blank verse.

Satire has been a common subject for discursive poetry since classical times. The satires of the Roman poets, Horace and Juvenal, inspired many 18th century poets, such as Jonathan Swift, author of the prose satire *Gulliver's Travels*, who was also known for writing satires in verse such as the 'Satirical Elegy on the Death of a Late Famous General'. The contemporary poet Tony Harrison is also known for writing gritty satires such as his controversial poem 'v'.

Although little of this type of verse is written today, discursive poetry was common from at least Greek and Roman times until the 18th century: famous examples include the Roman writer Lucretius' long poem about 'the nature of things' (*De Rerum Natura*), and the 18th century English poet Alexander Pope's 'Essay on Man', a reflection on the relationship between science and religion.

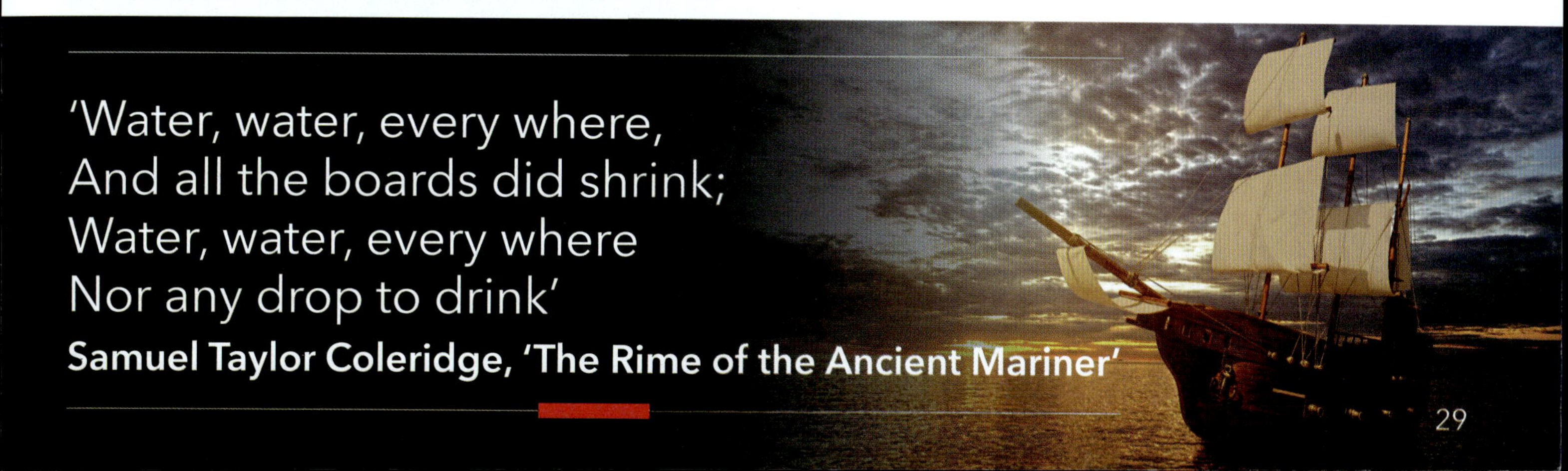

'Water, water, every where,
And all the boards did shrink;
Water, water, every where
Nor any drop to drink'

Samuel Taylor Coleridge, 'The Rime of the Ancient Mariner'

Key terms

discursive poetry: poetry that discusses, makes arguments about and/or satirises philosophical, historical and political ideas and topics

satire: humorous or ironical comment on topical issues, often intended to ridicule and expose the failings of individuals and societies

2.2.4 Modernism: breaking with tradition

Until the 20th century, almost all poems were written according to a set of conventions developed over many centuries. Poems were expected to use elegant language and be beautiful to listen to. They were also expected to be set out in a regular form using techniques such as rhyme, metre and stanzas in a traditional way.

However, in the early 20th century, the advent of modernism brought about unprecedented change in the way that much poetry was written, reflecting a modern age of challenge and experimentation. In all the expressive arts - music, visual art, dance, drama, poetry and fiction - artists began to push at the boundaries of convention, moving away from the traditional forms and rules that had governed art for centuries.

See 3.3.6 and 8.2.4 for more on modernism

2.2.5 Poetry today

The influence of T.S. Eliot and the other modernist poets has been immense throughout the 20th century and into the 21st. Today, poets write in a variety of styles and forms from the highly traditional to the highly experimental. Many adopt a course somewhere in between, borrowing ideas from traditional verse and from modernist verse. Contemporary poetry publishing is thriving, poetry readings are more popular than they have ever been, and many poets are well-known national figures - such as Simon Armitage and Carol Ann Duffy, the current UK **Poet Laureate**.

In recent decades, especially since the rise of pop music in the 1960s and 70s, and the development of hip-hop during the 1980s, popular poetry performance has also become a vibrant feature of the poetry scene. A new form of oral culture has grown up centred on **poetry slam** performances and competitions. These can take in a wide range of styles of poetry, from improvised rap to more traditional kinds of poetry. As a result, writing and improvising poetry has hugely increased in popularity with young people.

The art of writing song lyrics has also increased massively since the 1960s, with many young people following the example of the singer-songwriters and bands who have written highly poetic song lyrics over the last half century.

Key terms

Poet Laureate: the official national poet

poetry slam: a competition or performance at which poets recite or improvise their poems, especially popular with young people

2.3 Approaching poetry

You might be tempted to see poems as awkward puzzles with irritatingly difficult meanings that need to be solved like crosswords. But remember that poets

'Under the brown fog of a winter dawn,
A crowd flowed over London Bridge,
 so many,
I had not thought death had undone
 so many.'

T.S.Eliot, 'The Waste Land'

enjoy shaping language in expressive ways to help convey meanings and ideas as effectively as possible. Don't feel that you have to get 'the right answer' and reduce a poem to little more than a paraphrased meaning. Instead look at ambiguity of meaning and language play as part of what makes poetry interesting and pleasurable.

Another temptation to be avoided is treating poems as a kind of collection of random literary devices and techniques that have to be identified and listed, without any real sense of how all these things connect to convey the thoughts, feelings and ideas that the poet wants to express in a particular and effective way.

Exploring ways of looking at poetry

A poem that has become very popular in recent years is 'Introduction to Poetry' by the contemporary American poet and English teacher Billy Collins. In it, he says he wants his students, among other things, to 'waterski across the surface of the poem'. Instead, they seem to want to 'tie the poem to a chair with rope' and 'torture' it in order to 'find out what it really means'. Look for the whole poem on the Poetry Foundation website or for Billy Collins on YouTube and TedTalks.

In this section of the unit, we encourage you to take a broader view of poetry to help you to understand better:

- the way in which poems function as complete works of art that have a pleasurable impact on the reader - rather like a painting in an art gallery
- the language 'game' that the writer plays with the reader in poetry, and the pleasure that this can produce.

2.3.1 Experiencing poetry: the art of the reader

More than any other form of literature, poetry is an *expressive* art - in some ways like painting, music or dance - designed to evoke an *aesthetic* response in the reader, a response by which the reader becomes aware of the beauty or power of the work and engages actively in interpreting it.

ACTIVITY 3

Responding to poetry as art

a Now look at Text 2B and think about your responses to it. As you read the poem, be sure to hear it dramatically in your head. What impact does it have on you? What do you think it might be about? How do you feel about the ambiguity of the poem?

b Look at the structure of the poem. What use is made of repetition as a device? What is the effect of this? How else is the poem structured? As you think about structural devices, what effect do you find they have on the mood or tone of the poem?

c Finally, think about what the poem means. Is it possible to assign clear meaning or meanings to the poem? If not, does it matter? If you're not sure about the meaning of the poem, would more information help you? What role might the title play, or knowing about the author?

Text 2B

In the beginning was Scream
Who begat Blood
Who begat Eye
Who begat Fear
Who begat Wing
Who begat Bone
Who begat Granite
Who begat Violet
Who begat Guitar
Who begat Sweat
Who begat Adam
Who begat Mary
Who begat God
Who begat Nothing
Who begat Never
Never Never Never

Who begat Crow

Screaming for Blood
Grubs, crusts

Anything

Trembling featherless elbows in the nest's filth

Check your response in the Ideas section on Cambridge Elevate

You may have identified several ways in which paintings and poems are similar and different. For instance, like paintings, poems often make use of a variety of aesthetic techniques with sensual effects – such as vivid imagery, shape, pattern and sound – to help convey meanings in a more powerful way than prose. These can be as powerful as, or more powerful than, the arguments or thoughts expressed in the poem, and make the experience of the poem memorable.

Another important point that might have emerged is the idea that meanings, whether in poetry or painting, cannot always be defined absolutely. In general, poems tend to have more concrete meaning than paintings, because words come with definitions, which by their very nature tend to tie down meaning to a greater extent than in art or music. Nevertheless, both painters and poets are often insistent that the 'point' of their work is not simply to express meaning, but also to convey atmosphere, mood and emotion in powerful ways.

Exploring sound in poetry

One vital aspect of poetry that does not feature in visual art is sound, which is a central part of its appeal. For this reason, it's important always to 'hear' a poem in your head when you read it. Sound can feature in several ways in poetry:

- Rhythm can be created by the use of metre, and also by various kinds of repetition – of words, sounds or structures.
- Rhyme often features in poetry, as well as other sound effects – **alliteration**, **assonance** and **consonance**, often having an **onomatopoeic** effect.
- The pace and mood of a poem – the speed and feeling with which it might be read – can be affected by the use of rhythm and rhyme, the length of the lines and stanzas, the choice of long or short words and so on.

Whichever techniques the poet uses to enhance the sound of the poem, the way a poem sounds often reflects and strengthens its meaning.

Many poets and painters are also clear that they want their work to provoke a variety of possible responses in the reader; and it's possible that some of those responses are not ones that the artist intended. In the end, whether the poet or painter had a specific meaning in mind or not, they are not usually available (or willing) to tell us what this might have been.

Key terms

alliteration: use of a repeated *letter* sound for effect (e.g. 'In sooth I know not why I am so sad')

assonance: the use of repeated identical or similar *vowel* sounds in nearby words (e.g. 'she needs cream for her feet')

consonance: repeated sounds produced by consonants at the beginning, middle or end of nearby words (e.g. 'he chuckled as he kicked the bucket')

onomatopoeia: when words sound like what they mean (e.g. clap, bark, whistle)

So we are left with the process of interpretation. In 'the real world', we weigh up our responses and come to decisions about what we think or feel. This does not mean, however, that, for the purposes of *studying* poetry, *any* meaning will do! In the literature classroom, you will learn how to *evaluate* interpretations using evidence from both inside and outside the text.

2.3.2 Creating poetry: the art of the writer

Your understanding and interpretation of poetry can be transformed by learning about what poets actually *do* when they write poetry. Poets use a wide range of literary techniques and devices to convey their meanings. Imagery is one of the most important because of its descriptive power; sound effects such as alliteration and assonance can also be very powerful. In addition, the poet's choice of words, and the way those words are put together, can create different styles, tones, modes and atmospheres. All these techniques are shared by poets and other writers. In the rest of this unit, we are going to focus on a set of techniques which is unique to poetry: the techniques of **poetic form**.

See 2.2.1 for more on the techniques writers use to shape meaning

Every poem and every poet has their own story, of course; but all poets work within and around a set of traditions and conventions which determine the shape and style of their poems. The decisions poets make when writing often involve using, rejecting or adapting these conventions in particular ways.

The combination of conventions used to shape a poem on the page is known as its **form**. We can describe the form of any poem by identifying the decisions the poet has made about how to shape the poem. But to really get to grips with poetry, and in addition to thinking about *why* poets decide to write using particular forms, we also need to consider the reader and its *effect* on the reader.

Key terms

poetic form: a set of techniques used by poets to give poems a particular shape and structure

form (of a poem): the particular shape and structure of an individual poem

Rhyme

A poem may be rhymed or unrhymed – or sometimes a mixture of the two. There are no hard and fast rules about the effect of using **rhyme** or not doing so: as with most literary devices, effects must be judged in the context of the poem as a whole. However, rhymed verse often (not always) produces a lighter, more lively mood than unrhymed verse, and is almost always used in humorous or comic verse.

The **rhyme scheme** of a poem is denoted by allocating a letter for each new set of rhymes. For instance the rhyme scheme of a **sonnet** might be denoted as follows: ABABCDCDEFEFGG. In this scheme – known as a Shakespearean sonnet – there are three rhyming units: ABAB/CDCD/EFEFGG.

We can describe the rhyming *units* according to the number of lines they have:

- two lines: **couplet**
- three lines: **tercet** or **triplet**
- four lines: **quatrain**
- five lines: **quintet** or **cinquain**
- six lines: **sestet**, **sextet** or **sexain**
- seven lines: **septet**
- eight lines: **octave** or **octet**
- above eight lines: no formal name is given.

Note that these rhyming units can occur *within* stanzas, or they can make up a whole stanza.

In the Shakespearean sonnet, there are two quatrains (four-line units, ABAB and CDCD) and one final sestet (a six-line unit, EFEFGG). Note, however, that although a sonnet is typically 14 lines long, it can use a variety of different rhyme schemes.

Exploring the sonnet

Some poetic forms have developed over time as specific genres in themselves. For instance, the 14-line sonnet was immensely popular in the Renaissance, when it was used exclusively for love poetry. The sonnet tradition still continues, now used for a wider range of subjects. The long 14-line stanza of the sonnet enables the poet to formulate a kind of mini-argument or narrative within the stanza that often involves a shift in meaning or approach – often a surprising conclusion – in the last six lines (sestet) or in the last couplet. This shift is often referred to as the **turn** in the poem.

ACTIVITY 4

Rhyme schemes

Read one of Shakespeare's most famous sonnets, Sonnet 18, in Text 2C. What is the rhyme scheme of this sonnet? Can you identify where the turn in the meaning of the poem occurs?

Text 2C

Sonnet 18

Shall I compare thee to a summer's day?
Thou art more lovely and more temperate.
Rough winds do shake the darling buds of May,
And summer's lease hath all too short a date.
Sometime too hot the eye of heaven shines,
And often is his gold complexion dimmed;
And every fair from fair sometime declines,
By chance, or nature's changing course, untrimmed;
But thy eternal summer shall not fade,
Nor lose possession of that fair thou ow'st,
Nor shall death brag thou wand'rest in his shade,
When in eternal lines to Time thou grow'st.
    So long as men can breathe, or eyes can see,
    So long lives this, and this gives life to thee.

William Shakespeare

Check your responses in the Ideas section on Cambridge Elevate

Key terms

rhyme: where two or more words at the end of lines of verse share the same sound

rhyme scheme: a regular pattern of rhyming throughout a poem

sonnet: a 14-line poem which can use a variety of rhyme schemes to make up the 14 lines

turn: a point towards the end of a sonnet or other poem where there is a shift in the direction of the poem's meaning

Unrhymed and half-rhymed verse

Where poems, like Sonnet 18, use rhymes throughout, the strong sound of the rhyming pattern can be an insistent, almost attention-seeking, feature of the verse. One reason why a poet might choose to write in unrhymed verse, therefore, is to create a more serious, reflective mood in which the reader's attention is directed more fully towards the poem's ideas, or other aspects of its language or form.

Furthermore, in long narrative or dramatic verse, too much rhyme can become wearing to listen to, so many poets use unrhymed verse for that reason. Most of Shakespeare's plays, for instance, were written in what we call **blank verse** – verse that has a regular metre but does not have any rhyme. Famously, Shakespeare often inserted rhyming couplets at the ends of scenes (or long speeches) of unrhymed blank verse to provide a memorable conclusion and to signal that the scene or speech had come to an end.

As an alternative to unrhymed verse, a poet might choose to use some form of **half rhyme**. Until the 20th century, rhymes were almost always full rhymes of the traditional sort, but the advent of modernism brought with it experimentation with new forms of rhyme:

- **half rhyme:** a rhyme where only the final consonant of the rhyming words is the same, not the vowel (e.g. ha**t** and co**t**, sha**pe** and kee**p**)
- **vowel rhyme**: a form of assonance where only the vowels in the rhyming words match each other (e.g. h**a**t and l**a**p, m**a**n and fl**a**t)
- **consonant rhyme**: a form of consonance where both consonants in the rhyming words match each other (e.g. **h**a**t** and **h**o**t**, **l**i**mp** and **l**u**mp**)
- **visual or eye rhyme**: where the words look the same but don't sound the same (e.g. c**ome** and h**ome**, g**ive** and d**ive**).

Using half rhyme provides both writer and reader with a rhyming structure while reducing its force. In some cases, the use of half rhyme might also reflect some aspect of the meaning of a poem, such as a sense of incompleteness or imperfection.

Exploring the effects of syllable rhyme

The number of syllables that rhyme in a word can also be significant. The more syllables that rhyme, in general, the lighter the effect. Where three syllables in a word rhyme, this is almost always used for comic effect! We describe these different quantities of rhyme as:

- single rhyme = one rhyming syllable (e.g. coat, boat)
- double rhyme = two rhyming syllables (e.g. bumper, jumper)
- triple rhyme = three rhyming syllables (e.g. jollity, quality).

Metre

Until the 20th century, all Western poetry was written using **metre**, a rhythmic pattern similar to beats and bars in music. Like rhyme, one of the functions of metre was originally to help reciters of verse to memorise it and pass it on. Even now, many poets still use rhyme and metre because of the pleasure that pattern, rhythm and structure can bring to both writers and readers.

Metre is described by identifying the number and pattern of stressed and unstressed beats in the lines of a poem. There are several different types of metre, but perhaps the most significant in English poetry has been the **iambic pentameter**, which is the metre used in Chaucer's *The Canterbury Tales* and Shakespeare's plays.

A **pentameter** is a line of poetry with five **feet** or measures (a foot being similar to a bar of music). An iambic pentameter is a line in which each foot is an **iamb** – a unit in which the first syllable is unstressed and the second syllable is stressed. We can show this pattern of stresses as follows, using a well-known line from *Romeo and Juliet:*

He **jests** / at **scars** / that **ne** / ver **felt** / a **wound**

You can see that there are five stressed (in bold) and five unstressed syllables in this line, creating the rhythmic pattern that is the metre of the line.

Exploring scansion

The process of measuring out or 'scanning' the metre of a line of poetry is called **scansion**. The symbols '—' and '◡' are marked above the words to mark out the stressed and unstressed syllables, while the symbol / is used to show the feet.

All metres can be described by naming the number of feet in the line (**dimeter**, **trimeter**, **tetrameter**, pentameter, **hexameter**, and so on), and the type of feet that are used. The four main metrical feet are iambs, **trochees**, **anapaests** and **dactyls**.

ACTIVITY 5

Writing iambic pentameters and tetrameters

One of the reasons why iambic pentameters have been so popular over many centuries for writing poetry (especially longer poetry) is that they are close to the natural rhythms of speech and writing in English. So you will find that it is not difficult to make up your own iambic pentameters: they trip off the tongue quite easily.

Look at the examples in Text 2D.

Text 2D

I **went** to **see** my **mo**ther **yes**ter**day**

But **when** I **got** there **she** had **gone** away

In **Lon**don, **there's** a **ri**ver **called** the **Thames**

With **bridg**es **you** can **cross** a**long** its **length**

a Try writing some examples of your own. See whether you can have a conversation with a friend in iambic pentameters.

b Now write some iambic tetrameters – with only four iambic feet. Look at the example in Text 2E.

Key terms

blank verse: unrhymed verse – usually, verse that has metre but no rhyme

half rhyme: where only the final consonant of the rhyming words is the same

vowel rhyme: where only the vowel of the rhyming words is the same

consonant rhyme: where the consonants at the beginning and end are the same in both rhyming words, but not the vowel

visual/eye rhyme: where the rhyming words look the same but don't sound the same

metre: a regular rhythm used to structure a whole line of verse

iambic pentameter: a metre consisting of five iambic feet

pentameter: a metre consisting of five feet

foot: a unit of rhythm in a metrical line

iamb: a metrical foot consisting of a short beat followed by a long beat (e.g. at**tempt**)

scansion: the system used to measure the metre of a line of verse

dimeter: a metre consisting of two feet

trimeter: a metre consisting of three feet

tetrameter: a metre consisting of four feet

hexameter: a metre consisting of six feet

trochee: a metrical foot consisting of a long beat followed by a short beat (e.g. **leg**end)

anapaest: a metrical foot consisting of two short beats followed by one long beat (e.g. under**foot**)

dactyl: a metrical foot consisting of one long beat followed by two short ones (e.g. **mur**muring)

Text 2E

My dog has eaten all my lunch

There's nothing left for me to eat

You will find that many poems you encounter during your course are written using iambic pentameters, tetrameters or trimeters – for instance, poems by

Geoffrey Chaucer (14th century); John Milton and John Donne (17th century); Jonathan Swift, William Blake and Robert Burns (18th century); John Keats, Robert Browning, Christina Rossetti, Lord Tennyson and George Crabbe (19th century); Thomas Hardy, W.B.Yeats, Robert Frost, W.H. Auden, John Betjeman and Tony Harrison (20th century).

Varying metre

Just as rhyme can dominate a poem if it is too heavy and unvaried, so metre can sometimes seem tediously rhythmic if it is not varied at times. So, poets have often tried to lessen the dominating effect of metre while at the same time retaining the essential rhythmic structure. Shakespeare, for instance, frequently and deliberately disrupted the flow of his chosen metre to create specific emphases in the verse, and to ensure that the verse did not become monotonous. For instance, in *Hamlet*:

To **be** / or **not** / to **be**: / **that** is the / **ques**tion.

Hamlet, Act 3, Scene 1, line 55

In this example, the first three feet are iambic feet, but Shakespeare varies the stress pattern in the fourth and fifth feet so that the stress is on the first syllable of each foot. This enables him to place a strong emphasis on the word 'that', so that one reads the line 'To be or not to be: **that** is the question.'

As well as creating emphasis on particular words or ideas, such variations in metre can sometimes reflect the meaning of a line or a whole poem, for instance by suggesting disruption or imperfection. The disrupted metres of Hamlet's speeches, for example, help to convey the passion, rage and madness that characterise him in the play.

Stanzas

As well as deciding on whether (and how) to use rhyme and metre, poets must make decisions about how to *arrange* the lines on the page. The traditional choices are either continuous verse (without stanzas) or **stanzaic verse**. Continuous verse is mainly used in longer narrative or dramatic texts; stanzas, on the other hand, though used in poems of all lengths, are generally associated with shorter, lyric verse.

Stanzas come in many forms and are used in various ways. These are some of the ways in which the form and use of stanzas may vary.

- **Number of lines:** Stanzas may be any number of lines long, from 2-line couplets to 14-line sonnets, and even longer. Stanzas between four and eight lines long are particularly common.
- **Rhyme and metre:** Some stanza forms use a regular rhyme scheme and/or metre; others do not use rhyme or metre at all.
- **Shape of stanza:** In some stanza forms, all the lines will be the same length and have the same metre in each stanza. In others, the stanza form may include lines of different lengths and metres. For example, in the four-line **ballad form**, the first and third lines are longer than the second and fourth and have a different metre, as in Text 2F from Coleridge's 'The Rime of the Ancient Mariner'.

Text 2F

And **now** there **came** both **mist** and **snow**,
    And **it** grew **won**drous **cold**:
And **ice**, mast-**high**, came **float**ing **by**,
    As **green** as **em**er**ald**.

Samuel Coleridge, 'The Rime of the Ancient Mariner'

- **Consistency of form:** In most stanzaic poems, all the stanzas will have the same number of lines and the same metrical and rhyming pattern (if they

'To sleep, perchance to dream: aye, there's the rub.'

William Shakespeare, *Hamlet*

have them). But in some poems, especially in modern free verse, the stanza form may differ from stanza to stanza.

As with rhyme and metre, poets' choices can have a major effect on the sound, the mood and sometimes even the meaning of the poem, although it's not usually possible to say that using a particular form will inevitably have a particular effect. While it's true that some forms have specific associations – for instance, the **limerick** is invariably comic – in general, poetic forms work in combination with all the other elements of a poem, and so must be judged in context.

Key terms

stanzaic verse: poetry written in stanzas

ballad form: a four-line rhyming stanza in which the first and third lines are a different length and metre from the second and fourth line

limerick: a five-line formulaic comic poem

Exploring the ballad

Ballads are popular narrative poems that were originally spoken or sung, and were handed down orally. They usually tell tales of doomed love affairs. They have a regular structure, consisting of four-line stanzas, an ABCB rhyming pattern, and a regular metre. The longer first and third lines are iambic tetrameters; the second and fourth lines are iambic trimeters.

Many folk ballads still exist from the medieval age, but poets have continued to use the ballad form to tell stories since then. They were particularly popular with the Romantic poets, especially Wordsworth and Coleridge, who were attracted by their relatively simple form and language.

ACTIVITY 6

Looking at stanzas

In the poem 'The Flea' by John Donne, there are three stanzas, each with nine lines. Look carefully at how one of the stanzas (shown in Text 2G) is constructed.

a What is the rhyme scheme?

b What metre or metres are used? Read the lines out loud and see whether you can feel the beats in each line. Does the rhythm match that of an iambic pentameter? If not, how is it different? Do all the lines have the same metre or do some of them have different metres? Can you see a pattern?

c You will notice that three of the lines are indented at the end of the stanza. Why might that be?

Check your responses in the Ideas section on Cambridge Elevate

Text 2G

Mark but this flea, and mark in this,
How little that which thou deniest me is;
It sucked me first, and now sucks thee,
And in this flea our two bloods mingled be;
Thou know'st that this cannot be said
A sin, nor shame, nor loss of maidenhead,
    Yet this enjoys before it woo,
    And pampered swells with one blood made of two,
    And this, alas, is more than we would do

John Donne, 'The Flea'

Lines: end-stopping, caesura and enjambement

As well as deciding on a form, the poet also needs to make decisions about how the words they use will *fit into* that form. In particular, the poet must decide on the relationship between the *lines* of the poem and the *sentences* that fit onto those lines.

In traditional verse, it is usual for the poet to mould sentences to single lines, couplets or stanzas, so that the grammar of the sentence fits in with the line breaks. In the simplest verse of this kind, full stops and commas almost always come at the end of a line, and there is usually a convenient grammatical pause at the end of each line. This is called **end-stopping**. The example in Text 2H is from 'The Passionate Shepherd to His Love' by Christopher Marlowe.

Text 2H

Come live with me and be my love,
And we will all the pleasures prove
That hills and valleys, dale and field,
And all the craggy mountains yield.

Christopher Marlow,
'The Passionate Shepherd to His Love'

In more complex poetry, there may be a more fluid relationship between sentences and lines. If a sentence ends in the middle of a line, this causes a **caesura**, an enforced pause in mid-line. Sometimes this can seem quite abrupt and surprising because it appears to be in the 'wrong' place. Shakespeare used this technique often, partly to emphasise certain words, and partly to make the experience of reading or listening to the verse more varied, imitating the variable rhythms of ordinary speech rather than constantly adhering to the patterns and rhythms of formal poetry.

Similarly, where a sentence does not stop or pause at the end of a line, but flows over to the next line in an unexpected way (often before or after a caesura), this is known as **enjambement**. As with caesura, and for the same reasons, Shakespeare often used enjambement.

You can see Shakespeare using a combination of caesura and enjambement in Text 2I, an extract from *Macbeth,* perhaps to reflect the chaos of the emergency that Macbeth faces at this moment in the play.

Text 2I

... – I have no spur
To prick the sides of my intent but only
Vaulting ambition which o'erleaps itself
And falls on th'other – How now! What news?

Macbeth, Act 1, Scene 7, lines 25-28

ACTIVITY 7

Enjambement and caesura in *Macbeth*

Look carefully at the lines from *Macbeth* in Text 2I. Find at least one surprising use of enjambement and one of caesura in these lines. Can you explain how these techniques help to convey Macbeth's stress at this moment?

In modern poetry, poets have often experimented with even more complex uses of enjambement and caesura. Like Shakespeare, they have tried to 'break out' of the rhythmic structure of their chosen form, for instance, by using enjambement to allow words to flow from one stanza to the next as if the stanza division were not there.

Key terms

end-stopping: where a unit of grammatical sense coincides with the end of a line of verse

caesura: where a unit of grammatical sense ends in the middle of a line of verse

enjambement: where a unit of grammatical sense flows over the end of a line of verse and onto the next line

Working with and rebelling against conventions

Finally, a crucial point about poetic form. We have seen how poets often use traditional elements of poetic form such as rhyme, metre, stanzas and lines, and yet at the same time seem to break or ignore the 'rules' of the forms they have chosen. Why do they do this? It might be tempting to think that it's because they 'couldn't make the words fit' into their chosen form: but in fact, poets make these choices very consciously.

Imagine a fountain consisting of a cascade of water from one vessel into another vessel and then more vessels. The water pours into one vessel, overflows that vessel and carries on into another vessel just below it, and so on. There is a special beauty to the way in which the flowing water moulds itself to the vessels and yet at the same time flows on past them. This tension between the containers that hold the water and the water itself is what makes the fountain so pleasing and surprising.

For many poets and readers, the tension between the form of the poem on the one hand and the words and meanings contained within that form on the other provides similarly pleasing and surprising sensations, which can enhance both the feeling and the meaning of the poem. This explains why many poets like to have their cake *and* eat it: to use the regular shapes of poetic form, but to break out of them or rebel against them at the same time.

Free verse

As we have seen, many modern poets continue to use the traditional elements of poetic form described in the previous section albeit in rather unusual ways. However, modern poets have another choice they can make: to abandon these elements of form altogether and write what is known as **free verse.** You will find that several of the modern poets you may study write in varieties of free verse – such as U.A Fanthorpe, Philip Larkin and Liz Lochhead.

In free verse, the poet does not have to abide by any rules or conventions about the shape of the poem. Rhyme and metre are not used. The lines and stanzas of the poem do not all have to be the same length. Sometimes the first letter of each line is not a capital letter. Poems written in free verse may feel more spontaneous, with the shape of the poem appearing to imitate the natural spontaneity of speech or thought.

Key terms

free verse: poetry written without rhyme, metre or regular length of lines and stanzas

Exploring poetic form

For a funny and accessible introduction to poetic form, see *The Ode Less Travelled* by Stephen Fry. *How Poetry Works* by Phil Roberts is another accessible book that explores many aspects of poetry including form and language.

2.4 Bringing it all together

2.4.1 How much do you know?

These questions ask you to bring together the elements you have studied in this unit. Look at Text 1J, Ted Hughes' poem 'Wind'. In it, Hughes describes the effect of a storm on a house, its inhabitants and the surrounding countryside.

1 Read the poem silently to yourself, but making sure you hear it in your head. Read it a second time, and this time try to hear it more dramatically. At this point, don't worry about the form of the poem or the techniques that the writer uses. Think about the kind of response to the poem that the poet might have wanted a reader to have. How would you describe the impact of the poem? What does it sound and feel like? What kind of poem is it?
2 Read the poem one more time and listen to the sounds it makes. Can you hear rhythms or patterns or sound effects (such as alliteration, assonance or onomatopoeia) in the poem? How do these seem to contribute to the way the poet describes the wind in the poem?
3 Now, think about the poet's use of imagery. Make a list of images in the poem: they might be metaphors, similes or simple descriptions. Think about each image separately. How do these images help us to visualise the scene and feel its power? Can you identify anything that connects the images?
4 Now, look carefully at:
   - the use of rhyme
   - the use of metre
   - the use of lines and stanzas.

   What techniques can you find being used? Do you feel that these elements of form contribute to the overall mood or meaning of the poem?

2.4.2 Assessment objectives

In relation to the assessment objectives, this unit has explored:

- how you as a reader can make personal, informed and creative responses to poetry. It has also introduced you to a range of essential terminology and concepts that you might use in thinking and writing about poetry (AO1)
- the ways in which poets shape meanings in verse texts through their use of a variety of conventions and techniques, including the use of poetic forms and structures (AO2)
- some of the history of poetry as a form, introducing some key contextual ideas such as oral culture, performance, reading for pleasure, and modernism (AO3)
- the key elements of the genre of poetry that can be found across a wide range of texts (AO4)
- the roles of interpretation and analysis in reading poetry, with special reference to ideas about pleasure and ambiguity (AO5).

Summary

In this unit, you have learned about:

- the three main types of verse - narrative, lyrical and discursive
- the radical way in which modernism changed poetry in the 20th century
- how poetry thrives today through performance as well as through reading
- the impact of poetry on readers as a form of art that is powerful and pleasurable
- the ways in which poets play games with language and work with the elements of poetic form - rhyme, metre, lines and stanzas.

BEGINNING

3 Drama

In this unit, you will:

- explore the ways in which readers respond to and interpret drama
- explore the ways in which dramatists craft their work and shape meaning
- explore the history of drama and the way it has changed over time.

3.1 Introduction to drama

In your A Level and AS Level courses you have to study and write about drama through the lens of Tragedy and Comedy. At A Level it is compulsory in Paper 1 and optional in Paper 2. At AS Level you will have to write about two drama texts on Paper 1. This unit will enable you to do some preparatory work on drama before you look at it though a specific optic.

Some of you will come to your A Level studies as regular theatre-goers and drama enthusiasts. Some of you will be keen actors yourselves, familiar with the theatre space and the processes involved in staging and enacting drama. Most of you will already have studied a number of Shakespeare plays and other drama texts like J.B. Priestley's *An Inspector Calls* or Arthur Miller's *The Crucible* and *A View from the Bridge*. As you progress to the study of drama texts at A Level, however, you will encounter new concepts about drama as a narrative form (in fact a dual narrative form!) and its functions within the literary and non-literary worlds, the ways in which dramatists tell their stories, and the ways in which these stories are mediated on the stage. You'll think about the differences between reading drama and watching drama (including the vast array of screen drama for both television and the large screen) and the ways in which dramatists, directors, actors and audiences collaborate in the creation of meanings from drama texts.

Drama in and out of the classroom

Most people are enthusiastic consumers of drama, though this is often not experienced in the theatre. Drama tends to be dominated by the prolific access we have to narrative drama on film and television. The Sunday night drama slot has seen extraordinary success for the dramatisation of classic novels such as Jane Austen's *Pride and Prejudice*, Charles Dickens' *Great Expectations* and John Galsworthy's *The Forsyte Saga*, as well as for original screen drama like *The Village* and *Downton Abbey*. There is also a world of popular television drama such as *Doctor Who*, *CSI*, *Inspector Morse*, *Buffy the Vampire Slayer* and *EastEnders,* which reaches mass audiences.

There is also, however, a vibrant theatre 'scene'. Most large towns have their own theatre, and village and church halls around the country regularly host amateur dramatic performances, while major cities have many theatres where an array of musicals, plays and performances of other kinds are staged.

ACTIVITY 1

Is theatre the same as drama?

Many events take place in theatres where an audience comes together to watch and/or participate in a shared experience focused on an event taking place on the stage (see Figure 3A).

Figure 3A

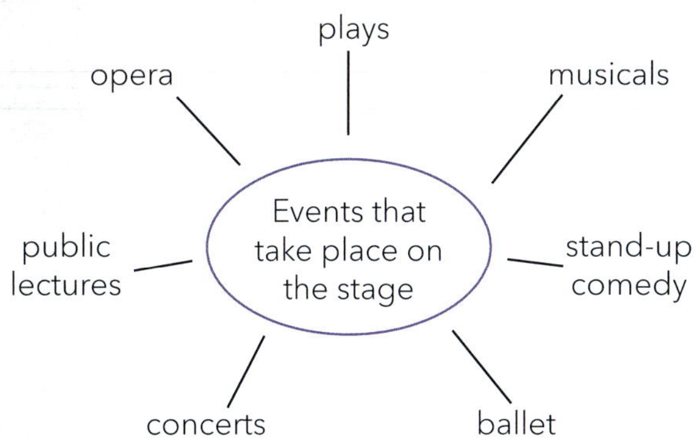

This raises some interesting issues. Jot down your thoughts about questions a–e:

a Are all productions that take place in theatres drama?
b Is there a difference between 'theatre' and 'drama'?
c How does the role of the audience differ in each kind of event?
d How does the role of the performer(s) differ in each case?
e Is there crossover between any of these forms of theatre? (For example, the musical *Les Misérables* might be considered drama and was initially performed by actors from the Royal Shakespeare Company.)

Before thinking about the ways in which you will encounter drama texts as part of your literary studies, think about your experiences of drama to date. Some of these experiences will have been as part of your previous English studies, but others will probably have been gained in other ways, not least by watching television, now one of the major media for the production and consumption of drama.

ACTIVITY 2

Experiences of drama

a Think about your own experience of drama in school, and out of school. How would you sum up your feelings about drama? What kind of experiences have you had over the years? What kind of drama have you enjoyed, or not? How are your experiences of drama different in and out of school?
b Look at the quotation in Text 3A from Joe Winston, an academic of drama education. How does this relate to your own experiences of drama, and how does it make you think about drama texts?

Text 3A

In a written story, context is defined through words alone. In drama, however, it is actually constructed from space, objects and people as well as words.

Joe Winston

3.2 Studying drama

Many parts of literary study are based on the relationship between a solitary reader and a text. That is, by and large, how readers experience novels, non-fiction and poetry. Drama, however, is different. Although you might read a drama text on your own – we'll look in more detail at that later – drama as an art form presupposes a shared, lived experience. Drama texts written for stage production (and in different ways for the screen) depend upon a dynamic interaction between various groups:

- the producer of text (the playwright)
- the mediators of text (a plethora of directors, designers, technicians and actors)
- the receivers of the text (an audience).

The ways in which meaning is created in drama texts, therefore, is rather different to the ways in which it's created in other literary forms. A range of processes go into the 'making' of drama as it lifts from the page, and this in its turn affects the ways in which drama texts need to be read.

The prime impulse for writing drama is generally for it to be viewed on stage or screen: to put it simply, plays are written to be watched, not read. Reading will play a central part in your study of drama, though, and you could argue that drama texts are most objectively approached in their written form.

ACTIVITY 3

Drama and objective reading

Think about the idea of reading a drama text rather than seeing a stage production or a screen adaptation of it. Maybe you could draw on your own prior experience of studying drama.

a What does reading alone allow you access to?
b What does viewing alone give you access to?
c What does viewing add to your ability to interpret?
d What does viewing take away from your ability to interpret?

Check your responses in the Ideas section on Cambridge Elevate

3.2.1 Reading drama texts

At its simplest, reading means the act of decoding and making sense of words on the page - what you're doing now. When you study drama texts, however, reading requires you to do other things as well. You need to visualise the play in performance:

- to imagine the possible effects of staging and stagecraft (for example, set, costume, music, use of stage space, use of props)
- to create characters' voices
- to 'hear' and weigh up different performances of particular lines in your head.

As you read the page, in other words, you need to have an eye on the stage.

You should also make sure that you see multiple stage and/or screen versions of the plays you're studying. Here is how the critic Jean Howard refers to stage productions: 'a particular succession of sights, sounds and events that create a unique theatrical experience with its own tempo, rhythm, and pauses, its own moments of engagement and detachment, and its own natural points of emphasis'.

No two productions of a drama text, in other words, are ever the same as each other. Watching stage and screen productions of the drama texts you're studying is, therefore, like watching creative 'readings'.

Whenever you see a production, you should consider not only *how* the play has been produced, but how it *might be* produced. Watching a variety of productions (and adaptations) of your drama texts will keep the potential meanings of the play alive in your mind and will encourage you to develop creative critical readings of the play for yourself.

Referring to particular productions

There is nothing wrong with making brief reference to staged versions of plays you are studying in a critical essay. However, you should give details of the production to which you're referring (for example, 'in Hytner's 2010 production of *Hamlet* ...') and make clear that this is what you're doing. You should treat the production as a creative critical 'reading' of the text in the same way as you might use critics' or theorists' views of a text.

Reading at one sitting

Lots of people will tell you that plays are meant to be watched not read, but reading is a crucial part of your study of drama texts. It's also the first thing that directors and actors do when they're putting on a play.

Unlike novels, it will only take you a couple of hours to read through most drama texts. If you can, it's really good to do an initial reading of the full play in one sitting. You might want to do this on your own, or you might want to join up with others and do it as a dramatic reading. Either way, an unbroken read through will allow you to:

- experience the play as a whole
- understand the time over which an audience will engage with the drama
- see clearly how the full narrative of the drama works.

Reading is a crucial part of studying drama texts

Don't worry at this stage if you don't understand it all and if some of the language is difficult. There is plenty of time later for scene-by-scene close reading of the play where these things can be sorted out.

3.2.2 From script to stage

We've already seen that studying drama texts involves thinking about the extra dimensions of drama – the ways in which plays have been, and could be, realised on stage. Watching live performances or examples of the many high-quality DVDs and online streamings of live performances provides a great opportunity to explore the translation of a script to the stage.

ACTIVITY 4

From script to stage

Watch one or more versions of a play you have studied or know well. Then write down your responses to questions a–f.

a Was the play in performance as you expected it to be or different?

b What aspects of the play came to life or made sense in production that did not when reading the script?

c Were there any differences between the script and the play in performance? Was anything added, left out or moved around?

d Were you surprised by any of the interpretations or staging?

e Did the staging support, challenge or even undermine your understanding of the play?

f What did the director choose to emphasise? Is this what you'd choose to emphasise? Does it matter if your views differ?

You may also find it useful to read reviews and programmes of different productions of any play you study. This has two obvious advantages: first, you become familiar with the way that critics write about drama and the theatre, and second you're introduced to a variety of ways of looking at the same play in varying performances.

Exploring stage 'languages'

According to Antonin Artaud (French playwright, poet, actor and theatre director), it is not only the words on the page that constitute the language of theatre. Theatre productions consist of more than the words on the page. Other kinds of theatre 'language' are also used, which may be suggested by the text, but which are effectively additions made by a director or a group of actors, artists or technicians. Think carefully about the role of these kinds of theatre 'language', using examples from your own experience of watching plays:

- scenery
- props
- lighting
- the 'period' of a production (historical, contemporary or even futuristic)
- costumes
- hair and make-up
- music
- sound effects.

Think carefully about stage productions you have seen and screen adaptations of plays you know well. How can these be considered as 'languages'? What does each mean? How do you 'read' these different 'languages'? How do they work separately and together to build meaning?

3.2.3 Mise en scène

Literally this means 'put in the scene'. Some dramatists are very specific about the details of what they want to happen on stage. At the beginning of *Look Back in Anger*, John Osborne provides very detailed stage directions, and so does J.B Priestley in *An Inspector Calls*. Shakespeare, on the other hand, provides little guidance – most of the stage directions in his plays are editorial, based on what is happening in the literary text.

Key terms

mise en scène: literally 'put in the scene'; an expression used to describe the design aspects of a stage or screen production

ACTIVITY 5

Mise en scène

Look carefully at Text 3B, an extract from the opening stage direction of *Death of a Salesman*, by Arthur Miller.

a What demands does this opening place upon the director and actors?

b How would you approach these scenes as a director or actor in terms of what the stage directions imply? What would you want to achieve?

Text 3B

A melody is heard, played upon a flute. It is small and fine, telling of grass and trees and the horizon. The curtain rises.

Before us is the SALESMAN'S *house. We are aware of towering, angular shapes behind it, surrounding it on all sides...*

Before the house lies an apron, curving beyond the forestage... This forward area serves as the back yard as well as the locale of all WILLY'S *imaginings...*

From the right, WILLY LOMAN, *the* Salesman, *enters, carrying two large sample cases... He is past sixty years of age, dressed quietly... A word-sigh escapes his lips – it might be* 'Oh boy, Oh boy'... LINDA, *his wife, has stirred in her bed at the right. She gets out and puts on a robe, listening. Most often jovial, she has developed an iron repression of her exceptions to* WILLY'S *behaviour...*

Arthur Miller, *Death of a Salesman*

3.2.4 Staging drama texts

An effective way of building your knowledge about how drama texts function is to think about developing your own staging of a play you are studying - or at least part of it.

ACTIVITY 6

Developing stage resources

Think about a play you know very well or perhaps a drama text that you're studying. Now develop your ideas for a set of resources for use in performance, to include:

- set designs
- costume designs
- props
- lighting
- incidental music (maybe pre-composed, for example, Jean Sibelius' *The Tempest* or Edvard Grieg's music for *Peer Gynt*, or music you choose)
- colour schemes for use in the production
- concepts surrounding a contemporary, other time period, modern-day or futuristic setting for the play.

Present your ideas to other students explaining how and why you believe they will work well in relation to the play's genre.

This will get you thinking creatively about your reading of drama texts as well as how the different component 'languages' of drama combine to create meaning. It will also allow you to consider issues relating to audience response. For example, how would you understand the Inspector in *An Inspector Calls* differently if he wore different kinds of coat? Or, what kind of drinking vessel could be used to poison Gertrude at the end of *Hamlet*?

ACTIVITY 7

Exploring staging

There are many other ways in which you could also approach this aspect of drama texts.

a Consider a character from a play you're studying as if you were an actor. Answer these questions in as much detail as possible.
   - What does my character say about him/herself?
   - What does my character say about other characters?
   - What do other characters say about my character?
   - What does my character do (for example, entering, exiting, shaking hands, drinking, kissing) and how would he/she do these things?
   - What does the playwright say about my character (for example, in notes on the cast list, in stage directions)?

b Read a range of reviews of stage performances of the play - where possible from different time periods. What do the reviewers say about the play and its production? How does this provide an insight into ways of reading the play?

c Look at photographs of stage productions or 'stills' from filmed live productions. In what ways do these images reflect the content of the text? What has the director or designer brought to the text? How are these likely to affect audience response?

d Listen to the incidental music to a play (for example, Felix Mendelssohn's for *A Midsummer Night's Dream*) and then read the relevant extract of the source text. How is such music likely to shape the way a play appears on the stage?

e Look at a variety of costumes for particular characters in a set text. What impact would these different costumes make on an audience? What different information would they give us about the character?

3.2.5 Doing drama

You can see that studying drama texts involves layers and dimensions not shared by prose fiction and poetry. A really useful way to develop your understanding of these extra dimensions and your engagement with them is to approach selected extracts of your drama texts as if you were going to stage them. Maybe you could *actually* stage them. By using a variety of drama approaches to text - either with or without your teachers - you can explore:

- how different dramatic techniques can be used to convey action, character, atmosphere and tension
- different ways in which words, actions, sound and staging combine to create drama
- how actors work with texts to build meaning and effective productions.

3.2.6 Going to the theatre

In order to familiarise yourself with the different potentials of the theatre and of drama as a form, it's worth going to the theatre as often as possible and seeing a wide variety of staged productions. Don't restrict yourself to seeing productions of the plays you're studying - the chances of there being any production of these in a live theatre near you are probably pretty small. But there are lots of benefits of seeing any play. You:

- broaden your experience of drama
- become familiar with a range of ways in which theatre can work and its effects
- learn to become more critical in comparing different productions of your set plays
- see the possibilities and limitations of different theatre spaces.

Exploring theatre space

It may seem an obvious point to make, but remember that plays are generally performed in theatres. Look at images of different theatre spaces (many available online), such as:

- Shakespeare's Globe
- the Sam Wanamaker Playhouse
- the amphitheatre at Epidaurus
- the Minack Theatre in Cornwall
- a 19th-century proscenium arch theatre (for example, the Theatre Royal in York)
- a theatre-in-the-round (for example, the Royal Exchange Theatre in Manchester).

Think about the different kind of relationship with the audience that these particular kinds of stage may encourage, and then think about how differently the drama texts you're studying could be represented in each space.

ACTIVITY 8

Going to the theatre

a Pay two visits to a local theatre – once when the theatre is empty and once for a live performance. On the first visit, reflect on these questions.

- How is the theatre laid out?
- How is seating arranged (if there is any)?
- What might this suggest about the relationship between the audience and the stage?
- What is the décor like?
- Is there natural light?

b When you see a performance, reflect on these points.

- How and when does the audience interact with the performance?
- When is it acceptable to make noise and what kinds of noise are acceptable?
- What kind of set is used (realistic or symbolic)? Does the set change? If so, how are set changes carried out?
- How are sound, lighting and special effects used?
- Is music live or recorded? What is its impact?

3.3 Drama through history

Why look at the history of drama? Although you don't need to know the history of the Western dramatic tradition in detail for your course, you may find it helpful to know something about the history of drama as a literary form. An understanding of the major trends of drama will help you to see the drama texts you study as part of a tradition rooted in symbol and ritual. This will help you to understand the ways in which drama seeks to represent the world through symbol, convention and **metaphor**, and how these in their turn relate to 'reality'. Drama is not and can never be **mimetic**. The relationship between the real world and the world of the play is complex.

Key terms

metaphor: when a word or phrase usually used for one meaning is used to denote another (for example, 'the men were trees in the mist') or when something is used to represent something else (for example, the flickering flame of a candle could be a metaphor for the fragility of human life)

mimesis [mimetic]: a straightforward imitation of reality

3.3.1 Classical theatre

Thespis, a Greek musician and actor from the 6th century BCE, is generally acknowledged as the first dramatist in the Western literary tradition and gives his name to the modern word 'thespian', meaning actor.

Thespis didn't write what we'd think of as conventional stage drama, but composed a series of musical 'dialogues' between a solo singer and a chorus of singer-dancers. As such, these first works of drama compare more closely to the world of opera or the musical theatre than they do to the mainstream stage. These works were often performed during religious celebrations (or rites), so from the outset drama was closely connected with ritual and symbolism rather than with simple representations of reality. Over time, these works changed in nature, relying less on music and more on the spoken word, and a set of recognisable character types began to emerge. Eventually these became known as tragedies and provided the foundation for the works of the Greek tragic playwrights. These actor-writers produced hundreds of plays, comparatively few of which have survived. Those that have, however, (32 plays by the three major dramatists – Aeschylus, Sophocles and Euripides) have been enormously influential. These plays retain a focus on ritual and symbol and deal with the interaction between human and divine worlds. A parallel classical tradition emerged in Ancient Rome. Here the major tragedian was Seneca, who would later exercise a profound influence on the works of Shakespeare. Comedy also flourished as a 'lighter' counterpart to the often deadly serious world of tragedy. In Greece, Aristophanes was a particularly talented comic dramatist, while the Roman tradition produced significant works by Plautus and Terence.

3.3.2 Medieval drama

After the collapse of the great classical civilisations of Greece and Rome, there was a long hiatus in the writing of drama. It was not until hundreds of years later that it re-emerged, again from the religious and ritualistic background. The established church had traditionally opposed any form of theatre as dishonest and immoral. Over time, however, it became a tradition – first at Easter, and later at Christmas – to introduce short dramatisations of biblical narratives into religious services. Over time, these short dramas became more elaborate until eventually they were presented on their own by secular actors outside the church, though they retained their close connection with their symbolic and religious roots. These plays became known as the morality, miracle and mystery plays of the medieval era. Cycles of plays from York and Wakefield (the 'Towneley plays') are perhaps the best known.

See 5.2.2, 6.2.2, 7.2.2 and 7.2.3 for more on medieval drama

The connection of theatre to religious ritual is still clear, but from the medieval era onwards, secular elements began to play a bigger and bigger part in drama until it emerged as a major literary (and secular) art form in its own right from the mid-16th century.

3.3.3 The Renaissance

By the beginnings of the early modern period, drama was a well-established and popular form; the religious authorities still, however, regarded it with plenty of moral scepticism. Although still in many ways conventional, drama had now established its own codes and conventions and had moved far from its original religious roots. Shakespeare is the titanic figure of the period, but there was a flowering of dramatic talent and an eager urban theatre-going public was served by a developing network of purpose-built and adapted theatres (for example, The Rose, The Swan, The Hope, and The Globe in London). Revenge tragedy was a very popular form, building on the bloodthirsty works of Seneca. The excessive violence and dubious ethical content of these plays – major examples of which were produced by Shakespeare, but also by John Ford, Cyril Tourneur, John Webster, Thomas Kyd, John Marston, Philip Massinger and others – no doubt added to the perceived suspicion of drama as a form. Comedy was also a thriving dramatic form. Shakespeare produced a string of well-known comedies while Thomas Dekker, Ben Jonson, Thomas Middleton, Francis Beaumont and John Fletcher, and others produced a large body of witty 'urban' comedies (for example, *The Shoemaker's Holiday*, *Bartholomew Fair*, *A Chaste Maid in Cheapside* and *The City Madam*).

ACTIVITY 9

Shakespeare in love

Tom Stoppard's 1998 film drama *Shakespeare in Love* provides a fascinating insight into the worlds of both Renaissance and contemporary drama. Watch the film and then think about the questions a–c.

a What do you learn from Stoppard's screenplay about Renaissance theatre?

b How does Stoppard adapt and use *Romeo and Juliet* in developing his own dramatic narrative?

c What do you learn about contemporary drama?

'I remember, the players have often mentioned it as an honour to Shakespeare, that in his writing (whatsoever he penned) he never plotted out a line.'

Ben Jonson, *Discoveries–De Shakespeare nostrat*

History plays focusing on the lives of the English monarchs and on classical subjects were also a common subject for the Renaissance stage. Shakespeare wrote plays on classical historical subjects such as *Coriolanus*, *Timon of Athens* and *Antony and Cleopatra* as well as sequences of English histories on various English kings. Other dramatists (for example, Christopher Marlowe's *Edward II* and George Peele's *Edward I*) also approached such historical subjects. Pastoral (for example, John Fletcher's *The Faithful Shepherdess* and Shakespeare's *Cymbeline* and *The Winter's Tale*) and masques (for example, John Milton's *Comus* and a long sequence of works by Ben Jonson) were also produced.

Although works such as Christopher Marlowe's *Doctor Faustus* and John Fletcher's *Four Plays in One* retain close links to the medieval morality and mystery plays, the Renaissance stage made a significant shift towards realism. Characters in these works are much more psychologically developed and defined than those in medieval drama, but theatrical 'types' remained important features, and declamatory dramatic verse continued to play a very significant role.

See 5.2.4 and 6.2.4 for more on Renaissance drama

3.3.4 The closure of theatres and the Restoration

Drama went through a brief enforced decline when the Puritans closed the theatres in 1642. They remained closed throughout the Civil War, but re-opened when Charles II returned from exile in 1660. At first the theatre relied on the pre-Civil War repertoire, but under the influence of Molière and other French dramatists (Charles II had been exiled to France) a new, more satirical and bawdier body of work emerged in reaction to the enforced restraints of the Puritans, more fitted to contemporary tastes than the Renaissance dramas. The Restoration stage took further steps towards the concerns of the 'real' world. The titles of works like *The Man of Mode* (George Etherege), *The Way of the World* (William Congreve), *The Recruiting Officer* (George Farquhar) and *The Country Wife* (William Wycherley) hint at the ways in which these plays related to the world around.

Aphra Behn – arguably the first female professional author – was also a very significant figure at this time, and her play *The Rover* has remained popular across the centuries.

Early in the 18th century, however, a resurgence of Puritanism clamped down on the free spirits and rough humour of the Restoration stage and turned towards more sentimental comedy and moralising domestic tragedy. The theatre experienced a significant resurgence in the hands of Colley Cibber (*Love's Last Shift* and *The Careless Husband*) and Henry Fielding (*The Temple Beau* and *Tom Thumb*), but then the Licensing Act of 1737 brought the theatres under the personal censorship of the Lord Chamberlain.

3.3.5 The Victorian stage

Domestic theatricals were very popular in the Victorian era. Wilkie Collins, in his novel *No Name*, gives an extended account of a domestic production of Richard Brinsley Sheridan's play *The Rivals*. Collins, Dickens and others also wrote original plays, but the novel was the driving literary force of the age and adaptations of many of the major fictional works of the era (such as Charles Dickens' *Great Expectations*, Charlotte Brontë's *Jane Eyre* and Wilkie Collins' *The Woman in White*) were very popular and tended to dominate the stage, which emphasises the interaction of the novel and drama as narrative forms. Few writers of serious drama emerged again in Britain until the beginning of the 20th century, although a thriving popular theatre scene in the form of melodrama and music hall developed. Oscar Wilde (*The Importance of Being Earnest*, *Lady Windermere's Fan* and *Salomé*) and George Bernard Shaw (*Mrs Warren's Profession*, *Arms and the Man* and *Major Barbara*) are major exceptions.

3.3.6 The modern theatre

Developments in drama over the last 150 years have seen further shifts towards realism, particularly under the influence of Scandinavian and European dramatists. Playwrights such as Henrik Ibsen, August Strindberg and Frank Wedekind have been powerful influences in this respect, as have directors such as Constantin Stanislavski.

ACTIVITY 10

Stanislavski on drama

Look at these ideas on drama, all from the Russian director Stanislavski. What does each add to your thinking about drama and how it interacts with the world?

- 'Painting creates an illusion of several planes. They recede into the canvas but the foreground comes out of the frame at us. These planes exist in our own speech and they lend perspective to the sentence. The key word is highlighted most clearly of all and comes right into the foreground of the sound-plane. The less important words create a series of deeper planes.'
- 'The main factor in any form of creativeness is the life of a human spirit, that of the actor and his part, their joint feelings and subconscious creation.'
- 'Unless the theatre can ennoble you, make you a better person, you should flee from it.'
- 'Our demands are simple, normal, and therefore they are difficult to satisfy. All we ask is that an actor on the stage live in accordance with natural laws.'

Bertolt Brecht, however, challenged the notion that drama should offer a window onto reality. He intentionally disrupted audiences' expectations and discouraged them from identifying with the characters on stage as if they were 'real' people. In the second half of the 20th century, the Theatre of the Absurd – associated with playwrights such as Samuel Beckett, Harold Pinter and Tom Stoppard, as well as Continental dramatists such as Eugène Ionesco, Jean Genet and Václav Havel – took this sense of estrangement to new extremes, depicting a world apparently lacking in meaning that resists any straightforward interpretation.

Major British figures in the 20th and 21st centuries have been T.S Eliot (who produced a sequence of plays, including the highly influential verse drama *Murder in the Cathedral*, dealing with the martyrdom of Thomas Becket in Canterbury Cathedral), John Osborne (*Look Back in Anger*), Shelagh Delaney (*A Taste of Honey*), Alan Bennett (*The History Boys* and *Talking Heads*), Caryl Churchill (*Top Girls*) and Alan Ayckbourn (*The Norman Conquests*).

3.4 Dramatic narrative

Drama is a narrative form and uses many of the same techniques as the novel, the short story and narrative poetry. However, narrative in drama is social, physical and visual in ways that prose fiction and poetry cannot be. Some of the features that distinguish dramatic narrative are as follows.

- Narrative in drama is often on a smaller scale than in novels and narrative poetry and is likely to employ fewer characters and settings.
- Often there is no narrator in drama. Stories are told almost entirely through dialogue. Settings, characters, costumes and gestures may be present in stage directions, but are rarely part of the verbal text the audience hears. Instead they form a 'visual' text that contributes to the narrative.
- The role of the audience – drama narrative is not designed to be consumed in private like novels or narrative poems. As the on-stage narrative unfolds, the audience becomes part of a secondary narrative – the narrative of what is happening in

Narrative in drama is social, physical and visual

the theatre. The direct communication between actors and audience, and the emotional effect of the live performance makes this possible. Some dramatic narrative techniques (for example, asides and soliloquies) are deliberate ways of involving audiences in the drama.

3.4.1 Voice

The concept of voice is particularly significant in drama texts. As we've already seen, dialogue is the primary vehicle for narrative in drama - the story in dramatic texts is 'told' in a rather different way than in prose fiction or narrative poetry. Different characters have their own voices and, as such, each adds a unique inflection to the part of the story they carry.

ACTIVITY 11

Dramatic voices

Using the passages from *Tamburlaine the Great* and *The Importance of Being Earnest* in Texts 3C and 3D, what do you notice about the voices of the different characters? Take each character in turn. What would you say about the voice of each? Using examples from the texts to support your argument, write a short paragraph about each.

3.4.2 Verse and prose

Dramatic narratives can be written in verse or prose (or both). Much Renaissance drama, for instance employs blank verse, developed initially by the playwright Christopher Marlowe. Text 3C is an example from his play *Tamburlaine the Great*.

Text 3C

Enter TAMBURLAINE leading ZENOCRATE, TECHELLES, USUMCASANE, AGYDAS, MAGNETES, LORDS, and SOLDIERS laden with treasure.

TAMBURLAINE
Come, lady, let not this appal your thoughts;
The jewels and the treasure we have ta'en
Shall be reserv'd, and you in better state
Than if you were arriv'd in Syria,
Even in the circle of your father's arms,
The mighty **Soldan of Aegyptia**.
ZENOCRATE
Ah, shepherd, pity my distressed **plight**!
(If, as thou seem'st, thou art so mean a man,)
And seek not to enrich thy followers
By lawless **rapine** from a silly maid,
Who, travelling with these Median lords
To Memphis, from my uncle's country of Media,
Where, all my youth, I have been governed,
Have pass'd the army of the mighty Turk,
Bearing his **privy-signet** and his hand
To safe-conduct us **thorough** Africa.
MAGNETES
And, since we have arriv'd in Scythia,
Besides rich presents from the **puissant** Cham,
We have his highness' letters to command
Aid and assistance, if we stand in need.

Christopher Marlowe, *Tamburlaine the Great*

'As far as the piano is concerned, sentiment is my forte. I keep science for Life.'

Oscar Wilde,
The Importance of Being Earnest

Glossary

Soldan of Aegyptia: Sultan of Egypt

plight: distressing circumstances

rapine: theft

privy-signet: a ring giving the bearer authority

thorough: through

puissant: powerful

Text 3D is an example of dramatic narrative in prose from Oscar Wilde's *The Importance of Being Earnest*.

Text 3D

Morning-room in Algernon's flat in Half-Moon Street. The room is luxuriously and artistically furnished. The sound of a piano is heard in the adjoining room.

[LANE is arranging afternoon tea on the table, and after the music has ceased, ALGERNON enters.]

ALGERNON: Did you hear what I was playing, Lane?

LANE: I didn't think it polite to listen, sir.

ALGERNON: I'm sorry for that, for your sake. I don't play accurately – anyone can play accurately – but I play with wonderful expression. As far as the piano is concerned, sentiment is my forte. I keep science for Life.

LANE: Yes, sir.

ALGERNON: And, speaking of the science of Life, have you got the cucumber sandwiches cut for Lady Bracknell?

LANE: Yes, sir. *[Hands them on a salver.]*

ALGERNON: *[Inspects them, takes two, and sits down on the sofa.]* Oh! . . . by the way, Lane, I see from your book that on Thursday night, when Lord Shoreman and Mr. Worthing were dining with me, eight bottles of champagne are entered as having been consumed.

LANE: Yes, sir; eight bottles and a pint.

ALGERNON: Why is it that at a bachelor's establishment the servants invariably drink the champagne? I ask merely for information.

LANE: I attribute it to the superior quality of the wine, sir. I have often observed that in married households the champagne is rarely of a first-rate brand.

ALGERNON: Good heavens! Is marriage so demoralising as that?

Oscar Wilde, *The Importance of Being Earnest*

ACTIVITY 12

Verse and prose in dramatic narrative

It's important to think about why some dramatists choose to use verse and others prose (or a mixture) and the impact of their choices.

Look again at the two extracts from *Tamburlaine the Great* and *The Importance of Being Earnest* in Texts 3C and 3D. How do the language of **blank verse** and the language of prose create differences in the drama?

Key terms

blank verse: unrhymed iambic pentameter (10 syllable lines)

See Metre in 2.3.2 for more on iambic pentameter

3.4.3 Stage directions

Playwrights also use stage directions as a means of telling their stories. These, of course, are available to you when you read a drama text, but are not if you are in an audience at a performance.

Let's think about stage directions for a moment; they fulfil a central function in establishing the world of the text, but are they actually a part of the literary text or are they something else? They contribute to the play's 'literary' qualities, but their language and style is obviously very different.

ACTIVITY 13

Writing about stage directions

Look back at the stage directions in the passages from *Tamburlaine the Great* and *The Importance of Being Earnest* in Texts 3C and 3D. Think about questions a-d.

a What is the function of this dimension of language in the drama text?

b How is this dimension of language different from the literary language the authors employ in their dialogue?

c Is this dimension of language any less important?

d Are there situations in which you would write about stage directions (for example, when discussing dramatic method or when thinking about how characters are represented)? Would you write about and analyse this dimension of language in the same way as you would about the dialogue playwrights use?

3.5 Symbolism and realism

Drama is a ritualised literary form and playwrights often appeal to their audiences' cultural and literary knowledge of symbol, ritual and theatrical history. Dialogue, costume, masks, music, the use of the stage, character types, dialogue and other dimensions of drama are all used in ritualised ways to create connections between the real world we inhabit and the imagined world of the drama. Playwrights place their work somewhere on a continuum between stylisation (highly artistically constructed dramatic worlds) and realism (based firmly on the everyday world). Table 3A shows some of the typical features of the two ends of the continuum.

Table 3A

Stylisation	Realism
Poetic language, music, dance	The language and movement of ordinary social life
Explicit symbolism in character and setting	Psychologically and socially specific characterisation and settings
Traditional fables, myths, legends	'Original' stories about invented characters

Even when plays appear to represent 'reality', you should look for the artistic, stylised elements and conventions they employ.

See 3.6 for more on drama conventions

Text 3E is the opening of *The Dog Beneath the Skin: or Where is Francis?* by Christopher Isherwood and W.H Auden.

Text 3E

The garden of the Vicarage at Pressan Ambo. The scene suggests the setting of a pre-war musical comedy. The stage is crowded with villagers of all classes, who promenade to the strains of a distant band. The characters, as they pass in turn along the footlights, address the audience.

VICAR: Here come I, the Vicar good
Of Pressan Ambo, it's understood;
Within this parish border
I labour to expound the truth
To train the tender plant of Youth
And guard the moral order.
CHORUS: With troops of scouts for village louts
And preaching zest he does his best
To guard the moral order.
GENERAL: General Hotham is my name.
At Tatra Lakes I won my fame,
I took the Spanish Lion.
In Pressan now my home I've made
And rule my house like a brigade
With discipline of iron.
CHORUS: Side by side his peacocks stride:
He rules them all at Conyers Hall
With discipline of iron.
GENERAL'S WIFE: Woman, though weak, must do her part
And I who keep the General's heart
Know well our island story
And do my utmost to advance
In India, Russia, Finland, France,
The just and English glory.
CHORUS: With subtle wile and female smile,
With speech and vote she will promote
The just and English glory.
IRIS: And here am I, Miss Iris Crewe,
I live in Pressan Ambo too,
The prize at village dances.
From Honeypot Hall, the haunt of doves,
In my blue Daimler and white gloves
I come to take your glances.
CHORUS: With nose and ear and mouth and hair
With fur and hat and things like that
She takes our loving glances.

Christopher Isherwood and W.H. Auden,
The Dog Beneath the Skin: or Where is Francis?

ACTIVITY 14

Stylisation and realism

Read the extract from *The Dog Beneath the Skin: or Where is Francis* in Text 3E. Which elements are stylised? Which are realistic? Where on the stylisation–realism continuum do you think this play probably sits?

Drama, like other literary forms, relates to but is not the same as the real world. It is a literary space where a number of different worlds meet: the fictional world of the play, the real-world event that is witnessed by the audience and the alternative worlds represented by the different possible interpretations of the play. Perhaps for this reason, dramatists often employ the metaphor of the stage within their own dramatic works. Texts 3F, 3G and 3H are just three examples, all from Shakespeare.

Text 3F

All the world's a stage,
And all the men and women merely players;
They have their exits and their entrances,
And one man in his time plays many parts,
His acts being seven ages. At first, the infant,
Mewling and puking in the nurse's arms.
Then the whining schoolboy, with his satchel
And shining morning face, creeping like snail
Unwillingly to school. And then the lover,
Sighing like furnace, with a woeful ballad
Made to his mistress' eyebrow. Then a soldier,
Full of strange oaths and bearded like the pard,
Jealous in honour, sudden and quick in quarrel,
Seeking the bubble reputation
Even in the cannon's mouth. And then the justice,
In fair round belly with good capon lined,
With eyes severe and beard of formal cut,
Full of wise saws and modern instances;
And so he plays his part. The sixth age shifts
Into the lean and slippered pantaloon,
With spectacles on nose and pouch on side;
His youthful hose, well saved, a world too wide
For his shrunk shank, and his big manly voice,
Turning again toward childish treble, pipes
And whistles in his sound. Last scene of all,
That ends this strange eventful history,
Is second childishness and mere oblivion,
Sans teeth, sans eyes, sans taste, sans everything.

As You Like It, Act 2, Scene 7

Text 3G

To-morrow, and to-morrow, and to-morrow,
Creeps in this petty pace from day to day,
To the last syllable of recorded time;
And all our yesterdays have lighted fools
The way to dusty death. Out, out, brief candle!
Life's but a walking shadow, a poor player,
That struts and frets his hour upon the stage,
And then is heard no more. It is a tale
Told by an idiot, full of sound and fury,
Signifying nothing.

Macbeth, Act 5, Scene 5

Text 3H

Now I am alone. O, what a rogue and peasant slave am I!
Is it not monstrous that this player here,
But in a fiction, in a dream of passion,
Could force his soul so to his own conceit
That from her working all his visage wann'd,
Tears in his eyes, distraction in's aspect,
A broken voice, and his whole function suiting
With forms to his conceit? and all for nothing!
For Hecuba!
What's Hecuba to him, or he to Hecuba,

'All the world's a stage'
William Shakespeare,
As You Like It

That he should weep for her? What would he do,
Had he the motive and the cue for passion
That I have? He would drown the stage with tears
And cleave the general ear with horrid speech,
Make mad the guilty and appal the free,
Confound the ignorant, and amaze indeed
The very faculties of eyes and ears. Yet I,
A dull and muddy-mettled rascal, peak,
Like John-a-dreams, unpregnant of my cause,
And can say nothing; no, not for a king,
Upon whose property and most dear life
A damn'd defeat was made. Am I a coward?
Who calls me villain? breaks my pate across?
Plucks off my beard, and blows it in my face?
Tweaks me by the nose? gives me the lie i' the throat,
As deep as to the lungs? who does me this?
Ha!
'Swounds, I should take it: for it cannot be.

Hamlet, Act 2, Scene 2

ACTIVITY 15

All the world's a stage

Think about Texts 3F, 3G and 3H:

- In what ways do you find the metaphor of life as 'drama' useful?
- In what ways does drama seem to reflect reality?
- In what ways does it diverge from reality?

3.6 Drama conventions

The presence of these dramatic metaphors points to the artifice that underlies all drama texts. Even where a play is very realistic, it is still only actors pretending to be real people, and their worlds and their words are not real but artistically created for them. Table 3B shows some of the major dramatic conventions and devices that dramatists employ.

See 5.1.2 for more on the unities

Table 3B
Some of the dramatic methods used by playwrights

Convention/ device	Function
Aside	When a character steps aside from the world of the drama and addresses the audience directly. The play is effectively interrupted, allowing the playwright to comment (often ironically or humorously) through the character on what is taking place.
Soliloquy	When a character speaks alone. This is another way that dramatists directly address the audience. Characters often reveal their inner thoughts, emotions or hidden motivations.
Chorus	Originating in classical Greek drama, the Chorus often provides a commentary on the events of the play, or moves the narrative of the drama on through space or time.
Masque	Masque is a kind of courtly musical theatre, highly stylised in form. Characters hide their faces under masks, which often represent stock character types.
Song	Songs in plays often reflect (seriously or ironically) on the main events of the drama.
Cross-dressing	Where characters of one gender dress (for a variety of reasons comic and serious) as the opposite.
Disguise	Disguises are often used as a dramatic device, but also reflect ironically on the whole nature of theatre with its use of artifice, pretence and deception.
Dramatic irony	This is when an audience is aware of information undisclosed to some or all of the characters on stage.
Unities	Three principles derived by French classicists from Aristotle's *Poetics*. In the unities, a play should have unity of action (a single plot), unity of place (a single location) and unity of time (take place in the course of a day).

ACTIVITY 16

Dramatic conventions and devices

Think carefully about the drama texts you are studying. Look through the dramatic conventions outlined in Table 3B, then answer questions a–d.

a Which of these conventions do the playwrights use?

b What effects do they achieve by using these effects?

c In what ways are the effects that the playwrights achieve similar and different from text to text?

d Are any of these effects also used in any of the poetry texts or prose texts you've studied?

3.7 Bringing it all together

3.7.1 How much do you know?

Questions 1–5 ask you to bring together the elements you have studied in this unit.

1 What additional dimensions do you need to consider when thinking about drama texts as compared to poetry and prose fiction?

2 What other kinds of 'language' are important when thinking about drama texts? How far are these languages present in the text and how far are they imported into the text?

3 What can you recall of the history of drama in English? How does this help you to contextualise the drama texts you are studying?

4 In what ways does narrative in drama differ from narrative in poetry and in prose fiction?

5 How much can you recall of the major conventions of drama texts and their functions?

3.7.2 Assessment objectives

In relation to the assessment objectives, this unit has explored:

- how you can develop and articulate informed personal responses to drama texts (AO1)
- the additional dimensions of drama texts, how these differ from poetry and prose fiction, and how structure, language and other dramatic methods are used to shape meaning in drama texts (AO2)
- issues surrounding the contexts in which drama texts are produced and received, how theatre spaces provide very particular contexts both for the production and reception of drama texts, and how the contexts of literary study of drama texts differ from theatrical representation (AO3)
- how to write in connected ways about literary texts (AO4)
- alternative ways of understanding drama texts, drama productions as creative-critical interpretations of literary text, and how and in what ways you can use such alternative perspectives in your own reading and writing (AO5).

Summary

In this unit, you have learnt about:

- the unique nature of drama as a literary form
- the historical development of drama
- how playwrights, directors, actors and audiences collaborate to create meaning in drama texts
- how drama productions represent creative-critical responses to drama texts
- key aspects of mise-en-scène, prose and verse dramatic narrative, the language and the conventions used in drama
- how dramatists shape meanings in their works.

BEGINNING

4 The novel

In this unit you will:

- explore the ways in which readers respond to and interpret novels
- explore the ways in which novelists craft their work and shape meaning
- explore the history of the novel and the way it has changed over time.

4.1 Introduction to the novel

In your A Level and AS Level courses you have to study and write about novels: at AS Level, through the lens of Tragedy and Comedy and, at A Level, Tragedy and Comedy and Crime Writing and Political and Social Protest Writing. At A Level it is optional in Paper 1 (Tragedy and Comedy) and compulsory in Paper 2: Texts and Genres, and also in the Non-exam Assessment (NEA). At AS Level, it is compulsory in Paper 2. This unit will enable you to do some preparatory work on novels before you look at it though a specific optic.

Many students embarking on A Level English Literature courses talk about the pleasure they have gained from reading novels. The novels they have encountered in their prior study of literature have often had an enormous impact on them, introducing them to characters and stories that stay in their minds long after they have finished reading. At A Level, your study of English Literature will encourage you to think about the ways in which novelists tell these stories, developing your understanding of the novel as a literary form and considering the craft of the novelist in detail.

4.1.1 The novel in and out of the classroom

The novel is the type of text you're most likely to turn to in your reading outside the classroom. Novels are a source of enjoyment and escapism, offering you a world that you can immerse yourself in and characters who can seem as rounded and absorbing as anyone you might meet in real life. However, the fact that we see novels as a source of pleasure can make studying them difficult. Often, we want to engage with novels as if they are an extension of reality: for instance, we talk about which characters we like and dislike, and discuss how they should react to the situations they are in. The ways in which we have to analyse novels in the classroom can seem very different to these more 'personal' readings. You might even have heard people complaining about having to 'dissect' novels, and how this 'spoils' them. (At one time, some people thought that novels shouldn't actually be studied at all, for this very reason.)

Figure 4A

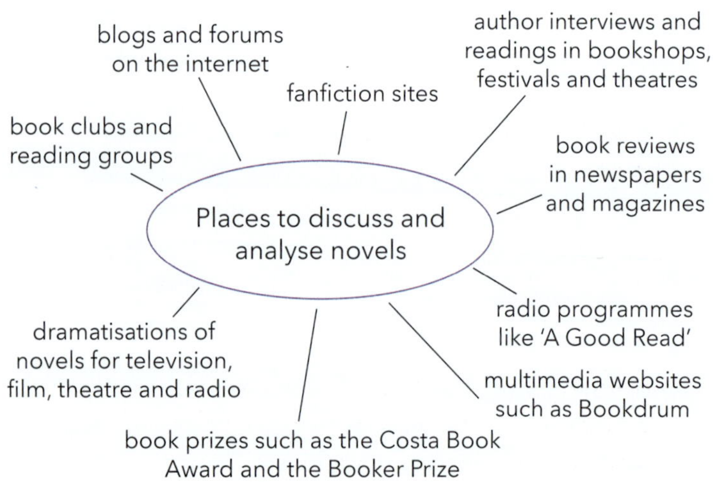

Nevertheless, studying novels doesn't *have* to dampen the pleasure you can gain from them. It can actually enhance it - by drawing your attention to the ways in which a few carefully chosen words, for instance, can reveal so much about characters and their motivations; or to the effects created by a novelist's decision to structure their narrative in an unconventional manner. As you become more experienced as a reader, you will find that thinking about novels in this way becomes second nature, and that it heightens your understanding of why novels affect us in the way that they do.

It's important to bear in mind that novels are discussed and analysed in other settings too - not just in the classroom (see Figure 4A).

During your A Level course, you should aim to explore some of these different ways of engaging with novels in order to broaden your experience of literature.

ACTIVITY 1

Experiences of the novel

a Think about your experience of reading novels for pleasure. How would you sum up your feelings about reading novels? What kinds of experiences have you had over the years? Which novels have you particularly enjoyed? Which novels have you found most inspiring, challenging or thought-provoking? In what ways have your tastes changed as you've grown older?

b Think about your experiences of reading novels in school. Have these experiences differed from your encounters with novels outside of school? If so, how?

c How do you feel about studying novels? Why do you think some people find the experience of studying novels frustrating? Can you think of any times when studying a novel has increased your understanding of it? Can you think of any times when studying a novel has enhanced your *enjoyment* of it?

4.1.2 Studying the novel

If novels are intended to be read for pleasure, why do we study them? Why have novels been given such an important role in the teaching of English literature?

First, novels are an enormous part of our culture. They offer perspectives on the experiences of different people at different times, and are a form in which ideas have been discussed and debated. They have introduced us to memorable characters and stories that continue to resonate with people today. It's important that you understand why novels are so powerful and why they've had such an impact on the people who've read and enjoyed them.

Studying novels alerts us to the ways in which narratives are constructed and the ways in which they might give particular perspectives more emphasis than others. This, in turn, might encourage us to think about stories in the wider world: how history can be rewritten, and how replacing one story with another can help us to consider alternative points of view.

Exploring the rewriting of history: *Animal Farm*

George Orwell's novel *Animal Farm* (1945) gives us several examples of the rewriting of history, offering valuable insights into the ways in which narrative can be used to control the ways in which people see the world.

- The Seven Commandments are changed as the original ideals of the farm are replaced by selfishness and greed.
- Squealer persuades the animals that Snowball's actions at the Battle of the Cowshed were not heroic, as they initially appeared, but cowardly.
- The slogan 'Four legs good, two legs bad' is replaced by 'Four legs good, two legs better'.
- Napoleon uses his power, enforced by threats and brutality, to change the animals' perceptions of the past.

We hope, then, that this unit will get you to think about novels and what they do, considering the reasons why the novel is such an important cultural form and the place that novels occupy in our emotional and imaginative lives. We believe that in order to do this, it is important to look beyond the individual novels you study in class and think about the novel more widely, exploring it within the literary tradition and as an art form.

4.2 The novel through history

People have always told stories, but the novel as a literary form is a relatively recent invention. For many centuries most narratives were told in verse, in the form of poetry or verse drama. They were spoken – or acted – rather than read, with rhythm and rhyme being used as an aid to memory. They were, therefore, part of a culture that was oral rather than written. Even though some narratives were written down, and even though some of these were written in prose, it took many centuries for these prose narratives to evolve into the novel.

See 2.2.1, 3.4.2 and 6.2.8 for more on narratives in verse or poetry

4.2.1 The rise of the novel

The rise of the novel is often linked to the emergence of a modern, **industrial-capitalist society**, as opposed to the **agrarian society** of the past.

Key terms

industrial-capitalist society: a society in which industry, technology and trade are the main sources of wealth

agrarian society: a society in which most people cultivate the land and produce only what they need in order to stay alive

This might seem strange. We tend to think of the production of a novel as a purely literary process – one of writing a narrative. However, a novel is also a physical object that has to be created and reproduced. Moreover, it is also a commercial object: novelists (and publishers) have to succeed in the marketplace in order to make a living. Novels therefore need to be promoted and sold. And, of course, they have to be read. In order for novels to exist in the form that we know them today, then, a number of things have to happen.

- Print technology has to develop to the point where it can be used to create books that are relatively small, portable and cheap to produce. In the past, the printing process was laborious and time-consuming, meaning that books were luxury objects available only to the rich.
- Paper has to be cheap enough for books to be relatively affordable.
- People have to be able to read. The rise of the novel depended on the spread of literacy.
- People have to have *time* to read. In the agrarian societies of the past, there would have been little time for leisure. The rise of industrial capitalism led to the emergence of a new middle class who earned a living through trade and employed servants to do domestic work. Middle-class women, in particular, were the target audience of many early novelists.

ACTIVITY 2

The novelty of the novel

The word 'novel' also means 'new'. Using a good dictionary, such as the online version of the Oxford English Dictionary, find out what you can about the origins of the word 'novel', including its French and Latin roots. Why might people consider it important for novels to be 'novel'? Why might novelty be linked to commercial success?

Now find out the French word for what we call the novel. What are the origins of this word? What might this suggest about the roots of the novel in France?

The emergence of the novel can therefore be linked to a number of social, technological and economic factors. As we shall see in the brief history of the

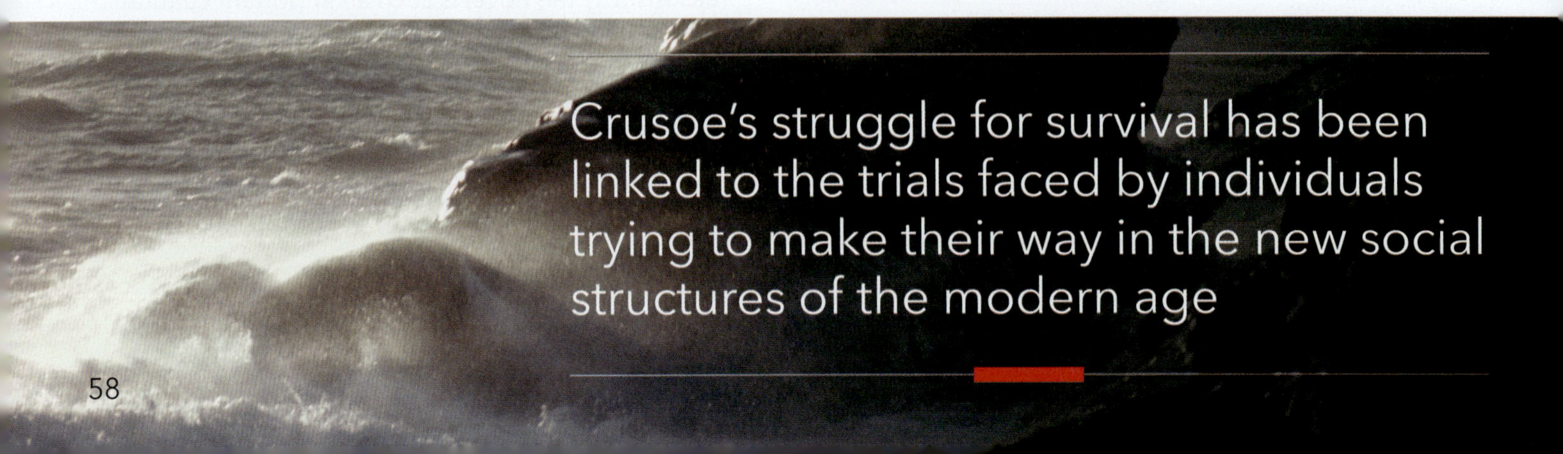

Crusoe's struggle for survival has been linked to the trials faced by individuals trying to make their way in the new social structures of the modern age

novel in 4.2.2, these factors have continued to play a part in the novel's development.

4.2.2 The development of the novel

The importance of the individual

One strand of the novel's history concerns the importance of the individual. The prose narratives that preceded the novel tended to focus on stock characters or stories drawn from mythology. The novel, in contrast, turned its attention to particular characters in particular circumstances. This concentration on the individual is often seen as having its roots in the philosophical changes that took place during the Renaissance, when thinkers across Europe were examining what it meant to be human. The text that is generally accepted as the first novel written in English, Daniel Defoe's *Robinson Crusoe* (1719), is about a castaway who spends 28 years on a remote island. Crusoe's struggle for survival has been linked to the trials faced by individuals trying to make their way in the new social structures of the modern age: in this new world, people needed to fend for themselves in order to survive.

Exploring history and the novel

In the early years of the novel, the form was often accused of being trivial and frivolous – it lacked the seriousness and solidity of poetry and drama. These claims took a long time to disappear. The American novelist Henry James wrote in 1884 that 'the old superstition about fiction being "wicked"' still lingered. In view of this, it is interesting to note that many novels of the 18th and 19th centuries included phrases such as 'The History of …' and 'The Life of …' in their titles. Some examples are Henry Fielding's *The History of Tom Jones* (1749), Frances Burney's *Evelina, or the History of a Young Lady's Entrance into the World* (1778), Charles Dickens' *The Life and Adventures of Nicholas Nickleby* (1839) and William Makepeace Thackeray's *The History of Henry Esmond* (1852). The full title of Jonathan Swift's novel *Gulliver's Travels* (1726) is *Travels into Several Remote Nations of the World. In Four Parts. By Lemuel Gulliver, First a Surgeon, and then a Captain of Several Ships*. It is as though these writers wanted to give their novels the outward appearance of being true stories.

Rogues and adventurers

An important influence on these early novels was the genre of the **picaresque**, which originated in Spain in the 16th century. Its name comes from the Spanish word *picaro*, meaning 'rogue'. Picaresque novels told the story of a low-born hero who had to live by his wits, making his way through a foolish, corrupt society in a series of loosely related adventures. The hero's actions were often immoral, but were depicted in a humorous manner. The novels of Henry Fielding and Charles Dickens show many traces of the picaresque. Many protagonists of picaresque novels were male, but some authors chose to focus on female characters: two significant picaresque heroines are Moll in Daniel Defoe's *Moll Flanders* (1722) and Becky Sharp in William Makepeace Thackeray's *Vanity Fair* (1847–48).

The sentimental novel

Another key genre that emerged in the 18th century was the **sentimental novel**, which focused – as its name suggests – on emotion. Its characters were often presented as having extreme reactions to their experiences, and feelings were elevated over reason and logic. Famous sentimental novels include Samuel Richardson's *Pamela* (1740) and Laurence Sterne's *A Sentimental Journey* (1768). The sentimental novel was satirised by some writers, but its emphasis on the emotions of the individual would influence many of the great 19th-century novelists.

The exploration of society

A further important aspect of the novel is its exploration of society. The novelist Jane Austen focused on what she described as 'three or four families in a country village', using wit and **satire** to highlight the shortcomings of many of her characters. Austen's works, such as *Pride and Prejudice* (1813), *Emma* (1815) and *Persuasion* (1818), are often viewed as typically 'feminine', with their emphasis on marriage. Nevertheless, they highlight the restrictions facing many young middle-class women in the early 19th century, when marriage was often the only way of achieving financial security. Behaving in a way that was deemed 'acceptable', according to the narrow codes of polite society, was vital if one was to secure a husband.

Key terms

picaresque: a novel that focuses on the adventures of a roguish character, who has to use his or her wits to survive

sentimental novel: a genre that focused on the emotional responses of its characters

satire: humorous or ironical comment on topical issues, often intended to ridicule

A focus on the self

The great age of the novel in England – the 19th century – was also the age of the ***Bildungsroman*** or 'novel of experience', which focused on its central character's development from childhood to maturity. Examples include Charlotte Brontë's *Jane Eyre* (1847), Charles Dickens' *David Copperfield* (1850) and *Great Expectations* (1861), and George Eliot's *The Mill on the Floss* (1860). Such novels reflected a growing concern with the thoughts, emotions and motives of individuals that would eventually lead to the emergence of the **psychological novel** – a genre that concentrates on the inner lives of characters, depicting the workings of the human mind in great detail. Perhaps the most unusual novel to emerge from the Victorian era was Emily Brontë's *Wuthering Heights* (1847), with its complex narrative style and depiction of raw passion and brutality.

The 19th-century novel also explored broader processes of social change, and how these affected the individuals caught up in their midst. Perhaps the greatest example of this is George Eliot's *Middlemarch* (1871–72), the story of a town in the Midlands, but also important was the so-called 'Condition of England' novel, which highlighted the effects of the Industrial Revolution on ordinary men and women. Examples include Benjamin Disraeli's *Sybil* (1845), Elizabeth Gaskell's *Mary Barton* (1848) and *North and South* (1854–55), and Charles Dickens' *Hard Times* (1854). Towards the end of the 19th century, Thomas Hardy gave the novel a new direction by drawing on elements of tragedy, exploring the conflicts between characters and their circumstances in novels such as *The Return of the Native* (1878), *Tess of the D'Urbervilles* (1891) and *Jude the Obscure* (1895).

Exploring titles

Notice that the titles of many of the novels mentioned in this section – *A focus on the self* – highlight a common set of concerns: with individuals, the concepts that define them and the locations in which their stories take place. As you encounter different texts, think about their titles and what they suggest.

Innovation and experiment

A further strand of the novel's history concerns experimentation. In the early years of the novel, Laurence Sterne drew attention to the impossibility of representing an individual's experiences in their entirety: his comic novel *Tristram Shandy* (1759–67) claims to tell its eponymous hero's life story, but contains digressions, repetitions and even blank pages as Tristram agonises over the hopelessness of his task.

Writers of the early 20th century, such as James Joyce and Virginia Woolf, continued this experimentation through the technique of **stream of consciousness**. Their novels – such as *Ulysses* by James Joyce (1922) and *Mrs Dalloway* by Virginia Woolf (1925) – might seem very different from the works of Jane Austen or Charles Dickens, but they can still be seen as part of the novel's attempt to represent the experiences of particular characters in particular circumstances.

Key terms

Bildungsroman: a novel dealing with a character's development from childhood into adulthood

psychological novel: a genre that focuses on the inner workings of the minds of its characters

stream-of-consciousness: a writing technique that attempts to capture the movements of the mind and the way it filters different impressions and experiences

In the 20th century, authors such as D.H. Lawrence, Evelyn Waugh and Graham Greene continued to explore the relationship between individuals and their background and society – often through the prism of religion. The last few decades of the 20th century saw the influence of novelists from around the world – including the Commonwealth and former colonies – who introduced distinctive new voices and drew attention to experiences of the world beyond the British Isles. Examples include Salman Rushdie, Margaret Atwood, J.M. Coetzee and Peter Carey.

Experiments with form and style continued in the late 20th century in the work of authors such as Julian Barnes, Ian McEwan, Angela Carter and Martin Amis. The novel continues to offer scope for innovation: one of the most striking novels to have been written in the new millennium is David Mitchell's 2004 novel *Cloud Atlas*, a series of interlocking stories that travel across time, place and genre. Yet novels also continue to look to the past for inspiration. Hilary Mantel's novels *Wolf Hall* (2009) and *Bring Up The Bodies* (2012) offer a richly detailed version of events at the court of King Henry VIII, focusing on the rise and fall of Thomas Cromwell.

ACTIVITY 3

Exploring different novels

Choose two of the novelists mentioned in section 4.2.2. Try to select novelists whose work is separated by at least 50 years. Find one novel by each of these novelists, and read the first chapter.

a How do the novelists introduce their narratives?
b Where are the novels set?
c Which characters stand out?
d Which aspects of each novelist's style are most distinctive?
e Which first chapter do you prefer, and why?

4.2.3 The novel on stage and screen

Novels have been adapted for the screen ever since the earliest days of film and television. Even before then, stage adaptations of novels were a highly popular form of entertainment in Victorian Britain, and audiences flocked to see theatrical versions of novels such as Mary Shelley's *Frankenstein*, Charlotte Brontë's *Jane Eyre* and **novellas** such as Charles Dickens' *A Christmas Carol*.

Screen and stage adaptations can be very useful accompaniments to your study of a novel, as well as being entertaining in their own right. However, stage and screen adaptations of novels are, of course, very different from the texts themselves. (A highlight of the BBC's 1995 serialisation of Jane Austen's novel *Pride and Prejudice* was an incident where Colin Firth, who played 'Mr Darcy', emerged dripping from a lake after going for a swim – an incident that does not appear anywhere in Austen's original text.) It is useful, then, to consider some of the differences between the novel on the page, and the novel on stage or screen.

Key terms

novella: a short novel or a long short story

ACTIVITY 4

Adaptations of the novel

Think of a novel that you have both read and watched as a stage or screen adaptation.

a Did you read the novel before seeing the adaptation, or the other way round? Would you rather have read the novel first? Why/why not?
b What differences did you spot between the original and its adaptation?
c What kinds of decisions would the production team have had to make? Think, for instance, about choice of location, costumes, props, music, sound effects and so on. How do these influence your viewing of the adaptation?
d Which key elements of the novel were emphasised most strongly in the adaptation? In what ways was the director able to do this? (For example, Cary Fukunaga's 2011 film version of *Jane Eyre* emphasises the bleakness and isolation of the landscape in which the events unfold. John Boulting's 1947 film adaptation of Graham Greene's novel *Brighton Rock* uses tightly-framed shots to build a sense of claustrophobia, as if Pinkie's world is closing in on him.)
e How did the adaptation dramatise the key incidents in the novel? In what ways did these incidents affect you?
f Did anything surprise you? Did anything disappoint or irritate you?
g Which version did you prefer, and why?
h Why do you think novels are adapted for stage and screen so frequently?

Remember, also, that just like the production of a play, a stage or screen adaptation of a novel is a director's *interpretation* of that particular text. Part of your study of English literature at A Level involves exploring the ways in which texts have been interpreted by different readers. If you are studying a text that has been adapted a number of times, it is interesting to compare these adaptations - perhaps focusing on the ways in which key incidents are presented. Even if only one adaptation exists - as in the case of Ian McEwan's novel *Atonement* (2001), which was adapted for film in 2007 - it can still add another dimension to the way you see the text, offering a different view of a particular character or drawing your attention to themes and symbols you had not previously considered.

4.3 Approaching the novel

Many students say that reading novels is much easier than reading poetry or drama - after all, a novel is the kind of text we're most likely to pick up and read in our spare time. But studying novels can seem much harder. For one thing, the novels you encounter during your A Level course will be much longer than any of the poems you study, and they will probably be longer than the plays, too. The American novelist Henry James (1843–1916) referred to the long novels of the 19th century as 'loose, baggy monsters', and it's true that novels can seem unwieldy in comparison to poems and plays. It can seem much more difficult to identify relevant authorial methods in the novel, where narratives and characters clamour for attention.

In this section of the unit, we introduce you to some key elements of the novelist's craft that can help to shape and convey meanings in the novel.

4.3.1 Understanding the craft of the writer

Henry James' description of novels as 'loose, baggy monsters' could be taken to mean that novels lack structure: that their authors simply begin at the beginning and end at the end. However, controlling the shape and structure of the novel - deciding how to begin, what kind of narrative voice to use, when to introduce key characters and where to place important incidents - is a complex undertaking. The decisions novelists make will involve careful consideration of a range of techniques, with different options being selected or rejected for a number of potential reasons.

ACTIVITY 5

Novelists on the novel

Texts 4A–4C are extracts from interviews with four contemporary novelists. What insights do these extracts give you into the ways in which they approach the writing process? Think about:

- where their initial ideas come from
- how they develop these ideas
- the drafting process
- the difficulties of writing.

If you are a creative writer yourself, how do these extracts compare with your experiences of the writing process?

Text 4A

Kazuo Ishiguro, author of *Never Let Me Go* (2005), described in an article by Tim Adams of *The Observer*

He spends, he says, around five years on each of his books and the first couple of these years, each time, involves little circumnavigations of the imaginative space of his novel, marking boundaries, testing structures, making himself at home. All of his quietly unsettling, intimate vantages have foundations in the voices that narrate them and he spends a good deal of time, too, 'auditioning' these voices, listening to different possibilities, before he settles on one.

Novels also continue to look to the past for inspiration

Text 4B

Rose Tremain, author of *The Road Home* (2007), a novel about an Eastern European immigrant trying to make a new life for himself in the UK

The most important piece of research I did for *The Road Home* was to interview Polish field-workers in Suffolk. I learned a lot from them – about what they hoped to achieve in England, how they viewed the people here, and how much they worried about their parents at home, left adrift – after 40 years in a Communist political system – in a world they might never fully understand. I also read many books about life in post-1989 Eastern Europe and returned to my own notes made on earlier visits to East Berlin and Russia.

Text 4C

Mark Haddon, author of *The Curious Incident of the Dog in the Night-Time*, talking about his 2012 novel, *The Red House*

I don't even know where I started in the book, really. Things just slowly and painfully coalesce over a long time. *The Red House* came from a previous novel I half-wrote and then threw away. For me, books never have a single story – never have a single moment of beginning. Some things I find to be hanging around for many years before I get around to using them. I have the characters and images in the back of my mind, waiting for a home. Much of *The Red House* was born in this previous novel, which was about lost children, dead children, and absences in family. The novel didn't work because it was too grandiose and overcomplicated. I abandoned the novel, but the central idea stayed with me.

In order to get to grips with the novels you're studying, you need to consider not just what stories they tell, but how these stories are told - how story is transformed into narrative, and how the author's use of language creates a distinctive style, tone and atmosphere. Sections 4.3.2–4.3.7 will introduce you to some key aspects of the novel.

4.3.2 Understanding setting, character and dialogue

As we saw earlier in this unit, setting and character are fundamental aspects of the novel - a form that focuses on the experiences of particular individuals in particular places at particular times. Dialogue, in turn, helps to convey character and is often important in helping the plot of the novel to unfold.

ACTIVITY 6

Setting, character and dialogue in the novel

Think about one of the novels you are studying.

a Where and when is the novel set? How is this setting established? Does this setting have any particular significance? For example, the first part of Sebastian Faulks' novel *Birdsong* (1993) is set in the city of Amiens, in northern France, in 1910. Faulks' descriptions of the river Somme, which runs through the city, foreshadow the horror and destruction that would take place there during World War I, just a few years later.

b How are characters created and conveyed? How important are names and physical appearance? Do you notice anything significant about the patterning of characters? Does the novel contain a **protagonist** and an **antagonist** or **foil**? Are there parallel characters in different generations or different parts of the text?

c How is dialogue used? Is it used, for instance, to reveal character or further the plot? Is speech **attributed** or **unattributed**? **Direct** or **reported**? Is there anything significant about which characters speak and which ones don't?

d Are there any significant patterns of imagery, recurring symbols or extended metaphors?

Faulks' descriptions of the River Somme in *Birdsong* foreshadow the horror and destruction that would take place just a few years later

Key terms

protagonist: the central character

antagonist: the central character's opponent or rival

foil: a character who contrasts in some way with the protagonist, emphasising particular aspects of the protagonist's personality

attributed speech: where the author makes it clear who is speaking, using words such as 'he said' or 'she explained'

unattributed speech: where the author does not make it clear who is speaking

direct speech: the actual words used by a character, enclosed in speech marks

reported speech: when the words used by a character are reported by another character or the narrator, e.g. *He said that he would be back later*

4.3.3 Understanding the language of prose

Certain features might be used to create significant effects in the novels you are studying.

Paragraph and sentence length

- The use of single-sentence paragraphs, simple sentences or multi-clausal complex sentences can be used to create particular effects.
- Many single-sentence paragraphs or simple sentences together often have a very noticeable effect, indicating a slow or fast pace, irony or humour.
- Many multi-clausal sentences and multi-sentence paragraphs together usually result in writing that is strongly descriptive.
- However, the effects of these techniques can only be judged in the context of the whole piece of writing.

Sentence structure

- Sentences may follow conventional structures approximate to ordinary simple speech, or they may use more complex, unusual or artificial structures.
- There may be symmetry or balance in the structure of a sentence. Does the sentence fall into two or three deliberately balanced parts? (Some sentences can be described as **bipartite** or **tripartite**, for instance.)
- The word order in the sentence may be conventional or unusual.
- Punctuation may be used deliberately as an aid to reading to create interest or surprise.

Rhetorical devices

Rhetorical devices are methods of arranging words for particular effect. They are particularly associated with speech-making, but are often used in written prose. They may include such things as:

- rhetorical questions
- exclamations
- repetition
- use of imagery, including metaphor and simile
- sound effects (**alliteration**, **assonance**, **consonance**, rhyme, **onomatopoeia**)
- **enumeration**
- **allusion**.

The presence or absence of any of these rhetorical devices might contribute to the overall 'style' of the writing.

Key terms

bipartite: a sentence that is divided into two deliberately balanced parts

tripartite: a sentence that is divided into three deliberately balanced parts

rhetorical device: a method of arranging words for particular effect

alliteration: use of a repeated *letter* sound for effect (for example, 'In sooth I know not why I am so sad')

assonance: the use of repeated identical or similar *vowel* sounds in nearby words (for example, 'she needs cream for her feet')

consonance: repeated sounds produced by consonants at the beginning, middle or end of nearby words (for example, 'he chuckled as he kicked the bucket')

onomatopoeia: when words sound like what they mean (for example, clap, bark, whistle)

enumeration: the listing of examples

allusion: the use of indirect references to people, places, ideas or other literary texts

See 1.5.5 for more on rhetoric

See 1.5.6 for more on imagery

See 2.3.2, 'Rhyme', for more on rhyme

4.3.4 Understanding narrative voice and perspective

Narrative voice is usually first person or third person.

First person	Third person
Tells the story as 'I'	May be invisible
Can share their thoughts and feelings directly with the reader	May comment on the narrative as if they are the author
Can be involved in the narrative as a character	Is not involved in the narrative as a character
May be unreliable - their knowledge and opinions are not necessarily to be trusted	Can be **omniscient** (all-knowing) - meaning that they can enter into the thoughts and feelings of other characters
Can occasionally enter into the thoughts of other characters	

Notice that with a first-person narrator, the perspective or point-of-view that we read is usually that of the character who is the narrator. With a third-person narrator, the point of view may shift as the narrator writes from the perspective of different characters, or from a neutral perspective. When a third-person narrator writes from the perspective of one particular character, this is known as **focalisation**. For example, in Text 4D from Pat Barker's novel *Regeneration* (1991), the focaliser is the military psychologist, Rivers. Rivers is visiting an unfamiliar hospital.

Text 4D

He took the lift to the third floor. He pushed through the swing doors on to a long, empty, shining corridor, which, as he began to walk down it, seemed to elongate. He began to be afraid he was really ill. This deserted corridor in a hospital he knew to be overcrowded had something eerie about it.

Pat Barker, *Regeneration*

Sometimes, a third-person narrator might adopt the language and attitudes of one character, as well as writing from their point of view. This is known as **free indirect discourse** (or free indirect narrative). For example, in Text 4E from David Lodge's novel *Nice Work* (1988), a character called Vic Wilcox is lying awake in the early hours of the morning, wondering how long it will be until his alarm clock goes off. Notice how the extract begins with Vic simply as the focaliser (like Rivers in the previous extract). As the extract continues, however, the questions indicate that the third-person narrator has entered Vic's mind in order to convey his thoughts.

Text 4E

How long he has to wait he doesn't know. He could easily find out by groping for the clock, lifting it to his line of vision, and pressing the button that illuminates the digital display. But he would rather not know. Supposing it is only six o'clock? Or even five? It could be five. Whatever it is, he won't be able to get to sleep again.

David Lodge, *Nice Work*

Another example of free indirect discourse can be found a few pages later (see Text 4F), when Vic reflects on the fact that while he has to get up and go to work, his family can stay in bed.

Text 4F

A few weeks before, he'd returned home soon after getting to work because he'd left some important papers behind, and found the house totally silent, all three children and their mother sound asleep at 9.30 in the morning. No wonder the country is going to the dogs.

David Lodge, *Nice Work*

The attitude expressed in the final sentence is not the narrator's, but Vic's: the use of free indirect discourse allows the author to give the reader an insight into his character's exasperation.

A few writers have used second-person narratives, in which the reader - or another character within the narrative - is addressed as 'you'. A famous example of this is Italo Calvino's novel *If on a Winter's Night a Traveler* (1979), which begins as shown in Text 4G.

Text 4G

You are about to begin reading Italo Calvino's new novel, *If on a Winter's Night a Traveler*. Relax. Concentrate. Dispel every other thought. Let the world around you fade. Best to close the door; the TV is always on in the next room. Tell the others right away, 'No, I don't want to watch TV!' Raise your voice – they won't hear you otherwise – 'I'm reading! I don't want to be disturbed!' Maybe they haven't heard you, with all that racket; speak louder, yell: 'I'm beginning to read Italo Calvino's new novel!' Or if you prefer, don't say anything; just hope they'll leave you alone.

Italo Calvino, *If on a Winter's Night a Traveler*

You might also encounter a novel with a dual (or multiple) narrative. In this type of novel, the story might be told from two (or more) different narrative viewpoints or perspectives. Alternatively, two (or more) different stories might be intertwined. You might also read **epistolary novels** that incorporate letters and other documents, or novels told wholly or partly in the form of a diary.

Key terms

omniscient: all-knowing

focalisation: when a third-person narrator tells the story from the perspective of one particular character

free indirect discourse: when a third-person narrator adopts the language and attitudes of one particular character

epistolary novel: a novel told in the form of a series of letters

4.3.5 Understanding narrative structure

Novels can be structured in any number of ways - from a simple linear narrative in which the story moves chronologically from beginning to end, to a much more complex, multi-layered narrative involving numerous shifts in time. They can also be organised in different ways - in parts, chapters and so on. It is likely that you will need to consider these questions.

- What do you notice about the beginning of the novel? How does the author set the scene?
- How is the plot developed? What are the key turning points and climaxes?
- What can you say about the organisation of the novel into parts and/or chapters? Do chapters begin and end in similar ways? Can you spot any patterns in the ways that chapters are organised?

For example, in Mark Haddon's novel *The Curious Incident of the Dog in the Night-Time* (2003), chapters are used alternately to tell the story and allow Christopher, the narrator, to reveal aspects of his interests, personality and inner life.

In Graham Swift's novel *Waterland* (1983), chapters often end with a sentence that flows over into the beginning of the next chapter. Sometimes, the title of the next chapter is part of the sentence. The example in Text 4H is from the end of Chapter 2 and the beginning of Chapter 3.

Text 4H

And since a fairy-tale must have a setting, a setting which, like the settings of all good fairy-tales, must be both palpable and unreal, let me tell you

3

About the Fens

Which are a low-lying region of eastern England, over 1,200 square miles in area, bounded to the west by the limestone hills of the Midlands, to the south and east by the chalk hills of Cambridgeshire, Suffolk and Norfolk.

Graham Swift, *Waterland*

This helps to create the sense of a haunting, insistent narrative voice and mirrors a central theme of the novel - the interconnectedness of events through history. It also keeps you reading!

In Kazuo Ishiguro's novel *Never Let Me Go* (2005), many chapters begin with the narrator, Kathy H, hinting at what is to come and marking where she is in her narrative, as if she feels the need to keep her story tightly controlled. Text 4I is an example from the beginning of Chapter 7.

Text 4I

I want to move on now to our last years at Hailsham. I'm talking about the period from when we were thirteen to when we left at sixteen. In my memory my life at Hailsham falls into two distinct chunks: this last era, and everything that came before. The earlier years – the ones I've just been telling you about – they tend to blur into each other as a kind of golden time, and when I think about them at all, even the not-so-great things, I can't help feeling a sort of glow. But those last years feel different.

Kazuo Ishiguro, *Never Let Me Go*

ACTIVITY 7

Thinking about narrative structure

Think about a novel you are studying. What kinds of structural devices are used in it? Can you identify their effects?

Using the ideas in this section, identify between three and five significant aspects of narrative structure in your chosen text. Write one paragraph about each of these, identifying the specific structural devices the author uses and the effects these devices have.

4.3.6 Understanding time in narratives

Novelists can use time in different ways. Here are some examples.

- **Linear** or **chronological narrative:** the story moves from beginning to end in chronological order.
- **Fragmented** or **non-chronological narrative**: the story moves between past, present and future and challenges the reader to piece the parts together.
- **Foreshadowing** (sometimes called **flashforward** or **prolepsis**): the narrative refers to something that has not happened yet but will happen later. This could be in the form of a hint that is not intended to be understood until later, or it may be an explicit reference to something that is going to happen, though we do not yet know how or why it is going to happen.
- **Flashback** (sometimes called **analepsis**): the narrative moves back in time to refer to something that has already happened.
- A **narrative frame** might be used to enclose the story and give you a sense of the importance of the events that will unfold. An example of a narrative frame in a novel you might study at A Level is in F. Scott Fitzgerald's *The Great Gatsby*, which begins with the narrator, Nick Carraway, hinting at why the events that he is about to narrate had such an effect on him.

4.3.7 The sense of an ending

One further aspect of narrative that you need to consider is how the novel ends. Does the novel reach a satisfying conclusion? Does the ending seem convincing? Are all the loose ends tied up, or is there a sense that some things are left unresolved? Would a different ending have been more satisfying?

An interesting perspective on endings is offered by David Lodge's novel *Changing Places* (1975). In the novel, a character called Morris Zapp, a lecturer in English Literature, finds a book called *Let's Write a Novel*. It contains the advice in Text 4J.

Text 4J

There are three types of story, the story that ends happily, the story that ends unhappily, and the story that ends neither happily nor unhappily, or, in other words, doesn't really end at all. [...]The best kind of story is the one with a happy ending; the next best is the one with an unhappy ending; and the worst kind is the story that has no ending at all. The novice is advised to begin with the first kind of story. Indeed, unless you have Genius, you should never attempt any other kind.

David Lodge, *Changing Places*

'The best kind of story is the one with a happy ending; the next best is the one with an unhappy ending; and the worst kind is the story that has no story at all.'

David Lodge, *Changing Places*

Interestingly, *Changing Places* itself is a novel that lacks a clear sense of an ending! Its final chapter is told in the form of a film script, and ends by freezing the action in mid-frame just as a character is reflecting on the artificial nature of endings – a form of **metafiction**.

Key terms

foreshadowing (flashforward/prolepsis): a technique in which narrative refers to something that has not yet happened but will happen later

flashback (analepsis): a technique in which narrative moves back in time to refer to something that has already happened

narrative frame: a literary device used to enclose a story to give a sense of importance the events that will unfold

metafiction: fiction that self-consciously draws attention to the act of writing, for example, by commenting on the process or difficulty of writing fiction

ACTIVITY 8

Exploring endings

Think about the endings of some of the novels you have read. Do they end happily or unhappily? Do they tie the plot up neatly, or leave questions unanswered? Do they have a moral? Does the novel take you on some kind of journey? What kind of ending do you prefer, and why?

4.4 Bringing it all together

4.4.1 How much do you know?

Questions 1–3 ask you to bring together the elements you have studied in this unit.

1 Summarise what you can remember about the historical development of the novel.

2 Explain the meanings of these terms:
   - first-person narrator
   - third-person narrator
   - omniscient narrator
   - free indirect discourse
   - focaliser
   - linear narrative
   - fragmented narrative
   - foreshadowing
   - flashback
   - direct speech
   - reported speech
   - narrative frame
   - metafiction.

3 Identify two or three of the key narrative methods used to shape meanings at different points in two different novels you have read. In coherent prose, describe these methods, give examples, and explain their effects.

4.4.2 Assessment objectives

In relation to the assessment objectives, this unit has explored:

- how you as a reader can make personal, informed and creative responses to the novel. It has also introduced you to a range of essential terminology and concepts that you might use in thinking and writing about the novel (AO1)
- the ways in which writers shape meanings in the novel through their use of a variety of conventions and techniques (AO2)
- some of the development of the novel as a literary form and the ways in which it has been adapted by different writers and received by different readers at different times (AO3)
- the key aspects of the novel form which can be found across a wide range of texts (AO4)
- the roles of interpretation and analysis in reading the novel (AO5).

Summary

In this unit, you have learnt about:

- the novel as a literary form
- the historical development of the novel
- key aspects of narrative used in the novel
- how the authors of novels shape meanings in their works.

DEVELOPING

5

Tragedy

In this unit, you will:

- find out about the literary genre of tragedy
- explore how the authors of literary texts use different aspects of tragedy in their works
- develop your ability to write about tragedy.

5.1 Introduction to tragedy

What does the word 'tragedy' mean to you? Nowadays, this term is used in a wide range of different circumstances. Take a look at any newspaper, and you'll see it being applied to a variety of situations, from unexpected deaths and

Set text focus

Aspects of Tragedy is one of the options in the Literary Genres components for A Level and AS Level. The set texts for this option are listed here.

At AS Level, if you choose the Aspects of Tragedy option for Papers 1 and 2 you must study one Shakespeare text, one other drama text, one poetry text and one prose text. At A Level, if you choose the Aspects of Tragedy option (Paper 1 only) you must study one Shakespeare text, one other drama text and one other text from any genre. One of these last texts must have been written before 1900.

A Level and AS Level

Othello by William Shakespeare
King Lear by William Shakespeare
The Great Gatsby by F. Scott Fitzgerald
Tess of the D'Urbervilles by Thomas Hardy
'Lamia' by John Keats
'Isabella; or, The Pot of Basil', 'La Belle Dame Sans Merci', and 'The Eve of Agnes' by John Keats
Death of a Salesman by Arthur Miller
Richard II by William Shakespeare

AQA English Literature B Poetry Anthology (Tragedy): Extracts from the Prologue of 'The Monk's Tale' and 'The Monk's Tale' by Geoffrey Chaucer; 'Jessie Cameron' by Christina Rossetti; Extract from *Paradise Lost* by John Milton; 'Tithonus' by Alfred, Lord Tennyson; 'The Convergence of the Twain' by Thomas Hardy; 'The Death of Cuchulain' by W.B. Yeats; 'Out, out...' by Robert Frost; 'Death in Leamington' by John Betjeman; 'Miss Gee' by W.H. Auden

AS Level only

A Streetcar Named Desire by Tennessee Williams

The Remains of the Day by Kazuo Ishiguro

Selected poems by Thomas Hardy: 'A Sunday Morning Tragedy', 'At An Inn', 'Tess's Lament', 'Under the Waterfall', 'Lament', 'Rain on a Grave', 'Your Last Drive', 'The Going', 'The Haunter', 'At Castle Boterel', 'A Trampwoman's Tragedy', 'The Frozen Greenhouse', 'The Forbidden Banns', 'The Mock Wife', 'The Flower's Tragedy', 'After a Journey', 'The Newcomer's Wife' environmental disasters to a missed goal at a penalty shootout and a politician's taste in clothes. As a student of literature, however, you need to learn that 'tragedy' has a much more specific set of meanings. These will give a shape to your study of tragedy and provide you with a lens through which to view the texts you study as part of this unit. However, they will not necessarily be present to the same degree in every text. Writers subvert literary genres as well as follow them, and you might find that the texts you are studying challenge, overturn or even omit different aspects of tragedy. Part of your study of these texts will involve considering why their authors treat the genre in the way they do, and what effects they achieve.

Tragedy has its roots in the ritualised dramas of Ancient Greece. It developed as a way of exploring the relationship between humans and the gods, the limits of human power and the workings of **fate**.

Key terms

fate: the name given to a power that predetermines the course of events; also used to refer to the outcome of a predetermined course of events: you might refer, for example, to King Lear's fate

Exploring the Fates in mythology

In Greek mythology, the Fates were three goddesses who were able to decide what people's destiny would be. Each had a different role in this process. Clotho, the spinner, created the thread of life; Lachesis, the measurer, decided how long the thread would be; and Atropos cut the thread off with her shears at the end.

Later dramatists have used the genre to ask questions about their own societies and concerns, and have been accompanied by poets and novelists, who have used other literary forms to explore ideas related to tragedy: error, guilt, suffering and death. Today, tragedy is just as powerful, and just as relevant, as it was in the newly democratic society of Athens in the 5th century BCE.

Exploring ritual madness and shedding identity

Dionysus was the god of wine, festivity, agriculture and fertility. He is often associated with ritual madness, and with the shedding of one's normal identity.

5.1.1 The earliest forms of tragedy

The original meaning of 'tragedy' was the rather bizarre-sounding 'goat song'. This term's precise meaning is unclear, but what is known is that it has its origins in the dramas that were performed at a number of annual festivals in Ancient Greece, particularly the festival of Dionysus, which took place in the spring. These dramas were very different to theatrical performance today. They were performed in open-air amphitheatres, in front of vast audiences (the amphitheatre at Epidaurus, now a UNESCO World Heritage Site, can seat up to 14,000 people). Attendance was part of the duty of a citizen: the theatre was not mere entertainment, but a place where important issues could be raised and discussed.

'Goat song', then, might refer to the goatskin trousers worn by the actors playing the satyrs – creatures that were human from the waist up and goat from the waist down, often depicted as lustful and unruly.

Exploring satire

The satyr play gave rise to another literary genre, the **satire**. Satire is a subversive genre that aims to challenge and overturn established values.

5.1.2 Classical aspects of tragedy

The most important name in the history of tragedy is that of the Greek writer Aristotle, who lived in the 4th century BCE. Aristotle was a philosopher, not a dramatist, but his work *Poetics*, written in about 335 BCE, is one of the most important texts ever written about the genre of tragedy. In it, Aristotle described the characteristics of the tragic dramas he had seen performed. The aspects he described have become a staple of the way that later dramatists and critics have thought about tragedy.

- Central to Aristotle's description of tragedy was the role of the **tragic protagonist**. This was a man of high status (such as a king) who also possessed what Aristotle termed **megalopsychia** or 'greatness of soul'.
- The action of the tragedy focuses on the tragic protagonist's downfall from this initial high status. Aristotle's term for this reversal of fortune was **peripeteia**.
- This downfall was not the result of accident or chance: it was brought about by an error of judgement committed by the protagonist. This error of judgement, which Aristotle termed **hamartia**, was often the result of **hubris** or excessive pride. It set in motion a chain of events that led to the protagonist's inevitable death.
- Crucially, at some point before his death, the protagonist experiences a period of **anagnorisis** in which he recognises what he has done wrong. This results in an increase of self-knowledge and a new understanding of the truths of existence, especially of the relationship between humans and the gods.
- The effect on the audience is a purging of the emotions, drawing out feelings of fear and pity and bringing about a new sense of clarity. Aristotle termed this process **catharsis**.

The emotional impact of tragedy is what gives the drama its power. In *Shakespearean Tragedy* (1904), the literary critic A.C. Bradley said that when watching tragedy 'we realise the full power and reach of the soul, and the conflict in which it engages acquires that magnitude which stirs not only sympathy and pity, but admiration, terror, and awe'.

Exploring the 'fatal flaw'

A.C. Bradley's work has been very influential. One of Bradley's central concepts was that of the **fatal flaw**, a fault within the tragic protagonist's personality that set in motion the chain of events that would lead to his or her downfall. [The fatal flaw is sometimes confused with Aristotle's concept of hamartia.]

Key terms

satire: a genre that aims to challenge and overturn established values

tragic protagonist: the most important character, usually a person of high status

megalopsychia: the 'greatness of soul' that the tragic protagonist should possess

peripeteia: the reversal of fortune experienced by the tragic protagonist

hamartia: the error of judgement committed by the protagonist that sets his or her reversal of fortune in motion

hubris: an excess of pride or self-confidence that often leads the protagonist to commit his or her hamartia

anagnorisis: the point at which the protagonist recognises what he or she has done wrong and gains a new insight into the truths of existence

catharsis: the purging of the emotions experienced by the audience when watching tragedy

'I am in blood
Stepp'd in so far that, should I wade no more,
Returning were as tedious as go o'er.'

William Shakespeare, *Macbeth*, Act 3, Scene 4

ACTIVITY 1

Thinking about tragedy

You might have explored a tragic drama at some point in your prior studies. If so, think back to see whether you can identify the aspects of tragedy that Aristotle described.

Check your responses in the Ideas section on Cambridge Elevate

Aspects of classical tragedy can also be detected in more recent plays. In Arthur Miller's play *All My Sons* (1947) the actions of the tragic protagonist, the businessman Joe Keller, bring about the deaths of 21 young pilots whose planes have been fitted with faulty engine parts supplied by Keller's company. Keller could have prevented the parts from being sold, but was more concerned with safeguarding the material wealth of his family. Towards the end of the play, he recognises that the pilots who died were 'all my sons' - an acknowledgement of the responsibility that we bear to the wider society as well as to our own families.

Two other Aristotelian concepts may be relevant to your study of tragedy.

The unities

In *Poetics*, Aristotle stated that the action of tragic drama was intensified if it had a single focus, occurred in one location and took place between the hours of sunrise and sunset on one day. These have come to be termed the **unities of plot, place and time**.

Key terms

unity of plot: a focus on one plot, with no sub-plot to complicate the action

unity of place: a single location in which all the action of the play takes place

unity of time: limiting the action of a play so that it takes place on a single day

Many dramatists have violated these unities. Shakespeare's tragedy *King Lear* (1605) has a main plot (concerning Lear and his daughters) and a sub-plot (concerning Gloucester and his sons). In *Othello* (1604) the action begins in Venice and then moves to Cyprus. Nevertheless, some dramatists adhere to the unities: in *All My Sons*, the action takes place in the Keller family's back garden, starting in the early morning of a Sunday in August and ending in the evening of the same day.

The chorus

In Ancient Greek tragedy, the chorus was a group of people who appeared onstage between the main episodes of the tragedy to narrate and interpret certain aspects of the plot. The chorus sometimes represented groups of citizens, and offered a voice of 'common sense', able to comment on the action but not to intervene. One key feature of the chorus is its breaking of the **fourth wall**, the imaginary boundary between the audience and the events onstage.

Again, modern dramatists have adapted this idea for their own purposes, using different characters to perform the role of the chorus. The lawyer Alfieri, for example, acts as a chorus in Arthur Miller's play *A View from the Bridge* (1955), while in Alan Bennett's *The History Boys* (2004), this function is performed by the students in Hector's class.

Key terms

fourth wall: the imaginary barrier separating the events onstage from the audience

Watch tutorial video, Catharsis, on Cambridge Elevate

Exploring the aspects of tragedy that give it lasting power

The lasting power of tragedy has been summed up by the critic Robert N. Watson: 'Even two thousand years before Shakespeare, drama portrayed human traits and situations that still seem very familiar: fascism and democracy struggling for political power, with recognizable kinds of schemers and idealists on both sides; married couples squabbling over money and the perpetual lure of infidelity; sibling rivalries and … oedipal conflicts; losses that are still agonizing and (perhaps most remarkable) jokes that are still funny'. How many of these aspects can you identify in the tragedies you are studying?

5.2 Development of tragedy

5.2.1 Classical drama

Tragedy has its roots in the ritualised dramas of Ancient Greece. Very few of these ancient tragedies are still in existence, but there are three great dramatists whose work has survived: Aeschylus, Sophocles and Euripides. Their plays date from the 5th and 4th centuries BCE, and focus on a number of common themes as shown in Figure 5A.

Many of these early plays draw on a much older set of myths, often relating to the Trojan and Theban wars. These myths are, however, used to dramatise contemporary concerns about the nature of citizenship, duty and freedom. These were important concerns for the people of Athens, which had become a democracy in the 5th century BCE. The critic Simon Goldhill sees the theatre as playing an important role in the proceedings of democracy: 'The Greeks … had a word for it: *es meson*, which means 'put into the public domain to be contested'. Democracy prides itself on its openness to questioning. Tragedy is the institution which stages this openness in the most startling fashion.'

Figure 5A

As an example, let's look at one famous classical Greek tragedy, *Antigone*.

ACTIVITY 2

Antigone

Antigone was written in about 441 BCE by the dramatist Sophocles. It is set against the backdrop of the Theban wars. Read the summary of *Antigone* in Text 5A.

Text 5A

The play opens with the news of the deaths of two brothers, Polynices and Eteocles. Polynices attempted to seize the city of Thebes from Eteocles, its ruler. In the battle that followed, both brothers were killed. Thebes' new ruler, Creon, has declared that because of his treachery, Polynices cannot be given a proper burial: instead, his body must be left as carrion for wild animals. In saying this, Creon is defying religious custom and setting himself up in opposition to the gods.

Polynices' sister, Antigone, defies Creon and buries her brother. When Creon finds out, he orders Antigone's arrest. Antigone states that she chose to disobey him because her loyalty to her brother and to the gods is greater than her loyalty to Creon. Creon, who is trying to unify Thebes after the crisis it has experienced, refuses to pardon Antigone and sentences her to be walled up alive.

Creon's son Haemon, who is engaged to Antigone, pleads for her release, but to no avail. The elders of Thebes are also on Antigone's side. Creon only relents when the blind prophet Tiresias warns him that he has provoked the anger of the gods. However, it is too late: Antigone has killed herself in prison. Haemon, who found her, stabs himself, and Creon's wife Euridyce also commits suicide.

The tragedy of *Antigone* raises a number of issues.

1 Who is the tragic protagonist of this play? Is it Antigone, or could it be Creon?
2 From the summary in Text 5A, can you identify what the tragic protagonists' hamartia might be?
3 In what ways does *Antigone* explore the relationship between the gods, the state and the individual?

Check your responses in the Ideas section on Cambridge Elevate

The tragedies of Ancient Rome were heavily influenced by their Greek predecessors. Nevertheless, theatre did not hold the same importance for the Ancient Romans as it did for the Greeks: to a Roman, the theatre was principally a form of entertainment. As a result, tragedy became dominated by visual display rather than playing the sophisticated philosophical role that it had occupied in Ancient Greece. The main tragic dramatist of Ancient Rome was Seneca, who worked in the 1st century CE. His tragedies were just as influential as their Greek counterparts, but for very different reasons.

Senecan tragedy is characterised by its focus on bloodshed and horror. It is set in a nightmarish world in which evil has the power to destroy good, and contains graphic descriptions of horrific scenes. In his tragedy *Thyestes*, for example, Thyestes' young sons are murdered by their uncle, Atreus, who roasts their bodies and feeds them to their father. Often, Seneca's tragedies present humans as trapped in a world in which they cannot escape their fates: all they can do is wait for events to unfold.

Seneca's tragedies had an enormous influence on tragedy in the Renaissance period. Aspects of Senecan drama can be seen in the revenge tragedies of dramatists such as John Webster, Thomas Kyd and Thomas Middleton. It can also be seen in a number of Shakespeare's plays. Shakespeare's most gruesome tragedy, *Titus Andronicus*, owes an obvious debt to the violence of Seneca, with its shocking scenes of murder, mutilation and cannibalism. (During the 2014 Globe Theatre production of *Titus Andronicus*, a number of audience members fainted.) The revenge-plot of *Hamlet* also has Senecan origins.

5.2.2 Tragedy in medieval literature

After its initial flourishing in classical Greece and Rome, tragic drama received little attention during the medieval period. The rise of Christianity meant that plays featuring non-Christian belief systems (such as the Greek and Roman gods of classical tragedy) were frowned upon. In England, the dramas of the medieval period tended to be small in scale, often performed in the streets rather than in the great theatres of Ancient Greece and Rome. Many of these plays were comic in nature and heavily influenced by Christian mythology. One extremely popular form of drama during this period was the **mystery play**. These plays dramatised Bible stories such as the Creation, the Flood, the Nativity and the Crucifixion.

See 6.2.2 for more on comedy in the medieval period

This does not mean that tragedy was completely absent from the medieval period. Many writers told stories that explored the consequences of error, combining aspects of Christian belief with aspects of tragedy. One important genre of the medieval period was that of the **de casibus story**. This stemmed from the work of the Italian poet Giovanni Boccaccio (1313–75), who wrote a series of narratives based on the calamities and disasters that befell various great men as a result of their folly and sinfulness. Boccaccio's stories acted as **cautionary tales**, offering a warning of the catastrophes that might happen if people acted unwisely. They influenced the work of the English writers Geoffrey Chaucer and John Lydgate.

Set text focus: 'The Monk's Tale' and Prologue

Geoffrey Chaucer began to write *The Canterbury Tales* around 1387. Rather than writing in the French spoken at the English court, he chose to write in vernacular English that could be enjoyed by ordinary English people. His satire of the aristocracy and clergy permeates the whole of *The Canterbury Tales*, which was written at a time of peasant rebellion, when the traditional estates of nobility, Church and peasantry were breaking down. Indeed, 'The Monk's Tale' tells of famous noble characters who were brought down and that wealth and position in this world are pure illusion. The extract from the Prologue to 'The Monk's Tale' offers a definition of the genre of tragedy; the extract from the Tale itself describes the fall of Lucifer and Adam's expulsion from Eden.

Although not an exhaustive list, the following aspects of tragedy could be explored in relation to 'The Monk's Tale':

- the poem as a classical tragedy about public figures (see 5.2.4, *King Lear*)
- classical aspects of tragedy (see 5.1.2)
- the heroes' fatal flaws (see Activity 6; 5.3.1; 5.3.6)
- aspects of good and evil (see Activity 5)
- the roles of fate, inevitability and free will (see Activity 4; 5.3.4; 5.3.5)
- the structural pattern of the extract (see 5.2.7)
- the way language is used to heighten tragic experiences (see 5.2.4, *Dr Faustus*)
- the effects on the audience/reader (see 5.1.2; 5.3.8).

The poem could be read from the perspective of:

- value and the canon (see 5.4.5, Critical lens; 9.3)
- narrative theory (see 5.3.8, Critical lens; 9.4).

ACTIVITY 3

The Monk's* (cautionary) *Tale

Geoffrey Chaucer's poem *The Monk's Tale* recounts the tragic endings of a range of historical and mythological characters, from Lucifer and Adam to Alexander the Great and Julius Caesar. If you are studying *The Monk's Tale*, you will need to make notes on what Adam and Samson do and what happens to them. Use the table to structure your notes.

Character	Actions	Consequences	Key quotations

The cautionary tale implies that humans are at least partly to blame for their own downfall. One key medieval image, however, suggests otherwise. This is the image of the **wheel of fortune**, often represented by the female figure Fortuna. In medieval philosophy, all humans - from beggars to kings - are subject to the turning of the wheel of fortune. Sometimes, you are at the top of the wheel: sometimes, you are at the bottom. Crucially, there is nothing you can do to speed up or slow down the wheel of fortune. Its movement is inevitable.

Key terms

mystery play: a play, usually part of a longer sequence, that dramatises stories from the Bible and was performed during religious festivals

***de casibus* story:** a story that used tales of the disasters that befell great men as examples of how to behave

cautionary tale: a story that contains a warning, showing the consequences of some kind of error

wheel of fortune: a medieval image of a wheel that represented good and bad luck and the inevitability of change. If you are at the top of the wheel, you are experiencing a period of good luck: if you are at the bottom, you are experiencing bad luck. The wheel's turning is inevitable and cannot be halted

ACTIVITY 4

The wheel of fortune

Research the medieval wheel of fortune, or *rota fortuna*. Shakespeare's plays contain many references to the wheel of fortune.

a Which characters welcome and accept fortune? Which characters reject or challenge her?

b What observations can you make about the depiction of fortune as a woman? (Think, in particular, about the way she is described as a lover, a goddess, a 'false housewife' and a whore.)

c Is the idea of the wheel of fortune – whose inevitable turning will both favour everyone and bring everyone low – incompatible with the idea that tragedy stems from individual actions?

Exploring Shakespeare's use of fortune

***Hamlet*:** In his famous soliloquy, Hamlet refers to 'the slings and arrows of outrageous fortune'. He also calls fortune a 'strumpet'. The First Player asks the gods to 'break all the spokes and fellies from her wheel'.

***King Lear*:** Kent, imprisoned in the stocks, bids fortune 'good night', and asks her to 'smile once more, turn thy wheel!' King Lear describes himself as being 'bound upon a wheel of fire', while Gloucester's scheming son Edmund, just before the battle that will cost him his life, states that 'The wheel is come full circle'.

***Macbeth*:** The Sergeant who describes Macbeth's victory over the Thane of Cawdor describes fortune as 'like a rebel's whore'. Later, the lord who describes the turmoil that follows the death of Duncan refers to 'the malevolence of Fortune'.

***Coriolanus*:** The general Lartius calls upon 'the fair goddess, Fortune' to 'fall deep in love' with his fellow solider Caius Marcius.

***Antony and Cleopatra*:** As her lover Mark Antony lies dying, Cleopatra begs Mark Antony to let her speak so loud that it will break Fortune's wheel (see Text 5B).

Text 5B

let me speak, and let me rail so high,
That the false housewife Fortune break her wheel,
Provoked by my offence.

Antony and Cleopatra, Act 4, Scene 15, lines 52–4

Another way in which tragedy was explored in medieval literature was through the **morality play**. As the name suggests, the morality play presented its audience with religious and ethical problems, dramatising the choices made by humans in their journey through life. Significantly, the morality play belonged to a world that was firmly Christian. It had a number of key features.

- It focused on a struggle between good and evil.
- It was allegorical rather than naturalistic: characters were not individuals, but representations of ideas or values (such as Virtue, Slander and Perseverance).
- The main character represented humanity. In *The Castle of Perseverance* (c.1405), this character is called Mankind; in *Everyman* (c.1510), it is called Everyman.
- It often had a character or characters who fulfilled the role of chorus.
- The main character had to negotiate his or her way through life, facing various trials and being tempted by sin.
- Eventually, the main character renounces temptation, is pardoned by God and assured of salvation in heaven.

After the complexity of classical drama, morality plays can seem highly simplistic. It can also be difficult to see how they can be linked to the genre of tragedy. Nevertheless, one of their most important functions was to remind audiences that their actions could end in eternal damnation. Mankind, in *The Castle of Perseverance*, is accompanied by good and bad angels who stand on either side of him. Look at his comments in Text 5C.

Key terms

morality play: a genre of medieval and early Tudor theatrical entertainment in which the characters represent abstract qualities or concepts, such as humanity, virtues: good and evil, vices, or death

Text 5C

Two such has every man alive
To rule him and his wits five.
When man does evil, one would him **shrive**,
The other draws him to ill.

Anon, *The Castle of Perseverance*

Glossary

to shrive: to gain forgiveness for one's sins, usually as a result of the Christian sacrament of confession. It is most commonly found today in the form of Shrove Tuesday, the day before the first day of Lent.

While they invariably ended happily, with the main character rejecting sin and achieving redemption, the possibility of hell has to be present in order for the drama to have its force.

ACTIVITY 5

Moral aspects

There are aspects of the morality play in many later tragedies. As you read the tragedies you are studying, look for examples of:

a good and bad angels
b protagonists reflecting on the moral choices they must make
c characters acting as advisors or confidantes to the protagonist as he or she makes these choices
d images of hell and damnation.

5.2.3 The first English tragedies

Towards the end of the medieval period, dramatists began to turn their attention to individuals, rather than character-types. One of the earliest English tragedies is *Gorboduc* by Thomas Norton and Thomas Sackville, which was first performed in 1561. It tells the story of a king who ignores the advice of the wise and divides his kingdom between his sons. His decision leads to war, bloodshed and death. *Gorboduc*, and other early tragedies such as *Cambises*, are seen today as relatively simplistic, unsophisticated plays. In just a few decades, however, they would be eclipsed by the tragic dramas of the major Renaissance dramatists, who would take aspects of both classical and medieval tragedy and fuse them into plays that offered a richer and more fully developed vision of the relationship between humans and the gods.

5.2.4 Tragedy in Renaissance drama

The word Renaissance means 'rebirth'. It denotes a period of intellectual and cultural transformation that began in Italy in the 14th century and spread to the rest of Europe. The Renaissance saw a renewal of interest in the classics of Greek and Roman literature. It is also associated with the development of humanism – an interest in the abilities of the human mind and a new sense of what it was to be a thinking, learning, reflecting individual.

Exploring the development of tragedy

Look back at sections 5.1 and 5.2.1. What scope do the tragedies of Ancient Greece and Rome offer to explore the human mind? Can you think of ways in which Renaissance dramatists might have built on the work of their classical predecessors?

One key aspect of the Renaissance, then, was the potential of the individual self. It was also a time of discovery, invention and exploration in many areas of life.

- Johannes Gutenberg invented the printing press.
- Nicolaus Copernicus developed the theory that the earth revolves around the sun.
- Dissection and examination led to the growth of knowledge about the human body.
- Artists developed linear perspective, thus allowing the world to be represented in more accurate ways.
- The invention of the telescope enabled Galileo Galilei to observe the movements of the stars.
- The newly developed mariner's astrolabe allowed sailors to navigate the oceans more easily.
- Leonardo da Vinci produced designs for a number of inventions, including dams, bridges, parachutes, steam cannons, hydraulic pumps and musical instruments.

Nevertheless, humans were constantly encountering barriers, being brought up short by the restrictions of technology, the weather, social and political factors, their own minds – and, of course, by the greatest limiting factor of all, that of mortality. The critic Robert N. Watson sees English Renaissance tragedy as a reflection of the conflict that results from this combination of aspiration and limitation: 'A remarkable number of the memorable heroes are destroyed by … this confrontation between the desiring personal imagination and the relentless machinery of power, whether social, natural, or divine.'

For Watson, the tragic protagonist's ambitions might well be flawed, but they still represent an important part of what it is to be human.

ACTIVITY 6

Human struggles

Think about the tragedies you are studying. What kinds of aspirations do their protagonists embody? What limitations do they come up against? To what extent are they destroyed by the confrontation that Watson describes?

You could keep a record of quotations, like Watson's, that make statements about aspects of tragedy.

A complete survey of Renaissance tragedy is beyond the scope of this book. Nevertheless, a detailed summary of three particular tragedies – *Dr Faustus* by Christopher Marlowe (1588), *King Lear* by William Shakespeare (1605) and *The Duchess of Malfi* by John Webster (1614) – will help to highlight some of the major themes and debates that shaped tragic drama at this key period of its history.

Dr Faustus

In many ways, Dr Faustus can be seen as an embodiment of the intellectual daring of the Renaissance. Faustus, whose story is based on a German legend, is a scholar whose thirst for knowledge is so strong that it ultimately condemns him to hell. He conjures up a devil, Mephistopheles, and makes a pact with him: Mephistopheles will do Faustus' bidding for 24 years and, at the end of this time, he will receive Faustus' soul. Rather than using this time to accomplish something of worth, Faustus fritters it away. He plays tricks on people (including the Pope and a horse dealer), and has sex with a demon that he believes to be Helen of Troy. Eventually, Mephistopheles arrives to claim Faustus' soul.

Exploring the life and work of Christopher Marlowe

Christopher Marlowe, the author of *Dr Faustus*, was born in 1564, the same year as William Shakespeare. He was a playwright, poet and translator, and was suspected of being a spy and a heretic (a supporter of beliefs that challenged orthodox religion). He was killed in a fight in a tavern in Deptford, London, in May 1593.

One famous study of Marlowe and his works is Harry Levin's book *The Overreacher*, whose title refers to the towering ambitions of Marlowe's tragic protagonists. Some critics argue that this title could equally apply to Marlowe himself.

Faustus was described by the literary critic William Hazlitt as 'a personification of the pride of will and eagerness of curiosity'. It is easy to identify his hamartia – his decision to make his pact with Mephistopheles – and, from then on, his peripeteia is clear, a simple matter of the passage of the 24 years until his death. While Faustus claims not to believe in hell, and refuses the chance to repent, he faces his death in a state of torment that can be seen as his moment of anagnorisis. And while he often appears comic – his antics are undoubtedly foolish – his language as he confronts his death has a grandeur that draws out the pity and fear necessary for the process of catharsis (see the quote in Text 5D).

Text 5D

FAUSTUS Ah, Faustus,
Now hast thou but one bare hour to live,
And then thou must be damn'd perpetually!
Stand still, you ever-moving spheres of heaven,
That time may cease, and midnight never come;
Fair Nature's eye, rise, rise again, and make
Perpetual day; or let this hour be but
A year, a month, a week, a natural day,
That Faustus may repent and save his soul!
O lente, lente currite, noctis equi!
The stars move still, time runs, the clock will strike,
The devil will come, and Faustus must be damn'd.

Christopher Marlowe, *Dr Faustus*

Glossary

O lente, lente currite, noctis equi!: Run slowly, slowly, horses of the night!

Nevertheless, some critics have argued that Faustus' damnation is predestined, rather than the result of his own choice. The doctrine of predestination was the subject of widespread debate at the time *Dr Faustus* was written. It was based on the teachings of John Calvin, who believed that God had chosen some people to be saved and others to be condemned to hell. The individual, therefore, has no control over his or her spiritual fate. Debates about predestination are closely linked to the topic of free will.

See 5.3.4 and 5.3.5 for more on free will

King Lear

King Lear is one of Shakespeare's four major tragedies. It is often seen as being unbearably bleak. The eighteenth-century critic Samuel Johnson was so appalled by its ending that he could hardly bring himself to read it a second time, and for over a century the play was performed only in a heavily rewritten form.

Barbara A. Mowat and Paul Werstine, in their introduction to the Folger Shakespeare Library edition of *King Lear*, highlight the play's bleakness: 'It is a play that relentlessly challenges its readers and … audiences with the magnitude, intensity, and sheer duration of the pain that it represents.'

Watching *King Lear* is certainly an uncomfortable experience. Lear curses and disowns his daughters, children plot against their parents and the elderly Duke of Gloucester has his eyes torn out in a scene of horrific viciousness. However, it also exemplifies the ways in which Renaissance tragedy combined aspects of classical drama with detailed psychological exploration.

King Lear is the oldest and the most distinguished of Shakespeare's tragic heroes: unlike Macbeth, who attains power during the play, Lear is coming to the end of his powers. At the beginning of the play, Lear has decided to abdicate and divide his kingdom between his three daughters, who must offer him a public declaration of their love in order to determine which portion of the kingdom they will receive. Goneril and Regan make eloquent speeches telling Lear of their apparent love for him, but their younger sister, Cordelia, refuses to take part. The enraged Lear banishes her from his kingdom.

Lear plans to divide his time alternately between Goneril and Regan's homes, but his increasingly irascible temper leads them to lose patience with him. They refuse to give him and his entourage a place to stay, and he curses them for their lack of respect. Meanwhile, the country descends into chaos.

The third act of the play sees the homeless Lear wandering on a heath as a violent storm breaks. He rages at the elements and at the gods above, but in his madness he gains a new insight into the injustices that took place during his reign - and into his own shortcomings.

Towards the end of the play, Lear is reunited briefly with Cordelia, but she is then killed. The play's emotional climax occurs when Lear carries the dead Cordelia on stage, desperately searching for signs of life - and then dies himself (see Text 5E).

Text 5E

LEAR: No, no, no life?
Why should a dog, a horse, a rat have life,
And thou no breath at all?

King Lear, Act 5, Scene 3, lines 279–81, Cambridge School Shakespeare

It is easy to find in *King Lear* the aspects of tragedy described by Aristotle. The hamartia, or error of judgement, takes place in the very first scene, with Lear's division of his kingdom, the staging of the 'love-trial', and his subsequent exiling of Cordelia. This whole process is driven by hubris - Lear's conviction that his daughters will not fail to express their love for him. From this point onwards, Lear's downfall, or peripeteia, is all too apparent, as he alienates Goneril and Regan and descends into madness. The most powerful aspect of *King Lear*, however, is the detailed depiction of Lear's anagnorisis - his recognition of the truth of his own situation, including the pain he has caused and his place within the universe. Such is the intensity of Lear's experience on the heath that the audience is utterly absorbed: the play cannot fail to bring about catharsis.

Set text focus: *King Lear*

Shakespeare wrote *King Lear* some time around 1605. Many members of his audience would have been aware of two legal cases in which elderly men were poorly treated by their daughters, as happens to Lear. This story might also be said to reflect the concerns of the nation when a potential power struggle was narrowly avoided by the childless Elizabeth I's nomination of James I as heir to her throne.

Although not an exhaustive list, the following aspects of tragedy could be explored in relation to *King Lear*:

- the play as a classical tragedy about public figures (see 5.2.4)
- classical aspects of tragedy (see 5.1.2)
- settings of time and place (see 5.1.2, The unities)
- use of nature and the supernatural (see 5.3.14)
- Lear's journey towards death (see 5.2.4, *King Lear*; 5.3.1; 5.3.6; 5.3.13)
- Lear's potential and sense of personal dignity (see 5.2.4 , *King Lear*; Activity 9)
- Lear's error of judgement or fatal flaw (see Activity 6; 5.2.4, *King Lear*; 5.3.1; 5.3.6)
- the role of real and metaphorical blindness (see 5.3.6)
- Lear's insight and self-knowledge (see 5.2.4, *King Lear*; 5.3.6)
- how Lear's behaviour creates chaos and suffering (see 5.2.4, *King Lear*; 5.3.7; 5.3.8)
- aspects of good and evil (see Activity 5)
- the role of tragic villain (see 5.3.2, The malcontent)
- the role of fate, the wheel of fortune, inevitability and free will (see Activity 4; 5.3.4; 5.3.5)
- the role of deception (see 5.3.10)
- significance of family and social class (see 5.2.4, *King Lear*; Activity 35; 5.4.4)
- the role of the fool (see 5.3.3)
- treatment of female characters (see 5.2.4, *The Duchess of Malfi*, Exploring…; Activity 34)
- structural pattern of the play (see 5.1.2; Activity 25)
- use of plots and sub-plots (see 5.1.2, The unities; 5.3.12)
- how language is used to heighten tragic experiences (see 5.2.4, *Dr Faustus*; 5.2.4, *The Duchess of Malfi*, Exploring…; 5.3.3)
- effects on the audience (see 5.1.2; 5.2.4, *King Lear*; 5.3.8).

The play could be read from the perspective of:

- value and the canon (see 5.4.5, Critical lens; 9.3)
- narrative theory (see 5.3.8, Critical lens; 5.3.12, Critical lens; 9.4)
- feminist theory (see 5.2.4, *The Duchess of Malfi*, Exploring…; 5.4.1; 9.5)
- Marxist theory (see 5.4.2, Critical lens; 9.6)
- eco-critical theory (see 5.3.14, Critical lens; 9.7).

ACTIVITY 7

Lear's anagnorisis

In many tragedies, the process of anagnorisis is one that the protagonist does not undergo until a relatively late stage. In *King Lear*, however, this process begins much earlier.

Find evidence of Lear's recognition of his mistakes. When does he acknowledge that his treatment of Cordelia was wrong? At which point in the play do you start to feel most sympathy for Lear?

Exploring more of Shakespeare's plays with tragic aspects

Shakespeare's major tragedies are considered to be *King Lear, Macbeth, Hamlet* and *Othello*. Try reading or watching a performance of one of Shakespeare's other tragedies – *Romeo and Juliet, Titus Andronicus, Timon of Athens, Coriolanus, Antony and Cleopatra* or *Julius Caesar*. One of Shakespeare's history plays, *Richard II*, could also be seen as a tragedy (its original title was, in fact, *The Tragedy of King Richard the Second*). *Richard III* also contains some aspects of tragedy.

If you read or watch one of Shakespeare's other tragedies, identify ways in which it differs from the tragedy you are studying.

The Duchess of Malfi

The Duchess of Malfi shows the influence of an important subgenre of tragedy, the revenge tragedy. Revenge tragedies were often set in the Mediterranean climates of Italy and Spain, which, for audiences in Renaissance England, had connotations of exoticism, hot-bloodedness and intrigue.

See 5.3.9 for more on revenge tragedy

The Duchess of Malfi, set in southern Italy, is full of cruelty and corruption. Its heroine, the Duchess, is a beautiful young widow whose brothers, Ferdinand and the Cardinal, want to prevent their sister from marrying again. However, she is in love with her steward, Antonio, and the two marry and have children in secret. Ferdinand employs a spy, Bosola, to keep watch over his sister. When the Duchess's marriage is uncovered, Ferdinand has her arrested. In a series of horrific scenes, he tortures her by giving her a dead man's hand to kiss and showing her images of the dead bodies of Antonio and her children. The play ends in carnage, with Bosola strangling the Duchess and her children and killing Antonio, Ferdinand and the Cardinal before receiving a fatal wound.

As well as being an important example of revenge tragedy, *The Duchess of Malfi* is also notable for its exploration of relationships between the sexes.

- The Duchess is trapped in a patriarchal world in which she is governed by powerful men.
- She embodies virtue, love and tenderness in a world that is otherwise corrupt.
- Her *hamartia*, or error of judgement, is her decision to marry Antonio, against the orders of her brothers.

The German philosopher Georg Hegel (1770–1831) saw tragedy as the result of a clash of values. For Hegel, the tragic protagonist is caught between two sets of principles that are mutually exclusive (that is, in order to follow one set of principles, you must reject the other). The Duchess can be seen as a perfect example of this: in order to follow her own private desires and marry the man she loves, she must disobey her brothers' commands.

See 5.4.1 to explore the Duchess's relationship with her brothers

Exploring the treatment of female characters in tragedy

There's plenty of scope for reflection on the way tragedies treat their female characters. If you're studying *King Lear*, think about the way Lear controls his daughters' behaviour through the love trial, and the violence of his language as he curses them (plus the way in which some of his curses hint at a fear of their sexuality). If you're studying *Tess of the D'Urbervilles*, consider Angel's reaction to Tess when she tells him her story. If you are studying Keats' poetry, think about the depiction of characters such as Isabella in 'Isabella; or, The Pot of Basil', Madeline in 'The Eve of St Agnes', Lamia in 'Lamia' and the Belle Dame in 'La Belle Dame Sans Merci'.

5.2.5 Restoration to Victorian drama

In 1642, the theatres were closed by order of the Puritan parliament. They reopened in 1660 when the English monarchy was restored under King Charles II, but the tragedies that emerged from this restoration period displayed little of the richness and complexity of their Renaissance forebears. Instead, they were formal, stylised and conventional.

One of the most successful Restoration tragedies was *Venice Preserv'd* by Thomas Otway, first performed in 1682. Its plot turns on corruption, promiscuity and conspiracy, and closely paralleled contemporary political events.

Perhaps of more significance is the way in which some older tragedies were treated during the 17th and 18th centuries. One of the most popular plays of this period was Nahum Tate's adaptation of *King Lear*. Tate gave Shakespeare's play a happy ending, in which Lear and Cordelia do not die. Lear is restored to the monarchy, and Cordelia marries Edgar. Tate's version – which he called *The History of King Lear*, as it was, of course, no longer a tragedy – was first performed in 1681, and is believed to have replaced Shakespeare's play completely until the mid-19th century.

In the 19th century, the theatre became an increasingly grand, social affair that focused on spectacle and display. It aimed to entertain and to impress, rather than to ask the difficult questions posed by the tragedies of the Renaissance period. One important 19th-century genre was that of the well-made play, which featured a complex plot, a build-up of suspense, a climactic scene in which loose ends were resolved neatly and a happy ending. This appealed to audiences' desire to be amused and intrigued without threatening the order and security of their world.

Set text focus: *Richard II*

Shakespeare wrote *Richard II* in the late 1590s, near the end of Elizabeth I's reign. At that time, there was much concern about the power struggle that might ensue when Elizabeth died, leaving no heir to the English crown. It was generally held that the monarch was appointed by God, which raised questions about the succession and whether it was a sin to relieve a monarch of the right to rule, especially if that monarch, like Shakespeare's Richard II, proved incapable of ruling effectively. Although Shakespeare was careful to praise the Tudor monarchs when speaking directly (through his characters) about his own times, *Richard II* is one of various plays that explores these concerns in the safe environment of another time and place.

Although not an exhaustive list, the following aspects of tragedy could be explored in relation to *Richard II*:

- the play as a classical tragedy about public figures (see 5.2.4)
- classical aspects of tragedy (see 5.1.2)
- use of nature and the supernatural (see 5.3.14)
- Richard's journey towards death (see 5.2.4; 5.3.1)
- Richard's potential and sense of personal dignity (see 5.2.4; Activity 9)
- Richard's fatal flaw (see Activity 6; 5.3.1; 5.3.6)
- Richard's self-knowledge as a man (see 5.3.6)
- how Richard's behaviour creates disorder (see 5.3.7; 5.3.14, Activity 30)
- the role of Richard as tragic villain (see 5.3.2, The malcontent)
- the role of fate and free will (see 5.3.4; 5.3.5)
- treatment of female characters (see 5.2.4, *The Duchess of Malfi*, Exploring…; Activity 34).

The play could be read from the perspective of:

- value and the canon (see 5.4.5, Critical lens; 9.3)
- narrative theory (see 5.3.8, Critical lens; 9.4)
- feminist theory (see 5.4.1; 9.5).

Set text focus: 'The Eve of St Agnes'

The Eve of St Agnes is on 20 January and commemorates a young girl who died as a martyr in the fourth century and became the patron saint of virgins. The poem is based on the superstition that if a young woman performed particular rites on this celebration, she would see her future husband in a dream. It tells the story of the forbidden love between Madeline and Porphyro, set against a richly-detailed background. John Keats wrote the poem in 1819 just after he and Fanny Brawne had fallen in love, which might account for his desire to celebrate romantic love and focus on the senses in a wealth of description, rather than tell a thrilling story.

Although not an exhaustive list, the following aspects of tragedy could be explored in relation to 'The Eve of St Agnes':

- classical aspects of tragedy (see 5.1.2)
- settings or time and place (see 5.1.2, The unities)
- tragic narratives in poetry (see 5.2.7)
- nature of suffering in the poem (see 5.3.7)
- the role of deception (see 5.3.10)
- treatment of female characters (see 5.2.4, *The Duchess of Malfi*, Exploring…; Activity 34)
- how language is used to heighten tragic experiences (see 5.3.4).

The poems could be read from the perspective of:

- value and the canon (see 5.4.5, Critical lens; 9.3)
- narrative theory (see 5.3.8, Critical lens; 9.4)
- feminist theory (see 5.2.4, *The Duchess of Malfi*, Exploring…; 5.4.1; 9.5).

Domestic tragedy

Towards the end of the 19th century, however, tragedy resurfaced in a manner that aimed to shake audiences out of their complacency. Rather than focusing on the lives of great rulers, it turned its attention to domestic matters - to the lives of ordinary people.

The three most important writers associated with this development in tragedy were from continental Europe:

Playwright	Country	Dates	Key works
Henrik Ibsen	Norway	1828–1906	*A Doll's House*, *Hedda Gabler*, *Ghosts*
August Strindberg	Sweden	1849–1912	*Miss Julie*
Anton Chekhov	Russia	1860–1904	*The Cherry Orchard*, *The Seagull*, *Three Sisters*, *Uncle Vanya*

In the words of Sean McEvoy, their plays 'adopted many of the forms of tragedy and created works in which real lives are lived realistically, in all their ugly glory'. They focused not on public events but on issues of private discontent: infidelity, suffocation, lack of fulfilment. Often, they touched on matters that many people would prefer to ignore, with characters making choices that would shock audiences. At the end of Ibsen's *A Doll's House* (1879), Nora, the protagonist, leaves her husband and children in order to find fulfilment. As she leaves, she slams the door behind her: this door slam was, as one critic put it, 'heard around the world'.

Significantly, these tragedies did not necessarily end with a death. Nora does not die at the end of *A Doll's House*. Nevertheless, she does give up her marriage, her children - and her respectability.

ACTIVITY 8

Metaphorical tragedy?

Does tragedy have to end in the death of a person? Can it end with some other kind of death - the death of an ideal, or a principle, or a way of life? Can you think of any other metaphorical 'deaths' in texts that you've read or studied? Think, for instance, of moments when characters realise that a particular dream is never going to come true, or when a belief they hold is destroyed. If you've studied Harper Lee's novel *To Kill a Mockingbird* (1960), one possible metaphorical death is represented by the ending of the trial, when Tom Robinson is found guilty. Scout's faith in human nature is challenged by the jury's decision to ignore the evidence that points to Tom's innocence. In William Golding's novel *Lord of the Flies* (1954), Ralph's tears at the end are partly for 'the darkness of man's heart' - the events that have taken place have taught him that people are innately savage.

If you're studying *A Streetcar Named Desire*, the idea of a metaphorical 'death' is an important one, as Blanche does not actually die. At the end of the play, however, she is committed to a mental institution. In what ways does this act as a kind of death for Blanche? Similarly, Stevens in Kazuo Ishiguro's *The Remains of the Day* does not die. However, the novel could be seen as the story of a number of metaphorical deaths. What kinds of values, ideals and hopes 'die' during *The Remains of the Day*? To what extent is the novel about the death of a particular way of life?

Another important aspect of many 19th-century European tragedies was their refusal to come to a clear conclusion. This was in keeping with their **realist** principles: their ambivalent endings reflect the fact that life is complex. They also challenged the conventions of the 'well-made play', with its neat resolution and tying-up of loose ends. However, they often adhered to classical principles: *Miss Julie*, for example, obeys the unities of plot, place and time.

Key terms

realism: a movement in drama to represent life in as realistic a way as possible. It was driven partly by a desire to explore the details of everyday life, including the ways in which people think, behave and express themselves

5.2.6 Modern drama

In the 20th century, dramatists continued to explore the tragic potential of the lives of ordinary people. Like their predecessors, they focused on clashing values, thwarted emotions and uncomfortable secrets; on personal fulfilment and on the events that unfold when truths that are suppressed finally bubble up to the surface.

Set text focus: *The Remains of the Day*

The Remains of the Day (1989), written by Kazuo Ishiguro, is a story of regret, an emotion the author knew well after, as a child, leaving his grandfather in Japan never to see him again. Stevens, the novel's protagonist, places great value in how he performs his job as a butler, foregoing emotion and romance, which he later regrets. Instead he gives total loyalty to his master, Lord Darlington, a man who makes huge mistakes, including, in common with quite a few of the British aristocracy in the early 1930s, taking a pro-German stance, as Germany struggled to make an economic recovery despite the punitive peace settlement dictated by the Allies in 1919.

Although not an exhaustive list, the following aspects of tragedy could be explored in relation to *The Remains of the Day*:

- the novel as a tragedy about ordinary people (see 5.2.5; 5.3.15)
- Stevens' journey towards self-knowledge and regret (see 5.2.4; 5.3.1; 5.3.13)
- the role of metaphorical tragedy (see Activity 8)
- Stevens' sense of personal dignity (see 5.2.4; Activity 9)
- Stevens' error of judgement and blindness to what is happening around him (see Activity 6; 5.3.1; 5.3.6)
- significance of social class (see Activity 35)
- treatment of female characters (see 5.2.4, *The Duchess of Malfi*, Exploring…; Activity 34).

The novel could be read from the perspective of:

- value and the canon (see 5.4.5, Critical lens; 9.3)
- narrative theory (see 5.3.8, Critical lens; 9.4)
- feminist theory (see 5.2.4, *The Duchess of Malfi*, Exploring…; 5.4.1; 9.5)
- Marxist theory (see 5.4.2; 9.6).

American tragedy

Two of the greatest tragic dramatists of the 20th century were the American playwrights Tennessee Williams (1911–83) and Arthur Miller (1915–2005). Both focused on the family and its frustrations, giving their plays a heightened intensity by drawing on classical principles.

- Williams' first major success, *The Glass Menagerie* (1944), obeys the unities of plot, place and time.
- The action of Williams' play *Cat on a Hot Tin Roof* (1955) takes place in real time, exploring tensions within the Pollitt family as they gather in one room on one long, hot, uncomfortable evening.
- Miller's plays *All My Sons* (1947) and *Death of a Salesman* (1949) both concentrate on the last day of their tragic protagonists' lives as they confront truths that they have previously denied.
- Williams' *A Streetcar Named Desire* (1947) obeys the unity of place, with the action happening inside and outside the Kowalskis' apartment in a run-down area of New Orleans.
- Miller's *A View from the Bridge* (1955) uses the character of Alfieri, a lawyer, as a chorus to guide the audience's reaction to the character of Eddie Carbone and his frustrated feelings for his niece, Catherine.

ACTIVITY 9

Personal dignity

Arthur Miller argued in his essay 'Tragedy and the Common Man' (1949) that tragedy did not only have to be about kings or nobles. What mattered was not status, but the character's strength of principle, a 'sense of personal dignity' for which he is willing to sacrifice anything – even his life.

Sean McEvoy has referred to the way in which 20th-century tragedies explore 'those small-scale, crushing disappointments that happen … in the gap between ambition and reality'.

1 Consider these two perspectives on tragedy in relation to the tragic protagonists of the texts you are studying.
2 Begin by identifying what each protagonist's 'sense of personal dignity' rests on. Is it a particular set of values? Is it their self-image? Is it their reputation? Is there a difference between the 'sense of personal dignity' felt by public figures such as King Lear or Othello, and that felt by

Set text focus: *Death of a Salesman* and *A Streetcar Named Desire*

Arthur Miller wrote *Death of a Salesman* in the post-war America of 1949. At that time, various writers, including Miller, were exploring the way the vision of the original American Dream was being undermined. It seemed that the Dream had been subverted to the relentless pursuit of material success, whilst the comfortable classes were losing sight of moral values, feeling threatened by communism and ignoring the inequalities within society.

Although not an exhaustive list, the following aspects of tragedy could be explored in relation to *Death of a Salesman*:

- the play as a tragedy about ordinary people (see 5.2.5; 5.3.1; 5.4.2)
- classical aspects of tragedy (see 5.1.2)
- settings of time and place (see 5.1.2, The unities; 5.3.13)
- Loman's journey towards death (see 5.2.4; Activity 6; 5.3.1)
- Loman's sense of personal dignity (see 5.2.6; Activity 9; 5.4.2)
- Loman's error of judgement or fatal flaw (see Activity 6; 5.3.1; 5.3.6)
- Loman's lack of insight (see 5.3.6)
- the role of fate, inevitability and freewill (see 5.3.4; 5.3.5)
- the role of deception (see 5.3.10)
- significance of family and social class (see 5.4.2; 5.4.4)
- treatment of female characters (see 5.2.4, *The Duchess of Malfi*, Exploring…; Activities 34, 38).

The play could be read from the perspective of:

- value and the canon (see 5.4.5, Critical lens; 9.3)
- narrative theory (see 5.3.8, Critical lens; 9.4)
- feminist theory (see 5.4.1; 9.5)
- Marxist theory (see 5.4.2; Activity 35; 9.6).

Tennessee Williams' *A Streetcar Named Desire* premiered in New York in 1947. It shows the conflict between the masculine, machine-drive world of post-war America, symbolised by Stanley, the ex-soldier expecting to throw his weight around having returned from a victorious war, and the vanishing, aristocratic culture of the southern states, represented by Blanche. Williams used his own experience to model his characters: his father's alcoholism, the breakdown of his family life, the mental illness of his mother and older sister, and his own frustrated desires and loneliness.

Although not an exhaustive list, the following aspects of tragedy could be explored in relation to *A Streetcar Named Desire*:

- the play as a tragedy about ordinary people (see 5.2.5)
- classical aspects of tragedy (see 5.1.2)
- settings of time and place (see 5.1.2, The unities)
- the role of metaphorical death (see Activity 8)
- Blanche's potential and sense of personal dignity (see Activity 9; 5.4.2)
- Blanche's fatal flaw and lack of insight (see Activity 6; 5.3.1; 5.3.6)
- how Blanche's behaviour creates suffering for herself and others (see 5.3.7; 5.4.4)
- the role of Stanley as tragic villain (see 5.3.2, The malcontent)
- the role of fate and freewill (see 5.3.4; 5.3.5)
- treatment of female characters (see 5.2.4, *The Duchess of Malfi*, Exploring…; 5.4.1)
- structural pattern of the play and restoration of order (see 5.1.2; 5.3.8)
- effects on the audience (see 5.1.2; 5.3.8).

The play could be read from the perspective of:

- value and the canon (see 5.4.5, Critical lens; 9.3)
- narrative theory (see 5.3.8, Critical lens; 9.4)
- feminist theory (see 5.2.4, *The Duchess of Malfi*, Exploring…; 5.4.1; 9.5)
- Marxist theory (see 5.4.2; 9.6).

ordinary people, such as Tess in *Tess of the D'Urbervilles*, Stevens in *The Remains of the Day*, Willy Loman in *Death of a Salesman* or Blanche Dubois in *A Streetcar Named Desire*? Does this sense of dignity rest on different things?

3 What kinds of ambitions do each tragic protagonist have? What kinds of disappointments do they suffer in trying to achieve these ambitions? Are these large-scale, public disappointments, or McEvoy's 'small-scale, crushing disappointments'?
4 Find quotations and examples from each text to support and illustrate your ideas.
5 Now write up your ideas in coherent paragraphs, using one paragraph for each text. Try to refer back to Miller and McEvoy's ideas. As an example of how this could be done, read Text 5F, about Arthur Miller's play *A View from the Bridge*.

Text 5F

Eddie Carbone's 'sense of personal dignity' is bound up with his image of himself as the centre of his family, a hardworking man who is adored by both his wife Beatrice and his niece Catherine. Catherine's devotion to him is shown very early in the play, in the way she attends to him when he comes home from work: she shows off her new skirt, leads him to his armchair and, later, lights his cigar. Nevertheless, Miller makes it clear that Eddie's feelings for Catherine go beyond those which might be expected. He is extremely protective of her, and at times, this protectiveness shades over into possessiveness – as in his criticism of her for 'walkin' wavy' and his unhappiness over her decision to leave school and get a job. The arrival of Beatrice's cousins, Marco and Rodolpho, highlight the complexity of Eddie's feelings by challenging his status within his own household. The attention that Catherine pays to Rodolpho could be seen in the light of the 'small-scale, crushing disappointments' referred to by Sean McEvoy. By the end of the cousins' first night in New York, Eddie's face is 'puffed with trouble' – a trouble that, as Alfieri tells us, 'will not go away'.

Social and political tragedy

Many modern tragedies engage with contemporary social and political issues. For example, Alan Bennett's *The History Boys* (2004) explores the clash between two opposing educational philosophies, represented by two very different teachers: the elderly traditionalist, Hector, and his ambitious young antagonist, Irwin.

Set text focus: *Tess of the D'Urbervilles*

The cliffhangers throughout *Tess of the D'Urbervilles* by Thomas Hardy, first published in 1891, are typical of the serialised stories of its day. It was a time of great social change, when old rural traditions were being replaced by a new industrial existence. The novel suggests that Tess's family's desire for an aristocratic family history is completely misplaced and shows Hardy's sympathy for lower class women victimised by the rigid, self-righteous attitudes of Victorian society.

Although not an exhaustive list, the following aspects of tragedy could be explored in relation to *Tess of the D'Urbervilles*:

- the novel as a tragedy about ordinary people (see 5.2.5; 5.4.2)
- classical aspects of tragedy (see 5.1.2; Activity 14)
- settings of time and place (see 5.1.2, The unities; 5.3.13)
- use of nature and the supernatural (see 5.3.14)
- Tess's journey towards death (see Activity 6; 5.2.8; 5.3.1; 5.3.13)
- Tess's sense of personal dignity (see Activity 9)
- Tess's error of judgement or fatal flaw (see Activity 6; 5.2.8; 5.3.1)
- the role of order and disorder (see 5.3.8)
- significance of violence and revenge (see 5.3.9)
- nature of Tess's suffering (see 5.3.7)
- the role of fate, inevitability and freewill (see 5.2.8; 5.3.4)
- significance of family and social class (see 5.4.2; 5.4.4)
- treatment of female characters (see 5.2.4, *The Duchess of Malfi*, Exploring…; see 5.2.8, Critical lens; Activity 15; 5.4.1)
- structural pattern of the play (see 5.1.2)
- how language is used to heighten tragic experiences (see 5.3.4)
- effects on readers (see 5.1.2; 5.3.8).

The novel could be read from the perspective of:

- value and the canon (see 5.4.5, Critical lens; 9.3)
- narrative theory (see 5.3.8, Critical lens; 9.4)
- feminist theory (see 5.2.8, Critical lens; Activity 15; 5.4.1; 9.5)
- Marxist theory (see 5.4.2; 9.6)
- eco-critical theory (see 5.3.14, Critical lens; 9.7).

ACTIVITY 10

Character names

Find out about the character of Hector in Greek mythology. What values does he represent? What does the name Alan Bennett has chosen for his tragic protagonist contribute to the tragedy?

Now choose one of the listed characters. Explore the origins and associations of this character's name.

1. Angel Clare (*Tess of the D'Urbervilles*)
2. Willy Loman (*Death of a Salesman*)
3. Blanche and/or Stella (*A Streetcar Named Desire*)
4. Cordelia (*King Lear*)

How could you use what you've learned about this character's name in your written work? Try to summarise your knowledge in just one sentence.

For example: *In calling Lear's youngest daughter Cordelia, Shakespeare signals the goodness of her heart.*

5.2.7 Tragic narratives in poetry

We tend to think of tragedy as primarily a dramatic form. However, poetry offers a huge amount of scope for exploring aspects of tragedy. 'Tragedy' in its loosest sense - sadness, loss and trauma - has been a staple topic for poets for centuries. Poetry also addresses the themes of guilt and responsibility that are central to the literary genre of tragedy.

One type of poem that lends itself to tragedy is the ballad, a story told in verse that blurs the boundaries between poetry and song. Ballads were originally spoken rather than written, and were handed down through the oral tradition.

See Stanzas in 2.3.2 for more on ballads

Many ballads tell tales of forbidden or unrequited love and the heartbreak and deaths that ensue. In his poem 'La Belle Dame Sans Merci' (1819), John Keats depicts a young knight who has fallen in love with a beautiful young lady, entered a nightmarish dream-world populated by those who have loved this lady in the past, and wakes to find himself alone on a 'cold hill-side'.

ACTIVITY 11

Exploring 'La Belle Dame Sans Merci'

Read Keats' poem. As you read, pay attention to the effects of the regular rhyme and metre. In what ways do they contribute to the sense of inevitability that is part of tragedy?

Now think about whether the poem contains the different aspects of classical tragedy shown in the table.

Aspect of tragedy	Evidence in the poem
Tragic protagonist	
Hamartia	
Peripeteia	
Anagnorisis	

'And there she lulled me asleep,
And there I dream'd–Ah! woe betide!
The latest dream I ever dream'd
On the cold hill's side.'

John Keats, 'La Belle Dame Sans Merci'

The knight in Keats' poem does not die, but he does suffer as a result of his love. How does Keats convey a sense of his suffering? Think about how Keats describes a) the knight's dream and b) the landscape at the end of the poem.

Exploring critics' responses

Martin Earl suggests that 'La Belle Dame Sans Merci' bears traces of John Keats' own impending death from tuberculosis, a disease whose victims are often depicted as pale, wasted and feverish: 'Keats' knight is lost, abandoned, and already living a posthumous existence, which is how the poet himself would eventually refer to the last months of his life just two years later.'

Set text focus: 'La Belle Dame Sans Merci'

The Romantic poet John Keats wrote the ballad 'La Belle Dame Sans Merci' in 1819. The relatively simple form of the medieval ballad, revived by the Romantic poets, belies the fascinating sense of intrigue and enigma in this poem.

Although not an exhaustive list, the following aspects of tragedy could be explored in relation to 'La Belle Dame Sans Merci':

- classical aspects of tragedy (see 5.1.2)
- the poem's setting (see 5.1.2, The unities)
- use of nature and the supernatural (see Activity 31)
- the role of deception (see 5.3.10)
- treatment of female characters (see 5.4.1)
- structural pattern of the poem (see 5.2.7).

The poem could be read from the perspective of:

- value and the canon (see 5.4.5, Critical lens; 9.3)
- narrative theory (see 5.3.8, Critical lens; 9.4)
- feminist theory (see 5.3.10, Critical lens; 5.4.1; 9.5).

Set text focus: 'Paradise Lost'

The epic poem written in English, *Paradise Lost* by John Milton, was originally published in 1667. Although originally a Protestant, Milton eventually embraced many ideas that were contrary to the orthodox position. He despised the Church's apparent corruption and the way organised religion seemed to him to get in the way of true faith. His very individual interpretation of Christianity makes *Paradise Lost* both personal and universal. The poem expresses the idea that human beings need to show true repentance and faith, even in the face of widespread condemnation, in order to be better Christians. In the extract featured in the Anthology, Satan, newly arrived in Hell, announces that he is going to embrace evil and the freedom it will bring him: 'Better to reign in Hell, than serve in Heav'n'.

Although not an exhaustive list, the following aspects of tragedy could be explored in relation to *Paradise Lost*:

- the poem as a classical tragedy about public figures (see 5.2.4; 5.2.5; 5.4.2)
- classical aspects of tragedy (see 5.1.2)
- use of nature and the supernatural (see 5.3.14)
- Satan's potential and sense of personal dignity (see 5.2.4; Activity 9)
- how much Satan can be seen as a tragic hero (see Activity 6; 5.3.1; 5.3.6)
- aspects of good and evil (see Activity 5)
- the role of fate, inevitability and free will (see 5.3.4; 5.3.5)
- the role of deception (see 5.3.10)
- structural pattern of the poem (see 5.2.7).
- how language is used to heighten tragic experiences (see 5.2.4, *Dr Faustus*).

The poem could be read from the perspective of:

- value and the canon (see 5.4.5, Critical lens; 9.3)
- narrative theory (see 5.3.8, Critical lens; 9.4)

Two further narrative poems that you might be studying also draw on the ballad tradition, but in different ways. Christina Rossetti's poem 'Jessie Cameron' recounts the scorn of a young woman for the man who loves her. As the two stand on a beach, the young man pleading with Jessie to return his love, the tide sweeps in and drowns them. Thomas Hardy's poem 'The Convergence of the Twain' is about the sinking of the *Titanic*. Hardy also uses elements of the ballad form in poems such as 'A Trampwoman's Tragedy', 'A Sunday Morning Tragedy', 'The Mock Wife' and 'The Newcomer's Wife'.

Set text focus: 'Jessie Cameron' and Thomas Hardy's poems

'Jessie Cameron' was first published in a collection of poems in 1866. Its author, Christina Rossetti, drew on aspects of the ballad form, such as the regular rhyming pattern, the story of unrequited love and the deaths of Jessie and her lover. Jessie's 'careless, fearless' nature can also be seen as a challenge to the conventional views of women.

Although not an exhaustive list, the following aspects of tragedy could be explored in relation to 'Jessie Cameron':

- the poem as a classical tragedy about ordinary people (see 5.2.5)
- classical aspects of tragedy (see 5.1.2)
- the poem's setting (see 5.1.2, The unities)
- the journey towards death (see 5.2.4; 5.3.1)
- Jessie's sense of personal dignity (see Activity 9)
- the role of fate, inevitability, free will and the natural world (see 5.3.4; 5.3.5; 5.3.14)
- Jessie's fatal flaw and self-knowledge (see Activity 6; 5.3.1; 5.3.6)
- how Jessie's behaviour creates suffering (see 5.3.7)
- the role of fate and the wheel of fortune (see Activity 4; 5.3.4)
- treatment of female characters (see Activity 34)
- structural pattern of the poem (see 5.2.7; 5.3.8, Critical lens).

The poem could be read from the perspective of:

- value and the canon (see 5.4.5, Critical lens; 9.3)
- narrative theory (see 5.3.8, Critical lens; 9.4)
- feminist theory (see 5.2.8, Critical lens; 9.5)
- eco-critical theory (see 5.3.14, Critical lens; 9.7).

Thomas Hardy grew up in 19th-century Dorset, a county that had changed little in centuries and remained one of the poorest in England. This place, which he labelled 'Wessex', after one of the Anglo-Saxon kingdoms of Britain, and its country folk provided much of the inspiration for his novels and poems. His writing is deeply rooted in the Dorset countryside, but is also known for its pervasive fatalism. Many of his poems were written after the sudden death of his first wife Emma in 1912. Although their married life was far from happy, he lamented her death and the loss of his early love for her.

Although not an exhaustive list, the following aspects of tragedy could be explored in relation to the selected poems:

- classical aspects of tragedy (see 5.1.2)
- settings of time and place (see 5.1.2, The unities)
- nature of regret and suffering (see 5.3.7)
- the role of human struggle and inevitability (see Activity 6; 5.3.4)
- treatment of female characters (see 5.2.4, *The Duchess of Malfi*, Exploring…; Activity 34)
- structural patterning of the poems (see 5.2.7).

The poems selected for the AS Level specification could be read from the perspective of:

- value and the canon (see 5.4.5, Critical lens; 9.3)
- narrative theory (see 5.3.8, Critical lens; 9.4)
- feminist theory (see 5.2.4, *The Duchess of Malfi*, Exploring…; 5.4.1; 9.5)
- eco-critical theory (see 5.3.14, Critical lens; 9.7).

Set text focus: 'The Convergence of the Twain'

Thomas Hardy wrote 'The Convergence of the Twain' in response to the loss of the luxury liner *Titanic* in 1912, with most of her passengers and crew, on hitting an iceberg. Rather than an elegy to those who lost their lives, he wrote about the futility of human ambition in fashioning a luxury liner, and other material goods, when nature, and death, are much more powerful.

Although not an exhaustive list, the following aspects of tragedy could be explored in relation to 'The Convergence of the Twain':

- classical aspects of tragedy (see 5.1.2)
- the ship's journey towards destruction and death (see 5.2.4; 5.3.1)
- the fatal flaw (see Activity 6; 5.3.1; 5.3.6)
- the role of fate and inevitability (see 5.3.4)
- structural pattern of the poem (see 5.2.7).

The poem could be read from the perspective of:

- value and the canon (see 5.4.5, Critical lens; 9.3)
- narrative theory (see 5.3.8, Critical lens; 9.4)
- eco-critical theory (see 5.3.14, Critical lens; 9.7).

ACTIVITY 12

Verse form in narrative poetry

1. For each of the poems you are studying, work out:
   - the rhyming pattern
   - the number of lines in each stanza
   - the number of stresses in each line.
2. Do the poems use a traditional ballad metre?
3. What effects are conveyed by the verse forms chosen by Rossetti and Hardy? In what ways could these effects be seen as important to an interpretation of these poems as tragedy?

5.2.8 Tragic narratives in the novel

The novel lends itself perfectly to the kind of psychological exploration that late 19th-century dramatists such as Ibsen and Strindberg had brought into the theatre. Novels such as Gustave Flaubert's *Madame Bovary* (1856), George Eliot's *The Mill on the Floss* (1860), Leo Tolstoy's *Anna Karenina* (1873–77) and Edith Wharton's *The House of Mirth* (1905) all contain aspects of tragedy and can be seen to be plotted along Aristotelian lines, with a protagonist whose downfall is brought about by a tragic error.

Often these protagonists are in conflict with the moral codes of the societies in which they live. Lily Bart, the protagonist of *The House of Mirth*, falls out of favour with her social circle after a series of disasters and scandals. Early in the novel, when Lily's reputation is at its height, the narrator comments that 'society is a revolving body which is apt to be judged according to its place in each man's heaven; and at present it was turning its illuminated face to Lily'. This description echoes the medieval image of the wheel of fortune: sometimes you are at the top of society's wheel; sometimes at the bottom.

Novelists can use a whole host of narrative techniques to explore aspects of tragedy.

- First-person narration can take us directly into the mind of the tragic protagonist and give us an insight into his or her experiences (including, potentially, the lack of self-knowledge that initiates the protagonist's peripeteia).
- An **omniscient narrator** can hint at larger forces at work in the universe that bring about the tragic protagonist's inevitable end.
- The novel, as a more expansive form than the drama, can build a detailed picture of the context in which tragic narratives take place, including the social forces in which protagonists are caught up.
- Framing devices, such as intrusive narrators and the use of the story-within-a-story, can guide the reader's reactions to events.

As an example of how these techniques can guide the reader's response to the tragedy, look at Activity 13.

Key terms

omniscient narrator: a third-person narrator who is all-seeing and all-knowing

ACTIVITY 13

Narrating tragedy

In the first chapter of F. Scott Fitzgerald's novel *The Great Gatsby* (1925), the novel's narrator, Nick Carraway, reflects on his relationship with the enigmatic millionaire Jay Gatsby.

1. What hints does Nick Carraway give us as to the kind of story he is about to tell?
2. What do we learn about Gatsby's personality?
3. What kind of effect did Gatsby have on Carraway?

4 In what ways does F. Scott Fitzgerald prepare us for the fact that this will be a tragic narrative? Can you find any evidence of the different aspects of tragedy?
5 What connections can you make between Nick Carraway and the idea of the chorus in classical tragedy?

Check your responses in the Ideas section on Cambridge Elevate

One of the most important tragic novelists is Thomas Hardy (1840–1928), whose novels, in which the action takes place in the fictionalised region of Wessex, set their characters' struggle against their social circumstances in the context of the wider workings of fate. Hardy also draws on elements of the ballad tradition: the critic Philip V. Allingham comments on Hardy's most famous novel, *Tess of the D'Urbervilles* (1891), that 'the story of Tess, in particular, smacks of an oral tradition, the seduction of a maid in a great house'.

Nevertheless, it is difficult to see Hardy's protagonists as responsible for their own downfalls. Tess, for example, is the victim of all manner of circumstances.

- She is sent by her parents to the D'Urbervilles, in the mistaken belief that their families are related.
- She is raped by Alec D'Urberville, and becomes pregnant as a result.
- Her baby dies in infancy.
- She falls in love with Angel Clare, but makes the mistake of telling him about her past, and is abandoned by him.
- Her family is left destitute after the death of her father.

In view of this, her decision to go to Sandbourne with Alec can be seen as a rational course of action: it could be argued that there is little else that she can do. What do you think?

Set text focus: *The Great Gatsby*

The Great Gatsby by F. Scott Fitzgerald was published in 1925. Many aspects in the novel mirror Fitzgerald's own life: in seeking to please his wife Zelda, Fitzgerald sought out fame, wealth and a decadent life style but, although he chronicled the prosperity and parties of 1920s America, he seemed to be aware of a lack of morality in that life style that he despised.

Although not an exhaustive list, the following aspects of tragedy could be explored in relation to *The Great Gatsby*:

- classical aspects of tragedy (see 5.1.2)
- settings of time and place (see 5.1.2, The unities; 5.3.13)
- Gatsby's journey towards death (see Activity 13; 5.3.1)
- Gatsby's potential and sense of personal dignity (see Activities 6, 9, 13)
- Gatsby's error of judgement or fatal flaw (see Activity 6; 5.3.1)
- the role of blindness (see 5.3.6)
- the role of order and disorder (see 5.3.8)
- aspects of morality (see Activity 5)
- the role of tragic villain (see 5.3.2, The malcontent)
- the role of fate, inevitability and free will (see 5.3.4; 5.3.5)
- the role of disguise and reinvention (see 5.3.10)
- significance of family and social class (see Activity 35)
- treatment of female characters (see Activity 34)
- use of plot, framing devices and ending (see 5.1.2, The unities; 5.2.8; Activities 24, 29)
- effects on readers (see 5.2.8).

The novel could be read from the perspective of:

- value and the canon (see 5.4.5, Critical lens; 9.3)
- narrative theory (see 5.3.8, Critical lens; 9.4)
- feminist theory (see 5.4.1; 9.5)
- Marxist theory (see 9.6).

Critical lens: feminist theory

Feminist literary theory encourages us to analyse the representation of gender in literature, including the ways in which female characters are presented as being controlled by the expectations of others.

As you read *Tess of the D'Urbervilles*, think about the ways in which both Alec and Angel treat Tess. What expectations do they have of her and the role she should play in their relationships? In what ways does Tess suffer as a result of these expectations?

See 9.5 for more on feminist theory

ACTIVITY 14

Tess and tragedy

If you are studying *Tess of the D'Urbervilles*, think about which aspects of classical tragedy you can detect in her story.

5.3 Aspects of tragedy

5.3.1 Heroes

As we have seen, the tragic heroes of Ancient Greece possessed a number of clear characteristics. They were people of high status who also possessed a greatness of soul or megalopsychia. However, they also possessed a certain amount of hubris or excessive pride. As a result of this hubris, the protagonist made an error of judgement - a hamartia - that led to their downfall and death. In the early 20th century, the critic A.C. Bradley introduced the idea of the fatal flaw, which suggests that the tragic hero's error of judgement comes about because of some kind of deep-seated weakness in his character.

As part of your study of tragedy, try to apply the key concepts of megalopsychia, hubris, hamartia and the fatal flaw to the characters you are studying.

Try also to trace their peripeteia and identify the moment of their anagnorisis. For example:

Othello's hubris is conveyed in his very first appearance in Shakespeare's play, in the way he responds to the news that Brabantio is angry at his marriage to Desdemona:

> Let him do his spite;
> My services which I have done the signiory
> Shall out-tongue his complaints.

In *Death of a Salesman* by Arthur Miller, Willy Loman is an ordinary salesman who does not possess the high status of the classical tragic hero. However, he has devoted his whole working life to trying to build a career and providing for his family. This, in itself, could be seen as evidence of megalopsychia. His status within his own family is reflected in an early flashback sequence when his sons Young Biff and Young Happy vie for his approval, showing off their skills in exercising and polishing the family car.

ACTIVITY 15

Tragic heroes

a Use a table like Table 5A to make notes on how the key concepts of tragedy can be applied to the protagonists of the texts you're studying.

b Identify quotations or examples that illustrate these concepts. These will help you to write about the protagonists of your set texts.

c If one or more of these aspects seems to be missing from a text you've studied, think about what effect this might have. For instance, are we able to sympathise with a tragic protagonist who does not appear to experience a moment of anagnorisis? And what are we to make of a text that doesn't appear to have an actual protagonist at all - like Thomas Hardy's poem 'The Convergence of the Twain'?

d Write up your observations. Explore each of the key terms in a separate paragraph, including quotations and examples.

Set text focus: *Othello*

Othello was first performed in 1604, at the court of King James I. Although the description of Othello as a 'Moor' indicates his African roots, the black and white imagery in the play was not necessarily as racially specific in Shakespeare's day as it seems now, since Elizabethans often referred to dark-haired or dark-skinned Europeans as 'black'.

Although not an exhaustive list, the following aspects of tragedy could be explored in relation to *Othello*:

- the play as a classical tragedy about public figures (see 5.2.4)
- classical aspects of tragedy (see 5.1.2)
- settings of time and place (see 5.1.2, The unities)
- Othello's journey towards death (see 5.2.4; 5.3.1)
- Othello's potential and sense of personal dignity (see 5.2.4; Activity 9)
- Othello's error of judgement or fatal flaw (see Activity 6; 5.3.1; 5.3.6)
- Othello's blindness to what is happening around him (see 5.3.6)
- Othello's insight and self-knowledge (see 5.3.6)
- how Othello's behaviour creates suffering for himself and others (see 5.3.7)
- the role of ethnicity and suspicion (see 5.4.3)
- aspects of good and evil (see Activity 5)
- the role of Iago as tragic villain (see 5.3.2)
- the role of fate, the wheel of fortune, inevitability and free will (see Activity 4; 5.3.4; 5.3.5)
- the role of Iago's deception (see 5.3.10)
- treatment of female characters (see 5.2.4, *The Duchess of Malfi*, Exploring…; Activity 34)
- structural pattern of the play (see 5.1.2)
- use of plots and sub-plots (see 5.1.2, The unities; 5.3.12)
- how language is used to heighten tragic experiences (see 5.2.4, *Dr Faustus*; 5.4.3, Critical lens)
- effects on the audience (see 5.1.2; 5.3.8).

The play could be read from the perspective of:

- value and the canon (see 5.4.5, Critical lens; 9.3)
- narrative theory (see 5.3.8, Critical lens; 5.3.12, Critical lens; 9.4)
- feminist theory (see 5.2.4, *The Duchess of Malfi*, Exploring…; 5.4.1; 9.5)
- post-colonial theory (see 5.4.3; 9.8).

Table 5A

Concept	How can this be applied to the protagonist of my set text?	Quotations and examples
Megalopsychia		
Hubris		
Hamartia		
Fatal flaw		
Peripeteia		
Anagnorisis		

5.3.2 Villains

Tragedy also possesses **villains** or **antagonists**, although these are not as common as you might imagine. (It could be argued, for instance, that many tragic protagonists are their own worst enemies.) These villains often have distinctive, mercurial personalities that make them absorbing to watch. Edmund, in *King Lear*, is frequently played as a much more charismatic and attractive character than his brother Edgar.

Tragic villains often possess traits of two particular types of character: the **Machiavel** and the **malcontent**.

Key terms

villain: an evil character who the protagonist must battle against and who contributes to the tragic hero's fall

antagonist: a character (or an institution or group of characters) that opposes the protagonist

Machiavel: a character who is prepared to behave in an immoral way in order to achieve what he or she wants

malcontent: a character who is dissatisfied because of some unfair treatment, often as a result of a decision made by the protagonist

The Machiavel

The Machiavel is based on a historical figure: the Florentine statesman Niccolò Machiavelli (1469–1527), whose treatise *The Prince* analysed the ways in which political power is won and lost. One of Machiavelli's key teachings was that people sometimes need to act in apparently immoral ways if they are to maintain their power.

Machiavelli's teachings exerted such a powerful influence throughout Western Europe that his name has given us the adjective 'Machiavellian' as well as a theatrical archetype. Christopher Marlowe's play *The Jew of Malta* (c.1589) features a character called 'Machevill', and in the play's Prologue, its protagonist Barabas is described as 'a sound Machevill'.

Probably the best-known Machiavel, however, is Iago in William Shakespeare's *Othello*. Iago speaks more lines than Othello: the part of Iago is actually one of the longest parts in any of Shakespeare's plays. He is scheming, manipulative, and so slippery and dishonest that one production (the Synetic Theater production of 2010) cast three performers in the role of Iago, with all three appearing on stage simultaneously to convey the multiplicity of Iago's character.

The malcontent

Iago's complaints in Act 1, Scene 1 about Othello's failure to promote him mean that he can also be seen as a malcontent. In Renaissance tragedy, malcontents were characters who perceived themselves to be slighted, and were intent on gaining revenge for this. In Thomas Middleton's play *The Revenger's Tragedy* (1606) the malcontent is called, appropriately, Vindice – a name that conveys his vindictive nature. Edmund in *King Lear* is a malcontent, as is, arguably, Bolingbroke in *Richard II*. What about other characters you've encountered? (Could Tom Buchanan, in *The Great Gatsby*, be considered a malcontent? How about Stanley Kowalski in *A Streetcar Named Desire*?)

Watch tutorial video, Villains in Tragedy, on Cambridge Elevate

5.3.3 The fool

The fool was based on the jester, a character employed by many rich households to provide both entertainment and satirical commentary. In tragedy, the key role of a fool is, paradoxically, to provide a voice of wisdom. In *King Lear*, the Fool's riddles highlight themes of injustice, oppression and poor judgement, reminding Lear of his folly (see Text 5G).

The fact that the Fool's language sometimes seems nonsensical is significant. In the topsy-turvy world that results from Lear's division of his kingdom, accepted values are turned on their head. If you are studying *King Lear*, look out for examples of the Fool's inverted logic and the ways that he uses it to comment on Lear's actions.

Text 5G

When thou clovest thy crown i'th'middle and gav'st away both parts, thou bor'st thine ass on thy back o'er the dirt. Thou hadst little wit in thy bald crown when thou gav'st thy golden one away.

King Lear, Act 1, Scene 4, lines 123–6,
Cambridge School Shakespeare

Significantly, the Fool is one of the few characters to remain loyal to Lear. He accompanies Lear on the heath, and the tenderness that Lear shows to the Fool at the height of the storm is one of the first indications that Lear has started to look beyond himself to the plight of others.

Exploring depictions of Shakespeare's fools

Productions of *King Lear* often experiment with the part of the Fool. Some recognise the fact that Cordelia and the Fool never appear on stage together by casting the same actor in both roles. One production underlined the connection between the two by opening with a tableau of both characters with their heads inside a hangman's noose – a terrifying foreshadowing of Lear's line 'And my poor fool is hanged'.

Use the Royal Shakespeare Company's website to examine some of the ways in which the Fool has been depicted.

Visit the Royal Shakespeare Company's website via Cambridge Elevate

5.3.4 Fate and inevitability

The trajectory of tragedy always involves some measure of inevitability – a sense that once the protagonist's downfall has been set in motion, its course cannot be changed or halted. Protagonists often express a sense of this inevitability: some accept it, others fight against it. What about the protagonists of the texts you are studying?

Dr Faustus is probably the clearest example of this sense of inevitability. As soon as he makes his pact with Mephistopheles, Faustus knows that in 24 years' time, the Devil will claim his soul. At the end of Act 5, Scene 2, there is a chilling countdown towards Faustus' death (see Text 5H).

Text 5H

The stars move still, time runs, the clock will strike.
The devil will come, and Faustus must be damned.

Christopher Marlowe, *Dr Faustus*

This sense of inevitability is often linked to the natural world. In both 'Jessie Cameron' by Christina Rossetti, and 'The Death of Cuchulain' by W.B. Yeats, it is bound up with the movement of the tides. In Thomas Hardy's poem 'The Convergence of the Twain', the building of the *Titanic* is given a parallel in the inexorable growth of the iceberg (see Text 5I).

Text 5I

And as the smart ship grew
In stature, grace, and hue,
In shadowy silent distance grew the Iceberg too.

Thomas Hardy, 'The Convergence of the Twain'

Watch tutorial video, Tragic Inevitability, on Cambridge Elevate

Set text focus: 'The Death of Cuchulain'

The legend of Cuchulain is a major theme in W.B. Yeats' poems and plays. It features strongly in a cycle of work that began with 'The Death of Cuchulain' (also called 'Cuchulain's Fight with the Sea') in 1892. At a time when Irish political nationalism was growing, Yeats used ancient Celtic legend, capturing moments of intense feeling in Cuchulain's story that resonated with the day-to-day struggles of the Irish, to inspire a new faith in what Ireland could be in the modern world.

Although not an exhaustive list, the following aspects of tragedy could be explored in relation to 'The Death of Cuchulain':

- classical aspects of tragedy (see 5.1.2)
- use of nature (see 5.3.14)
- Cuchulain's fatal flaw (see 5.3.1; 5.3.6)
- the role of fate, inevitability and free will (see 5.3.4; 5.3.5)
- the role of deception (see 5.3.10)
- treatment of female characters (see Activity 34).

The poem could be read from the perspective of:

- value and the canon (see 5.4.5, Critical lens; 9.3)
- narrative theory (see 5.3.8, Critical lens; 9.4)
- feminist theory (see 5.4.1; 9.5)
- eco-critical theory (see 5.3.14, Critical lens; 9.7).

In *Tess of the D'Urbervilles*, meanwhile, Thomas Hardy uses the powerful image of Stonehenge to convey a sense of Tess's impending fate. The ancient stone circle is described in language that highlights its mysterious links with the eternal movement of the sun, as shown in Text 5J.

'The eastward pillars and their architraves stood up blackly against the light, and the great flame-shaped Sun-stone beyond them; and the Stone of Sacrifice midway.'

Thomas Hardy, *Tess of the D'Urbervilles*

Text 5J

The band of silver paleness along the east horizon made even the distant parts of the Great Plain appear dark and near; and the whole enormous landscape bore that impress of reserve, taciturnity, and hesitation which is usual just before day. The eastward pillars and their architraves stood up blackly against the light, and the great flame-shaped Sun-stone beyond them; and the Stone of Sacrifice midway. Presently the night wind died out, and the quivering little pools in the cup-like hollows of the stones lay still. At the same time something seemed to move on the verge of the dip eastward – a mere dot. It was the head of a man approaching them from the hollow beyond the Sun-stone. Clare wished they had gone onward, but in the circumstances decided to remain quiet. The figure came straight towards the circle of pillars in which they were.

Thomas Hardy, *Tess of the D'Urbervilles*

ACTIVITY 16

The Sun-stone

Find out about the significance of the Sun-stone (also called the Heel Stone) at Stonehenge. Why do you think Hardy chose to depict the first member of the arresting party as appearing from beyond the Sun-stone?

Inevitability is a key part of the sense of fate that is also integral to tragedy. In *Shakespearean Tragedy* (1904), A.C. Bradley described fate as 'a mythological expression for the whole system or order, of which the individual characters form an inconsiderable and feeble part ... [Fate is] so vast and complex that they can scarcely at all understand it or control its workings.'

Bradley argued that fate is essential to give tragedy its emotional impact: 'If we do not feel at times that the hero is, in some sense, a doomed man; that he and others drift struggling to destruction like helpless creatures borne on an irresistible flow towards a cataract; that, faulty as they may be, their fault is far from being the sole or sufficient cause of all they suffer; and that the power from which they cannot escape is relentless and immovable, we have failed to receive an essential part of the full tragic effect.'

A text that offers a different perspective on inevitability is Robert Frost's poem 'Out, out -'. In this poem, a boy dies after losing his hand in an accident with a buzz saw. The events depicted in 'Out, out -' are certainly tragic in the general sense of the word. What can you bring to this poem by interpreting it through the lens of the literary genre of tragedy?

ACTIVITY 17

Fate

a How is a sense of fate conveyed in the tragedies you are studying? Are its workings referred to explicitly, or hinted at in a more subtle manner?

b Do the characters accept fate, or resist it? Is there a difference between the kinds of characters who accept fate and the kinds of characters who resist it?

c What kind of imagery is used to convey a sense of fate? Is it personified, or expressed through particular chains of metaphor such as that of the wheel of fortune?

Set text focus: Robert Frost 'Out, out...'

Robert Frost wrote 'Out, out...' in 1916, apparently based on the true story of a friend's son. However, it was also the year after he had to move back to America because of the onset of World War I, which robbed many innocent young boys of their childhoods and lives.

Although not an exhaustive list, the following aspects of tragedy could be explored in relation to 'Out, out...':

- classical aspects of tragedy (see 5.1.2)
- use of nature (see 5.3.14)
- the laying of blame (see Activity 6; 5.3.6)
- the boy's sense of personal dignity (see Activity 9)
- the role of fate and inevitability (see 5.3.4)
- structural pattern of the poem (see 5.2.7)
- how language is used to heighten tragic experiences (see 5.2.4, *Dr Faustus*).

The poem could be read from the perspective of:

- value and the canon (see 5.4.5, Critical lens; 9.3)
- narrative theory (see 5.3.8, Critical lens; 9.4)
- eco-critical theory (see 5.3.14, Critical lens; 9.7).

5.3.5 Free will

If human fate is predetermined, the choices that individuals make are not truly their own. In such a situation, the tragic protagonist would suffer not as a result of his or her own actions, but as a result of forces that he or she was powerless to change. On the other hand, the notion that humans make their own choices – **free will** – could be seen as fundamental to the very notion of tragedy, which rests on the tragic protagonist's error of judgement.

Key terms

free will: the capacity to make one's own choices in life, rather than having the course of one's life determined by a higher power

ACTIVITY 18

Free will and tragedy

Think about the implications of free will for the genre of tragedy. In the Aristotelian model of tragedy, the tragic protagonist's downfall results from his or her own choices.

a How important is it that the tragic protagonist is responsible for his or her own fate?

b Why do we feel sympathy for the tragic protagonist? Would this change if the tragic protagonist was simply a victim of forces beyond his or her control?

5.3.6 Pride and folly, insight and blindness

Hubris can be translated as 'pride' – an overweening sense of self-confidence and a belief in the importance of one's own self-image. The other side of this, of course, is folly – an inability to see one's own faults. What evidence of pride can you see in the tragic protagonists you are studying? How is their folly displayed?

Dr Faustus, for example, sees himself as being too good for the drudgery of the study of medicine and the law. The law is 'too servile and illiberal for me', while medicine would only attract him if it would give him the ability to raise the dead. Instead, he turns to divinity, and in particular to a branch of divinity called necromancy (the ability to communicate with and resurrect the dead), which he believes will give him the power he desires (see Text 5K).

Text 5K

Oh, what a world of profit and delight,
Of power, of honour, of omnipotence,
Is promised to the studious artisan!

Christopher Marlowe, *Dr Faustus*

As a result, he enters into a pact with the demon Mephistopheles, who will grant him the power he desires in return for his soul. However, Faustus squanders this power, using it to play tricks on people. Both his pride, and his folly, are established in the play's prologue, by the Chorus.

ACTIVITY 19

***Dr Faustus*: pride and folly**

a Read the Chorus' opening speech. What does it tell us about Faustus' origins? What might this suggest about the reasons for his pride?

b What image from classical mythology does the Chorus use to illustrate Faustus' fall from grace?

c In this speech, Marlowe uses images of greed and overeating. Identify these images. What do they suggest about Faustus?

In *Richard II*, Shakespeare explores the concept of the 'divine right of kings' – the belief that the monarch derives his authority from God alone. This belief means that Richard II possesses a huge amount of hubris, being so concerned with his own image of himself as king that he is unable to rule effectively. He exercises power in an arbitrary fashion (such as when he halts the duel between Bolingbroke and Mowbray) and ignores the advice of wiser men, such as the Duke of York's warning of what will happen if he confiscates Bolingbroke's lands. In essence, Richard believes that because he is king, he can do anything.

ACTIVITY 20

Richard II: Hubris

a Read *Richard II*, Act 1, Scene 3. In what ways might Richard's status as monarch be conveyed to the audience?

b What do you notice about the ways in which Richard exercises his power? Does he always seem fair?

In Thomas Hardy's poem 'The Convergence of the Twain', hubris is conveyed in a different way. The poem sets the building of the ocean liner *Titanic* against the growth of the iceberg with which it collided on its fatal voyage in 1912. Hubris is associated not with a single person, but with human ambition and vanity. Ship and iceberg are, unknown to anyone, 'twin halves of one august event'. The inability of humans to exert absolute control is shown in the poem's final stanza (see Text 5L).

Text 5L

Till the **Spinner of the Years**
Said "Now!" And each one hears,
And **consummation** comes, and jars two **hemispheres**.

Thomas Hardy, 'The Convergence of the Twain'

Glossary

Spinner of the Years: a reference to the Fates in Classical mythology

consummation: completion

hemisphere: half of a sphere

Do tragic protagonists ever recognise what they have done wrong? In classical tragedy, protagonists should experience a period of anagnorisis, when they gain a new insight into both their initial pride and the folly that resulted from it. King Lear's anagnorisis is lengthy. It can be seen as early as Act 1, Scene 5, after Lear's violent cursing of Goneril, when he admits to the Fool that 'I did her wrong'. A few lines later, Lear makes a plea for sanity that is emphasised by a shift from prose to verse (see Text 5M).

Text 5M

O let me not be mad, not mad, sweet heaven!
Keep me in temper, I would not be mad.

King Lear, Act 1, Scene 5, lines 37–8

In other tragedies, however, the protagonist's anagnorisis is much shorter. In *Othello*, it comes just before Othello's suicide, when he recognises that Iago has deceived him and tells Lodovico and Cassio what he wants his epitaph to be (see Text 5N).

Text 5N

Then must you speak
Of one that loved not wisely but too well,
Of one not easily jealous but, being wrought,
Perplexed in the extreme; of one whose hand,
Like the base Indian, threw a pearl away
Richer than all his tribe …

Othello, Act 5, Scene 2, lines 339–44,
Cambridge School Shakespeare

Images of blindness are often used to highlight the lack of insight shown by the protagonist in the period leading up to this moment of anagnorisis. In *King Lear*, these images take on a hideous reality when Gloucester's eyes are torn out by Regan and Cornwall. Many tragic protagonists suffer from an inability to 'see' the truth: Stevens, in *The Remains of the Day*, shows a blind loyalty to his employer Lord Darlington and does not recognise the true nature of his feelings for Miss Kenton. Willy Loman, for example, fails to recognise his lack of success, and has existed for years in a state of denial.

ACTIVITY 21

Seeing and not seeing in *Death of a Salesman*

One form of metaphorical blindness that exists in many tragedies is the protagonists' tendency to surround themselves with illusions. The critic Matthew C. Roudané points out that the Lomans' lives are full of illusions: 'Illusions appear so suffused within the psychodynamics and vocabulary of the family that the Lomans, we realise, have slipped years ago into a psychotic denial, hoping all along that outer events will somehow right themselves.'

- What does Roudané mean by 'psychodynamics' and 'psychotic denial'?
- What evidence can you find within the play of the illusions with which the Lomans have surrounded themselves?
- At what point do these illusions begin to slip?

Another key image relating to sight in tragic literature is that of the eyes of Doctor T.J. Eckleburg in *The Great Gatsby*, staring out 'blue and gigantic' - but, of course, completely unseeing - from the giant billboard that looms above the Valley of Ashes. What do these eyes symbolise?

Exploring the link between tragedy and blindness

The link between tragedy and blindness stretches back to Sophocles' play *Oedipus Rex* (c.429 BCE). In the play, Oedipus ignores the words of the blind prophet Tiresias: later, when he realises that Tiresias was speaking the truth, Oedipus blinds himself.

5.3.7 Suffering and chaos

It should go without saying that suffering is an integral part of tragedy, but this suffering takes on a number of different forms. As part of your study of tragedy, you should consider:

- what kinds of suffering the protagonists undergo (for example, the rape of Tess, Othello's mental torment at Desdemona's supposed infidelity, the grief depicted by Thomas Hardy in his poems, Isabella's suffering after the death of Lorenzo, Tithonus' weariness of immortality and desire for the release of death)
- what kinds of suffering they inflict on others (Faustus' trickery, Lear's banishment of Cordelia)
- what kinds of suffering others experience (the blinding of Gloucester, the death of Myrtle Wilson)
- how others react to the suffering (the indifference of Gatsby's acquaintances and of the onlookers at the end of 'Out, out –').

Set text focus: 'Tithonus'

'Tithonus', by Alfred, Lord Tennyson, was completed in 1859. Tennyson wrote the original version after the death of a very close friend and the poem might be said to reflect his own suffering in losing a friend and the necessity of accepting the inevitability of death.

Although not an exhaustive list, the following aspects of tragedy could be explored in relation to 'Tithonus':

- classical aspects of tragedy (see 5.1.2)
- use of nature and the supernatural (see 5.3.14)
- Tithonus' journey towards wishing for death (see 5.2.4; 5.3.1)
- Tithonus' fatal flaw (see Activity 6; 5.3.1; 5.3.6)
- the role of fate and inevitability (see 5.3.4)
- treatment of female characters (see Activity 34)
- structural pattern of the poem (see 5.2.7)
- use of plots and sub-plots (see 5.1.2, The unities; 5.3.12)
- how language is used to heighten tragic experiences (see 5.2.4, *Dr Faustus*)
- effects on readers (see 5.1.2; 5.3.8).

The poem could be read from the perspective of:

- value and the canon (see 5.4.5, Critical lens; 9.3)
- narrative theory (see 5.3.8, Critical lens; 9.4)
- feminist theory (see 5.4.1; 9.5)
- eco-critical theory (see 5.3.14, Critical lens; 9.7).

ACTIVITY 22

Suffering in tragedy

Choose one of the tragedies that you have studied. Explore the role played by suffering in this text. Think about these points.

a How is the suffering depicted? Does it take place on stage? Is it reported or glossed over, or described in graphic detail? If it is described in detail, why do you think this is?

b When does this suffering occur? Is it near the beginning of the text, or closer to the end?

c Do we react to mental suffering in a different way to the way in which we react to physical suffering?

d Do we react to the protagonist's suffering in a different way if we feel that it is self-inflicted?

Set text focus: Isabella; or, The Pot of Basil

'Isabella; or, The Pot of Basil' was written by John Keats in 1818. It is based on a story that appears in *The Decameron*, a collection of stories by the 14th-century Italian author Giovanni Boccaccio. The poem's medieval setting and its association of love with suffering are typical of Keats.

Although not an exhaustive list, the following aspects of tragedy could be explored in relation to 'Isabella; or, The Pot of Basil':

- classical aspects of tragedy (see 5.1.2)
- Isabella's journey towards metaphorical death (see Activity 6; 5.3.1)
- nature of Isabella's suffering (see 5.3.7)
- the role of deception (see 5.3.10)
- significance of family and social class (see Activity 35; 5.4.4)
- treatment of female characters (see 5.2.4, *The Duchess of Malfi*, Exploring…; Activities 34, 37).

The poem could be read from the perspective of:

- value and the canon (see 5.4.5, Critical lens; 9.3)
- narrative theory (see 5.3.8, Critical lens; 9.4)
- feminist theory (see 5.4.1; 9.5)
- Marxist theory (see 9.6).

Exploring language

Today, we think of the word 'chaos' as referring to any state of disorder, but in Christian mythology it has a much more specific meaning, denoting the formless state that existed before the creation of the universe, and which some people believe will return when the world ends.

In classical tragedy, the protagonist's hubris is seen as an offence against the gods, for which the protagonist must be punished. In the Renaissance, tragic protagonists often committed acts that contravened the **Great Chain of Being**. The gods' displeasure is often shown through disturbances in nature, such as the storms in both *King Lear* and *Othello*. In *Macbeth*, there is not only a storm, but other disturbances in nature too: the Old Man, in Act 2, Scene 4, reports that Duncan's horses have eaten each other. In the Quarto text of *King Lear*, there is an echo of this in Albany's ominous prediction that if the heavens do not punish Regan and Cornwall for their blinding of Gloucester, 'Humanity must perforce prey upon itself / Like monsters of the deep'.

Key terms

Great Chain of Being: a strict hierarchy encompassing everything that existed, ordered in ranks with God at the top

Exploring the Great Chain of Being

Commonly, representations of the Great Chain of Being placed God at the top, followed by the different orders of archangels and angels, and then by humans, ordered in ranks with kings, princes and nobles above ordinary people and peasants. After humans come animals, trees and other plants, then precious stones, metals and minerals.

ACTIVITY 23

Exploring chaos

What other examples of chaos and disorder can you find in the texts you are studying?

Is this chaos seen as the result of the protagonist's actions? Is it some kind of punishment for what the protagonist has done?

5.3.8 Order and disorder

Chaos is closely linked to disorder – the state that ensues once the protagonist's hamartia has set the plot in motion. An important part of tragedy is, therefore, the restoration of order. The process of catharsis, in fact, depends on this restoration: in order for catharsis to take place, members of the audience must experience a rebalancing of their emotions. In what ways is this achieved in the tragedies you have studied?

In some of Shakespeare's tragedies, the play ends with a sense of the new order that will replace the previous disorder: *Macbeth*, for instance, concludes by looking forward to the coronation of Malcolm. In others, this resolution is more ambiguous.

ACTIVITY 24

Endings

a There are two versions of *King Lear*: the Quarto version (1608) and the First Folio version (1623). Who speaks the final lines in the Folio version? What about the Quarto version? If you wanted to convey the sense of order being restored at the end of the play, which version would you choose? Why is this?

b What kind of restoration of order takes place at the end of *The Great Gatsby*? What about *Tess of the D'Urbervilles*?

c *A Streetcar Named Desire* ends with an image of Stanley comforting Stella as she cradles their baby. How convincing is this image of togetherness?

d The deaths of Angela and the Beadsman are mentioned briefly at the end of 'The Eve of St Agnes'. In what ways are their deaths linked to the elopement of Madeline and Porphyro? Is it significant that their deaths occupy so little space in the poem?

Exploring the First Folio and Quarto versions

See the Cambridge School Shakespeare edition of *King Lear* for an exploration of the differences between the two versions of the play.

Exploring form

In *Macbeth*, the restoration of order at the end of the play is reinforced by Malcolm's use of rhyming couplets in the last four lines (see Text 5O). Does a similar kind of stylistic resolution take place in the tragedies you have studied?

Text 5O

… this, and what needful else
That calls upon us, by the grace of Grace,
We will perform in measure, time and place:
So, thanks to all at once and to each one,
Whom we invite to see us crown'd at Scone.

Macbeth, Act 5, Scene 9, lines 37–41

Critical lens: narrative theory

Narrative theory encourages us to look at the endings of texts and consider the extent to which they resolve the questions and loose ends raised by the plots. As you study your set texts, think about whether their endings provide a sense of resolution and completeness – or whether they leave certain questions unanswered.

See 9.4 for more on narrative theory

'This is the excellent foppery of the world, that when we are sick in fortune… we make guilty of our disasters the sun, the moon, and the stars; as if we were villains by necessity, fools by heavenly compulsion, knaves, thieves, and treachers by spherical predominance, drunkards, liars, and adulterers by an enforced obedience of planetary influence'

William Shakespeare, *King Lear*

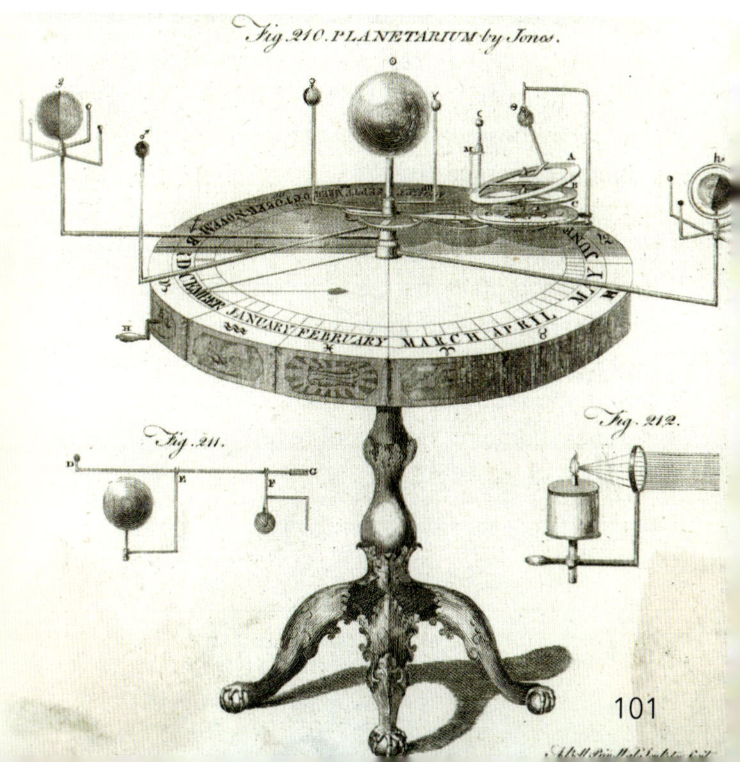

5.3.9 Violence and revenge

The notion of revenge, in tragedy, has its roots in the Senecan drama of Ancient Rome. Seneca's bloody, vengeance-driven plays gave rise to the genre of revenge tragedy. Revenge tragedies had a number of common features.

- They were usually set in Italy or Spain, partly to place themselves at a safe distance from England (and therefore avoid accusations of political sedition, or rebellion against authority) and partly so that they could draw on the stereotypes of passion, hot-bloodedness and deceit that were associated with the 'Latin temperament'.
- Their protagonists were typically noblemen who were driven to avenge a terrible wrong through what the essayist Francis Bacon (1561–1626) described as 'a kind of wild justice'.
- The plays are dominated by the pursuit of this revenge.
- Characters are often **archetypes** rather than individuals (in Thomas Middleton's *The Revenger's Tragedy*, they are given names like Vindice ('vindictiveness'), Ambitioso ('ambition') and Spurio ('the illegitimate one').
- They deal with themes of lust and corruption.
- Revenge is often exacted through highly macabre means (in *The Revenger's Tragedy*, Vindice uses the poisoned skull of his murdered fiancée to kill her murderer).

Key terms

archetype: a character who represents a particular characteristic. In some texts, as in *The Revenger's Tragedy*, these characters' names reflect their defining characteristics

Revenge tragedy certainly influenced many other Renaissance dramatists, and it could be argued that characters such as Edmund and Iago are motivated by vengeance. What about other texts you have read? Could you argue that *Tess of the D'Urbervilles*, for instance, contains aspects of revenge tragedy?

5.3.10 Disguises, deceptions and discoveries

There are obvious examples of disguise and deception in tragedy. Sometimes, disguise is a means of self-preservation. Kent and Edgar, in *King Lear*, disguise themselves (as the servant Caius and as Poor Tom, respectively) to protect themselves after they are cast out: both, nevertheless, are able to use their new identities in order to help both Lear and Gloucester. In other cases, however, deception is more morally ambiguous.

Jay Gatsby in *The Great Gatsby*, for instance, turns out to be not Jay Gatsby at all, but James Gatz, a working-class farmer's son from North Dakota. His reinvention of himself contributes to the mystery that surrounds him, and is important to understanding the novel.

ACTIVITY 25

From James Gatz to Jay Gatsby

a Why do you think James Gatz created a new identity for himself?

b What does he gain as a result of this new identity?

c What does F. Scott Fitzgerald suggest about the morality of what James Gatz does? Is it morally wrong – or a legitimate response to the age in which he lives?

Another ambiguous example of deception occurs in John Keats' poem 'Lamia'. The beautiful serpent, Lamia, wants to assume human form in order to make the youth, Lycius, fall in love with her. We might expect her actions to be presented in a disapproving light. How does Keats depict Lamia? Are we supposed to disapprove of what she does or to view her more sympathetically?

Other instances of deception are more clear-cut, leaving us in no doubt as to their negative effects. The Belle Dame, in John Keats' poem 'La Belle Dame Sans Merci', appears innocent – 'a faery's child' – but the sleep into which she lulls the knight-at-arms is a nightmarish one, leaving him death-like and pale. Lady Macbeth's advice to 'Look like the innocent flower, but be the serpent under't' is a clear guide to her malign intent. And Iago – who states openly in Act 1, Scene 1 of *Othello* that 'I am not what I am' – is at that point very clear as to what he wants his deception to achieve.

ACTIVITY 26

Discovery

Examine the moments in tragedies you have studied where disguises and deceptions are uncovered. In what ways are these moments important to their respective plots? What do they reveal about the discoverer?

Critical lens: feminist theory

Feminist literary theory invites us to look at the ways in which female characters are given particular qualities - for instance, they might be idealised, or viewed with suspicion.

Lady Macbeth, Lamia and the Belle Dame are all depicted as presenting a false image in order to deceive other characters. To what extent is their deceptiveness linked to the fact that they are female? Can you think of male characters who behave in similar ways?

See 9.5 for more on feminist theory

5.3.11 Mistakes and misunderstandings

Errors are, of course, central to tragedy - hamartia, after all, means an 'error of judgement'. In the tragedies you are studying, what kinds of mistakes do the protagonists make? Why do they make these mistakes?

5.3.12 Parallels and subplots

Tragedies that obey the unity of plot focus on one central plotline, concentrating the action on the story of the protagonist's downfall in order to increase its intensity. Some tragedies, however, contain subplots that allow the playwright to create parallels with the main plot. *King Lear*, in which the story of Lear and his daughters is paralleled by that of Gloucester and his sons, is one such example.

ACTIVITY 27

The subplot of *King Lear*

How does Shakespeare use the subplot of *King Lear*? What would be lost (or gained) if Gloucester and his sons were cut from the play?

Critical lens: narrative theory

Narrative theory encourages us to think about the ways in which narratives are structured, including how they use main plots and subplots to highlight particular issues and themes.

Can you think of any other texts in which a subplot is used as a parallel to the main plot? How is this text structured? In what ways does the author invite you to make links between the subplot and the main plot?

See 9.4 for more on narrative theory

5.3.13 Settings, journeys, escapes, returns

Ancient Greek tragedy, as described by Aristotle, observed the unity of place, concentrating the action into one specific setting. As we have seen, some dramatists have used the unity of place to great effect - Arthur Miller, for instance, uses it in *Death of a Salesman*, and in *All My Sons* and *A View from the Bridge*, and Tennessee Williams uses it in *A Streetcar Named Desire*, as well as in *The Glass Menagerie* and *Cat on a Hot Tin Roof*.

If you are studying Arthur Miller, pay careful attention to the way he describes the settings of his plays in the opening stage directions. His descriptions are extremely detailed and help you to visualise what the stage would look like, if you are unable to see a production. They often employ symbolism: the Keller backyard in *All My Sons* contains 'plants whose season is gone' and the stump of an apple tree with fruit still clinging to its branches (we find out later that the tree was planted as a tribute to the Keller's older son Larry, who went missing in action in World War II). In addition, the descriptions can be highly lyrical. The opening directions for *Death of a Salesman*, for instance, state that 'An air of the dream clings to the place, a dream rising out of reality'. What does this suggest to you about the Loman family and the values that their lives are built on?

However, many tragedians use different settings - and the journeys in between them - to symbolise different stages in the protagonist's downfall. There could be no starker contrast than the pomp and ceremony of the opening scene of *King Lear* - when the 'love trial' is preceded by a trumpet fanfare, and by the arrival of Lear with all his train – and the scenes on the heath, when Lear is finally able to acknowledge the plight of the 'poor naked wretches' who, like him, have nowhere to shelter from the storm. In *Tess of the D'Urbervilles*, meanwhile, the lush surroundings of Talbothays Dairy and the 'starve-acre' Flintcomb-Ash represent the changes in Tess's fortunes. Hardy also uses settings in his poetry as a backdrop to his reflections on the death of Emma Gifford, his first wife. Poems such as 'At Castle Boterel' and 'After a Journey' have vividly-evoked settings that have a clear emotional resonance.

In *The Great Gatsby*, setting is used to different effect. The East Coast, for Nick Carraway, represents an escape from his everyday life in the Midwest, which seems like 'the ragged edge of the universe' for him after his return from the Great War. The East has connotations of wealth, opportunity and sophistication: it is where the American dream can be realised. Nevertheless, F. Scott Fitzgerald hints that Carraway's desire to escape to the East is based on an illusion. Fashionable West Egg is described in terms that highlight this illusoriness: its 'white palaces … glittered along the water'. Gatsby's mansion is described as 'a factual imitation of some Hôtel de Ville in Normandy, with a tower on one side, spanking new under a thin beard of raw ivy, and a marble swimming pool, and more than forty acres of lawn and garden'. The beginning of Chapter 3, where Fitzgerald describes one of Gatsby's lavish parties, continues this theme of superficiality and illusion.

ACTIVITY 28

Gatsby's party

Examine the description of Gatsby's party at the beginning of Chapter 3. What kind of atmosphere does Fitzgerald create? What techniques does he use in order to do this?

Significantly, by the end of the novel, Carraway is relieved to return to the Midwest, saying that the East 'had always for me a quality of distortion'.

ACTIVITY 29

Escapes, returns and narrative framing

In *The Great Gatsby*, Fitzgerald makes use of a narrative frame, in which Nick Carraway tells the story in retrospect. The Midwest, from where he tells his story, is contrasted with the East, where the events of the story actually take place.

What is the effect of this framing of Carraway's narrative? In what ways does it heighten the contrast between East and West?

In *The Remains of the Day*, Kazuo Ishiguro uses a journey in a different way. Stevens' tour of the West Country forms the backdrop to his reminiscences about his past at Dartington Hall. As he approaches his meeting with his former colleague Miss Kenton, he reflects on the events that took place at the Hall, his loyalty to Lord Darlington and his relationship with Miss Kenton herself – a relationship that lies at the heart of the novel's tragedy.

Arthur Miller often employs symbolism in his stage settings

5.3.14 Nature and the supernatural

The action of tragedy is frequently set against a backdrop of ideas relating to what is natural and what is unnatural. Sometimes, these ideas are stated explicitly. Look at these examples, all taken from *King Lear*.

- Edmund (Gloucester's illegitimate son) declares 'Thou, Nature, art my goddess'.
- Lear calls Cordelia 'a wretch whom nature is ashamed / Almost t'acknowledge hers'.
- Lear invokes Nature when he curses Goneril. (See Text 5P.)
- When Goneril and Regan try to persuade Lear that he does not need his knights, he responds 'Allow not nature more than nature needs, / Man's life is cheap as beast's'.
- Musing on the actions of his daughters to Poor Tom, Lear says 'Is there any cause in nature that makes these hard-hearts?'

At other times, these ideas are implicit. Many tragedies contain a sense that the protagonist's hamartia is an offence against a natural order that must then be restored. Lear's abdication - which overturns the order of succession - is one instance of this. Another example is Cuchulain's killing of his son, in W.B. Yeats' 'The Death of Cuchulain'. Some tragedies also hint at the disorder that is unleashed when the natural order is ignored.

Text 5P

Hear, Nature, hear, dear goddess, hear:
Suspend thy purpose, if thou didst intend
To make this creature fruitful.

King Lear, Act 1, Scene 4, lines 230–2, Cambridge School Shakespeare

ACTIVITY 30

John of Gaunt's speech

In Act 2, Scene 1 of *Richard II*, John of Gaunt makes a speech about the state of the kingdom. Part of this speech is frequently quoted to evoke feelings of patriotism and national pride, but its concluding lines - omitted from such quotations - make it clear that John of Gaunt is protesting about the disorder that has resulted from Richard's ineffective rule. Read the speech in Text 5Q and examine the way in which Shakespeare uses images of nature.

Text 5Q

This royal throne of kings, this **scepter'd** isle,
This earth of majesty, this seat of **Mars**,
This other **Eden**, **demi-paradise**,
This fortress built by Nature for herself
Against infection and the hand of war,
This happy breed of men, this little world,
This precious stone set in the silver sea,
Which serves it in the office of a wall,
Or as a moat defensive to a house,
Against the envy of less happier lands,
This blessed plot, this earth, this realm, this England,
This nurse, this **teeming** womb of royal kings,
Fear'd by their breed and famous by their birth,
Renowned for their deeds as far from home,
For Christian service and true chivalry,
As is the **sepulchre** in stubborn Jewry,
Of **the world's ransom**, blessed Mary's Son,
This land of such dear souls, this dear dear land,
Dear for her reputation through the world,
Is now leased out, I die pronouncing it,
Like to a **tenement** or **pelting** farm:
England, bound in with the triumphant sea
Whose rocky shore beats back the envious siege
Of watery **Neptune**, is now bound in with shame,
With inky blots and rotten parchment bonds:
That England, that was wont to conquer others,
Hath made a shameful conquest of itself.

Richard II, Act 2, Scene 1, lines 40–66, Cambridge School Shakespeare

Glossary

scepter'd: a sceptre is an ornate metal rod that symbolises the power of the monarch

Mars: the Roman god of war

Eden: reference to the Garden of Eden in the Book of Genesis in the Bible

demi-paradise: one of two paradises (Gaunt is comparing England to the Garden of Eden)

teeming: full of

sepulchre: a tomb (here, the tomb in which Jesus was buried after his crucifixion)

the world's ransom: Christ's death on the Cross which, according to Christian doctrine, gave all people the chance of eternal life in Heaven

tenement: a rented property

pelting: (archaic) mean or miserable

Neptune: the Roman god of the sea

Critical lens: eco-critical theory

Eco-critical theory invites us to consider the ways in which the natural world is used in literary texts. In John of Gaunt's speech, for example, images of beauty are contrasted with more negative depictions of the state to which England has been reduced. Can you think of other examples of the ways in which images of the natural world are used to highlight particular aspects of the tragedies you are studying? (If you're studying *Tess of the D'Urbervilles*, for example, what can you say about the contrast between Talbothays and Flintcomb-Ash?)

See 9.7 for more on eco-critical theory

The supernatural is also a frequent presence in tragedy, from the angels and devils of *Dr Faustus* and the mysterious transformation of Lamia to the haunting presence of the pagan gods at the end of *Tess of the D'Urbervilles*.

ACTIVITY 31

The supernatural

What examples of the supernatural can you find in the tragedies you are studying? If the tragedy takes place in a religious universe, is this Christian, pre-Christian – or some other kind of power? Can tragedy take place in a universe without gods?

5.3.15 Tragedy in miniature

Many of the tragedies discussed in this unit take place on a grand scale, involving forces beyond human control. A different kind of tragedy can be seen in the poems 'Miss Gee' by W.H. Auden and 'Death in Leamington' by John Betjeman. Both poems depict lives that seem characterised by narrowness and a lack of fulfilment. This is represented by the 'lonely crochet' of 'Death in Leamington' (see Text 5R), and by the sense that Miss Gee is ignored by the world, despite her charitable acts.

Text 5R

Miss Gee looked up at the starlight
    And said, 'Does anyone care
That I live on Clevedon Terrace
    On one hundred pounds a year?'

W.H. Auden, 'Miss Gee'

Making connections between these poems and the wider genre of tragedy might seem difficult at first. Think, however, about the domestic tragedies of the late 19th century and about Sean McEvoy's description of tragedy as exploring 'those small-scale, crushing disappointments that happen… in the gap between ambition and reality'.

ACTIVITY 32

'Small-scale disappointments': 'Miss Gee' and 'Death in Leamington'

Remind yourself of those aspects of life explored by the 19th-century tragedians Ibsen, Strindberg and Chekhov.

a What connections can you make between the concerns of these tragedians, and the lives depicted by Auden in 'Miss Gee' and Betjeman in 'Death in Leamington'?

b How do Auden and Betjeman use language to shape meanings? Think, in particular, about the words and phrases they use to conjure up a sense of their protagonists' lives.

c If 'Miss Gee' and 'Death in Leamington' represent tragedy on its smallest scale, which texts would you argue represent tragedy on its largest scale?

Set text focus: 'Lamia'

'Lamia' was written in 1819 at a time when the poet, John Keats, was in love with Fanny Brawne. From his letters, it seems that he knew he was obsessed by her and Brawne's biographer, Joanna Richardson, has said that he transformed her in his imagination into 'the very symbol of beauty'. 'Lamia' might suggest that passionate love is an illusion, and will disappear.

Although not an exhaustive list, the following aspects of tragedy could be explored in relation to 'Lamia':

- classical aspects of tragedy (see 5.1.2)
- tragic narratives in poetry (see 5.2.7)
- the role of fate and inevitability (5.3.4)
- the role of pride and folly, insight and blindness (5.3.6)
- use of nature and the supernatural (see 5.3.14)
- the journey towards death and destruction (see 5.3.1)
- the role of deception (see 5.3.10)
- treatment of female characters (see 5.2.4, *The Duchess of Malfi*, Exploring…; Activity 34).

The poem could be read from the perspective of:

- value and the canon (see 5.4.5, Critical lens; 9.3)
- narrative theory (see 5.3.8, Critical lens; 9.4)
- feminist theory (see 5.4.1; 9.5)
- eco-critical theory (see 5.3.14, Critical lens; 9.7).

Set text focus: 'Death in Leamington' and 'Miss Gee'

John Betjeman probably wrote 'Death in Leamington' in the early 1930s. In it, he shows his concern for the passing of a life – the death of a lonely old lady and the decaying of her world – which no one seems to recognise had real meaning. Later in the same decade, W.H. Auden interpreted the same theme in 'Miss Gee', an unmarried woman whose life and death seem insignificant.

Although not an exhaustive list, the following aspects of tragedy could be explored in relation to 'Death in Leamington' and 'Miss Gee':

- the poem as a tragedy about ordinary people (see 5.2.5; 5.3.15; Activity 32)
- classical aspects of tragedy (see 5.1.2)
- the role of fate and inevitability (see 5.3.4)
- treatment of female characters (see Activity 34)
- structural patterning of the poems (see 5.2.7)
- how language is used to heighten tragic experiences (see Activity 33).

The poems could be read from the perspective of:

- value and the canon (see 5.4.5, Critical lens; 9.3)
- feminist theory (see 5.4.1; 9.5)
- narrative theory (see 5.3.8, Critical lens; 9.4).

5.4 Voices and perspectives in tragedy

Now that you've explored the concept of tragedy, and analysed the different aspects of the tragedies you're studying, this section will encourage you to think about issues of voice and perspective. Who do tragedies focus on, and who do they ignore? To whom do they offer a voice? Whose perspectives do they emphasise, and whose perspectives are pushed to the sidelines?

See 4.3.4 for more on voice and perspective

One way of approaching this notion of voice and perspective is through looking at two opposing theories of tragedy, the *idealist* and the *materialist*. Regardless of which texts you're studying, these theories can offer you interesting ways of exploring tragedy.

Idealist tragedy: Idealist interpretations see tragedy as representing a struggle between forces that are beyond the comprehension of man. Each tragic drama involves a certain set of individuals, but it also reflects a wider and more mysterious conflict between good and evil.

Materialist tragedy: In contrast to idealist tragedy, materialist interpretations of tragedy emphasise the facts of human existence. They state that tragedy is not the product of a struggle between metaphysical forces but the result of the actions of human beings and the conditions and societies in which they live. If we are to understand tragedy, we must understand what it is about the lives of the protagonists that drive them to act in the ways they do.

Until the late 20th century, most critical studies of tragedy were idealist in nature. In the 1960s and 70s, however, a number of critics began to offer alternative views - reflecting the growing political consciousness of the age in which they lived. J.W. Lever, writing in 1971, argued that tragic drama involved the condemnation of societies, not individuals: that conflict and suffering are brought about not by cosmic powers, but by social and historical forces. In 1994, the critic Jonathan Dollimore published a highly influential study called *Radical Tragedy*, in which he argued that the tragedies of the early 17th century gave dramatists the chance to question existing hierarchies and beliefs.

As part of your study of tragedy, you should try to identify and explore what these hierarchies and beliefs might be (see Figure 5B).

Figure 5B

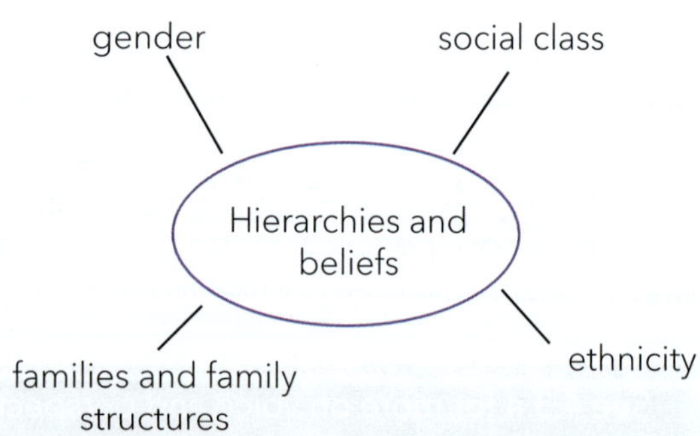

5.4.1 Gender

Most tragic protagonists are men. Aristotle, in his *Poetics*, stated that the protagonist should enjoy 'prosperity and a high reputation', and it is fair to say that throughout history, it is men who have occupied the kinds of roles that give them this 'high reputation' - and the power and prosperity that go with it. In addition, until the 19th century, the vast majority of published authors were men - and we could assume, therefore, that it would be much more likely for them to concentrate on male characters. Nevertheless, some tragedies do focus on women. Earlier, we looked at the ancient Greek tragedy *Antigone*, and you may be studying *Tess of the D'Urbervilles* or *A Streetcar Named Desire*, whose protagonists are two of the most striking tragic heroines in literature.

Often, the relationships between men and women allow dramatists to explore issues of power and the abuse of power, reflecting a range of social attitudes and beliefs.

ACTIVITY 33

Power and control

John Webster's play *The Duchess of Malfi* deals extensively with issues related to gender. The Duchess is a young widow whose brothers, the Cardinal and Ferdinand, want to prevent her from remarrying.

Read Act 1, Scene 2, lines 216–62 of *The Duchess of Malfi* and consider the questions that follow.

a In what ways do the Cardinal and Ferdinand assert their control over the Duchess?
b What do the Cardinal and Ferdinand suggest about widowhood? Why do they want to prevent the Duchess from remarrying?
c How many lines does the Duchess speak? What do you notice about the ways in which many of her lines end?
d Many of Webster's verse lines are split between the Cardinal and Ferdinand. What does this suggest about their relationship?
e Think about other female characters in the tragedies you are studying. In what ways are they also subject to male control?

Check your responses in the Ideas section on Cambridge Elevate

ACTIVITY 34

Gender in tragedy

Think about these questions.

a What kinds of roles do men and women play?
b Which is the more powerful gender? How is this this power demonstrated?

c Is it possible to generalise about the male / female characters in the tragedy you're studying? (If you can, it's likely that the characters are being presented as types rather than individuals.)
d What kinds of values do the male / female characters embody? Do these seem to be stereotyped? (Do women, for instance, represent values such as purity, innocence and gentleness?)
e Are women the victims of male actions?
f What sacrifices do women have to make?
g Are women seen as dangerous? Is female sexuality a threat to male order?
h Are women punished by the action of the tragedy?

Exploring the perspectives of women in tragedy

One powerful way of exploring the perspectives of women in tragedy is to try to re-tell the story from the point of view of a female character. Jane Smiley's novel *A Thousand Acres* (1991), for example, transplants the story of *King Lear* to a farm in the American Midwest. Smiley's novel is narrated from the point of view of an elderly farmer's oldest daughter, who recounts her struggles with her father's disintegrating mental state and her family's troubled past. This is an example of what the critic Terry Eagleton would describe as reading 'against the grain' – looking at a text from a different angle in order to investigate the world-view it presents.

Critical lens: feminist theory

Feminist literary theory often involves questioning male-centred views of the world, replacing them with an emphasis on women's experiences.

The questions in Activity 34 invite you to look at tragedy through the lens of feminist literary theory – and to re-write tragedy from the point of view of female characters. What might Desdemona, in *Othello*, say about her experiences? What about the Belle Dame, Lamia, or Daisy Buchanan?

See 9.5 for more on feminist theory

See 10.7 for more on creative responses to literature

5.4.2 Social class

Just as early tragedies focused on men, they also focused on *important* men – those of high status, whose errors of judgement posed a threat to the stability of the wider societies over which they ruled. As we have seen, however, tragedians from the 19th century onwards turned their attention to ordinary people. In *Death of a Salesman*, Arthur Miller creates a tragic protagonist who is an ordinary working man, desperate to uphold his sense of dignity in the face of the knowledge that his life has not amounted to what he wanted it to. Blanche Dubois, in *A Streetcar Named Desire*, is similarly haunted by her sense that life has not brought her the love, wealth and status that she craves.

ACTIVITY 35

Social class and tragedy

How do the tragedies you are studying treat different social classes? How do they depict social structures?

a Which classes hold most power? How do they treat those who are less powerful?
b How do the less powerful suffer as a result of the action of the tragedy? Do they gain anything?
c Are the less powerful given a voice? Do they appear as individuals, or are they simply there in the background? (Do they appear at all?)
d Do the most powerful learn anything about the lives of the less powerful? In *King Lear*, for instance, Lear comes to recognise the plight of the 'poor naked wretches' who must 'bide the pelting of this pitiless storm'. (See Text 5S.)
e Does the end of the tragedy offer the possibility of change?

Text 5S

How shall your houseless heads and unfed sides,
Your looped and windowed raggedness, defend you
From seasons such as these? Oh, I have ta'en
Too little care of this!

King Lear, Act 3, Scene 4, lines 30–3,
Cambridge School Shakespeare

Critical lens: Marxist theory

A key theme of Marxist literary theory is that of alienation – the state experienced by workers who are not in control of their lives.

Willy Loman, in *Death of a Salesman*, is marked out by his job. Is this job a source of pleasure and fulfilment, or a treadmill that he is unable to escape? How much control has he been able to assert over his life? Is he free to make decisions – or trapped by forces beyond his control?

See 9.6 for more on Marxist theory

5.4.3 Ethnicity

In *Othello*, the protagonist's ethnicity is constantly emphasised as a source of both difference and suspicion. Othello is continually described in terms of his colour: he is referred to as 'the Moor' rather than by name, and in Act 1, Scene 1 he is referred to as 'the thick-lips' and as the 'old black ram' in contrast to the 'white ewe' that is Desdemona. Would Othello be treated differently by the other characters – especially Iago – if he were white?

ACTIVITY 36

Othello's ethnicity

If you're studying *Othello*, explore the ways in which various directors have used Othello's ethnicity.
In some productions, the actor playing Othello is physically imposing, with the character using his physical presence to assert his power in the face of the opposition of the white characters. In others, he is slighter and less intimidating.

a What effects might be created by these different ways of portraying Othello?

b Think also about the ways in which other characters treat Othello's ethnicity. In what ways does Othello lack power?

c Do you agree with C.L.R. James' argument that ethnicity is irrelevant to *Othello*? Why/why not?

d Could the part of Othello be played by a white actor? What effects might be achieved by casting a white actor in this role?

Critics are divided as to whether *Othello* is a racist play – and even as to whether it is about race at all. The Caribbean writer C.L.R. James saw *Othello* as a play about jealousy: for him, the characters' ethnicity did not matter. Other people, however, have disagreed. Jyotsna Singh points out that during the course of the play, Othello 'self-destructively internalizes the prevailing racism' in Venetian society, coming to equate the colour black with all that is negative.

Critical lens: post-colonial theory

Post-colonial theory encourages us to consider the ways in which ethnicity is used in literary texts – how it marks particular characters out as 'other'.

As you read *Othello*, think about the language used by other characters to describe Othello and highlight his position as an outsider. How does Othello respond to these descriptions?

See 9.8 for more on post-colonial theory

'Arise, black vengeance, from thy hollow cell!'

William Shakespeare, *Othello*

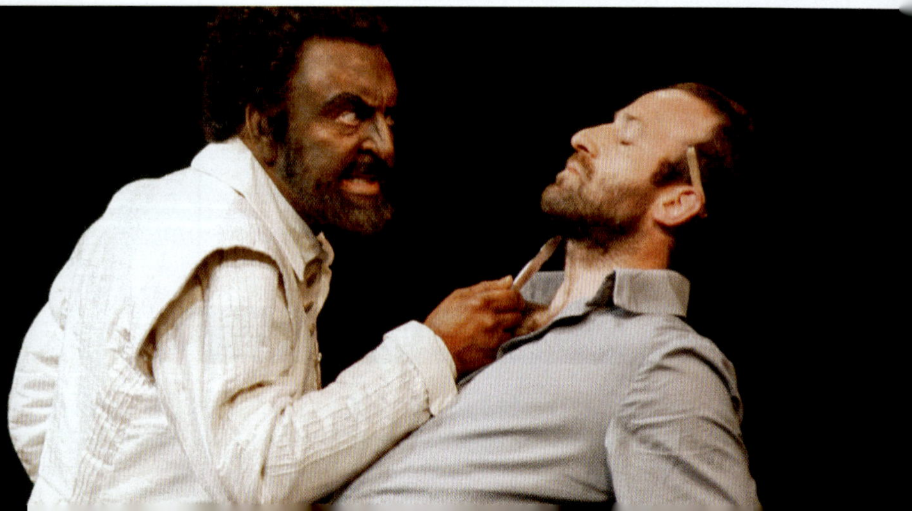

5.4.4 Families and family structures

Power is often seen in terms of society as a whole - the rulers and the ruled; the dominant social classes and the subordinates. Yet issues of power are also at the heart of our most intimate social structure - that of the family. Tragedies certainly have a lot to say about the relationships between husbands and wives, fathers and daughters, fathers and sons - and, increasingly, about mothers and sons.

ACTIVITY 37

Tragedy and the family

What can you say about how power operates within the family structures of the tragedies you are studying? What kinds of duties, for instance, are members of families seen as owing to each other? Think about the bullet points that are relevant to your studies:

- Lear's expectations of his daughters, and his rage at having these expectations disrupted
- the worries and fears of Linda Loman, in *Death of a Salesman*
- the effect of Blanche's arrival on the relationship between Stella and Stanley, in *A Streetcar Named Desire*
- the sacrifices that Tess makes in *Tess of the D'Urbervilles* in order to support her parents and siblings
- the power exerted over Isabella, in 'Isabella; or, The Pot of Basil', by her brothers
- whether characters are constrained by their families, or able to follow their own hopes and desires
- whether characters fulfil their responsibilities, or pursue freedom at all costs.

Whether you are thinking about gender, social class, ethnicity or the family, you should also consider the effect to which the text you are studying upholds traditional power structures or challenges them. Is the status quo reinforced, or overturned?

5.4.5 Literary tragedy and 'everyday' tragedy

We began this unit by reflecting on the different meanings of the word 'tragedy', and the fact that its broader, non-literary meaning encompasses events that seem very far removed from the literary genre of tragedy. In his play *Educating Rita* (1980), the playwright Willy Russell discusses this gap between literary tragedy and 'everyday' tragedy through the character of Rita, a hairdresser who has decided to pursue an Open University degree in English literature.

Critical lens: value and the canon

The 'canon' is the name given to the body of texts that are considered most valuable and important - the texts often seen as being most worthy of study. When we explore the canon, we think about the reasons why certain kinds of text are considered more valuable than others.

Rita, in Text 5V, is clearly intrigued by the fact that she can see 'all sorts of things' in *Macbeth*. Do we place a greater value on texts that we can see 'all sorts of things' in? Why do you think this might be the case?

See 9.3 for more on value and the canon

5.5 Bringing it all together

5.5.1 How will this unit be assessed?

A Level

This unit will be assessed through a closed-text exam of 2 hours 30 minutes. The exam will consist of three sections:

Section A: One passage-based question on your set Shakespeare play. This question will ask you to read a passage taken from your set play and explore the significance of this passage to the tragedy of the play as a whole. The passage will be approximately 40-45 lines long. There will be no choice of questions.

Section B: One essay question on your set Shakespeare play. There will be a choice of two questions on each of the set plays. Each question will invite you to discuss the extent to which you agree with a critical statement about your set play, including relevant comment on Shakespeare's dramatic methods.

Section C: One essay question linking your other two set texts, one of which will be drama. There will be a choice of two questions. Both will invite you to discuss a statement about tragedy with reference to your two set texts. You are reminded to include relevant comment on the ways the writers have shaped meanings. One of the texts you write about must be a drama text and one of the texts you write about must have been written before 1900. If *Richard II* is chosen both rules are satisfied.

Each section is worth 25 marks and this unit is worth 40 per cent of your overall A Level grade.

AS Level

This unit will be assessed through two exams.

Paper 1: Literary Genres: Drama

This is a closed-text exam of 1 hour 30 minutes. There are two sections:

Section A: One passage-based question on a Shakespeare text. This question will ask you to read a passage taken from your set play and explore the significance of the aspects of dramatic tragedy in this passage in relation to the play as a whole. Bullet points providing suggestions for consideration will be included to help you. The passage will be approximately 40–45 lines long. There will be no choice of questions.

Section B: One essay question on your other set play. This question will invite you to explore a critical statement about your set play. You will be reminded to include in your answer relevant comment on the playwright's dramatic methods. There will be no choice of questions.

Each section is worth 25 marks and this paper is worth 50 per cent of your overall AS Level grade.

Paper 2: Literary Genres: Prose and Poetry

This an open-text exam of 1 hour 30 minutes. There are two sections:

Section A: One essay question on your set poetry text. The question will invite you to analyse a critical statement about your set poetry. You will be reminded to include in your answer relevant comment on the poet's authorial methods. The question will include a short extract from the set text and you will need to refer to this extract in your answer. There will be no choice of questions.

Section B: One essay question on your set prose text. The question will invite you to explore a critical statement about your set prose text. You will be reminded to include in your answer relevant analysis of the author's methods. There will be no choice of questions.

Each section is worth 25 marks and this paper is worth 50 per cent of your overall AS Level grade.

For guidance on preparing for the exams, see Unit 11

5.5.2 How much do you know?

These questions ask you to bring together the aspects you have studied in this unit.

1 What can you remember about these concepts?
- the tragic protagonist
- megalopsychia
- hamartia
- peripeteia
- anagnorisis
- catharsis
- the chorus
- the unities
- machevils and malcontents
- pride and folly
- blindness and insight
- suffering
- fate and inevitability.

2 Identify how any five of the tragic aspects listed in question 1 are used in the tragedies you are studying. Summarise your findings in clear prose.

3 If any of the tragic aspects listed in question 1 aren't used in the texts you're studying, consider why this might be and what effects it might have. For example, *King Lear* does not obey the unity of plot, but this allows Shakespeare to use the Gloucester subplot to mirror and provide a commentary on aspects of the main plot. *Tess of the D'Urbervilles* does not obey the unity of place but, instead, Hardy uses different locations to mark out the different stages of Tess's tragic journey. 'The Convergence of the Twain' does not have a tragic protagonist, but this allows Hardy to focus on the larger forces at work in the universe.

4 Identify two or three of the key dramatic methods used to shape meanings at different points in the texts you are studying. In coherent prose, describe these methods, give examples and explain their effects.

5 Read the Texts 5T and 5U containing quotations about tragedy.

Text 5T

The argument of Tragedies is wrath, crueltie, incest, injurie, murther eyther violent by sworde, or voluntary by poyson. The persons, Gods, Goddesses, Juries, friends, Kinges, Queenes, and mightie men.

Stephen Gosson, *Playes Confuted in Five Actions* (1582)

Text 5U

Tragedie is to seyn a certeyn storie,
As olde bokes maken us memorie,
Of him that stood in greet prosperitee
And is y-fallen out of heigh degree
Into miserie, and endeth wrecchedly.

Geoffrey Chaucer, Prologue to 'The Monk's Tale'

Which of these quotations seems most relevant to each of the tragedies you have studied? Explain your answer, in coherent, continuous prose, with reference to each of your set texts. Write one paragraph for each text.

5.5.3 Assessment objectives

In relation to the assessment objectives, this unit has explored:

- how you as a reader can make personal, informed and creative responses to tragedy, using a range of essential terminology and concepts (AO1)
- the ways in which writers shape meanings in tragedy through their use of a variety of conventions and techniques, including the ways in which they use key aspects of the tragic genre (AO2)
- some of the development of tragedy as a genre, introducing some key contextual ideas such as the genre's origins in Ancient Greece and Rome and the ways in which it has been adapted by different writers at different times (AO3)
- the key aspects of the genre of tragedy, which can be found across a wide range of texts (AO4)
- the roles of interpretation and analysis in reading tragedy, with special reference to different perspectives on the nature of tragedy and the actions of the tragic protagonist (AO5).

Summary

In this unit, you have learned about:

- the literary genre of tragedy
- the development of tragedy over time
- key aspects of tragedy
- how the authors of literary texts use different aspects of tragedy in their works
- voices and perspectives in tragedy.

DEVELOPING

6

Comedy

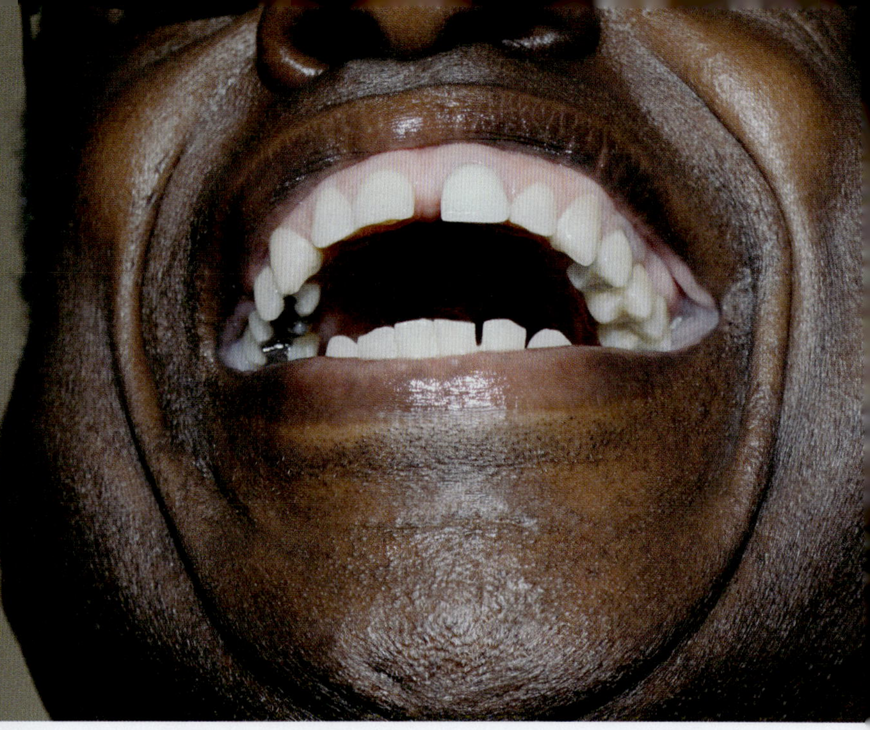

In this unit, you will:

- find out about the literary genre of comedy
- explore how the authors of literary texts use different aspects of comedy in their works
- develop your ability to write about comedy.

6.1 Introduction to comedy

The word 'comedy' implies something funny – something light-hearted or something that makes us laugh. We might describe various things as 'comic' – for instance:

- real-life situations where things go wrong in a hilarious way
- funny performances of various kinds (from stand-up comedy to comedy sketches and plays)

Set text focus

Aspects of Comedy is one of the options in the Literary Genres components for A Level and AS Level. The choice set texts for this option are listed here. At AS Level, if you choose the Aspects of Comedy option for Papers 1 and 2 you must study one Shakespeare text, one other drama text, one poetry text and one prose text. At A Level, if you choose the Aspects of Comedy option (Paper 1 only) you must study one Shakespeare text, one other drama text and one other text from any genre.

A Level and AS Level

The Taming of the Shrew by William Shakespeare
Twelfth Night by William Shakespeare
Emma by Jane Austen
'The Nun's Priest's Tale' by Geoffrey Chaucer
She Stoops to Conquer by Oliver Goldsmith
Small Island by Andrea Levy
The Importance of Being Earnest by Oscar Wilde

AQA English Literature B Poetry Anthology (Comedy): 'The Flea' by John Donne; 'Tam o' Shanter' by Robert Burns; 'A Satirical Elegy on the Death of a late Famous General' by Jonathan Swift; 'Sunny Prestatyn' by Philip Larkin; 'Mrs Sisyphus' by Carol Ann Duffy; 'Not My Best Side' by U.A. Fanthorpe; 'My Rival's House' by Liz Lochhead

AS Level only

Educating Rita by Willy Russell
Wise Children by Angela Carter

Selected poems by John Betjeman: 'The Arrest of Oscar Wilde at the Cadogan Hotel', 'Upper Lambourne', 'In Westminster Abbey', 'A Subaltern's Love Song', 'Christmas', 'The Licorice Fields at Pontefract', 'Senex', 'Diary of a Country Mouse', 'An Edwardian Sunday, Broomhill, Sheffield', 'Slough', 'On a Portrait of a Deaf Man', 'Ireland with Emily', 'The Village Inn', 'Hunter Trials', 'Lenten Thoughts of a High Anglican', 'Executive', 'Advertising Plays', 'Late-Flowering Lust'

- funny stories and pieces of writing (including anecdotes, journalism, poems and novels).

As a student of literature, however, you'll learn that 'comedy' has a specific set of meanings relating to the literary *genre* of comedy. These will give shape to your study of comedy and provide you with a lens through which to view the texts you study. However, they will not necessarily be present to the same degree in every text. Writers subvert literary genres as well as follow them, and you might find that the texts you are studying challenge, overturn or even omit different aspects of comedy. Part of your study of these texts will involve considering why their authors treat the genre in the way they do, and what effects they achieve.

Like tragedy, the genre of comedy has its roots in the ritualised dramas of Ancient Greece. Like tragedy, too, it evolved as a way of exploring the nature of human existence and society, and the workings of **fate** and choice in our lives. But comedy also has another mission: to make us laugh and feel happy, by making fun of (and ultimately perhaps helping us to come to terms with) the ridiculousness of our lives. In literature, dramatists, poets and novelists throughout history have used aspects of comedy to ask questions about their own societies and concerns, and to help us to laugh at the human condition.

Key terms

fate: the name given to a power that predetermines the course of events; also used to refer to the outcome of a course of events

See 5.1 for more on the Fates in mythology

Defining comedy as a genre

Comedy is a tricky word to define. Although many kinds of narrative and writing (including poems, novels and articles) can incorporate aspects of comedy, comedy as a literary genre originated in drama. When we speak of 'comedy' today, we are usually referring to a performance of some sort - but we might be referring to a wide range of types of performance:

- a single person on a stage telling jokes to an audience
- a series of short funny dramatic sketches
- a television or radio sitcom
- a funny film
- a funny play for the theatre, television or radio.

In this sense, comedy, then, is a performance of something funny, but can draw on a wide range of forms and narrative types, from a series of jokes to the extended dramatic play.

If we add the indefinite article 'a', and talk about '*a* comedy', the definition is narrowed. '*A* comedy' probably only refers to the last three of the five preceding bullet points:

- a sitcom
- a funny film
- a funny play.

We wouldn't refer to a stand-up comedian as 'a comedy', but as 'comedy'. '*A* comedy', then, suggests an extended *dramatic* performance of some kind rather than simply someone on stage telling jokes or a group of people performing comic sketches. It can still cover a range of things - from a television sitcom or a 'rom com' film to a Shakespearian play or a trouser-dropping **farce**. Whereas it is relatively easy to define 'a tragedy' - a play with a hero or heroine

The idea of comedy is not only applicable to comic performance

that involves a series of tense dramatic scenarios that culminate in the death (or degradation) of the hero or heroine – it's much more difficult to compose a similar simple definition for 'a comedy', which can imply a range of different types of comic drama and narrative.

Also, the idea of comedy is not only applicable to comic *performance*. Although it originated in drama, it can also be applied to other non-dramatic literary forms. We can describe the narrative of a comic novel or poem as 'a comedy', or say that they are comic, incorporating *aspects* of comedy. In addition, aspects of comedy may be found in literary works that are *not* comedies: for instance, there are comic scenes in a number of Shakespeare's *tragedies*. Finally, we can use the word 'comedic' , rather than 'comic', to refer to aspects of the genre of comedy that are not necessarily funny.

In this unit, we will explore these various different meanings of the word 'comedy', beginning with the idea of comedy as drama.

Key terms

farce: a kind of energetic comedy that employs **caricature**, **slapstick**, fast action and unlikely events

caricature: exaggerated portrayal of character for comic effect

slapstick: physical humour involving people falling, being hit and so on

ACTIVITY 1

Comedy in a range of literary forms

Think about texts you have studied or read in a range of forms:

- drama (stage, film or television)
- novels and stories
- poetry
- non-fiction writing (for example, articles, autobiography, letters).

In each category, think of a couple of examples of texts that you would describe as comedy or comic. How would you describe what makes each one comic?

Critical lens: Value and the canon

Your set texts for studying aspects of comedy are drawn from a body of comic works generally considered appropriate for A Level study. This literary canon does not include texts such as scripts for television sitcoms or comedy sketch shows. However, many critics and academics argue that such texts are equally valid objects of study. Do you think such texts are worth studying? Think about:

- what they might tell us about our society
- what kind of literary skill the writers are using
- whether you think these texts are more or less valuable or significant than your set texts.

See 9.3 for more on value and the canon

Dramatic comedy

As we have seen, the origin of comedy as a literary genre is in drama. In this very specific sense, we can define 'a comedy' as a funny, light-hearted or romantic play. Even here, though, there are few hard-and-fast rules about what we can expect to *find* in a comedy of this sort. It might, or might not, feature a variety of elements including jesters, slapstick, jokes, sexual innuendo, mistaken identity, love, marriage, **satire**, and many other things. A comedy in this sense might be rip-roaringly hilarious from beginning to end, setting out to make the audience laugh continuously; or it might just be 'light-hearted' or romantic, with a few laughs along the way. (In the latter case, it would be more appropriate to describe it as 'comedic' rather than 'comic'.)

Key terms

satire: a genre that aims to challenge contemporary events, values and attitudes by making fun of them

What almost all dramatic comedies have in common is that they have 'a happy ending' (though we can even find occasional exceptions to this rule too). Before the happy ending arrives, characters are likely to experience a series of conflicts, misadventures and chaotic situations, and experience various kinds of disorder, confusion and even suffering. These events might happen because of the foolishness or ridiculousness of the characters, or because they are shown to somehow fall foul of the complex workings of a world that they do not understand and cannot control.

One important thing to notice is that the typical narrative structure of a comedy is not substantially different from that of a tragedy. Like tragedy, comedy seems to warn us of the pitfalls and problems of life, and 'holds up a mirror' to our world. Many of the events in a comedy are potentially tragic but are usually – because this is comedy – presented in a light-hearted way, with disaster ultimately averted. Perhaps part of the power of comedy lies in the audience's relief at the ending – stemming from their awareness that things could have turned out far worse.

ACTIVITY 2

Comic narratives in drama

Look carefully at the descriptions of dramatic comedy in this section, and then think about any comedies you have studied or seen. (This could include comic films and sitcoms as well as the more traditional play.) To what extent do these descriptions apply to the comedies you have identified?

- It contains hilarious comedy from beginning to end.
- It is light-hearted with a few laughs along the way.
- It includes an element of love, sex or marriage.
- It contains jokes or witty use of language.
- It includes slapstick, caricature or fast-paced physical action.
- It includes an element of confusion, error, or mistaken identity leading to conflict.
- It includes foolish or arrogant behaviour on the part of one of the main characters.
- Some kind of disaster is averted.
- It has a happy ending.

Remember that not all of these descriptions apply to every comedy.

6.1.1 The earliest forms of comedy

The origins of the idea of comedy lie in Ancient Greece. The word 'comedy' comes from the Greek words *komos* and *oide* – meaning 'revel' and 'song'. So a comedy was a 'revel song', probably referring to the drunken revels in Ancient Greek festivals.

Dramatic performances often took place in these festivals, especially in Athens at the festival of Dionysus, in the 5th century BCE. Playwrights entered plays in competitions: three tragedies and a shorter, lighter 'satyr play', which was a kind of light relief version of the full tragedies. It is from these plays that we get the modern idea of satire; the sending up of something serious and topical.

The comedies performed at the festival were quite unlike tragedies or satyr plays. Whereas tragedies and satyr plays were concerned with the relationships between gods and humans as played out in the lives of kings, queens, heroes (and satyrs), Greek comedy was much more down-to-earth.

Exploring satyrs and satyr plays

The word 'satyr' refers to the half-human, half-goat characters who in Greek myth were companions of Dionysus and appeared as the chorus in the satyr plays. Satyrs were mischievous and lewd, and the plays often involved depictions of drunkenness, vulgarity, sexual arousal (with phallic props) and trickery – rather like some controversial modern comedies such as, for instance, the cartoon *South Park*.

'Comedy aims at representing men as worse, Tragedy as better than in actual life.'

Aristotle, *Poetics*

6.1.2 Aristotle and Plato on comedy

The Greek philosopher Aristotle, who lived in the 4th century BCE, was a philosopher who included literature among his topics. His work *Poetics* is the first great work of literary criticism, and discusses the principles of both tragedy and comedy, although there is relatively little about comedy in the book.

See 5.1.2 for more on Aristotle's views on tragedy, in comparison to comedy

In *Poetics*, Aristotle writes that comedy is 'an imitation of inferior people' who are seen to perform 'an error or disgrace that does not involve pain or destruction', but that is 'laughable'. There is a clear contrast here with Aristotle's view of tragedy as focusing on the errors of noble, heroic people, which *do* finally cause pain and destruction.

In other works, Aristotle and another great Greek philosopher, Plato, write about the dangers of comedy. Plato, for instance, in his great work *The Republic*, which describes an ideal republic, says that one should avoid 'abandoning oneself to great laughter' - warning that it is a sign of lack of self-control. In other works, he writes of the dangers of mockery and ridicule, suggesting that the law should have the right to see these as potentially disruptive behaviours.

ACTIVITY 3

Exploring Aristotle and Plato on comedy

Again, think of examples of comedy you know.

a To what extent do you think Aristotle's description of comedy as 'an imitation of inferior people' is reasonable?

b Does Aristotle's idea that the errors made by characters in comedy do not cause 'pain or destruction' but are 'laughable' seem true?

c Is Plato right to suggest that comedy has the potential to be socially dangerous or disruptive?

d Do you agree with Plato's argument that comedy should therefore be avoided?

Check your responses in the Ideas section on Cambridge Elevate

6.2 Development of comedy

6.2.1 Classical comedy

Very few of the Ancient Greek comedies have survived. The only surviving whole plays are eleven by Aristophanes. These plays, such as *The Birds*, *The Frogs*, *The Wasps*, and, perhaps most famously, *Lysistrata*, were political satires that contained a great deal of farce and sexual humour.

Lysistrata, for instance, is about an attempt by a group of Athenian women to bring about the end of the Peloponnesian War (between Athens and Sparta) by refusing to have sex while it continues. The plot is as described in Text 6A.

Text 6A

Plot of *Lysistrata*

Lysistrata leads the women of Athens in rebellion against the warring men. She persuades her followers to swear to abstain from sex. The young women confer, and the old women seize the Acropolis, the seat of power and site of the city treasury. A chorus of old men arrives and tries to burn the women out, but the old women douse the men with cold water, driving them back.

A magistrate arrives and announces that men must keep women in their place; it is their own fault if the women take over. His men try to break into the treasury but fail. Lysistrata tells him that women could govern well enough, but he replies that he would never take orders from a woman. The women put a veil on him, and Lysistrata lectures him again. He goes for reinforcements. The old men attack again, and each group strips for battle. The men start to become desperate for sex. One of the women, Myrrhine, teases her fully aroused husband, promising sex but deliberately delaying it.

The Spartans, whose wives have also gone on a sex-strike, arrive, all with erections. The Spartans and the Athenians agree to make peace, and everyone dances to celebrate. Lysistrata brings out a beautiful naked woman, and names her Peace. Everyone prepares for the feast. Once they get drunk, they discover they love one another, and sing to their former enemies.

Although at a superficial level, the play may seem to have a feminist message, it must be borne in mind that the women in the play are continually seen to be weak-willed and unequal to the task, and Lysistrata

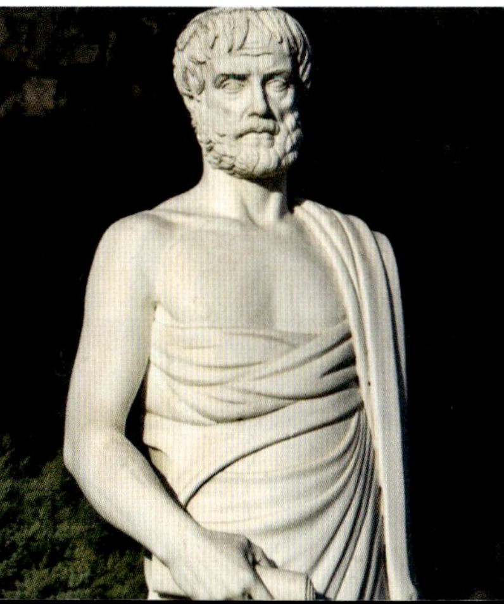

has to work hard to stop them from giving in to the sexual demands of their husbands. Nevertheless, it's undeniable that it is perhaps the earliest example of a play that confronts gender roles in society head-on.

ACTIVITY 4

Lysistrata

a To what extent does this, one of the earliest comedies in existence, seem to be similar to or different from modern comedies? Are you surprised by any aspects of the comedy?

b Can you identify elements in *Lysistrata* that remind you of any of the comedies you know?

c Does the emphasis on politics, or sex and gender roles in society, feature in any of those comedies?

Old comedy and new comedy

Aristotle distinguishes between the 'old comedy' of Aristophanes in the 5th century BCE and the 'new comedy' which developed in the 4th century BCE, of which Menander is the main playwright. The only surviving play of this genre is Menander's *The Misanthrope*. The plot is as shown in Text 6B.

Text 6B

Plot of *The Misanthrope*

In *The Misanthrope*, the wealthy young gentleman, Sostratos, falls in love with the nameless daughter of the misanthropic peasant, Knemon, who will not allow anyone near his daughter. Helped by Knemon's stepson, Gorgias, Sostratos dresses up as a rough labourer in order to be near her, and ends up helping to rescue Knemon from the well he has fallen down. Although Sostratos nearly kills Knemon in the process, because he is too busy admiring the daughter to focus properly on the rescue, Knemon is so grateful that he gives him his daughter's hand in marriage. Sostratos also persuades his father Kallippides to allow his sister to marry the man who helped him, Gorgias. After his recovery from his injuries, Knemon is as misanthropic as ever, but is persuaded to join in the celebration of the impending marriages.

New comedy was very different from old comedy. Gone are the sexual innuendo and political satire. Instead, these plays focus on a complex plot - not unlike the plot of a tragedy, involving lovers, family relationships, misunderstandings and mistaken identities - at the end of which members of a family separated by events are reunited.

ACTIVITY 5

The Misanthrope

Look at the plot of *The Misanthrope*.

a To what extent does it seem similar to any modern comedies you know? What aspects of the comedy are familiar from later comedies?

b To what extent does this comedy satisfy Aristotle's idea that comedy is about 'inferior people' whose actions are 'laughable'?

Roman comedy

Greek plays continued to be performed in Rome, and Roman writers continued the traditions of both tragedy and comedy, often developing them in new ways. The most famous of Roman plays are the comedies of Plautus (3rd century BCE) and Terence (2nd century BCE) - both of whom adapted and reworked ideas from Greek comedy. Six plays by Terence and twenty by Plautus still survive. The plays of Plautus were a particular influence on Shakespeare, who adapted Plautus' comedy *The Menaechmi* in his own *The Comedy of Errors*.

At the height of the age of Roman comedy, a Roman audience could expect to see some or all of these things in a comedy, some drawn from Greek new comedy, and some developed by Roman playwrights:

- a single domestic setting (following the Greek idea of **unity of place**) and events that take place in quick succession on one day (**unity of time**)
- parallel plots and **subplots**, which might overlap with the main plot and come together at the end (a rejection of the traditional Greek **unity of plot**)
- division of the play into acts and scenes
- a delight in playing with language
- mistaken identities, coincidences and overheard conversations that cause confusion and propel the plot forward
- stock characters such as comic servants and bad-tempered masters, strict fathers, bossy wives and mothers, young lovers, swaggering soldiers, and prostitutes
- reunion of long-lost family members at the end of the play.

Key terms

unity of place: a single location in which all the action of the play takes place

unity of time: limiting the action of a play so that it takes place on a single day

subplot: a secondary plot which is often related to the main plot thematically or becomes caught up in the main plot as the narrative progresses

unity of plot: a focus on one plot, with no subplot to complicate the action

ACTIVITY 6

Aspects of Roman comedy

Think about each of the aspects of Roman comedy. Try to match each one with an example from a modern comedy you know. Draw on your knowledge of comedy from Shakespeare to sitcom and comic films.

6.2.2 Medieval comedy

The comedies of ancient Rome survived beyond the medieval period – roughly a thousand years, from the fall of Rome in the 6th century CE to the Renaissance (at its height in the 15th century CE).

However, during the medieval period itself, there was little performance of these old comedies, and little writing of extended dramatic comedies.

That does not mean that comic drama did not exist in this period. Drama of many sorts continued to be performed by small groups of 'players' in the streets or in inn courtyards, often using wagons or carts as a stage, and sometimes in the great halls of the nobility.

Mummers, mysteries, miracles and morality

Sometimes these mobile plays were relatively small-scale comic performances that included a great deal of clowning and trickery, such as **mummers plays**. More spectacular and more serious were the **mystery plays**, **miracle plays** and **morality plays** of the later medieval period, which told stories from the Bible, stories of the lives of saints, and stories intended to teach good Christian behaviour.

Although these were essentially serious religious plays, many of them contained comic scenes that were very popular with audiences. Stories such as Mary telling Joseph that she was pregnant with Jesus, or Noah announcing to his wife that they had to live in a boat, provided the material for these comic scenes. Comic interludes were often performed in the breaks in these plays, too.

Key terms

mummers play: a short comic medieval folk play performed on streets and in inns by a troupe of actors known as mummers or guisers

mystery play: a medieval play that dramatises stories from the Bible

miracle play: a medieval play that dramatises stories of the lives of the saints

morality play: a medieval play that dramatises moral values such as good and evil

'I have everything, yet have nothing; and although I possess nothing, still of nothing am I in want.'

Terence, *Eunuchus*. Act ii. Sc. 2, 12.

6.2.3 The first English comedies

In 16th-century England, major changes occurred which led to the revival of comic drama as a genre in its own right. As the mystery plays grew more spectacular and more highly staged, as the power of the Church began to wane, and as interest in Greek and Roman culture revived, theatre companies developed, especially in London, and playwrights flourished. A new tradition of tragedy and comedy, strongly influenced by the classical world, began to grow. The comedies of Terence and Plautus were rediscovered and began to be performed again, prompting contemporary writers to write new comedies in which they combined aspects of the comic interludes of the medieval era with aspects of the classical comedies. Such a play was the first English comedy, *Ralph Roister Doister*, which built on the medieval tradition of clowning but also returned to the comic structures, settings, themes and characters of Roman comedy.

ACTIVITY 7

Ralph Roister Doister

a Read the extract from the Prologue of *Ralph Roister Doister* in Text 6C. Although there are one or two tricky words, the ideas are quite straightforward. What does Udall say are the benefits and purposes of comedy, and what kind of comedy does he indicate to be acceptable?

b Now look at the plot of *Ralph Roister Doister* in Text 6D. What familiar aspects of comedy can you see in this plot? To what extent does the plot reflect Aristotle's idea that comedy is 'an imitation of inferior people' who perform 'an error or disgrace that does not involve pain or destruction' but that is 'laughable'?

Text 6C

What creature is in health, either young or old,
But some **mirth** with modesty will be glad to use –
As we in this interlude shall now unfold?
Wherein all **scurrility** we utterly refuse,
Avoiding such mirth wherein is abuse;
Knowing nothing more commendable for a man's recreation
Than mirth which is used in an honest fashion.
For mirth prolongeth life, and causeth health
Mirth recreates our spirits, and **voideth pensiveness**,
Mirth increases **amity**, not hindering our wealth...

Nicholas Udall, *Ralph Roister Doister*

Glossary

mirth: laughter

scurrility: something offensive or shocking

voideth pensiveness: stops quiet thoughtfulness

amity: friendship

Text 6D

Plot of *Ralph Roister Doister*

In *Ralph Roister Doister*, the cunning Matthew Merrygreek convinces the foolish and arrogant Ralph Roister Doister to try his luck with Dame Custance. He writes her a letter and sends gifts to her. However, she is engaged to Gawyn Goodluck and rejects Ralph's advances. In a series of comic scenes, Merrygreek eggs Ralph on to follow up his initial advances in several absurd ways, culminating in Ralph marching to Custance's house and demanding entry, whereupon he is beaten back by her female servants. Meanwhile, Goodluck, Custance's fiancé, hears about Ralph's advances from his servant and misunderstands the situation, accusing Dame Custance of cheating on him. Eventually, Custance and Goodluck marry and Ralph is forgiven.

6.2.4 Comedy in Renaissance drama

The process of cultural development described in the previous section, involving the rediscovery of Greek and Roman ideas and culture, is known as the Renaissance. It denotes a period of intellectual and cultural transformation that began in Italy in the 14th century and spread to the rest of Europe. *Ralph Roister Doister* was the beginning of a Renaissance golden age for English comedy, which saw comedy develop in a number of different ways.

The most celebrated writers of comedy during this period were William Shakespeare and Ben Jonson, both of whom emerged on the dramatic scene in the 1590s. By the time of Shakespeare's and Jonson's first comedies, a professional theatre with new theatre buildings was well established in London: the first theatre to open in London was 'The Theatre' in c.1576.

Shakespeare and farce

Shakespeare's earliest comedy, *The Comedy of Errors* (c. 1590), is an adaptation of a Roman play by Plautus. It is Shakespeare's purest farce, a delightfully knockabout spectacle focused on the misunderstandings that occur when two sets of identical twins are set loose on an unsuspecting city. It still has the power to make audiences roar with laughter today.

Although most of Shakespeare's later comedies are not pure farces, most of them also contain significant *elements* of farce – misunderstandings resulting in domestic confusion, played out through slapstick and fast physical action. For instance, think of the rough wooing of Kate in *The Taming of the Shrew*; the confusion of the lovers and the 'rude mechanicals' in *A Midsummer Night's Dream* caused by Titania's magic and Puck's antidote to it; and the 'gulling' (deception) of Malvolio in *Twelfth Night*.

Exploring farce

Farce is a form of comedy in which the emphasis is on complex, confusing and unlikely plots and situations. Aspects of farce include:

- misunderstandings, mistaken identities, disguises and attempts to avoid discovery, which lead to confusion, conflict and absurd situations
- fast-paced action in which characters enter and leave the stage suddenly and in quick succession, often chasing or running away from each other
- the involvement of innocent parties who do not know what is going on
- slapstick and visual humour caused by people falling over, things coming off, and other physical problems.

Set text focus: *Twelfth Night*

William Shakespeare wrote *Twelfth Night, or What You Will* in the middle of his career, probably in 1601. The play includes various stock features – separated twins, disguise, obstacles to love – set within the context of the title, which probably refers to the twelfth night of the Christmas celebration, when society was turned upside down. Confusion and comedy result when Shakespeare disturbs traditional gender and class roles by disguising Viola as a man – who promptly falls in love with a man, and is fallen in love *with* by a woman; and by showing the humiliation of a servant (Malvolio) who seeks to rise above his own social position.

Although not an exhaustive list, the following aspects of comedy could be explored in relation to *Twelfth Night*:

- the type of comedy (see 6.1; 6.2.4)
- settings of time and place (see Activity 6; 6.3.5)
- the protagonists' journey towards knowledge and happiness (see Activity 10; 6.2.4, Shakespeare's romantic comedies; 6.3.3, *Errors*…; 6.3.5, Journeys…; 6.3.7)
- the role of the comic hero/heroine (see 6.3.2, Heroes…)
- the role of the comic villain, adversary or rival (6.3.2, Villains…)
- significance of human folly, trickery and deceit (see 6.3.3, *Trickery*…)
- the inclusion of clowns and fools, physical and visual humour (6.3.2, Natural fools…; 6.3.3, *Slapstick*…)
- use of disguise and discovery (6.3.3, *Disguise*…; 6.4.1)
- structural pattern of the play: disorder and order, rule and misrule (see 6.3.1; 6.3.3, Misrule…; 6.3.7)
- use of complex plots, framing and sub-plots (see Activities 6, 10; 6.3.6)
- how language is used to heighten the comedy (see Activity 27; 6.3.4)
- effects on the audience (see 6.1; 6.3.2, Clowns…).

The play could be read from the perspective of:

- value and the canon (see 9.3)
- narrative theory (see 6.3.6, Critical lens; 9.4)
- feminist theory (see 6.3.3, Critical lens; 6.4.1; 9.5)
- Marxist theory (see 6.3.2, Critical lens; 6.4.2; 9.6)
- eco-critical theory (see Activity 32; 9.7).

ACTIVITY 8

Aspects of farce

Look at the list of aspects of farce in the box Exploring farce. To what extent are they a feature of any comedies you know?

Shakespeare's romantic comedies

After *The Comedy of Errors*, Shakespeare gradually moved away from hilarious physical farce to a gentler form of comedy that contained strong elements of romance.

His second comedy, *The Taming of the Shrew* (c. 1592), retains some of the farcical atmosphere of *The Comedy of Errors*, its plot similarly revolving around a set of fast-paced domestic scenes focused on one household. However, at the heart of *The Taming of the Shrew*, unlike *The Comedy of Errors*, is a story of love. We'd be hard-pressed to call the play a romance: there's very little that's romantic about Petruchio's rough wooing of Kate. Nevertheless, the ending of the play is marked by the flowering of love between two people, which is also the central element of many of the later comedies.

A Midsummer Night's Dream (believed to have been written in the mid-1590s) is perhaps the first of Shakespeare's comedies in which the driving force of the plot is the idea that 'the course of true love never did run smooth', as Lysander says in the play. The central narrative direction of the play is towards the eventual realisation of love following a series of difficulties which threaten to thwart it - also a feature of most of Shakespeare's later comedies, including *Much Ado About Nothing* (c. 1598), *As You Like It* and *Twelfth Night* (the two great romantic comedies of 1600-01), and *The Tempest* (c. 1611, possibly his last play).

Although these plays move away from the dominant slapstick, farce and bawdiness of classical comedy, they still contain elements of all these. But on the whole, in these **romantic comedies**, Shakespeare seems to develop comedy into something gentler, darker and more emotional, concerned less exclusively with raw laughter, and more with exploring the mystery of the journey of life.

Although love plays a central part in Shakespeare's romantic comedies, it would be a mistake to think

Set text focus: *The Taming of the Shrew*

The Taming of the Shrew is one of Shakespeare's earliest plays, written in the early 1590s. In it, he examines society's attitudes to women and how they were supposed to behave, at a time when views were already beginning to change. 'Shrews' (or 'scolds') were often punished publicly for resisting their husbands' authority and daughters could be more or less sold off to the highest bidder, as Kate's father does. Shakespeare portrays the battles of will and wit that might take place between daughters and fathers, and wives and husbands, within such a system, whilst nevertheless acknowledging the ultimate authority of the men.

Although not an exhaustive list, the following aspects of comedy could be explored in relation to *The Taming of the Shrew*:

- the type of comedy (see 6.1; 6.2.4)
- settings of time and place (see Activity 6; 6.3.5)
- the protagonists' journey towards knowledge and happiness (see 6.2.4, Shakespeare's romantic comedies; 6.3.3, *Errors*…; 6.3.5, Journeys…; 6.3.7)
- the role of the hero or heroine (see 6.3.2, Heroes…)
- the role of the comic villain, adversary or rival (6.3.2, Villains…)
- the inclusion of clowns and fools, physical and visual humour (see 6.3.2, Clowns… and Natural fools…; 6.3.3, *Slapstick*…)
- use of disguise (6.3.3, *Disguise*…)
- structural pattern of the play, disorder and order, rule and misrule (see 6.3.1; 6.3.3, Varieties of confusion…; 6.3.6; 6.3.7)
- use of complex plots, framing and sub-plots (see Activity 6; 6.3.6)
- how language is used to heighten the comedy (see 6.3.4)
- effects on the audience (see 6.1; 6.3.2, Clowns…).

The play could be read from the perspective of:

- value and the canon (see 9.3)
- narrative theory (see 6.3.6, Critical lens; 9.4)
- feminist theory (see 6.3.3, Critical lens; 6.4.1; 9.5)
- Marxist theory (see 6.3.2, Critical lens; 6.4.2; 9.6)
- eco-critical theory (see 6.3.5, Critical lens; Activity 32; 9.7).

that they are only about love. These plays also return repeatedly to themes of family relationships, exile and homecoming, power and powerlessness, fate, and so on. Even *The Comedy of Errors*, Shakespeare's most farcical and least romantic comedy, ends with an intensely moving scene of a family reconciled after having been separated in tragic circumstances many years earlier.

Key terms

romantic comedy: a kind of comedy that focuses humorously, and more gently than farce, on love, relationships and other aspects of characters' lives

ACTIVITY 9

***Wise Children* and Shakespeare**

The world of Shakespearean comedy – and of *A Midsummer Night's Dream* in particular – plays a major role in Angela Carter's 1991 novel *Wise Children*. If you are studying the novel, think carefully about these questions.

- How does Carter make use of elements of Shakespearean comedy (e.g. doubling of characters, bawdy humour, mistaken identity) in her novel? You might relate these to specific plays or refer to Shakepseare's work more generally.
- How does she use characters' names to comic effect?
- How does the narrative of *A Midsummer Night's Dream* – and the production of the film version of it – interact with the narrative of the Chance sisters?

ACTIVITY 10

***Twelfth Night* and the development of romantic comedy**

Read the plot of *Twelfth Night* in Text 6E and compare it with the earlier plot of *Ralph Roister Doister*.

a How are the two plots different or similar in the kind of characters and action they contain?

b To what extent does *Twelfth Night* satisfy Aristotle's idea that comedy is 'an imitation of inferior people' who perform 'an error or disgrace that does not involve pain or destruction' but that is 'laughable'?

Set text focus: *Wise Children*

Angela Carter wrote her last novel, *Wise Children*, in 1991, a year before she died of lung cancer, which makes the repeated refrain in the novel – 'What a joy it is to dance and sing!' – even more poignant. Her writing is often remarkable for its energetic exuberance. Carter is also well known for her darkly comic vision of the world, which in many ways relates closely to the gothic tradition.

Femininity is a frequent topic of concern in her work, and she often explores the macabre and dark elements of female experience and sexuality; the emerging sexual freedom of the 1960s is an important element of *Wise Children*. In this novel, juxtaposition of pairs or opposites, and elements from music hall and Shakespearian comedy vie with each other as Carter explores the relationship between legitimacy and illegitimacy, reality and illusion, and the idea of being on the 'wrong side'.

Although not an exhaustive list, the following aspects of comedy could be explored in relation to *Wise Children*:

- the type of comedy (see 6.2.7)
- settings of time and place (see Activity 6; 6.3.5)
- the protagonist's journey towards knowledge and discovery (see 6.3.3)
- the role of the comic heroine (see 6.3.2, Heroes…)
- the role of the comic villain (6.3.2, Villains…)
- structural pattern of the novel (see 6.3.1; 6.3.3; 6.3.7)
- how language is used to heighten the comedy (see 6.3.4).

Other comedic aspects to consider in relation to the novel could be the use of the absurd, pantomimic scenes, family relationships, sexual encounters, mistaken identities, and the use of sets of twins.

The novel could be read from the perspective of:

- value and the canon (see 9.3)
- narrative theory (see 6.3.6, Critical lens; 9.4)
- feminist theory (see 6.4.1; 9.5)
- Marxist theory (see 6.4.2; 9.6).

Text 6E

Plot of *Twelfth Night*

In *Twelfth Night*, Viola and her twin brother, Sebastian, are shipwrecked off the coast of Illyria, and separated from each other, each believing the other dead. At the beginning of the play, Viola finds herself on the shore of Illyria. Uncertain of her safety, she disguises herself as a boy, called Cesario, and enters the service of the duke Orsino. The duke sends Cesario with messages of love to a lady, Olivia, on his behalf. Olivia, however, falls in love with Cesario (Viola), not realising that he is in fact a woman. At the same time, Viola (Cesario) falls in love with Orsino.

Meanwhile, at Olivia's house, members of her household – her servant Maria, her kinsman Sir Toby Belch, his friend Sir Andrew Aguecheek and the jester Feste – are plotting the humiliation of Malvolio, Olivia's steward. Malvolio is a pompous and snobbish character who disapproves of their riotous behaviour around the house. Maria and her co-plotters persuade Malvolio that Olivia is in love with him and that he should woo her appropriately. In doing so, he makes a fool of himself and realises that he has been tricked.

Viola's twin brother, Sebastian, now arrives in Illyria, having been saved by the sea captain, Antonio. Olivia meets Sebastian and, thinking he is Cesario, arranges for them to be secretly married. Several incidents of mistaken identity occur causing chaos and confusion among all the characters in relation to both the main plot and the subplot.

Finally, the two twins meet each other and realise what has happened. With the identities of the twins revealed, Olivia is free to marry Sebastian, while Orsino realises that his true love is his confidante Viola (Cesario). At the end of the play, the two couples are married. However, Malvolio, who has been seriously humiliated by the members of Olivia's household, has the last word, swearing to take revenge on them all.

Check your responses in the Ideas section on Cambridge Elevate

Exploring romance

Romance is a complicated concept. In the medieval era, the word referred to stories of heroic adventure, often stories about King Arthur and the Knights of the Round Table. Many of the stories in Chaucer's *The Canterbury Tales* are romances, as is the narrative poem 'Sir Gawain and the Green Knight'. Love for or enchantment by a beautiful woman is usually an important part of the narrative, but the main focus is on the heroic quest of the knight. In 'The Nun's Priest's Tale' in *The Canterbury Tales*, Chaucer even parodies the romance, portraying Chauntecleer the cock and Pertelote the hen satirically as a romantic hero and heroine.

During the Renaissance, the meaning of the word 'romance' began to change. It was still applied to stories of travel and adventure, but there was a greater focus on the element of love in them. In this sense, many of Shakespeare's comedies are described as romances, distinguishing them from more farcical and satirical types of comedy. Later the word was applied to many of the great novels of the 19th century, with their continuing emphasis on both adventure and love.

It wasn't until the 20th century that the word began to mean a simple love story or a love affair, with the element of travel or adventure.

'Of charity, what kin are you to me?'

William Shakespeare, *Twelfth Night*

Set text focus: 'The Nun's Priest's Tale'

Geoffrey Chaucer began to write *The Canterbury Tales* around 1387. Rather than writing in the French that had traditionally been spoken at the English court, he chose to write in vernacular English, which was increasingly being recognised as the language of public discourse. 'The Nun's Priest's Tale' is based on an older folklore tale of Chanticleer and the Fox, which made an appearance in literature in *Le Roman de Renart* in 1170. Chaucer cleverly parodies the popular theme of courtly love of medieval and Renaissance literature by setting his tale in a barnyard. In folklore, Reynard the fox is a peasant hero in stories that satirise the aristocracy and clergy, an element that permeates the whole of *The Canterbury Tales*, which was written at a time of peasant rebellion when the traditional estates of nobility, Church and peasantry, were breaking down.

Although not an exhaustive list, the following aspects of comedy could be explored in relation to 'The Nun's Priest's Tale':

- the type of comedy (see 6.2.4, Exploring romance; 6.2.8)
- settings of time and place (see Activity 6; 6.3.5)
- the protagonist's journey and escape (see 6.3.5; 6.3.7)
- the role of the comic hero (see 6.3.2, Heroes…)
- the role of the comic villain (6.3.2, Villains…)
- significance of trickery and deceit (see 6.3.3, *Trickery*…)
- structural pattern of the poem (see 6.3.1; 6.3.6; 6.3.7)
- mockery of pride (see 6.1.2)
- use of complex plots, framing and sub-plots (see Activity 6; 6.3.6; 6.4.1)
- how language is used to heighten the comedy (see 6.3.4).

Other comedic aspects to consider in relation to the poem could be the use of animals, birds and allegory, sexual encounters, absurdity, farce, and mockery of pride.

The poem could be read from the perspective of:

- value and the canon (see 9.3)
- narrative theory (see 9.4)
- feminist theory (see 6.4.1; 9.5)
- Marxist theory (see 9.6)
- eco-critical theory (see 6.3.5, Critical lens; Activity 32; 9.7).

ACTIVITY 11

Comedy – laughter or love?

As we have seen, comedy as a genre encompasses a range of types of narrative and action. Greek and Roman comedies were essentially farce. Greek 'old comedy' was characterised by riotous political satire and sexual innuendo, while Greek 'new comedy' and Roman comedy focused more on families, mistaken identities, complex misunderstandings and so on. Shakespeare then moved away from farce towards a gentler and darker form of comedy, with strong elements of romance, combining jokes and physical humour with a focus on love and fate.

a Think about comedies you have seen or studied, including comedies written for television, film and theatre. On a piece of paper, write 'farce' at the top and 'romance' at the bottom, and try to plot the comedies that you know, with the most farcical near the top and the most romantic near the bottom.

b What do you think makes the most satisfying comedy – riotous farce or gentler romance?

6.2.5 Restoration to Victorian drama

The extraordinary flowering of theatre, which had taken place in the second half of the 16th century and the first half of the 17th century, came to an abrupt end in 1642, when the theatres were closed by order of the Puritan parliament, not reopening until 1660 when the English monarchy was restored under King Charles II. However, following the restoration of royal power in 1660, a new golden age of English comedy began which lasted until the early decades of the next century.

The most significant form of comedy during this period was the **comedy of manners**, which satirised the behaviour and attitudes of the sophisticated upper classes, at the same time ridiculing them *and* celebrating their wit and ingenuity. This kind of comedy, in various forms, continued to be popular until early in the 20th century. The greatest examples are the plays of William Wycherley (for example, *The Country Wife)* and William Congreve (for example *The Way of the World*) during the Restoration, Oliver Goldsmith (*She Stoops to Conquer*) and Richard Sheridan (for example, *The Rivals*) in the Georgian age, and Oscar Wilde (for example, *The Importance of Being Earnest*) in the late Victorian age.

Set text focus: *She Stoops to Conquer* and *The Importance of Being Earnest*

Oliver Goldsmith's *She Stoops to Conquer* was first performed in 1773, two years after it was first written. The reluctance to produce it on stage may have been because his previous play was not well received. He wanted to satirise what he called the 'weeping sentimental comedy so much in fashion at present' and produce a new type of comedy, which he called 'laughing comedy'. His primary aim was to produce laughter, by featuring middle and lower class people, speaking in natural dialogue, to expose human folly.

Although not an exhaustive list, the following aspects of comedy could be explored in relation to *She Stoops to Conquer*:

- the type of comedy (see 6.1; 6.2.4, Exploring farce; Activity 8; 6.2.5)
- settings of time and place (see Activity 6; 6.2.5; 6.3.5)
- the protagonists' journey towards knowledge and happiness (see 6.2.5; 6.3.1; 6.3.3, *Errors*...; 6.3.5, Journeys...; 6.3.7)
- the role of the comic hero/heroine (see 6.3.2, Heroes...)
- significance of human folly and trickery (see 6.2.5; 6.3.3, *Trickery*...)
- use of disguise (6.3.3, *Disguise*...)
- structural pattern of the play and use of a sub-plot (see Activity 6; 6.3.1; 6.3.3, Varieties of confusion...; 6.3.6; 6.3.7)
- how language is used to heighten the comedy (see 6.2.5)
- effects on the audience (see 6.1; 6.3.2, Clowns...).

The play could be read from the perspective of:

- value and the canon (see 9.3)
- narrative theory (see 6.3.6, Critical lens; 9.4)
- feminist theory (see 6.4.1; 9.5)
- Marxist theory (see 6.3.2, Critical lens; 6.4.2; 9.6)
- eco-critical theory (see Activity 32; 6.3.5, Critical lens; 9.7).

Oscar Wilde's *The Importance of Being Earnest* was first performed in London in 1895. Sentimental comedy had dominated the theatre for many generations and Wilde retained some of its elements in this play - abandoned children, secrets from the past, mistaken identity. But he deliberately exaggerated and satirised the shallowness of the form to great comic effect. He pushed it to extremes, used language wittily and added the character of the 'dandy' - rather like himself - in all, ridiculing the hypocrisy and rigid rules of Victorian society, whilst ultimately bringing about a resolution in which established values are satisfied.

Although not an exhaustive list, the following aspects of comedy could be explored in relation to *The Importance of Being Earnest*:

- the type of comedy (see 6.1; Activity 11; 6.2.5)
- settings of time and place (see Activity 6; 6.2.5; 6.3.5)
- the protagonists' journey towards knowledge and happiness (see 6.2.5; 6.3.5, Journeys...; 6.3.7)
- the role of the comic hero/heroine (see 6.3.2, Heroes...)
- significance of trickery and deceit (see 6.3.3, *Trickery*...)
- structural pattern of the play (see 6.3.1; 6.3.6; 6.3.7)
- use of complex plots and sub-plots (see Activity 6; 6.3.6)
- how language is used to heighten the comedy (see 6.3.4)
- effects on the audience (see 6.1; 6.3.2, Clowns...).

The play could be read from the perspective of:

- value and the canon (see 9.3)
- feminist theory (see 6.4.1; 9.5)
- Marxist theory (see 6.3.2, Critical lens; 6.4.2; 9.6)
- eco-critical theory (see 6.3.5, Critical lens; 9.7).

The Restoration and the comedy of manners

The comedy of manners was not an entirely new form. Its use of boisterous farce, and its focus on the love affairs of the upper classes, and their propensity for arrogance and foolishness, can be seen in many earlier comedies from Ancient Greece through to Shakespeare and Jonson, especially the 'city comedy' which Jonson popularised.

However, there are several features of the comedy of manners that are characteristic:

- a celebration of the flamboyance, sophistication and wit of the upper classes, including the elegance of their behaviour, language, and dress

- ridicule of those who pretend to be what they are not or who do not conform to the expectations of society
- a tension between the polite public manners and wit of upper-class characters and their private desires and behaviours
- a focus on sexual innuendo and the **rakish** sexual behaviour of upper-class men
- a sense of celebration of the excitement of sexual exploration, particularly through escaping the routine and respectability of marriage
- a contrast between the sophistication of the city and the court and the dull simplicity of the country.

By the beginning of the 18th century, the bawdy sexual farce of the Restoration comedy of manners was becoming less fashionable, reflecting an increased sense of social disapproval of such immoral and riotous behaviour. Gradually, during the 18th and 19th centuries, **sentimental** romantic comedies (nowadays generally considered to be inferior works) began to fill the playhouses instead. However, the comedy of manners never completely disappeared, and there were two particular periods of revival, towards the end of the 18th century and towards the end of the 19th century. Although the comedies of manners written during these periods placed less emphasis on bawdiness and sexual promiscuity than the Restoration comedies, they nevertheless maintained many of the features of those plays.

Key term

comedy of manners: a kind of comedy that focuses on the behaviour, attitudes and love affairs of the upper classes, featuring elements of farce

rakish: with an air of decadence, immorality and sexual promiscuity, from the noun **rake**

rake: a decadent upper-class man of dubious morality who is witty and charming, sexually promiscuous, and often careless with money

sentimental: appealing to the emotions in a rather indulgent way

ACTIVITY 12

She Stoops to Conquer* and *The Importance of Being Earnest

Read the plot summaries of Goldsmith's *She Stoops to Conquer* (Text 6F) and Wilde's *The Importance of Being Earnest* (Text 6G), both often classified as comedies of manners. To what extent do these plots seem to embrace the conventions of the comedy of manners? What other aspects of comedy do you see in them?

Text 6F

Plot summary of *She Stoops to Conquer*

In *She Stoops to Conquer*, Charles Marlow and his friend George Hastings, young city gentlemen, visit the home of the country gentleman, Mr Hardcastle. Hardcastle has invited Marlow to visit hoping that he will like and marry his daughter Kate. At the same time, Hastings wants to see Constance Neville, who lives with her cousin Kate Hardcastle. Hastings and Constance, having met previously elsewhere, are secretly in love.

Marlow and Hastings become lost on the journey to the Hardcastles, and stop at an alehouse to ask for directions. Here they encounter Tony Lumpkin, half-brother to Kate and cousin to Constance, a man of coarse country manners and interests. Lumpkin, deciding to play a practical joke on the refined city visitors, allows them to think that they are so far from their destination that they will have to stay overnight at a local inn. He gives them directions to the inn – which is really not at an inn at all, but the Hardcastles' home – warning them of the eccentricity of the landlord and his family.

On arriving at the 'inn', Marlow and Hastings, believing that the country-dwelling Hardcastles are innkeepers with pretensions above their class, treat them with disdain and amusement. On seeing his lover Constance, Hastings realises what is going on, but he and Constance decide to trick Marlow by continuing the pretence. They introduce Marlow to Kate, saying that by coincidence she is also staying in the inn.

Marlow – who is extremely shy with ladies of his own class, but very flirtatious with those of a lower class – finds it difficult to talk to Kate, so Kate – told of Marlow's 'problem' with women by Constance and Hastings – appears later as a barmaid. Believing her to be of lower class, Marlow flirts with Kate, showing himself to be witty and charming. Eventually, the two declare their love for each other.

After a number of farcical complications, the truth is revealed, and the two young couples are set to be married.

Text 6G

Plot summary of *The Importance of Being Earnest*

In *The Importance of Being Earnest*, we meet Jack Worthing and Algernon Moncrieff, two young gentlemen, in Algernon's London home. Algernon lives in London, but has invented an imaginary friend – Bunbury, who is an invalid – who lives in the country, and who gives Algernon an excuse to leave town whenever he wants to avoid the social obligations of the city. Jack lives in the country and has invented a younger brother – Ernest, who is always getting into trouble – who gives Jack an excuse to go to London whenever he wants to have fun in the city.

Jack wants to marry the sophisticated Gwendolen, Algernon's cousin, but Gwendolen's mother Lady Bracknell – who discovers that Jack does not know who his parents are, having been abandoned as a baby in a handbag at Victoria Station – refuses to allow him to marry Gwendolen unless he provides evidence of respectable parents.

Meanwhile, Algernon is fascinated by Jack's accounts of his young ward Cecily, a country girl with little knowledge of the city, who is intrigued by Jack's imaginary city cousin Ernest, whom she has never met. Algernon, pretending to be Ernest, goes to Jack's country home while Jack is in London and introduces himself to Cecily, whereupon the two fall in love.

After a number of farcical complications, the identity of Jack's parents is revealed as Lady Bracknell's own sister and brother-in-law, leaving the two sets of lovers free to marry each other.

Sentimental and laughing comedies

You have already discovered a recurring division in the genre of comedy between plays that tend towards boisterous farce and those that tend towards romantic comedy - although there are usually elements of both in all comedies. The move away from the comedy of manners to sentimental comedy that took place during the 18th and 19th centuries is another example of this division at work.

In 1773, Goldsmith, in the same year that his play *She Stoops To Conquer* was first performed, wrote an essay comparing the two forms of comedy, which he called 'laughing comedy' and 'sentimental comedy'. He was particularly responding to the inferior sentimental comedies that dominated the theatre at the time, which were quite different from the brilliant romantic comedies of Shakespeare. However, his argument about the distinction between the two types of comedy is interesting.

Goldsmith argues that modern writers of comedy have betrayed the principles of classical comedy by turning attention away from the primary purpose of comedy, which should be aimed 'only at rendering folly or vice ridiculous', as in the manner of Greek and Roman comedy. He continues as in Text 6H.

'To be born, or at any rate bred in a handbag ... seems to me to display a contempt for the ordinary decencies of family life which reminds one of the worst excesses of the French revolution, and I presume you know what that unfortunate movement led to?'

Oscar Wilde, *The Importance of Being Earnest*

Text 6H

Yet notwithstanding this weight of authority, and the universal practice of former ages, a new species of dramatic composition has been introduced under the name of 'sentimental comedy', in which the virtues of private life are exhibited, rather than the vices exposed; and the distresses rather than the faults of mankind make our interest in the piece. These comedies have had of late great success, perhaps from their novelty, and also from flattering every man in his favourite foible. In these plays almost all the characters are good... If they happen to have faults or foibles, the spectator is taught not only to pardon, but to applaud them, in consideration of the goodness of their hearts, so that folly, instead of being ridiculed, is commended, and the comedy aims at touching our passions without the power of being truly pathetic. In this manner we are likely to lose one great source of entertainment on the stage; for while the comic poet is invading the province of the tragic **muse**, he leaves her lovely sister quite neglected.... It will be allowed that... these sentimental pieces often amuse us; but the question is whether the true comedy would not amuse us more? ... It would be but a just punishment that when ... we have banished humour from the stage, we should ourselves be deprived of the art of laughing.

Oliver Goldsmith

ACTIVITY 13

The feelgood factor

Here, Goldsmith complains about what today we might call 'the feelgood factor' in comedy, suggesting that audiences are encouraged to identify with and feel for the characters in comedy rather than laugh at, ridicule and eventually forgive them. Thinking of comedies you know, in which plays (or films or television series) do you think you are encouraged to ridicule the main characters, and in which do you think you are encouraged to sympathise with them? Is it fair to suggest, as Goldsmith does, that one is less 'comic' than the other?

19th-century comedy and the well-made play

As we have seen, much of 18th- and 19th-century British theatre was dominated by sentimental comedy, most of which has been forgotten. In the second half of the 19th century, however, there was a Victorian revival of the comedy of manners in a form that became known as **the well-made play**.

Key terms

muse: in ancient Greece, the Muses were the goddesses of literature, science and the arts

well-made play: a kind of comedy of manners popular in the 19th century

Like the comedy of manners, and its predecessors in classical and Renaissance drama, the well-made play relied on farce, involving a range of eccentric characters, and a series of misunderstandings, mistaken identities and unexpected revelations. It was seen as 'well-made' because it was felt to have a particularly tight structure that delighted audiences. The plays often featured:

- a series of relevant events that happened in the past, before the action of the play, the full details of which are not revealed until the end
- a set of revelations brought about by the discovery of a lost letter or set of papers, which give full details of these events
- the discovery that one or more of the main characters are not in fact who they were thought to be, or who they thought themselves to be.

By the end of the 19th century, well-made plays, though still popular with many, were often criticised for being too concerned with farce and comic effect and too little with the reality of the social world. Set in the drawing rooms of the Victorian upper classes, the plays were felt by some to be shallow and irrelevant.

The playwright Oscar Wilde, however, deliberately exaggerated and satirised the shallowness of the form, as well as the conventional and conservative attitudes of the time, especially in his comedy *The Importance of Being Earnest*. While still using the features of the well-made play to great comic effect, he pushed it to extremes, using language wittily and sometimes absurdly to ridicule the hypocrisy of contemporary manners.

Watch tutorial video, Complications in Comedy, on Cambridge Elevate

ACTIVITY 14

Marriage in *The Importance of Being Earnest*

Read the two extracts from the first scene of *The Importance of Being Earnest* in Texts 6I and 6J. What attitudes to class, love and marriage seem to be expressed, and how might they be seen as satirical?

Text 6I

ALGERNON. Why is it that at a bachelor's establishment the servants invariably drink the champagne? I ask merely for information.

LANE. I attribute it to the superior quality of the wine, sir. I have often observed that in married households the champagne is rarely of a first-rate brand.

ALGERNON. Good heavens! Is marriage so demoralising as that?

LANE. I believe it IS a very pleasant state, sir. I have had very little experience of it myself up to the present. I have only been married once. That was in consequence of a misunderstanding between myself and a young person.

ALGERNON. *[Languidly.]* I don't know that I am much interested in your family life, Lane.

LANE. No, sir; it is not a very interesting subject. I never think of it myself.

ALGERNON. Very natural, I am sure. That will do, Lane, thank you.

LANE. Thank you, sir. *[LANE goes out.]*

ALGERNON. Lane's views on marriage seem somewhat lax. Really, if the lower orders don't set us a good example, what on earth is the use of them? They seem, as a class, to have absolutely no sense of moral responsibility.

Oscar Wilde, *The Importance of Being Earnest*

Text 6J

ALGERNON. My dear fellow, the way you flirt with Gwendolen is perfectly disgraceful. It is almost as bad as the way Gwendolen flirts with you.

JACK. I am in love with Gwendolen. I have come up to town expressly to propose to her.

ALGERNON. I thought you had come up for pleasure? ... I call that business.

JACK. How utterly unromantic you are!

ALGERNON. I really don't see anything romantic in proposing. It is very romantic to be in love. But there is nothing romantic about a definite proposal. Why, one may be accepted. One usually is, I believe. Then the excitement is all over. The very essence of romance is uncertainty. If ever I get married, I'll certainly try to forget the fact.

JACK. I have no doubt about that, dear Algy. The Divorce Court was specially invented for people whose memories are so curiously constituted.

ALGERNON. Oh! there is no use speculating on that subject. Divorces are made in Heaven...

Oscar Wilde, *The Importance of Being Earnest*

6.2.6 Comedy in 20th- and 21st-century drama

During the 20th and 21st centuries, the two traditions of farce and romantic comedy have continued to exist in parallel in the theatre, often combining in various different ways. Both farce and romantic comedy have proliferated in the cinema and on television and radio, too, during this time. There has also been a revival in political comedy and satire both on stage and on screen.

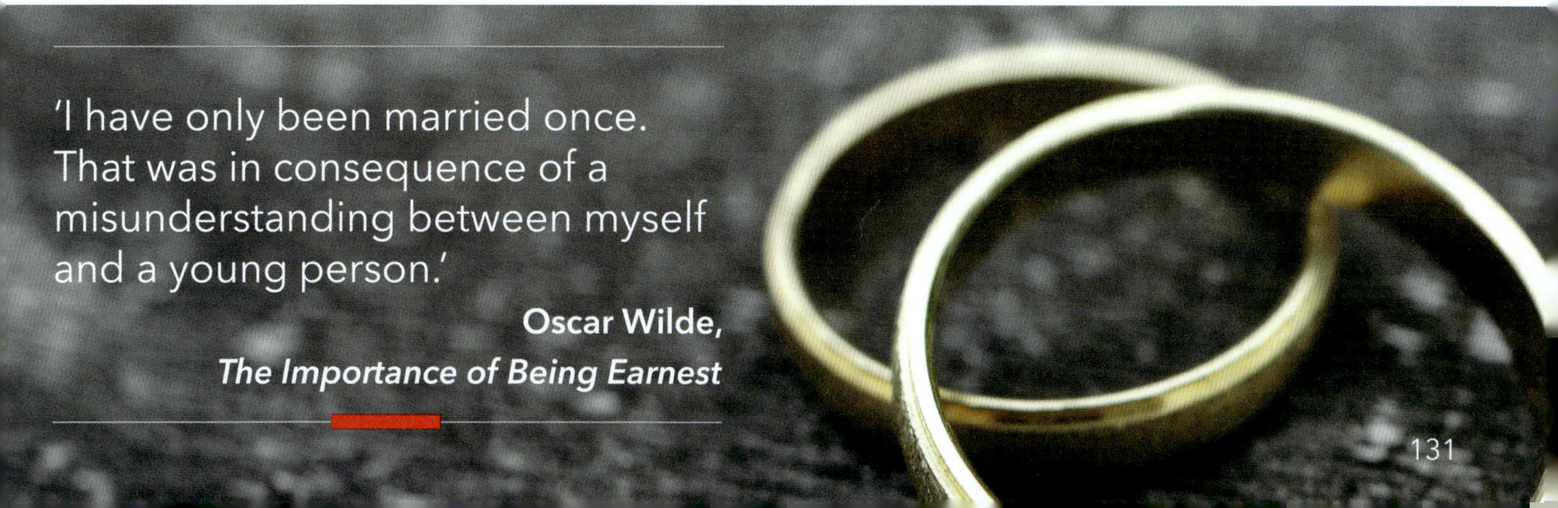

Farce

Farce has continued to be popular in various forms, notably the **bedroom farce**, a form that focuses on the embarrassments which might occur as characters attempt to move discreetly around various bedrooms in a house or hotel.

Emerging from France in the late 19th century (and sometimes known as 'French farce'), this type of farce built on the delight in sexual misbehaviour in comedy that was central to the satyr plays and the plays of Aristophanes in Ancient Greece, and also to a great deal of Renaissance and Restoration drama. All of these contained elements of bawdy humour and language, and a focus on the sexual desires of some of the characters.

Bedroom farce – as in the plays of the French playwright Georges Feydeau in the 1890s and the English Ben Travers in the 1920s and 1930s – involves a lot of running between bedrooms, along corridors and into cupboards to hide, resulting in ever more complex situations and much physical and visual humour. There are significant elements of bedroom farce in the work of the prolific contemporary playwright Alan Ayckbourn. Michael Frayn's farce *Noises Off* (1982) cleverly satirises bedroom farce at the same time as employing all its techniques to masterly effect.

The popularity of farce today has recently been demonstrated by the success of Richard Bean's *One Man, Two Guvnors* (2011), itself an adaptation of the 18th-century Italian farce the *Servant of Two Masters* by Carlo Goldoni.

Black comedy and theatre of the absurd

During the second half of the 20th century, many writers experimented with dark and disturbing comedy about serious or taboo issues such as aspects of death, political power and sexuality. While comedy has always tackled serious issues at some level, and has sometimes combined aspects of tragedy with aspects of comedy (as, for instance in some of Shakespeare's plays), the **black comedy** of this time was often both comic and shocking at the same time.

The dark farces of Joe Orton, such as *Loot* (1965) and *What the Butler Saw* (1969), and the sinister comedies of Martin McDonagh, such as *The Lieutenant of Inishmore* (2001) and the film *In Bruges* (2008) are good examples of this. Elements of farce were also employed in the **theatre of the absurd**, a form of drama that combines comedy and tragedy by focusing on a world that seems bleakly surreal, absurd and meaningless, but at the same time comic. The classic of this genre is Samuel Beckett's *Waiting for Godot* (1953).

The plays of Tom Stoppard, such as *Rosencrantz and Guildenstern Are Dead* (1969), and Harold Pinter, such as *The Homecoming* (1964), are often identified as containing strong aspects of black comedy and the theatre of the absurd. Pinter's plays have also been described as '**the comedy of menace**'.

Key terms

bedroom farce: a kind of farce that focuses on comic aspects of relationships and often takes place in bedrooms and corridors of a house

black comedy: comedy that treats very serious issues with humour

theatre of the absurd: a kind of drama that uses surreal and absurd dialogue and action to highlight the absurdity of life

comedy of menace: a kind of black comedy in which comedy merges with the threat of danger

Romantic comedy

Gentler forms of comedy have remained popular, too, and have thrived particularly in 'rom com' on film and 'sit com' on television. In the theatre, during the 20th century, there was a steady move away from the elegant upper-class wit of the comedy of manners and the well-made play towards a greater focus on the lives of middle- and working-class people.

The plays of George Bernard Shaw combined elements of social satire with romantic comedy, as for instance in *Pygmalion* (1912), a play about social class. Later in the century, the plays of Willy Russell, such as *Educating Rita* (1980) and *Shirley Valentine* (1986) also combined class and gender issues with comic love stories, while Alan Bennett's comedies, such as the *Talking Heads* monologues (1988) and *The History Boys* (2004) drew gently comic portraits of the lives of flawed characters against the backdrop of their social relationships.

Set text focus: *Educating Rita*

Willy Russell's *Educating Rita* premiered in London in 1980. Although the play is not autobiographical, many aspects are drawn from Russell's own experience of life - a working-class background, an early career in hairdressing, a late return to education and a father with alcohol problems. He has said that he wants 'to talk about things that matter' and writing about things that matter to women in particular, drawing on his childhood spent in the company of women, has produced convincing female characters and plays that are popular around the world.

Although not an exhaustive list, the following aspects of comedy could be explored in relation to *Educating Rita*:

- the type of comedy (see 6.2.6)
- settings of time and place (see Activity 6; 6.3.5)
- the protagonists' journey towards knowledge and happiness (see 6.2.7, 20th and 21st century…; 6.3.1; 6.3.5, Journeys…; 6.4.2)
- the role of the comic heroine (see 6.3.2, Heroes…)
- significance of human wisdom and foolishness (see 6.3.2)
- structural pattern of the play (see 6.3.1; 6.3.7)
- how language is used to heighten the comedy (see 6.3.4)
- effects on the audience (see 6.1; 6.3.2, Clowns…).

The play could be read from the perspective of:

- value and the canon (see 9.3)
- feminist theory (see 6.4.1; 9.5)
- Marxist theory (see 6.3.2, Critical lens; Activity 23; 6.4.2; 9.6).

Political comedy and satire

Explicit satire on contemporary political events and figures has rarely featured in comic drama since the plays of Aristophanes in Ancient Greece. Shakespeare included elements of such satire in his plays but, through the centuries, more often than not, satire in drama has had to be implied and suggested indirectly rather than aimed directly. However, there has been some revival of political satire during the last 50 years, perhaps particularly on television in the form of comedies such as *Yes Minister* and *The Thick of It*.

In the theatre, royalty and politicians have been a frequent focus for satire, most recently in Mike Bartlett's *King Charles III* (2014), a play about the future of the monarchy. Other plays have used comedy to explore the social and political state of the nation more broadly, for instance Jez Butterworth's recent *Jerusalem* (2009), an exploration of English society and values.

ACTIVITY 15

Comedy in modern theatre, film, and television drama

a Make a list of modern comic drama that you have experienced in the theatre, film, television and radio. The dramas could be full-length films or plays, or television or radio drama and situation comedy.

b Copy Table 6A and decide which category you might place each of your examples in.

c If it's difficult to decide on a category for any of the titles, this is probably because, as in many comedies, there is a balance between different types of comedy. What different types of comedy can you see at play in each title?

Table 6A

Farce	Black comedy and the theatre of the absurd	Romantic comedy	Political comedy and satire

6.2.7 Comedy in the novel

So far you have explored comedy as a dramatic genre. However, many of the aspects of comedy may also be found in other literary forms.

The novel might be seen as a kind of drama intended to be read in private rather than acted on a stage. It's not surprising, then, that, since its origin in the 18th century, the novel has produced narratives that contain many of the aspects of tragedy and comedy. Also, just as tragedy and comedy on stage deal with similar life experiences but with a different emphasis, so tragic and comic narratives in the novel represent the range of human experience from different perspectives.

The comic novel

As with dramatic comedy, comic elements manifest themselves in the novel in many different ways, from riotous farce through to gentle romantic comedy. The term 'the **comic novel**' can refer to novels that are exuberantly comic and satirical from beginning to end, using elements of farce and caricature throughout. However, it can also refer to novels that explore love, relationships, and other aspects of the journey of life in a gentler way than through the sustained exaggerations of farce, caricature and satire, rather as Shakespeare did in his romantic comedies. Such novels often contain many comic elements – comic characters, events, attitudes – without being wholly comic in tone and content; indeed, they often also contain quite moving, even at times potentially tragic, representations.

Key terms

comic novel: a novel that is predominantly humorous, or in which aspects of comedy predominate

ACTIVITY 16

Types of comedy in comic novels

Think back over novels you have read and studied. Can you identify:

a elements of farce, caricature and satire in any of the novels?

b aspects of romantic comedy in any of the novels?

c novels that contain aspects of tragedy despite having happy endings and comic elements?

18th- and 19th-century comic novels

The earliest comic novels were riotous, biting satires on contemporary social and political life, such as the novels of Henry Fielding, the first comic novelist. His first novel *Shamela*, published in 1741, was a parody of Samuel Richardson's novel *Pamela* (1740), sending up Richardson's melodramatic style and sentimental morality. Fielding went on to write the two great comic novels *Joseph Andrews* (1742) and *Tom Jones* (1749). In many respects, these novels are similar to the satirical stage comedies of the previous century.

The novels of Jane Austen, written half a century later, are regarded as comic novels, but they are gentler comedies than the riotous works of previous novelists such as Henry Fielding. Like many of Shakespeare's comedies, these novels focus on love and conclude with happy endings, usually involving weddings; but they also offer the reader a range of mildly satirical portrayals of social attitudes and behaviour, often focusing on attitudes to wealth, social status and relationships.

Charles Dickens – writing later in the 19th century – is famous for his many wonderful comic characters with extraordinary ways of speaking and attitudes, and frequently with absurd names such as Mr Pumblechook (in *Great Expectations*), Mr Micawber (in *David Copperfield*) and Mrs Crummles (in *Nicholas Nickleby*).

ACTIVITY 17

Comic characters in the novel

As with dramatic comedy, comedy in the novel is often populated by richly comic characters who speak and behave in richly comic ways.

a Read Texts 6K and 6L , extracts taken from Jane Austen's novels. In what way are these situations comic? How does Austen portray Miss Bates in *Emma* and Mrs Bennet in *Pride and Prejudice* as comic characters:

- through the way they speak
- through the way others speak to them
- through the way the story is narrated?

b Choose quotations to support your ideas for each bullet point, and then organise your thoughts into six paragraphs, three on *Emma* and three on *Pride and Prejudice*.

c For instance, you might start your section on *Emma* as follows: 'One of the ways in which Austen presents Miss Bates as a comic character is through the dialogue she gives her. Her speech is characterised by the over-use of exclamations and self-interruptions, which makes her seem ridiculously excitable…'

Set text focus: *Emma*

Emma was published in 1815, but Jane Austen's concern with domestic events in the lives of well-bred women owes more to the 18th-century comedy of manners, with its wit, polished manners and refined elegance, than to the intense emotion displayed by writers of the early 19th-century Romantic period. Perhaps that is not surprising at a time when most upper-class women still led very restricted lives and marriage was practically the only sphere in which they could come into their own. However, the intelligent and spirited heroines in Austen's novels might still be said to challenge the constraints of their conservative world.

Although not an exhaustive list, the following aspects of comedy could be explored in relation to *Emma*:

- the type of comedy (see 6.1; 6.2.5; 6.2.7)
- settings of time and place (see Activity 6; 6.3.5)
- the protagonist's journey towards knowledge and happiness (see 6.2.7; 6.3.1; 6.3.3, *Errors*…; 6.3.5, Journeys…; 6.3.7)
- the role of the comic heroine (see 6.3.2, Heroes…)
- the role of the comic adversary or rival (6.3.2, Villains…)
- structural pattern of the novel (see 6.3.1; 6.3.6; 6.3.7)
- use of complex plots, framing and sub-plots (see Activity 6; 6.3.6)
- the way that language is used to heighten the comedy (see 6.2.5; Activity 17; 6.3.4)
- effects on readers (see 6.1; 6.3.2, Clowns…).

The novel could be read from the perspective of:

- value and the canon (see 9.3)
- narrative theory (see 6.3.6, Critical lens; 9.4)
- feminist theory (see 6.4.1; 9.5)
- Marxist theory (see 6.4.2; 9.6)
- eco-critical theory (see Activity 32; 9.7)
- post-colonial theory (see 6.4.3; 9.8).

Text 6K

Full of thanks, and full of news, Miss Bates knew not which to give quickest. Mr. Knightley soon saw that he had lost his moment, and that not another syllable of communication could rest with him.

"Oh! my dear sir, how are you this morning? My dear Miss Woodhouse – I come quite overpowered. Such a beautiful hind-quarter of pork! You are too bountiful! Have you heard the news? Mr. Elton is going to be married."

Emma had not had time even to think of Mr. Elton, and she was so completely surprised that she could not avoid a little start, and a little blush, at the sound.

"There is my news: – I thought it would interest you," said Mr. Knightley, with a smile which implied a conviction of some part of what had passed between them.

"But where could <u>you</u> hear it?" cried Miss Bates. "Where could you possibly hear it, Mr. Knightley? For it is not five minutes since I received Mrs. Cole's note – no, it cannot be more than five – or at least ten – for I had got my bonnet and spencer on, just ready to come out – I was only gone down to speak to Patty again about the pork – Jane was standing in the passage – were not you, Jane? – for my mother was so afraid that we had not any salting-pan large enough. So I said I would go down and see, and Jane said, 'Shall I go down instead? for I think you have a little cold, and Patty has been washing the kitchen.' 'Oh! my dear,' said I – well, and just then came the note. A Miss Hawkins – that's all I know. A Miss Hawkins of Bath. But, Mr. Knightley, how could you possibly have heard it? for the very moment Mr. Cole told Mrs. Cole of it, she sat down and wrote to me. A Miss Hawkins –"

"I was with Mr. Cole on business an hour and half ago. He had just read Elton's letter as I was shewn in, and handed it to me directly."

"Well! that is quite – I suppose there never was a piece of news more generally interesting. My dear sir, you really are too bountiful. My mother desires her very best compliments and regards, and a thousand thanks, and says you really quite oppress her."

Jane Austen, *Emma*, Chapter 21

Text 6L

"Oh! Mr. Bennet, you are wanted immediately; we are all in an uproar. You must come and make Lizzy marry Mr. Collins, for she vows she will not have him, and if you do not make haste he will change his mind and not have HER."

Mr. Bennet raised his eyes from his book as she entered, and fixed them on her face with a calm unconcern which was not in the least altered by her communication.

"I have not the pleasure of understanding you," said he, when she had finished her speech. "Of what are you talking?"

"Of Mr. Collins and Lizzy. Lizzy declares she will not have Mr. Collins, and Mr. Collins begins to say that he will not have Lizzy."

"And what am I to do on the occasion? It seems an hopeless business."

"Speak to Lizzy about it yourself. Tell her that you insist upon her marrying him."

"Let her be called down. She shall hear my opinion."

Mrs. Bennet rang the bell, and Miss Elizabeth was summoned to the library.

"Come here, child," cried her father as she appeared. "I have sent for you on an affair of importance. I understand that Mr. Collins has made you an offer of marriage. Is it true?" Elizabeth replied that it was. "Very well – and this offer of marriage you have refused?"

"I have, sir."

"Very well. We now come to the point. Your mother insists upon your accepting it. Is it not so, Mrs. Bennet?"

"Yes, or I will never see her again."

"An unhappy alternative is before you, Elizabeth. From this day you must be a stranger to one of your parents. Your mother will never see you again if you do NOT marry Mr. Collins, and I will never see you again if you DO."

Elizabeth could not but smile at such a conclusion of such a beginning, but Mrs. Bennet, who had persuaded herself that her husband regarded the affair as she wished, was excessively disappointed.

"What do you mean, Mr. Bennet, in talking this way? You promised me to INSIST upon her marrying him."

"My dear," replied her husband, "I have two small favours to request. First, that you will allow me the free use of my understanding on the present occasion; and secondly, of my room. I shall be glad to have the library to myself as soon as may be."

Jane Austen, *Pride and Prejudice*, Chapter 20

20th- and 21st-century comic novels

Riotous and absurd comedy has continued to be popular throughout the 20th century and on to the present day. Perhaps most popular, especially since the mid-20th century, has been a gentler comic approach to writing about people's lives that combines aspects of romantic comedy with elements of the ***Bildungsroman*** – comic novels which tell the story of characters' progress through life, balancing aspects of comedy with a focus on love, relationships and broader social relationships.

Highly popular novels of this sort from the last 25 years include Kate Atkinson's *Behind the Scenes at the Museum* (1995), Jonathan Coe's *The Rotter's Club* (2001), Helen Fielding's *Bridget Jones's Diary* (1996), Louis De Berniere's *Captain Corelli's Mandolin* (1994), Andrea Levy's *Small Island* (2004) and Zadie Smith's *White Teeth* (2000). Angela Carter's *Wise Children* (1991), with its darkly comic combination of

The heroines in Austen's novels might still be said to challenge the constraints of their conservative world

outrageous Shakespearean comedy, surrealism and magic realism, is a particularly interesting example. As with many dramatic comedies, not everything in these novels is funny: some are more comic than others; some are more romantic than others; some are more satirical than others. It is the lighter, less serious tone and perspective of these narratives that distinguishes them as comic, rather than their funniness.

Set text focus: *Small Island*

Andrea Levy's father came to England from Jamaica on the *Empire Windrush* in 1948, so she was born and brought up black in a very white England. She has said that she grew up thinking she was 'worthless' and that the story of the Caribbean and the people from there was 'worthless'. So initially she was more than pleasantly surprised to find out that many people wanted to know about the Caribbean British experience in 1950s Britain portrayed in *Small Island*. The novel explores how immigration changes the lives of both immigrants and the indigenous people, and specifically how World War II was a catalyst on the path of today's multi-cultural Britain.

Although not an exhaustive list, the following aspects of comedy could be explored in relation to *Small Island*:

- the type of comedy (see 6.1; 6.2.7)
- settings of time and place (see Activity 6; 6.3.5)
- the protagonists' journey towards knowledge and happiness (see 6.2.7; 6.3.3, *Errors…*; 6.3.7)
- the role of the comic hero/heroine (see 6.3.2, Heroes…)
- structural pattern of the novel (see 6.3.1; 6.3.6; 6.3.7)
- use of complex plots, framing and sub-plots (see Activity 6; 6.3.6)
- how language is used to heighten the comedy (see Activity 18; 6.3.4)
- effects on readers (see 6.1; 6.3.2, Clowns…).

The novel could be read from the perspective of:

- value and the canon (see 9.3)
- narrative theory (see 6.3.6, Critical lens; 9.4)
- feminist theory (see 6.4.1; 9.5)
- Marxist theory (see 6.4.2; 9.6)
- post-colonial theory (see 6.3.3, Critical lens; 6.4.3; 9.8).

6.2.8 Comedy in poetry

In poetry, comic narrative and satire are ancient genres, stretching back in time almost as far as dramatic comedy.

Satire in poetry

Satire – political and social – was a major subject of poetry in the classical world. The Roman poets Juvenal and Horace were particularly famous as writers of satirical verse. In turn, their work influenced a revival of satire in the Renaissance. The form once more flourished in the late 17th and 18th centuries, when distinguished poets such as John Dryden, Alexander Pope and Jonathan Swift used satirical poetry to comment on many political and social issues and attitudes, sometimes in book-length poems, sometimes in very short ones. Swift's 'Satirical Elegy on the Death of a Late Famous General', composed on the death of the Duke of Marlborough in 1722, is a good example of a short satirical verse that uses **ironic humour** to deliver a judgement on the character and behaviour of a major public figure of the time.

Key terms

***Bildungsroman*:** a novel dealing with a character's development from childhood to adulthood

ironic humour: humour that relies on irony for its effect, often featuring a comic difference between what is said and what is actually meant

Comic narratives in poetry

Comic scenes in narrative verse were also popular in the classical world, featuring, for instance, in Homer's epic poems *The Odyssey* and *The Iliad*. Comic narrative verse flourished again in the late medieval and Renaissance periods. Geoffrey Chaucer's *The Canterbury Tales* includes several comic tales; the narrators of his tales are also often comic characters in their own right, whose way of telling the tales is sometimes as comic as the tales themselves, as, for instance, in 'The Miller's Tale'. A number of other poets have also written popular examples of comic narrative verse over the centuries since Chaucer – notably Robert Burns' 'Tam o' Shanter' (1790) and Hilaire Belloc's *Cautionary Tales for Children* (1907).

Set text focus: 'A Satirical Elegy on the Death of a Late Famous General'

Jonathan Swift wrote 'A Satirical Elegy…' in 1722 on the death of John Churchill, the first Duke of Marlborough. The duke had led British forces against Louis XIV of France, who laid claim to the Spanish throne and empire. Churchill had had a chequered diplomatic and military career, earning Queen Anne's gratitude in the form of his title and land, but eventually being accused of misuse of public money. As editor of the Tory paper, *The Examiner*, Swift had written strenuously against continuing the war and against the duke's role in it. Swift, known as a great prose satirist, combines stark anger and satire in this poem.

Although not an exhaustive list, the following aspects of comedy could be explored in relation to 'A Satirical Elegy on the Death of a Late Famous General':

- the type of comedy (see 6.1; 6.2.8)
- the role of the comic hero (see 6.3.2, Heroes…)
- the role of the comic villain (6.3.2, Villains…)
- how language is used to heighten the comedy (see Activity 17; 6.3.4)
- effects on readers (see 6.1; 6.3.2, Clowns…).

The poem could be read from the perspective of:

- value and the canon (see 9.3).

Comedy in lyric verse

Although satire and narrative verse have been major vehicles for comedy in poetry throughout history, a great deal of comic verse does not fit into those genres. Poetry of many kinds, including love poetry and other sorts of lyric poetry, contains comic aspects – for instance the use of comic voices and perspectives, imagery, word choice, sound effects and so on. Many poets – from Catullus in ancient Rome to Shakespeare and John Donne in the 17th century, Byron and Browning in the 19th century, and on to modern poets such as John Betjeman, Philip Larkin, U.A. Fanthorpe, Liz Lochhead and Carol Ann Duffy – have employed such techniques in a variety of types of poem, ultimately intended to amuse and delight readers with their ironic attitudes, wit and inventiveness.

Set text focus: 'Tam o'Shanter'

Robert Burns wrote his narrative poem 'Tam o' Shanter' in 1790 to accompany a drawing of Alloway Kirk, published in his friend Francis Grose's *The Antiquities of Scotland* in 1791. Burns took his inspiration from several local legends in the Ayrshire of his birth to give a comic picture of the drinking classes in late 18th-century Scotland, with gothic overtones.

Although not an exhaustive list, the following aspects of comedy could be explored in relation to 'Tam o' Shanter':

- the type of comedy (see 6.2.8)
- the protagonist's journey (see 6.3.5, Journeys…)
- the role of the comic hero/heroine (see 6.3.2, Heroes…)
- use of the supernatural (6.3.3, *The supernatural*…)
- how language is used to heighten the comedy (see Activity 18; 6.3.4)
- effects on readers (see 6.1; Activity 18; 6.3.2, Clowns…).

The poem could be read from the perspective of:

- value and the canon (see 9.3)
- narrative theory (see 9.4)
- feminist theory (see 6.4.1; 9.5)
- Marxist theory (see 9.6)
- eco-critical theory (see 6.3.5, Critical lens; 9.7).

ACTIVITY 18

Comic effects in verse

a Read the extracts from Swift's 'Satirical Elegy on the Death of a Late Famous General' (Text 6M) and Burns' 'Tam o' Shanter' (Text 6N), U.A. Fanthorpe's 'Not My Best Side' (Text 6O), and Betjeman's 'In Westminster Abbey' (Text 6P). In each one, can you suggest:

- i what might be seen as comedic about the content of the poem?
- ii what might be seen as comedic about the voice in which it is spoken?
- iii what elements of language and form contribute to the comic feel of the poem?

b Find quotations from each text to illustrate your ideas. Then write up your ideas on each poem in coherent paragraphs.

Check your responses in the Ideas section on Cambridge Elevate

Set text focus: John Betjeman's poetry

John Betjeman was appointed Poet Laureate in 1972 and is well known for his wry humour and gentle satirising of the English moneyed classes. In contrast with most of the 21st century's well-known poets, Betjeman used poetic form, rhyme and metre in a strictly traditional way throughout his work, and his poetry is often classified as 'light verse'. He seemed to be most at home in an England that was slipping away and said that he preferred places and faces to 'abstract things'. His poems address a number of themes, including his wistful longings about appealing women, his concerns that the Christian 'story' might not be true and his love of the ancient landscapes of the towns and countryside of England.

Although not an exhaustive list, the following aspects of comedy could be explored in relation to the selected poems:

- the type of comedy (see 6.2.8, Comedy in lyric verse)
- settings of time and place (see 6.3.5)
- significance of human folly (see 6.2.8)
- the role of comic characters (see 6.3.2)
- disorder, confusion and misunderstanding (see 6.3.3)
- comedy in miniature (see 6.3.8)
- structural patterning of the poems (6.3.1)
- how language and form is used to heighten the comedy (see Activity 18; 6.3.4; Activity 37).

Other comedic aspects to consider in relation to the selection could be gender, romance and sex. The poems selected for the AS Level specification could be read from the perspective of:

- value and the canon (see 9.3)
- narrative theory (see 6.3.6, Critical lens; 9.4)
- feminist theory (see 6.4.1; 9.5)
- Marxist theory (see 6.4.2; 9.6)
- eco-critical theory (see 6.3.5, Critical lens; 9.7).

Text 6M

His Grace! impossible! what dead!
Of old age too, and in his bed!
And could that mighty warrior fall?
And so inglorious, after all!
Well, since he's gone, no matter how,
The last loud trump must wake him now:
And, trust me, as the noise grows stronger,
He'd wish to sleep a little longer.
And could he be indeed so old
As by the newspapers we're told?
Threescore, I think, is pretty high;
'Twas time in conscience he should die
This world he cumbered long enough;
He burnt his candle to the snuff;
And that's the reason, some folks think,
He left behind so great a stink.

Jonathan Swift, 'Satirical Elegy on the Death of a Late Famous General', lines 1–16

Text 6N

O Tam! had'st thou but been sae wise,
As ta'en thy ain wife Kate's advice!
She tauld thee weel thou was a **skellum**,
A blethering, blustering, drunken **blellum**;
That frae November till October,
Ae market-day thou was nae sober...

She prophesied that late or soon,
Thou would be found deep drown'd in **Doon**;
Or catch'd wi' **warlocks** in the mirk,
By Alloway's auld haunted kirk.

Ah, gentle dames! it **gars me greet**,
To think how mony counsels sweet,
How mony lengthen'd, sage advices,
The husband frae the wife despises!

Robert Burns, 'Tam o' Shanter', lines 17–22 and 29–36

Glossary

skellum: rascal

blellum: rascal

Doon: the River Doon

warlocks: sorcerers

gars me greet: it makes me cry

Text 6O

I have diplomas in Dragon
Management and Virgin Reclamation.
My horse is the latest model, with
Automatic transmission and built-in
Obsolescence. My spear is custom-built,
And my prototype armour
Still on the secret list. You can't
Do better than me at the moment.
I'm qualified and equipped to the
Eyebrow. So why be difficult?
Don't you want to be killed and/or rescued
In the most contemporary way? Don't
You want to carry out the roles
That sociology and myth have designed for you?
Don't you realize that, by being choosy,
You are endangering job prospects
In the spear- and horse-building industries?
What, in any case, does it matter what
You want? You're in my way.

U.A. Fanthorpe, 'Not My Best Side', stanza 3

Text 6P

Gracious Lord, oh bomb the Germans,
Spare their women for Thy Sake,
And if that is not too easy
We will pardon Thy Mistake.
But, gracious Lord, whate'er shall be,
Don't let anyone bomb me.

John Betjeman, 'In Westminster Abbey', lines 7–12

Set text focus: 'Mrs Sisyphus'

'Mrs Sisyphus' was published in 1999 in *The World's Wife*, a collection of poems that looks at men from a new perspective, in Carol Ann Duffy's typical feminist way. She has said that she likes to 'use simple words, but in a complicated way' and that her aim is 'trying to reveal a truth'. Duffy was appointed Britain's first woman Poet Laureate in 2009.

Although not an exhaustive list, the following aspects of comedy could be explored in relation to 'Mrs Sisyphus':

- the type of comedy (see 6.2.8)
- the role of the comic hero/heroine (see 6.3.2, Heroes…)
- significance of human folly (see 6.3.2, Clowns…)
- how language is used to heighten the comedy (see Activity 18; 6.3.4).

Other comedic aspects to consider in relation to the collection could be role reversal, and the debunking of conventional ideas about virtue. The poem could be read from the perspective of:

- value and the canon (see 9.3)
- narrative theory (see 6.3.6, Critical lens; 9.4)
- feminist theory (see 6.4.1; 9.5).

'But, gracious Lord, whate're shall be, Don't let anyone bomb me.'
John Betjeman, 'In Westminster Abbey'

Set text focus: 'Not My Best Side'

U.A. Fanthorpe used 'Saint George and the Dragon', painted by Paolo Uccello, circa 1470, as the basis for her poem 'Not My Best Side', published in the volume *Side Effects* in 1978. In it, she parodies the traditional roles shown in the painting, giving a monologue from each of the characters in the painting, starting with the dragon. Her simple, understated language belies a sharp wit and thought-provoking ideas, and the poem exemplifies the feminist perspective that often informed her writing.

Although not an exhaustive list, the following aspects of comedy could be explored in relation to 'Not My Best Side':

- the type of comedy (see 6.1; 6.2.8)
- the role of the comic hero/heroine (see 6.3.2, Heroes…)
- the role of the comic villain (6.3.2, Villains…)
- how language is used to heighten the comedy (see Activity 18; 6.3.4).

Other comedic aspects to consider in relation to the poem could be the use of the non-human dragon who is given a voice, and the subversion of traditional expectations of sex and romance. The poem could be read from the perspective of:

- value and the canon (see 9.3)
- feminist theory (see 6.4.1; 9.5).

6.3 Aspects of comedy

6.3.1 The structure of comedy

As we have seen, one of the key things that a comic narrative generally has is a happy ending, especially for the **protagonists** of the comedy – the comic heroes or heroines. A comedy, whether a play, novel or narrative poem, generally charts the progress of the protagonist(s) through a series of confusing situations (which may have been brought about by their own error or by circumstances beyond their control), towards a state of understanding and happiness – often involving the realisation of love or marriage. The narrative structure of a comedy, then, is strongly related to the progress of the protagonists through the story.

In this way, comedy is very similar to tragedy. In tragedy, just as in comedy, the narrative direction of the story follows the progress of the hero or heroine through a set of conflicts that lead eventually to the ending. One of the main differences between tragedy and comedy is the nature of that ending – a tragic ending in tragedy, in which the protagonist often dies, having, at least to some extent, understood and accepted his or her fate; a comic ending in comedy. Even here, however, there are similarities, as both endings involve a transformation in which the protagonists come to some state of knowledge.

Like any narrative, the structure of a comedy encompasses these elements.

- **Exposition or state of harmony:** in which the audience or reader learns of the situation that exists at the beginning of the narrative, the *status quo*. Although at this point, there is probably no direct conflict in progress, there is likely to be a problem of some kind that is expressed and that may need to be solved.
- **Development** or **complication:** in which an event or events occur that act as a catalyst to further events, upsetting the balance that existed at the beginning and prompting some change that is likely to bring about conflict or confusion. This change is likely to exacerbate whatever problem was expressed in the exposition.
- **Climax** or **crisis:** in which the chain of events that has been set in motion comes to a head.
- **Resolution** or **denouement:** in which the crisis is resolved (including the starting problem) and a new situation, or *status quo*, is established.

Note that, although comedy often involves radical and subversive challenges to the conventional social order, the resolution of a comedy is often in fact very conservative, eventually re-establishing and confirming the social order.

Key terms

protagonist: the most important character in a play or novel

exposition: Part of a narrative which introduces background information or explains a situation

denouement: the resolution of a narrative

ACTIVITY 19

The structure of comedy

Look back at the plots of comedies in the previous section – *Lysistrata, The Misanthropist, Ralph Roister Doister, Twelfth Night, She Stoops to Conquer* and *The Importance of Being Earnest.* Can you identify the parts of each plot that relate to each of the four narrative elements listed in 6.3.1? Can you also apply the same exercise to your set texts?

6.3.2 Comic characters

Comic narratives are peopled by a wide range of different kinds of characters, many based on character types that originate in Greek and Roman comedy. Some of these characters will be characters whom we are expected to find lovable, some foolish, some villainous, some clever; some, we will be expected to laugh *at*, some to laugh *with*.

Figure 6A

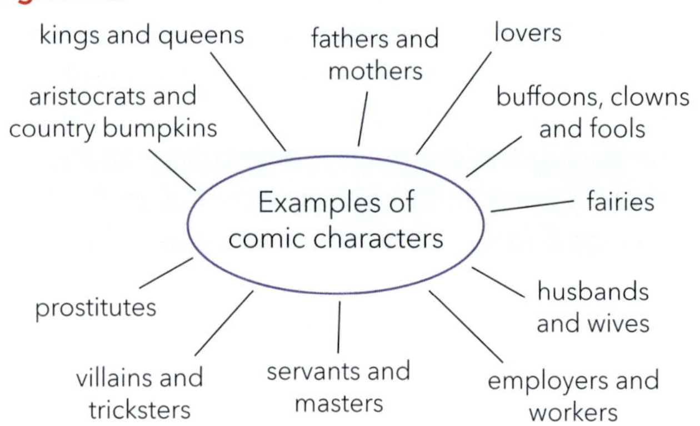

It's most important to realise that every comic narrative is different in the way it uses these characters. While we can usually identify certain characters as belonging to certain comic types or categories, there is no clear set of rules: each comic text has its own particular dynamic. Nevertheless, it's worth looking at some of the character types that occur in many comedies.

Heroes and heroines

Whereas a tragic hero or heroine is generally clearly defined, it is often harder to define a comic protagonist. Indeed, especially in comic drama, we may even have difficulty in identifying one specific character who is the hero or heroine. In general, however, we might define the protagonist of a comedy as the character or characters whose progress or plight we feel most concerned about following, and whose perspective we are most keenly aware of. Often, this is the character or characters who are in love and who will be married at the end of the narrative.

In many comedies, we feel a great deal of sympathy for the protagonist, and are delighted when they eventually fall in love, marry, overcome problems and achieve knowledge or happiness. The extent to which this is true, however, depends on the type of comedy. In the kind of comedy suggested by Aristotle, for instance, we may find the main characters 'inferior' and 'laughable'; in more romantic comedies we may feel far more sympathetic towards them or their plight. Whatever the case, the happy ending is likely to bring some sense of redemption or success to the protagonist, which we, the audience or readers, can celebrate.

ACTIVITY 20

Heroes and heroines

a In the comedies you are studying, which characters might you define as heroes or heroines? What kind of heroes or heroines are they? In what sense are they *comic* heroes or heroines?

b If you're studying 'The Nun's Priest's Tale' by Chaucer, look carefully at the depiction of the cock, Chauntecleer, and the hen, Pertelote, as a romantic hero and heroine. Describe the ways in which this depiction might be seen as comic. Don't forget to consider:
- the depiction of the setting of the tale
- the way Chauntecleer and Pertelote speak and behave
- the way the animal fable is framed by Chauntecleer and Pertelote's discussion.

c If you're studying Shakespeare's *The Taming of the Shrew*, think about the depiction of Petruchio and Katerina. They are clearly the protagonists of the play but in what sense might we describe them as the hero and heroine?

Villains, rogues, rivals and adversaries

The **antagonist** in a literary comedy – the character who seems to act against the protagonist – is unlikely to be a stereotypical comic villain, a moustache-twirling evil genius such as we might associate with comics and cartoons. It is usually more productive to think in terms of characters who are in some way rivals or adversaries of the hero or heroine, and who appear to stand in the way of the happy ending that we anticipate. The antagonist may or may not be a funny or an evil character, but is clearly in some sense in conflict with the protagonist.

In many comedies, this character is a rival in love, or someone who in some way tries to stop a love affair from developing. Antagonists may also resort to disguise, deceit or trickery in order to have their way. Usually, their influence is eventually defeated to make way for the happy ending.

In *Twelfth Night*, for instance, Malvolio fulfils many of these roles. He is not evil, but he is puritanical, pompous and arrogant, over-concerned with his duty to his mistress, condescending to others, and full of self-regard because of his position. At the same time, however, Malvolio is also a buffoon, because of his pompous manner and the way he is tricked, and a victim, the object of a humiliating revenge carried out mainly by Feste and Maria.

Key terms

antagonist: a character (or an institution or group of characters) that opposes the protagonist

ACTIVITY 21

Heroes and villains in three poems

Three of the poets mentioned in 6.2.8 are in the AQA Anthology.

a In Liz Lochhead's poem 'My Rival's House', we learn of the delicate relationship between a daughter-in-law and a mother-in-law. This is not a comic poem in the sense that it is full of humour, but what aspects of comedy can you see at work in it? In what sense is the mother-in-law a 'rival'?

b In 'Not My Best Side', U.A. Fanthorpe presents three characters from the legend of George and the Dragon – hero, villain and victim – using comic language and a comic perspective. How do the language and perspective for each character differ from what we might expect of these roles?

c In Jonathan Swift's 'Satirical Elegy…', there is a transformation in our view of the general between the beginning and the end of the poem. At what point do we cease to view him as a hero and begin to see him as a villain, and how does Swift use structure and language to make this shift?

Set text focus: 'My Rival's House'

Liz Lochhead, poet and playwright, was appointed Scots Makar (maker), Scotland's national poet, in 2011. Her poems often have a distinctive female voice, but she has said that she doesn't want to be confined by either her gender or her nationality. She acknowledges her Scottish literary heritage, but says she is also very keen on American poetry, and on the Liverpool poets Adrian Henri, Brian Patten and Roger McGough. She also sees performing poetry, which she began in the 1970s, as essential. She says 'for me, writing poetry has always been about putting sounds down in black and white… if it's a proper poem, it should be performable'.

Although not the only one, the following aspect of comedy could be explored in relation to 'My Rival's House':

- the role of the comic villain rival (6.3.2, Villains…)
- how language is used to heighten the comedy (see 6.3.4).

Other comedic aspects to consider in relation to the poem could be the use of situation, setting and voice. The poem 'My Rival's House' could be read from the perspective of:

- value and the canon (see 9.3)
- feminist theory (see 6.4.1; 9.5).

Clowns, fools and buffoons

Just as we are attracted to tragedies partly by the sense of **catharsis**, we feel when we realise that we have managed to avoid the kind of terrible fate that befalls the tragic hero, so we are attracted to comedies partly by the feeling that we have managed to avoid making a fool of ourselves in the way that many comic characters do.

Key terms

catharsis: the purging of the emotions experienced by the audience when watching tragedy

Almost all comedy places human folly at its centre. Whether riotous farce or gentle romance, comedy delights in the foolishness of people and the ridiculousness of their behaviour, and encourages us to laugh at it – and *with* it, as we recognise the same potential for folly in ourselves. Whether it's because the person we laugh at is stupid, or deceived, or arrogant, or unaware, or confused, comedy explores what happens when we fall into life's traps. Fools and buffoons, then – or people behaving like fools and buffoons – play a major role in comic narratives, and are strongly related to the ancient character of the clown, the ridiculous character who does all the things that sensible people usually try to avoid.

Fools and buffoons can play many different roles in a comic narrative, however.

- Sometimes, the comic protagonist might be a buffoon, a kind of anti-hero – one of Aristotle's 'inferior' characters who performs 'laughable' acts, but who in the end realises their stupidity, or finds their way to a happy resolution in some other way.
- Sometimes, such characters play only minor roles and simply bring laughter and elements of satire to the narrative.
- Whether a protagonist or not, the character might be a lovable buffoon – someone who is foolish but good-natured; or they might be an irritating buffoon – laughable rather because of their pompousness or arrogance or lack of self-awareness.
- At other times, we witness more heroic or romantic characters finding themselves behaving like buffoons because they have found themselves in an embarrassing or confusing situation, or perhaps because they are in love.

Exploring clowns

Clowning is an ancient form of comedy that celebrates the ridiculous, the absurd and sometimes also the taboo. Using mainly non-verbal action, clowns make people laugh by carrying out actions that everyone knows will go wrong in some way, or which break the normal rules according to which society runs. Sometimes clowns will act as though they are unaware that what they are doing is stupid and bound to fail; at other times, they mischievously push the boundaries of acceptable behaviour to see what will happen. The physicality of clowning is at the heart of farce, and works partly by showing what might happen when we lose the ability to reason with words and rely instead purely on action.

Although most characters in comic narratives are not actually clowns, we can see how their behaviour performs a similar function to clowns but in a literary context, by comically showing us behaviour which in some way challenges what is considered normal.

Natural fools and licensed fools

There is one further significant way of discussing the role of fools in comedy – by distinguishing between the 'natural' fool and the 'licensed' fool. Natural fools are characters who act foolishly because they don't know how – or are for various reasons unable – to do otherwise in the situation in which they find themselves.

Licensed fools, on the other hand, are jesters or clowns – characters who are *paid* to 'play the fool'. Fools of this kind are associated mainly with a number of plays by Shakespeare – both comedies

'This fellow is wise enough to play the fool;
And to do that well craves a kind of wit'

William Shakespeare, *Twelfth Night*

(Feste in *Twelfth Night*, Touchstone in *As You Like It*) and tragedies (The Fool in *King Lear*). These characters are employed (within the fiction of the plays) by aristocratic or royal masters in order to entertain them, and are generally addressed by their employers as 'fool'.

However, licensed fools go beyond mere entertainment: they also provide a satirical commentary on what they see as the foolish behaviour of their employers. The fools' role here is to be ironically wise; despite their inferior social position, they are able to use humour to point out the foolishness of their superiors, 'speaking truth to power' in a way that other characters cannot.

In these cases, fools play a role that is a kind of foreshadowing: they tell truths which are to be significant in the narrative as a whole, but - rather like an oracle or soothsayer in classical mythology - the character to whom they speak the truth is often unaware that what they say is significant.

Occasionally, the role of the *natural* fool is also used to convey truths or wisdom. In *Hamlet*, for instance, the gravedigger (labelled 'Clown' in the original text of the play) is a comic working-class character who, as he digs Ophelia's grave, makes simple but wise jokes about death, which echo the serious themes of death and mortality in the play as a whole. Comic working-class characters of this sort - whose dialogue contains elements of satirical truth - also feature in a number of other Shakespeare plays, for instance the servants Grumio in *The Taming of the Shrew* and the two Dromios in *The Comedy of Errors*.

ACTIVITY 22

Natural and licensed fools in *Twelfth Night*

Twelfth Night contains a licensed fool and at least one natural fool.

a In what ways does Feste conform to the convention of the licensed fool?

b To what extent do you think these characters might fit the characteristics of the natural fool - Olivia, Orsino, Malvolio, Sir Andrew Aguecheek, Sir Toby Belch?

c Would you agree that these characters do *not* exhibit the characteristics of a natural fool - Viola, Sebastian, Antonio, Maria, Feste? If so, why?

ACTIVITY 23

Education, class and comedy in *Educating Rita*

Willy Russell's *Educating Rita* does not contain fools or clowns in the traditional dramatic sense, but it does, like Shakespeare's plays, set ideas about wisdom and foolishness against a background of class and power relationships. Frank, Rita's university lecturer, is a highly educated middle-class man, whereas Rita is a working-class woman with little experience of education. The play explores, among other things, the way in which social status and education are connected. In becoming educated, the play suggests, Rita risks losing the earthy humour and wisdom of her class and the freshness of her perspective on literature and learning.

- Identify examples of Rita's wisdom and perceptiveness in the play.
- How does she change when she has been educated? How much of this change is good and how much not so good?
- Why do you think Frank values Rita's fresh approach so much and why is he so disappointed when she changes?
- Do you think the play's representation of the connection between class and education is accurate?

Critical lens: Marxist theory

Marxist theory focuses on the representation of class and social power in literature. A key issue is the extent to which working-class characters' voices and perspectives are heard in literature. Many of Shakespeare's plays feature lower-class characters who, although they are often portrayed as less serious than upper-class characters, nevertheless play a significant role in the narrative. As you read *Twelfth Night* or *The Taming of the Shrew*, think about the relationships between the classes in these plays, and their attitudes towards each other.

Class is also a major issue in *She Stoops to Conquer, The Importance of Being Earnest* and *Educating Rita*. Again, consider the way class relationships are portrayed in these plays.

See 9.6 for more on Marxist theory

6.3.3 Disorder, confusion and misunderstanding

Whether tragedy or comedy, the central sections of most narratives contain scenes in which an initially ordered situation changes, causing disorder, confusion or conflict of some sort. Such a situation might be brought about by the intrusion of a character or event that brings an unexpected change, and it might be exacerbated by elements of disguise, trickery or misunderstanding.

In comedy, this element of disorder and confusion is especially important. A significant part of the art of the writer of comedy is to make this central element as entertaining and often as complex as possible, finding ways of making the disorder multiply, and keeping the audience or readers guessing as to how the confusion will eventually resolve itself and order will return.

However, although the situations that arise as a result of disorder and confusion might be extremely comic, it's crucial too to notice that they are often potentially challenging, dangerous or emotional situations, which suggest significant tensions and conflicts within our lives.

Misrule and disorder

The pleasure audiences and readers might get from confusion and disorder is crucial to comedy. One of the great attractions of comedy is that we are given permission to laugh at the kind of ridiculous behaviour that in real life we would probably find threatening and embarrassing rather than amusing. In Shakespeare's day, this phenomenon was known as **misrule**, a kind of special dispensation to misbehave under certain circumstances, especially at festivals and carnivals.

Key terms

misrule: bad behaviour, disorder or lawlessness

In the medieval age, it was the role of the Lord of Misrule to encourage celebrations, giving permission to the community to suspend some of the normal rules of behaviour. The Lord of Misrule was most associated with the festivities of the twelve days of Christmas, especially the Feast of Fools and Twelfth Night. Shakespeare's *Twelfth Night* is certainly linked with these festivities, and other comedies might also have been linked with feast days.

Whatever the exact connections between Shakespeare's comedies and the festivities of the time, it should be clear that the idea of 'misrule' is relevant to all comedy, which gives us permission to laugh in a controlled way at absurd and sometimes wild, dangerous and subversive behaviour, and the way it challenges those in power.

Exploring misrule and Shakespeare's *Twelfth Night*

Twelfth Night is the festival that takes place at Epiphany, the twelfth night of Christmas (6 January), and was certainly associated with the Lord of Misrule in Shakespeare's time. The play itself, although called *Twelfth Night*, makes no mention at all of Twelfth Night, but depicts the kind of farce, clowning and foolery that would have been associated with such a festival, so it is thought that it may well have been written for performance as part of festivities on that night. We do know that *Twelfth Night* was performed on other festivals: for instance, Shakespeare's company performed it in 1602 in the Inns of Court on the festival of Candlemas.

The full title of the play is *Twelfth Night, or What You Will* – the second part of which also suggests the kind of freedom and suspension of rules that was associated with festivals. Furthermore, the character of the fool in the play is called Feste, a clear reference to the idea of festival. He is often seen as playing a kind of Lord of Misrule in the play, ultimately controlling the potentially dangerous behaviour that leads to the humiliation of Malvolio.

Varieties of confusion and disorder

The title of Shakespeare's *The Comedy of Errors* uses the single word 'errors' to identify one of the central aspects of comedy that contribute to its sense of disorder. While *The Comedy of Errors* focuses mainly on accidental misunderstandings, many comedies also contain elements of deliberate trickery, deceit and disguise that cause errors, misunderstandings and consequently confusion.

ACTIVITY 24

Varieties of confusion and disorder

Before reading the next sections, think about what kinds of confusion are present in comedies you know. Think about your set texts, but also think about other comedies such as film and television comedies.

Errors and misunderstandings

Simple errors are sometimes the catalyst for the confusing situations that occur in comedy. Errors made because of incompetence are often crucial. In Michael Frayn's superb 20th- century farce *Noises Off*, often described as the funniest play ever written, the characters are amateur actors who are incapable of remembering their lines, their entrances, or the props they are meant to bring on stage. This sets off a series of very funny events that lead to a disastrously out-of-control performance of a play within the play, which at the same time becomes confused with the dramas that are playing out in the characters' real lives.

But not all such situations arise because of incompetence: sometimes they are the result of accidents or misunderstandings that cannot be controlled or foreseen. In *The Comedy of Errors*, for instance, the entire narrative is driven by the misunderstandings that occur when two sets of identical twins are found in the streets of the same city. The inhabitants of the city, unaware that there are two sets of twins, continually believe that they are dealing with two people rather than four, and only the audience is aware of the reason for the confusion that ensues. Similar misunderstandings occur in *Twelfth Night*, which also features a set of identical twins who are mistaken for each other with comic effect.

Two elements are at play here: coincidence - the coincidence of two sets of identical twins being in the same city unknown to each other - and the mistaken identity that follows as a result. Both elements feature often in comedy. In the novel *Small Island*, for instance, we see both occurring together when it transpires that Hortense's cousin, Michael, and her husband, Gilbert, both from Jamaica, have separately and coincidentally befriended Queenie (unknown to each other and to Queenie) while living in London. This coincidence comes about partly because of mistaken identity caused by the similarity in looks between Michael and Gilbert. As a result, the novel ends with Hortense looking after a baby who she does not realise is, in fact, her cousin's child. Similar treatment of issues of identity is also central in the novel *Wise Children*, where Angela Carter explores the comic (and not-so-comic) potential of twins within literary texts.

Such coincidences and misunderstandings may seem far-fetched, but few of us get through life without experiencing occasional situations that seem almost supernatural in their unlikeliness and sometimes puzzling in their implications. Exploring the consequences of such events is not only full of comic potential, but is also perhaps a way of coming to terms with the workings of fate and fortune and of thinking about what happens when we realise that we are not always in full control of our lives.

It's also typical of comedy that it exploits the potential for comic confusion that might result from, say, the existence of twins, but is equally concerned with the psychological narrative of twins being separated from each other and then emotionally reunited. Thus, *The Comedy of Errors* and *Twelfth Night* are capable of making audiences both laugh and cry by means of the same device.

ACTIVITY 25

Errors and misunderstandings in *Small Island*, *Wise Children* and *Emma*

a The character in *Small Island* who is most notable for making comic errors is Hortense. How does Levy exploit the comic potential of being a stranger in a foreign land through the errors that Hortense makes?

b In *Emma*, it is Emma herself whose errors dominate the novel. How does Austen exploit the comic potential of Emma's flawed character in the novel?

c In *Wise Children* twins play an important narrative function. How does Carter use twins and the idea of twinning or doubling in the narrative to create comedy and confusion?

Critical lens: post-colonial theory

Post-colonial theory encourages us to consider the ways in which ethnicity is used in literary texts - how it marks particular characters out as 'other'. As you read *Small Island*, think about the language and behaviour of white characters towards Hortense. How do these highlight her role as an outsider and how does she respond?

See 9.8 for more on post-colonial theory

Trickery, deceit and revenge

Deliberate acts of trickery and spite can also form the starting point for comic confusion. In *Twelfth Night*, for instance, members of Olivia's household plot their revenge on the pompous killjoy Malvolio by tricking him into believing that Olivia is in love with him and will respond positively if he courts her, a plot that leads to one of the greatest comic scenes in Shakespeare's plays, but also eventually to Malvolio's humiliation. Similarly farcical scenes occur in Goldsmith's *She Stoops to Conquer* when Tony Lumpkin tricks Marlow and Hastings into believing that the house they have arrived at is an inn rather than the home of their genteel hosts. In this case, the trick is initiated out of pure mischief rather than revenge, however. Trickery is also central, of course, to Chaucer's 'The Nun's Priest's Tale'.

Other comedies focus on what happens when people tell lies that get out of control. A good example of this is in *The Importance of Being Earnest*, the plot of which revolves around the imaginary friends invented independently by both Jack and Algernon to provide them with an excuse to escape various social obligations. The play focuses on the web of complications that is constructed when they go a step too far in elaborating the existence of these non-existent characters.

Again, comic as these situations might be, they also deal with fundamental issues to do with the nature of reality - whether what appears to be true *is* true, and what happens when we become involved in webs of deceit.

ACTIVITY 26

Deceit and the potential for tragedy in comedy

Trickery, deceit and revenge are often central to tragedy - and yet they are often central to comedy too. Why then, do we find these potentially dangerous activities funny in comedy when they can have such devastating consequences in tragedy? Identify examples of trickery, deceit and revenge in the comic texts you are studying. In each case, why do we, as audience or readers, feel able to laugh at these dangerous things?

Disguise and cross-dressing

A further form of deceit common in comedy is disguise. Sometimes disguise is a ploy adopted as a form of trickery; at other times, however, it is more to do with the need for self-preservation.

A classic example of disguise used for trickery is in Ben Jonson's comedy *Volpone,* in which the cunning Volpone (whose name means 'fox' in Italian) dresses up in various ways in order to swindle the greedy characters Voltore, Corbaccio and Corvino (whose names mean 'vulture', 'crow' and 'raven'). Disguise is also used for the purpose of trickery in *The Taming of the Shrew*, in which a number of characters disguise themselves as tutors to Bianca to try to get closer to her romantically. In both these plays, as in many other works of literature, disguise is used as a means of circumventing certain social conventions as a means to an end - whether that end is ultimately honest or dishonest.

In two of Shakespeare's comedies, *Twelfth Night* and *As You Like It*, a particular form of disguise is used: cross-dressing. In both these plays, a female character disguises herself as a man in order to be safe when travelling in unknown territory. Although in both cases the disguise is carried out for fear of danger, the comic consequences of the disguise revolve around the gender confusion that occurs as a result. In *Twelfth Night*, for instance, Viola, disguised as a man, Cesario, falls in love with Duke Orsino but is unable to tell him because she is disguised as a man, while the lady Olivia in turn falls in love with Viola, believing that she is a man.

The comedy of cross-dressing is amplified when the cross-dressing female characters are played by men or boys (as they would have been in Shakespeare's day.) In *As You Like It,* this gender comedy is taken a step further: a male actor would have played the female character Rosalind, who disguises herself as a man, who at one point in the play pretends to be a woman, creating four different identities in one character.

All these instances of disguise produce moments of fine comedy, but they also suggest many issues to do with the way in which we form and perform our identities in real life. In particular, cross-dressing addresses, in a light-hearted way, a range of issues to do with the ways in which gender and sexuality work in our lives.

Critical lens: feminist theory

Feminist theory focuses on the portrayal of gender and sexuality in literary texts. In many of Shakespeare's comedies, the relationships between men and women, and perceptions of male and female behaviour, are central concerns. In *Twelfth Night* and *The Taming of the Shrew*, for instance, what attitudes to and expectations of female behaviour are displayed by the characters?

See 9.5 for more on feminist theory

ACTIVITY 27

Viola and the language of gender ambiguity in *Twelfth Night*

Look at the extracts from *Twelfth Night* in Texts 6Q–U. How does Shakespeare make the most of the comic potential of Viola being a woman but having to speak and behave as a man here?

Text 6Q

VIOLA I'll do my best
To woo your lady. *[Aside]* Yet a **barful** strife!
Whoe'er I woo, myself would be his wife.

Twelfth Night, Act 1, Scene 4, lines 39–41

Text 6R

VIOLA What will become of this? As I am a man,
My state is desperate for my master's love;
As I am a woman – now alas the day! –
What thriftless sighs shall poor Olivia breathe?
O time, thou must untangle this not I;
It is too hard a knot for me t'untie.

Twelfth Night, Act 2, Scene 2, lines 33–38

Text 6S

ORSINO My life upon't, young though thou art, thine eye
Hath stay'd upon some favour that it loves:
Hath it not, boy?
VIOLA A little, by your favour.
ORSINO What kind of woman is't?
VIOLA Of your complexion.
ORSINO She is not worth thee, then. What years, i' faith?
VIOLA About your years, my lord.

Twelfth Night, Act 2, Scene 4, lines 21–28

Text 6T

VIOLA Ay, but I know—
ORSINO What dost thou know?
VIOLA Too well what love women to men may owe:
In faith, they are as true of heart as we.
My father had a daughter loved a man,
As it might be, perhaps, were I a woman,
I should your lordship.

Twelfth Night, Act 2, Scene 4, lines 100–106

Text 6U

VIOLA By innocence I swear, and by my youth
I have one heart, one bosom and one truth,
And that no woman has; nor never none
Shall mistress be of it, save I alone.

Twelfth Night, Act 3, Scene 1, lines 142–45

Glossary

barful: full of 'bars' or obstacles, difficult

The supernatural

Beyond the world of human error, there is another element that can cause confusion: the supernatural. Elements of the supernatural are used in several of Shakespeare's comedies - for instance in *As You Like It, The Tempest* and *A Midsummer Night's Dream*.

ACTIVITY 28

'Tam o' Shanter' and the supernatural

The supernatural is central to the narrative of Burns' narrative poem 'Tam o' Shanter'. How does Burns use the witches and warlocks in the poem for comic effect?

Slapstick: physical and visual humour

A major feature of the disorder that occurs in comedy is the physical and visual humour that results from it - and often creates further disorder. Perhaps the most significant element here is slapstick, an important part of farce - the humour that arises when people unexpectedly fall over things, bang into things, are hit by things, walk into the wrong places, or otherwise perform the wrong actions for the situation they are in. Slapstick can also refer to deliberate actions such as characters comically throwing things at or hitting each other. More broadly, physical and visual humour can result from the way people dress, the way they walk, the way they sound, and so on.

Exploring slapstick

Slapstick has been a hugely popular form of comedy throughout history. Recent examples in popular culture include the television comedies *Mr Bean* and *Miranda*. Such comedy relies heavily on the audience's recognition of the way in which these characters comically fall into the physical traps that we all hope to avoid in our daily lives, such as slipping on banana skins (the classic slapstick move) or of the enjoyment that characters get from the physical release of letting rip at each other.

ACTIVITY 29

Physical and visual humour

What elements of physical and visual humour have you found in your set texts? Note that slapstick is particularly associated with drama, but there are often elements of such physical humour in novels and verse narratives too.

Watch tutorial video, Physical and Visual Humour, on Cambridge Elevate

6.3.4 Jokes, wit and wordplay

Many kinds of language are used in comedy, but there is one kind of language that is especially associated with comedy: unsurprisingly, this is humorous or comic language. Jokes, wit and wordplay of various kinds are, of course, not exclusive to comedy: they are used in many other forms of literature. But they have a special place in comedy, helping to make the audience or readers laugh, and to establish the comic and playful tone of the narrative. The use of comic language can also be part of the sense of misrule and disorder in comedy.

Figure 6B

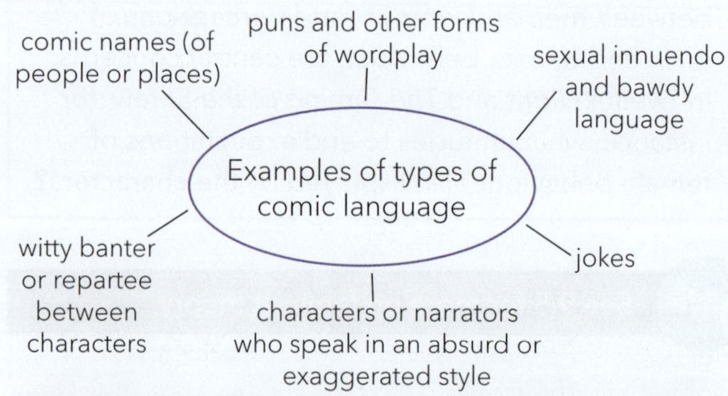

Watch tutorial video, Comic Language, on Cambridge Elevate

ACTIVITY 30

Comic language in comedy

Consider the texts you are studying. Which of the six types of language in Figure 6B are used in each one? Are there any other types of comic language in your texts? Find good examples of whichever types feature in your text and try to explain how language is used in a comic way in each example.

6.3.5 Settings, journeys and the passage of time

Classical drama generally conformed to the unities of plot, place and time, according to which the action of drama is intensified if it has a single focus, occurs in one location and takes place between the hours of sunrise and sunset in one day. In comic drama, sticking to these rules *can* add to the pace and complexity of the comedy, as for instance in

'There is something in the wind, that we cannot get in'

William Shakespeare, *The Comedy of Errors*

Shakespeare's *The Comedy of Errors,* one of only two plays in which he sticks to these rules. By contrast, novels often take place across very long periods of time in many settings and with many subplots.

In general, even if drama does not conform to the unities, it tends to remain fairly close to the *spirit* of the unities: too many plots and settings spread over too many time periods would result in less effective drama. However, many comic playwrights over the centuries *have* used different time settings and locations, as well as subplots, to great effect.

Time settings

Many comic writers - playwrights, novelists and poets - use the passage of time to structure their writing and to highlight some of their themes, often through emphasising the ways in which characters and situations change over time. In the comedy *As You Like It,* for instance, Shakespeare sets the first part of the play in winter, and the second part in spring, symbolically suggesting the rebirth of the characters and the reconciliations which take place towards the end of the play. He also uses the seasons as metaphors for the characters' experiences.

Sometimes different time settings can suggest parallels rather than change. In the modern comedy *Arcadia* (1993), Tom Stoppard sets the play in two different time periods - 1809 and 1993 - but in the same location, a country house in Derbyshire. The scenes of the play alternate between the two different sets of characters in the different time periods, gradually revealing unexpected parallels between them. In the last scene of the play, the two sets of characters occupy the stage at the same time. Although neither set of characters is aware of the other's presence on stage, their narratives have become so close that their dialogue at times merges.

ACTIVITY 31

Time settings in *Small Island* and *Emma*

The novels *Small Island* and *Emma* take very different approaches to telling a story over an extended period of time. *Small Island* is a fragmented narrative that ranges across two time settings, 'Before' and '1948', while Emma is a more traditional linear narrative.

- If you are studying *Small Island*, look at the way the 'Before' and '1948' sections are interwoven throughout the book. Can you see a logic to the structure? What are the effects of these structural choices?
- If you are studying *Emma,* look closely at the way Austen manages time in the novel. What periods of time elapse between the different chapters and sections of the novel, and how long does the action of the novel take altogether?

Locations

Comedies are almost always located in domestic settings, whether in the city, town, village or countryside. As we have seen, Shakespeare's *The Comedy of Errors* takes place in just one location - the public spaces of the Greek city of Ephesus. Much of the farcical humour of the play relies on the misunderstandings that occur as various characters rush off to another part of town, leaving the audience to watch what happens in the static location of the play. As characters return to this location, they are unaware of what has happened meanwhile; the audience, however, has seen it, creating the comic dramatic irony that farce often relies on.

The Comedy of Errors also makes much use of the contrast between action that is simultaneously taking place in public spaces and private spaces - for instance the inside and outside of Antipholus' house. The action that takes place outside the house can be seen by the audience and the characters outside the house, but they cannot see - they can only hear - what is happening inside the house.

Similar comic techniques have been used many times by the playwright Alan Ayckbourn, who specialises in farce. His comedies *House* and *Garden* (1999) take place in two different settings - one inside a house, the other in the garden of the house. The action of the two plays takes place simultaneously with the same characters but in two different locations. They are also written in such a way that they can be *acted* simultaneously in two neighbouring theatre spaces for two different audiences, with the actors moving between the two stages. The comedy here is created partly by the effect of the revelations that take place when *both* plays have been seen, and partly by the effect of the audience knowing that different action is going on elsewhere at the same time.

Exploring green worlds

The critic Northrop Frye, in his *Anatomy of Criticism* (1957), recognised this pattern within Shakespeare's comedies and described the progress characters in the plays make to a 'green world' that represents a metaphorical spring time or period of growth in the characters' lives leading to a positive resolution of problems and a happy ending. Frye's analysis is often applicable to the work of other playwrights, as well as to comic novels and poems.

Frye referred to 'green worlds' because in Shakespeare's comedies (and also in some of the tragedies), the place in question was often (though not always) a pastoral retreat, or a wild place. Such a green world might also be a place:

- where awareness of time is less important
- where youth and love have freedom to flourish
- where the concerns of a previous life can be set aside
- where many of the normal rules of society are relaxed
- which may be confusing at times.

Journeys, escapes and returns

Many comic narratives feature journeys away from a starting location to a secondary location that provides a realm of escape, retreat and perhaps renewal for the characters. This secondary location is often a place where exploration, discovery and change can take place. At the end, characters often move back to the starting location, which is in some sense transformed by the events that have taken place.

ACTIVITY 32

Green worlds and journeys of transformation

Significant journeys take place in a number of the set texts. If you are studying *Twelfth Night*, *The Taming of the Shrew*, *She Stoops to Conquer*, *The Importance of Being Earnest*, *Small Island*, or 'Tam o' Shanter', identify the journey or journeys that take place in the text. What transformations do these journeys bring about? Do any of them seem to fit the description of 'green worlds' in the 'Exploring green worlds' feature?

Critical lens: Eco-critical theory

Eco-critical theory invites us to consider the ways in which the natural world is used in literary texts. One important concept here is the Pastoral, an idealised view of the countryside often used in literature as a contrast with the stresses of city life. How is the countryside represented in your set texts? If you're studying *She Stoops to Conquer* or *The Importance of Being Earnest*, for instance, what attitudes towards the city and country are expressed by the characters in the plays?

See 9.7 for more on eco-critical theory

6.3.6 Plots, subplots, frames and parallels

Many comic narratives – whether in drama, the novel or poetry – are linear, satisfying the classical idea of the unity of action by presenting one plot or action that has a single, uninterrupted narrative drive from beginning to end. However, many other comic narratives take a quite different approach, using one or more of a number of methods of interweaving

A 'green world' that represents a metaphorical spring time in Shakespeare's characters' lives different plots, or framing a plot, in order to create resonant parallels or foreshadowing.

Subplots, multiple plots and frames in drama

Although subplots and **multiple plots** may be used in both tragedies and comedies, their use in comedies often adds to the comic effect of the narrative, not only by creating parallels and echoes between different plots, but also by amplifying the sense of confusion and disorder in the narrative.

In Shakespeare's *A Midsummer Night's Dream*, for instance, three separate plots are interwoven throughout the play – the argument between the fairies Titania and Oberon, the dramatic pursuits of the 'rude mechanicals' (Bottom and his colleagues), and the love plight of the four young lovers, Hermia, Helena, Lysander and Demetrius. Although these plots are quite separate, the events of each plot interconnect, spilling over from one to another in unexpected ways, heightening the sense of confusion. In the end, all three plots end happily, are resolved simultaneously and are shown to be connected through the idea that 'the course of true love never did run smooth'.

Furthermore, the three plots of *A Midsummer Night's Dream* are brought together by a fourth plot which acts as a **framing** device for the other three plots – the wedding of Theseus and Hippolyta. The plans for this wedding start the play, the wedding itself ends the play, and all the characters are, one way or another, to be guests at the wedding (although the fairies are arguably there in spirit only!). Thus the wedding initiates and draws together all the interwoven plots, providing both a thematic link – love and marriage – and a classic comic happy ending.

One of the most unusual examples of a framing device is in Shakespeare's *The Taming of the Shrew*, in which the 'Induction' is a short separate play in itself, a kind of prologue that appears unrelated to the main plot, although it sets up the main plot as a performance put on for the protagonist of the Induction, the drunken tinker Christopher Sly. It is not clear exactly what the relationship between the Induction and the main play is, but several critics have drawn attention to similarities in theme between the induction and the main plot, perhaps intended by Shakespeare as a parallel.

The Taming of the Shrew also makes use of a subplot (involving the marriage of Bianca) which, as in *A Midsummer Night's Dream*, appears in many respects quite separate and different from the main plot, despite the interweaving of the two plots at a narrative level. However, the two plots parallel each other in interesting ways, and, again, Shakespeare draws the two threads together powerfully in the final scene.

Chaucer's 'The Nun's Priest's Tale' provides another intriguing use of a framing device. Here, Chaucer adds several layers of complexity to a simple animal fable by framing it with an extended portrayal of the cock, Chauntecleer, as a mock-romantic hero in a **mock-heroic** setting, using mock-heroic language, telling his own story – all set within a hen-house in the meagre yard of a poor old lady. The comic and ironic use of parallels and contrasts between humans and animals in the tale make this a particularly interesting tale to interpret.

In addition, it's worth noting that 'The Nun's Priest's Tale' is itself framed by all the other tales in *The Canterbury Tales*. Chauntecleer is telling his own tale, but the Nun's Priest is telling Chauntecleer's tale, and Chaucer's narrator is in turn telling 'The Nun's Priest's Tale'.

Key terms

multiple plots: a series of plots that eventually become interwoven with each other

framing: the part of a literary text that may occur at the beginning (and sometimes also the end) in order to frame the main plot

mock-heroic: the application of the conventions of heroic narrative and language to a trivial subject

ACTIVITY 33

Subplots, multiple plots and framing plots in drama

The Taming of the Shrew, Twelfth Night, She Stoops to Conquer and *The Importance of Being Earnest* all have subplots or interwoven plot threads. Consider the play or plays you are studying. How are the two plots connected, and what are the parallels or differences between them?

Multiple plots in comic novels

Novels often contain many interconnected plot strands. Sometimes, the different elements of narrative in a novel are presented entirely from the perspective of a single narrator as part of a linear narrative, as in Jane Austen's *Emma*. In modern novels, the interconnectedness of different narrative threads is often emphasised by the use of fragmented narratives in which different characters' stories are told from different perspectives or in different sections of the book, but eventually merge in the reader's mind to make one complete narrative. Andrea Levy's *Small Island* is a good example of this kind of novel and Angela Carter's *Wise Children* is awash with multiple stories, digressions and flashbacks with the action in the narrative present taking place on one day.

Critical lens: narrative theory

Narrative theory is concerned with the ways in which writers weave together events in literary texts using a range of narrative devices. One significant issue is the extent to which readers or audiences are guided by the perspective of particular characters or narrative voices. Think about the texts you are studying. How might they seem different if the dominant perspectives were those of different characters?

See 9.4 for more on narrative theory

Prologues and epilogues

Narratives of all kinds are sometimes framed by **prologues** and/or **epilogues**, which may serve the purpose of introducing the themes, characters or events of the narrative, or rounding off, and perhaps reflecting on, the narrative in some way. Sometimes these are written in the voice of one of the characters, sometimes in the voice of a narrator, or even perhaps in the voice of the author. In Shakespearean comedy, the epilogue may also sometimes be used to ask the audience for their applause.

In comedy, prologue and epilogue also often help to set the comic tone of the work, or to confirm the comic nature of the ending. In Shakespeare's *As You Like It*, for instance, the epilogue, spoken by Rosalind, the female protagonist of the comedy, not only asks the audience for applause, but also plays humorously with one of the main themes of the play – the relationships between men and women – and one of the main devices in the play – a male actor playing a female character disguising herself as a man.

In Chaucer's *The Canterbury Tales*, the tales are framed by prologues and epilogues in which we learn something of the tellers of the tales, their reasons for telling them, and the way in which the tales are received by their audience. These prologues and epilogues not only suggest ways of interpreting the tales, but also help to link the tales together, making the whole text a detailed portrait of the social and cultural attitudes of the time.

Key terms

prologue: an introductory speech, scene, chapter or verse at the beginning of a play, novel or poem

epilogue: a concluding speech, scene, chapter or verse at the end of a play, novel or poem

ACTIVITY 34

The prologue in *Small Island*

If you are studying *Small Island*, remind yourself of the prologue. This is the only chapter which is set outside the 'Before' and '1948' sections. How does this chapter affect your reading of the novel and in what ways does it set the comic tone of the novel from the start?

6.3.7 Happy endings, marriages and resolutions

The happy ending that characterises most comedy often (especially in romantic comedy) involves a marriage, or the prospect of a marriage in the future. In more general terms, however, the ending of a comedy – whether in the form of a love union or a different kind of union or reconciliation – seems to represent an optimistic view of the world that is intended to send audiences home feeling that they can emerge positively from whatever troubles life throws at them and that life's troublesome loose ends have a chance of being tied up. As Shakespeare put it in the title of one of his comedies: *All's Well That Ends Well.*

In this sense, the ending of a comedy and of a tragedy, although quite different, nevertheless might be viewed as fulfilling similar functions. Most tragedies end not only with a death (or deaths) but also, like comedies, with a sense of problems resolved and a more orderly future to follow. There is often, too, a sense of moral lessons to be learned in both tragedy and comedy. Coincidence, misunderstanding and accident might account for a great deal of the confusion in comedy, but there is also usually – to a greater or lesser extent – some element of personal failing: arrogance, pompousness, vanity, naivety, prejudice, greed and so on. The happy ending often shows that we can overcome our failings and learn from our mistakes.

At the same time, we should also be aware that the neat happy endings of comedies might be interpreted as conveniently pushing aside many difficult questions about life. In general in life, problems are not so easily solved. In this respect, it's important to note that not all happy endings in comedies are unreservedly happy. The happy endings of several of Shakespeare's plays, for instance, contain quite stark elements of sadness among the general celebrations, or with a sense that the happy resolution has been achieved at a cost. In *Twelfth Night*, the happy ending is tempered by Malvolio's vow to avenge himself on those who have humiliated him, while in *The Taming of the Shrew*, Katerina's final submission to Petruchio (if that is how we interpret it) often leaves a bitter taste in the audience's mouth.

ACTIVITY 35

Happy endings – marriages and morals

Consider the endings of the texts you are studying.

a Which texts end in marriage or a love union of some sort?

b To what extent do characters learn from their mistakes in the resolution of the narratives?

c To what extent are all problems resolved satisfactorily? Are there any elements of sadness or unresolved issues at the end?

6.3.8 Comedy in miniature

Many of the comic texts discussed in this unit are broad comic narratives in the form of extended plays, novels or long poems. However, some of the aspects of comedy can also be seen at work in shorter texts, even if they do not employ the full range of comic narrative devices.

Such texts include short poems, some of which are comic in tone and content, or use aspects of comedy. These short texts often present what might be seen as a snapshot of a comic situation, and use comic language in a very concentrated and sometimes exaggerated fashion to appeal to the audience or readers' sense of humour. In this sense they are not unlike comedy sketches.

ACTIVITY 36

Comic situations in lyric poetry

Read Philip Larkin's 'Sunny Prestatyn' and John Donne's 'The Flea' (both in the AQA Anthology). In what ways would you say these two poems might be considered to use aspects of comedy? Consider:

- the situations described
- the way the poems are structured
- the imagery used
- the poet's choice of words.

Set text focus: 'Sunny Prestatyn'

'Sunny Prestatyn' was published in Philip Larkin's collection of poetry, *The Whitsun Weddings*, in 1964. It starts with a quotation from the type of hoarding poster that would have been common in the 1950s. This one advertises the seaside resort of Prestatyn, but the initial humour and image of perfection rapidly turns much darker to shocking words and violence, as though society can tolerate a disease like cancer more easily than perfection. The poem is typical of the work of Larkin and other writers of 'The Movement', using plain language and elements of realism in a reaction against the complex poetic language and imagery of the modernist poets.

Although not an exhaustive list, the following aspects of comedy could be explored in relation to 'Sunny Prestatyn':

- the type of comedy (see 6.3.8)
- how language is used to heighten the comedy (see 6.3.4; 6.3.8, 6.4.1).

Other comedic aspects to consider in relation to the poem could be gender issues and laughing at British culture and attitudes. The poem could be read from the perspective of:

- value and the canon (see 9.3)
- narrative theory (see 9.4)
- feminist theory (see 6.4.1; 9.5).

Set text focus: 'The Flea'

John Donne's poem 'The Flea' was first published posthumously in 1633. He is generally acknowledged to be the most accomplished of the metaphysical poets, whose work flourished in the late 16th- and early 17th centuries. The flea had been thought of as an erotic image since medieval times, since it is able to feed on the human lover at any time, but Donne uses a particularly elaborate extended metaphor and ingenious arguments to great effect in his erotic metaphysical poem.

Although not the only one, the following aspect of comedy could be explored in relation to 'The Flea':

- how language is used to heighten the comedy (6.3.4; 6.3.8).

Other comedic aspects to consider in relation to the poem could be situation comedy, playful bantering and sexual innuendo. The poem could be read from the perspective of:

- value and the canon (see 9.3)
- feminist theory (see 6.4.1; 9.5).

6.4 Voices and perspectives in comedy

Now that you've explored the concept of comedy and analysed the different aspects of the comedies you're studying, this section will encourage you to think about issues of voice and perspective. Who do comedies focus on, and who do they ignore? To whom do they offer a voice? Whose perspectives do they emphasise, and whose perspectives are pushed to the sidelines? Here, you are invited to think particularly about the way in which gender, social class and ethnicity are represented in the comedies you have studied.

6.4.1 Gender

The relationships between men and women are central to many of the texts you might be studying, and have been central to much comedy throughout the history of the genre. In Shakespeare's comedies, for instance, explorations of male and female behaviour, characteristics and relationships are often either central to the plot of the play (as in *The Taming of the Shrew* or *Much Ado About Nothing*), or are the subject of much comic discussion, as for instance in *As You Like It* and *Twelfth Night*).

However, it's not necessary for a text to have male and female relationships as a central theme in order to think critically about the way gender is represented in it. Whether the protagonist of the text is male or female, and whether the text explicitly discusses gender or not, it's always worth considering how the text you're studying treats the different genders.

ACTIVITY 37

Gender in comedy

Think about these questions in relation to the texts you are studying.

a What kinds of roles do men and women play?
b To what extent are women presented as protagonists or as subsidiary characters?
c Which is the more powerful gender? How is this power demonstrated?
d Is it possible to generalise about the male/female characters in the comedies you're studying, or do some or all of the characters display gender characteristics in a more complex and variable way?
e What kinds of values do the male/female characters embody? Do these seem to be stereotypes? (To what extent do women, for instance, represent values such as purity, innocence and gentleness?)
f Are women the victims of male actions?
g What sacrifices do women have to make?
h Are women seen as dangerous? Is female sexuality a threat to male order?
i Are women liberated by the action of the comedy?
j How are gender roles represented through aspects of comedy? To what extent does this comic presentation risk trivialising issues of gender?
k What do the representations of women and men in the comedy suggest about the created world of the text and about the author's own world?

Check your responses in the Ideas section on Cambridge Elevate

Critical lens: feminist theory

Feminist theory focuses on the portrayal of gender and sexuality in literary texts. A central concern is the extent to which women's voices and perspectives are heard in literature. In this regard, it's interesting that women characters play a far more active part in Shakespeare's comedies than in Shakespeare's tragedies, and their voices are heard a great deal more. Why do you think this might be?

See 9.5 for more on feminist theory

6.4.2 Social class

Comic drama from the 17th to the 19th centuries focused overwhelmingly on the upper classes. However, at other times comedy has been more representative of the range of social class in society. One of the critical issues about the representation of class in comedy is not only *whether* different classes have been included, but *how* they are portrayed. Often, for instance, upper class characters are portrayed as more dignified or noble than those of lower status. It's not necessary for a text to have class as a theme in order to think critically about the representation of class in it.

ACTIVITY 38

Class in comedy

How do the comedies you are studying treat different social classes? How do they depict social structures?

a Which classes hold most power? How do they treat those who are less powerful?

b Are the less powerful given a voice? Do they appear as individuals, or are they simply in the background? (Do they appear at all?)

c Do the most powerful learn anything about the lives of the less powerful?

Check your responses in the Ideas section on Cambridge Elevate

Critical lens: Marxist theory

Marxist theory focuses on the representation of class and social power in literature. A significant concern is the extent to which working-class characters display *false consciousness,* accepting their social inferiority without protest, or instead rebel in some way against their social inferiority. To what extent do working-class characters in your texts display either of these attitudes?

See 9.6 for more on Marxist theory

'PETRUCHIO: Come, come, you wasp, i'faith you are too angry.
KATHERINE: If I be waspish, best beware my sting.'

William Shakespeare, *The Taming of the Shrew*

6.4.3 Ethnicity

In many respects, it is not surprising that a great deal of English literature until the late 19th century did not feature people of different ethnicities because there was relatively little immigration to Britain until that time. Nevertheless, British explorers and travellers were in regular contact with people in many continents from at least the 15th century onwards, and Jewish people had lived in and visited Britain since the 11th century. Thus, for instance, we find the representation of a Jewish character as the protagonist of Shakespeare's *The Merchant of Venice*.

Nevertheless, there are some omissions. For instance, there are no black characters in any of Jane Austen's novels, and yet the slave trade - the centre of which was in Bristol, not far from Bath, where Austen lived for six years - was at its height at the time.

The 20th century has seen a rapid growth in literature dealing with issues of race, immigration, colonialism and so on, and in such texts it is always important to consider how they treat people of different ethnicities. It's also important to think critically about the reasons for the inclusion or exclusion of different ethnicities from particular texts.

ACTIVITY 39

Race in *Small Island*

Clearly, race is the central theme of *Small Island*. There are a number of important issues to consider.

a How is racial prejudice in the three countries in the book - Britain, Jamaica and the USA - presented differently?

b To what extent do you feel that Britain has moved on in its attitudes to race since 1948?

c How do you feel about Queenie's treatment of the black characters in the book?

d What difference does the inclusion of the story of Bernard's time in India make to the book? How do you feel about Bernard's views on the British Empire and the people he encounters in India?

Critical lens: post-colonial theory

Post-colonial theory encourages us to consider the ways in which colonialism has had lasting effects on both the colonised and the colonisers. As you read *Small Island*, think about the depiction of the British Empire. What attitudes to the Empire do the British and the Jamaican characters seem to have?

See 9.8 for more on post-colonial theory

6.5 Bringing it all together

6.5.1 How will your studies on Aspects of Comedy be assessed?

Aspects of Comedy is one of the two options for AS Level Papers 1 and 2, and for A Level Paper 1. Your knowledge will be tested by the exam.

For guidance on preparing for the exams, see Unit 11

6.5.2 How much do you know?

These questions ask you to bring together the elements you have studied in this unit.

1 What can you remember about these concepts?
- farce
- romantic comedy
- the unities of time, action and place
- natural and licensed fools
- green worlds
- cross-dressing
- comedy of manners
- disguise
- coincidence
- mistaken identity
- slapstick
- bawdy
- comic language.

2 Identify how any five of the concepts listed in question 1 are used in the comedies you are studying. Summarise your findings in clear prose.

3 If any of the concepts listed in question 1 aren't used in the texts you are studying, consider why this might be and what effects the concept might have. Also consider whether a similar concept or

device is used instead. For example, there is no disguise in *Small Island*, but Bernard does hide for a considerable period of the narrative, which might be seen as a form of disguise or lost identity. There is no cross-dressing in *The Importance of Being Earnest*, but gender roles are nevertheless a major issue in the play.

4 Identify two or three of the key dramatic methods used to shape meanings at different points in the texts you are studying. In coherent prose, describe these methods, give examples, and explain their effects.

5 Read the quotations in Texts 6V and 6W about comedy.

Text 6V

Comedy is an imitation of the common errors of our life

Sir Philip Sidney, *The Defense of Poesy* (1581)

Text 6W

All's well that ends well

William Shakespeare (c. 1604)

How true do you think these are, and which of the quotations seem most relevant to each of the comedies you have studied?

6.5.3 Assessment objectives

In relation to the assessment objectives, this unit has explored:

- how you as a reader can make personal, informed and creative responses to comedy. It has also introduced you to a range of essential terminology and concepts that you might use in thinking and writing about comedy (AO1)
- the ways in which writers shape meanings in comedy through their use of a variety of conventions and techniques, including the ways in which they use key aspects of the comic genre (AO2)
- some of the development of comedy as a genre, including the ways it has been adapted by different writers and received by different readers at different times (AO3)
- the key aspects of the genre of comedy that can be found across a wide range of texts (AO4)
- the roles of interpretation and analysis in reading comedy, with special reference to different perspectives on the nature of comedy and the actions of comic characters (AO5).

Summary

In this unit, you have learned about:

- the literary genre of comedy
- the development of comedy over time
- key aspects of comedy
- how the authors of literary texts use different aspects of comedy in their works
- voices and perspectives in comedy.

DEVELOPING

7

Crime writing

In this unit, you will:

- find out about major concepts surrounding crime and society
- explore how writers in a variety of genres have explored crime
- develop your abilities to think critically about literary representations of crime.

Set text focus

Elements of Crime Writing is one of the options in the Texts and Genres component for A Level. The set texts for this option are listed here. To see how these texts might fit into your course, look back at the Introduction to this book.

A Level

When Will There Be Good News? by Kate Atkinson
The Murder of Roger Ackroyd by Agatha Christie
'The Rime of the Ancient Mariner' by Samuel Taylor Coleridge
'Peter Grimes' by George Crabbe
'The Laboratory' by Robert Browning
'My Last Duchess' by Robert Browning
'Porphyria's Lover' by Robert Browning
'The Ballad of Reading Gaol' by Oscar Wilde
Oliver Twist by Charles Dickens
Brighton Rock by Graham Green
Atonement by Ian McEwan
Hamlet by William Shakespeare

7.1 Introduction to crime writing

Writing about crime has a long and illustrious tradition in English - and indeed world - literature. The best known manifestations of crime writing are perhaps the great crime sensation novels of the Victorian era, the cultural phenomenon that is Sherlock Holmes, and the detective novels, films and television series of our own time, but crime has been an enduring element of literary creation dating back to the very earliest known texts. Central elements of writing about crime are: transgression, violence, guilt, investigation, revenge, judgement and punishment. Crime writing also has characteristic structural patterns, affects readers in particular ways, comments on society and concerns itself with how society is affected.

As you work through this unit, you'll develop an understanding of how authors have incorporated crime elements and the impact of criminal behaviour upon individuals and their societies. We provide you with some ways to read crime texts. All set texts have a crime at their heart but writers work creatively within literary genres, so don't be surprised to find that texts you study play with, directly challenge or even totally ignore some of the elements of crime writing that we explore. Writers and the texts they produce are the products of context, and the same is true of readers. As a student of literature, you are involved in a process of recreating meaning from literary texts, and exploring the ways in which writers and readers work in context will help you think about different ways in which texts are produced and received.

It is also important to note that crime writing is not the same as crime fiction. The texts for study in this unit include some conventional crime fiction, but cover a wider variety of texts, all of which have at their heart crimes of some magnitude. In all cases, concepts related to crime are significant in driving their narrative and content.

ACTIVITY 1

Thinking about concepts

Think back over your reading to date. Jot down examples of where you've encountered transgression, guilt, investigation, revenge, judgement and punishment. Try to define what these concepts mean to you.

Several well-known stories from the Bible deal with issues of crime and its consequences.

- In *Genesis*, Adam and Eve commit a crime against God by eating the fruit of the forbidden tree and as a consequence they are expelled from the Garden of Eden.
- Cain murders his brother Abel and in punishment God places a mark upon him and he is driven out to live a life of wandering.
- Joseph is imprisoned after being falsely accused of committing adultery with Potiphar's wife.
- In the book of *Exodus*, Moses murders an Egyptian slave-driver and as a result is not allowed to enter the Promised Land as his punishment by God.

There are also many examples in literary texts.

- In Sophocles' play *Oedipus Rex*, the eponymous hero unknowingly murders his father and sleeps with his mother.
- In *Beowulf* (author unknown), the warrior Beowulf avenges the foul crimes of the beast Grendel and his mother.
- The **revenge tragedies** of the Renaissance era are intensely and darkly fascinated with human sin, crime and vengeance.
- In Christopher Marlowe's *Dr Faustus* and John Milton's *Paradise Lost*, Faustus and Satan respectively are punished for their flagrant challenges to God's authority.
- **Gothic fiction** could not exist without notions of crime and punishment.

See 5.3.9 for more on revenge tragedy; see 7.2.8 for more on gothic fiction

Watch tutorial video, Crime and Love, on Cambridge Elevate

Long before the rise of crime fiction in the mid-19th century, therefore, the seeds of the form were already flourishing.

For that reason this unit does not deal solely - or even largely - with conventional crime and detective fiction. Some examples do draw on the core detective **canon** (such as Agatha Christie's classic of the genre, *The Murder of Roger Ackroyd*), but many other examples draw on the elements of crime writing more broadly. As you read, you will be introduced to the wider range of ideas and concerns that underlie the representation of crime in literature and how this relates to a range of contextual, moral and societal concerns.

'Therefore the Lord God sent him forth from the garden of Eden'

Genesis 3:23, *King James Bible*

Legal and social definitions of what constitutes crime often vary. Legally, crime can be defined as acts that contravene the law of the land – although even this is open to challenge, as events in courtrooms all over the world demonstrate every day. In social terms, crime is harder to tie down. Definitions may:

- be based on unwritten social and cultural codes
- assume shared understanding and mutual respect
- see crime as any action that breaks mutual trust within society
- assume a body of 'normal' or 'acceptable' behaviours.

Key terms

revenge tragedy: a form of tragedy particularly concerned with crime and vengeance

gothic fiction: a form of fiction that frequently deals with horror, the supernatural and socially unacceptable and criminal behaviour

canon: a core and established body of literary texts

ACTIVITY 2

What do you already know about crime writing?

Think back over your study of literature to date and over your own personal reading and viewing. What stories, novels, plays, poetry, films, TV series and other kinds of writing have you come across that deal with crime? Do they all involve a detective or is your experience of crime writing wider than this?

7.1.1 What constitutes crime?

The answer to the question 'What is crime?' may at first seem self-evident, but in fact the notion of crime is quite complex. Different social and religious systems have different ways of understanding what constitutes crime and of dealing with it. There are also significant differences between what is *legally* criminal and what might be considered *socially* or *morally* criminal.

ACTIVITY 3

What is social 'law'?

The idea of social 'law' is important but often problematic.

a Is crime simply an anti-social act? For example, consider the idea of anti-social behaviour orders (or ASBOs).

b Is crime a violation of 'normal' and 'acceptable' behaviour? Who establishes what this means?

c Is crime social or behavioural deviance? Does deviance have levels of severity? At what point does deviance become crime?

d Is crime a threat to social order or morality? Where does that leave the right for challenges to the status quo, tradition and authority?

In *Tess of the D'Urbevilles*, Thomas Hardy explores just such ideas in relation to his heroine, Tess. Although she is the victim of rape, Tess is harshly judged by society, which sees her as guilty of having sex outside of marriage. Hardy uses her rejection by society to reflect philosophically on 'natural' and social law. In the passage shown in Text 7A, Tess considers society's views of her actions.

Text 7A

It was they that were out of harmony with the actual world, not she. Walking among the sleeping birds in the hedges, watching the skipping rabbits on a moonlit warren, or standing under a pheasant-laden bough, she looked upon herself as a figure of Guilt intruding into the haunts of Innocence. But all the while, she was making a distinction where there was no difference. Feeling herself in antagonism, she was quite in accord. She had been made to break an accepted social law, but no law known to the environment in which she fancied herself such an anomaly.

Thomas Hardy, *Tess of the D'Urbervilles*

ACTIVITY 4

The idea of crime

The word 'crime' is used in a wide range of different contexts as can be seen in Figure7A.

Figure 7A

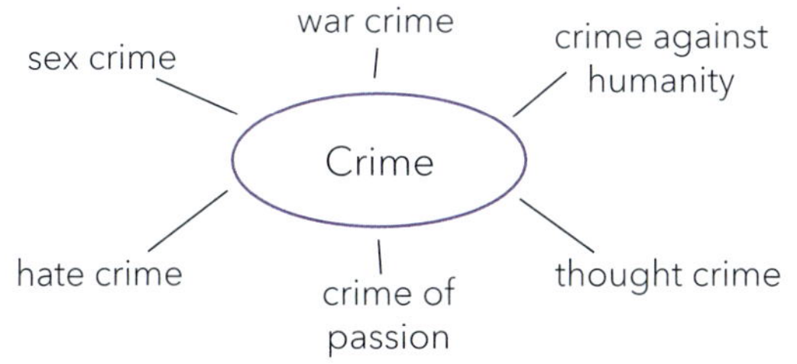

Feel free to add examples of your own. Now think about these questions.

a What does each of these types of crime entail?
b Are they all equally serious?
c How do they help you to see crime in different ways?
d What kinds of activity do these crimes involve?
e How might the notion of crime be open to interpretation and perhaps abuse?
f What are the roles of society, the authorities and the individual in establishing what constitutes crime?

7.1.2 Religious perspectives on crime

The major religions - and major world views such as Marxism or capitalism - have clear stances on crime and punishment. Naturally, these religious perspectives reflect varied societal and cultural formations. However, as globalisation leads to increasingly multicultural, multi-ethnic and multi-faith societies, the idea that we can assume shared understanding of what constitutes criminal behaviour and how such behaviour should be punished is increasingly problematic.

See 9.6 for more on Marxism

When thinking about crime in English literature, a useful starting point is The Ten Commandments (Exodus 20) shown in Text 7B, which are the bases of the Jewish and Christian traditions.

Text 7B

The Ten Commandments

1 You shall have no other gods before me.

2 You shall not make for yourself an image in the form of anything in heaven above or on the earth beneath or in the waters below. You shall not bow down to them or worship them…

3 You shall not misuse the name of the Lord your God, for the Lord will not hold anyone guiltless who misuses his name.

4 Remember the Sabbath day by keeping it holy. Six days you shall labour and do all your work, but the seventh day is a sabbath to the Lord your God. On it you shall not do any work … the Lord blessed the Sabbath day and made it holy.

5 Honour your father and your mother, so that you may live long in the land the Lord your God is giving you.

6 You shall not murder.

7 You shall not commit adultery.

8 You shall not steal.

9 You shall not give false testimony against your neighbour.

10 You shall not covet your neighbour's house. You shall not covet your neighbour's wife, or his male or female servant, his ox or donkey, or anything that belongs to your neighbour.

Exodus 20

ACTIVITY 5

The Ten Commandments – Defining crime

Think about how these commandments relate to the idea of crime. Which relate to religious expectations? Which relate to social crime? Which relate to legal crime?

7.1.3 Why do people read crime writing?

People read about crime – and often extremely brutal crime – as a way of exploring what they do not wish to experience or enact in their own lives. W.H Auden writes interestingly about this: 'I suspect that the typical reader of detective stories is, like myself, a person who suffers from a sense of sin. From the point of view of ethics, desires and acts are good or bad, and I must choose the good and reject the bad, but the I which makes this choice is ethically neutral; it only becomes good or bad in its choice. To have a sense of sin means to feel guilty at there being an ethical choice to make, a guilt which, however "good" I may become, remains unchanged. As St. Paul says: "Except I had known the law, I had not known sin."'

It is interesting to think about our own motivations as readers and to think about how this positions us in relation to what we are reading.

ACTIVITY 6

Readers of crime

Think over your reading and viewing about crime.

a How do you feel about the characters you encounter – detectives, criminals, victims of crime?

b How do your feelings vary from one text to another? Why?

c Do you sometimes relate more naturally to the perpetrator rather than the victim of crime? What are the ethical implications of this?

7.1.4 Crime writing and cultural value

Like such forms as thrillers, westerns and horror writing, crime writing is often dismissed as 'lowbrow' culture. However, crime writing has immense power to capture and hold the imagination, and serious writers produce crime writing. Ian Fleming's *James Bond* novels and John le Carré's *Smiley* books are classics of criminal espionage. Likewise Graham Greene wrote many novels dealing with crime and criminality (e.g. *Brighton Rock* and *A Gun for Sale*).

Set text focus: *Brighton Rock*

Graham Greene published his classic crime thriller *Brighton Rock* in 1938. It perfectly captures the dark and brooding menace of the pre-war world of the late 1930s. The novel relates closely to the film noir genre, which was emerging in pre-World War II crime melodramas such as *City Streets* (1931, directed by Rouben Mamoulian), and *Fury* (1936) and *You Only Live Once* (1937), both directed by Fritz Lang. Greene was a Roman Catholic and *Brighton Rock* obsessively explores notions of good and evil, the influence of Roman Catholicism, the nature of sin, and the basis of morality.

Although not an exhaustive list, the following elements of crime writing could be explored in relation to *Brighton Rock*:

- the type of text (see 7.2.8, The 20th century novel)
- transgressions against law and order; concepts of right and wrong (see 7.1.2; 7.2.3; 7.3.2)
- inclusion of violence and murder (see 7.3.6)
- guilt and remorse (see 7.3.3)
- creation of the criminal (7.5.3)
- creation of the investigator/detective (see 7.4.5; 7.5.1; 7.6.1)
- how the text is structured, from crisis to order (see Activity 14; see 7.4)
- effects on readers (see 7.1.3; Activity 15; 7.4.5).

The novel could be read from the perspective of:

- value and the canon (see 9.3)
- narrative theory (see 7.3.1, Critical lens; 7.4; 9.4)
- feminist theory (see 7.4.7, Critical lens; 7.6.1; 9.5)
- Marxist theory (see 7.5.1, Critical lens; 7.6.2, Critical lens; 9.6).

7.2 Development of crime writing

Although crime fiction as a literary genre did not develop until the 19th century, literature dealing with crime is as old as literature itself. In this section, we explore the different ways writers of poetry, drama and the novel have written about crime from the classical era to the present day.

7.2.1 Classical tragedy, comedy and verse narrative

Ancient Greek and Roman theatre may seem distant from what we think of as crime writing, but provides some interesting examples.

Classical tragedy and comedy typically deal with the relationship between humans and higher powers (e.g. the state or the gods). In both instances, humans find themselves at the mercy of inevitable fate. This often creates conflicts of loyalty and forces us to consider where the boundary lies between:

- the demands of society and the desires of the individual
- what is right and what is wrong
- the motivations of actions and their consequences.

The connection of all of these to the idea of crime is evident.

See Unit 5 for more on classical tragedy; see Unit 6 for more on classical comedy

Let's think about the example of Sophocles' play *Oedipus Rex* in more detail.

ACTIVITY 7

***Oedipus Rex* and crime**

The tragedy of Oedipus (see the summary in Text 7C) relates interestingly to the idea of crime writing. Think about these questions:

a What crimes does this play deal with?
b What is the role of punishment in this narrative?
c How does this narrative deal with some elements of crime writing?

Text 7C

It is over a decade since Oedipus became King of Thebes. Before becoming king, he has killed a man in a fight, but after successfully answering the riddle of the sphinx he becomes king and marries Jocasta – the recently widowed queen. He is determined to save the city from the anger of the gods as the previous king has been murdered and no one has brought the criminal to justice. Oedipus vows to track down and punish the killer no matter who it is.

Tiresias, a seer, tells Oedipus to stop looking for the killer, but when the king ignores him, Tiresias claims that Oedipus himself is the murderer and that he has killed his father and married his own mother. This reinforces a prophecy Oedipus has previously received while living in Corinth, but as Tiresias also claims the murderer was born in Thebes, the King refuses to believe the evidence points to him.

Jocasta encourages his disbelief until a messenger arrives carrying the tidings that Oedipus' father is dead. The burden of evidence increases when a shepherd arrives and tells the tale of his discovery of an infant abandoned in the wilderness outside Thebes – that infant was Oedipus who was taken in by adoptive parents in Corinth.

Oedipus now has to face up to the evidence – that the man he killed was none other than his father, King Laius, and that the woman he has married is his own mother, Laius' wife Jocasta. Jocasta hangs herself, and Oedipus gouges his own eyes out with the pins from her dress and walks away from the city to wander blindly around Greece as a wretched example to others.

Check your responses in the Ideas section on Cambridge Elevate

You could try looking at summaries for a range of other classical tragedies, comedies and verse narratives and think about the different ways in which they approach ideas relating to crime. Good texts to consider would be:

- the bloodthirsty plays of Seneca
- a comedy such as Aristophanes' *Lysistrata*
- major verse narratives such as Homer's *Iliad* or Virgil's *Aeneid*.

In his essay 'The Guilty Vicarage', W.H. Auden draws specific parallels between the characters of classical tragedy and of the detective story: 'Greek tragedy and the detective story have one characteristic in common, in which they both differ from modern tragedy, namely, the characters are not changed in or by their actions: in Greek tragedy because their actions are fated, in the detective story because the decisive event, the murder, has already occurred.'

ACTIVITY 8

Character and verisimilitude

a Read again what W.H Auden says about characters in crime writing. Characters in literary texts do not always rely on realistic details (**verisimilitude**). What other concerns might drive an author's representation of character? Do characters have to be believable to function effectively?

b Think about any investigator figures (e.g. Sherlock Holmes, Inspector Morse or Jack Bauer) or criminal figure you know from your own reading or viewing. In what ways are they 'real'? In what ways are they 'unreal'? How does this relate to their function in the text?

Key terms

verisimilitude: literally this means likeness to truth and may be summarised as 'truth to life'

7.2.2 Old English and medieval quest narratives

Beowulf, the longest and greatest of Old English poems, tells the tale of Beowulf, who leads the quest to capture the beast, Grendel, and his mother. They have been responsible for murderous raids on King Hrothgar's hall and have killed many of his finest men. As a criminal outsider, Grendel is overtly compared to Cain - the first murderer, whose tale is told in the book of *Genesis* (see Text 7D).

Text 7D

Grendel this monster grim was called,
march-riever mighty, in moorland living,
in fen and **fastness**; **fief** of the giants
the hapless **wight** a while had kept
since the Creator his exile doomed.
On kin of Cain was the killing avenged
by sovereign God for slaughtered Abel.
Ill fared his feud, and far was he driven,
for the slaughter's sake, from sight of men.
Of Cain awoke all that woeful breed,
Etins and elves and evil-spirits,
as well as the giants that warred with God
weary while: but their wage was paid them!

Anon, *Beowulf*

Glossary

march-riever: rover of the moors and fen

fastness: wilderness

fief: slave

wight: being

etin: monster

Exploring language

With its references to 'exile', 'killing', 'feud[ing]', 'slaughter', conflict and punishment, the connections to crime writing in 'Beowulf' are clear.

The verse narratives of the Middle Ages also often deal with crime and misdoing. Within the context of a feudal society, these narratives focus especially on ideas of transgression, honour and restitution, although some, like William Langland's epic *Piers Plowman*, are religious in focus. Inspired by the book of *Revelation*, Langland envisages the end of the world and vividly imagines the sins and depredations that are its precursors.

Sir Gawain and the Green Knight is a classic quest narrative, which has been summarised in Text 7E:

Text 7E

Sir Gawain takes up the brutal challenge of a mysterious green-clad knight: he must strike off the Green Knight's head in a single blow, but must in his turn face a single return blow from the Green Knight in a year's time. Perceiving no risk, Gawain decapitates the Green Knight only to see him rise to his feet, pick up his severed head and leave, ordering Gawain to seek out the Green Chapel to receive his return blow. Gawain lives the year in fear.

As the year draws to its close, he sets out on his quest and is invited to stay at an isolated castle. His host proposes an agreement: that Gawain should stay in the castle while the host hunts, but at the end of each day they must exchange whatever they have gained. The mistress of the castle tries to seduce Gawain; he resists, except for kissing and is honest in repaying his host the kisses he has received. On the third day, Gawain accepts the gift of a magic belt that will preserve his life. Gawain keeps silent about this.

Gawain meets the Green Knight at the chapel. Twice the Green Knight holds back his blow, but with the third he cuts the side of Gawain's neck. The first two blows represent Gawain's honesty in repaying the stolen kisses; the cut is for concealing the gift of the belt. Gawain is overcome with shame and wears the belt to remind him of his fault.

ACTIVITY 9

Sir Gawain and the Green Knight

The anonymous Gawain poet touches on crime writing in a number of interesting ways typical of the medieval romances. Read the summary of the poem in Text 7E, then jot down your thoughts about how the text uses:

a honour
b fear
c regret and guilt
d consequences and punishment
e temptation
f deception
g guilt.

How do these ideas relate to other crime texts you have read or seen?

Chaucer, the best known of the medieval poets, tells a number of stories in *The Canterbury Tales* – some tragic and some comic – that deal with issues relating to crime. In 'The Pardoner's Tale', he regales us with the darkly comic story of three roisterers who try to kill Death only to come to a sticky end themselves. 'The Reeve's Tale' and 'The Miller's Tale' are bawdy comedies dealing with adultery and its consequences. More seriously, we may think, the knight in 'The Wife of Bath's Tale' commits rape and is taught to reshape his attitude towards women. Crime within medieval society is thus a recurring theme in Chaucer's major work.

7.2.3 Medieval morality and mystery plays

Criminal desire and moral ambiguity are often explored in the **morality plays** and **mystery plays** of the medieval era. Like more modern crime writing, such as Fyodor Dostoevsky's novel *Crime and Punishment* or Graham Greene's *Brighton Rock*, religious faith is significant in the exploration and experience of crime. Significant issues relating to crime writing are:

- the conflict between good and evil
- the exploration of abstract social ideas and values related to the representation of crime in society (e.g. vice, justice and equity).

As in classical tragedy and the **classic detective novel**, characters tend not to develop but remain abstract 'types'.

- The main character faces a variety of ethical trials and temptations.
- In the end evil is defeated, sin is renounced and goodness is restored on earth.

Key terms

morality play: a medieval play that dramatises moral values such as good and evil

mystery play: a play performed by the medieval trade guilds – from the French *métier*, meaning line of work or trade

classic detective novel: a crime fiction genre that emerged as a recognisable literary genre in the mid-19th century

'Of Cain awoke all that woeful breed, Etins and elves and evil-spirits'

Beowulf

See 7.3.1 for more on *Crime and Punishment*; see 7.3.2 for more on *Brighton Rock*

7.2.4 Renaissance tragedy

The works of the major Renaissance dramatists represent a considerable development. While the classical, Old English and Middle English authors dealt with ideas about crime, the writers of the Renaissance tragedies (and especially the revenge tragedies) delve deep into the psychology of crime and its impact, from the perspectives of both the perpetrators and the victims of crime. Characters in these plays move far beyond the flat 'types' typical of earlier drama and much classic detective fiction - they live, breathe and have their being.

In *Othello* we are privy to Iago's criminal machinations and follow the terrible inevitability of Othello's descent from noble moor to murderer of Desdemona. Similarly, in *King Lear*, we observe the criminal means by which Goneril, Regan and Edmund further their own ends after Lear has 'criminally' given away his kingly powers. *Titus Andronicus* is a catalogue of crime: psychological torment, rape, dismemberment and murder.

Hamlet, which provides us with one of the great catchphrases of crime writing - 'murder most foul' (Act 1, Scene 5, line 27) - is another excellent example as we see the eponymous hero struggling to come to terms with the murder of his father and seeking to avenge his death. As the play progresses, Shakespeare explores a wealth of ideas relating to crime, including the elements of crime writing shown in Figure 7B.

In the passage in Text 7F, Hamlet reflects upon the possibility of murdering his stepfather Claudius while he is praying. Note how transgression and confession in both their criminal and religious senses are important.

Watch tutorial video, Guilt, Confession and Remorse, on Cambridge Elevate

Figure 7B

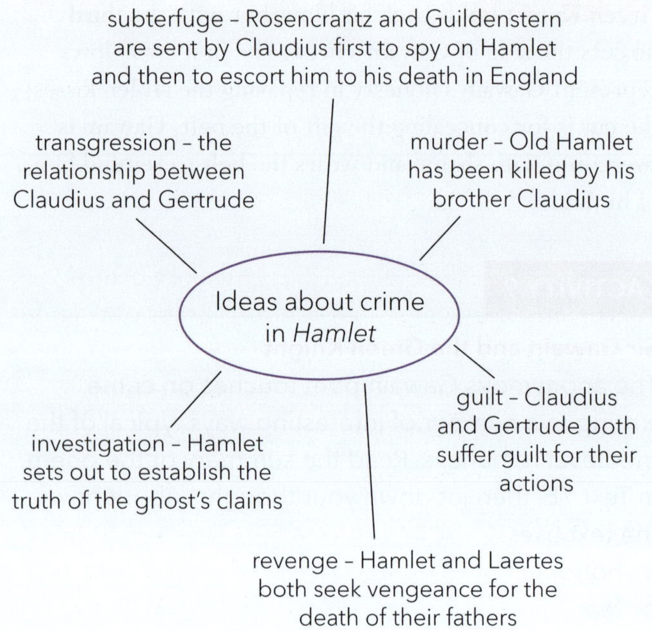

Text 7F

Now might I do it pat now he is praying,
And now I'll do it, and so he goes to heaven.
And so am I revenged, that would be scanned.
A villain kills my father; and for that,
I, his sole son, do this same villain send to heaven.
O, this is hire and salary, not revenge.
He took my father grossly, full of bread -
With all his crimes broad blown, as flush as May.
And how his audit stands, who knows save heaven?
But in our circumstance and course of thought,
'Tis heavy with him, and am I, then, revenged;
To take him in the purging of his soul,
When he is fit and seasoned for his passage?
No.
Up, sword, and know thou a more horrid **hent**:
When he is drunk asleep or in his rage;
Or in the incestuous pleasure of his bed;
At gaming, swearing or about some act
That has no relish of salvation in it.
Then trip him, that his heels may kick at heaven,
And that his soul may be as damned and black
As hell, whereto it goes.

Hamlet, Act 3, Scene 3

Glossary

hent: occasion or opportunity

ACTIVITY 10

The language of crime

Read the extract from *Hamlet* in Text 7F. Write down all the words that relate directly to ideas of crime and punishment.

a Which of these words relate to religious ideas of crime?

b Which words relate to secular ideas of crime?

c How do the two groups of words cross over and interact with each other?

d What is the effect of this on you as a reader?

7.2.5 Crime in poetry

After the Renaissance era, when the Puritans closed the theatres, narrative poetry continued to be a popular form - and continued to deal with issues of crime.

Paradise Lost by John Milton (1608–74) is a significant example. Like Langland's *Piers Plowman*, this is inspired by the Bible. Satan and a group of angels rebel against God. Banished from Heaven as a consequence, Satan travels to Earth in search of God's newest creation - humans. He seeks vengeance by causing the humans to sin against God. He successfully tempts Eve - and through her, Adam - into eating the forbidden fruit of the Tree of the Knowledge of Good and Evil. God detects their sin and, in spite of their grief and sorrow, they are punished by expulsion from the Garden of Eden.

See 7.2.2 to compare Satan's quest on Earth with medieval quest narratives

In the 19th century, the Romantics' emphasis on individual liberty (see the ideas of philosophers such as Jean-Jacques Rousseau and Emmanuel Swedenborg) provides an interesting development when thinking about crime writing. By elevating the importance of individual experience, personal ethics and moral choices, the impact these have upon others and upon society become important. As a result, the notion of crime and other related concepts is frequently important when we read the Romantics.

Set text focus: *Hamlet*

When *Hamlet* was first performed in 1602, revenge plays were hugely popular. Hamlet has every opportunity to kill Claudius - who he believes has killed his father. Instead of taking decisive action to avenge the murder, he delays, deliberating at length about the uncertainties - the truth of the Ghost's accusation, whether his mother is equally guilty and, ultimately, whether revenge is morally justified. In presenting Hamlet's character and dilemmas in this way, Shakespeare explores the nature of crime and the rights of humans to intervene in its punishment. This echoes the religious and emerging humanist ideas of his day about the difficulty of seeing past outward appearances and of knowing the truth about other people's inner selves.

Although not an exhaustive list, the following elements of crime writing could be explored in relation to *Hamlet*:

- the type of text (see 7.2.4)
- transgressions against law and order (see 7.1.1; 7.1.2; 7.2.1; 7.3.2)
- inclusion of deception, violence and murder (see Activities 9, 12; 7.2.4; 7.3.6)
- the role of reconstruction of crime (see 7.4.6)
- guilt, remorse and confession (see Activity 9; 7.2.4; 7.3.3)
- relationship between revenge and madness (see 7.3.5)
- creation of the criminal (see 7.3.5; 7.5.3)
- creation of the investigator (see 7.5.1)
- how the text is structured, from crisis to order (see 7.4)
- how language is used (see Activity 10)

The play could be read from the perspective of:

- value and the canon (see 7.4.1, Critical lens; 9.3)
- narrative theory (see 7.3.1, Critical lens; 7.4; 9.4)
- feminist theory (see 7.4.7, Critical lens; 7.6.1; 9.5).

Coleridge's 'The Rime of the Ancient Mariner' is an excellent example. An ill-fated mariner is made to pay the consequences through a life of guilt and suffering for his killing of an albatross. Wordsworth and Blake were almost revolutionary in their focus on social justice; their exposure of 'criminal' social ills (e.g. the conditions of the labouring poor, child labour, racial inequality) is almost an act of detection and exposure.

Other poets, such as Robert Browning, focus on the psyche of the criminal. In a sequence of dramatic monologues, Browning delves into the criminal mind; 'The Laboratory', 'Porphyria's Lover' and 'My Last Duchess', for instance, deal with crime within relationships.

The poet George Crabbe in 'Peter Grimes' explores the personal and social consequences of crime. The eponymous 'hero', Grimes, is accused of abusing and killing a sequence of apprentices. Crabbe provides a fascinating psychological profile of the criminal outsider who displayed violent tendencies even as a child. In Text 7G Grimes recalls his father's ominous warning, which foreshadows Grimes' eventual fate:

Text 7G

How he had oft the good old man reviled,
And never paid the duty of a child;
How, when the father in his Bible read,
He in contempt and anger left the shed:
"It is the word of life," the parent cried;
"This is the life itself," the boy replied;
And while old Peter in amazement stood,
Gave the hot spirit to his boiling blood:
How he, with oath and furious speech, began
To prove his freedom and assert the man;
And when the parent check'd his impious rage,
How he had cursed the tyranny of age, –
Nay, once had dealt the sacrilegious blow
On his bare head, and laid his parent low;
The father groan'd – "If thou art old," said he,
"And hast a son – thou wilt remember me:"

George Crabbe, 'Peter Grimes'

Set text focus: Robert Browning's poetry

Robert Browning wrote 'The Laboratory', 'Porphyria's Lover' and 'My Last Duchess' in the early Victorian era. These three poems, in the form of dramatic monologues, allowed Browning to explore various issues, including men's desire to control female sexuality, the moral difference between sensuality and violence, and the blurring of lines between ordinary life and insanity.

Although not an exhaustive list, the following elements of crime writing could be explored in relation to all three poems:

- the type of text (see 7.2.5)
- settings of time and place (see 7.3.3, Critical lens)
- transgressions against law and order (see 7.1.1; 7.1.2)
- inclusion of murder (see 7.3.6)
- guilt and confession (see 7.4.7)
- creation of the criminal and their motivation (see 7.3.5)
- the role of the narrator (see 7.4.7)
- representation of women (see 7.6.1)
- effects on readers (see 7.1.3; 7.4.5).

All three poems could be read from the perspective of:

- value and the canon (see 9.3)
- narrative theory (see 7.3.1, Critical lens; 7.4; 9.4)
- feminist theory (see 7.4.7, Critical lens; Activity 29; 9.5).

In addition 'Porphyria's Lover' could be read from the perspective of:

- eco-critical theory (see 7.3.3, Critical lens; 9.7).

ACTIVITY 11

Individual against society

Read again the extract from *Peter Grimes* in Text 7G.

a How does Crabbe use language and dialogue to demonstrate the ways in which an individual reacts against his or her society?

b How do we see the impact of Grimes' reaction?

Check your responses in the Ideas section on Cambridge Elevate

Exploring the work of George Crabbe

'Peter Grimes' is only one section of a much longer collection, entitled *The Borough*, by the regional East Anglian poet George Crabbe. The poem is best known as the source of one of the greatest 20th century British operas by the composer Benjamin Britten. Why not listen to some or all of the opera in which Britten brilliantly captures the enigmatic, misunderstood yet disturbing figure of Grimes?

Set text focus: 'Peter Grimes'

'Peter Grimes' was published in 1810 as Letter XXII of *The Borough*, a collection of poems based on society, trades and places in Aldeburgh. The poet, George Crabbe, was a clergyman and lifelong naturalist. Crabbe's son claimed the story of the fisherman Grimes was inspired by a real Aldeburgh fisherman, whose apprentices all died in suspicious circumstances.

Although not an exhaustive list, the following elements of crime writing could be explored in relation to 'Peter Grimes':

- settings of time and place (see 7.3.3, Critical lens)
- transgressions against law and order (see 7.1.1; 7.1.2)
- inclusion of violence and murder (see 7.2.5; 7.3.6)
- the role of remorse and punishment, resolution and death (see 7.3.1)
- whether there is a moral and restoration of order (see 7.3.3)
- creation of the criminal (7.5.3; Activity 31)
- how the text is structured, from crisis to order (see 7.4)
- how language and poetic form are used (see 7.2.5)
- social consequences of crime (see 7.2.5)
- effects on readers (see 7.1.3; 7.4.5).

The poem could be read from the perspective of:

- value and the canon (see 9.3)
- narrative theory (see 7.3.1, Critical lens; 7.4; 9.4)
- Marxist theory (see 7.5.1, Critical lens; 7.6.2; 9.6).

Oscar Wilde's *The Ballad of Reading Gaol* (1898), written after Wilde had been incarcerated for homosexuality, gives us an insight into the harsh realities of prison life. Stripped of the gloss of humour that characterises Wilde's other works, this poem exposes the tormented shadowlands of the poet's personality and experience. The poem conveys a wealth of personal emotion and torment and portrays the horrors of execution.

Set text focus: 'The Ballad of Reading Gaol'

At the height of his career in the early 1890s, Oscar Wilde's plays were hugely successful. However in 1895, he was convicted of homosexual practices, sentenced to two years' hard labour and imprisoned in Reading Gaol. During his time there, he wrote his last major work, the poem 'The Ballad of Reading Gaol', centred around the real-life hanging of Charles Woodbridge for murdering his wife. Wilde left prison a sick and broken man, and died just two years later at the age of 46.

Although not an exhaustive list, the following elements of crime writing could be explored in relation to 'The Ballad of Reading Gaol':

- settings of time and place (see 7.3.3, Critical lens)
- transgressions against law and order (see 7.1.1; 7.1.2; 7.3.2)
- inclusion of violence and murder (see 7.3.6)
- justice, the legal system, imprisonment and punishment (see 7.3.1)
- creation of the criminal (see 7.5.3)
- effects on readers (see 7.1.3; 7.4.5).

The poem could be read from the perspective of:

- value and the canon (see 9.3)
- narrative theory (see 7.3.1, Critical lens; 7.4; 9.4).

7.2.6 Crime in drama

In earlier sections we looked at classical, medieval and Renaissance drama. It was not really until the Victorian era that stage crime re-emerged. It was often poor quality **melodrama** that has not survived the passage of time. However, a substantial body of stage adaptations of **sensation fiction** were highly popular. These paved the way for the modern theatre, which has produced many works dealing with ideas of crime. *Miss Julie* (1888) by the Swedish playwright August Strindberg presents an obsessive and oppressive insight into the dark corners of the human psyche, and Ibsen in *Hedda Gabler* (1890) and *A Doll's House* (1879) inhabit similar territory.

Key terms

melodrama: a sensational form of drama with exaggerated characters and exciting events

sensation fiction: a form of fiction dealing with sensational crimes and their detection

The Irish dramatist Sean O'Casey in plays like *Juno and the Paycock* and *The Shadow of a Gunman* deals with the idea of crime against the troubled political background of 20th-century Ireland. The same Irish troubles are the canvas for Brian Friel's *Translations*. In England, George Bernard Shaw and J.B. Priestley, following in the tradition of poets like Blake, Coleridge, Wordsworth and the political thinker and novelist William Godwin (author of *An Enquiry Concerning Political Justice*), explore issues of social 'crime'.

Another important strand of crime writing in the 20th and 21st centuries has been writing for the screen. Many crime series or films are adaptations of works of fiction – for example, *Inspector Morse*, *A Touch of Frost* and *Rebus*. In the case of Morse, a major industry of spin-off series, *Lewis* and *Endeavour,* has developed. Television has taken up Sherlock Holmes in the modern-day rewriting, *Sherlock*, and there have been recent films starring Robert Downey Jr. Related genres such as political crime thrillers (e.g. the Bourne films, *24*, *Homeland*), police dramas (e.g. *The Bill*), gangster narratives (e.g. *The Godfather*, *The Sopranos*) and real-life crime (e.g. *In Cold Blood*, *JFK* and *Frost/Nixon*) also abound.

ACTIVITY 12

Crime on screen

Watch selected examples of crime writing for the screen suggested in the previous paragraph. As you watch, think about how they treat some of the major elements in Figure 7C.

Figure 7C

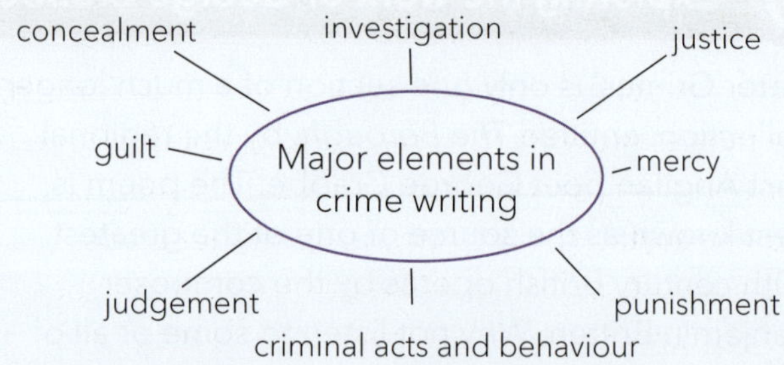

Do you see any major similarities and differences in the approach to crime in this medium?

7.2.7 Early crime narratives

A major source of early crime narrative is the notorious *Newgate Calendar*. Readers were regaled with semi-fictionalised accounts of crime. Unlike later crime writing, which tends to steer clear of punishment, these accounts revel in it, often presenting gory executions. It is punishment rather than detection that is the focus. Text 7H is an extract from the account of Catherine Hayes 'Who with Others foully murdered her Husband, and was burned alive on 9th of May, 1726'.

Text 7H

[the prosecution] did all in their power to convince the Court and jury that the most striking example should be made of one who had so daringly defied the laws of God and man. The indictment being opened, and the witnesses heard, the jury, fully convinced of the commission of the fact, found her guilty … Mrs Hayes entreated that she might not be burnt, according to the then law of petty treason, alleging that she was not guilty, as she did not strike the fatal blow; but she was informed by the Court that the sentence awarded by the law could not be dispensed with.

On the day of her death Hayes received the sacrament, and was drawn on a sledge to the place of execution … When the wretched woman had finished her devotions, an iron chain was put round her body, with which she was fixed to a stake near the gallows … this woman was literally burnt alive: for the executioner letting go the rope sooner than usual, in consequence of the flames reaching his hands, the fire burnt fiercely round her, and the spectators beheld her pushing away the faggots, while she rent the air with her cries and lamentations.

From *Newgate Calendar*

Critical lens: feminist theory

In the extract from the *Newgate Calendar* in Text 7H, the perpetrator of the crime is a woman. Think about the way in which her crime is presented. Is there anything more terrible about her crime because she is a woman? What expectations does society have of women? How does the idea of crime relate to these views? How does the writer use language in relation to the female criminal?

See 9.5 for more on feminist theory

7.2.8 The rise of crime writing

The developing form of the novel continued to demonstrate a peculiar fascination with crime. One of the most notorious criminals of 18th-century London, Jonathan Wild, is the subject of a fiction bearing his name by Henry Fielding, and other narratives such as Daniel Defoe's *Moll Flanders* deal energetically with the criminal underground of the rapidly expanding 18th-century urban society.

Exploring the life and work of Henry Fielding

Henry Fielding (1707–54), author of what is commonly recognised as the first novels in the English language – *Joseph Andrews* and *Tom Jones* – was closely connected with the world of crime. In 1749 he founded The Bow Street Runners, the precursors of Robert Peel's Metropolitan Police Force, and he was a high court justice.

The focus of these narratives continued to be a named individual, and this trend continued with the development of the novel and in particular the ***Bildungsroman***.

Key terms

Bildungsroman: a novel dealing with a character's development from childhood into adulthood

Literature and the formation of police and detective forces

The rise of crime writing coincided with the social formulation of crime and criminal detection in the establishment of police and detective forces around the world as shown in Table 7A.

Table 7A

Date	Force	Details
1749	Bow Street Runners (London)	• Founded by novelist and Justice Henry Fielding • Investigation of crime and writing about crime are connected from the outset
1812	Sûreté (Paris)	• Founded by criminal and criminologist Eugène Vidocq • A body of plainclothes police officers in Paris • Followed in 1833 by *Le bureau des renseignements* – a detective force • Vidocq believed the best people to detect and prevent crime were people who knew the criminal world from the inside
1829	The Metropolitan Police (London), also known as 'Peelers' or 'Bobbies'	• Founded by Robert Peel • 3500 uniformed officers in London • A brief to capture criminals, but also to prevent crime • Followed by forces in other areas; 13,000 police throughout England and Wales by 1851
1842	Detective division (London)	• Small elite plainclothes detective division • Formed to investigate murders and other serious crimes
1850	Pinkertons Detective Agency (US)	• Founded by Allan Pinkerton • Formed to track down counterfeiters • During American Civil War his agency headed up espionage

Gothic novels

A significant sub-genre of crime, gothic novels deal extensively with issues related to crime. The critic David Punter comments on the 'jagged' and 'fragmentary' nature of gothic texts. He relates this to the fact that gothic texts deal with the uncomfortable edges – including the criminal edges – of human experience. As a result, gothic novels and tales tend to differ from crime novels by dealing with discomfort, pain, abuse, brutality, forbidden behaviours, guilt and fear. William Godwin in *Caleb Williams* (1794) and Ann Radcliffe in a sequence of novels (e.g. *The Mysteries of Udolpho* and *The Romance of the Forest*) both deal with criminal abuse of power, often by predatory males. In *Frankenstein*, Mary Shelley explores a scientist's 'crime' in seeking to usurp the place of God.

ACTIVITY 13

Gothic and crime

Think about any gothic texts you've studied up to now. In what ways did they present and deal with crime? Create a spider diagram of your ideas, then develop a coherent paragraph outlining how you feel the gothic and crime elements relate.

The Victorian novelists produced a plethora of works exploring criminality. George Eliot, George Meredith, Elizabeth Gaskell and Anthony Trollope all provide us with large social canvases on which they explore the legal and moral concerns of their time. *Jane Eyre* by Charlotte Brontë and *Wuthering Heights* by Emily Brontë, deal with criminal behaviour and brutality within marriage. Charles Reade's *It is Never too Late to Mend* (1856) was written specifically to challenge abuses in prison discipline and the maltreatment of criminals. Charles Dickens frequently inhabits the seedy Victorian underworld (e.g. *Oliver Twist*, *Nicholas Nickelby* and *The Mystery of Edwin Drood*) and crime and its investigation are often present. Dickens' close friend Wilkie Collins was a prolific crime writer, developing claustrophobic worlds where criminality and domesticity meet (e.g. *The Woman in White*, *No Name*, *Armadale* and *The Moonstone*). Other classic sensation novels include Mrs Henry Wood's *East Lynne* and Mary Elizabeth Braddon's *Lady Audley's Secret* and *Aurora Floyd*. Towards the end of the Victorian era, decadent gothic texts such as Bram Stoker's *Dracula*, Robert Louis Stevenson's *The Strange Case of Dr Jekyll and Mr Hyde* and Oscar Wilde's *The Picture of Dorian Gray* explore the potent threat of crime within the apparently orderly world of late Victorian society.

Detective fever

After the formation of the Metropolitan Police Force and the London detective branch, public fascination with the idea of crime and the emerging 'science' of detection proliferated. In *The Moonstone* by Wilkie Collins, Franklin Blake (a gentleman) and Betteredge (a servant) discuss the psychological grip of an apparently insoluble mystery (see Text 7I).

The turn of the century saw the further rise of the detective story. Its most famous representatives are no doubt Sherlock Holmes, the lead character of a substantial set of tales and novels by Sir Arthur Conan Doyle, and Father Brown in the tales of G.K. Chesterton.

'My gloves of white, my coat of blue,
my dignity increase,
And every gesture shows to you, that I'm
one of the new police.'

'The New Police', satirical poem published 1835–1850

Text 7I

"How are you this morning, Betteredge?"

"Very poorly, sir."

"Sorry to hear it. What do you complain of?"

"I complain of a new disease, Mr. Franklin, of my own inventing. I don't want to alarm you, but you're certain to catch it before the morning is out."

"The devil I am!"

"Do you feel an uncomfortable heat at the pit of your stomach, sir? And a nasty thumping at the top of your head? Ah! not yet? It will lay hold of you at Cobb's Hole, Mr. Franklin. I call it the detective-fever; and I first caught it in the company of Sergeant Cuff."

Wilkie Collins, *The Moonstone*

Golden Age detective fiction

The 1920s and 1930s are generally recognised as the golden era of detective fiction. Agatha Christie, Dorothy L. Sayers and others built upon the foundations established by Collins, Conan Doyle and Chesterton to forge the classic detective form. In the wake of World War I, the detective story perhaps offered a sense of control – a world where guilt and horror were containable and the brilliant detective could restore peace and balance.

In 'The Guilty Vicarage', W.H Auden expressed the opinion that 'detective stories have nothing to do with works of art'. The detective story interests him because it explores 'the **dialectic** of innocence and guilt'. He goes on to define what he sees as two related formulae at play in detective narratives as shown in Figure 7D.

Key terms

dialectic: the art of formal reasoning, the logical structure that holds an argument together

Figure 7D

Peaceful state before the murder (false innocence)
↓
Murder (revelation of presence of guilt)
↓
False clues, secondary murders etc. (false location of guilt)
↓
Solution (location of real guilt)
↓
Arrest of murderer (catharsis)
↓
Peaceful state after arrest (true innocence)

ACTIVITY 14

Auden's formula

Look again at Auden's formula. How far and in what ways does this 'dialectic' of innocence and guilt relate to the presentation and investigation of crime as you see it in your own reading?

The 20th-century novel

As the 20th century progressed, detective fiction lost none of its appeal. Morse, Frost, Rebus, Dalziel and Pascoe, Barnaby and a host of others are household names. While the basic form of classic detective fiction has not changed, it has, of course, evolved to take account of the continuing developments in forensic science and the technology of detection.

The 20th century has also given rise to a vast array of writing that deals with crime, but which is not conventional crime fiction. In *Animal Farm*, George Orwell explores political abuse and crime through a thinly veiled fable of the Russian Revolution. In *1984*, Winston Smith lives in an absolute **dystopian** society where deviance from accepted thinking is considered 'thought crime'. *In Cold Blood* by Truman Capote deals with a real-life crime, the capture of the perpetrators and their experiences on death row. Ian McEwan, in *The Innocent*, *Saturday*, *Amsterdam* and *Atonement*, has produced a sequence of novels delving into criminal activity and psychology.

While in most crime writing the detective casts light, makes sense of confusion, and re-establishes order, **postmodern** interpretations of the role can be much less reassuring. In *Hawksmoor*, Peter Ackroyd's detective investigates a series of brutal ritual murders at churches designed by Nicholas Dyer. The more the detective becomes immersed in the historical world of Nicholas Dyer, the less he is able to establish order. Ackroyd seems deliberately to challenge the moral and societal certainties that underpin traditional crime writing. Similarly in *City of Glass*, *Ghosts* and *The Locked Room*, Paul Auster self-consciously plays with the increasingly indistinct role of the detective (the 'reader') and the author (the 'writer').

Key terms

dystopian: literary works describing a nightmarish world or state in which conditions are very bad

postmodern: a late 20th-century concept in the arts, characterised by self-conscious undermining of previous forms and structures

In *Brighton Rock*, Graham Greene plays with the idea of 'reading' and how we construct meaning from what we read. The process of investigation is an act of 'reading'. The police adopt a 'closed book' policy once they are convinced that Hale has died of natural causes. Ida Arnold, however, refuses to accept the apparent certainties of their reading and continues to seek her own interpretations.

ACTIVITY 15

Reading and writing in crime writing

Look at Table 7B and think about these participants in crime writing and how they 'read' and 'write' events. Some example ideas are included.

Table 7B

	... as reader	... as writer
Author		
Reader		makes predictions
Detective	'reads' clues	
Criminal		

Other novels deal with crime in a variety of contexts. Ian McEwan's *Atonement*, as the title suggests, is a study of guilt and restitution; Brian Moore's *Lies of Silence*, set in Belfast and London during the days of the IRA (Irish Republican Army), deals with ideologically motivated terrorist crime; Anthony Burgess's *A Clockwork Orange* takes us straight into the criminal underworld of Alex and his gang who commit a string of the most brutal crimes as a statement of their imagined independence from the normal moral constraints of society.

Set text focus: *Atonement*

Ian McEwan's novel *Atonement,* written in 2001, was shortlisted for various prizes in the same year, including the Booker Prize for Fiction. Among other prizes, it won the 2002 Los Angeles Times Book Prize for Fiction and the 2004 Santiago Prize for the European Novel. It inhabits the same morally ambiguous territory that typifies much of Ian McEwan's writing: the searching exploration of the impact of love and loss on people's lives, of moral dilemmas and dubious ethical decisions, and of the tortuous space of dysfunctional family relationships. McEwan's own father was abusive and his mother suffered from vascular dementia, as Bryony does in the novel.

Although not an exhaustive list, the following elements of crime writing could be explored in relation to *Atonement*:

- the type of text (see 7.2.8, The 20th century novel)
- what constitutes crime and transgressions against law and order (see 7.1.1; 7.1.2; 7.3.2)
- inclusion of deception (see Activity 9)
- guilt, remorse, confession and the desire for restitution and liberation (see Activities 9, 16; 7.3.3)
- the nature of right and wrong (7.3.2)
- crime and punishment (see 7.3.1)
- how the text is structured, from crisis to order (see 7.4)
- the role of the narrator (see 7.4.4; 7.4.7)
- effects on readers (see 7.1.3; 7.4.5).

The novel could be read from the perspective of:

- value and the canon (see 9.3)
- narrative theory (see 7.3.1, Critical lens; 7.4; 9.4)
- feminist theory (see 7.4.7, Critical lens; 9.5)
- Marxist theory (see 7.6.2, Critical lens; 9.6).

ACTIVITY 16

Crime as freedom

Think about any texts you've read in your studies to date. In what ways is crime seen as an act of protest or liberation, or as a statement of independence?

7.3 Elements of crime writing

7.3.1 Crime and punishment

When a crime has been committed, people expect to see justice done - and by justice they often mean punishment. Political parties at general election time battle to appear 'tough on crime', and the redtop press are vocal against lenient sentences and 'weak' community service. Summary (and illegal) vengeance such as lynchings and tit-for-tat killings are a visceral form of punishment. The world of revenge tragedy, for instance, is full of this kind of punishment.

The literary critic, John Scaggs, points out that punishment is rarely found in classic detective fiction, which is interested in the commission of crime, its motives and its detection, but has little interest in looking beyond. Where punishment does occur in such texts, it tends to be either:

- summary and violent (e.g. suicide, death or maiming), or
- 'divine' intervention (e.g. insanity or 'accidental' deaths).

The classic detective novel is actually a very conservative form. It does not seek to challenge the status quo but to reinforce it so that readers can go to their beds in the safe knowledge that crime has been defeated.

ACTIVITY 17

Crime - aesthetics and ethics

For W.H. Auden, the solution of the crime is a moment of artistic resolution when the 'aesthetic' (outward appearance of the world) and 'ethical' (moral framework of that world) are realigned having been thrown out of joint by the commission of the original crime.

a How do you feel about this idea?

b Look at Table 7C and use it to identify examples and relevant quotations from the texts you've studied.

c Write a separate response to this idea for each text you've studied.

d Now write a longer response in which you explore comparisons and contrasts between the texts you've studied. Remember, you are free to challenge and disagree with Auden's proposition.

Table 7C

Text	Aesthetic dimension	Ethical dimension

In the real world, of course, punishment does matter.

- Criminals live beyond their crimes, serve their punishment and are released into society again.
- Victims of crime have to live with the personal and sometimes physical consequences of transgression.

These are areas that other literary texts often explore. In Fyodor Dostoevsky's *Crime and Punishment*, Raskolnikov seeks to commit the perfect undetectable crime. Dostoevsky plays with the detective genre; we know who the criminal is from the start. Our interest is not in the investigation of the murder but in the exploration of guilt. In Text 7J, Dostoevsky suggests that crime and its consequences are their own punishment.

Text 7J

What was taking place in him was totally unfamiliar, new, sudden, never before experienced. Not that he understood it, but he sensed clearly, with all the power of sensation, that it was no longer possible for him to address these people in the police station, not only with heartfelt effusions, as he had just done, but in any way at all, and had they been his own brothers and sisters, and not police lieutenants, there would still have been no point in this addressing them, in whatever circumstances of life.

Fyodor Dostoevsky, *Crime and Punishment*

Punishment is also of central concern in Oscar Wilde's *The Ballad of Reading Gaol*. Written in France when the poet was living in self-imposed exile following his release from gaol, the poem deals with the execution of Charles Robert Wooldridge for murdering his wife. Wilde swiftly moves away from a specific focus, however, and the poem becomes an exploration of punishment and the ways in which it brutalises both those who experience it and those who mete it out. The poem is an intensely personal and philosophical testimony of the effects of crime, punishment and guilt as Wilde sought to rebuild his own life.

Critical lens: narrative theory

Narrative theory encourages us to look at the endings of texts and consider the extent to which they resolve the questions and loose ends raised by the plot. Think about whether the endings of the texts you are studying provide a sense of resolution and completeness – or whether they leave certain questions unanswered.

See 9.4 for more on narrative theory

7.3.2 Right/wrong – good/evil

We have already seen how closely religious and social perspectives are involved in defining what constitutes crime. Right and wrong (social concepts) and good and evil (spiritual concepts) are powerful ideas.

In Graham Greene's *Brighton Rock*, the relationship of faith and crime comes to the fore. Ida Arnold holds firm to Old Testament principles of justice – an eye for an eye (Exodus 21: 24) – as she investigates Charles Hale's mysterious death. Ida has strong personal moral certainties based on principles of right and wrong. Pinkie (the leader of the gang that has murdered Hale) and Rose (his girlfriend, then wife), however, have both been brought up as Roman Catholics. For them the idea of transgression and punishment are much stronger concepts than they are for Ida. For Pinkie, for instance, sex poses more of a moral problem (is a greater 'crime') than murder. As Text 7K demonstrates, he and Rose are driven not by 'weak' moral compasses like right and wrong, but by what Greene sees as more powerful guides – good and evil.

Text 7K

'Why don't you lift a finger to stop him [Pinkie, Rose's husband] killing you?'

'He wouldn't do me any harm.'

'You're young. You don't know things like I do.'

'There's things *you* don't know.' …

'I know one thing you don't. I know the difference between Right and Wrong. They don't teach you *that* at school.'

Rose didn't answer; the woman was quite right; the two words meant nothing to her. Their taste was extinguished by stronger foods – Good and Evil. The woman could tell her nothing she didn't know about these – she knew by tests as clear as mathematics that Pinkie was evil – what did it matter in that case whether he was right or wrong?

Graham Greene, *Brighton Rock*

This is also a key distinction in works like *Crime and Punishment* and in *Hamlet*, where Hamlet refuses to exact his revenge on Claudius while Claudius is at prayer in case the 'good' of prayer should outweigh the 'right' act of revenge.

See 9.6.2 for more discussion of this scene in *Hamlet*

7.3.3 Guilt

Guilt is a concept naturally attached to the idea of crime. It is important in two ways.

- **Factual guilt:** juries return verdicts of 'guilty' or 'not guilty', according to their understanding of the established facts of a case. In a sense, this is also the function of crime writing. Such guilt is a purely factual state.

'You're young. You don't know things like I do.'
Graham Greene, *Brighton Rock*

- **Emotional guilt:** this relates to whether the perpetrators of crime feel remorse for their actions. Sometimes this also relates to the victims of crime - as in the notion of 'survivor guilt'.

Not all criminals, of course, feel guilt for their actions; sometimes they do not even see their actions as crimes. Terrorists, for instance, regard their actions as politically and socially justifiable and therefore may not associate them with any need for guilt. Sometimes criminals display shameless bravado: In Bram Stoker's *Dracula*, the Count shamelessly runs amok; Professor Moriarty in the Holmes stories is persistent (even strangely admirable) and shows no remorse for his crimes; the hard-nosed organised crime boss, Colleoni, in *Brighton Rock* contrasts starkly with the guilt-ridden Pinkie. These are perpetrators of crime who feel justified in their actions rather than suffering from guilt because of them.

By contrast, victims of crime sometimes suffer from feelings of guilt, as if they are somehow culpable. In Kate Atkinson's *When Will There Be Good News?*, Joanna, the only survivor of an attack in which her mother, sister and baby brother have been killed, suffers from a mixture of emotions, including guilt (see Text 7L).

Text 7L

Later, when it was dark, other dogs came and found her. A stranger lifted her up and carried her away. 'Not a scratch on her,' she heard a voice say. The stars and moon were bright in the cold, black sky above her head.

Of course, she could have taken Joseph with her, she could have snatched him from the buggy, or run with the buggy (Jessica would have). It didn't matter that Joanna was only six years old, that she would never have managed running with the buggy and that the man would have caught her in seconds, that wasn't the point. It would have been better to have tried to save the baby and been killed than not trying and living. It would have been better to have died with Jessica and her mother rather than being left behind without them. But she never thought about any of that, she just did as she was told.

'Run, Joanna, run,' her mother had commanded. So she did.

It was funny but now, thirty years later, the thing that drove her to distraction was that she couldn't remember what the dog was called. And there was no one left to ask.

Kate Atkinson, *When Will There Be Good News?*

Critical lens: eco-critical theory

Eco-critical theory invites us to consider how the natural world is used in literary texts. Although crime writing is often set in urban contexts, the horrific murder that opens *When Will There Be Good News?*, for instance, takes place on an isolated country lane and *The Murder of Roger Ackroyd* is set in a rural community. Think about the crime writing you've read. Where does crime take place? Do you perceive it differently according to whether the setting is urban or rural? In what ways? How do crime writers use these different contexts to create differing effects?

See 9.7 for more on eco-critical theory

It is also important to note the connection between legal guilt and religious guilt. This is neatly captured in this extract from Ian McEwan's novel *Atonement*. In Text 7M Briony, the central perspective of the novel, reflects on her actions as a child when she wrongly accused Robbie Turner of a sexual assault.

Text 7M

Her memories of the interrogation and signed statements and testimony, or of her awe outside the courtroom from which her youth excluded her, would not trouble her so much in the years to come as her fragmented recollection of that late night and summer dawn. How guilt refined the methods of self-torture, threading the beads of detail into an eternal loop, a rosary to be fingered for a lifetime.

Ian McEwan, *Atonement*

ACTIVITY 18

Guilty as charged?

Think about your crime reading or viewing. Draw up a list of examples of the different types of guilt that characters (both criminals and victims) feel. How would you explain the use that crime writers make of guilt as a concept? Gather a body of evidence, including quotations you might use to illustrate your argument.

Set text focus: *When Will There Be Good News?*

When Will There Be Good New? is the third of the Jackson Brodie novels, written in 2008. The author, Kate Atkinson's driving interest seems to be character, not the typical plot and 'picking up clues' of mainstream crime writing. In an interview with *The Scotsman* she said, 'If you write [characters] from the inside, you can avoid a lot of the clichés and home in on how people are feeling, how they see life.' This approach results in strong female characters and, in Brodie, a male private investigator who becomes so much more than a stock figure.

Although not an exhaustive list, the following elements of crime writing could be explored in relation to *When Will There Be Good News?*:

- settings of time and place (see 7.3.3, Critical lens)
- transgressions against law and order (see 7.1.1; 7.1.2; 7.3.2)
- the role of violence and murder (see 7.3.6)
- the role of guilt (see Activities 12, 14, 18; 7.3.3)
- creation of the criminal (see 7.3.5; 7.5.3)
- creation of the investigator or detective hero (see Activity 8; 7.5.1; 7.6.1; Activity 31)
- how the text is structured, from crisis to order (see Activity 12; 7.4)
- victims of crime (see 7.1.3; 7.3.1; 7.3.3)
- how language and register are used (see 7.2.7, Critical lens)
- effects on readers (see 7.1.3; 7.4.5).

The novel could be read from the perspective of:

- value and the canon (see 9.3)
- narrative theory (see 7.3.1, Critical lens; 7.4; 9.4)
- feminist theory (see 7.4.7, Critical lens; 7.6.1; 9.5)
- Marxist theory (see 7.5.1, Critical lens; 9.6)
- eco-critical theory (see 7.3.3, Critical lens; 9.7).

7.3.4 Crime and fear

Fear is a powerful emotion. In crime writing, fear often does not come from 'without' - it is not random acts of violence - but rather from 'within' - it is often preconceived and deliberately targeted or committed within intimate settings (e.g. the family or the home). Kate Summerscale's *The Suspicions of Mr Whicher* explores the infamous murder at Road Hill House, a true story of the murder of a four-year-old boy in his own home by one of his own family. This bears close relation to the 'locked room' murder of classic detective fiction where a seemingly impossible murder is solved by investigating the 'insiders' of the tale.

Henry James, reviewing the works of Mary Elizabeth Braddon, identifies the power of 'those most mysterious of mysteries, the mysteries that are at our own doors … the terrors of the cheerful country house, or the busy London lodgings'. He recognises the pleasant chill of fear when the criminal is brought into the realm of the familiar. The sensation novels of the 1860s in this sense represented a departure from the more distant 'crimes' of the classic gothic canon, bringing acts of crime and the perpetrators of crime to the hearth and home of Victorian England.

Exploring ghost stories

Henry James was the author of *The Turn of the Screw*. The ghost story, in which readers are guided to understand the incursion of the supernatural into the natural world, is a sub-genre of detective and crime writing.

The philosopher Henry Mansel recognised the significance of the sensation crime novels of the Victorian era. He described them as 'indications of a widespread corruption, of which they are in part both the effect and the cause: called into existence to satisfy the cravings of a diseased appetite, and contributing themselves to foster the disease, and to stimulate the want they supply'.

Robert Audley, the amateur detective in Braddon's *Lady Audley's Secret*, reflects on the effect of crime upon the investigator: 'but am I to be tormented all my life by vague doubts, and wretched suspicions, which may grow upon me till I become a monomaniac'. And he goes on to consider the impact of actually solving the crime: 'why should I try to unravel the tangled skein, to fit the pieces of the terrible puzzle, and gather together the stray fragments which when collected make such a hideous whole?' He identifies, as does Mansel, the loving-loathing relationship with crime that typifies the crime genre. T.S. Eliot separates the English crime novel from the writings of crime writers such as Edgar Allan Poe. The distinction he draws is clear: 'The detective story, as created by Poe, is something as specialized and intellectual as a chess problem; whereas the best English detective fiction has relied less on the beauty of the mathematical problem and much more on the intangible human element (from 'Wilkie Collins and Dickens').

7.3.5 Crime and madness

The connection of crime with madness is firmly established. Diminished responsibility on the grounds of loss of sanity is sometimes claimed in courts of law and is an important feature of much crime writing. In *Hamlet*, Shakespeare explores the relationship between sanity, insanity and vengeance, and in *Macbeth* Lady Macbeth, consumed by guilt for her role in the murder of King Duncan, goes mad. In Victorian times, crime and madness were closely connected and 'insanity' is also criminally used as a means of removing unwanted people (e.g. Anne Catherick in Collins' *The Woman in White*).

The connection is easily understood. If crime is a deviance from social norms, then any kind of deviance can be construed as insanity, because such acts cannot be seen as the acts of 'normal' and 'right-thinking' people. In *Lady Audley's Secret* by Mary Elizabeth Braddon, Lucy, Lady Audley defines her criminality in just such terms: '"Yes, a madwoman. When you say that I killed George Talboys, you say the truth. When you say that I murdered him treacherously and foully, you lie. I killed him because I AM MAD! because my intellect is a little way upon the wrong side of that narrow boundary-line between sanity and insanity."'

In *When Will There Be Good News?*, Kate Atkinson also deals with this idea. Detective Chief Inspector Louise Monroe says the following, speaking of the man who has murdered a mother and two of her three children in cold blood: '"The man who was convicted of her murder was called Andrew Dekker," Louise said. "He was declared fit to plead. If stabbing her mother and two children is sane then what's the definition of insane? Makes you wonder, doesn't it?"'

Here the detective voices the mantra that murderers must be *de facto* insane. This is to suppose, however, that criminal acts cannot be the end of a process of rational thought. It is 'safe' for society to write deviant criminal behaviour off as madness, especially where it is violent. It is important to remember that most criminal acts – even violent ones – are committed by perfectly sane people for reasons that they consider perfectly good.

ACTIVITY 19

Crime and insanity in poetry

Read 'The Laboratory' and 'Porphyria's Lover' by Robert Browning. In these poems, he demonstrates the perfect logic that a killer might apply in deciding to commit murder (although in 'Porphyria's Lover' it is rather different as the lover has already committed the murder). In what ways do the personae of these poems appear 'rational' and in what ways 'insane'?

Differently in *Hamlet*, but still closely exploring the intimate connection between sanity and insanity, Hamlet feigns madness in order to cover his path towards vengeance for his father's murder.

Exploring the panopticon

Bentham's panopticon was a means of allowing the guards in a prison to look out on all the prisoners who would be housed in cells surrounding the central panopticon. The 'panopticon' function in detective fiction is normally fulfilled by the all-seeing and all-wise detective whose superior mental functions allow him (and of recent times also her) to overcome the forces of evil, which are often equated with madness.

7.3.6 'Murder most foul'

In classic detective fiction, murder is the crime *par excellence* – nothing less will do. W.H Auden sets murder in a category all of its own as an offence against God and society, because: ' [m]urder is unique in that it abolishes the party it injures, so that society has to take the place of the victim and on his behalf demand restitution or grant forgiveness.'

The crime writer S.S. van Dine also humorously observes the essential presence of murder:

> 'No lesser crime than murder will suffice. Three hundred pages is far too much pother for a crime other than murder. After all, the reader's trouble and expenditure of energy must be rewarded. Americans are essentially humane, and therefore a tiptop murder arouses their sense of vengeance and horror. They wish to bring the perpetrator to justice; and when "murder most foul, as in the best it is," has been committed, the chase is on with all the righteous enthusiasm of which the thrice gentle reader is capable.'

Murder remains at the heart of most contemporary crime writing, whether on the page or on the screen. A substantial body of literature about crime exists, however, where murder is not the primary focus. The long poem 'Peter Grimes' from George Crabbe's *The Borough*, deals with the crimes of neglect and abuse as Grimes maltreats a sequence of apprentices purchased from London workhouses. Coleridge's 'The Rime of the Ancient Mariner' deals with the sailor's crime of slaying the albatross and the consequences he has to live with as a result. In other texts, such as Graham Greene's *Brighton Rock*, readers are faced with a criminal underworld of gangland violence and racketeering.

Set text focus: 'The Rime of the Ancient Mariner'

'The Rime of the Ancient Mariner' was first published in 1798 in *Lyrical Ballads*, which is often regarded as marking the beginning of English Romantic literature. Samuel Taylor Coleridge collaborated with William Wordsworth to present a new type of poetry. But rather than Wordsworth's emphasis on simple commonplace things and the plainness of common speech, Coleridge represented the world of the imagination and showed his respect for nature in strange, unsettling tales full of fantastic imagery, revelling in the musical effects of poetry. He later wrote that 'my endeavours should be directed to persons and characters supernatural, or at least Romantic' to embody 'a semblance of truth sufficient to procure … that willing suspension of disbelief… which constitutes poetic faith.'

Although not an exhaustive list, the following elements of crime writing could be explored in relation to 'The Rime of the Ancient Mariner':

- the type of text (see 7.2.5)
- settings of time and place (see 7.3.3, Critical lens)
- transgressions against law and order (see 7.1.1; 7.1.2; 7.2.1; 7.3.2)
- inclusion of murder (see 7.3.6)
- the role of resolution and punishment (see 7.3.1)
- guilt and remorse, confession and the desire for forgiveness (see 7.3.3)
- whether there is a moral and restoration of order (see 7.3.3)
- how the text is structured, from crisis to order (see 7.4)
- the role of the narrator (see 7.4.7)
- how poetic form is used (see 7.2.5)
- effects on readers (see 7.1.3; 7.4.5).

The poem could be read from the perspective of:

- value and the canon (see 9.3)
- narrative theory (see 7.3.1, Critical lens; 7.4; 9.4)
- eco-critical theory (see 7.3.3, Critical lens; 9.7).

'A building circular…
The prisoners in their cells,
occupying the circumference–
The officers in the centre'

Jeremy Bentham, 1798

Interestingly, while the earliest recognised example of the detective fiction form – Edgar Allan Poe's 'The Murders in the Rue Morgue' – involves the crime of murder, many of the earliest detective fictions do not. Wilkie Collins' famous sequence of novels deal with a variety of crimes, none of which is murder: *The Woman in White* (wrongful incarceration on the grounds of insanity and fraud), *No Name* (an attempt to overturn an unjust will), *Armadale* (deception) and *The Moonstone* (robbery). And as George Orwell in 'Raffles and Miss Blandish' points out, not all of the Sherlock Holmes stories deal with murder, and in fact several do not even deal with indictable crime.

7.4 Narrative form and plot devices in crime writing

It is important to think carefully about how literary texts are constructed. Different genres have different formal requirements and are structured according to varied sets of 'rules'. The same is true for crime writing texts. In the section that follows, several formal and structural issues are considered. Some of the examples given in this section are from traditional crime fiction texts, but it is important to bear in mind that you are studying texts that deal with crime in a variety of ways.

7.4.1 Circular narratives

It can often help to think about narrative structure in terms of shape. Figure 7E illustrates a typical circular 'shape' for crime narratives.

Figure 7E

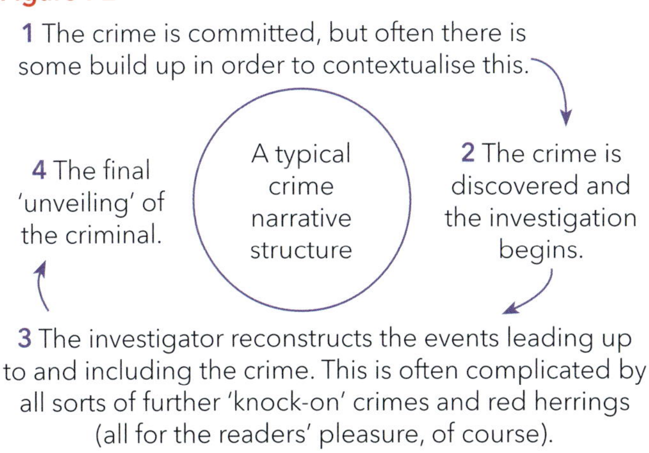

Critical lens: narrative theory

Think about the texts you've read that deal with crime. In what ways do they use this kind of circular narrative form? In what ways do they deviate from it? Do they use subplots either to parallel or to distract readers from the main plot? How is the use of subplots structured? In what ways does the author help you to make links between the subplot and the main plot, and in what ways conceal them?

See 9.4 for more on narrative theory

7.4.2 Dual narrative in crime writing

Crime writing usually incorporates two separate but interrelated narratives. This is outlined by Tzvetan Todorov in *The Poetics of Prose*. Crime narratives, he argues 'contain not one but two stories: the story of the crime and the story of the investigation'.

ACTIVITY 20

The two narratives of crime writing

Think back over any crime writing or viewing you have experienced to date.

a Select some of the texts you've studied and perhaps also a screen narrative you know particularly well.
b For each text, write two bullet point summaries – one for the 'story of the crime' and one for 'the story of the investigation'.
c Now think: in what ways are they distinct from each other? In what ways do they relate to each other?
d Develop your ideas into a spider plan responding to this question: 'Crime narratives contain not one, but two stories: the story of the crime and the story of the investigation.' How far is this true of the crime texts you have studied?
e Now use your spider plan to develop a full written response.

7.4.3 Bidirectional narrative

These related narratives tend to operate in opposite directions:

the narrative of the detection and investigation of the crime, which moves forward in time – from its first event (the discovery of the crime) to its final event (the detective's unmasking of the villain or perpetrator) →

← the narrative of the crime, which moves in a reverse direction backwards through time from its final event (the commission of the crime) through the reverse chain of intervening events to its first event (the motivation for the crime itself)

In *The Seville Communion*, Arturo Pérez-Reverte gives a fictional account of this kind of narrative method in a discussion between the detective, Father Lorenzo Quart, and César, in which the former comments on his methods of detection – in effect his reconstruction (or rewriting) of the already 'written' story of the crime (see Text 7N).

Text 7N

'It's called retrograde analysis.'

'What kind of analysis?'

'Retrograde. It involves taking a certain position on board as your starting point and then reconstructing the game backwards in order to work out how it got to that position. A sort of chess in reverse, if you like. It's all done by induction. You begin with the end result and work backwards to the causes.'

'Like Sherlock Holmes,' remarked Cesar, visibly interested.

'Something like that.'

Arturo Pérez-Reverte, *The Seville Communion*

As in any well-established genre, there is a danger that crime writing becomes formulaic, and detective stories often are. T.S. Eliot states this danger explicitly: 'The contemporary 'thriller' is in danger of becoming stereotyped; the conventional murder is discovered in the first chapter by the conventional butler, and the murderer is discovered in the last chapter by the conventional inspector – after having been already discovered by the reader.' Genres evolve and are refereshed by writers who challenge the rules.

ACTIVITY 21

Bending and breaking the rules

How far and in what ways do the ideas explored in this section relate to the texts you are studying? Look for examples of where writers have adopted the typical formal and structural elements of crime writing. Also look for places where authors have bent or broken the rules, or even where they have ignored the rules entirely. Why do you think they have done this? What effect is this likely to have upon readers?

7.4.4 'Rules' for the classic detective story

Table 7D lists some key 'rules' for Golden Age detective fiction summarised from writings by Ronald Knox and S.S. van Dine, both of whom were crime writers.

Crime writing, however, is not all detective fiction. Where writers employ the elements of crime writing for different purposes and in different ways, a much more generous range of material emerges.

ACTIVITY 22

Crime writing – a formula?

Look again at Todorov's, Eliot's, Knox's and van Dine's views and 'rules' of crime narratives. How far and in what ways do you think the crime writing that you've read or seen is formulaic? Where texts divert from the traditional formula, what is the impact on you as a reader?

7.4.5 Red herrings, MacGuffins and false trails

One of the major features of any crime narrative is the variety of ways in which writers and characters deceive and conceal. To keep the reader completely in the dark would be, of course, an act of unfair deception by the author – readers must stand at least a reasonable chance of understanding what the investigator understands. Information, in other words, must not be unreasonably withheld, and once the true solution of the crime is revealed, readers should be able to look back through events and see that they could have drawn the same conclusions as the investigator. That said, part of the pleasure of crime writing is the sense that we are dealing with a puzzle, and all good puzzles are hard to solve.

Table 7D

Knox	van Dine
The criminal must be someone mentioned in the early part of the story, but must not be anyone whose thoughts the reader has been allowed to follow.	The reader must have equal opportunity with the detective for solving the mystery.
No accident must ever help the detective, nor must he ever have an unaccountable intuition which proves to be right.	The author must not deceive the reader unless using deceptions legitimately played by the criminal on the detective.
All supernatural or preternatural agencies are ruled out as a matter of course.	Neither the detective nor any of the official investigators, should turn out to be the culprit.
The detective must not himself commit the crime.	The culprit must be determined by logical deductions – not by accident or coincidence or unmotivated confession.
The detective must not light on any clues that are not instantly produced for the inspection of the reader.	The problem of the crime must be solved by strictly naturalistic means. Such methods for learning the truth as slate-writing, ouija-boards, mind-reading, spiritualistic seances, crystal-gazing, and the like, are taboo.
The stupid friend of the detective must not conceal any thoughts which pass through his mind; his intelligence must be slightly, but very slightly, below that of the average reader.	Secret societies, camorras, mafias, et al., have no place in a detective story. A fascinating and truly beautiful murder is irremediably spoiled by any such wholesale culpability.
	The truth of the problem must at all times be apparent – provided the reader is shrewd enough to see it.

ACTIVITY 23

'Red herrings' and false trails

Writers about crime often mislead the reader: many crime texts involve 'red herrings' and false trails. These are a deliberate game played with the reader.

Drawing on your own reading and viewing, recount a variety of examples of methods that writers use to mislead their readers. How do you feel about each example?

Alfred Hitchcock, one of the greatest exponents of mystery and crime of the 20th century, insisted upon the importance of a plot device he called the **MacGuffin**.

Key terms

MacGuffin: a goal, desired object or motivator often pursued with little or no explanation

Exploring MacGuffins

On Open Culture, you can see a short video clip of Hitchcock defining a MacGuffin.

What 'MacGuffins' can you identify in the crime writing you've read, and how are they used?

Find and watch Hitchcock explain the MacGuffin via Cambridge Elevate

7.4.6 (Re)constructions of crime

One of the staple plot devices of crime writing is the staged reconstruction. In Agatha Christie's novel *The Murder of Roger Ackroyd*, Hercule Poirot stages a reconstruction of the events that surround Roger Ackroyd's death. He calls this a 'little comedy' and it is an explicit attempt to:

- prompt the memory of the participants
- stimulate guilt in the perpetrator of the crime.

Such reconstructions were not Christie's invention. In *Hamlet*, Hamlet uses the device of the play within the play to re-enact what he sees as the likely events surrounding the mysterious death of his father, Old Hamlet. The staging of the play, which Hamlet calls 'The Mouse-Trap' is an explicit attempt to 'catch the conscience of the king'. In *The Moonstone*, Wilkie Collins uses a similar reconstruction in order to demonstrate Franklin Blake's innocence in the theft of the diamond rather than proving his guilt.

Exploring connections

The Mousetrap is also the title of Agatha Christie's record-running play in the West End.

7.4.7 The teller of the tale

The figure of the narrator holds an interesting place in crime writing. Usually the telling of the tale lies with either:

- the detective - the first-person detective narratives of Bernie Gunther by the novelist Philip Kerr are an excellent example
- a third-person narrator close to the detective - as, for example, Dr Watson, the narrator of the Sherlock Holmes tales, or
- sometimes, as in the novels of Wilkie Collins or Bram Stoker's *Dracula*, the narrative is distributed between various characters involved in the tale.

This is not always the case, however. Sometimes the narrator is the criminal. Robert Browning's poems 'The Laboratory', 'My Last Duchess' and 'Porphyria's Lover' are all written from the criminal's perspective. As such, these poems take on something of the form of a confession. In 'The Laboratory' (see Text 7O), the narrator prepares to enact her revenge upon her lover's mistress.

Text 7O

Now that I, tying thy glass mask tightly,
May gaze thro' these faint smokes curling whitely,
As thou pliest thy trade in this devil's-smithy---
Which is the poison to poison her, prithee?
He is with her, and they know that I know
Where they are, what they do: they believe my tears flow
While they laugh, laugh at me, at me fled to the drear
Empty church, to pray God in, for them! – I am here.

Robert Browning, 'The Laboratory'

Similarly, the narrator of 'Porphyria's Lover' builds to his final admission in Text 7P.

Text 7P

all her hair
In one long yellow string I wound
Three times her little throat around,
And strangled her.

Robert Browning, 'Porphyria's Lover'

Critical lens: feminist theory

In 'My Last Duchess' and 'Porphyria's Lover', women are presented as both the cause and the victim of crime. In each case the narrative voice, however, is male. 'The Laboratory' is different, as one woman is the partial cause and another the perpetrator of the planned crime. Is it right and fair to say that the world of crime writing is a masculine world? How are males and females represented in the texts you've read? Are these representations prejudicial to women?

'Which is the poison to poison her, prithee?'
Robert Browning, 'The Laboratory'

See 9.5 for more on feminist theory

E.W. Hornung wrote a series of stories and one novel about the cricketer and gentleman thief Arthur J. Raffles. These tales are told from the criminal's eye view. This, of course, changes readers' perspective of the crime, as they are placed in the position of empathy with the criminal. A similar example can be found in the series of Flashman novels by George MacDonald Fraser. Agatha Christie's *The Murder of Roger Akroyd* provides a particularly interesting example of the criminal telling their own tale. The narrator of this murder mystery, Dr Sheppard, works closely alongside Hercule Poirot only to be revealed at the denouement as the murderer himself. Poirot has been invited to read the developing narrative of this self-appointed 'Watson' that, as Sheppard informs his readers in the final chapter, he had 'intended … to be published some day as the history of one of Poirot's failures!'

Exploring confession

It is interesting to consider confession in its religious sense. Where those who commit acts of crime feel guilt, this might lead to a religious confession, either in the confessional or its secular equivalent, the witness stand of a court, where confession of guilt might be made to a judge and jury. It is not necessary, however, to approach confession in its religious sense; instead, we can understand this as the criminal's need to voice guilt, even if only to a reader.

ACTIVITY 24

The criminal speaks

Confessions of this sort are often used in crime writing to provide us with an insight into the criminal's mind - to help us understand their motivations and actions.

a Think about the texts you have studied. How and in what ways are the criminal characters given 'voice'?

b Look closely at the criminal characters and think about how they speak about their actions. Do they at any point - either to themselves or to the investigator - make any kind of confession?

Set text focus: The Murder of Roger Ackroyd

When Agatha Christie started writing, in response to a challenge by her sister, detective fiction was a well-established genre with definite rules. However in 1926, her novel *The Murder of Roger Ackroyd*, although a classic in many ways, subverted some of those rules with an elegant twist that had a significant impact on the genre. The narrator was revealed as the killer, making it very difficult for the unsuspecting reader to solve the crime alongside the inimitable detective Hercule Poirot.

Although not an exhaustive list, the following elements of crime writing could be explored in relation to *The Murder of Roger Ackroyd*:

- the type of text (see 7.2.8, Golden Age…)
- settings of time and place (see 7.3.3, Critical lens)
- transgressions against law and order (see 7.1.2)
- inclusion of murder (see 7.3.6)
- detection and reconstruction of the crime (see 7.4.6)
- the role of resolution and punishment (see 7.3.1)
- the role of confession and guilt (see 7.3.3)
- creation of the criminal (see 7.5.3)
- creation of the detective hero and his sidekick (see Activity 8; 7.5.1; 7.5.2)
- how the text is structured, from crisis to order (see Activity 14; 7.4)
- the role of the narrator (see 7.4.7)
- effects on readers (see 7.1.3; 7.4.5).

The novel could be read from the perspective of:

- value and the canon (see 9.3)
- narrative theory (see 7.3.1, Critical lens; 7.4; 9.4)
- feminist theory (see 7.4.7, Critical lens; Activity 30; 9.5)
- Marxist theory (7.6.2, Critical lens; 9.6)
- eco-critical theory (7.3.3, Critical lens; 9.7).

c Plan an essay response in which you explore the different ways in which crime writers use the voice of the criminal and the idea of confession.

7.5 Character types in crime writing

7.5.1 The investigator

Investigators in crime writing come in three general categories.

- **Professional investigators:** often these are police officers or police detectives (e.g. D.I. Frost, Inspector Morse, Lieutenant Columbo or Detective Chief Inspector Louise Monroe), but sometimes a professional private investigator (e.g. Sherlock Holmes).
- **Interested and talented amateurs:** (e.g. Robert Audley in *Lady Audley's Secret*, Marion Halcombe and Walter Hartwright in *The Woman in White*, Father Brown, Gervase Fen, Lord Peter Wimsey, Hercule Poirot and Miss Marple, or Ida Arnold in *Brighton Rock*). These investigators are not driven by payment but by other personal motivations, perhaps related to specific crimes or perhaps more generally related to personal principles or interests. The motivations of these investigators vary:
  - Father Brown investigates crime out of his spiritual motivations as a priest - he wishes to find the criminals and to allow them the opportunity to repent of their actions.
  - Sherlock Holmes investigates out of a dual motivation - the desire to establish incontrovertible truth and the need to avoid his personal boredom.
  - Ida Arnold in *Brighton Rock* refuses to believe that Hale died of natural causes and goes on a personally motivated investigation of the unsatisfactory events surrounding his death.
  - In *Hamlet*, Hamlet, set on the trail of Claudius after a visit by the ghost of his dead father, investigates out of an obligation to avenge his father's murder; Polonius also acts as an investigator and is killed while spying on Hamlet and Gertrude behind the arras; Rosencrantz and Guildenstern are sent by Claudius to keep a close eye on Hamlet and to investigate his erratic behaviour.
- **'Hard-boiled' detectives emerging from the American detective tradition:** (e.g. Dashiel Hammett's Sam Spade and Continental Op, Raymond Chandler's Philip Marlowe, and Mickey Spillane's Mike Hammer - typically a right-wing, mysogynistic investigator who often himself (and it is almost always a 'he') engages in (semi-)criminal behaviour in unearthing the truth. More recent versions of this form can be found in the novels of Philip Kerr (Bernie Gunther) and Martin Cruz Smith (Arkady Renko).

Exploring investigators

Investigators of classic crime writing are often quite 'flat' characters who do not develop over time, even though they are typically the subject of long series of books. Agatha Christie, for instance, wrote 39 Poirot novels, and four collections of stories and 12 novels featuring Miss Marple; Edmund Crispin wrote 11 Gervase Fen books, including two sets of stories; Colin Dexter has written 12 Inspector Morse novels and one collection of stories. The detective's function is not to interest us as a character - if they did that too much they would take away from the primary interest - the crime they have to solve.

ACTIVITY 25

Private eyes and the police

Sometimes conflict exists between private investigators and the police. In 'The Murders in the Rue Morgue', 'The Mystery of Marie Roget' and 'The Purloined Letter', Auguste Dupin is pitted against the Paris police; in *Brighton Rock*, Ida Arnold finds herself in conflict with the police as she investigates Hale's death; Sherlock Holmes has a dubious relationship with Inspector Lestrade; and in *The Suspicions of Mr Whicher*, Kate Summerscale recounts the troubled relationship between Detective Whicher and the Somerset Police.

What other examples can you think of from your own reading and viewing? What effects does the writer achieve by these conflicts?

In the case of some detective novels (e.g. the Morse or the Frost novels - technically known as **police procedurals**), investigators are part of the established police force but the idea of conflict is still significant. The irascible and idiosyncratic detective with a tendency to bend or break the rules is set against the rigid procedures of the uniformed officers. Likewise Bernie Gunther, in Philip Kerr's entertaining series of crime novels set in and around Nazi Germany (and other examples of the hard-boiled criminal detective) finds himself in frequent collision with the demands of the authorities.

Key terms

police procedural: crime writing involving police detectives as opposed to private investigators or other self-appointed investigators

The ways in which investigators are presented is important. So readers believe in the capacity of the investigator – as a somehow superior being capable of solving mysteries that we could not – writers often adorn these figures with eccentric characteristics or interests.

- Sergeant Cuff has a passion for growing roses.
- Sherlock Holmes is a violin-playing recreational cocaine user.
- Inspector Morse is an avid Wagner fan.

Text 7Q shows how Dr Watson introduces Holmes in *A Study in Scarlet*.

Text 7Q

As the weeks went by, my interest in him and my curiosity as to his aims in life, gradually deepened and increased. His very person and appearance were such as to strike the attention of the most casual observer. In height he was rather over six feet, and so excessively lean that he seemed to be considerably taller. His eyes were sharp and piercing, save during those intervals of torpor to which I have alluded; and his thin, hawk-like nose gave his whole expression an air of alertness and decision. His chin, too, had the prominence and squareness that mark the man of determination. His hands were invariably blotted with ink and stained with chemicals, yet he was possessed of extraordinary delicacy of touch, as I frequently had occasion to observe when I watched him manipulating his fragile philosophical instruments.

Arthur Conan Doyle, *A Study in Scarlet*

Text 7R shows how G.K Chesterton introduces Father Brown, a vertically challenged, umbrella-wielding Roman Catholic priest-detective in 'The Blue Cross'.

Text 7R

The little priest was so much the essence of those Eastern flats [Essex]; he had a face as round and dull as a Norfolk dumpling; he had eyes as empty as the North Sea; he had several brown paper parcels, which he was quite incapable of collecting. … He had a large, shabby umbrella, which constantly fell on the floor. He did not seem to know which was the right end of his return ticket. He explained with a moon-calf simplicity to everybody in the carriage that he had to be careful, because he had something made of real silver "with blue stones" in one of his brown-paper parcels.

G.K Chesterton, 'The Blue Cross'

By stark contrast, Text 7S shows Philip Marlow introducing himself in *The Big Sleep*.

Text 7S

I was wearing my powder-blue suit, with dark blue shirt, tie and display handkerchief, black brogues, black wool socks and dark blue clocks on them. I was neat, clean, shaved and sober, and I didn't care who knew it. I was everything the well-dressed private detective ought to be. I was calling on four million dollars.

Raymond Chandler, *The Big Sleep*

Different again is the way Graham Greene draws Ida Arnold in Text 7T.

Text 7T

Ida blew into the police-station with a laugh to this man and a wave of the hand to that. She didn't know them from Adam. She was cheerful and determined, and she carried Phil along in her wake.

'I want to see the inspector,' she told the sergeant at the

'I was neat, clean, shaved and sober, and I didn't care who knew it.'

Raymond Chandler, *The Big Sleep*

desk. 'He's busy, ma'am. What was it you wanted to see him about?'

'I can wait,' Ida said, sitting down between the police capes. 'Sit down, Phil.' She grinned at them all with brassy assurance. 'Pubs don't open till six,' she said. 'Phil and I haven't anything to do till then.'

'What was it you wanted to see him about, ma'am?'

'Suicide,' Ida said, 'right under your noses and you call it natural death.'

The sergeant stared at her, and Ida stared back. Her large clear eyes (a spot of drink now and then didn't affect them) told nothing, gave away no secrets. Camaraderie, good nature, cheeriness fall like shutters before a plate-glass window. You could only guess at the goods behind: sound old-fashioned hallmarked goods, justice, an eye for an eye, law and order, capital punishment, a bit of fun now and then, nothing nasty, nothing shady, nothing you'd be ashamed to own, nothing mysterious.

Graham Greene, *Brighton Rock*

Critical lens: Marxist theory

Social distributions of power play an important part in Marxist theory. Think about the relationship between the police sergeant and Ida Arnold in the extract from *Brighton Rock* in Text 7T. Who should have power? Who in fact seems to have power? How does Greene use these ideas to create effect? Think about how ideas of power and the subversion of power relate more widely to the world of crime writing.

See 9.6 for more on Marxist theory

ACTIVITY 26

Presenting investigators

Reread Texts 7Q, 7R, 7S and 7T. Comment in detail on the ways in which the writers present their investigators. You may wish to comment on their use of these points - and more:

a language
b 'voice'
c physical detail
d surroundings.

7.5.2 The investigator's sidekick

The investigator's sidekick is another important figure: Holmes has Watson, Morse has Lewis, Poirot has Hastings. Sometimes this sidekick serves as a foil for developing ideas and sometimes emphasises, by their bumbling inefficiency, the brilliance of the detective. The investigator, however, cannot always be right, in spite of Poirot's inflated claims in *The Murder of Roger Ackroyd*, that he understands everything. Investigators often fall prey to incorrect assumptions, deliberate deception, 'red herrings', personal failings and so on, and when that happens the sidekick often comes to the rescue. As T.S. Eliot observes, 'the best heroes of English detective fiction have been, like Sergeant Cuff, fallible; they play their part, but never the sole part in the unravelling'. So Dr Sheppard, narrator of *The Murder of Roger Ackroyd*, comments on the roles of the respective characters in piecing together the investigation of the murder: 'Everyone had a hand in the elucidation of the mystery. It was rather like a jig-saw puzzle to which everyone contributed their own little piece of knowledge or discovery. But their task ended there. To Poirot alone belongs the renown of fitting their pieces into their correct place.'

As Poirot insists, '[e]verything is simple, if you arrange the facts methodically'.

7.5.3 The criminal

Criminals hold an interesting role in crime writing. They are first and foremost the opposite number of investigators. The investigator represents 'law' and 'right', whereas the criminal represents 'illegality' and 'wrong'. The distinction between these two character types is not always so easily defined, however. Investigators in crime writing can often be quite unappealing characters, while the criminal can (and often does) have a devil-may-care charm.

ACTIVITY 27

Criminals and investigators

Take two or three crime texts you have read or watched and know very well. For each text, write two lists of characteristics: one for the criminals and one for the investigators.

In what ways are these two lists different? Are there any characteristics that appear on both lists? Are there some texts you've read where the distinction between the two lists is very stark? Are there any where there is little (if any) difference? What does this suggest about these texts and their relationship with crime?

In much of what is called '**hard-boiled**' crime fiction, the distinction between criminals and detectives is rather blurred. George Orwell in his essay 'Raffles and Miss Blandish' explores this idea: 'It is implied … that being a criminal is only reprehensible in the sense that it does not pay. Being a policeman pays better, but there is no moral difference, since the police use essentially criminal methods.'

He goes on to argue later in the essay: 'Today no one would think of looking for heroes and villains in a serious novel, but in lowbrow fiction one still expects to find a sharp distinction between right and wrong and between legality and illegality.'

Text 7U shows how the criminal in Kate Atkinson's novel *When Will There Be Good News?* is first introduced to us – a random and unexplained incursion of violence into an apparently idyllic country walk.

Text 7U

He seemed to come out of nowhere. They noticed him because the dog growled, making an odd, bubbling noise in his throat that Joanna had never heard before.

He walked very fast towards them, growing bigger all the time. He was making a funny huffing, puffing noise. You expected him to walk past and say 'Nice afternoon,' or 'Hello,' because people always said that if you passed them in the lane or on the track, but he didn't say anything. Their mother would usually say, 'Lovely day,' or 'It's certainly hot, isn't it?' when she passed people but she didn't say anything to this man. Instead she set off walking fast, pushing hard on the buggy. She left the plastic bags of shopping on the grass and Joanna was going to pick them up but her mother said, 'Leave it.' There was something in her voice, something in her face that frightened Joanna. Jessica grabbed her by the hand and said, 'Hurry up, Joanna,' sharply, like a grown-up. Joanna was reminded of the time their mother threw the blue-and-white-striped jug at their father.

Kate Atkinson, *When Will There Be Good News?*

Key terms

hard-boiled: a type of crime writing typically involving explicit violence in murky urban settings and where the distinction between criminality and the law is quite blurred

By contrast, consider Text 7V, a rather different passage from Charles Dickens' novel *Oliver Twist* (1838) in which Bill Sikes and Fagin, the two criminal villains of the piece, discuss a potential theft at Chertsey in the presence of Bill's girlfriend, Nancy.

Text 7V

'It's cold, Nancy dear,' said the Jew, as he warmed his skinny hands over the fire. 'It seems to go right through one,' added the old man touching his side.

'It must be a piercer, if it finds its way through your heart,' said Mr. Sikes. 'Give him something to drink, Nancy. Burn my body, make haste! It's enough to turn a man ill, to see his lean old carcase shivering in that way, like a ugly ghost just rose from the grave.'

'Everything is simple, if you arrange the facts methodically.'

Agatha Christie, *The Murder of Roger Ackroyd*

Nancy quickly brought a bottle from a cupboard, in which there were many: which, to judge from the diversity of their appearance, were filled with several kinds of liquids. Sikes pouring out a glass of brandy, bade the Jew drink it off.

'Quite enough, quite, thankye, Bill,' replied the Jew, putting down the glass after just setting his lips to it.

'What! You're afraid of our getting the better of you, are you?' inquired Sikes, fixing his eyes on the Jew. 'Ugh!'

With a hoarse grunt of contempt, Mr. Sikes seized the glass, and threw the remainder of its contents into the ashes: as a preparatory ceremony to filling it again for himself: which he did at once.

The Jew glanced round the room, as his companion tossed down the second glassful; not in curiosity, for he had seen it often before; but in a restless and suspicious manner habitual to him. It was a meanly furnished apartment, with nothing but the contents of the closet to induce the belief that its occupier was anything but a working man; and with no more suspicious articles displayed to view than two or three heavy bludgeons which stood in a corner, and a 'life-preserver' that hung over the chimney piece.

Charles Dickens, *Oliver Twist*

As you read a variety of texts dealing with crime, think about the ways in which criminals are portrayed. In some of these texts, the 'crime' may not necessarily be an infringement of the law - it may be a moral, religious or personal infringement instead.

7.6 Representation in crime writing

It is interesting in concluding to think about some of the key issues of representation in crime writing.

7.6.1 Gender representation

Female investigators

The representation of women in crime writing is an important issue. Frequently women are portrayed as victims, but it is rarer to find females as major characters within the form. The figure of the investigator tends to be male - we can all easily reel off the names of countless male detectives - but with a few notable exceptions there is a distinct lack of well-known female detectives. Even where female detectives have become more common in the late 20th and 21st centuries, male detective figures still dominate the public imagination.

Set text focus: *Oliver Twist*

Charles Dickens experienced the appalling working conditions of the working class, and especially children, at first hand when, at 12 years old, he had to work in a blacking factory (which made boot polish) for a few months. That experience made a lasting impression and later work as a court reporter and journalist kept him informed about the living and working conditions of the poor. He was very disillusioned by 19th century society's punitive views about the poor, and at the ineffectual attempts to improve their conditions, and explored these injustices in *Oliver Twist* and other novels.

Although not an exhaustive list, the following elements of crime writing could be explored in relation to *Oliver Twist*:

- settings of time and place (see 7.3.3, Critical lens)
- transgressions against law and order (see 7.1.1; 7.1.2; 7.3.2)
- guilt and remorse (see 7.3.3)
- creation of the criminal and their motivation (see 7.5.3; 7.6.3; Activity 31)
- inclusion of violence and murder (see 7.2.5; 7.3.6)
- whether there is a moral and restoration of order (see 7.3.3)
- social consequences of crime (see 7.2.5)
- how the text is structured, from crisis to order (see 7.4)
- effects on readers (see 7.1.3; 7.4.5).

The novel could be read from the perspective of:

- value and the canon (see 9.3)
- narrative theory (see 7.3.1, Critical lens; 9.4)
- feminist theory (see 7.4.7, Critical lens; Activity 29; 9.5)
- Marxist theory (see 7.5.1, Critical lens; 7.6.2, Critical lens; 9.6)
- eco-critical theory (see 7.3.3, Critical lens; 9.7)
- post-colonial theory (see 7.6.3; 9.8).

ACTIVITY 28

Female investigators

Figure 7F is a diagram naming some well-known female investigators - some from conventional crime fiction, some from other writing dealing with crime. Add the names of any other female investigators you have come across.

Are there any ways in which the female investigators differ from their male counterparts? If so, why do you think this is the case? If not, does it matter that writers of crime do not make distinctions between male and female investigators?

Exploring female writers of Victorian detective fiction

Marion Halcombe is not the only example of the female detective in Victorian fiction - see *Sisters in Crime* the interesting anthology of short stories by female authors, some of which present women detectives.

Figure 7F

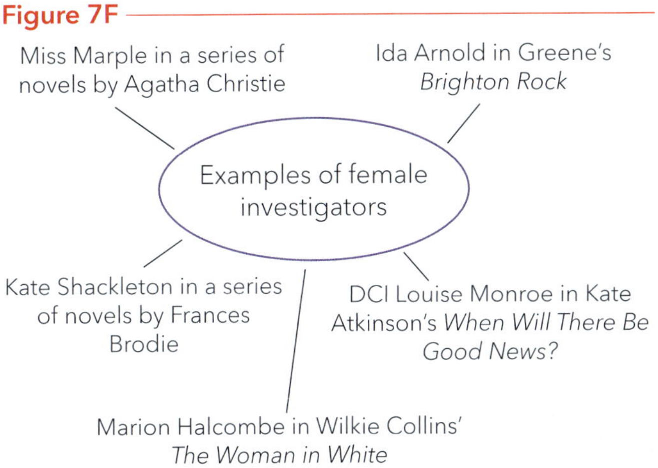

Misogyny in crime writing

Another important question to consider is misogyny. This is particularly evident in 'hard-boiled' detective fiction, where the male detective figure is often overtly sexist in his attitudes and where women are often subjected to criminal mistreatment. The representation of women as powerless victims and of males as the perpetrators of crime is an important issue to consider. In the classic canon of gothic fiction, for instance, it is often women who are the victims of abuse and crime - think of the heroines of Anne Radcliffe's gothic romances. An alternative issue is the representation of delinquent women and the additional horror that seems to attach to their criminal actions simply because they are women, as in Collins' representation of Lydia Gwilt (note the pun on Guilt) in *Armadale*, or the speaker in Browning's 'The Laboratory'.

ACTIVITY 29

Women in crime writing

Think about your own reading and viewing of crime writing.

a In what ways do female characters tend to be used?
b In what ways is their role important?
c Are they represented in positive or negative ways?
d In what ways do they hold power and in what ways are they disempowered?
e Is this different to the representation of males? If so, how?

Male and female 'voice' in crime writing

It is always important to consider the role of male and female 'voice' in literary texts, as it is central to issues of gender representation. In relation to this unit, it is important to think about the predominance of the 'male' voice in much crime writing. This is especially evident in the first- person narratives of much 'hard-boiled' crime fiction, where the predominant perspective of the narrative is male and where male issues seem to dominate.

Watch tutorial video, Women in Crime Writing, on Cambridge Elevate

ACTIVITY 30

Women crime writers

In some cases the female authors named in Figure 7G are the creators of female detectives, but in other cases they write male detectives. What do you make of this? Does it matter? How does this affect your view of male and female 'voice' in crime writing?

Figure 7G

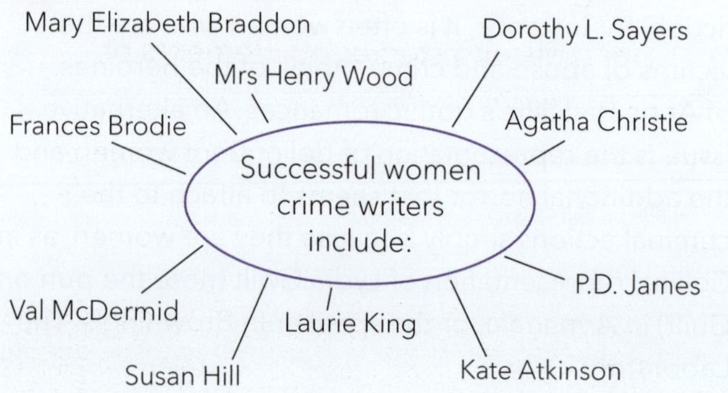

7.6.2 Social class and function

The representation of social class and function is another interesting issue to consider. As we explored earlier, detective figures are often somehow set apart.

- Father Brown is a priest.
- Cadfael is a monk.
- Miss Marple is a woman.
- Hercule Poirot is Belgian.
- Sherlock Holmes is an eccentric genius.

Social function is, therefore, one means by which writers distinguish their detective figures. Another way they achieve this is through social class. The upper-class male detective is a well-known character in much classic crime writing. Think, for example, about Lord Peter Wimsey, the aristocratic hero of Dorothy L. Sayers' novels or of Gervase Fenn, the well-heeled English don who stars in a sequence of novels by Edmund Crispin.

It is also interesting to think about how this relates to the perpetrators of crime. How are these people set apart? Again social function and social class are often used to do this. Francis Davey, the central criminal figure in Daphne du Maurier's *Jamaica Inn*, for example, is a vicar. Count Dracula in *Dracula* is, as his title suggests, an aristocrat. Many of the central villains of the gothic canon are aristocrats who abuse their position. Sir Hugo Baskerville is the perpetrator of a brutal historical killing that paves the way for Stapleton's crime in *The Hound of the Baskervilles*. Heathcliff, a character of dubious social roots who has become a gentleman, is the towering central figure of *Wuthering Heights* by Emily Brontë.

Critical lens: Marxist theory

A key focus of Marxist literary theory is the relationship between social classes and their respective functions in society. Characters in texts dealing with crime are frequently divided along lines of social class. How do the texts you're studying deal with issues of social class? What functions do different social classes play in the narrative? How and in what ways does this affect the ways in which you read texts dealing with crime?

See 9.6 for more on Marxist theory

ACTIVITY 31

Detectives, criminals and society

Detectives and criminals in crime writing are often set apart from the majority of humanity.

a Think back over your reading and viewing. In what ways are detective figures and criminals set apart from the rest of society?

b Are there any examples of detectives and criminals who are portrayed as normal people? If so how does this have an impact on your perceptions as a reader?

c Draft a written response exploring the ways in which authors use social class and function within crime writing.

7.6.3 Ethnicity

Representation of ethnicity is also important in crime writing. We have seen that detective figures and criminals are often distinguished from the rest of society. Because of this, we need to think about how ethnicity as a distinguishing feature is treated in crime writing.

As with the representation of women, ethnicity has sometimes been pejoratively used within crime writing. Criminal outsiders are sometimes distinguished by ethnicity, as in these examples.

- Tom Robinson in *To Kill a Mockingbird* is assumed by many of the white population of the town to be guilty of an attack on Mayella Ewell simply because he is black, and indeed he is convicted by a court in a sham trial.

- Othello becomes the victim of racially motivated crime at the hands of his servant Iago.
- Shylock and the Jewish race he represents in *The Merchant of Venice* is perceived as criminal because of his lending of money at interest and is himself the victim of abuse solely on account of his ethnicity.
- Fagin, the disturbingly comic child gang-master in Dickens' *Oliver Twist*, is frequently identified as 'the Jew'.
- The Count in *Dracula* comes from Transylvania, a remote area of Romania, and he is closely associated with the gypsies, another frequently mistrusted ethnic group.

Critical lens: post-colonial theory

Post-colonial theory encourages us to consider the ways in which ethnicity is used in literary texts – how it marks particular characters out as 'other'. As you read texts dealing with crime, think about the characters' ethnicity. Are there characters from a variety of ethnic groups? If not, does this matter? If there are, what function do these characters play in the text and how are they presented? Look at the kinds of language used by other characters when referring to characters from different ethnic backgrounds.

See 9.8 for more on post-colonial theory

ACTIVITY 32

Representation of ethnicity in crime writing

Think back over your crime reading and viewing.

a In what ways are characters of different racial and ethnic backgrounds represented?

b Are they represented positively or negatively?

c Can you recall any investigators who come from minority ethnic groups?

d How do you respond to this?

7.7 Bringing it all together

7.7.1 How will your studies on Elements of Crime Writing be assessed?

Elements of Crime Writing is one of the two options for A Level Paper 2. Your knowledge will be tested by exam.

For guidance on preparing for the exams, see Unit 11

7.7.2 How much do you know?

These questions ask you to bring together the elements you have studied in this unit.

1 Write notes on your responses to these key concepts:
   - what constitutes crime?
   - guilt in crime writing
   - punishment in crime writing
   - confession in crime writing
   - concealment in crime writing
   - transgression in crime writing
   - social and religious views of crime
   - investigation in crime writing
   - mercy in crime writing.

2 Identify how the concepts listed in question 1 are used in the crime writing texts you are studying, but also range more widely in your reading and viewing of crime texts. Develop your ideas in more extended prose, summarising how these issues relate to your understanding of the functions of crime writing.

3 Some of these concepts appear more often than others. Consider why this might be. What does this suggest about the reasons why writers produce crime texts and the reasons why readers read them? Develop your ideas in the form of extended prose.

4 Read 'The Laboratory' by Robert Browning. How does the poet use language to provide us with an insight into the mind of the criminal?

Consider each of these quotations in turn. How far is each true of the variety of crime texts you have studied and of your wider understanding of crime writing?

7.7.3 Assessment objectives

In relation to the assessment objectives, this unit has explored:

- how you as a reader can make personal, informed and creative responses to crime writing. It has also introduced you to a variety of terminology and key concepts relating to the idea of crime and to associated ideas. These will help you in your thinking about a variety of crime writing texts both traditional and non-traditional (AO1)
- a variety of ways in which authors working in variety of genres shape meanings in texts dealing with crime. It has introduced you to conventions and techniques within crime writing, including structural and formal properties (AO2)
- the development of writing about crime from its appearance in the earliest literary texts through to the contemporary, introducing some key social, religious and literary contexts that underpin texts dealing with crime, and including the development of crime writing as a form in the mid-19th century (AO3)
- the key elements of crime writing across a wide range of literary works in each of the major genres - poetry, drama and prose fiction - and relating it to other narrative forms, such as literary non-fiction and writing for the screen (AO4)
- the roles of interpretation and analysis in reading crime writing. It has also considered questions relating to the literary and cultural value of some crime writing texts (AO5).

Summary

In this unit, you have learned about:

- the way crime writing is approached in a variety of genres
- the development of crime writing over time
- key elements of crime writing and the key concepts that crime writing addresses
- how the authors of literary texts use different elements of crime writing in their works
- narrative structure and form in crime writing
- voices, perspectives and representation in crime writing.

DEVELOPING

8

Political and social protest writing

In this unit, you will:

- find out about major concepts surrounding politics and social protest
- explore how writers in a variety of genres have examined political issues and social protest
- develop your abilities to think critically about literary representations of political issues and social protest

Set text focus

Elements of Political and Social Protest Writing is one of the options in the Texts and Genres component for A Level. The set texts for this option are listed here. To see how these texts might fit into your course, look back at the Introduction to this book.

A Level
The Handmaid's Tale by Margaret Atwood
Songs of Innocence and of Experience by William Blake
Harvest by Jim Crace
Hard Times by Charles Dickens
Selected poems by Tony Harrison: 'v', 'National Trust', 'Them and [uz]', 'Divisions', 'Working', 'Marked with D'
The Kite Runner by Khaled Hosseini
A Doll's House by Henrik Ibsen (translated by Michael Meyer)
Henry IV Part I by William Shakespeare

8.1. Introduction to political and social protest writing

Politics and political issues – for instance power and powerlessness, government and social control, protest and rebellion, and war – are at the heart of a great deal of English – and world – literature, and have been since the earliest known texts.

As you work through this unit, you'll develop an understanding of how authors across time have returned to concepts related to political and social protest writing, protest and power, and the impact of such issues on individuals and society more broadly. This will provide you with a variety of lenses through which to read texts dealing with political and social protest writing, although not all will be present in all texts. Writers work creatively within literary genres, so don't be surprised to find that texts you study play with, directly challenge or even totally ignore some of the elements of political writing we will explore. Writers and the texts they produce all exist in a context, and the same is true of readers. As a student of literature, you are involved in a process of recreating meaning from literary texts, and exploring the ways in which writers and readers work in context will help you to think about different ways in which texts are produced and received.

Watch tutorial video, Political and Social Protest Writing, on Cambridge Elevate

ACTIVITY 1

Thinking about concepts

a Think about these elements:
- power and powerlessness
- equality and inequality
- freedom and slavery
- democracy and corruption
- war and peace
- protest and rebellion
- government and law
- patriotism and nationalism

b Try to define what these concepts mean to you.

8.1.1 Politics and social protest in literature

Exploration of the workings of power in society dates back to many of the most ancient literary works in Western culture:

- The Bible frequently deals with political issues and contexts, such as the way in which the kings of the biblical lands used their power, and the way in which popular leaders such as Moses and Jesus challenged it.
- In Ancient Greece, a central focus of many tragedies is the power of kings over their people and power struggles within social elites.

This trend continues in many of the great texts of English literature:

- In *Beowulf*, we see the power structures of an Anglo-Saxon community in which kings, tribes and warriors play a significant part.
- Shakespeare's history plays follow the politics of Britain throughout the medieval age, focusing particularly on ideas about the nature of leadership and kingship.
- Jonathan Swift's famous work *Gulliver's Travels*, often thought of as a children's book, is in fact a complex exploration of different social and political theories.
- The work of the Romantic poets was often inspired by and portrayed the plight of the poor and powerless in society.
- Modern political novels and drama range across many different aspects of politics, often depicting the way in which political issues and struggles impact on individual lives.

This unit draws on many examples of political writing. As you read, you will be introduced to a wide range of ideas and concerns that underlie the representation of politics in literature and how this relates to a range of social and political issues.

ACTIVITY 2

What do you already know about political and social protest writing?

Think back over your study of literature to date, and over your own personal reading and viewing. What stories, novels, plays, poetry, films, TV series and other kinds of writing have you come across that deal with politics?

a How many of them depict the work of governments and politicians?

b How many involve kings, queens, dictators and other unelected leaders?

c How many depict the oppression or struggle for freedom or rights of particular groups of people?

d How many focus more on political *issues* than on politicians and political institutions?

8.1.2 What constitutes politics?

Often, when we speak of politics, we mean the world of government, parliament and politicians – the people and institutions who make decisions about laws, taxes, schools, health and so on. However, politics also is concerned with the many and varied ways in which power operates within society, beyond the daily workings of government and politicians. There is not always agreement about exactly what is and is not political – but the use and distribution of *power* in society is always a central issue in politics and social protest.

Exploring the personal and the political

'The personal is political' is a phrase that became popular in the 1960s, a time when many groups in society were protesting against social injustice and fighting for their rights – women, black people, gay people, and so on. The phrase expresses the idea that we make political statements daily by the way we choose to live our lives. It also reminds us that our personal lives are affected by politics and that we as individuals have the power to exercise our political rights.

ACTIVITY 3

What is political?

Many people would claim to have little or even no interest in politics. However, as we have seen, the personal and the political are often related, and we all confront issues of power and politics in our daily lives. In what ways do you think the following aspects of our lives might be seen as political?

a The way we react to our own – or other people's – class, race, gender or sexuality, and the kind of language we use to talk about these things.

b The choices we make about whether or not to comply with laws or social conventions.

c The choices we make about where to shop, what to buy, how to eat, how to dress, how to dispose of waste, which schools and hospitals to use and so on.

d The social causes we choose to support.

Power and leadership: government, tyranny, royalty, nationhood, war

One key concern of politics is the institutional structures of power, leadership and government. How are leaders made, chosen or elected? What makes a good leader? What makes a tyrant? How are governments formed? How can a government be a force for good or evil? What is the role of royalty in leading a nation? How are nations defined and to what extent are they a force for good? To what extent are wars just or necessary instruments of national or international power?

ACTIVITY 4

Power and leadership

Think carefully about each of the questions in the section 'Power and leadership'. How do you think they are relevant to current or recent political events, either in Britain or in the world more generally?

Power and the people: freedom, democracy, equality, protest, rebellion

Another main concern of politics is the relationship between those in power and the people they lead. What kinds of freedom should all individuals expect? To what extent do individuals have the freedom to participate in politics, by exercising democratic rights such as the right to vote or to protest? To what extent does the government or political system treat individuals and groups of people fairly and justly, without discrimination? To what extent does the government of a nation act to protect and help its citizens? To what extent is the legal system fair? What happens when the people rebel against unjust leadership?

ACTIVITY 5

Politics and protest

Social protest is a crucial means of bringing about change in society, presenting views that often run counter to the conventional political wisdom of their times. Look closely at these quotations, all from well-known social protestors. What messages do their words seem to convey? In what ways do they seem to challenge conventional political wisdom? In what ways are their views challenging and/or threatening?

- 'The fundamental values of a democracy cannot be changed because we are provoked by terrorists.' (Shami Chakrabarti, civil rights activist)
- 'Power is of two kinds. One is obtained by the fear of punishment and the other by acts of love. Power based on love is a thousand times more effective and permanent than the one derived from fear of punishment.' (Gandhi, Indian political leader)
- 'Nobody can give you freedom. Nobody can give you equality or justice or anything. If you're a man, you take it.' (Malcolm X, American black community leader)

Social protest is a crucial means of bringing about change in society

- 'There really can be no peace without justice. There can be no justice without truth. And there can be no truth, unless someone rises up to tell you the truth.' (Louis Farrahkan, leader of the Nation of Islam)

How do you respond to what they say?

Check your responses in the Ideas section on Cambridge Elevate

8.1.3 Politics, social protest and literature: changing the world?

The issues mentioned in 8.1.2 will be central to your study of political and social protest writing - and you will find that there are many different kinds of literature dealing with them. Some literature is explicitly political writing about political movements and beliefs, governments and the institutions of power. Much other literature, however, is political in a more personal way, often dealing with the plight of individuals who are powerless in the face of injustice, and showing how politics and the individual are connected.

A major issue that you will encounter often is the extent to which political and social protest writing can itself affect politics and help to create a better world. Literature is a hugely powerful and influential medium for the communication of important ideas about society and politics, and has provided inspiration to politicians and ordinary citizens throughout history. How and to what extent does it have the power to actually change society?

ACTIVITY 6

Literature and politics

Think about these questions.

a In what ways do you think literature has the power to change society? To what extent do you think literature can help to determine people's social and political beliefs?

b On many occasions in history, governments or authorities have tried to ban works of literature. Why do you think this might be?

8.2 Development of political and social protest writing

In this part of the unit, we explore the different ways that writers of poetry, drama and the novel have written about politics and social protest, from the classical era to the present day.

8.2.1 Politics and social protest in classical narratives

Ancient Greece - especially Athens - is considered the birthplace of modern ideas about democracy. The rise of democracy in Athens coincided exactly with the development of drama, so it's not surprising that Greek tragedy and comedy are frequently concerned with ideas about politics.

The political concerns of Greek tragedy can be seen particularly in the relationship between the **choruses** and the heroes of the plays. The earlier epic poems of Homer - *The Odyssey* and *The Iliad* - present the heroes of Greek history as brave adventurers. In tragedy, however, those same heroes are treated as powerful ruling figures whose actions directly affect the welfare of the people, with the chorus expressing the communal fears of the citizens about what will happen as a consequence of those actions.

This strong sense of a relationship between powerful leaders and powerless citizens **foreshadows** the concerns of much political writing through the centuries, notably perhaps Shakespeare's history plays, in which the playwright contrasts powerful figures - kings and princes - with the ordinary people who are caught up in their wars - most famously, perhaps, in *Henry V*.

Key terms

chorus: a group of people who appear on stage between the main episodes of the play to narrate and interpret certain aspects of the plot

foreshadowing: a technique in which narrative refers to something that has not yet happened but will happen later

Satire, commenting on a range of social and political issues, was also popular in classical times. One of the earliest explicitly political writers in Western literature was the Greek playwright Aristophanes, whose satirical comedies commented on the nature of government and the work of politicians and other leading figures. His play *Lysistrata* imagines what might happen if women took over Athens, an early example of a play exploring issues of gender equality and social protest.

Key terms

satire: use of humour, irony, exaggeration or ridicule to expose and criticise foolishness or vice, especially in relation to contemporary topical issues and politics

For more on Aristophanes' play, Lysistrata, see 6.2.1

8.2.2 Politics and social protest in medieval narratives

Social structures and power relationships are key issues in many medieval English texts. *Beowulf*, for instance, explores what happens when the well-ordered world of Hrothgar's court is thrown into disarray by the attacks of the monster Grendel and his mother. The Arthurian legends and related texts, such as *Sir Gawain and the Green Knight* and Malory's *Le Morte d'Arthur,* explore central medieval values such as kingship, loyalty and chivalry.

Literature (and literacy) were largely the preserve of the upper classes at this time. Therefore, explicitly political texts and works representing the point of view of the mass of society are rare. One exception is William Langland's long poetic narrative *Piers Plowman*, a satire on medieval society written from the perspective of a labouring man. Chaucer also made use of working people, such as the miller and the cook, in *The Canterbury Tales*.

Religious authority was also central to medieval society. The Church in England was led by the Pope in Rome, and this posed a potential threat to the powers of the English monarchy and aristocracy. Perhaps for this reason, priests and religious authority were often satirised in medieval literature, as in both *Piers Plowman* and *The Canterbury Tales*.

ACTIVITY 7

Politics, religion and literature

a What contemporary examples of the role of religion in politics can you think of, either in Britain or internationally?

b In which works of literature that you have read or studied has religion been a political issue?

c If you have studied Blake's *Songs of Innocence and of Experience*, Atwood's *The Handmaid's Tale* or Hosseini's *The Kite Runner*, write a paragraph or two explaining how religion and politics are connected in those texts.

Check your responses in the Ideas section on Cambridge Elevate

8.2.3 Politics and social protest in drama

Shakespeare's political theatre

The tragedies (and sometimes the comedies) of the Renaissance theatre revelled in colourful, action-packed representations of kings and queens and other political and religious leaders, bringing questions about power and politics to the stage in dynamic ways. Conflicts in court and between courts, such as those in Shakespeare's *Hamlet, King Lear, Macbeth* and *Julius Caesar*, provided the backdrop not only for powerful dramas of personal tragedy, but also for an examination of ideas about leadership, nobility, power, corruption and justice, in an age where the monarchy and the Church still wielded enormous power.

Of particular significance for the development of political writing is the genre of the history play, which originated in Britain in the late 16th century. Histories tell the story of real figures - usually kings - from relatively recent history (as opposed to legendary or classical tales), focusing particularly on their political leadership of the nation, and often combining elements of both tragedy and comedy. Shakespeare's histories are the most famous of this genre: ten plays telling the stories of seven English kings, from King John to Henry VIII. Eight of the plays - *Richard II; Henry IV Parts 1 and 2; Henry V; Henry VI Parts 1, 2 and 3;* and *Richard III* - form a cycle that is sometimes referred to as *The Wars of the Roses*.

Set text focus: *Henry IV Part I*

Probably written in 1596–97, *Henry IV Part I* is one of William Shakespeare's history plays, the second part of a four-part series. Set in 1402–03, the play generally portrays real events and people, although Shakespeare makes Hotspur and Prince Harry the same age and creates the characters of Mortimer and Falstaff from various real figures and also, in the latter's case, stock characters. The history plays deal with the rise and fall of the house of Lancaster, and a pervading dilemma of the age – whether the monarch is appointed by God and whether it is a sin to remove a monarch from office. This question casts a shadow over the two Henry IV plays, as Henry is haunted by his responsibility for Richard II's death.

Although not an exhaustive list, the following elements of political and social protest writing could be explored in relation to *Henry IV Part I*:

- the type of text (see Activity 6; 8.2.3)
- settings of time and place (see Activity 8)
- the nature of the power struggle, including warfare (see 8.2.1; 8.2.3; 8.3.3)
- behaviours of those with power (see 8.1.2; 8.2.3; 8.3.2, Kings…)
- behaviours of protestors, in pursuit of power and rebellion (see 8.1.2; 8.2.3; 8.3.2, Rebels…; 8.3.3)
- corruption and abuse of power (see 8.2.3)
- issues of gender and sexuality (see 8.4.1)
- issues of social class (see Activity 28)
- how the text is structured, tensions heightened and resolved (see 8.3.3)
- how language is used (see Activity 23)
- representation of society in a particular historical period (see 8.2.3)
- effects on the audience (see 8.1; 8.3.2, Kings…; 8.3.2, Critical lens).

The play could be read from the perspective of:

- value and the canon (see 8.2.3, Critical lens; 9.3)
- narrative theory (see 8.3.2, Critical lens; 9.4)
- feminist theory (see 8.4.1, Critical lens; 9.5)
- Marxist theory (see 8.2.4, Critical lens; 9.6).

Henry IV Part 1

Henry IV Part 1, one of the most popular of the history plays, illustrates many of these plays' concerns and methods. In the characters of Henry IV, the young prince Hal, the heroic rebel Hotspur, the anti-heroic Falstaff, and others, we see a group of noblemen reacting in different ways to their political responsibilities, some of them portrayed comically. The play explores a range of political ideas. Some examples are shown in Figure 8A.

Figure 8A

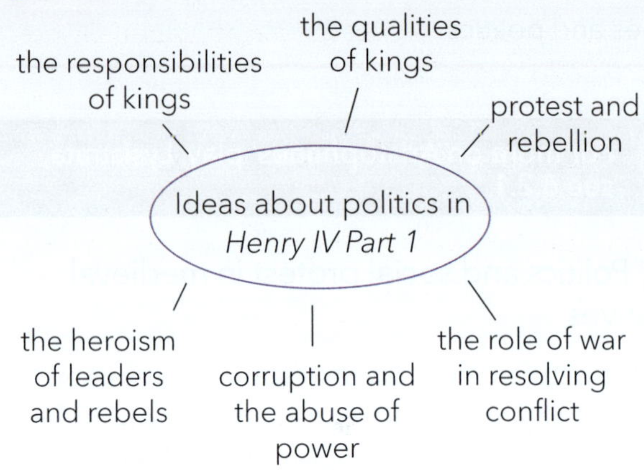

ACTIVITY 8

History into drama – Henry IV and Prince Hal

Henry IV's reign (1399–1413) was plagued by plots, rebellions and assassination attempts, especially repeated revolts by Owain Glyndŵr, who declared himself Prince of Wales in 1400. Henry Percy, Earl of Northumberland, led a sequence of rebellious attempts, culminating in the Battle of Shrewsbury in 1403. In 1405, Richard le Scrope, Archbishop of York, led a rebellion in northern England. Henry successfully put down these rebellions, but this was largely owing to the military prowess of Prince Henry of Monmouth, his eldest son. Monmouth later became King Henry V, but effectively wrested much power from his father in 1410.

a In what ways does Shakespeare present these historical events during *Henry IV Part 1*?

b Are historical events accurately portrayed or are they adapted for the purposes of the developing drama?

c What political messages emerge through the characters of Henry and Hal?

ACTIVITY 9

History into drama – Falstaff

One of Henry V's courtiers was Sir John Falstaff, who fought in many military campaigns but was accused of and gained a reputation for cowardice – although he was in fact acquitted of the accusation. Another of his courtiers – and a good friend of Henry in his early years as prince – was Sir John Oldcastle, another controversial character, who was eventually hanged for treason and heresy. In the early versions of the play, the character John Falstaff was called Oldcastle, but this was later changed to Falstaff after protests from the Oldcastle family.

a How does Shakespeare use the stories of these two men to form the character of Falstaff?

b In what ways does Falstaff represent the political status quo? In what ways does he challenge it?

c How does his character shape your view of the political themes of the play?

From the Restoration to the 19th century, 1660–1843

The golden age of Renaissance political drama was brought to an end by the closure of the theatres in 1642, following the execution of King Charles I. After the restoration of the monarchy in 1660, the theatres were re-opened, and a dynamic revival of drama took place. At this politically sensitive time, however, the focus of the drama was largely on upper-class comedy, and on grand musical entertainments such as the new Italian opera, rather than on serious drama.

For more on the closure of the theatres, see 3.3.4

In the early decades of the 18th century, a number of writers sought to produce a more directly political drama. *The Beggar's Opera* by John Gay (1728) is the most famous work of this time, a kind of anti-elite folk opera – which he called a 'ballad opera' – in which the characters are ordinary people rather than kings and heroes, and in which the music and words are based on the ballads of popular culture rather than the florid and refined arias of fashionable Italian opera. In itself this was a political statement, giving the working classes representation in the theatre. However, the play was also a political satire on the behaviour of the current government, with the character Peachum representing the Prime Minister, Horace Walpole.

For more on the ballad form, see 2.2-2.3

Critical lens: value and the canon

The literary canon is a group of works that is agreed to be of particular literary value. Many critics, however, argue that it operates as a form of unofficial censorship, a form of discrimination against the work of authors who are not or have not been socially approved. It is unlikely, for instance, that you will study popular blockbuster novels in your A Level course, or the scripts of TV soap operas. However, you could choose a non canonical text for your non-exam assessment and use 'Value and the canon' to defend it. Do you think such texts are worth studying?

For more on value and the canon, see 9.3

Social realism, 1843–1945

After the Theatres Act of 1843, the potential for government censorship was much reduced and non-musical drama was once more allowed to be performed in all theatres, a situation that led to a boom both in theatre-going and play-writing, and a revival of serious drama.

Whereas the popular drama and music theatre of the day were formulaic and dominated by **caricature** and spectacle, some writers began to experiment with dramatic **realism** – an attempt to make stage settings, speech and action appear more like the real world – and to deal with contemporary social and political issues. The combination of these techniques is known as **social realism**.

Key terms

caricature: an exaggerated or unrealistic representation of character

realism: a movement in art and literature to represent life in as realistic a way as possible

social realism: a form of realism that focuses on contemporary social and political issues

Exploring realism

Realism was a major movement in literature and the arts that dominated the second half of the 19th century and has remained powerful into the 21st. Realism seeks to represent society accurately, reflecting the understanding that people are the products of their social and economic contexts and their genetic and psychological inheritances. Realist writers seek to examine the detailed domestic reality of modern lives and identify how individuals can act in the circumstances in which they find themselves. *Social* realism in particular explores the social, political and economic realities of the less powerful in society.

Realism in drama has been immensely influential; it is the style of much contemporary drama and most film and television drama. Realist drama is likely to contain these features:

- believable characters, usually middle or working class, dressed in lifelike clothes and in a lifelike setting, often a domestic scene
- realistic dialogue and action, with no direct address to the audience
- a narrative that reflects a concern with the psychology and relationships of the characters in their social and economic context, often dealing with social and political issues.

It's important to recognise that *realism* is not the same as *reality*: the narratives, characters and dialogue of realist drama are all inevitably shaped for the stage in ways that are ultimately artificial. Realist dialogue, for instance, although far more like reality than the drama of previous ages, rarely if ever has the fragmented and improvised quality of real speech.

Ibsen, *A Doll's House* and social realism

One playwright was more influential than any other in the Victorian move towards political drama and social realism – the Norwegian playwright Henrik Ibsen; indeed, he has often been described as the 'father of realism' and consequently of modern theatre. His work remains immensely popular internationally. Ibsen's pioneering works, however, initially shocked audiences around Europe because of the ways in which his characters – especially the female characters (notably in *A Doll's House* 1879 and *Hedda Gabler* 1889) – challenged social conventions and the values of the establishment, as well as the conventions of traditional drama.

Ibsen has been particularly associated with the rise of feminism in Europe; his plays were ground-breaking in the way they questioned gender roles, allowing strong women characters to give voice to the frustrations that arose from their lack of social freedom and political power within the confines of marriage. *A Doll's House,* for instance, with its shocking ending in which Nora, unable to tolerate her marriage to Torvald any more, walks out of her house, slamming the door behind her, deals explicitly with the economic limitations of married women at the time.

Ibsen's drama also firmly established the dramatic conventions of realism – for instance, his use of middle-class domestic settings and costume, and the minutely detailed stage directions in which he described them, as in the opening of *A Doll's House;* and his use of intimate and relatively realistic dialogue.

After the Theatres Act of 1843, the potential for government censorship was much reduced

Set text focus: *A Doll's House*

The Norwegian playwright Henrik Ibsen is regarded as the 'father' of realism and modern prose drama. He worked in theatres in Bergen and what is now Oslo from 1851 to 1864. In 1858 he married Suzannah Thoreson, horrifying polite society by advocating that husband and wife should live together as equal, but independent human beings. Norwegian society also often disapproved of his plays because the characters – typically strong, independent women – challenged social values and conventions of the day, including gender roles. *A Doll's House* was published in 1879, after Ibsen had moved to Italy, and particularly reflects his association with the rise of feminism in Europe.

Although not an exhaustive list, the following elements of political and social protest writing could be explored in relation to *A Doll's House*:

- the type of text (see Activity 6; 8.2.3, Ibsen…)
- settings of time and place (see 8.2.3, Ibsen…)
- the nature of the power struggle (see 8.3.3)
- behaviours of those with power (see 8.1.2; 8.3.2, Kings…)
- behaviours of those without power (see 8.1.2; 8.3.2, Servants…)
- behaviours of protestors (see 8.1.2; 8.3.3)
- connections of the smaller world to the larger world (see Activity 3; 8.2.3, Exploring realism; 8.2.3, Ibsen…)
- issues of gender and sexuality (see 8.2.3, Ibsen…; 8.4.1)
- issues of social class (see Activity 28)
- how the text is structured, tensions heightened and resolved (see 8.3.3)
- how language is used (see 8.2.3, Ibsen…; Activity 23)
- representation of society in a particular historical period (see 8.4.1)
- effects on the audience (see 8.1; 8.2.3, Exploring realism; 8.3.2, Critical lens).

The play could be read from the perspective of:

- value and the canon (see 8.2.3, Critical lens; 9.3)
- narrative theory (see 8.3.2, Critical lens; 9.4)
- feminist theory (see 8.3.1, Critical lens; 9.5)
- Marxist theory (see 8.2.4, Critical lens; 9.6).

Ibsen's influence was to be seen over the next 60 years in the work of many major playwrights – most notably, in Britain, Oscar Wilde (*Lady Windermere's Fan* 1892, *A Woman of No Importance* 1893), George Bernard Shaw (*Mrs Warren's Profession* 1902, *Pygmalion* 1912) and J.B. Priestley (*Time and the Conways* 1937, *An Inspector Calls* 1945), and, in the United States, Eugene O'Neill (*Mourning Becomes Electra* 1931, *Long Day's Journey into Night* 1941), all of whom, in different ways, continued his work of exploring the uncomfortable realities of domestic life (especially for women) and the hypocrisies of social class and convention.

ACTIVITY 10

Social realism and soap opera

Social realism has probably had more influence on TV drama, with its intimate, close-up social portrayals, than on any other form – and especially on soap opera. However, while soap opera includes many of the classic features of realism, it is also in some senses less realistic than other types of realist drama.

a Think about the soap operas you know. Using the list of features of dramatic realism in the box 'Exploring realism', decide in what ways they might satisfy the definition of realism, and in what ways they might not.

b What political and social issues are addressed by the soap operas you know?

After World War I, there was a growing concern in theatre with the representation of the struggles of ordinary people, and with making theatre more accessible to ordinary people. In response, a new form of political theatre grew in Europe in the 1920s and 30s, sometimes known as **agitprop theatre**.

Key terms

agitprop theatre: theatre of an explicitly political nature designed to show the struggles of the working classes; from the words 'agitation' and 'propaganda'

Exploring agitprop theatre

Agitprop theatre abandoned elaborate sets and plush theatre settings and took theatre to the people on the streets, in warehouses and small theatres and so on. It used physical theatre techniques such as improvisation, music and clowning to communicate its political messages, often in the form of satire.

The Workers' Theatre Movement pioneered many of the methods of agitprop in Britain in the 1930s, making direct political comment a popular focus of drama – and in 1945, a new company, Theatre Workshop, emerged from it.

The rise of modern political theatre: 1945–2000

Since World War II, there has been a massive growth in political theatre of many kinds in Britain, reflecting the radical social and political changes resulting from the conflicts of the first half of the 20th century.

In 1955, Theatre Workshop staged the first British performance of *Mother Courage and Children,* the most famous political play of the influential left-wing German playwright Bertolt Brecht. The company also premiered two of the most important British political plays of the century – *A Taste of Honey* by Shelagh Delaney (1958) and *Oh What A Lovely War,* developed by Theatre Workshop's director Joan Littlewood and the cast of the play (1963) – both of which broke new ground in the theatre.

Oh What A Lovely War draws directly on the pioneering techniques of agitprop theatre, in the form of a satirical anti-war musical condemning World War I. *A Taste of Honey* is a ground-breaking social realist drama dealing with a range of contemporary issues connected with class, race, gender and sexuality, and set in a working-class flat in the North of England – a type of drama that became known as **kitchen sink realism**.

Key terms

kitchen sink realism: a form of social realist drama depicting the domestic lives of working-class people, often set in small flats or rooms in working-class areas

1940s–1960s: The Angry Young Men and the American realists

Kitchen sink realism was one style adopted by a group of left-wing playwrights in the 1950s and 1960s known as the 'Angry Young Men', most notably in the play *Look Back in Anger* by John Osborne (1956). The work of this group (which also included Harold Pinter, John Arden and Arnold Wesker) was motivated by anger at the class division and snobbery of Britain at the time. The plays often feature young, educated male characters who rebel against the conservative conventions of the middle-class culture around them.

In the United States, realist drama at this time similarly reflected disillusionment with social division and the conservative establishment, most notably in the work of Tennessee Williams and Arthur Miller. Although Williams was a less explicitly political – and more poetic – playwright than Miller, his plays (such as *The Glass Menagerie* 1944, *A Streetcar Named Desire* 1947 and *Cat on a Hot TIn Roof* 1955) reveal a profound empathy for those alienated by society's power structures and social divisions. Miller tackled political issues more directly, for instance capitalism, justice and immigration (*Death of a Salesman* 1949, *The Crucible* 1953, *A View From the Bridge* 1955).

'Ibsen's drama…firmly established the dramatic conventions of realism'

Henrik Ibsen, *A Doll's House*

1970s-1990s: Radical political theatre

During the 1970s and 1980s, radical new political theatre companies dedicated to depicting political struggles developed, focusing on issues such as political power, class, race, gender and sexuality. The major playwrights of this movement, many still writing today, included Edward Bond (*Lear* 1971), David Edgar (*Destiny,* 1976), David Hare and Howard Brenton (*Pravda,* 1985) and Caryl Churchill (*Top Girls,* 1982). David Hare has continued to explore and examine issues of power, for instance in his trilogy of plays examining the Church, the law and government, *Racing Demon* (1990), *Murmuring Judges* (1991) and *The Absence of War* (1993).

During the 1990s too, **verbatim theatre** was invented, a form of political drama that uses the words from real interviews and political events as dialogue to confront the public with political truths. Two important verbatim plays are Richard Norton-Taylor's *The Colour of Justice* (1999), and Robin Soans' *Talking to Terrorists* (2005), both of which explore issues to do with racism and racial discrimination in contemporary Britain.

Key terms

verbatim theatre: a form of political theatre that uses the words from real interviews as dialogue

Political theatre today

Political theatre continues to thrive in Britain. The national theatre companies, and numerous other companies around Britain, champion the work of the current generation of political playwrights, such as Mark Ravenhill (*The Cut*, 2006), Jez Butterworth (*Jerusalem*, 2009), Gregory Burke (*Black Watch*, 2010), David Greig (*Dunsinane*, 2010), Richard Bean (*Great Britain*, 2014) and Mike Bartlett (*King Charles III*, 2104). More mainstream writers such as Alan Bennett and Michael Frayn also produce work with significant political messages, such as Bennett's *The Madness of George III* (1991) and *The History Boys (2004),* and Frayn's *Copenhagen* (1998) and *Democracy* (2004).

ACTIVITY 11

King Charles III

Read the plot of *King Charles III* in Text 8A, a play premiered in London in 2014.

a What are the key political issues in contemporary Britain that this play deals with? Who has power and who wants power in the play? In what sense might it be seen as satire?

b What do you think are important issues about power in contemporary Britain? Consider what kind of play might effectively portray those issues.

c Unusually for a modern play, *King Charles III* is written in iambic pentameters rather than prose, and echoes elements of Shakespearean drama in several respects. Can you see any similarities in the plot with any Shakespeare plays you know?

Text 8A

At the beginning of the play, Queen Elizabeth II has died and been succeeded by King Charles III. Charles and Prince William have separately seen the ghost of Princess Diana, who promises both that they will become 'the greatest king of all'. In his first weekly audience with the prime minister, Charles discusses his doubts about a new bill for regulation of the press to which he has to give his assent. Charles worries that the law restricts press freedom, potentially allowing governments to censor news and hide abuses of power. The prime minister refuses to alter the bill and it seems that Charles has no alternative but to sign it. The next day, however, Charles returns the bill to 10 Downing Street unsigned. The prime minister tries to persuade Charles to sign, but he continues to refuse, whereupon the prime minister threatens to pass a new law getting rid of the need for royal assent. Charles, however, dissolves parliament. There are protests across the country and the army has to give Charles increased protection. Meanwhile, Prince Harry, who is going out with a republican, Jess, decides he wants to become a commoner. Charles agrees to Harry's request. Kate, the Duchess of Cambridge, suggests that Prince William should mediate between parliament and his father. Charles reacts angrily and is eventually forced to abdicate in favour of William, who is prepared to sign the press bill. The play ends with William and Kate's coronation.

Politics in TV drama

TV has provided a powerful and popular medium for political drama since the 1960s.

ACTIVITY 12

Politics in TV drama

Before continuing your reading, think about TV drama you have seen that includes coverage of political issues and struggles. What different types of drama can you think of, and what kinds of political issue are dealt with?

The 1960s to 1980s are often identified as a 'golden age' of political drama on television. Playwrights writing for TV pioneered a social realism style that is now often referred to as **gritty realism**, depicting the sometimes harsh and brutal truths of social inequality and injustice in Britain at that time. The most famous of all these plays was Jeremy Sandford's *Cathy Come Home* (1966), a play about homelessness.

An important group of radical political playwrights emerged on TV at this time, including Dennis Potter (*Stand Up Nigel Barton*, 1965), Alan Bleasdale (*Boys from the Blackstuff* 1982) and Trevor Griffiths (*Oi For England* 1982). These plays, like the work of the theatre playwrights of the time, explored the full range of social and political issues in Britain, and are still considered classic works of political drama.

Since the 1980s, there has been more of an emphasis on political drama serials, many of them thrillers, examining the work of politicians, police, soldiers, spies, journalists, civil servants and lawyers, and often covering issues to do with corruption and democracy, terrorism, religious fundamentalism and the environment. Significant examples include *House of Cards* (Michael Dobbs, 1990), *Our Friends in the North* (Peter Flannery, 1996) and *State of Play* (Paul Abbott, 2003). American political drama series such as *The West Wing* and *Homeland* have also been influential.

Key terms

gritty realism: a form of social realism investigating the extremes of poverty and social alienation

ACTIVITY 13

Political issues in tv drama

Read about the TV dramas mentioned in the section 'Politics in TV drama'. Which of them deal with the following issues: corruption, democracy, government, religion, class, race, gender and sexuality, social justice, inequality, terrorism, war?

8.2.4 Politics and social protest in poetry

The Romantics and the French Revolution

Some of the most influential political verse in the history of English poetry is the work of the Romantic poets in the late 18th and early 19th centuries. The Romantics were in fact often inspired and motivated by radical social and political beliefs, frequently

TV has provided a powerful and popular medium for political drama since the 1960s

focusing on the struggle of the individual for freedom and expression in an oppressive world.

The French Revolution in 1789 was a highly significant moment for the Romantics (as well as a crucial event in the development of modern politics). Initially, many of the radical thinkers and writers of the time supported the French Revolution, seeing it as the overthrow of a powerful, oppressive and exploitative monarchy by the people. Their hopes for a truly democratic and equal society, in which the masses were relieved from poverty and exploitation and granted fundamental social rights such as a fair legal and political system, were to be disappointed by the events of the 'Reign of Terror' that followed in France. Nevertheless, they continued to be inspired by the ideal of a more equal society characterised by social justice.

Wordsworth, Coleridge and the *Lyrical Ballads*

One of the most significant literary works of the early Romantic period in Britain is the *Lyrical Ballads* (1798), a collection of poetry jointly written by two of the most important writers of the age, William Wordsworth and Samuel Taylor Coleridge. Both writers were deeply committed to the ideals of democracy and social justice, which they had championed during the French Revolution.

A landmark in the history of English poetry, the *Lyrical Ballads* set out to challenge the elitist intellectualism and literary style of many of the writers of the preceding decades, instead representing the experience of ordinary people in language that would be accessible to ordinary readers. Central to Wordsworth and Coleridge's project was the use of simple, popular and traditional song forms such as the ballad. This use of ballad form and simple style can be seen in Coleridge's 'The Rime of the Ancient Mariner', the longest poem in the *Lyrical Ballads*, for instance, in the first stanza of the poem shown in Text 8B.

Text 8B

It is an ancient Mariner,
And he stoppeth one of three.
'By thy long grey beard and glittering eye,
Now wherefore stopp'st thou me?'

Samuel Taylor Coleridge,
from 'The Rime of the Ancient Mariner'

For more on ballad, see 2.2-2.3

The Romantics and the Industrial Revolution

An important message as, for example, in Coleridge's 'The Dungeon' is to do with the purity and power of nature. This was a central idea of Romanticism. The idea of the power of nature to bring about personal and social improvement was not new in literature: it stretches back at least as far as the **pastoral** poetry of Ancient Greece. It can also be seen in English literature throughout the medieval era and the Renaissance; for instance, in the story of Robin Hood and in Shakespeare's pastoral comedy *As You Like It*. However, in the late 18th century, the pastoral ideal achieved new political significance, in the face of the Industrial Revolution.

Key terms

pastoral: a type of literature concerned with the beauty of the countryside and the healing power of nature

Exploring the Industrial Revolution

The first steam engine was patented in 1698, marking the beginning of the age of industry in Britain. From about 1750 to about 1850, the spread of industry, and the social change it brought about, became so extensive that the period became known as the Industrial Revolution. One of the main consequences was urbanisation and population growth on a massive scale.

Many thousands of people left the countryside and moved to cities where work opportunities in factories were multiplying. There, working and living conditions were often extremely poor, exacerbated by the pollution caused by thousands of smoky factories. The threat both to the health and welfare of the working classes and to the environment were of great concern to many. At the same time, industrial landscapes began to invade the countryside, and rural poverty increased as economic activity shifted to the cities.

For the Romantic poets, such as Wordsworth and Coleridge, social, political and environmental issues came together in the face of the spread of industry.

The economic exploitation of the masses, their lack of social and political rights, the polluted urban environments in which they increasingly lived, and the degradation of the countryside formed a network of concerns, which they expressed in verse through powerful ideas about the links between nature, love, beauty and the intellectual, spiritual, and social welfare and freedom of the individual.

Critical lens: Eco-critical theory

Eco-critical theory invites us to consider the ways in which the natural world is used in literary texts. One important concept here is the pastoral, an idealised view of the countryside often used in literature as a contrast with the stresses of city life. How are city and countryside represented in your set texts? If you're studying *Harvest*, *Hard Times* or *Songs of Innocence and of Experience*, for instance, what attitudes towards the city and country are expressed?

For more on eco-critical theory, see 9.7

Blake and *Songs of Innocence and of Experience*

Such ideas were central to another of the most important works of the period, William Blake's *Songs of Innocence and of Experience* (1794), in which he set poems expressing a version of the pastoral ideal (*Songs of Innocence*) against poems expressing a view of reality as a corruption of that ideal (*Songs of Experience*). Like Wordsworth and Coleridge, Blake used simple song forms and simple but powerful language and imagery to make the works accessible and relevant to ordinary people. He also used visual images in the original versions of the poems, embedding each poem in a framework of his own drawings.

In many of these poems, especially in *Songs of Experience*, you can see Blake's political concerns about the way that the institutions of Church and government oppress the people, and about the poor urban conditions prevalent in early industrial London. There is a particular concern, too - shared also by Wordsworth and Coleridge in *Lyrical Ballads* - with the plight of children in society. By contrast, in *Songs of Innocence*, Blake presents an idealised view of nature and childhood as states of purity and innocence that are inevitably corrupted by age and the experience of social and political reality.

The oppressive influence of the Church in society is a particularly frequent theme in these poems, seen for instance in 'Holy Thursday', 'The Chimney Sweeper', 'The Garden of Love', 'A Little Boy Lost', and 'The Little Vagabond' (see Text 8C).

Text 8C

The Little Vagabond

Dear Mother, dear Mother, the Church is cold,
But the Ale-house is healthy & pleasant & warm;
Besides I can tell where I am used well,
Such usage in Heaven will never do well.

But if at the Church they would give us some Ale,
And a pleasant fire our souls to regale,
We'd sing and we'd pray all the live-long day,
Nor ever once wish from the Church to stray.

Then the Parson might preach, & drink, & sing,
And we'd be as happy as birds in the spring;
And modest Dame Lurch, who is always at Church,
Would not have bandy children, nor fasting, nor birch.

And God, like a father rejoicing to see
His children as pleasant and happy as he,
Would have no more quarrel with the Devil or the Barrel,
But kiss him, & give him both drink and apparel.

William Blake

'Dear Mother, dear Mother, the Church is cold'
William Blake, 'The Little Vagabond'

Set text focus: William Blake's 'Songs of Innocence and of Experience'

William Blake began his working life as an illustrator and engraver in 18th-century London. At the same time he wrote poems, eventually publishing *Songs of Innocence* in 1789, followed by *Songs of Experience* in 1793, illustrated with his own images, which he thought of as an intrinsic part of his work. The poems were combined in 1794 in a volume entitled *Songs of Innocence and of Experience showing the Two Contrary States of the Human Soul*. Although in his lifetime Blake was seen as an eccentric, politically radical and disapproving of rationalism and organised religion, he is now highly regarded for his unique expressiveness and creativity.

Although not an exhaustive list, the following elements of political and social protest writing could be explored in relation to *Songs of Innocence and of Experience*:

- the type of text (see Activity 6; 8.2.4, Blake…)
- settings of time and place (see 8.3.1)
- the nature of the power struggle (see 8.2.1 (background); 8.3.3)
- workings of the ruling political and religious classes (see Activities 4, 7; 8.2.4, Blake…)
- behaviours of those with power (see 8.1.2)
- behaviours of those without power (see 8.1.2; 8.3.2, Servants…)
- corruption of ideals (see 8.2.4, Blake…)
- connections of the smaller world to the larger world (see Activity 3)
- issues of social class (see 8.2.4, The Romantics…; Activity 28)
- how the text is structured, tensions heightened and resolved (see 8.3.3)
- how language is used (see 8.2.4, Blake…; Activity 19)
- representation of society in a particular historical period (see 8.2.4, Blake…)
- effects on readers (see 8.1; 8.3.2, Critical lens).

The poems could be read from the perspective of:

- value and the canon (see 8.2.3, Critical lens; 9.3)
- narrative theory (see 8.3.2, Critical lens; 9.4)
- Marxist theory (see 9.6)
- eco-critical theory (see 8.2.4, Critical lens; 8.3.1, Critical lens; 9.7).

ACTIVITY 14

Songs of Innocence and of Experience

Carefully read Blake's 'The Little Vagabond' in Text 8C.

a In the last stanza, what does Blake seem to suggest about the relationship between God, the Devil and drink? What does Blake suggest about the Church as an institution and its relationship with the people?

b This poem was omitted from the first edition of the book in 1839, and yet other poems in the book also criticise the Church. Why do you think this poem in particular might have been seen as unacceptable?

c What similarities are there in the political ideas in this poem and in Coleridge's 'The Dungeon'?

d In his book *The Marriage of Heaven and Hell*, Blake writes: 'Prisons are built with stones of Law, Brothels with bricks of Religion.' What does he mean by this, and how does it help you to understand both 'The Dungeon' and 'The Little Vagabond'? Write a paragraph explaining how this proverb connects the two poems, using evidence from both texts to support your argument.

Exploring Blake, religion and politics

Although Blake was a Christian, he believed that the Church, like many institutions, was an oppressive force in society, exerting power over ordinary people by forbidding them from enjoying natural pleasures and freedoms. He also rejected conventional ideas about religious authority, believing that God exists in all of us. In *Songs of Innocence*, he expresses this in 'The Divine Image', where he describes Love as 'the human form divine'.

Modernism

The first half of the 20th century was a period of immense political upheaval as the world faced the turmoil of two world wars. During this period, too, **modernism**, with its many artistic and literary movements, emerged. Modernist literature often reflected the chaotic political state of the world, with writers developing challenging literary forms to communicate their ideas. The work of the major modernist poets – notably Ezra Pound, T.S. Eliot, D.H. Lawrence and W.B. Yeats – reflected this upheaval with their rejection of traditional poetic language and form, and their themes of social and cultural fragmentation.

Some of these writers became caught up in the extreme and often brutal politics of the period. Pound, Eliot and Lawrence were all at various points connected unfavourably with **fascism**. Another major modernist poet, W.H. Auden, was associated strongly with the political left, even fighting against the fascists during the Spanish Civil War. He expressed his anti-fascist ideals in poems such as '1st September, 1939', written on the first day of World War II.

Politics in modern poetry

Since World War II, poets writing in English around the world have written extensively about political issues and struggles in many different ways.

Key terms

modernism: a literary and artistic movement that challenges traditional forms and conventions

fascism: an extreme right-wing political movement

ACTIVITY 15

Reading modern political poems

Find as many of the poems written by the poets mentioned in the previous three paragraphs as you can. Many can be found on the internet.

a In what ways would you say that each poem is political, and what political issues does it deal with?

b How do the form and language of each poem contribute to conveying the political ideas the poem deals with?

Set text focus: Tony Harrison's poetry

Tony Harrison, poet and playwright, was born and educated in Leeds. He is a major contemporary political poet, known for his controversial views on language, class, culture and politics. His poems, such as 'Them and [uz]', often explore his own sense of class identity: brought up in a working-class home, further education changed his language and culture. Written in 1985 during the miners' strikes, 'v' is one of the most significant political poems of the last few decades. It describes Harrison's visit to his parents' graves in a Leeds cemetery, defaced by litter and graffiti, and explores the language of graffiti and reflects on political conflicts in Britain at that time.

Although not an exhaustive list, the following elements of political and social protest writing could be explored in relation to the selected poems:

- the type of text (see Activities 6, 15)
- settings of time and place (see Activity 20)
- the nature of the power struggle, (see 8.2.1 (background); 8.3.3)
- behaviours of those with and without power (see 8.1.2)
- connections of the smaller world to the larger world (see Activity 3; 8.2.4, Politics in modern poetry; 8.4.2)
- issues of social class and racism (see 8.4.2)
- how the text is structured, tensions heightened and resolved (see 8.3.3)
- how language and form are used (see Activities 15, 19, 23)
- commentary on society (see 8.2.4, Politics in modern poetry)
- effects on readers (see 8.1; 8.3.2, Critical lens).

The poems selected for the A Level specification could be read from the perspective of:

- value and the canon (see 8.2.3, Critical lens; 9.3)
- narrative theory (see 8.3.2, Critical lens; 9.4)
- Marxist theory (see 8.2.4; 9.6).

Critical lens: Marxist theory

Marxist theory focuses on the representation of class and social power in literature. A key issue is the extent to which working-class characters' voices and perspectives are heard in literature. Poems like 'The Six O'Clock News' and 'Half-Caste' use spoken accents and dialects in first-person narration to strengthen the authenticity of working-class voices. Where else in your set texts do you hear working-class voices, and do they use spoken language, or written Standard English?

For more on Marxist theory, see 9.6

8.2.5 Politics in the novel

Since its origins in the 18th century, the novel has portrayed politics and political issues time and time again. The rise of the novel coincided with a time of great political turbulence (the Industrial Revolution), the development of the powerful ideology of **socialism**, and the development of a modern conception of parliamentary democracy. Thus power and powerlessness in many forms have been central concerns for novelists over the last three centuries.

Key terms

socialism: a left-wing political movement that aims to increase the economic and social power of ordinary people

Early political fiction

Some of the earliest prose fiction was fashioned around strongly political ideas. Jonathan Swift's *Gulliver's Travels* (1726), for instance, is a satirical work (written just before the development of the novel) that uses the structure of a travel narrative to explore different political philosophies and ways of organising society. Novels of the Romantic period often dealt with political issues - most notably William Godwin's *Caleb Williams* (1794) and Mary Shelley's *Frankenstein* (1818), which set out to explore the relationship between the individual and society, examining ideas about justice, politics and nature, and reflecting similar themes in the work of the Romantic poets.

Exploring William Godwin and Mary Wollstonecraft

Mary Shelley grew up in a home steeped in radical politics and literature. Her father William Godwin was closely connected with radical political causes such as the Chartists, fighting for electoral reform, while her mother was the radical feminist Mary Wollstonecraft, author of *A Vindication of the Rights of Women*. They were close friends of Byron, Shelley and Coleridge.

The Victorian novel

All the great novelists of the Victorian era - the Brontë sisters, George Eliot, Charles Dickens, Thomas Hardy, Anthony Trollope, and others - reflected the political ideas and movements of their time in their works, often dealing with significant social and political themes, and setting their stories against the backdrop of political events and ideas. The novels of Thomas Hardy, for instance, often focus on social attitudes towards women (e.g. *Under the Greenwood Tree* and *Tess of the D'Urbevilles*) and other under-represented groups such as the working class (e.g. *Jude the Obscure*). George Eliot's novel *Felix Holt, The Radical* is set against a strongly political backdrop, and her novels often deal with issues of social injustice, whether related to gender, class or race (as in her Zionist novel, *Daniel Deronda*).

Perhaps the most explicitly political of Victorian novelists, however, were Charles Dickens, Anthony Trollope, Wilkie Collins and Benjamin Disraeli.

Charles Dickens

Politics and social protest were central to the novels of Charles Dickens, who began his career as a political reporter. As a teenager, he began work for *The Mirror of Parliament*, responsible for producing word-for-word accounts of the business of Parliament. Such reports were massively popular: literary historians estimate that they were regularly read by as many as two million readers. According to the young Dickens, 'I have worn my knees by writing on them on the old back row of the old gallery of the House of Commons.' In so doing, he covered some of the most significant events of his time, such as The Great Reform Act (1832) - which substantially improved the process of democratic elections – and The Poor Law (1834) – which established workhouses for the poor. The influence of these experiences were later to influence his fiction.

Dickens felt that politicians spent much of their time speaking 'sentences with no meaning in them'. And so he turned to his own writing as a means of effecting political and social change. Throughout his fiction, he challenged what he saw as glaring social injustices. He wrote *A Christmas Carol* in response to a visit to a ragged school in London, where he was deeply shocked by the conditions of the poor. *Oliver Twist* exposes the evils of the workhouse system and the abuse of children by unscrupulous criminal gangs. In *Nicholas Nickleby* he takes on, and is often credited with single-handedly closing down, a group of notoriously appalling Yorkshire boarding schools. *Hard Times* also portrays the injustices of the education system. And in *A Tale of Two Cities,* he provides us with a vivid representation of the French Revolution.

In Text 8D, from *The Pickwick Papers*, his first novel, we are treated to events in the run-up to a political by-election in the wonderfully named borough of Eatanswill.

Text 8D

'You have come down here to see an election – eh? Spirited contest, my dear sir, very much so indeed. We have opened all the public-houses in the place. It has left our opponent nothing but the beer-shops. Masterly policy, my dear sir, eh?' The little man smiled complacently, and took a large pinch of snuff.

'And what is the likely result of the contest?' inquired Mr. Pickwick.

'Why, doubtful, my dear sir, rather doubtful as yet,' replied the little man. 'Fizkin's people have got three-and-thirty voters in the lock-up coach-house at the White Hart.'

'In the coach-house!' said Mr. Pickwick, much astonished.

'They keep 'em locked up there till they want 'em,' resumed the little man. 'The effect, you see, is to prevent our getting at them. Even if we could, it would be of no use, for they keep them very drunk on purpose. Smart fellow, Fizkin's agent very smart fellow indeed.'

'We are pretty confident, though,' said Mr. Perker, his voice sinking almost to a whisper. 'We had a little tea-party here, last night – five-and-forty women, my dear sir – and gave every one 'em a green parasol when she went away. Five and-forty green parasols, at 7/6d each. Got the votes of all their husbands, and half their brothers. You can't walk half a dozen yards up the street, without encountering half a dozen green parasols.'

'Is everything ready?' said Samuel Slumkey to Mr. Perker.

'Nothing has been left undone, my dear sir. There are twenty washed men at the street door for you to shake hands with; and six children in arms that you're to pat on the head, and ask the age of. Be particular about the children, my dear sir. It always has a great effect, that sort of thing.

'And perhaps if you could manage to kiss one of 'em, it would produce a very great impression on the crowd. I think it would make you very popular.'

'Very well,' said Samuel Slumkey, with a resigned air, 'then it must be done. That's all.'

Charles Dickens, *The Pickwick Papers*

'And perhaps if you could manage to kiss one of 'em, it would produce a very great impression on the crowd.'
Charles Dickens, *The Pickwick Papers*

ACTIVITY 16

Political satire

Read Dickens' account of political electioneering from *The Pickwick Papers* in Text 8D.

a What is the impression you gain of the election at Eatanswill?

b How does Dickens use language to engage us in the behaviour and attitudes of the interested parties?

c In what ways does Dickens' comedy aim to create a political impact on us as readers?

Check your responses in the Ideas section on Cambridge Elevate

Collins, Trollope and Disraeli

Wilkie Collins was a close friend of Charles Dickens, and the two men occasionally collaborated. Collins was deeply engaged with the social and political issues of his time, and often explores social and legal injustice in his works. In *The Woman in White*, for instance, he explores the legal position of women and the abuses they could suffer at the hands of their husbands, while in *No Name* he takes on the plight of illegitimate children in Victorian England.

Anthony Trollope wrote extensively not only on political issues but also about parliament and politicians. Novels such as *Phineas Finn* (1868), *Phineas Redux* (1873), *The Prime Minister* (1876) and *The American Senator* (1877) explore the careers and beliefs of politicians and the way they function in and out of government. *The Way We Live Now* (1875) explores more broadly the social evils of greed and corruption and their implications for society. Trollope was often outspoken on political topics, and in *An Autobiography* he proclaimed that '[a] man who entertains in his mind any political **doctrine**, except as a means of improving the condition of his fellows, I regard as a political intriguer, a **charlatan**, and a conjuror'.

Benjamin Disraeli holds a unique position in the English literary canon as the only serving prime minister who was also a major literary figure. He was a prolific author in spite of his onerous duties as a politician. His most famous novel is *Sybil*. Bearing the sub-title *The Two Nations*, the novel is in essence a fictional exploration of Disraeli's political beliefs, looking at the social implications of a divided society.

Glossary

doctrine: a belief or set of beliefs

charlatan: a person who falsely claims to have particular skills or knowledge

20th-century and contemporary political fiction

The tumultuous political events and debates of the 20th and early 21st centuries have been strongly reflected in the novels and stories of this period, with fiction of many different kinds including elements of political writing. In this part of the unit, we discuss three genres in which politics is particularly significant.

Dystopian and science fiction

From its beginnings in the 18th and 19th centuries, fiction that imagines the future and the effects of technological change has dealt with major issues to do with the organisation of society and the freedom of the individual. In the last century, the potential of technology to control and manipulate data and processes, and to become a dynamic tool in the hands of those who seek power, has increased massively, so it is not surprising that science fiction has often also been highly political.

Most significant has been the growth of **dystopian fiction**, which explores the effects of new social and power structures in oppressive societies of the future, often providing a metaphorical reflection on the political dangers that exist in the real, contemporary world. The most famous of all these novels is *1984* by George Orwell (1948), in which Orwell – informed by the oppressive communist state in Russia in the 1940s – warns of the dangers of **totalitarian regimes** by painting a picture of a society that controls people's minds as well as their actions. Other notable examples of this genre include Aldous Huxley's *Brave New World* (1931), Anthony Burgess's *A Clockwork Orange* (1962), Margaret Atwood's *The Handmaid's Tale* (1985) and China Miéville's *The City and The City* (2009).

Set text focus: *The Handmaid's Tale*

Margaret Atwood is a Canadian poet, novelist and environmental activist, who published her first novel *The Edible Woman* to wide acclaim in 1969. *The Handmaid's Tale* quickly became a bestseller after publication in 1986. In it, Atwood offers a feminist vision of dystopia – a world of subjugation, infertility and pollution. This was perhaps inspired by various trends in the 1980s – a revival of conservative values; criticism of feminism and the sexual freedom born in the 1960s; fears about declining birth rates and the dangers of nuclear power; and fears for the environment.

Although not an exhaustive list, the following elements of political and social protest writing could be explored in relation to *The Handmaid's Tale*:

- the type of text (see Activity 6; 8.2.5, Dystopian…)
- settings of time and place (see 8.2.5, Dystopian…; 8.3.1)
- the nature of the power struggle (see 8.3.3)
- workings of the ruling political and religious classes (see Activities 4, 7)
- behaviours of those with power (see 8.1.2; 8.3.2, Kings…)
- behaviours of those without power (see 8.1.2; 8.3.2, Servants…)
- behaviours of protestors, in pursuit of rebellion (see 8.1.2)
- corruption, conspiracy and control (see Activity 17)
- connections of the smaller world to the larger world (see Activity 3)
- focus on human organisation: in the home, work place, government (see 8.1.2)
- issues of gender and sexuality (see 8.2.5, Social issues…; 8.4.1)
- how the text is structured, tensions heightened and resolved (see 8.3.3)
- how language is used (see Activity 23)
- representation of society in a particular historical period (see 8.2.5; 8.4.1)
- effects on readers (see 8.1; 8.3.2, Critical lens).

The novel could be read from the perspective of:

- value and the canon (see 8.2.3, Critical lens; 9.3)
- narrative theory (see 8.3.2, Critical lens; 9.4)
- feminist theory (see 8.3.1, Critical lens; 9.5)
- eco-critical theory (see 8.3.1, Critical lens; 9.7).

Key terms

dystopian fiction: literary works dealing with nightmare worlds

totalitarian regime: a non-democratic political system in which a dictator or single political party has complete power

ACTIVITY 17

Surveillance, control and power

Both the dystopian novel and the political thriller deal head on with issues about surveillance and social control. These issues remain highly controversial in the contemporary world and have been major news items in the last few years:

- the use of CCTV cameras to combat crime
- the secret surveillance of digital data (such as emails and social media) to combat terrorism
- the leaking of top secret data to the public by organisations such as Wikileaks
- the use of undercover police to infiltrate groups of political activists.

What do you know about these four issues? Investigate them further, perhaps using news websites, personal blogs, YouTube footage and so on for a variety of different representations of them. Why are they controversial and what political issues do they raise? Finally, think about how each of these issues might form the starting point for the plot of a novel. How do related issues to do with surveillance and control feature in your set texts?

The historical novel

Novels about historical people, events or movements have been popular since the works of Walter Scott in the 19th century, and many have a sharp political focus. Portraying the structures of society and channels of power at particular moments in history from the perspective of the future, they often tell us as much about our political concerns in the present as they do about the way we perceive the politics of the past.

Recent historical novels have explored a wide range of periods and societies – for instance 16th- century England (*Harvest*, Jim Crace, 2013), 17th-century

Holland (*The Girl with The Pearl Earring*, Tracey Chevalier, 1999), 18th-century France (*Pure*, Andrew Miller, 2011) and 19th-century Tasmania (*English Passengers*, Matthew Kneale, 2000). Perhaps the most successful historical novels of the last decade have been Hilary Mantel's trilogy of novels about the political landscape of the reign of Henry VIII, *Wolf Hall, Bring Up the Bodies* and *The Mirror and the Light* (2009–2015), which have been acclaimed for their attempt to portray the lived experience of complex events and power struggles of the past in a politically and psychologically convincing way.

Social issues in the modern novel

Another way of thinking about the varieties of political fiction of the last century is to focus on writing – some historical, some satirical, some romantic, some tragic – which sets out to tackle specific social issues with political implications. In particular, we can identify major trends in writing about the politics of race, class and gender.

- **Writing about race:** novels focusing on issues to do with race, colonialism, slavery and immigration. Many of the influential works of this genre are American, for instance Harriet Beecher Stowe's *Uncle Tom's Cabin* (1852), Harper Lee's *To Kill a Mockingbird* (1960), Alice Walker's *The Color Purple* (1982), and Khaled Hosseini's *The Kite Runner* (2003). Among the significant British novels of the past 40 years are Salman Rushdie's *Midnight's Children* (1981), Hanif Kureishi's *The Buddha of Suburbia* (1990), and Zadie Smith's *White Teeth* (2000).
- **Writing about class:** novels focusing on portrayals of class conflict and the experience of the working class. Many Victorian and early 20th-century novelists dealt with issues of class (e.g. Dickens and Lawrence). In more recent times, writers such as the Scots novelist James Kelman (*How Late it Was How Late* 1994) have used first-person dialect narratives to give a more authentic voice

Set text focus: *Harvest*

After graduating in 1968, Jim Crace travelled around Africa, producing educational TV programmes in Sudan and teaching in Botswana. He wrote *Harvest*, which he has said will be his last novel, in 2013. It was shortlisted for the 2013 Man Booker Prize, among others, and won the 2013 James Tait Black Memorial Prize. The novel deals with a recurring theme in Crace's novels – a society on the brink of great change, although the villagers are unaware that the commercial world of wool production is about to displace the old way of life of subsistence agriculture. Although presumably set in 16th-century England, it addresses issues that are still relevant around the world today.

Although not an exhaustive list, the following elements of political and social protest writing could be explored in relation to *Harvest*:

- the type of text (see Activity 6; 8.2.5, The historical novel)
- settings of time and place (see Activity 30)
- the nature of the power struggle (see 8.3.3)
- behaviours of those with power (see 8.1.2; 8.3.2, Kings…; 8.4.2)
- behaviours of those without power (see 8.1.2; 8.3.2, Servants…; 8.4.2)
- connections of the smaller world to the larger world (see Activity 3)
- issues of social class (see 8.2.5, Social issues…; 8.4.2)
- how the text is structured, tensions heightened and resolved (see 8.3.3)
- how language is used (see Activity 30)
- representation of society in a particular historical period (see 8.2.5; 8.4.2)
- effects on readers (see 8.1; 8.3.2, Kings…; 8.3.2, Critical lens).

The novel could be read from the perspective of:

- value and the canon (see 8.2.3, Critical lens; 9.3)
- narrative theory (see 8.3.2, Critical lens; 9.4)
- Marxist theory (see 8.4.2, Critical lens; 9.6)
- eco-critical theory (see 8.2.4, Critical lens; 8.3.1, Critical lens; 9.7).

to working-class characters. Other significant portrayals of the relationships between working and upper classes in the past 40 years include Kazuo Ishiguro's *The Remains of the Day* (1983), Pat Barker's *Regeneration* (1991) and Jim Crace's *Harvest* (2013).

- **Writing about gender and sexuality** – novels focusing on issues to do with gender roles in society, and attitudes to sex and sexuality. While many 19th-century novelists deal with gender issues (notably George Eliot *in Middlemarch* and Thomas Hardy in *Tess of the D'Urbervilles*), D.H. Lawrence was perhaps the earliest to deal explicitly with the expression of sexuality, for instance in the controversial *Lady Chatterley's Lover* (1928). In more recent decades, novels such as Margaret Atwood's *The Handmaid's Tale*, Angela Carter's *The Bloody Chamber* (1973) and Jeanette Winterson's *Oranges are Not the Only Fruit* (1985) have explored gender and sexuality from feminist and gay perspectives.

We will explore some of the ways in which modern novels represent such political issues in the next part of this unit.

Watch tutorial video, Women in Political and Social Protest Writing, on Cambridge Elevate

8.3 Elements of political writing

8.3.1 Political settings: real nations, imagined dystopias

Political and social issues belong to the real world, but they also form a powerful part of the imagined worlds of literary texts. The settings that writers adopt when writing about political and social issues are therefore very significant. Sometimes writers use real-world settings, drawing directly on the political issues and structures of those settings. Sometimes, however, they choose to use imagined worlds, with fictional political landscapes. Sometimes these imagined worlds relate closely to the real world, but at other times they are more distant and relate to our world in potentially more disturbing ways.

Songs of Innocence and of Experience

In his *Songs of Innocence and of Experience*, William Blake employs a variety of settings, real and imagined. 'London' is firmly rooted in a real place inhabited by real people as you can see in Text 8E.

Text 8E

I wander through each charter'd street
Near where the chartered Thames doth flow
And mark in every face I meet
Marks of weakness, marks of woe.

William Blake, from 'London'

The 'black'ning church', the 'palace walls' and the busy city streets where the sufferings of life are enacted are clearly very much real places; as are the church of the 'Holy Thursday' poems and the chapel in 'The Garden of Love'. Elsewhere, however, Blake opts for a variety of imagined settings. The misty and ethereal woods of 'The Little Boy Lost', the mythical lands of 'The Little Girl Lost', the primeval forests of 'Introduction' to *The Songs of Experience* and 'Earth's Answer' and the forge of 'The Tiger' in which the fearsome beast of the title is created, bear a more tangential relationship to the real world. By adopting a variety of settings within the poems, Blake affords himself the opportunity to approach his social and political concerns from a variety of angles.

The Kite Runner

In *The Kite Runner*, Khaled Hosseini deals with a real-world location – Afghanistan. As the novel progresses he uses the city of Kabul, Taliban-controlled Afghanistan and the USA as a means of representing the nightmarish descent of his homeland from comparative freedom into a fundamentalist religious state.

ACTIVITY 18

Setting in *The Kite Runner*

Read the quotations from the novel in Text 8F–8H. How, in each case, does Hosseini use location to capture the social and political realities Amir faces?

Text 8F

Kabul had become a city of ghosts to me. A city of hare-lipped ghosts. America was different. America was a river, roaring along, unmindful of the past. I could wade into this river, let my sins drown to the bottom, let the waters carry me someplace far. Someplace with no ghosts, no memories, and no sins.

Khaled Hosseini, *The Kite Runner*

Text 8G

'You want to know?' he sneered. 'Let me imagine, Agha sahib. You probably lived in a big two- or three-storey house with a nice backyard that your gardener filled with flowers and fruit trees. All gated, of course. Your father drove an American car. You had servants, probably Hazaras. Your parents hired workers to decorate the house for the fancy mehmanis they threw, so their friends would come over to drink and boast about their travels to Europe or America. And I would bet my first son's eyes that this is the first time you've ever worn a pakol.'

He grinned at me, revealing a mouthful of prematurely rotting teeth. 'Am I close?'

'Why are you saying these things?' I said.

'Because you wanted to know,' he spat. He pointed to an old man dressed in ragged clothes trudging down a dirt path, a large burlap pack filled with scrub grass tied to his back. 'That's the real Afghanistan, Agha sahib. That's the Afghanistan I know. You? You've always been a tourist here, you just didn't know it.'

Khaled Hosseini, *The Kite Runner*

Set text focus: *The Kite Runner*

Khaled Hosseini was born in Kabul, Afghanistan in 1965. His father was a diplomat, his mother a teacher, so he grew up in a privileged home, when Kabul was a cosmopolitan city. As a boy, he enjoyed Western films as well as traditional kite-fighting. Having been relocated to Paris in 1976, the Hosseinis were ready to return home in 1980, but Afghanistan had been invaded by the Soviet Army. The family was given asylum in California, but it wasn't easy to adjust to the new culture at first and Hosseini remembers working in the local flea market with his father. Eventually Hosseini qualified as a doctor, but now writes full time. *The Kite Runner* was published in 2003 to international acclaim and won various prizes, in the midst of the war against the Taliban in Afghanistan. In 2006, Hosseini became a Goodwill Envoy for the United National Refugee Agency and now the Khaled Hosseini Foundation helps vulnerable people in Afghanistan.

Although not an exhaustive list, the following elements of political and social protest writing could be explored in relation to *The Kite Runner*:

- settings of time and place (see 8.3.1)
- the nature of the power struggle (see 8.2.1; 8.3.3)
- workings of the ruling political, religious and ethnic classes (see Activities 4, 7)
- behaviours of those with power (see 8.1.2; 8.3.2, Kings…)
- behaviours of those without power (see 8.1.2; 8.3.1; 8.3.2, Servants…)
- issues of social class (see 8.2.5, Social issues…; Activity 28)
- issues of ethnicity (see 8.4.3)
- how the text is structured, tensions heightened and resolved (see 8.3.3)
- representation of society in a particular historical period (see 8.2.5; Activity 32)
- effects on readers (see 8.1; 8.3.2, Critical lens).

The novel could be read from the perspective of:

- value and the canon (see 8.2.3, Critical lens; 9.3)
- narrative theory (see 8.3.2, Critical lens; 9.4)
- feminist theory (see 8.3.1, Critical lens; 9.5)
- post-colonial theory (see 8.4.3, Critical lens; 9.8).

'Kabul had become a city of ghosts to me.'
Khaled Hosseini, *The Kite Runner*

Text 8H

I sat against one of the house's clay walls. The kinship I felt suddenly for the old land… it surprised me. I'd been gone long enough to forget and be forgotten. I had a home in a land that might as well be in another galaxy to the people sleeping on the other side of the wall I leaned against. I thought I had forgotten about this land. But I hadn't. And, under the bony glow of a halfmoon, I sensed Afghanistan humming under my feet. Maybe Afghanistan hadn't forgotten me either. I looked westward and marvelled that, somewhere over those mountains, Kabul still existed. It really existed, not just as an old memory, or as the heading of an AP story on page 15 of the *San Francisco Chronicle*. Somewhere over those mountains in the west slept the city where my hare-lipped brother and I had run kites. Somewhere over there, the blindfolded man from my dream had died a needless death.

Khaled Hosseini, *The Kite Runner*

Hard Times

In *Hard Times*, Dickens creates a location with an imaginary name - Coketown - but one that is firmly rooted in the real world of Victorian Britain, clearly suggesting life in the industrial towns (specifically Preston) of the North at the height of the Industrial Revolution. Consider the opening description of Coketown shown in Text 8I.

Text 8I

It was a town of red brick, or of brick that would have been red if the smoke and ashes had allowed it; but as matters stood, it was a town of unnatural red and black like the painted face of a savage. It was a town of machinery and tall chimneys, out of which interminable serpents of smoke trailed themselves for ever and ever, and never got uncoiled. It had a black canal in it, and a river that ran purple with ill-smelling dye, and vast piles of building full of windows where there was a rattling and a trembling all day long, and where the piston of the

Set text focus: *Hard Times*

Charles Dickens experienced the appalling employment conditions of the working class, and especially children, at first hand when, at 12 years old, he had to work in a blacking factory (which made boot polish) for a few months. That experience made a lasting impression and later work as a court reporter and journalist kept him informed about the living and working conditions of the working classes. He was very disillusioned by Victorian society's ineffectual attempts to improve education and working conditions for the working classes, and explored these injustices in *Hard Times* and other novels.

Although not an exhaustive list, the following elements of political and social protest writing could be explored in relation to *Hard Times*:

- the type of text (see Activity 6; 8.2.1; 8.2.5, Charles Dickens)
- settings of time and place (see 8.3.1)
- the nature of the power struggle (see 8.2.1; 8.3.3)
- behaviours of those with power (see 8.1.2)
- behaviours of those without power (see 8.1.2; 8.3.2, Servants…)
- connections of the smaller world to the larger world (see Activity 3)
- focus on human organisation: in the home, work place, government (see 8.1.2; 8.2.5)
- issues of social class (see 8.2.5, Charles Dickens; Activity 28)
- how the text is structured, tensions heightened and resolved (see 8.3.3)
- how language is used (see Activity 19)
- representation of society in a particular historical period (see 8.2.5)
- effects on readers (see 8.1; Activity 19; 8.3.2, Critical lens).

The novel could be read from the perspective of:

- value and the canon (see 8.2.3, Critical lens; 9.3)
- narrative theory (see 8.3.2, Critical lens; 9.4)
- feminist theory (see 8.3.1, Critical lens; 9.5)
- Marxist theory (see 8.2.4, Critical lens; 8.4.2, Critical lens; 9.6)
- eco-critical theory (see 8.2.4, Critical lens; 8.3.1, Critical lens; 9.7).

steam-engine worked monotonously up and down, like the head of an elephant in a state of melancholy madness. It contained several large streets all very like one another, and many small streets still more like one another, inhabited by people equally like one another, who all went in and out at the same hours, with the same sound upon the same pavements, to do the same work, and to whom every day was the same as yesterday and to-morrow, and every year the counterpart of the last and the next.

Charles Dickens, *Hard Times*

Watch tutorial video, Political Writing and Social Class, on Cambridge Elevate

ACTIVITY 19

Language and setting

a Read the extract from *Hard Times* in Text 8I closely. What do you notice about Dickens' use of language? How does he use this to convey to his readers a sense of the place? What social and political issues can you identify in the passage? How are settings used as a method of political or social protest?

b If you have also read Blake's *Songs of Innocence and of Experience*, what similarities do you notice between the language and ideas of Blake's and Dickens' texts?

Critical lens: Eco-critical theory

Eco-critical theory invites us to consider the ways in which the natural world is used in literary texts. One significant topic is the way in which the natural world is perceived as a resource for humanity to exploit rather than use in a balanced and respectful way. What attitudes to the co-existence of nature and humanity do you see in your set texts – especially *Songs of Innocence and of Experience*, *Hard Times*, *The Handmaid's Tale* and *Harvest*?

For more on eco-critical theory, see 9.7

The Handmaid's Tale

In *The Handmaid's Tale* Margaret Atwood creates the fearsome dystopian world of Gilead, a fundamentalist religious state – in this case based on extreme Christian beliefs. Although this is an imagined world, it reflects elements of the real world. Her depiction of Gilead is in some ways similar to Hosseini's treatment of Afghanistan in *The Kite Runner*. Both present us with distorted social visions of the world in which women, minority groups or those unwilling to support the powers that be are subject to fearsome and brutal oppression. Both Atwood's and Hosseini's fictional visions present us with 'before and after' perspectives on their respective societies as a means of allowing us a critical insight into the motivations and effects of social and political change. Atwood's vision, however, having no actual parallel in historical events in the USA, remains a fully dystopian rather than a real-world setting.

ACTIVITY 20

Real and imagined worlds

Select three or four texts you've read – or screen dramas you've seen – that deal with social and political issues. For each of these texts, think about the differing ways in which the writers have used setting.

a Is it an actual place? In what ways does the writer use the recognisable features of this place?

b Is it a fictional, but evidently 'real' setting (e.g. Coketown in *Hard Times*)? How does the writer use the features of the real world in creating the fictional space? Why do you think the writer opted to create a 'real' setting rather than using an actual place?

c Is it a real but unfamiliar setting (e.g. Kabul in *The Kite Runner*)? How does the writer use familiarity and unfamiliarity in creating your sense of place?

d Is it a completely imagined world (e.g. Gilead in *The Handmaid's Tale*)? How does the writer create such a setting? In what ways does it relate to the recognisable 'real' world and in what ways does it diverge from it?

e In questions a–d, how do the social and political issues the texts deal with relate to the setting? Or how does the setting affect your view of the issues covered in the text? What kinds of social and political issues are the writers highlighting? How do you feel this affects their choice of setting?

Critical lens: feminist theory

Feminist theory focuses on the portrayal of gender and sexuality in literary texts. In many political texts, the relationships between men and women, and perceptions of male and female behaviour, are central concerns. In *A Doll's House*, *The Handmaid's Tale* and *The Kite Runner*, for instance, what attitudes to and expectations of female behaviour are displayed by the characters?

For more on feminist theory, see 9.5

8.3.2 Political characters: people and power relationships

Political narratives contain a range of types of political character, representing those who *have* power, those who *lack* power, and those who try to *gain* power. Just as the settings of political and social protest writing explore political systems and social conditions by presenting a mixture of real and imagined worlds, so the characters in political narratives explore the qualities of participants in politics and social protest by combining elements of reality and imagination.

Kings, tyrants, leaders: the powerful

As we have seen, political and social protest writing is concerned with the ways in which power operates in society. A common feature of political narratives, then, is an exploration of the people who wield power - whether they are royalty, aristocracy, politicians, religious leaders, the social elite, the wealthy, or simply those who have power within communities and families. The institutions that support these powerful people - from the monarchy to parliament, and from the Church to marriage - are also important elements of many political narratives.

In general, the powerful fall into two camps - the benevolent and the malevolent: the good leader and the tyrant or villain. In *Henry IV Parts I* and *2*, for instance, and in *Henry V*, we are presented with an image of royalty as heroic and responsible, and of the monarchy as crucial to the health of the nation. Similarly, In Jim Crace's *Harvest*, Master Kent is portrayed as a benevolent lord who has the best interests of his people at heart. In both cases, however, as modern readers, we might also want to ask important questions about the vested interests of these leaders and about the extent to which their authority is democratically authorised.

Shakespeare's kings are not always benevolent, however. Sometimes they are tyrants or villains - as for instance in *Richard III*. In *Richard II* and *Henry IV Part 2*, audiences often feel ambivalence to Bolingbroke's actions and it is questionable how far his behaviour is heroic and responsible. Perhaps he is intended to capture a newly defined type of 'political' king rather than a stock 'good' or 'bad' monarch.

Political villains like Richard III are powerful and threatening figures in political and social protest writing. They serve as a focal point for the reader's dislike, even hatred, as they come to represent the evil of the forces of misrule or threat. The character O'Brien in *1984* captures perfectly the amoral, power-fuelled aspiration of this character, as does Rosa Klebb in Ian Fleming's *From Russia with Love*.

Other powerful characters are more ambivalent, combining sympathetic or heroic qualities with flaws of various kinds, or aspects of villainy with redemptive qualities - Macbeth and King Lear, for instance. Often, the ambivalence of such characters is a result of their obedience to the social roles they have inherited or worked in - Torvald in *A Doll's House* and The Commander in *The Handmaid's Tale*, for instance.

ACTIVITY 21

Authority figures in political narratives

Think about the characters in the texts you have studied. Which ones hold power within the institutions or relationships portrayed? Which of these descriptions is appropriate for each character?

Figure 8B

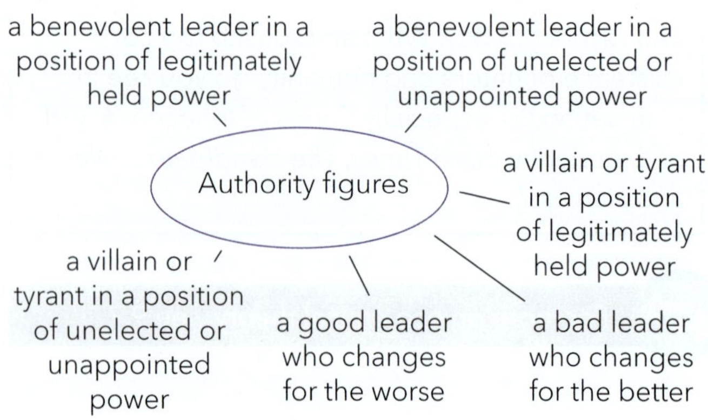

How do the writers portray the powerful status of the characters through the way they speak and act, through the way others behave towards them, and through the narrative voice or voices in the text?

Servants, slaves and victims: the powerless

By contrast, political narratives also often feature depictions of the powerless - either the completely powerless (slaves or the victims of tyrants), or the relatively powerless - those whose democratic rights are not granted, or who are unjustly disadvantaged by their class, race, gender, or other social category.

ACTIVITY 22

Protecting the powerless

Think about the characters in your set texts who might be defined as powerless. Why are they powerless? Is their powerlessness just or unjust? To what extent are their freedoms portrayed as restricted by individuals or by systems and institutions? How might they be granted more power, and how would this create a better society?

In his review of Crace's *Harvest*, Adam Mars-Jones writes: 'The absence of institutions is the most startling thing about the world of this book. There are law courts and civil authorities somewhere, with relevant powers and responsibilities, but they're so far out of reach they might as well not exist. There's no church, although a site has been set aside for one. The nearest place of worship is a long day's travel away, as is the nearest alehouse.'

To what extent are the powerless in your texts effectively protected by social or political institutions and systems? If not, why not?

Rebels, challengers, conspirators: the protesters

Often acting in direct defiance of established leaders in political narratives are challengers to or rebels against their power - who may be principled social protestors, or rivals who seek merely to take power for themselves. Such characters might act for themselves or represent an institution or movement, and they may be supported by a group of conspirators who act together to rebel against and seize power from the established leader.

Whether they rise up from among the ranks of the powerless, or whether they are already powerful but seek more power, they are likely to have many of the qualities of leadership already discussed. The established leader and the challenger are likely to fulfil the roles of protagonist and antagonist in the narrative, though which is which will depend on the exact dynamics of the text, for instance whose perspective the narrative focuses on.

In *Henry IV Part 1*, for instance, although we might identify several leaders and challengers in various parts of the play, we might argue that in the central narrative Prince Hal is represented as the protagonist, in this case the established leader, while Hotspur is the antagonist, the challenger. One of the main themes of the play is the heroism that leadership requires, and note that both leader and challenger are portrayed as heroic (in different ways). This affects how the audience will respond to the protestor and his motivation, and to the established leader's resistance.

The dynamics of the relationship between leader and protester play out very differently in other texts. In *A Doll's House*, for instance, we might argue that Torvald is the established leader in their relationship, representing the institution of marriage, and his wife Nora, the challenger, a social protester representing new ideas about women's roles in society and seeking to wrest power from her husband. Which one we might define as protagonist and which antagonist is perhaps less clear here, because, although she is the challenger, we see Nora as the principal actor in events throughout the play. Here, too, the way we see her role and her husband's affects our response to the protest portrayed.

ACTIVITY 23

Rebels and the language of political rebellion

Think about the roles of challengers or rebels in the texts you have studied. How many challengers or rebels are there? Who supports them? Which takes a leading or heroic role? Is there a clear protagonist and antagonist in the narrative? Which - if any - is presented as acting for or against justice?

The language used to describe the actions and character of rebels and protestors, and to suggest who we should support or feel sympathy with, is a significant issue in political narratives, as it is in real-world politics. Often, the ways we view political events determines the kind of language we use about them, and people's differing views will lead to differing representations. Think, for example, about the following words: 'terrorist', 'guerrilla', 'revolutionary', 'rebel', 'protestor', 'freedom fighter'.

a What does each of these terms mean for you? What characteristics do you associate with each? Could they all be applied to one person or group?

b Which of the words listed in the introduction to this activity would you apply to the following individuals and why: Osama bin Laden, Nelson Mandela, Vladimir Lenin, Che Guevara, Robert Mugabe, Martin Luther King? Note that all these individuals are historically important challengers to established power, and all have been viewed as political heroes and as political criminals by different groups of people at different times.

c Which characters in the texts you have studied might be labelled with one or more of these words? What language is used to suggest which characters have justice or morality on their side?

Critical lens: narrative theory

Narrative theory is concerned with the ways in which writers weave together events in literary texts using a range of narrative devices. One significant issue is the extent to which readers or audiences are guided by the perspective of particular characters or narrative voices. Think about the texts you are studying. What narrative perspectives are used? How might they seem different if the dominant perspectives were those of different characters?

For more on narrative theory, see 9.4

8.3.3 Political narratives: conspiracy, protest, rebellion and war

Political and social protest literature takes many forms, so it is difficult to make generalisations about narrative structures in such writing. However, we *can* say that its narratives are often marked by conflict or tension between opposing political viewpoints or forces, and by the escalation and resolution of those conflicts or tensions – just as in real-world politics.

In political literature, conflict or tension might take the form of something personal – a conflict within a relationship, for instance – or something more public – a conspiracy or rebellion, a protest or a war, for instance. Whichever it is, the private and the public are often entangled, and both private and public actions are likely to have political implications. In such oppositions, it is often the case that one side is an oppressive force and the other side is seeking freedom; however, many political narratives are more complex.

ACTIVITY 24

Conflict and resolution in political and social protest narratives

Consider the texts you have studied. In each one, what would you identify as the main political conflict or tension? To what extent would you say that that conflict or tension drives the narrative? What are the moments of crisis during the narrative, and to what extent is the conflict or tension resolved?

8.4 Representation in political writing

8.4.1 Gender and sexuality

The politics of gender, and more recently sexuality, have been central concerns of political writers since the rise of feminism in the late 18th and 19th centuries, although of course the discussion of gender roles in literature goes back further than that, at least as far as 'The Wife of Bath' in Chaucer's *Canterbury Tales* and Kate in Shakespeare's *Taming of the Shrew*. Debate about the nature of gender and the representation and allocation of gender roles is often described as 'gender politics'.

ACTIVITY 25

Gender politics in literature

To what extent would you say that gender or sexuality are issues in the texts you have studied? If they are, are the issues raised explicitly as political or social protest issues in the narrative, or is it left to the reader to interpret them as political issues?

The Handmaid's Tale and *A Doll's House*

Gender is a particularly prominent issue in Atwood's *The Handmaid's Tale* and Ibsen's *A Doll's House*. Read the passages from the two texts in Texts 8J–8M and consider the ways that the authors represent women.

Text 8J

Helmer [*calls out from his room*]. Is that my little lark twittering out there?
Nora [*busy opening some of the parcels*]. Yes, it is!
Helmer. Is it my little squirrel bustling about?
Nora. Yes!
Helmer. When did my squirrel come home?
Nora. Just now. [*Puts the bag of macaroons into her pocket and wipes her mouth.*] Come in here, Torvald, and see what I have bought.
Helmer. Don't disturb me. [*A little later, he opens the door and looks into the room, pen in hand.*] Bought, did you say? All these things? Has my little spendthrift been wasting money again?

Henrik Ibsen, *A Doll's House* (from the beginning of Act 1)

Text 8K

Nora. What do you consider my most sacred duties?
Helmer. Do I need to tell you that? Are they not your duties to your husband and your children?
Nora. I have other duties just as sacred.
Helmer. That you have not. What duties could those be?
Nora. Duties to myself.
Helmer. Before all else, you are a wife and a mother.
Nora. I don't believe that any longer. I believe that before all else I am a reasonable human being, just as you are – or, at all events, that I must try and become one. I know quite well, Torvald, that most people would think you right, and that views of that kind are to be found in books; but I can no longer content myself with what most people say, or with what is found in books. I must think over things for myself and get to understand them.

Henrik Ibsen, *A Doll's House* (From late in Act 3)

Text 8L

Women were not protected then.

I remember the rules, rules that were never spelled out but that every women knew: don't open your door to a stranger, even if he says he is the police. Make him slide his ID under the door. Don't stop on the road to help a motorist pretending to be in trouble. Keep the locks on and keep going. If anyone whistles, don't turn to look. Don't go into a Laundromat by yourself at night.

I think about Laundromats. What I wore to them: shorts, jeans, jogging pants. What I put into them: my own clothes, my own soap, my own money, money I had earned myself. I think about having such control.

Now we walk along the same street, in red pairs, and no man shouts obscenities at us, speaks to us, touches us. No-one whistles.

There is more than one kind of freedom, said Aunt Lydia. Freedom to and freedom from. In the days of anarchy, it was freedom to. Now you are being given freedom from. Don't underrate it.

Margaret Atwood, *The Handmaid's Tale*, Chapter 5

Text 8M

But what else do we know about her... ? She does not see fit to supply us with her original name, and indeed all official records of it would have been destroyed upon her entry into the Rachel and Leah Re-education Centre. 'Offred' gives no clue, since, like 'Ofglen and Ofwarren', it was a patronymic composed of the possessive preposition and the first name of the gentleman in question. Such names were taken by these women

'I believe that before all else I am a reasonable human being...'
Henrik Ibsen, *A Doll's House*

upon their entry into a connection with the household of a specific Commander, and relinquished by them upon leaving it.

Margaret Atwood, *The Handmaid's Tale*, Historical Notes

ACTIVITY 26

Women in Ibsen and Atwood

a How do Ibsen and Atwood use language to represent women's voices and the role of women in society here - through dialogue and stage directions (in the Ibsen) and first-person narration (in the Atwood)?

b What political issues are raised here in relation to gender? What is the significance of the idea of 'freedom to and freedom from' in relation to both these texts?

Women as authors, actors and characters

Gender politics is not only an issue in relation to the representation of characters in literature, but also in relation to the relative roles of men and women in producing and performing in works of literature. For instance, as in many other art forms, there were few published women writers until the second half of the 20th century, and in the 19th century many women (for instance George Eliot and the Brontë sisters) had to use male pseudonyms when they published their work. Similarly, women were not allowed to act on a stage until the late 17th century, so there are relatively few women's roles in much classic theatre - and, where women's roles do exist, even in relatively modern drama, they are frequently less interesting than men's roles because of the restrictions placed on women in real life.

ACTIVITY 27

Henry IV - a man's world?

A 2014 production of *Henry IV* at the Donmar Warehouse employed an all-female cast. Think about the following:

a In what ways does the use of an all-female cast change your perceptions of the play?

b To what extent was the director's choice to use an all-female cast in itself a political act?

c In Shakespeare's day, casts were all male. How do you respond to the 'political' reversal of genders?

d Think about the major political concerns of the play (kingship, nationhood, political motivation, manhood and so on). Does the fact that these were enacted entirely by women rather than men change your perceptions? In what ways and why?

Critical lens: feminist theory

Feminist theory focuses on the portrayal of gender and sexuality in literary texts. A central concern is the extent to which women's voices and perspectives are heard in literature. In this regard, it's interesting that women characters play a relatively small role in Shakespeare's histories. Why do you think this might be? What roles do you see female characters playing in *Henry IV Part 1*?

For more on feminist theory, see 9.5

8.4.2 Social class

As with gender, issues of class have been central concerns of political writers since the rise of socialism in the 19th century - although of course the discussion and depiction of class relationships has also been an important element of literature for centuries - at least as far back as Chaucer's *The Canterbury Tales* and the plays of Shakespeare. Debate about class and class conflict is often described as 'class politics'.

ACTIVITY 28

Class politics

To what extent would you say that class is an issue in the texts you have studied? If it is, is it raised explicitly as a political or social protest issue in the narrative, or is it left to the reader to interpret it as political issue?

Class in the poetry of Tony Harrison

As you saw in the poetry unit, Tony Harrison is a major contemporary political poet. His long poem 'v' (written in 1985) is one of the most significant political poems of the last twenty years, a complex reflection on language, class, culture and politics. 'v' describes a visit Harrison makes to his parents' graves in a cemetery in Leeds, and is a reflection both on political conflict in Britain at the time and on Harrison's own sense of class identity.

Close to Leeds United's football grounds, the gravestones in the cemetery are daubed with graffiti ranging from football matches ('Leeds v. Derby') to racist slogans. Harrison draws parallels between the conflict of football matches (such as Leeds v. Derby) and the more serious political conflicts that are implied by the racist graffiti. He reflects on the miners' strike and the mass unemployment of the time suggesting that these hardships have contributed to the alienation the working classes feel and that has fed their racist attitudes. He also reflects on his own working-class past, and the way his language and culture have changed as a result of his education. Ultimately, he reflects on how poetic art and crude graffiti can both emerge from the same starting point, and whether poetry can adequately represent or overcome social division of this sort.

ACTIVITY 29

The language of 'v'

Language is significant in many different ways in 'v'. The poem is partly *about* language, and it also *uses* language in interesting ways.

a Why do you think Harrison uses so much 'bad language' in the poem? Did this language surprise you? Do you think such language is acceptable in a poem like this? What arguments might you put for and against using such language in the poem? Why does he place some of the swear words in capital letters?

b In what ways is the voice of the skinhead used as a means of conveying protest?

c How might you sum up the political message of the poem, and how might the use of 'bad language' like this help to convey that message?

d What do you notice about the form of the poem - its rhyme scheme, its metre, its stanzas and the organisation of its lines? In what ways might this form help to convey protest in the poem?

Check your responses in the Ideas section on Cambridge Elevate

For more on poetic form, see 2.3.2

Class relationships in *Harvest*

One of the central themes of Jim Crace's novel *Harvest* is class and power relationships in a village in Tudor England at the time of the land enclosures of that period. In particular, the novel explores the vulnerability of ordinary people with few rights in a society controlled by a small but powerful elite of wealthy landowners.

Exploring enclosure

Enclosure is the name given to the removal of the rights of ordinary people to freely use common land. In many cases, this land was enclosed by fences, to prevent its common use and to keep grazing animals in. During the Tudor period, whole villages were often enclosed by landowners so that they could farm sheep, which were immensely profitable. This often led to unemployment and poverty for villagers, many of whom had to leave to seek a living elsewhere. Enclosure was also common during the Industrial Revolution, when land surrounding cities became valuable for urban development.

Read the passages in Texts 8N and 8O from *Harvest* and think about the ways that Crace represents class relationships.

Text 8N

It is only now I can address myself to… Master Kent's request, instruction actually…. I have seldom disappointed him before. I take great pride in that. My father was his father's clerk. My mother was his milk nurse. We are almost of an age and so must have been ear-to-ear when we were nuzzling infants, growing plump on the same breasts. I do not want to say he is my brother; our stations are too different. But we were playmates in his father's yards….

I will not forget those early playmate days or my family debt to Master Kent… I have always taken it as my particular duty to speak up on his behalf amongst my neighbours, if anyone's disgruntled… I have been sensible – and loyal, in both our interests. *To all of our advantages*, let's say… I have warranted his respect by always helping him. So he relies on me…

Jim Crace, *Harvest*, Chapter 3

Text 8O

[Master Jordan] is maddened by our way of life. He is exasperated by the disarray he has discovered in our village. He sighs dramatically to leave us in no doubt. We've brought these troubles on ourselves. And he will bring them to a sudden and impatient end if needs be. 'So, Walter Thirsk', he says, just listing me. He's wondering I think how useful I might be…

Again he circles, but this time he is smiling… 'Nothing but sheep' he says, and laughs out loud. His joke, I think is this: we are the sheep, already here and munching at the grass. There's none more pitiful than us, he thinks. There's none more meek. There's none to match our peevish fearfulness, our thoughtless lives, our vacant, puny faces, our dependency… He will replace us with a nobler stock.

Jim Crace, *Harvest*, Chapter 7

ACTIVITY 30

Class and power in harvest

a How does Crace use comparison and contrast to represent the power relationships between Walter Thirsk and his two masters in the passages in Texts 8N and 8O? How are his relationships with the two men similar and different?

b Although *Harvest* is apparently a historical account of class relationships in Tudor England, it might also be read as an **allegory** about human behaviour, especially in the face of fear of the unknown and outsiders and threats to our security. Rob Nixon, in the *New York Times*, calls it a 'novel of social decomposition… a perfect fit for our unstable, unforgiving age'. Do you think Crace might have intended us to read the book in this way? What parallels with contemporary society might we see in the narrative?

Key terms

allegory: a literary work in which the apparent meaning of characters and events symbolises a deeper moral or spiritual meaning

Critical lens: Marxist theory

Marxist theory focuses on the representation of class and social power in literature. A significant concern is the extent to which working-class characters display *false consciousness,* accepting their social inferiority without protest, or instead rebel in some way against their social inferiority. To what extent do working-class characters in your texts display either of these attitudes?

For more on Marxist theory, see 9.6

8.4.3 Ethnicity

Representations of race relationships and different ethnicities have featured in English literature at various times over the centuries. The most famous historical examples are probably Shakespeare's *Othello* and Harriet Beecher Stowe's anti-slavery novel *Uncle Tom's Cabin* (1852). It was not, however, until widespread immigration and the growth of the civil rights movement in the 20th century that ethnicity became a central concern of many political and social protest writers.

Debates about race relationships are often called 'racial politics' – although it is important to note that the concept of 'race' is itself highly controversial, since 'the human race' (*homo sapiens*) is one species and there are no clear genetic boundaries between different ethnic groups. The word 'ethnicity' is more appropriate because it recognises that social and

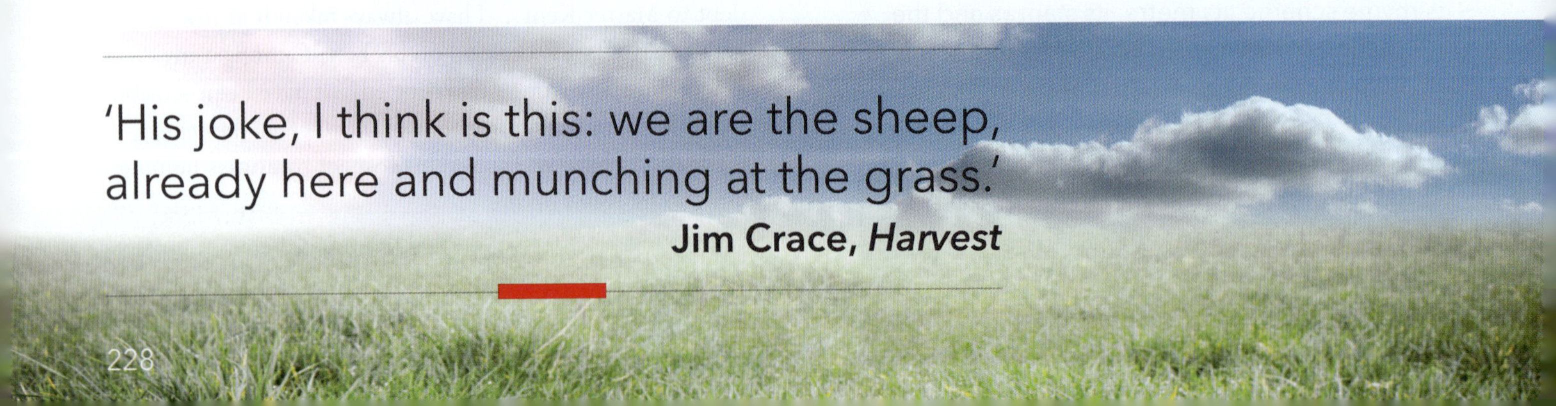

cultural differences between groups of people are more significant than biological differences.

ACTIVITY 31

Racial politics

To what extent would you say that race is an issue in the texts you have studied? If it is, is it raised explicitly as a political or social protest issue in the narrative, or is it left to the reader to interpret it as political issue?

The Kite Runner

Read the passage in Text 8P from Chapter 2 in Hosseini's novel *The Kite Runner,* which examines the racial and political tensions in modern Afghanistan.

Text 8P

They called him "flat-nosed" because of Ali and Hassan's characteristic Hazara Mongoloid features. For years, that was all I knew about the Hazaras, that they were Mogul descendants, and that they looked a little like Chinese people. School text books barely mentioned them and referred to their ancestry only in passing. Then one day, I was in Baba's study, looking through his stuff, when I found one of my mother's old history books. It was written by an Iranian named Khorami. I blew the dust off it, sneaked it into bed with me that night, and was stunned to find an entire chapter on Hazara history. An entire chapter dedicated to Hassan's people! In it, I read that my people, the Pashtuns, had persecuted and oppressed the Hazaras. It said the Hazaras had tried to rise against the Pashtuns in the nineteenth century, but the Pashtuns had "quelled them with unspeakable violence." The book said that my people had killed the Hazaras, driven them from their lands, burned their homes, and sold their women. The book said part of the reason Pashtuns had oppressed the Hazaras was that Pashtuns were Sunni Muslims, while Hazaras were Shi'a. The book said a lot of things I didn't know, things my teachers hadn't mentioned. Things Baba hadn't mentioned either. It also said some things I *did* know, like that people called Hazaras *mice-eating, flat-nosed, load-carrying donkeys*. I had heard some of the kids in the neighborhood yell those names to Hassan.

Khalid Hosseini, *The Kite Runner*

ACTIVITY 32

Race in *The Kite Runner*

What are the political issues raised in Text 8P? How does it combine personal experiences, political events, and ideas about race? How does Khaled Hosseini use the first-person narrative of Amir to bring these different things together?

Critical lens: post-colonial theory

Post-colonial theory encourages us to consider the ways in which imperialism and international warfare has had lasting effects on the world. As you read *The Kite Runner*, think about the depiction of the USSR and the USA, and their roles in the war in Afghanistan. How are they portrayed in the novel? To what extent do you think their interventions in the country are shown to have had positive or negative effects?

For more on post-colonial theory, see 9.8

8.5 Bringing it all together

8.5.1 How will your studies on Elements of political and social protest writing be assessed?

Elements of political and social protest writing is one of the two options for A Level Paper 2. Your knowledge will be tested by exam.

For guidance on preparing for the exams, see Unit 11

8.5.2 How much do you know?

The following questions ask you to bring together the elements you have studied in this unit.

1 Write notes on your responses to the following key concepts:
- what constitutes politics?
- power and powerlessness in political and social protest writing
- leadership and kingship in political and social protest writing
- religion in political and social protest writing
- protest and rebellion in political and social protest writing

- equality and social justice in political and social protest writing
- war in political and social protest writing
- private and public lives in political and social protest writing
- politicians and political institutions in political and social protest writing.

2 Identify how the concepts listed in question 1 are used in the political and social protest writing texts you are studying, but also range more widely in your reading and viewing of political and social protest texts. Develop your ideas in more extended prose, summarising how these issues relate to your understanding of the functions of political and social protest writing.

3 Political and social protest writing in literature is a broad category that includes writing in a wide range of different forms and genres. Reflecting on the issues that you have read about in this unit, what do you think identifies a text as political or social protest literature? What are the main elements of political and social protest literature that you might expect to find in these texts? Develop your ideas in the form of extended prose.

4 Read 'Divisions', 'Working' and 'Marked with D' by Tony Harrison. How does the poet use language to shape political meanings in these three poems?

Consider each of these quotations in turn. How far do you think each is relevant to the texts you have studied and to your wider understanding of political writing?

8.5.3 Assessment objectives

In relation to the assessment objectives, this unit has explored:

- how you as a reader can make personal, informed and creative responses to political and social protest writing. It has also introduced you to a variety of terminology and key concepts relating to the idea of politics and to associated ideas. These will help you in your thinking about a variety of political writing texts both traditional and non-traditional (AO1)
- a variety of ways in which authors working in a variety of genres shape meanings in texts dealing with politics and social protest. It has introduced you to conventions and techniques within political writing, including structural and formal properties (AO2)
- the development of writing about politics and social protest from its appearance in the earliest literary texts through to the contemporary, introducing some key social and political contexts that underpin texts dealing with politics (AO3)
- the key elements of political and social protest writing across a wide range of literary works in each of the major genres – poetry, drama and prose fiction – and relating it to other narrative forms, such as writing for the screen (AO4)
- the roles of interpretation and analysis in reading political and social protest writing (AO5).

Summary

In this unit, you have learned about:

- the way political and social protest writing is approached in a variety of genres
- the development of political and social protest writing over time
- key elements of political and social protest writing and the key concepts it addresses
- how the authors of literary texts use different elements of political writing in their works
- narrative structure and form in political and social protest writing
- voices, perspectives and representation in political and social protest writing.

DEVELOPING

9 Literary theory

In this unit, you will:
- explore the idea of literary theory
- explore a range of theoretical approaches
- apply these approaches to a number of different texts.

9.1 What is literary theory?

A Level English Literature can be described as an exploration of meaning: much of what you do involves discussing what various texts might mean. However, studying literature also involves exploring the concept of 'meaning' itself. On a simple personal level, you'll probably be aware of the ways in which the meanings of a text can change: a poem that you studied four years ago can take on new resonances when you read it from an older and more knowing perspective, and a story that appeared relatively straightforward when you read it as a child can seem entirely different – and much more complex – when you revisit it as an adult. But 'meaning' is even more slippery than this, as the same text can be read and interpreted in different ways by different people, depending on their experiences, beliefs, perspectives and contexts. The study of these different ways of reading is called **literary theory**.

Your non-exam assessment will involve learning about some of the different approaches to literature that literary theory can involve, informed by your study of the Critical Anthology. You will apply at least two of these approaches to two texts (one poetry, one prose) of your choice. As you approach this assessment, it's important that you think carefully about the questions and insights raised by literary theory, and relate these questions and insights to some of the texts that you have encountered in your independent reading.

See 9.9,11.1.2 and 11.3.3 for more on the non-exam assessment

9.1.1 Theoretical questions

You have probably started to think about literary theory already, without actually realising it. Have you ever wondered, when you're studying a text, whether the author meant you to interpret it in the way you have? Have you ever thought that a particular way of interpreting a text is 'reading too much into it'? Have you ever heard anyone say that 'Poems can mean whatever you want them to mean'? All three of these examples raise questions that literary theorists are interested in. The first concerns the idea of **authorial intention** and whether our interpretations of a text should be constrained by its author. The second and third address the issue of whether there are any limits to interpretation – or whether a text has as many possible meanings as it has readers (or, indeed, as many possible meanings as it has read*ings*, because the same person can interpret the same text in different ways at different times).

Key terms

literary theory: the study of the ways in which we interpret literary texts

authorial intention: what an author intended his or her work to mean

Some authors have given us very clear messages as to how they want their texts to be interpreted. In his essay 'Tragedy and the Common Man' (1949), Arthur Miller set out his belief that ordinary people were just as suitable as subjects for tragedy as kings and great rulers, setting his own plays in the context of classical drama. However, there are many authors who have left no such statements (Shakespeare is one key example). In addition, some critics have argued that these messages should not be used as a guide for interpreting or evaluating texts. W.K. Wimsatt and Monroe C. Beardsley wrote in their essay 'The Intentional Fallacy' (1946) that 'the design or intention of the author is neither available nor desirable as a standard for judging the success of a work of literary art'. What do you think?

Exploring the relationship between author and reader

The French literary theorist Roland Barthes (1915–80) said that 'The birth of the reader must be at the cost of the death of the Author'. What do you think he meant by this?

ACTIVITY 1

Where is the meaning of a text?

One way of approaching literary theory is by thinking about the diagram in Figure 9A.

Where is the meaning of the text? Put a cross where you think the meaning is. Is it located in the words on the page – waiting to be extracted through a complex process of interpretation? Is it in the mind of the reader? In the mind of the author? Or somewhere else? Where else might it be? Should your English teacher be able to tell you what the meaning of a text is? Where would you put your teacher on this diagram?

Figure 9A

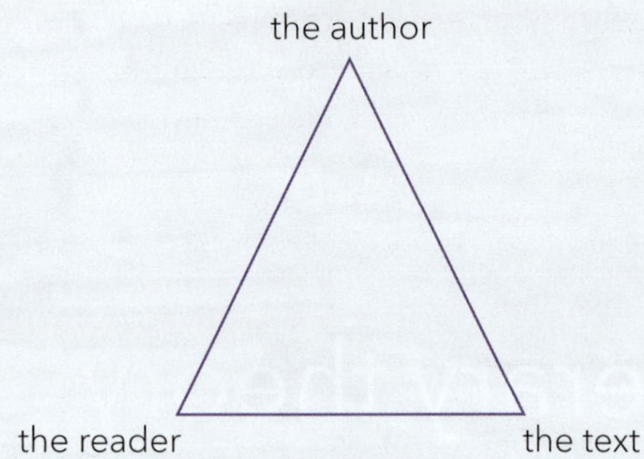

You might decide, for instance, that the meaning is somewhere in the middle. The author's ideas are obviously important, because they determine what the text actually says (and you might also be able to find out what the author wanted his or her works to mean). Equally, the words on the page shape the ways in which you interpret the text, but this doesn't mean that the text has only one possible meaning. These words will be interpreted in different ways by different readers (and individual readers might be able to perceive multiple meanings in the same text at the same time). But there are other factors that matter too. For example, how does your English teacher influence the way you read?

9.1.2 The importance of context

You might think that your English teacher doesn't really influence the way you read at all. However, the fact that you are studying texts in preparation for an A Level in English Literature will undoubtedly be an important factor in the way you experience these texts. In other words, it's one of the contexts that will shape your reading. None of us exists in a vacuum: we are all shaped by our gender, our upbringing, the society we live in and a host of other factors. What else might influence your interpretation?

ACTIVITY 2

Exploring the context of the reader

Draw a person in the centre of a piece of paper. Use this person as the middle of a spider diagram. Think of the different factors that might shape the way people interpret literary texts. Add these to your spider diagram. Use the example in Figure 9B as a starting point.

Now read the poem 'Pied Beauty' in Text 9A, by the poet Gerard Manley Hopkins (1844–89). Then think about how the factors you identified might influence the way readers interpret 'Pied Beauty'.

Figure 9B

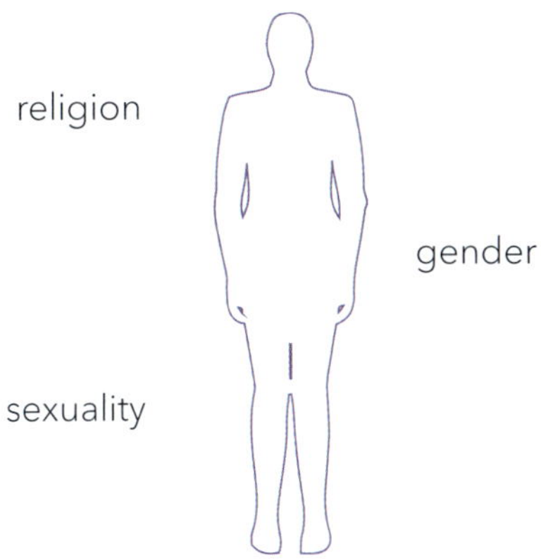

Text 9A

Pied Beauty

Glory be to God for dappled things –
    For skies of couple-colour as a **brinded** cow;
    For rose-moles all in stipple upon trout that swim;
Fresh-firecoal chestnut-falls; finches' wings;
    Landscape plotted and pieced – fold, fallow, and plough;
    And all trades, their gear and tackle and trim.
All things counter, original, spare, strange;
    Whatever is fickle, freckled (who knows how?)
    With swift, slow; sweet, sour; adazzle, dim;
He fathers-forth whose beauty is past change:
        Praise him.

Gerard Manley Hopkins

Glossary

brinded: marked with patches, spots or stripes

Check your responses in the Ideas section on Cambridge Elevate

9.1.3 Writers and their contexts

Of course, the kinds of factors that influence readers also influence writers as well. If you study the work of Charlotte Brontë, for instance, you will almost certainly consider the ways in which her work was shaped by the following:

- Brontë was a woman with little money and few social connections, living at a time when there were few options available to women of her particular social class.
- She was deeply affected by the deaths of her two older sisters from an illness caught at a charity school, run on strict religious principles that denied its pupils warmth, comfort and a proper diet.
- She saw herself as plain and undesirable, and during her life she fell in love with a number of men who were not in a position to return her affections.

In *Jane Eyre*, Brontë's most famous novel, you'll recognise the traces of these experiences in her depiction of Jane's suffering at Lowood, her struggle for independence and her relationship with Mr Rochester. Some critics would argue that such knowledge has no place in literary study, as the figure of the author seems so powerful that it limits the text's potential interpretations. The French philosopher Michel Foucault (1926–84) described

'For rose-moles all in stipple upon trout that swim'
Gerard Manley Hopkins, 'Pied Beauty'

the author as 'the ideological figure by which one marks the manner in which we fear the proliferation of meaning': in other words, a way of making the text more 'safe' and manageable by restricting its potential meanings to those related to the author's life and intentions. Others, however, would say that some texts are simply impossible to interpret without a certain amount of biographical knowledge.

ACTIVITY 3

The figure of the author

Think of an author you've studied. What do you know about this author's life? How does this knowledge help you to interpret his or her work? What have you gained – or lost – as a result?

Both reader and author, then, can be seen as being influenced by a number of different contexts: social, cultural, historical and so on. All of these contexts will influence them in different ways (and in ways that they might not necessarily be aware of). And, in addition, the text itself can be situated in particular literary contexts. You'll know from your prior study of literature that your reading of a play like *Twelfth Night* or *King Lear* will be influenced by your knowledge of the generic conventions of comedy or tragedy.

Let's look at an example of how these issues might relate to a particular poem. 'Anthem for Doomed Youth' in Text 9B was written by Wilfred Owen in 1917. Owen was a second lieutenant in the Manchester Regiment who fought in northern France during World War I. In 1916 he was diagnosed with shell shock, and was admitted to Craiglockhart War Hospital in Edinburgh. This poem was written during Owen's time as a patient there.

Text 9B

Anthem for Doomed Youth

What passing-bells for these who die as cattle?
Only the monstrous anger of the guns.
Only the stuttering rifles' rapid rattle
Can patter out their hasty **orisons**.
No mockeries now for them; no prayers nor bells,
Nor any voice of mourning save the choirs,
The shrill, demented choirs of wailing shells;
And **bugles** calling for them from sad **shires**.

What candles may be held to speed them all?
Not in the hands of boys, but in their eyes
Shall shine the holy glimmers of goodbyes.
The pallor of girls' brows shall be their **pall**;
Their flowers the tenderness of patient minds,
And each slow dusk a drawing down of blinds.

Wilfred Owen

Glossary

orisons: prayers

bugles: wind instruments made of brass, traditionally used in the army as signal-horns

shires: rural counties of England

pall: a shroud used to wrap a dead body or cover a coffin

ACTIVITY 4

Exploring interpretations

How might your reading of this poem be influenced by:

- your gender?
- your experiences of war?
- your political beliefs?
- your religious beliefs?
- what you know about Wilfred Owen?
- what you know about World War I?
- your understanding of the sonnet form?

See Rhyme in 2.3.2 for more on the sonnet form

9.2 Theoretical perspectives

As part of your study of A Level English literature, you will be exploring a number of different theoretical perspectives, representing particular ideas about the interpretation of literary texts. The Critical Anthology contains a range of accessible, thought-provoking extracts designed to introduce you to the following ideas.

- **Narrative theory** (sometimes called narratology) focuses on the ways in which narratives are constructed, paying attention to the ways in which the reader's perspectives are shaped by narrative perspective, sequence and style.

- **Feminist** and **Marxist theory** both draw attention to issues of power, looking at how literary texts reflect and explore the struggles between genders and social classes for fairness and equality.
- **Eco-critical theory** looks at the relationship between humans and the natural world, highlighting the way the natural world is depicted and the values associated with it.
- **Post-colonial theory** explores texts written in, and about, nations that have been colonised by others, and by writers whose roots are in these nations. It looks at questions of power, identity and exploitation, and offers a counter-narrative to challenge the narratives offered by those who have historically held most power.

As a starting point, you will look at one of the most fundamental questions asked by literary theory: what *is* literature? This involves questions concerning value and the canon – the group of texts considered most central to our idea of literature.

See 9.3.1 for more on the canon

9.3 Value and the canon

What is literature? If you look up the word 'literature' in a dictionary, you will probably get a very lengthy definition that encompasses a number of meanings. Figure 9C contains the entry for 'literature' in the Oxford English Dictionary.

Figure 9C

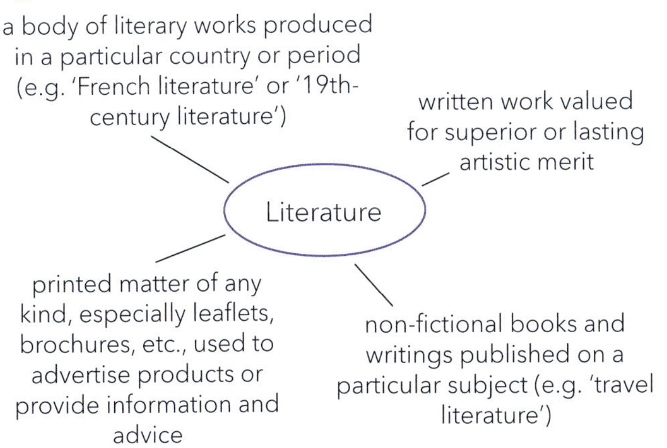

When we talk about 'the study of English literature', we might think we're using the word in the first of these senses (although we need to clarify what we mean by 'English', as you might well have studied the work of writers who are American or Irish, for example: what we mean is, of course, 'the study of literature written in English'). However, the second sense – 'written work valued for superior or lasting artistic merit' – is also an important one. Who decides which works have 'superior or artistic merit'? What is 'artistic merit', anyway?

ACTIVITY 5

Exploring the idea of literature

Think about the following questions. They encourage you to consider what 'literature' is, what values it represents and what it means to study literature.

a How would you define 'literature'?
b What is the difference between 'literature', and 'fiction' or 'drama'? (*Is* there a difference?)
c Is soap opera literature? Is *Harry Potter* literature?
d Is there a particular kind of language which is only found in literature?
e What is the point of studying literature?
f Is it more important to study old texts or new?
g What benefit is there for society in the study of literature?
h What benefit is there for the individual in studying literature?
i How do you evaluate whether a literary text is good or not?
j Is it possible to dislike or disapprove of a text but still think it is 'good' (or to enjoy a text but still think it is 'bad')?

Several of the questions in Activity 5 asked you to reflect on your own study of literature. Students are often unaware of the decisions that underpin the courses they're studying. However, every one of your A Level courses will be the result of months of discussion, with committees having to decide what students will study, how they will study it and how their work will be assessed. In English Literature, these discussions are particularly heated. There are endless debates about which literary texts should be studied in schools, and whether particular texts have 'sufficient literary merit' to be considered worthy of study.

In Texts 9C and 9D, you will find two articles about the teaching of English Literature in schools. Read the articles and then do Activity 6.

Text 9C

Teach Jane Austen, state schools to be told

State schools will be told to teach the classic English novels they currently ignore in a radical overhaul of what is taught in the classroom.

The move comes after a survey carried out for ministers found state secondary schools tend to teach children aged 11 to 14 works by contemporary writers such as Louis Sachar and John Boyne, rather than classic authors such as Jane Austen and William Golding.

Ministers now want to see more challenging texts introduced in state schools to mirror what is taught in private schools, where pupils are much more likely to read dead authors whose work has stood the test of time.

Changes to English lessons will form a central plank of the proposals to be made in a sweeping review of the national curriculum which will report in the New Year.

They are expected to specify the key authors, as a minimum, that pupils should read in each year of schooling.

The survey by the Department of Education shows that two thirds of the books studied in a sample of more than 100 state secondary schools had been written in the last twenty years.

Plans to make English more challenging underline the determination by Michael Gove, the education secretary, to deal with what he believes is a lack of rigour in schools.

'The academic demands placed on children in state schools have been too low for too long', said a Government source. 'Schools need to raise the bar by requiring pupils to read a larger selection of books.'

Julie Henry *Daily Telegraph*, 6 November 2011

Text 9D

Gove kills the mockingbird with ban on US classic novels

The John Steinbeck novella *Of Mice and Men*, and other American classics including Arthur Miller's play *The Crucible* and the Harper Lee novel *To Kill a Mockingbird*, have been dropped from new English literature GCSEs after Michael Gove, the education secretary, insisted teachers should study works by British writers.

Three-quarters of the books on the Government-directed GCSEs, which will be unveiled this week, are by British authors and most are pre-20th century.

'*Of Mice and Men*, which Michael Gove really dislikes, will not be included. It was studied by 90% of teenagers taking English literature GCSE in the past', said OCR, one of Britain's biggest exam boards. 'Michael Gove said that was a really disappointing statistic.'

OCR added: 'In the new syllabus 70–80% of the books are from the English canon.'

University professors have warned that teenagers will be turned off studying English literature by the new exams.

Bethan Marshall, senior lecturer in English at King's College, London and chairwoman of the National Association of the Teaching of English, said: 'It's a syllabus out of the 1940s and rumour has it Michael Gove, who read literature at university, designed it himself. Schools will be incredibly depressed when they see it.

'Kids will be put off doing A Level literature by this. Many teenagers will think that being made to read Dickens aged 16 is just tedious. This will just grind children down.'

Another academic source added: 'The change is from a modern exam covering lots of authors still alive today, as well as the American greats, to a very traditional, old-fashioned one, featuring largely dead British authors. It's very disappointing.'

Pupils will still be able to study one or two modern works, but these too are by British writers. Willy Russell's play *Educating Rita* is understood to be on one exam board's syllabus.

'Why is *Educating Rita* better than *The Crucible*? It isn't – it's just it was written in Britain', said Marshall. 'The fact it was written in Britain should not be a factor.'

Sian Griffiths *Sunday Times*, 25 May 2014
[Note that, at the time of writing, Michael Gove is no longer the Education Secretary]

ACTIVITY 6

Debates about literature

a What do you think of the arguments put forward in the articles in Texts 9C and 9D?

b Should children be taught 'classic' novels rather than contemporary texts?

c Why might people consider it important to read texts that have 'stood the test of time'? On the other hand, why might people consider contemporary texts more appealing?

d Are 'classic texts' harder to study than contemporary ones? Is Michael Gove right to equate contemporary novels with a lack of rigour?

9.3.1 The literary canon

The article in Text 9D refers to **the canon**. This important term comes originally from religion, where it refers to 'the collection or list of books of the Bible accepted by the Christian Church as genuine and inspired' (Oxford English Dictionary). In English literature, the word 'canon' has come to mean the body of literary texts considered most worthy of study, because of their importance, quality and value.

It's easy to think of authors who belong, very firmly, within the English literary canon: Geoffrey Chaucer, John Milton, William Wordsworth, Jane Austen, etc. Nevertheless, the canon is notoriously slippery. Some authors who appear to have an established place on the canon did not achieve this status until relatively recently (when the study of English Literature in the universities first began, in the late 19th century, novels were not considered worthy of study). Others have lost their place in the canon as a result of changing fashions and tastes. And there are other texts whose value is being reconsidered, not because they contain some kind of eternal truth or beauty, but because of what they might tell us about particular social groups or historical periods.

Key terms

the canon: the body of literary texts considered most worthy of study, because of their importance, quality and value

ACTIVITY 7

Exploring the canon

Here is a list of 12 texts. Which ones do you think should belong to the canon, and which should be outside it? Put the texts into a rank order from the most to the least canonical.

- *How to be a Domestic Goddess*, by Nigella Lawson (2003). Recipe book that was described by one reviewer as 'the bible for the yummy-mummy generation'.
- *Oliver Twist*, by Charles Dickens (1838). Dickens' second novel and one of the most popular and enduring books of the 19th century, adapted countless times for film, stage and television.
- *Lyrics: 1962–2001,* by Bob Dylan (2006). The collected lyrics of one of the 20th century's leading musicians.
- *Persepolis,* by Marjane Satrapi (2008). Graphic novel whose author describes her experience of growing up in Iran after the Islamic Revolution of 1979.
- *Hamlet*, by William Shakespeare (1602). Renaissance tragedy; one of the most influential plays in the English language.
- *Silent Spring,* by Rachel Carson (1962). Non-fiction book about environmentalism credited with alerting the world to the dangers of pesticides in farming.
- *The Rover,* by Aphra Behn (1677). The most famous play by one of the first women to earn a living from her writing.
- *Casino Royale,* by Ian Fleming (1952). The first James Bond novel and the text that sparked one of the longest-running film series in history.

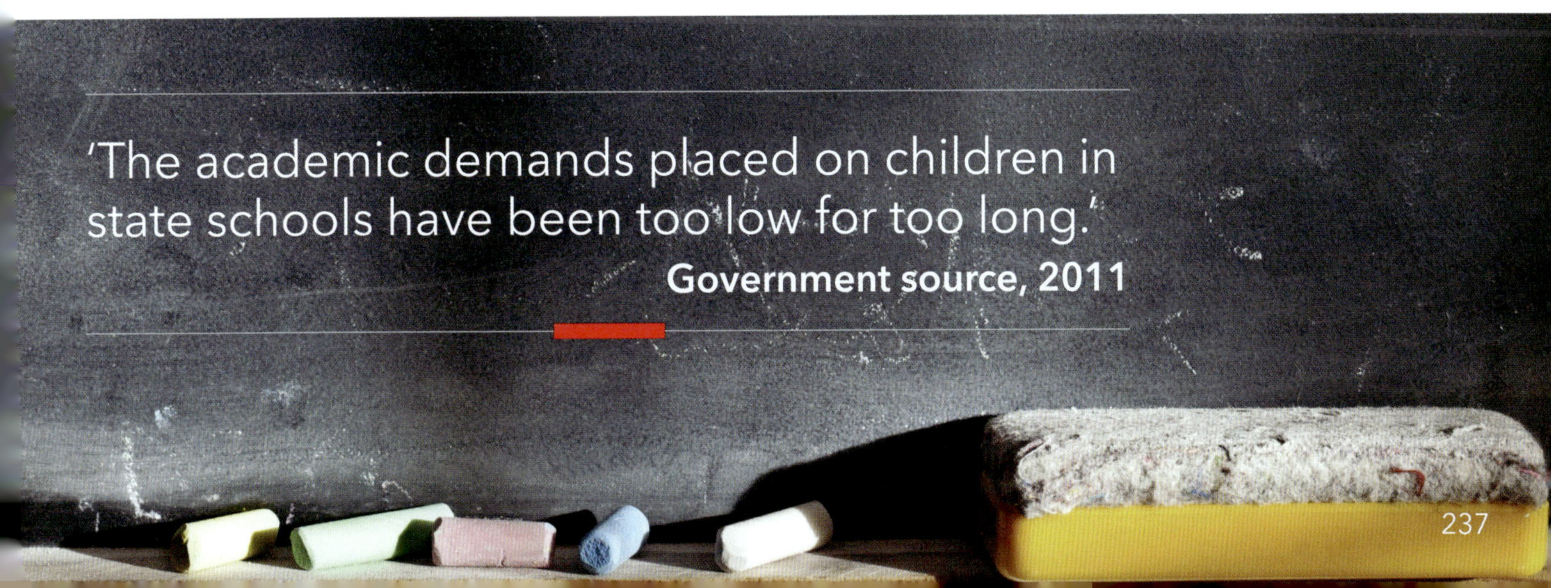

- *Lyrical Ballads*, by William Wordsworth and Samuel Taylor Coleridge (1798). Collection of poems that challenged prevailing fashions in poetry, professing to use 'a selection of the real language of men'.
- *Winnie-the-Pooh*, by A.A. Milne (1926). Enormously popular children's book whose characters are loved by children around the world.
- *Lady Chatterley's Lover*, by D.H. Lawrence (1928). Novel about the relationship between an upper-class woman and a gamekeeper that was the subject of a famous obscenity trial.
- *Twilight*, by Stephenie Meyer (2005). Young adult vampire romance that was one of the biggest-selling novels of the early 21st century.

Check your responses in the Ideas section on Cambridge Elevate

9.3.2 Value and the canon: taking it further

Virginia Woolf on 'rubbish-reading'

The novelist Virginia Woolf was firmly committed to the importance of non-canonical texts. In her 1926 lecture 'How Should One Read a Book?' she argued against the idea of an established canon, saying that 'The only advice … that one person can give another about reading is to take no advice, to follow your own instincts, to use your own reason, to come to your own conclusions'. She attempted to celebrate what she referred to as 'rubbish-reading': the minor and forgotten texts that were not viewed as 'literature'. For Woolf, these obscure authors and marginal genres still had a contribution to make to the sum of human experience (see Text 9E).

Text 9E

If you give yourself up to the delight of rubbish-reading you will be surprised, indeed you will be overcome, by the relics of human life that have been cast out to moulder. It may be one letter – but what a vision it gives! It may be a few sentences – but what vistas they suggest!

Virginia Woolf, 'How Should One Read a Book?'

Woolf's views on 'rubbish-reading' have an interesting parallel in the lost and forgotten texts that have been rediscovered by publishers such as Persephone, Girls Gone By and Hesperus Press, all of which aim to draw attention to neglected texts that exist at the margins of the traditional canon. Often, these publishers encourage us to think about the reasons why these texts have been neglected - which is often a question of who they were written by and what they are about, rather than their literary merit.

You could apply ideas about value and the canon to 'rubbish-reading' by:

- finding your own example of a text that has been 'cast out to moulder' - perhaps a book that an older relative read as a child that has fallen out of fashion, a book you find in a charity shop, or a book published by one of the publishers listed in the previous paragraph
- considering why this text has been neglected
- exploring what this text might have to offer to readers.

The 'test of time'

The critic Sir Frank Kermode described canons as 'instruments of survival built to be time-proof'. Earlier in this unit, you considered why some people consider it important for texts to 'stand the test of time'. How easy is it to predict which recent publications will stand up to this test?

You could apply ideas about value and the canon to the 'test of time' by:

- thinking about what kinds of qualities enable a text to 'stand the test of time'
- choosing a novel or collection of poetry published in the last ten years
- considering the extent to which it displays these qualities
- thinking about whether it might stand the test of time.

Outside the margins of the canon

There are some genres - science fiction, fantasy, thrillers, graphic novels - that stand outside the mainstream canon. These genres may have evolved canons of their own, but they are often looked down upon by people for whom Literature (with a very definite capital L) is dominated by the traditional classics. What do you think?

You could apply ideas about value and the canon to texts outside the mainstream by:

- finding an example of a text that belongs to a 'marginal' genre

- considering it in relation to a range of different definitions of 'literature'
- making a case as to why this text should, or should not, be considered part of the mainstream canon.

9.4 Narrative

Narrative theory explores the ways in which narratives convey meaning - in other words, the ways in which stories are told. It begins by looking at the idea of narrative itself and by creating a clear distinction between the concepts of 'narrative' and 'story' - two words that are often used interchangeably, yet which nevertheless refer to different ideas.

ACTIVITY 8

Story and narrative

To illustrate the difference between story and narrative, think of something you did yesterday. It could be something very mundane - getting out of bed, making a cup of coffee or walking to school. Write down the basic sequence of events that took place. This basic sequence of events is the **story**.

Now think about how you could retell these events to make them more interesting. You might decide, for instance, to introduce them in a particular way: 'It was an ordinary morning in the Smith household'. You might decide to tell them in the third person, or from a perspective that is not your own (could you describe making a cup of coffee from the point of view of the kettle?). You might borrow the features of a particular genre (try describing your journey to school in the style of a wildlife documentary!). This retelling of events - the product of ordering, editing and presenting them to the reader - is the **narrative**.

Key terms

story: the basic sequence of events

narrative: the way in which events are ordered, presented and retold

From this activity, you should be able to see that a narrative is much more complex than a story (see Figure 9D). A story will always take place in chronological order, and will include everything that actually happens. A narrative, on the other hand, will be a highly selective account.

Figure 9D

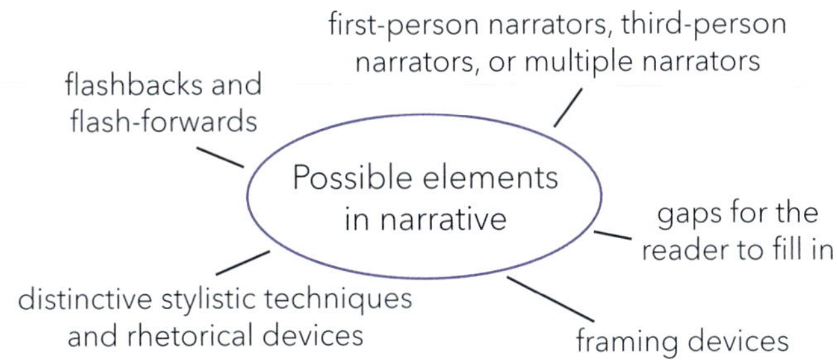

9.4.1 Experimenting with narrative

A good way of experimenting with narrative is to try telling a story in a number of ways. The French writer Raymond Queneau experimented with narrative in his book *Exercises de Style* (1947), in which the same story is told in 99 different ways. The basic story is a very simple one: the narrator gets on a bus, witnesses an argument between a man and another passenger, and then sees the same man two hours later at the Gare St-Lazare, where he is trying to sew a button onto his coat. However, Queneau's 'exercises in style' transform it in a range of interesting (and often bizarre) ways, including the following:

- telling it in rhyming slang, as a word game, as a cross-examination, in a sequence of haiku and as an ode
- rewriting it using a restricted range of letters, as a series of anagrams, in note form
- focusing on different senses (touch, taste, smell, hearing and sight)
- using reported speech, the active and passive voices, and the past and present tense.

ACTIVITY 9

Exercises in style

Take a children's story. You could use a short fairy tale, or a picture book such as *The Very Hungry Caterpillar* by Eric Carle or *We're Going on a Bear Hunt* by Michael Rosen. Rewrite this story in a number of different styles, using some of the suggestions from the bullet points in 9.4.1. What do these rewritings allow you to do? Which versions do you think are most interesting, and why?

9.4.2 Narratives in letters and diaries

As well as the narrative devices listed in this section, authors also make use of other techniques for telling their stories. In the 17th and 18th centuries, one popular genre was the **epistolary novel** – a novel told in the form of a series of letters. Some epistolary novels contain letters by just one correspondent; others contain letters by two or more correspondents, allowing the author to present different points of view and explore the differing opinions and experiences of these characters. Examples include Samuel Richardson's *Clarissa* (1749) and Frances Burney's *Evelina* (1778). Mary Shelley's most famous novel, *Frankenstein* (1818), contains a frame narrative in which a series of letters from a sea captain who encounters Victor Frankenstein on his travels, are used to present Frankenstein's story. More recent examples of the genre include Alice Walker's *The Color Purple* (1982), which consists mainly of a series of letters in which Celie, the protagonist, confides in God about the abuse she experiences at the hands of the man she believes to be her father.

Key terms

epistolary novel: a novel told as a series of letters

Narratives can also be told in the form of diaries, telegrams, police reports, emails and other documents. Charlotte Perkins Gilman's short story 'The Yellow Wallpaper' (1892), George and Weedon Grossmith's *The Diary of a Nobody* (1892) and Sue Townsend's extremely popular *Adrian Mole* series (1982–2009) are all told in diary form. Bram Stoker's *Dracula* (1897) consists of letters, diaries, extracts from newspaper articles, doctor's notes and telegrams. Julian Barnes' novel *Flaubert's Parrot* (1984) approaches the story of the French novelist Gustave Flaubert from a number of different angles, including conventional biography, extracts from Flaubert's letters and diary entries, a spoof version of his *Dictionary of Received Ideas*, and an examination paper.

Often, novels that make use of these different devices rely heavily on the reader to piece together the different documents they contain, detecting links, contradictions and omissions. As we read *Flaubert's Parrot*, for example, we come to see that the real story is only partly about Flaubert: it is also about the novel's middle-aged narrator, Geoffrey Braithwaite, who buries himself in his study of Flaubert because he is unable to come to terms with the death of his wife. Letters and diaries can also be a source of humour, as authors use them to hint at the shortcomings of particular characters and their lack of understanding of particular situations – as in the case of Sue Townsend's teenage intellectual Adrian Mole.

9.4.3 Unreliable narrators

Unreliable narrators present a particular challenge for the reader, because although their telling of the story is not to be trusted this is a deliberate part of the author's method that ultimately has a positive effect in the telling of the story. Unreliable narrators might simply be naive, and have a limited grasp of the story they are trying to tell (one such example is Huckleberry Finn, in Mark Twain's 1884 novel *The Adventures of Huckleberry Finn*; another is Christopher, in Mark Haddon's 2003 novel *The Curious Incident of the Dog in the Night-Time*). They might exaggerate their stories, or withhold information: they might depict other characters in a biased manner, or deliberately misrepresent their actions. Sometimes, the reader is aware of this from the start, but in some novels, this awareness emerges very gradually. Barbara Covett, the narrator of Zoe Heller's 2003 novel *Notes on a Scandal*, initially appears as a lonely woman in her early sixties, desperate to find a friend: as the novel progresses, however, Barbara's narrative reveals more and more of her obsessive nature. Meanwhile, Stevens, the butler who narrates Kazuo Ishiguro's novel *The Remains of the Day* (1989), has a different reason for concealing the truth: his code of loyalty, obedience and deference to his superiors prevents him from acknowledging that his employer, Lord Darlington, was a Nazi sympathiser.

Other narrators might not be quite so obviously unreliable, but their narratives might still contain odd gaps or places where they overemphasise some events at the expense of others. Charles Ryder, the narrator of Evelyn Waugh's *Brideshead Revisited* (1945), gives a highly detailed account of his friendship with Sebastian Flyte as an undergraduate at Oxford. However, he tells us very little about the details of his marriage. His wife is presented almost as an afterthought, and is rarely referred to by name.

This clearly reflects the relative importance of the two relationships to him, without stating it overtly.

9.4.4 Narrative: taking it further

Tristram Shandy: telling your story

Laurence Sterne's comic novel *Tristram Shandy* (1759–67) has been described as the first truly experimental novel in the English language. It grapples with the impossibility of telling the story of an individual's life. Its eponymous hero, Tristram, is trying to write his autobiography, but is met by repeated obstacles as he struggles to explain himself. His narrative contains digressions, repetitions and false starts: he is distracted by trivia and so anguished by the difficulty of his task that at times his narrative is interrupted by blank pages. A film adaptation, *A Cock and Bull Story*, was released in 2006.

You could apply a narrative approach to *Tristram Shandy* by:

- exploring how long it takes Tristram to tell the story of his conception, gestation and birth, and the different ways in which he tries (and fails) to do this
- charting the various ways in which Tristram's story is interrupted, and why these interruptions occur
- analysing Tristram's remarks about the difficulty of telling one's life story.

'Let me tell you ...': narrative in *Waterland*

The narrator of Graham Swift's novel *Waterland* (1983) is Tom Crick, a history teacher who is experiencing a number of personal crises. He is about to lose his job: the headteacher of his school has decided that history is no longer relevant to contemporary teenagers. He is also being challenged in class by a troubled pupil called Price who is concerned about the threat of nuclear war (a potent fear in the early 1980s). In addition, his wife, Mary, has abducted a baby from a supermarket and is now in a psychiatric hospital. To calm both himself and his students, Crick tells stories: about history, about the Cambridgeshire Fens where he grew up, and about his own past. His narrative voice allows Swift to explore both the nature of history, and the telling of stories.

You could apply a narrative approach to *Waterland* by:

- identifying the stylistic devices that Swift uses to create the sense of Tom Crick's narrative voice
- tracing the ways in which the different stories that are told in the novel intertwine and shed light on each other
- analysing the effects of Swift's manipulation of time.

Controlling your own story: *Personality*

Andrew O'Hagan's novel *Personality* (2003) is loosely based on the life of the Scottish singer Lena Zavaroni. It is about a child star, Maria Tambini, whose life is dominated by other people's desires and intentions for her. The narrative is divided between a number of different voices, including Maria's mother, her agent, her boyfriend, the host of the TV talent show on which she appears, and a fan who becomes her stalker. It is only at the end of the novel that Maria gets to tell her own story.

You could apply a narrative approach to *Personality* by:

- considering the effect of the different perspectives we get on Maria's life through the different narrative voices
- thinking about the effect of not allowing Maria to tell her own story until right at the end of the text
- giving Maria a voice by rewriting an earlier incident from the novel from her point of view.

9.5 Feminism

Feminism is a political and philosophical movement that focuses on the position of women in society. Its starting point is the idea that society is, and always has been, 'patriarchal' – that is, controlled by men, organised to a great extent for the benefit of men and designed to maintain the dominance of men. (This kind of power structure – where one social group has profound dominance over another – is known as a **hegemony**.)

One of the key elements of feminist analysis is the idea that the hegemony of men is perpetuated, often on a subconscious or unconscious level, through the operation of accepted social norms and conventions. These conventions are encoded in social, cultural and linguistic behaviours and discourses, and individuals who deviate from them, are punished – sometimes literally, but more often through earning the disapproval of those who seek to uphold the accepted beliefs.

The idea of **gender** is crucial to feminism. Feminism argues that power structures are maintained through the perpetuation of certain gender roles assigned to men and women in society.

Exploring gender

While **sex** refers to the physical sexual characteristics with which we are born ('male' or 'female'), gender refers to the socio-cultural behaviours that we display: 'masculine' or 'feminine'. While sex is biologically determined, ideas about gender – in particular what behaviours are considered typical or appropriate for the different sexes, what is masculine and what is feminine – are the product of particular cultures. Some aspects of gender roles might to some extent be related to sexual difference, such as the belief that women are more nurturing than men because they have traditionally been the main caregivers. However, these differences can be overstated. The role of cultural and environmental factors in determining what is 'masculine' and what is 'feminine' is vital, most obviously in relation to the way men and women are expected to dress and look, but in many other aspects of behaviour too. Indeed, the feminist philosopher Judith Butler (born 1956) has argued that gender is something that we *perform*, rather than something that we *are*.

Key terms

hegemony: a power structure in which one group has dominance over another

gender: the socio-cultural behaviours stereotypically associated with each sex

sex: the physical sexual characteristics with which we are born

9.5.1 The history of feminism

Historians of the feminist movement have identified three distinct phases, or waves, of feminist thought.

First-wave feminism, commonly associated with the late 19th and early 20th centuries, was concerned with securing equal rights for women, such as the right to vote, the right to an education and the right to enter professions such as medicine and the law.

Second-wave feminism, commonly associated with the 1960s and 1970s, explored the stereotypes and cultural constructions that underpinned society's ideas about women. It looked at the role of women within the family, and the ways in which women's potential was restricted by their traditional status as homemakers and caregivers. One of its aims was to liberate women from the expectation that they should be content to be wives and mothers (a name sometimes applied to this wave of feminism is the 'Women's Liberation movement', or 'Women's Lib'). It also examined the depiction of women by the media and by industries such as advertising and pornography, drawing attention to the ways in which women were presented as objects of male desire.

Third-wave feminism, which emerged in the 1990s, points out that the second wave was dominated by the voices of white, middle-class women. It therefore seeks to open up feminism to a wider range of voices, representing different ethnicities, social classes, sexualities and backgrounds. It argues that second-wave feminism often represented a highly restricted view of women's lives that ignored the experiences of many. One of its key points is that second-wave feminism could be just as oppressive as the views that it opposed. For instance, in saying that women should not be content to stay at home and raise children, second-wave feminism ignored the fact that for many women, this was a source of fulfilment. Third-wave feminism emphasises that women should be able to make positive choices rather than feeling pressurised by social expectations.

If you're considering feminist approaches to literature, an insight into these phases of feminism is extremely useful: it helps to highlight the concerns and priorities that feminists had at different times, and can illuminate the ways in which particular issues are depicted.

9.5.2 Feminist approaches to literature

Feminist literary theory sees literature as one of the crucial ways in which ideas about gender are spread throughout society. It is concerned with the ways in which women and gender roles are represented in literature, as well as in culture more widely (feminist approaches can also be applied to forms such as film, music and computer gaming). It is also interested in visibility: in whether women's experiences are considered worthy of exploration in literature and other cultural forms.

Exploring visibility

Visibility is a term that refers to the position of particular social groups. It stems from the observation that for many years, certain groups have been invisible: that is, they have been under-represented in public life and in the media. For example, there are very few television presenters with physical disabilities.

Approaching literature from a feminist point of view might involve:

- analysing the balance of power between men and women in the literary world (such as the obstacles that faced women writers in the past)
- exploring the representation of women's lives in literary texts.

It might also encompass the ways in which texts hide and reveal patriarchal power structures, for instance:

- through the use of male narrators, voices and viewpoints
- through language patterns and imagery
- through representations of behaviour and emotions.

ACTIVITY 10

Fairy tales and folk tales

One way of approaching feminist literary theory is by looking at the ways in which women are depicted in popular narratives such as fairy tales and folk tales. These often present us with clear stereotypes of feminine and masculine behaviour and of the ways in which female characters are expected to behave (and the ways in which they are punished for not complying with these expectations).

a Brainstorm as many fairy tales and folk tales as you can.

b Now put them into groups under the following headings:
 i Tales that have a woman as a victim who needs rescuing by a man
 ii Tales that have an evil female character
 iii Tales that have no significant female characters

'Thou, O Queen, art the fairest of all!'
The Brothers Grimm, *Little Snow White*

A tale may appear in both group i and group ii.

c Next, examine the women in each group.
- For group i, describe the general characteristics of the woman who is a victim.
- For group ii, describe the general characteristics of the evil woman.
- For group iii, if there are any woman characters, what roles do they tend to play?

What kinds of patterns do you notice?

1 Now look at the men in these stories. Do they share any common characteristics? What might this indicate about the ways in which society views men and women?

2 Finally, read some re-tellings of popular fairy tales and folktales, such as Angela Carter's *The Bloody Chamber* (1979) and Roald Dahl's *Revolting Rhymes* (1982). Carter and Dahl both rewrite the story of Little Red Riding Hood: Carter in 'The Werewolf' and 'The Company of Wolves', and Dahl in 'Little Red Riding Hood and the Wolf'. How do these interpretations challenge the depiction of Little Red Riding Hood in more traditional versions of the tale?

9.5.3 Virginia Woolf and *A Room of One's Own*

Virginia Woolf's *A Room of One's Own* (1929), based on a series of lectures that Woolf delivered at the University of Cambridge, has become a key text of feminist literary criticism. In it, Woolf discusses a number of issues relating to the history of women's writing. These include:

- the exclusion of women from higher education
- the fact that women and their experiences have, historically, been written about by men rather than by other women
- the lack of opportunities, encouragement and time available for women who want to write
- the subsequent lack of a tradition of women writers to act as role models for other women.

Woolf addresses the work of a number of women writers, including Aphra Behn, Jane Austen, Charlotte Brontë and George Eliot. She also explores two fictional figures. The first of these is Judith Shakespeare, an imaginary sister of William Shakespeare. Woolf compares Judith's experiences with those of her brother in Text 9F.

The second is an aspiring novelist called Mary Carmichael. Her first novel, *Life's Adventure*, is praised by Woolf for its depiction of the experiences of female characters. In a very famous passage from *A Room of One's Own*, Woolf muses on the way in which writers in the past have ignored the friendships that exist between women (see Text 9G).

Woolf also argued that women need to find their own way of expressing themselves rather than emulating masculine styles. This has led to the notion of the 'women's sentence', a mode of expression that allows women to articulate themselves more freely and precisely than that of the male-dominated literary tradition. Appropriately, *A Room of One's Own* is written in a highly unorthodox style. It begins in mid-conversation, and contains digressions, anecdotes and imaginary characters rather than the logic and facts that would be expected of an academic lecture. Woolf therefore resists the conventions of the male-dominated world of academia, drawing upon the resources of fiction to express herself in her own distinctive voice. Her desire was for all women writers to be able to do the same.

Exploring gender: The Bechdel test

In 1985, the American cartoonist Alison Bechdel proposed a test for gender bias that could be applied to works of fiction. Bechdel was interested in issues surrounding male dominance and female invisibility – specifically, the ways in which female characters are often marginalised or seen only in terms of their relationships with men. The test, which owes an obvious debt to Woolf, asks whether two female characters talk to each other about anything other than a man. If they do, the work passes the test.

Text 9F

She was as adventurous, as imaginative, as agog to see the world as he was. But she was not sent to school. She had no chance of learning grammar and logic, let alone of reading Horace and Virgil. She picked up a book now and then, one of her brother's perhaps, and read a few pages. But then her parents came in and told her to mend the stockings or mind the stew and not moon about with books and papers.

Virginia Woolf, *A Room of One's Own*

Text 9G

'Chloe liked Olivia,' I read. And then it struck me how immense a change was there. Chloe liked Olivia perhaps for the first time in literature. [...] All these relationships between women, I thought, rapidly recalling the splendid gallery of fictitious women, are too simple. So much has been left out, unattempted. And I tried to remember any case in the course of my reading where two women are represented as friends. [...] They are now and then mothers and daughters. But almost without exception they are shown in their relation to men. It was strange to think that all the great women of fiction were, until Jane Austen's day, not only seen by the other sex, but seen only in relation to the other sex. And how small a part of a woman's life is that; and how little can a man know even of that when he observes it through the black or rosy spectacles which sex puts upon his nose.

Virginia Woolf, *A Room of One's Own*

9.5.4 Feminist attitudes to the body

Many feminist writers have turned their attention to the issue of the body. Historically, the female body has been viewed as something that should be presented for male approval: it has been painted with make-up, adorned with jewellery, stripped of hair and modified in a host of other ways (in China, wealthy women had their feet bound to prevent them from growing). In many cultures, however, the female body has also been seen as a source of weakness and shame. Girls are told that they are not as strong as boys, that they cannot run as fast or climb as high: menstruation has been viewed as a taboo, and female sexual pleasure is treated as something to be disciplined, controlled or eradicated altogether.

Feminists have challenged these views by celebrating the female body and seeing it as a source of pride. They have argued that women should feel able to make choices about their bodies without being restricted by the judgements of others. They have focused on moments in texts where female characters attempt to evade the control of others, such as the incident in George Eliot's novel *The Mill on the Floss* (1860) when the headstrong Maggie Tulliver cuts off her hair because her curls annoy her.

Feminist theorists have also looked at the idea of the 'male gaze'. This idea originated from film theory, where it is used to describe the way in which the camera puts the audience into a male position (lingering on the female body, for instance, or following the movement of a female character). They have explored the value-judgements that society makes about the appearance of women, and how these are reflected in literary texts. One dominant theme of Charlotte Brontë's *Jane Eyre*, for instance, is that of the heroine's unattractiveness, and her feeling that she is less of a human being because of this.

ACTIVITY 11

Considering the body

a Think of a text you know well. Are female characters defined in terms of how attractive they are to men? Are women always seen through the eyes of male characters, or through the lens of a male-dominated view of 'beauty'? Are women active, or passive? What happens if the genders are reversed?

b Now find out about the context in which this text was written. Can you make any connections between the way it treats the female body and its context of production? For instance, we might expect a text written in the 19th century to treat female sexual desire very differently to a text written in the 21st century.

9.5.5 Feminist theory: taking it further

The Unlit Lamp: challenging convention

The Unlit Lamp (1924) was written by the novelist Radclyffe Hall, whose most famous novel, *The Well of Loneliness*, was the subject of a famous obscenity trial for its depiction of lesbian relationships. *The Unlit Lamp* is about a girl called Joan Ogden who must struggle against convention to fulfil her desire of studying medicine – an ambition that her middle-class parents consider 'indecent'. The novel focuses on Joan's attempts to free herself from the restrictions of family and society and shape a future for herself, guided by her beloved governess, Elizabeth. Hall's depiction of Joan invited readers to consider the experiences of a character who was not stereotypically feminine, and who was fundamentally unsuited to the role that society deemed appropriate for her.

You could apply a feminist approach to *The Unlit Lamp* by:

- exploring Hall's depiction of Joan's appearance, considering how it marks her out as being 'unfeminine'
- identifying the main obstacles to Joan's independence
- rewriting an incident from the point of view of one of Joan's parents, bringing out the beliefs and assumptions that shape their view of their daughter's behaviour.

Reading against the grain: *The Whitsun Weddings*

It is often interesting to apply feminist approaches to texts that do not explicitly deal with 'women's issues'. Such texts can often be highly revealing of particular attitudes towards women, whether these are held consciously or unconsciously. It can be intriguing to see how women are often placed in particular roles or depicted in particular ways.

Philip Larkin's collection *The Whitsun Weddings* (1964) is a good example of a text that conveys particular attitudes towards women. Larkin's own relationships with women were notoriously complex: he was highly resentful of his mother and older sister, and while he never married, he had long-term relationships with a number of women - often several at a time. Poems in *The Whitsun Weddings* depict women as partners, mothers, widows, objects of desire and objects of contempt. Women never speak for themselves in the poems, although their voices are sometimes parodied. The voice that narrates the poems is not necessarily Larkin's own, but it is nevertheless interesting to explore the poems in the context of what we know about his life, and the society in which he lived.

You could apply a feminist approach to *The Whitsun Weddings* by:

- exploring Larkin's depiction of women in poems such as 'Wild Oats' and 'Afternoons'
- identifying attitudes towards relationships, marriage and domesticity, from the point of view of both men and women
- writing a response to Larkin from one of the women he describes in his poems, exploring this woman's own perspective on the way she has been depicted.

The importance of the ordinary: *Unless*

Unless (2002) was the final novel by the Canadian writer Carol Shields. Its protagonist, Reta Winters, is a professional translator, working on the memoirs of a Holocaust survivor: she is also the author of light-hearted domestic novels. One day, her teenage daughter Norah drops out of university and decides to live on the streets of Toronto. Norah's rejection of the world prompts Reta to reflect on her own life and the choices available to women. She explores the ways in which women's achievements have been ignored or undermined, and considers, in particular, the view that women writers are doomed to be considered 'trivial', their concerns less important than those of their male counterparts.

You could apply a feminist approach to *Unless* by:

- tracing Reta's feelings about her identity as a woman and the way it has been shaped by different people and ideas
- examining what Reta says about her work as a writer, and about the judgements people make about 'women's writing'
- considering the significance of the letters Reta writes (but does not send) to various public figures, protesting about the treatment of women by society at large.

9.6 Marxism

As its name suggests, Marxist literary theory draws on the work of the German philosopher Karl Marx (1818–83). Marx's work focused on relationships between the social classes, and in particular, on the concept of class struggle - which he saw as the consequence of modern industrial capitalism.

Marxism's starting point is the idea that wealth in society is created by the working classes (the **proletariat**) but controlled by a few in the upper classes (the **bourgeoisie**) who own the means of production. (As with the dominance of men over women that we looked at in section 9.5 on Feminism, this kind of power structure is a hegemony.) Despite producing society's wealth, the working class receive the least payment for their work. The less numerous middle and upper classes, on the other hand, receive higher rewards. They also uphold social systems (such as the education system) that promote middle- and upper-class values and dismiss or undervalue those of the working class. Thus, the proletariat is controlled and exploited by the bourgeoisie.

Key terms

proletariat: the working classes of society

bourgeoisie: the upper classes of society

This might seem a long way from the study of literature. However, Marxism offers us a number of ways of approaching literary texts. At a simple level, Marxist literary theories are interested in the ways in which social power is represented in literature. This might include the following points.

- The representation of class in literary texts: how are the relationships between the proletariat and the bourgeoisie depicted?
- The balance of power between classes in the literary world: to what extent is literature dominated by the bourgeoisie? To what extent does literature reflect the voices of the proletariat?

It might also include the ways in which texts hide and reveal social and economic structures, for instance:

- through the use of bourgeois narrators, voices and viewpoints
- through the use of particular language patterns and imagery to depict class relationships
- through what is hidden or not said about the class struggle.

One of Karl Marx's most famous sayings was 'Religion is the opium of the people'. What he meant by this was that religion was one of the institutions that could be used to keep the proletariat in their place, enforcing particular codes of behaviour and demanding submission.

William Blake's 'Chimney Sweeper' poems offer an interesting way of exploring the relationship between religion and the proletariat. The first was published in *Songs of Innocence* in 1789; its companion was published in *Songs of Experience* in 1794. Both tell of the plight of young boys (sometimes as young as four or five) who were employed in sweeping chimneys. They also highlight the way in which religion was used to offer consolation to the young chimney sweeps.

ACTIVITY 12

'The Chimney Sweeper'

Read both 'Chimney Sweeper' poems and then consider the following questions.

a What does Blake tell us about the plight of the chimney sweeps? How are their lives depicted?

b How does Blake contrast the chimney sweeps' lives with the vision offered by the angel in the poem from *Songs of Innocence*?

c In what ways does religion operate as a means of control? What does it offer to the chimney sweeps and what do they have to do in order to get this?

d What is the effect of Blake's use of simple language and a childlike rhythm and rhyming pattern? In what ways does this underline what Blake is saying about the use of religion as a means of control?

Read both 'Chimney Sweeper' poems via Cambridge Elevate

To extend your study of these poems and to deepen your understanding of the conditions in which chimney sweeps worked, look at the *Report from the Committee On Employment of Boys in Sweeping of Chimneys* (1817). This will provide an additional dimension to Blake's poetry of protest.

Read the *Report from the Committee On Employment of Boys in Sweeping of Chimneys* via Cambridge Elevate

9.6.1 Alienation

A key element of Marxist analysis is the idea of **alienation**, the state experienced by workers who are not in control of their lives. Their work is often mechanical and monotonous, reduced to a small series of operations on a production line: they make money for their employers, but derive little financial reward themselves and gain no real sense of satisfaction. In an alienated society, work is routine, repetitive and tedious, and individuals are given few (if any) opportunities to grow, flourish or make meaningful choices about their working lives.

Key terms

alienation: the state experienced by workers who are not in control of their lives

9.6.2 Marxism and oppression

An important theme of Marxist theory is that of oppression: the way in which different social groups attempt to control others. Marxist theorists might consider how texts challenge the established forms of social and political control that are used to uphold particular kinds of order, offering new ways in which different social groups might interact. They might also explore the ways in which less powerful groups try to resist the methods of control that others try to use in order to assert power over them.

One text that involves issues of oppression and control is Shakespeare's play *Hamlet*. Hamlet's father, the King of Denmark, has been murdered; at the beginning of the play, Hamlet's recently widowed mother, Gertrude, marries his uncle, Claudius, the dead king's brother. Hamlet is visited by the ghost of his father, who reveals that Claudius was his murderer and charges Hamlet with the task of exacting revenge.

A Marxist analysis of the play would focus on the ways in which Hamlet tries to resist Claudius' authority, violating norms of polite behaviour. Look, for example, at Hamlet's first appearance. This occurs in Act 1, Scene 2, lines 64–120. Claudius, Gertrude, Hamlet and the Danish court assemble in a room of state for Claudius' first formal address to the court. After making his speech, and after speaking to Laertes (the son of Polonius, the Lord Chamberlain), Claudius turns to Hamlet.

ACTIVITY 13

Hamlet's resistance

Read lines 64–120 in Act 1, Scene 2 of *Hamlet* and answer the following questions.

a What do Claudius and Gertrude appear to be saying to Hamlet? How, in particular, do they think he should respond to his father's death?

b In what ways does Hamlet resist Gertrude and Claudius' attempts to control his behaviour? Think about the following:
- the fact that his first line (the first line he speaks in the whole play) is an aside
- the way he responds to the words Claudius and Gertrude use
- the way he responds to their advice about his father's death.

c How many lines do Claudius and Gertrude speak? How many lines does Hamlet speak? What might this indicate about Hamlet's behaviour?

Check your responses in the Ideas section on Cambridge Elevate

Exploring the character of Hamlet

When you are studying drama, it is important to be on the lookout for moments where the actors and director might offer particular interpretations of characters. For example, the stage direction at the beginning of Act 1, Scene 2 of *Hamlet* states 'Enter Claudius King of Denmark, Gertrude the Queen, Hamlet, Polonius, Laertes, Ophelia, Voltemand, Cornelius, Lords attendant'. However, the characters do not need to enter in this particular order. In fact, the earlier, Second Quarto version of the play puts Hamlet almost at the end of the list, after Polonius and Laertes but before the attendants. Could this indicate that Hamlet is hanging back, reluctant to take part in a ceremony that he obviously finds repugnant?

It is also worth noting that even though Hamlet enters at the beginning of the scene, he does not speak until line 65, after Claudius' long ceremonial speech and his conversation with Laertes. What might Hamlet be doing while all of this is going on? How might gesture and facial expression be used to convey his feelings about Claudius and Gertrude? And how could these feelings also be conveyed by costume? (For example, Hamlet could be depicted as a stroppy teenager, wearing his oldest and scruffiest clothes because he does not want to dress up for an occasion that marks the beginning of his uncle's rule.)

9.6.3 Marxist theory: taking it further

Alienation in *Hard Times*

Charles Dickens' novel *Hard Times* (1854) is a classic example of the 'Condition-of-England' novel – the name given to a group of texts written in the mid-19th century that dealt with the consequences of industrialisation. *Hard Times* was influenced by Dickens' visit to Preston in Lancashire, where he witnessed the conditions endured by workers in the cotton mills, the degradation of repetitive work and the dangers posed by heavy machinery and inadequate safety regulations – all driven by the desire for profit.

You could apply a Marxist approach to *Hard Times* by:

- exploring Dickens' portrayal of the lives of the workers, especially Stephen Blackpool
- analysing the philosophies of the factory owner Bounderby and the schoolmaster Gradgrind
- producing a first-person narrative from the point of view of one of the 'hands', exploring issues of alienation and monotony.

The language of class: Tony Harrison's 'Them & [uz]'

Tony Harrison was born into a working-class family in Leeds in 1937. He won a scholarship to the prestigious Leeds Grammar School and went on to read classics at university, at a time when relatively few students from working-class families went on to higher education. Harrison was acutely aware of the tensions that existed between the different cultures of family and school, and many of his poems explore this clash. In 'Them & [uz]', he writes of being made to feel self-conscious about his working-class accent. The poem consists of two **caudate sonnets**.

Key terms

caudate sonnet: a poem that follows a conventional sonnet form but adds one or more additional lines

You could apply a Marxist approach to 'Them & [uz]' by:

- exploring what Harrison says about the links between language and identity
- analysing the way in which culture is used to signify inclusion and exclusion
- considering the effect of Harrison's use of the sonnet form – in particular, why he uses caudate sonnets rather than the conventional 14 lines.

How Late It Was, How Late: Whose English literature?

The main character of *How Late It Was, How Late*, by the Scottish novelist James Kelman, is Sammy, an unemployed working-class Glaswegian man whose girlfriend has left him and who loses his sight as a result of a fight he gets into. The dialogue spoken by Sammy and other working-class characters throughout the book is an earthy Glaswegian dialect, with expletives used in almost every sentence, sometimes several times – a realistic representation of a mode of informal speech that is common in certain working-class areas of Glasgow.

The novel is narrated in the third person by an omniscient narrator, but closely tracking Sammy's perspective throughout. Highly unusually, this third-person narrator, although not a character in the book, also uses a working-class Glaswegian dialect, telling the story in the same dialect as the one with which Sammy speaks – almost as if he were telling the story

'A heart unfortified, a mind impatient,
An understanding simple and unschool'd'

William Shakespeare, *Hamlet*

informally to a friend. Consequently, the narrative uses as many swear words as the characters use in their dialogue.

It is very unusual for a third-person narration to be in a dialect other than Standard English. When we read the narrative of this book, we are made to realise that we generally don't question – or even notice – the middle-class bias of narrative voices: we accept unquestioningly that narratives of characters of all classes will be mediated by a middle-class narrator spoken in middle-class Standard English. Kelman seems to be saying that the third-person narrator is just as entitled to be working class as the characters in a novel.

An extraordinary and powerful work, *How Late It Was, How Late* won the Booker Prize in 1994 but caused outrage because of its prolific use of swear words. Many of the book's supporters pointed out that Kelman reveals the poetry behind the use of swear words in ordinary speech, demonstrating the powerful ways they can be used to emphasise and amplify emotion and experience. The book divided the Booker Prize judging panel, with one of the judges resigning in protest. Kelman, himself a working-class Glaswegian, criticised such middle-class protests in his acceptance speech, suggesting that they were a form of racism.

You could apply a Marxist approach to *How Late It Was, How Late* by:

- analysing the way Kelman uses dialect in the narrative and dialogue of the novel
- exploring Kelman's depiction of working-class experience, and the extent to which the third-person narrative affects our understanding of it
- producing your own narrative in a non-standard dialect of English, considering which aspects of character and community the use of non-standard English allows you to capture.

9.7 Eco-critical theory

Eco-critical theory is a relatively new way of looking at literary texts. As its name suggests, it emerged from the environmental movement. It focuses on the way that literature depicts the relationship between humans and the natural world, both celebrating nature and pointing out threats to it. Eco-critical theory often draws on the work of Romantic writers such as William Wordsworth, whose depictions of his beloved Lake District – and its effect on his growing mind – offer a powerful exploration of the interaction between the individual and the environment.

Another key genre for eco-critical theory is the genre of pastoral, which emerged in Ancient Greece. Much pastoral writing offers an idealised, nostalgic view of the countryside, seeing the natural world as an escape from everything that is wrong with the hustle and bustle of urban life. Eco-critical theory looks at the values invested in nature, which often becomes a repository for all manner of aspirations and ideals.

ACTIVITY 14

Escape to the country

a What values do we associate with the countryside? One popular daytime TV show, 'Escape to the Country', focuses on people who want to move to the countryside in search of a 'better' life. What is conveyed by this notion of 'escape'?

'You can only form the minds of reasoning animals upon Facts: nothing else will ever be of any service to them.'

Charles Dickens, *Hard Times*

b Read the poem 'The Lake Isle of Innisfree' in Text 9H. It was written in 1888. In it, W.B. Yeats describes his fantasy of living on Innisfree, an uninhabited island in Lough Gill, Ireland.

c What vision does the narrator of the poem give us of his life on Innisfree?

d What kind of language does he use? Is it simple or complex? Is there a regular rhyming pattern? Why might this be significant?

e What contrasts does Yeats draw in the final stanza between the country and the city? What does this suggest about the role of the natural world in his life?

Text 9H

The Lake Isle of Innisfree

I will arise and go now, and go to Innisfree,
And a small cabin build there, of clay and **wattles** made;
Nine bean-rows will I have there, a hive for the honey-bee,
And live alone in the bee-loud glade.

And I shall have some peace there, for peace comes dropping slow,
Dropping from the veils of the morning to where the cricket sings;
There midnight's all a glimmer, and noon a purple glow,
And evening full of the **linnet**'s wings.

I will arise and go now, for always night and day
I hear lake water lapping with low sounds by the shore;
While I stand on the roadway, or on the pavements grey,
I hear it in the deep heart's core.

W.B. Yeats

Glossary

wattle: a wall made from woven sticks and strips of bark

linnet: a small songbird

Eco-critical theory's revaluation of the natural world often places great emphasis on the meticulous observation of nature. Authors who describe the natural world in detail can be seen as showing a respect for plants and animals that might otherwise go unnoticed, drawing attention to the rich variety of life. In his book *The Song of the Earth* (2000), a key eco-critical text, Jonathan Bate writes of 'the capacity of the writer to restore us to the earth that is our home'. The two texts in Activity 15 ask you to consider how two very different writers achieve this restoration.

John Clare, the so-called 'peasant poet', was born in the village of Helpston, near Peterborough, in 1793. He was largely uneducated, but began to write poems about the countryside around his home, observing plants, animal and birds. Many of his poems trace the changes that resulted from the process of 'enclosure', which removed people's rights to graze their livestock on common land. In the poem 'Sonnet: I love to see the summer', written in 1841, he records his pleasure at the sights of early summer.

Text 9I

Sonnet: I love to see the summer

I love to see the summer beaming forth
And white wool sack clouds sailing to the north
I love to see the wild flowers come again
And mare blobs stain with gold the meadow drain
And water lillies whiten on the floods
Where reed clumps rustle like a wind shook wood
Where from her hiding place the Moor Hen pushes
And seeks her flag nest floating in bull rushes
I like the willow leaning half way o'er
The clear deep lake to stand upon its shore
I love the hay grass when the flower head swings
To summer winds and insects happy wings
That sport about the meadow the bright day
And see bright beetles in the clear lake play

John Clare

ACTIVITY 15

The importance of detail

Read Clare's sonnet in Text 9I and answer the following questions.

a How many different plants, creatures and other natural objects does Clare mention in this poem? What kind of language does he use to describe them?

b What kinds of flowers are 'mare blobs' and 'flags'? What is the effect of Clare's use of dialect words for these plants?

c There are many simple declarations of emotion ('I love … I love … I like'). What is the effect of this simplicity?

- d Comment on the lack of punctuation in this poem.
- e This poem is a sonnet – a form that could be seen as highly stylised and sophisticated. Can you suggest reasons why Clare might have used the sonnet form?

See Rhyme in 2.3.2 for more on the sonnet form

In Kate Grenville's novel *The Idea of Perfection* (2000), Douglas Cheeseman, an engineer, has been sent to a rural village in New South Wales to survey an ancient bridge that has been scheduled for demolition. Read the extract in Text 9J and consider the following questions.

- a What do you notice about the kinds of observations that Douglas makes about the bridge and its surroundings?
- b What can you say about the sequence and structure of the extract and the effects they have?
- c What techniques does Grenville use to draw the reader's attention to particular observations? (Look, for example, at how alliteration and assonance are used.)
- d In the third paragraph, the narration shifts slightly to the second person ('… like someone talking to you, keeping you company'). What is the effect of this?
- e This extract is partly about the destruction of nature (in the form of the trees that have been cut down to make the bridge). In what ways could it also be said to be about *respect* for nature?
- f Could the passage also be said to be about respect for other things? If so, what?

Text 9J

Under the bridge it was cool and dank, full of rich organic smells. He stood with his boots sinking in the soft sand. The piers spanned a small glassy pool, each one disappearing into its own reflection. He looked at them with sympathy. His own teeth were somewhat similar, ringbarked at gum-line from years of unscientific brushing.

Pale sand fanned out underwater where the current slowed and shelved away into deeper, darker brown water against the far bank. Over there a dragonfly danced above a pucker of current. Upstream and downstream of the pool, the water bubbled mildly down through slopes of rounded stones.

There was a quiet secretive feel under here, crouching on the strip of damp sand. It was like hide-and-seek. He had always preferred to be the one doing the hiding. The water bubbling through the stones was like someone talking to you, keeping you company. Pale bands and twists of light reflected upwards from the water, stippling and shimmering over the dark timbers, making a secret upside-down world.

As he watched, a leaf twirled down out of the trees. It floated under the bridge where the water went black, and he waited for it to come out into the light on the other side.

He looked at the uprights, each one a whole tree trunk. Even after a hundred years whole shreds of bark still clung to them in places, and you could still see the knobs where branches had been roughly lopped off. It was not so much a bridge made out of timber as a bridge made out of trees.

There was no great engineering in these old bridges but he had noticed how often there was exceptional workmanship. Here, for instance, a neat bit of squaring had been done on the timbers of a joint so each one slotted in snugly against the other. The long-dead men who had built this bridge had even gone to the trouble of countersinking the bolt-heads, pecking out a tidy hole to get it all as tight as a piece of cabinetwork. It was tricky, working hardwood like that, but they had thought it worth doing.

True was the word carpenters used. It was as if they thought there was something moral about it.

Kate Grenville, *The Idea of Perfection*

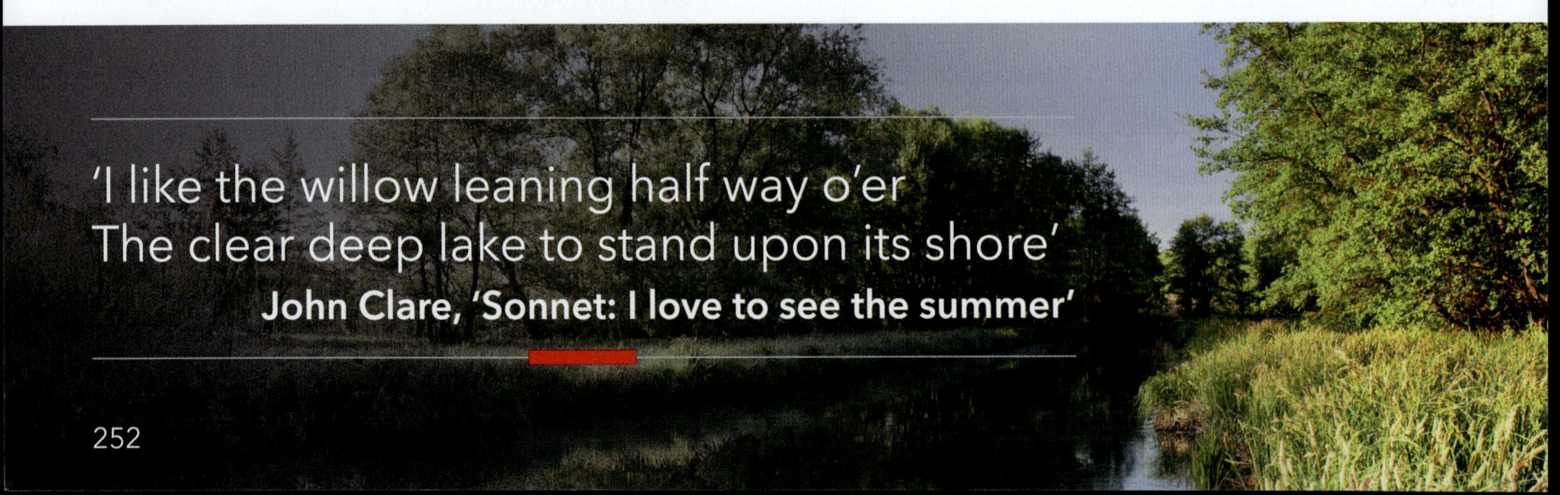

9.7.1 Stereotypes and the natural world

One complaint sometimes levelled at writing about the natural world is that it often glosses over the difficulties of living in the countryside. The genre of pastoral rests on an idealised view of nature that tends to present the countryside through rose tinted lenses – ignoring the fact that the natural world can be harsh, and that it does not always provide people with the peaceful retreat that they seek. The subgenre of anti-pastoral draws attention to the gap between ideal and reality. In the 18th century, the poet and clergyman George Crabbe wrote in his poem 'The Village': 'Can poets soothe you, when you pine for bread, / By winding myrtles round your ruin'd shed?' Crabbe was highlighting the plight of the rural poor, and the fact that poets wrote elevated verse about the lives of country villagers while ignoring the hardships that they suffered. Over 200 years later, the graphic novelist Posy Simmonds focused on a similar gap in *Tamara Drewe*, which first appeared as a comic strip in *The Guardian*. The novel, which is loosely based on Thomas Hardy's *Far from the Madding Crowd*, is set in a fictional Dorset village. The village is home to an author's retreat where stressed novelists can write in peace, uninterrupted by the hustle and bustle of urban life – yet the teenagers who grow up in the village have nothing to do and nowhere to meet except the village bus shelter.

9.7.2 Eco-critical theory: taking it further

Far from the Madding Crowd: pastoral and anti-pastoral

Thomas Hardy's novel *Far from the Madding Crowd* (1874) takes its title from a line in Thomas Gray's pastoral poem *Elegy Written in a Country Churchyard*. The title suggests a peaceful rural seclusion set apart from the hustle and bustle of the city. The text is packed with descriptions of English country life: it was the first of Hardy's works to be set in what he described as the 'partly real, partly-dream country' of Wessex, and in it Hardy records the details of a way of existence that he felt was being threatened by the advance of industrialisation. However, he also explores the complexities of rural life, drawing attention to the hardships experienced by characters such as Gabriel Oak, and the difficulties encountered by the novel's heroine, Bathsheba Everdene, as she attempts to run her own farm.

You could apply an eco-critical approach to *Far from the Madding Crowd* by:

- exploring Hardy's depiction of the traditions of Wessex country life
- analysing incidents that draw attention to the hardships and difficulties of rural life
- writing about rural isolation and poverty from the point of view of someone living in a rural area today.

Dylan Thomas: representation and reality

Dylan Thomas' much-anthologised poem, 'Fern Hill' (1945), depicts a landscape based on the poet's childhood visits to his aunt and uncle's farm in Carmarthenshire. It is idyllic and highly lyrical, evoking vivid impressions of a world in which the narrator was 'prince of the apple towns' (see Text 9K).

The farm described in 'Fern Hill' is also the subject of Thomas' short story 'The Peaches', published in his collection *Portrait of the Artist as a Young Dog* (1940). However, in 'The Peaches', the farm is portrayed very differently.

Text 9K

And once below a time I lordly had the trees and leaves
    Trail with daisies and barley
  Down the rivers of the windfall light.

Dylan Thomas, 'Fern Hill'

You could apply an eco-critical approach to 'Fern Hill' and 'The Peaches' by:

- exploring the ways in which each text depicts the farm, its inhabitants and the events that take place there
- considering whether biographical and historical evidence might shed light on why Thomas portrayed the farm in such different ways
- analysing the effects of form and style in both texts.

Nineteen Eighty-Four: eco-criticism and dystopia

The **dystopian** world of George Orwell's *Nineteen Eighty-Four* might initially seem to have very little to do with nature. London, the chief city of Airstrip One, is dominated by the trappings of The Party and its totalitarian rule: the posters of Big Brother, the huge telescreens used to monitor the population, the hidden microphones. The city is also ravaged by war and in a state of decay and disorder.

Significantly, when Winston Smith and Julia begin their relationship, they meet in the countryside, at a woodland clearing where they think they will be undetected by the Party. Ironically, the café in which Winston sits at the end of the novel is called the Chestnut Tree Café: a name whose overtones of rural peace contrast sharply with the café's drabness. Orwell plays on the idea that the countryside should offer a place of escape, suggesting that in the totalitarian world of Airstrip One, there is nowhere to go in order to get away from the all-pervasive Party.

You could apply an eco-critical approach to *Nineteen Eighty-Four* by:

- analysing Orwell's depiction of London
- considering what Orwell might be saying about the ecological effects of war and totalitarianism
- exploring the way Orwell uses images of the countryside.

9.8 Post-colonial theory

Post-colonial theory, which first emerged in the 1980s and 1990s, concentrates on the relationships between different cultures. It looks, in particular, at the legacy of **colonialism**. This process, identified largely with the period between the early 16th and mid-19th centuries, saw a number of western European countries establishing colonies in Africa, Asia, the Americas and Australasia. Over the years, these colonies were expanded, native populations were subjected to colonial rule, and natural resources were exploited. The process of colonialism was often justified through narratives that spoke of bringing 'civilisation' to parts of the world that lacked the sophistication and belief-systems of the colonial powers (sometimes referred to as imperial powers).

Post-colonial theory questions these narratives, and explores the impact they have had on the ways in which people in former colonies see themselves. These people, and the cultures to which they belong, are referred to as occupying a **subaltern** position. One key area of focus for post-colonialist theory is the way in which subaltern nations, and their inhabitants, have been depicted by writers from colonial powers. Eurocentric descriptions of the subaltern often depict non-European nations as savage, primitive and uncivilised: Europe, in contrast, is a model of sophistication. The non-European, in short, is the 'Other': unfamiliar, strange, and threatening.

Key terms

dystopian: an imaginary world in which everything is negative, distorted and terrifying

colonialism: the process by which nations have been conquered, ruled over and exploited by other nations

subaltern: originally a military term referring to members of the lower ranks; now a term used in post-colonial theory to refer to people ruled by colonial powers

9.8.1 Heart of Darkness

Joseph Conrad's novella *Heart of Darkness* (1899) tells a story of corruption and inhumanity; of violence, greed, short-sightedness, and evil. Its main narrator, Marlow, is a merchant seaman who is travelling upriver on a steamship to a remote trading station in the heart of the Belgian Congo. On his journey, he encounters a number of European traders who have all been corrupted, to varying degrees, by their experiences of colonialism and commerce. The most corrupt is Kurtz, head of the trading station, who rules with a combination of messianic zeal and utter savagery. Kurtz is dying: his final words, spoken in a whisper, are 'The horror! The horror!' Text 9L is taken from Part I of the novella, when Marlow is on his way to Africa.

ACTIVITY 16

***Heart of Darkness* and 'the dark places of the earth'**

a Pick out the descriptions of Africa. What kinds of imagery does Conrad use? To what extent do these descriptions support the Eurocentric stereotype of Africa as wild and uncontainable?

b Look at the descriptions of the African people. How are they depicted? Are they treated as individuals, or as a homogenous group? What does Marlow feel about them? Are his feelings based on stereotypes?

c In what ways does Conrad present Africa as the 'Other'?

d What attitudes towards colonialism do you think Marlow displays in this extract?

Text 9L

The best way I can explain it to you is by saying that, for a second or two, I felt as though, instead of going to the centre of a continent, I were about to set off for the centre of the earth.

I left in a French steamer, and she called in every blamed port they have out there, for, as far as I could see, the sole purpose of landing soldiers and custom-house officers. I watched the coast. Watching a coast as it slips by the ship is like thinking about an enigma. There it is before you – smiling, frowning, inviting, grand, mean, insipid, or savage, and always mute with an air of whispering, 'Come and find out'. This one was almost featureless, as if still in the making, with an aspect of monotonous grimness. The edge of a colossal jungle, so dark-green as to be almost black, fringed with white surf, ran straight, like a ruled line, far, far away along a blue sea whose glitter was blurred by a creeping mist. The sun was fierce, the land seemed to glisten and drip with steam. Here and there greyish-whitish specks showed up clustered inside the white surf, with a flag flying above them perhaps. Settlements some centuries old, and still no bigger than pinheads on the untouched expanse of their background. We pounded along, stopped, landed soldiers; went on, landed custom-house clerks to levy toll in what looked like a God-forsaken wilderness, with a tin shed and a flag-pole lost in it; landed more soldiers – to take care of the custom-house clerks, presumably. Some, I heard, got drowned in the surf; but whether they did or not, nobody seemed particularly to care. They were just flung out there, and on we went. Every day the coast looked the same, as though we had not moved; but we passed various places – trading places – with names like Gran' Bassam, Little Popo; names that seemed to belong to some sordid farce acted in front of a sinister back-cloth. The idleness of a passenger, my isolation amongst all these men with whom I had no point of contact, the oily and languid sea, the uniform sombreness of the coast, seemed to keep me away from the truth of things, within the toil of a mournful and senseless delusion. The voice of the surf heard now and then was a positive pleasure, like the speech of a brother. It was something natural, that had its reason, that had a meaning. Now and then a boat from the shore gave one a momentary contact with reality. It was paddled by black fellows. You could see from afar the white of their eyeballs glistening. They shouted, sang; their bodies streamed with perspiration; they had faces like grotesque masks – these chaps; but they had bone, muscle, a wild vitality, an intense energy of movement, that was as natural and true as the surf along their coast. They wanted no excuse for being there. They were a great comfort to look at. For a time I would feel I belonged still to a world of straightforward facts; but the feeling would not last long. Something would turn up to scare it away. Once, I remember, we came upon a **man-of-war** anchored off the coast. There wasn't even a shed there, and she was shelling the bush. It appears the French had one of their wars going on thereabouts. Her **ensign** dropped limp like a rag; the muzzles of the long six-inch guns stuck out all over the low hull; the greasy, slimy swell swung her up lazily and let her down, swaying her thin masts. In the empty immensity of earth, sky, and water, there she was, incomprehensible, firing into a continent. Pop, would go one of the six-inch guns; a small flame would dart and vanish, a little white smoke would disappear, a tiny **projectile** would give a feeble screech – and nothing happened. Nothing could happen. There was a touch of insanity in the proceeding, a sense of lugubrious drollery in the sight; and it was not dissipated by somebody on board assuring me earnestly there was a camp of natives – he called them enemies! – hidden out of sight somewhere.

Joseph Conrad, *Heart of Darkness*

Glossary

man-of-war: a battleship

ensign: the name given to a national flag when it is displayed on a ship

projectile: a missile

Exploring Joseph Conrad

Joseph Conrad was born in Poland, and spent part of his adolescence in France. English was his third language: he did not learn to speak it fluently until he was in his twenties. He was granted British nationality in 1886, but always regarded himself as Polish. In what ways might Conrad's own early life have influenced his attitudes towards other cultures?

9.8.2 'The Empire Writes Back'

One key work of post-colonialist theory is *The Empire Writes Back*, by Bill Ashcroft, Gareth Griffiths and Helen Tiffin. It takes its title from the name of the second Star Wars film, *The Empire Strikes Back*, and explores the influence of colonialism on the 'perceptual frameworks' of the inhabitants of colonised and previously colonised nations. By 'perceptual frameworks', Ashcroft, Griffiths and Tiffin mean the ways in which these people see themselves, their cultures and their relationship with their former rulers. (The relationship between colonisers and colonised is often described using terms such as 'the centre' or 'the metropolis' for the imperial powers, and 'the margins', 'the periphery' or 'the frontier' for the colonies – metaphors that underline a Eurocentric view of the world.) Colonialism is therefore a lens that shapes one's view of the world – even many years after previously colonised nations have gained their independence.

Ashcroft, Griffiths and Tiffin identify three stages in the development of writing about the colonies.

1 The first stage consists of writing produced by people from the imperial centre, such as the early European settlers and those involved in establishing and maintaining imperial rule. Writing from this stage tends to focus on the 'Otherness' of the new cultures, climates, landscapes and people encountered.
2 The second stage consists of writing produced 'under imperial licence'. This is the work of people from the subaltern culture who have entered what Ashcroft, Griffiths and Tiffin refer to as 'a special and privileged class': they have learned the language of their rulers, gained an education, and been able to have their work published and distributed by these rulers. In order for their work to be published, it must have earned the rulers' approval – by being in an appropriate style and by focusing on subjects and ideas deemed acceptable for 'natives' to write about. It must, therefore, have assimilated the values of the imperial culture.
3 The third stage is marked by the development of alternative voices that challenge and overturn the values of the imperial culture rather than accepting them. It might do this through its subject matter: by exposing the brutality that the process of colonialism often involved, or by questioning its results. Additionally, it might use non-standard English, reflecting the ways in which its writers have tried to find a voice and a language of their own. These linguistic experiments are sometimes referred to as hybrid forms.

This three-part model enables us to identify a number of issues that post-colonialist literary theory might focus on. These include:

- the ways in which early European settlers depicted non-European countries and cultures
- the ways in which people from subaltern cultures have had to assimilate the values of the dominant culture

'The word 'ivory' rang in the air, was whispered, was sighed. You would think they were praying to it.'

Joseph Conrad, *Heart of Darkness*

- the ways in which writers have experimented with language and style to produce hybrid forms of literature that blend elements of different languages and cultures.

Post-colonialist theory might also explore the work of writers from migrant communities.

Exploring *The Buddha of Suburbia*

The experience of growing up in a migrant community, and finding oneself caught between different cultures, is expressed in the first sentence of Hanif Kureishi's 1990 novel *The Buddha of Suburbia*: 'My name is Karim Amir, and I am an Englishman born and bred, almost'. Read Susie Thomas' essay on *The Buddha of Suburbia*, which explores the novel's setting.

Read Susie Thomas' essay on *The Buddha of Suburbia* via Cambridge Elevate

9.8.3 The scope of post-colonial theory

Post-colonial approaches can also be applied to texts that might appear, at first, to have very little to do with colonialism. Jane Austen's *Mansfield Park* (1814) is set on a country estate in Northamptonshire: the novel's heroine Fanny Price is sent there to live with her wealthy relatives, the Bertrams, because her impoverished parents cannot afford to look after all nine of their children. The Bertrams' riches come from the plantations they own on the island of Antigua, in the West Indies: at one point, Fanny asks her uncle Sir Thomas Bertram about his involvement in the slave trade, and parallels are drawn between slavery and the way that Fanny is treated by the Bertrams. In Text 9M from Chapter 1, Sir Thomas explains to his sister-in-law Mrs Norris that Fanny must not be allowed to see herself as a true member of the family.

Text 9M

'There will be some difficulty in our way, Mrs Norris,' observed Sir Thomas, 'as to the distinction proper to be made between the girls as they grow up: how to preserve in the minds of my daughters the consciousness of what they are, without making them think too lowly of their cousin; and how, without depressing her spirits too far, to make her remember that she is not a Miss Bertram. I should wish to see them very good friends, and would, on no account, authorise in my girls the smallest degree of arrogance towards their relation; but still they cannot be equals. Their rank, fortune, rights, and expectations will always be different.'

Jane Austen, *Mansfield Park*

The character of Bertha Mason, in Charlotte Brontë's *Jane Eyre* (1847), is also interesting to explore from a post-colonial perspective. Bertha is a Creole, the daughter of white European settlers in the West Indies. She has 'dark' hair and a 'discoloured', 'black' face: her parents wanted her to marry Rochester because he was 'of good race'. Even as a white Creole, Bertha would have been seen as 'alien'. In the 18th and 19th centuries, many Europeans associated Creoles with the Caribbean, distancing them from 'civilised' Europeans. This was particularly the case for Creole women, who were often depicted as strong-willed and unstable. The contrasts between Bertha and the 'grave and quiet' Jane are heightened by the gothic imagery that surrounds Bertha, who is described as a 'goblin' and a 'vampire'. In her 1966 novel *Wide Sargasso Sea*, Jean Rhys explored *Jane Eyre*'s colonial heritage in detail, focusing on Bertha's early life and experiences, and featuring Bertha – who she renamed Antoinette Cosway – as one of the novel's narrators.

9.8.4 Post-colonial theory: taking it further

Wuthering Heights: Who is Heathcliff?

The character of Heathcliff, in Emily Brontë's *Wuthering Heights* (1847), is endlessly intriguing. Heathcliff's background is a mystery. He is an orphan found on the streets of Liverpool by Mr Earnshaw, who rescues him and brings him home to Yorkshire to raise him alongside his own children. Mr Earnshaw describes Heathcliff as being 'as dark almost as if [he] came from the devil', and another character states that he could be a 'little Lascar or American castaway' (a Lascar was an Indian seaman employed on a European ship). Critics have speculated that Heathcliff may be of Gypsy or Indian origin, or a refugee from famine-stricken Ireland. Wherever he is from, Heathcliff is certainly depicted as 'Other', both ethnically and morally: his demonic behaviour places him outside the norms of civilised society. This makes him an excellent subject for post-colonial analysis.

You could apply a post-colonialist approach to the character of Heathcliff by:

- identifying the different ways in which he is described, and looking at the racial and moral implications of these descriptions
- exploring some illustrated versions of *Wuthering Heights* (such as those by Fritz Eichenberg and Barnett Freedman) to see how these aspects of Heathcliff have been exaggerated by artists
- finding out about the Liverpool slave trade and the Irish potato famine, and considering how this information could influence the way in which Heathcliff is interpreted.

The Poisonwood Bible: Africa answering back

Barbara Kingsolver's powerful novel *The Poisonwood Bible* (1998) explores the legacy of colonialism – and the painful process by which The Republic of the Congo, formerly the Belgian Congo, gained its independence. It is set in the early 1960s, at the time when the first democratic elections took place in the Congo, and focuses on Nathan Price, a Baptist missionary from the southern USA, who takes his family to Africa in an attempt to bring Christianity to the Congolese people. The story is told by five different narrators: Price's wife Orleanna, who gives her account of events in retrospect, and the four Price daughters, Rachel, Leah, Adah and Ruth May. The novel is highly critical of the American government's involvement in Congolese politics, and offers an interpretation of colonial rule that complicates and contradicts the 19th-century view of colonialism as bringing 'civilisation' to a 'dark continent'.

You could apply a post-colonialist approach to *The Poisonwood Bible* by:

- identifying the perspectives of different characters (both American and Congolese) on colonial rule, including its injustices and perceived benefits
- considering the effects of Kingsolver's use of multiple narrators
- exploring the instability of language and meaning (Rachel's **malapropisms**, Adah's **palindromes**, the fact that Congolese words can change their meanings if pronounced in a different way).

Key terms

malapropism: a word used mistakenly in place of another word with a similar sound

palindrome: a word or phrase that reads the same both forwards and backwards

Hybrid voices: the poetry of Daljit Nagra

Daljit Nagra was born in west London in 1966. His Punjabi Sikh parents came to Britain from India in the 1950s, and his poetry is inflected with the rhythms and speech-patterns of Punjabi. His first collection, *Look We Have Coming to Dover!* (2007) is an energetic, humorous exploration of the experience of people from the Sikh community who have come to live in Britain. Nagra says that *Look We Have Coming to Dover!* is 'heavily populated with first generation characters and their second and third generation descendants. I have sought to explore their thoughts, feelings and cultural attitudes towards their own community, other ethnic communities and the indigenous white population'.

You could apply a post-colonialist approach to Daljit Nagra's poetry by:

- exploring the poet's depiction of the experiences of first-generation immigrants and their descendants
- considering how these depictions challenge and complicate stereotypes of British Asian communities
- analysing the effect of Nagra's use of non-standard English to convey the different voices of his characters.

9.9 Approaching the non-exam assessment

Remember that you cannot base your non-exam assessment on a text that is set for any of the examined units for this A Level course, nor can you base it on drama. The poetry text that you choose must be substantial (for an idea of how many poems to focus on, look at the length of the poetry collections that AQA has set for the other units of this specification). Remember also that one of your responses can be a re-creative piece.

See 11.3 for more on re-creative responses to literature

This unit has introduced you to a range of different theoretical approaches, and given you some ideas as to how they could be applied to a variety of texts. How will you start work on your non-exam assessment?

Unit 10, Critical and creative responses to literature, gives you detailed guidance on the process of writing about literature – building your initial thoughts about a text, planning your response, and developing your ideas into an extended piece of critical or creative writing. It also contains a range of suggestions that will be particularly useful for the non-exam assessment. These include the following:

- engaging in a dialogue with a text (Activity 1): one of the main aims of literary theory is to get you to question and reply to what an author writes
- keeping a reading journal (section 10.3.1): this is a great way of developing your thoughts about the texts you have selected for your non-exam assessment, allowing you to capture ideas and impressions and return to them later
- setting up a wiki (section 10.3.2): this enables you to include other people in the dialogue you have entered into with your chosen text, meaning that you can test out your ideas (and giving you practice in explaining them coherently).

Your choice of texts and approaches will be important to you. The best texts to use are those that have challenged you personally to think about the issues raised by the different aspects of literary theory you've studied, such as a text that explores gender in an interesting way, or that challenges perceptions of a particular ethnic group or social class. Perhaps you could choose an issue that you feel strongly about, or a text that has been particularly controversial.

Bear in mind, too, that while some texts might seem to be suited to particular approaches, it can sometimes be much more productive (and interesting!) to approach them in a very different way. George Orwell's novel *Animal Farm*, for instance, might seem a natural topic for a Marxist approach – but what might you gain from reading it from a feminist perspective? The poetry of Seamus Heaney lends itself very readily to a post-colonialist approach – but what could you uncover from exploring it through the lens of eco-criticism? Remember that you can explore your chosen text from more than one perspective – it might be interesting to evaluate two very different critical approaches to the same text.

Crucially, you should be willing to read your chosen texts more than once. Figure 11A in section 11.2.1 highlights the circularity of the reading process, showing that you will need to revisit your chosen texts in the light of your critical and theoretical reading. Be prepared to spend time making notes, jotting down your thoughts and asking questions of the text and yourself before you start to plan your response.

See 11.2 for more on planning and structuring critical essays

9.10 Bringing it all together

9.10.1 How will the Theory and Independence component be assessed?

For the Theory and Independence component, you will study two texts (one poetry and one prose), informed by your study of the Critical Anthology. You will produce two essays, each of 1250–1500 words, responding to a different text and linking to a different aspect of the Critical Anthology.

One of the essays can be re-creative. This piece must be accompanied by a commentary.

Your essays will be assessed by your teachers in school and moderated by AQA. Each essay will be given a mark out of 25, to produce a total out of 50.

The Theory and Independence component is worth 20 per cent of your overall A Level grade.

For guidance on preparing for the exams, see Unit 11

9.10.2 How much do you know?

The following questions ask you to bring together the elements you have studied in this unit.

1. Explain what the term 'literary theory' means.
2. Explain the kinds of issues that the following approaches might focus on:
   - value and the canon
   - narrative
   - feminism
   - Marxism
   - eco-criticism
   - post-colonial criticism.

3 Choose two different critical approaches. Apply them to a text that you have studied for one of your other A Level English Literature units. For example, you could apply Marxist and feminist approaches to *King Lear*, or narrative and post-colonial approaches to *Small Island*. Write up your responses in coherent, continuous prose.

9.10.3 Assessment objectives

In relation to the assessment objectives, this unit has explored:

- how you as a reader can make personal, informed and creative responses to literary texts, drawing on a range of theoretical approaches to develop different readings of these texts. It has also introduced you to a range of essential terminology and concepts that you might use in thinking and writing about literature (AO1)
- how authorial methods shape meanings and convey particular views of the world (AO2)
- how texts are influenced by the contexts of both the author and the reader, including factors such as gender, ethnicity, social class, sexuality, and religious and political beliefs (AO3)
- how literary theory can inform your interpretation of literary texts and allow you to connect with other texts (AO4)
- how texts can be interpreted in different ways, drawing on a range of theoretical approaches (AO5).

Summary

In this unit, you have learned about:

- what literary theory is
- how literary theory can shape your interpretations of literary texts
- key elements of a range of different theoretical approaches
- how these approaches could be applied to a range of texts.

DEVELOPING

10

Critical and creative responses to literature

In this unit you will:

- consider what is meant by the idea of literary criticism
- explore how creative responses to literature can enhance critical understanding.

10.1 Introducing criticism and creativity

Unlike other subjects, written text is the primary focus in English. Writing is central to the study of English in three distinct ways:

- writing as a product – literary texts and **literary criticism**
- writing as a process – the ways in which writers construct literary texts
- the act of writing – as you produce critical and creative texts in response to your reading.

As you progress in your studies, you need to think carefully about how all kinds of text (literary texts, critical texts and the texts you write yourself) are produced and consumed. You will need, in other words, to develop understanding of how and why writers write and how and why readers read.

Key terms

literary criticism: the art of making judgements about and commenting upon the qualities and character of literary works

10.1.1 Critical, creative and re-creative responses to literary texts

People often treat 'critical' and 'creative' responses to literature as if they were different things. It's not that simple. Reading and writing are both creative *and* critical. Writing about literature inevitably explores the ways in which writers create meaning, and when you read any text you are creatively involved in building meaning.

See 9.1.1 to explore where the meaning of a text is located

Whenever you write – even if it is a critical essay – you are involved in creating meaning through your writing, so you need to develop the ways in which you work creatively with critical language, and you may also have the opportunity to do some creative writing of your own to explore a variety of issues and effects in the texts you are studying. Creative, re-creative and critical writing are closely related.

See 11.3 for more on re-creative responses to literature

10.2 Reading as a writer, writing as a reader

Think about your study of literature to date. By and large you have probably been taught how to read literary texts and how to write critical texts. You have probably spent much less time learning how to *read critical* texts, and even less on how to write literary texts.

Developing your confidence as a reader and increasing your confidence as a writer are related processes. The ideas in this unit are designed to help you explore your thinking through and about writing. This will take some practice and may result in some disappointment along the way - nobody gets it right all the time - but it will also be rewarding, fulfilling and even enjoyable. Reading and writing are closely related processes. Reading is not possible without a written text, and writing is generally undertaken so that somebody will read it! In other words, readers and writers are both involved in giving a text its life and in creating what it might mean. Text 10A shows what the poet Philip Larkin has to say, in 'The Pleasure Principle', about writing and reading.

Text 10A

It consists of three stages: the first is when a man becomes obsessed with an emotional concept to such a degree that he is compelled to do something about it. What he does is the second stage, namely, construct a verbal device that will reproduce this emotional concept in anyone who cares to read it, anywhere, any time. The third stage is the recurrent situation of people in different times and places setting off the device and re-creating in themselves what the poet felt when he wrote it. The stages are interdependent and all necessary. If there has been no preliminary feeling, the device has nothing to reproduce and the reader will experience nothing. If the second stage has not been well done, the device will not deliver the goods, or will deliver only a few goods to a few people, or will stop delivering them after an absurdly short while. And if there is no third stage, no successful reading, the poem can hardly be said to exist at all.

Philip Larkin, 'The Pleasure Principle'

As you work through your course, think carefully about how your development as a reader affects your development as a writer, and how the writing you do impacts upon you as a reader. See Table 10A for how we might summarise this.

Table 10A

Read like a writer	Think about how writers work for and with their readers. What is the purpose of the writing? What effects do writers achieve and how do they do so? How might you use these to develop your own writing?
Write like a reader	Think about how readers are likely to respond to what you write. Is your writing appropriate to the needs of whoever will be reading it? Are your ideas effectively argued, well expressed and sufficiently illustrated? Are spelling, punctuation and grammar accurate? Is handwriting legible?

These are important strategies to apply when you are reading and writing either literary or critical texts. By thinking in these ways, you will engage more closely with what readers, writers and critics do, and how you can do this yourself.

The Russian critic Mikhail Bakhtin (1975) talks of what he calls a 'dialogic' relationship between readers and authors centred on the text, and the French critic Roland Barthes (1973) suggests that texts are either 'readerly' - allowing readers few if any rights of interpretation - or 'writerly' - allowing readers the freedom to interpret widely. Creative and re-creative writing will allow you to explore your own 'dialogue' with literary texts and can really help in developing your understanding.

ACTIVITY 1

Exploring the idea of engaging in a 'dialogue'

In *The Dialogic Imagination*, Mikhail Bakhtin explores the idea that readers and writers engage in a 'dialogue' to create meaning from the text they share.

a In what ways do you as a reader engage in a dialogue with the texts you are studying?

b How does this change your understanding of your role as a reader?

c Dialogue implies a right of reply. In what ways can you as a reader 'reply' to what an author writes?

10.3 Reading

As you can see, reading and writing are closely inter-related processes, and as part of your studies you will have to read a lot - in terms of set texts, wider reading of literary texts and secondary reading such as context materials (relevant historical documents, author biographies, relevant religious or philosophical texts), literary criticism and the materials in the Critical Anthology. With this in mind, it is a good idea to think about how you feel about reading.

ACTIVITY 2

Exploring your views on reading

Think carefully about the following questions. It would be a good idea to draw up a table listing each of the 'rights' and then to think about how they relate to your views of reading for pleasure and reading for study.

a As a percentage, how much of your reading is for study and how much for pleasure? (For example, if 90 per cent of your reading is for pleasure, you would write '10%/90%'.)
b What is the difference between reading for pleasure and reading for study, if any?
c Which of the 'rights' in the cartoon do you allow yourself when you are reading for pleasure?
d Do you give yourself different 'rights' for reading different kinds of text? Think about your reading of prose fiction, drama, poetry, non-fiction, literary criticism.
e Which of these 'rights' have your teachers allowed you in your study of English to date? Why?
f Which of them have your teachers routinely denied you in the course of your studies? Why?
g How has this affected your views of reading (and writing)?
h Should it be this way?
i Do you think this situation will change now you are studying at A Level?

It would be a good idea to compare your views with those of other students in your group, and to discuss the outcomes of your thinking with your teacher(s).

10.3.1 Approaches to reading: keeping journals and blogs

Your thinking about the texts you are studying and your responses to them will naturally change over time. As you read more widely around a topic, you will begin to see it in new and more complex ways. For example, as you read poetry by a variety of poets you will begin to see interesting connections and contrasts with the work of other poets; when you read a narrative in drama form you will begin to see ways in which it both relates to and diverges from prose fiction narratives.

It is really useful to capture your developing thoughts and responses as you proceed through your course. Keeping journals or blogs relating to your study of particular texts, on bigger concepts relating to your study of literature (for example, ideas about tragedy, comedy, crime writing or social and political protest writing) and more general issues (for example, literary terminology, narrative forms) will provide you with a core body of material to draw on when you are talking and writing more formally about literature. Journals or blogs might also include extracts from your set texts and your wider reading that effectively illustrate the ideas you are exploring. In this way, you begin to get used to selecting and using quotation and other kinds of evidence from literary texts more effectively, ready for the process of writing. Journals and blogs might also contain things other than writing - such as appropriate photographs, colour schemes, paintings, stage sets, film extracts, music clips and so on - and the potential of blogs to store multimedia texts widens the possibilities still further.

10.3.2 Approaches to reading: setting up wikis

Journals and blogs will probably be personal documents, but setting up wikis to develop group responses and resources is also very useful and can prompt some fascinating debates about different ways of reading and approaching texts.

10.4 Writing

The main form of writing you'll be expected to produce is the critical essay. This may be in a more extended form for non-exam assessment or in a briefer form for timed examination. Fundamentally, however, the form remains the same, although the approaches you'll adopt when you have the time to develop a longer non-exam assessment response and those you'll adopt when producing a shorter timed response will obviously be different.

See 11.2 for more on writing critical essays

The important thing for now is to remember that you want to develop into the best writer you can become. Effective and exciting writers take risks with words and look for imaginative ways to convey and explore meaning. The best way to learn this is to write regularly. The more you write, the more familiar you will become with the process of writing and the less inhibiting it will be. We therefore recommend that you work regularly and often at your writing. This does not have to be in the form of full written essays all the time – we'll explore a variety of approaches in this unit. The important thing is that you make writing your friend rather than seeing it as an alien and intimidating process.

ACTIVITY 3

Your relationship with writing

Jot down your responses to the following questions.

a What is writing?
b Do you write regularly?
c Do you enjoy writing?
d What kinds of writing do you do?
e Are you a meticulous planner, or do you prefer to allow writing to emerge and develop more organically?
f What are your processes as a writer?
g Do you like or dislike redrafting your writing?
h How confident are you in your abilities as a writer?
i How does writing at this stage in your education differ from the writing you have done previously?
j What features of writing do you think are particularly important at this level?
k What kinds of writing would you like to do more of?
l What do you find particularly difficult as a writer?
m What skills and understanding do you wish to develop as a writer?

Why not use your thoughts as the basis for a 'writing biography' in which you trace your own personal relationship with writing? You could do this either as a factual or as a fictional piece of writing.

10.4.1 Types of writing

As a student you will write a lot for assessment purposes, and it's easy to think that this is all writing is for. In fact, much (even most) of the writing you do is not just about a final product for assessment – often writing is provisional and exploratory; a process through which you can develop your ideas. In many ways, it's a kind of thinking aloud on paper. Through writing, you can develop your own responses to literary texts and interact with a variety of critical ideas about literature as well as learning what it feels like to be a writer, making the kinds of choices made by the writers you are studying.

Table 10B shows some of the types of writing you're likely to do.

It is important to see these as part of your development as a writer. All of these are ways in which you can become more confident expressing your ideas in writing, and they will in their turn begin to have an impact on more formal written work.

Table 10B

note-taking	During taught sessions, you will take notes on what your teachers or peers say.
note-making	This is a more extended process when you make notes to summarise and respond to interesting ideas from your reading or viewing.
initial response writing	In this kind of writing, you will write free responses to your reading as you try to articulate what it means to you. These responses are likely to develop or even change completely as new evidence emerges and new ideas occur to you.
planning	In planning, you will write outlines in response to particular assessment tasks or ideas relating to the texts you are studying.
annotation	You may write in the margins of the texts you are studying as you try to capture meaning, gloss unfamiliar words, ask yourself prompt questions and so on.

Writing is not always a definitive end product. You might find it helps to know that a lot of the writing you do is provisional and exploratory.

10.4.2 Approaches to writing: working with others

You may think of writing as a solitary activity. This is partially true. Sometimes you definitely need to write alone and without distractions, but there are other times when it is useful – even important – to work with others on your course.

Writing is a formalised way of 'talking' about literature. Both critical and creative responses to literature are a kind of 'conversation' with the texts you've been studying – a way of expressing your personal and critically informed understanding of what they might mean. Sometimes – if, for example, you're asked to respond to a critical proposition about a text or group of texts – you have to demonstrate your ability to engage with others' points of view. The idea of dialogue is therefore very important, so it is essential that you take time to talk with others about your writing.

Writing workshops can be very helpful. Everyone supplies some writing they have done (this could be critical or creative writing). There follows a discussion of each piece of writing, considering its strengths and ways in which it could be developed. You may well feel uncomfortable and vulnerable at first, but as you come to know and trust your fellow students, discussing writing collaboratively is useful in many ways. Consider, for example,

- how effectively the response addresses the task set
- how ideas might be developed more effectively
- the sequence of arguments
- the effectiveness and precision of vocabulary choices
- how well quotation is used to support argument
- how effectively other forms of reference to text are employed.

An important principle in building trust and making sure that writing workshops are open, honest and constructive is to ensure that criticism is always positively intended. Of course the whole point of the exercise is to learn how your writing can improve, and it doesn't help anyone if the workshop becomes a mutual admiration society or a place where nobody can express honest views about ways in which writing can be improved. However, it is essential that nobody makes a criticism in order to belittle another student, so make it a rule that a criticism must always be accompanied by a positive suggestion. At first it might be helpful to use only published critical responses to the texts you are studying and then gradually begin to include texts of your own. By spending time talking about writing and the processes of writing, you will be taking crucial steps in developing as an independent writer.

Workshops work best when everyone contributes and when participants have had time to think in depth about the writing 'on the table'. Judgements are better informed and criticisms more thoughtful when you've taken time to form them, so make sure that work for consideration in a workshop is circulated at least a day in advance and that you always take the time to read others' work – you want them to pay your work the same respect.

ACTIVITY 4

Giving constructive criticism

Read the passage in Text 10B, which has been written as the opening to a thriller. Imagine that it is a piece that has been circulated by one of your group members for discussion at the next workshop.

You have been told to focus your comments on:

- pace
- atmosphere
- vocabulary
- uncertainty.

a What constructive criticisms would you make? Select specific examples and think carefully about what you want to say. Select examples you think are good and also examples you think could benefit from improvement – remember to have alternative suggestions for these.

b How do you think this process would benefit:
  - the writer of the passage?
  - other students in the group?
  - yourself?

Text 10B

Prologue – Events

He held the book in his hand and scanned the room. Light from the late afternoon sun filtered into the chamber through a dirty window high up on one wall. It would soon be dark. He had to be quick and he needed more light. He went to the table that stood in the middle of the room and lit a candle which had been crudely stuffed into the neck of a bottle.

That done, unhurried and calm, he turned his mind to the obvious question. Where should he leave it? He could not just leave it on some random shelf. The success of his plans depended on choosing precisely the right spot. He had to make his choice with the mind of the poet.

He did a quick circuit of the room. There were texts in all of the main European languages. The answer came to him easily enough. It would be best with the other texts in English.

He returned to the shelves where he had seen the English books and quickly read over the titles. Again the answer supplied itself. There was only one place it could go. Next to Milton.

Yes.

He slipped the book on to the shelf.

*

'Morose,' said The Poet, 'never seen him in any other state.'

The Dean, accompanying the great man nodded in a non-committal sort of way and sucked again at the rim of his crystal sherry glass. He flicked a glance across from under his peppery eyebrows to the person under discussion. Dr Marshall – rounded shoulders, gown sprinkled with dandruff, crumpled trousers. His dour eyes and hangdog expression, the thinning, once-ginger hair now grey, and his pallid-as-parchment face all certainly, the Dean had to admit, contributed to The Poet's observation that he was, indeed, morose. The Dean, however, did not necessarily subscribe to all The Poet's particular perspectives.

'Who's he with?' The Poet peered across the Hall, which was now concertedly rumbling with a hundred Donnish conversations.

The Dean peered with him, glad to escape the need to actually agree with The Poet. 'Looks like Freeman,' he said, correctly identifying the younger man in glasses who was dressed, beneath his gown, in a rusty corduroy suit and desert boots – his unruly, nut brown hair sprayed in all directions, making him look as if he'd only just got up.

Dr Marshall became aware that he was being watched. As his eyes latched onto The Poet's, his gloomy countenance was replaced by something not far from active dislike, if not venom. Although Dr Marshall, despite his demeanour, was probably not capable of actual venom. His was not an unkind soul. However, there was something about The Poet that rankled, and brought out the worst in him.

In fact, Dr Marshall, only a few minutes earlier, as they had wandered into Hall for the pre-dinner reception, had slid alongside The Poet and made clear his views.

'You have been weighed, tested and found wanting,' the academic had muttered to The Poet under his breath.

The Poet sneered in response, not deigning to turn and look at his accuser. He had initially taken the remark as a manifestation of jealousy. He was about to be honoured by his illustrious peers at this rather splendid dinner; glittering with silver and chandeliers. An honour he had,

it was true to say, felt he utterly deserved. It was doubtful Dr Marshall would ever be so honoured.

No wonder.

Miserable old fool.

Yet, on further reflection, The Poet had begun to question his initial reaction. Had the academic's bitter remark anything to do with previous conversations they'd had last year, during Trinity term?

And why was he now standing talking to Freeman?

It looked like conspiracy to The Poet. How much did Marshall know? How much was he telling Freeman?

Freeman of all people?

10.4.3 Approaches to writing: talk for writing

Another important thing to think about is the role of talk in developing your writing. Hopefully you will spend a lot of time in your lessons talking about the texts you are studying and a wide range of issues surrounding the study of literature. It is important that you see all this talk as essential preparation for your writing. You can use your talk to develop ideas about how to write and thoughts about what you want to communicate.

Although your course does not include any formal assessment of speaking and listening, this will be an essential part of your experience. You will do a lot of talking about books and about ideas relating to literature. It is a crucial means of setting out, expanding and clarifying your thinking before, during and after reading and writing. So, working in an effective atmosphere of discussion and collaboration is very important. You might use some of your study time to work in the ways suggested in Figure 10A with others on your course.

Figure 10A

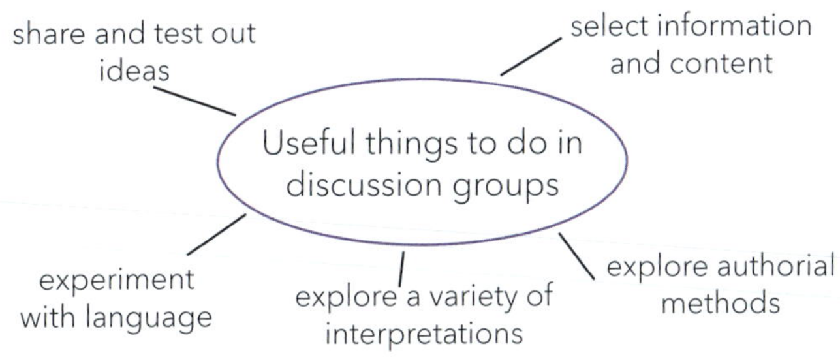

You could easily record your ideas and developing thoughts on your mobile or similar device whenever and wherever they occur to you and use these to inform or become part of your written work.

Summary

In this unit, you have learned about:

- the types of writing required in A Level literary study
- what we mean by critical and creative responses to literary texts
- the relationship between critical, creative and re-creative responses to literary texts
- how reading and talk feed into writing
- the relationship between writers and readers
- how to work collaboratively on developing writing.

DEVELOPING

11

Preparing for your exam

In this unit you will:

- understand the examined and non-examined assessment components for A and AS Level
- consider how to prepare for the exam and practise responding to sample exam questions
- develop the skills necessary for structuring and writing critical essays
- explore critical commentary and writing creative responses to literary texts
- learn how to use secondary sources and wider reading as a way of developing and communicating your understanding and ideas.

11.1 Examined assessment and non-exam assessment

Here are the different assessment components for AS Level and the full A Level:

AS Level	**Paper 1** **Literary Genres: Drama** **Aspects of Tragedy or Aspects of Comedy** Closed book 1½ hours 50% of AS Level	**Section A** One passage-based question on a set Shakespeare play (25 marks)	**Section B** One essay question on your other set play (25 marks)
AS Level	**Paper 2** **Literary Genres: Prose and Poetry** **Aspects of Tragedy or Aspects of Comedy** Open book 1½ hours 50% of AS Level	**Section A** One essay question on a poetry set text, with particular reference to a short extract (25 marks)	**Section B** One essay question on a prose set text (25 marks)

A Level	**Paper 1** **Literary Genres** **Aspects of Tragedy or Aspects of Comedy** Closed book 2½ hours 40% of A Level	**Section A** One passage-based question on a set Shakespeare play (25 marks)	**Section B** One essay question on a set Shakespeare play (25 marks)	**Section C** One essay question linking two texts (25 marks)
A Level	**Paper 2** **Texts and Genres** Open book 3 hours 40% of A Level	**Section A** One passage-based question on an unseen text (25 marks)	**Section B** One essay question on a set text (25 marks)	**Section C** One essay question linking two texts (25 marks)
A Level	**Non-exam assessment** **Theory and Independence** 20% of A Level Study of one poetry and one prose text	**Element 1** Critical essay of 1250–1500 words on one text		**Element 2** Critical essay OR re-creative writing task and accompanying commentary of 1250–1500 words on the other text

The different components make different demands on your writing. Clearly open-book exams allow you to look up and utilise quotation in ways not available to you in a closed-book exam and there is the expectation that specific sections of the set text will be selected to further the argument and for close consideration of key aspects of method, such as structural and organisational features. Also, for those of you taking the full A Level, the non-exam assessment is an opportunity to develop your independent thoughts at greater length and potentially in a greater variety of ways.

11.1.1 Examined assessment

Examined units offer different types of questions. You will be expected to demonstrate your response by writing in a variety of different ways:

- analysing text extracts
- approaching your chosen texts through the aspects and elements of genres, and so engaging with them
- commenting on how genres work
- exploring how genres inform reading
- debating critical viewpoints
- writing about some texts on their own
- writing about some texts in connection with each other (A Level only).

All the exam questions test all AOs, so if you answer the questions carefully, you will hit all four of these AOs.

The examiner will take AO1 into account when marking your work, so you must present your ideas accurately and coherently to give an informed, personal and creative response, using appropriate terminology and referring to appropriate concepts. You should focus on relevant contexts that arise out of the questions and the texts, and link them to the texts directly.

See 'How to Use This Book' for more on assessment objectives

In this section you will find more detailed information about each part of the exam, along with advice on how to prepare for the different types of question you will have to answer.

AS Level

The AS Level will be assessed through two exams: Paper 1 and Paper 2.

Paper 1: Literary Genres: Drama

This closed-book exam has two sections: A and B.

Section A

There will be one passage-based question on your set Shakespeare play. There will be no choice of questions on your play. The question will ask you to read an extract from your set play and explore the significance of the aspects of tragedy or comedy you find in the passage in relation to the play as a whole. Bullet points will guide the focus of your response and the passage will be approximately 40–45 lines long. The question tests your close reading abilities, focusing on issues of dramatic tragedy or comedy. It is also essential, however, that you demonstrate your understanding of how the passage relates to the tragedy or comedy of the whole play.

Section B

There will be one essay question on your other set play. There will be no choice of questions on your play. The question will invite you to discuss the extent to which you agree with a critical statement about an aspect of the tragedy or comedy of your play, and ask you to consider the author's dramatic methods. So you will write a critical essay to explore different possible meanings of your play. While taking the opportunity to draw on materials from the Critical Anthology to debate critical perspectives would be a very sound method, other approaches and your personal views are also valid.

Paper 2: Literary Genres: Prose and Poetry

This open-book exam has two sections: A and B.

Section A

There will be one essay question on your set poetry text. There will be no choice of questions on your text. The question will invite you to discuss the extent to which you agree with a critical statement about aspects of tragedy or comedy in your set text, considering the methods the author uses. The question will include a short extract from the set text and you will need to refer to this extract in your answer.

Section B

There will be one essay question on your set prose text. There will be no choice of questions on your text. The question will invite you to discuss the extent to which you agree with a critical statement about aspects of tragedy or comedy in your set text, considering the methods the author uses.

You will write a critical essay in response to both sections, A and B. As this is an open-book exam, you will be expected to make specific and detailed reference to your set texts.

A Level

The A Level will be assessed through two exams (Paper 1 and Paper 2) and non-exam assessment.

See 11.3.3 for more on the non-exam assessment

Paper 1: Literary Genres

This closed-book exam has three sections: A, B and C. In preparation, you will study three texts: one Shakespeare, a second drama and one further text, one of which must have been written before 1900.

Paper 1: Literary Genres

Section A

There will be one passage-based question on your set Shakespeare play. There will be no choice of questions on your play. The question will ask you to read an extract from your set play and explore the significance of the aspects of tragedy or comedy you find in the passage in relation to the play as a whole. The passage will be approximately 40–45 lines long. The question tests your close reading abilities, focusing on issues of dramatic tragedy or comedy. It is also essential, however, that you demonstrate your understanding of how the passage relates to the tragedy or comedy of the whole play.

Section B

There will be a choice of two essay questions on your play. Each question will invite you to discuss the extent to which you agree with a critical statement about an aspect of tragedy or comedy of your play, and ask you to include relevant comment on Shakespeare's dramatic methods. So you will write a critical essay to explore different possible meanings of your play. While taking the opportunity to draw on materials from the Critical Anthology to debate critical perspectives is a very sound method, other approaches and your personal views are also valid. Supporting your argument with well-selected reference to the text is essential and, even though this is a closed-book exam, quotation will be expected (though close references will be credited).

Section C

There will be one essay question linking your other two set texts. There will be a choice of two questions. Both will invite you to discuss to what extent you agree with a given view about an aspect of tragedy or comedy in relation to your two texts. You will be reminded to include in your answer relevant comment on the ways writers have shaped meanings. One of the texts you write about must be a drama text and one of the texts you write about must have been written before 1900.

You will write a critical essay, exploring a wider debate around aspects of tragedy or comedy. In writing about two texts in relation to the question, you will be making a connection between them, although explicit comparison of the two texts is not required. You don't have to spend equal amounts of time on each text, but you are expected to deal substantially with both.

Paper 2: Texts and Genres

This open-book exam has three sections: A, B and C. In preparation, you will study three texts: one prose text written after 2000; one poetry and one further text, one of which must have been written before 1900.

Section A
There will be one passage-based question on an extract from an unseen text in relation to the genre. There will be no choice of questions. The passage may be poetry, drama or prose. This question will ask you to read the passage and explore the significance of the crime writing or political and social protest writing elements in it. You will need to apply your ideas about your selected genre to the details of the passage. As the passage is unseen, there is no expectation that you will relate the passage to wider knowledge of the text, but you will be expected to demonstrate your understanding of the genre.

Section B
There will be a choice of questions on the set texts and you will need to choose one question. Each question will invite you to discuss the extent to which you agree with a critical statement about elements of crime or political and social protest writing in your set text. As this is an open-book exam, your critical essay will be expected to make specific and detailed reference to your chosen text. You will also need to consider how the form of the chosen text (poetry, drama or prose) affects representation and response in relation to the critical viewpoint.

For sections B and C combined, you must write about three texts, of which at least one must be poetry and at least one must be prose written after 2000. One text must have been written before 1900. In Section B, you must write about a text that you will **not** write about in Section C. Read Sections B and C carefully before making your choices.

Section C
You will write one essay question linking two of your set texts. There will be a choice of two questions, but you must write about two texts that you have **not** written about in Section B. Both questions will invite you to discuss a statement about crime or political and social protest writing with reference to the two set texts you choose. You do not need to write equal amounts on each text, but both should be covered substantially.

11.1.2 Non-exam assessment

For this component, you will study two texts: one poetry and one prose, which are **not** set texts for any of the examined units for A Level. These two texts must be studied in relation to at least two sections of the Critical Anthology. You will write a critical essay on one of the texts, and may choose to write a second critical essay, or a re-creative piece accompanied by a commentary, on the other text.

The non-exam assessment provides different writing opportunities. The title of this unit – 'Theory and Independence' – gives you some clues as to its philosophy and function. It allows you to read and explore texts of your own choice from differing critical and theoretical perspectives, drawing in detail on at least two sections of the Critical Anthology:

- narrative construction and how texts work (narrative theory)
- gender (feminist criticism)
- economics and social organisation (Marxist criticism)
- nationality, identity and power (post-colonial criticism)
- nature and the survival of the planet (eco-criticism)
- aesthetics and value (literary value and the canon).

See Unit 9 for more on critical theories

Both of the non-examined assessment pieces test all AOs so in planning and drafting your essays, you need to make sure that you hit all four of these AOs. Your teachers will take AO1 into account when marking your work, so you must present your ideas accurately and coherently to give an informed, personal and creative response, using appropriate terminology and referring to appropriate concepts.

As indicated by the word 'independence', you should be actively involved in making your own choices of texts, topics and tasks for this unit.

See 11.3 for more on re-creative writing options

11.1.3 Preparing for the exams

The examinations will test your knowledge of the appropriate genre and the ways in which you can apply your knowledge of your set texts to the genre. You will need to consider each text in relation to the framework in which you have studied it, reflecting on how it uses particular aspects of the tragic or comic genre, or elements of crime or political and social protest writing. Some of these aspects will be more in evidence in some texts than in others and you will need to explain how aspects are used, or indeed discarded, by the authors of the texts you have studied.

You will also need to consider literary form (drama, poetry or prose) so that you can assess and explain how this affects and shapes the texts you have studied. Drama, prose and poetry operate in rather different ways, and you will be expected to comment on how authors use aspects of their chosen form.

A third factor that will be assessed is your knowledge of the different ways in which your set texts can be interpreted. The 'Critical lens' boxes in units 5–8 will have raised some questions to get you thinking about these different interpretations, but during your course you should revisit your set texts in the light of your growing understanding of the range of potential meanings that literary works can have.

Remember, however, that while you need to know your set texts thoroughly, you don't need to know everything there is to know about them. As part of your exam preparation, you should make sure that you know what kinds of questions you will be asked and what kinds of knowledge you will need in order to tackle them.

It's vital that you spend some time practising how to answer exam questions under timed conditions. Your teacher will probably give you plenty of opportunities to do this in class, but it's also worth doing some exam practice in your own time. You could begin by using the practice questions in sections 11.1.4–11.1.8.

Once you've written an answer, mark it using the AQA mark scheme. You could, if possible, swap your essay with a partner and mark each other's work. Identify what you did well and what you need to develop, using the mark scheme to help you. Then rewrite your answer.

11.1.4 How should you approach a passage-based question on a set drama text?

The Section A questions in the AS Level Paper 1, and in the A Level Paper 1, follow a similar format. You will be given an extract from your set Shakespeare play (which will be printed in the exam paper). You will be asked to read the extract and explore it in relation to aspects of tragedy or comedy. At AS Level, you will focus on the extract itself, and will be given a number of bullet points to guide your response. At A Level, you will be asked to write about the significance of the extract to the tragedy or comedy of the play as a whole.

Practice A Level question on *King Lear*

The extract referred to is from 'Kent still in the stocks; Enter Lear, the Fool and a Gentleman; Lear: 'Tis strange that they should so depart from home' to 'Fool: Winter's not gone yet if the wild geese fly that way' in Act 2, Scene 4.

At AS Level: Explore the significance of the aspects of dramatic tragedy in the following passage in relation to the play as a whole.

You should consider the following in your answer:

- the relationship between Lear and Kent
- Shakespeare's use of dialogue
- the dramatic setting
- other relevant aspects of dramatic tragedy.

At A Level: Read the extract and then answer the question.

Explore the significance of this extract in relation to the tragedy of the play as a whole. Remember to include in your answer relevant analysis of Shakespeare's dramatic methods.

As this question involves close reading, you should spend time reading and annotating the extract and planning your response.

You will not know which extract will be set, so there is an 'unseen' element to this question. However, the extract will not be completely unseen, as you will have studied the play in considerable detail. The most important thing to recognise is that while the specific extract will differ, the task will follow the same format. At AS Level, you will be asked to explore the significance of the aspects of dramatic tragedy or comedy in the extract, guided by a number of bullet points. At A Level, you will be asked to analyse Shakespeare's dramatic methods and explore the significance of the extract to the tragedy or comedy of the play as a whole.

How should you tackle this question?

1 First, you are given the Act and scene and told to **read the extract**. In fact, you should aim to read the extract twice. This will give you the chance to familiarise yourself with it, and then to analyse it in more detail.

On your first reading, skim-read the extract to remind yourself of how it fits into the wider context of the play. Think first of all about when it occurs: towards the beginning, in the middle, or at the end? Which characters are involved? Is the tragic or comic protagonist one of these characters? Do you have any immediate thoughts about why this extract might be significant?

Remember that you are allowed to annotate the extract that is printed in the exam paper. You might want to take a pencil and highlighter into the exam to help you with this.

2 Once you've skim-read the extract, **remind yourself of the question**.

> At AS Level: Explore the significance of the aspects of dramatic tragedy in the following passage in relation to the play as a whole.

> At A Level: Explore the significance of this extract in relation to the tragedy of the play as a whole.
>
> Remember to include in your answer relevant analysis of Shakespeare's dramatic methods.

At AS Level, you will need to focus on the list of bullets providing guidance on how to form your response and:

- analyse Shakespeare's craft as a dramatist
- draw on your knowledge and understanding of different aspects of tragedy or comedy
- support your points with quotations, appropriately and succinctly.

At A Level, you will need to do this, but also:

- explore the significance of the extract to the whole tragedy or comedy
- refer to other parts of the play.

3 Now re-read the extract. On your second reading, think in more detail about Shakespeare's use of different aspects of tragedy or comedy, about his use of dramatic methods and about the significance of this extract to the tragedy or comedy as a whole. You might want to think, for instance, about:
   - where this extract fits into the tragic or comedic structure of the play
   - the way the extract begins and ends
   - where this extract is set, and the significance of this
   - what kind of scene it is (for example, a formal ceremony with lots of characters present, a more intimate scene with only two or three characters, a moment that is particularly shocking)
   - what kind of characters are present (for example, the protagonist, the antagonist, villains, victims, fools, innocent bystanders)
   - what kind of language is used (for example, controlled and heightened, disordered and chaotic, confiding and regretful, emotive or restrained; verse or prose; particular patterns of sound and/or imagery)
   - potential ambiguities or different interpretations.

(This list is not exhaustive: as your understanding of your set play develops, you should be able to think of the kinds of things you will need to look out for on this second reading.)

4 Now take a few minutes to plan your response.

5 Once you've planned your response, being careful to focus on what is most telling in terms of the ideas you are exploring, give yourself sufficient time to write your answer.

11.1.5 How should you approach a passage-based question on a poetry set text?

The Section A question in the AS Level Paper 2 follows a similar format, in that it will include a short extract from your set poetry text. However, it will also invite you to discuss the extent to which you agree with a critical statement about the genre of your set text (tragedy or comedy), considering the methods the author uses. Therefore, you will need to range wider in the play and not just write about the extract. Paper 2 also differs from Paper 1 in that it is an open-text exam.

Practice question on the Poetry Anthology (Tragedy)

The extract referred to in the question is from 'The Death of Cuchulain' by W.B Yeats: 'Again the fighting sped…' to 'In vain her arms, in vain her soft white breast'.

> Explore the view that poets writing in the tragic tradition always convey a deep sense of sadness.
>
> You must refer to 'The Death of Cuchulain' and **at least one** other poem.
>
> In your answer, you need to analyse closely the poets' authorial methods and include comment on the extract.

Practice question on the Poetry Anthology (Comedy)

The extract referred to in the question is from 'Not My Best Side' by U.A. Fanthorpe: 'Why, I said to myself …' to 'To show they were taking me seriously'.

> Explore the view that competition and rivalry created between characters in comedic poetry is always light hearted.
>
> You must refer to the poem **'Not my Best Side'** and at least one other poem.
>
> In your answer you need to analyse closely the poets' authorial methods and include comment on the extract below.

Again, you will need to read and annotate the extract.

However, you will also need to think about the critical statement in the question, and plan your response to this. In this question, comment on the extract will need to be built in to your response and you will also need to refer to your poetry text more widely.

1 First of all, read the question. Underline or highlight the key words and phrases in the critical statement. This will help you to focus on what it is that you need to consider. Look at the example in Text 11A.

Text 11A

Focus on aspects of tragedy: in what ways are the poets writing in the tragic tradition?

'Explore the view that poets writing in the tragic tradition always convey a deep sense of sadness.'

Always? Is this true?

Where do the poets convey 'a deep sense of sadness'? What methods do they use to do this?

2 Then read the example extract in Text 11B. This will be much shorter than the extract on the Drama paper. Use it as a focus for your initial response to the critical statement, remembering to bear in mind the poet's methods. In what ways could your reading of this extract – in the light of the critical statement – act as the basis of your essay?

Text 11B

Again the fighting sped,
But now the war rage in Cuchulain woke,
And through the other's shield his long blade broke,
And pierced him.
"Speak before your breath is done."
"I am Finmole, mighty Cuchulain's son."
"I put you from your pain. I can no more."
While day its burden on to evening bore,
With head bowed on his knees Cuchulain stayed;
Then Concobar sent that sweet-throated maid,
And she, to win him, his grey hair caressed:
In vain her arms, in vain her soft white breast.

Narrated in a very simple manner – rhyme gives a sense of inevitability

Structured through positioning connectives first in the line and using repetition

Seems very matter-of-fact: 'deep sadness'?

Stature of tragic hero

Sadness of Cuchulain at putting his son from pain. Link also to Cuchulain myth in Irish mythology

Repetition conveys sense of sadness and helplessness

3 Next, return to the critical statement. Think now about your poetry text as a whole. You will need to show that you have read the text with an awareness of the different meanings that are possible. You will also need to show your understanding of the methods used by your set poet(s) and how their work draws on aspects of tragedy or comedy. Can you think of examples that support the critical statement? What about examples that contradict it?

You will need to draw on your detailed knowledge and understanding of your set text, engage in debate and select appropriate references to support and illustrate your argument. Remember that you will have your set text with you in the exam, so you will be expected to focus on specific passages and discuss them in detail in terms of structure, organisation and language.

4 Once you have jotted down some ideas, take several minutes to plan your response.

5 Then give yourself enough time to write your answer.

11.1.6 How should you approach a passage-based question on an unseen text?

This section refers only to those of you studying for A Level.

There will be passages for both Elements of Crime Writing (Paper 2A) and Elements of Political and Social Protest Writing (Paper 2B). The difference with the questions in Section A of Paper 2 is that the passage you have to respond to will be a passage from a text you have not been taught. As with passage-based questions you'll encounter on Paper 1, an extract will be printed on the exam paper. You will be expected to read the extract carefully and respond to elements of crime writing or social and political protest writing in it. The passage may be poetry, drama or prose. You are advised to spend one hour on this question.

1 As the passage will be unknown to you, it is important that you read it through very carefully in order to gain an overview of what it is about before launching straight into thinking about crime or politics. You must understand the passage in its own terms as either crime or political writing before you relate to it in terms of the exam question.

2 An initial contextualising paragraph will be provided in order to give you a way into the passage. Here is an example contextualising paragraph for an unseen on Elements of Crime Writing:

> This extract is taken from the early part of Susan Hill's novel, *A Question of Identity* (published in 2012). The witnesses have just given their evidence in a murder trial. The accused, Alan Keyes, has pleaded not guilty. Two crime reporters, Charlie Vogt and Rod Hawkins, are awaiting the verdict with every expectation of a conviction.

You'll notice that this provides you with differing kinds of information:

- about the text: it is from a 2012 novel called *A Question of Identity* – the date provides useful contextual information so you know what period it is likely to be dealing with; the title points to certain issues relating to crime, such as identity, mystery, investigation etc.
- about the author: in this case the passage is by a woman named Susan Hill – this could be helpful in discussing, for instance gender issues relating to representation in crime writing
- narrative information: we know at what point in the narrative this extract comes (early in the novel) and that it comes from a trial; we are also told how the events we read of fit into the scheme of that trial
- character information: we are told the names and roles of the characters we encounter and are given suggestions about how they relate to one another
- likely outcomes: we are told that they are expecting a conviction.

Such information is obviously crucial in helping you to settle into your reading, so it is worth spending some time on such contextualising paragraphs, underlining key ideas.

Here is an example of a similar contextualising paragraph on Elements of Political and Social Protest Writing:

> The play *A Man for All Seasons* was written in 1960 about historical events in 1535 during the reign of Henry VIII. Sir Thomas More, Chancellor of England and a Catholic, has refused to endorse the king's wish to divorce his wife and to set himself up as head of the Church in England. Henry desperately wants More to support him because he likes him personally and he knows that the country greatly respects More, a man of conscience and integrity. At this point in the play, More is on trial for High Treason because he will not swear the Oath of Supremacy which puts Henry at the head of the Church, in defiance of the Pope's authority. Presiding over the trial is the Duke of Norfolk. More's chief accuser is Thomas Cromwell.

What kinds of key information does the example relating to *A Man for All Seasons* give you as a way into thinking about political elements?

3 The contextualising paragraph provides you with key information to help you read the main passage for the unseen passage. Here is the extract from *A Question of Identity*:

The court was full to overflowing, the public benches packed. Charlie and Rod stood pressed against the doors poised like greyhounds in the slips.

You never got over it, Charlie thought, your blood pressure went up with the tension and excitement. Better than any film, better than any book. There was just nothing to beat it, watching the drama of the court, eyes on the face of the accused when the word rang out. Guilty. The look of the relatives, as they flushed with joy, relief, exhaustion. And then the tears. These were the final moments when he knew why he was in his job. Every time.

Alan Keyes stood, face pale, eyes down, his police minder impassive.

Charlie's throat constricted suddenly as he looked at him, looked at his hands on the rail. Normal hands. Nothing ugly, nothing out of the ordinary. Not a strangler's hands, whatever they were supposed to look like. But the hands, resting on the rail, hands like his own, one beside the other resting on the rail, resting on the ... those hands had ... Charlie did not think of himself as hard-boiled but you did get accustomed. But nothing prepared you for the first time you saw the man in front of you, ordinary, innocent until proved guilty, however clear his guilt was, nothing prepared you for the sight of a man like Keyes, there in the flesh, a man who had strangled three elderly women. Nothing. He couldn't actually look at Keyes at all now.

The lawyers sat together, shuffling papers, fiddling with box lids, not looking at one another, not murmuring. Just waiting.

And then the door opened and they were filing back, concentrating on taking their seats, faces showing the strain, or else blank and showing nothing at all. Seven women, five men. Charlie was struck by the expression on the face of the first woman, young with dark hair pulled tightly back, bright red scarf round her neck. She looked desperate – desperate to get out? Desperate because she was afraid? Desperate not to catch the eye of the man in the dock, the ordinary-looking man with the unremarkable hands who had strangled three old women? Charlie watched as she sat down and stared straight ahead of her, glazed, tired. What had she done to deserve the past nine days, hearing appalling things, looking at terrible images? Been a citizen. Nothing else. He had often wondered how people like her coped when it had all been forgotten, but the images and the accounts wouldn't leave their heads. Once you knew something you couldn't un-know it. His Dad had tried to un-know what he'd learned about Hindley and Brady for years afterwards.

'All rise.'

The court murmured; the murmur faded. Everything went still. Every eye focused on the jury benches.

In the centre of the public benches a knot of elderly women sat together. Two had their hands on one another's arms. Even across the room, Charlie Vogt could see a pulse jumping in the neck of one, the pallor of her neighbour. Behind them, two middle-aged couples, one with a young woman. He knew relatives when he saw them, very quiet, very still, desperate for this to be over, to see justice being done. Hang in there, he willed them, a few minutes and then you walk away, to try and put your lives back together.

Schoolteacher, he thought, as the foreman of the jury stood. Bit young, no more than early thirties. Several of them looked even younger. When he'd done jury service himself, several years ago now, there had only been two women and the men had all been late-middle-aged.

'Have you reached a verdict on all three counts?'

'Yes.'

'On the first count, do you find the accused guilty or not guilty?' The first murder of Carrie Gage.

Charlie realised that he was clenching his hand, digging his nails into the palm.

'Not guilty.'

The intake of breath was like a sigh round the room.

'Is this a unanimous verdict?'

'Yes.'

'On the second count of murder, do you find the accused guilty or not guilty?' Sarah Pearce.

'Not guilty.'

The murmur was faint, like a tide coming in. Charlie glanced at the faces of the legal teams. Impassive except for the junior barrister of the defence who had put her hands briefly to her mouth.

'Is this verdict unanimous?'

'Yes.'

'On the third count, do you find the accused guilty or not guilty?'

His honour Judge Palmer was sitting very straight, hands out of sight, expression unreadable.

'Not guilty.'

'Is –

The gavel came down hard on the bench and the judge's voice roared out: 'Order…'

(Susan Hill, *A Question of Identity*, 2012)

4 When it comes to answering on unseen passages, it does not help to have a pre-learned list of features that you're trying to find. These will tend to limit what you're looking for and therefore what you see. Read with an open mind, not a checklist. In other words, don't try to force your knowledge of crime or political writing on to the unseen passage; approach the passage openly and apply it to your understanding of elements of crime or political and social protest writing. So, once you've read the passage through to gain an overview of what it has to say, think about the following:
- its crime or political/social protest elements
- its key events
- the characters and how they're represented
- the ideas it conveys
- its voices and setting
- the language it uses.

5 Now it's time to look closely at the question you have to answer and to think about how you can apply the passage to your knowledge of crime or political writing. Here is the question relating to *A Question of Identity*:

> Explore the significance of the crime elements in this extract. Remember to include in your answer relevant detailed analysis of the ways in which Hill has shaped meanings.

Firstly, identify the key words and see what they are asking you for. It is also useful to think how these words relate to the Assessment Objectives. In this case they are:
- analysing (AO1, AO2)
- methods (AO2)
- explore (AO1)
- significance (AO2, AO3, AO4, AO5)
- crime elements (AO2, AO3, AO4).

Now use these as the basis for a second targeted reading of the passage. As the primary component of this response is the 'crime elements', this is a good place to start your thinking. Once you've identified the elements you will be focussing on, go on to consider *how* the author has dealt with these (her 'methods'), *why they matter* (their 'significance'), and the meanings that arise from them.

Here is an example question for Elements of Political Writing. You can see that the phrasing and structure of the question is very similar to the question on Crime Writing:

> Explore the significance of the elements of political protest in this extract. Remember to include in your answer relevant detailed analysis of the ways in which Bolt has shaped meanings.

6 Use your thoughts about these as the basis for a plan. You have an hour to answer this question, so there is plenty of time, and a clear plan will help you to structure your response more effectively and will give you confidence as you move on to writing. Spend a few minutes on this.

7 Finally, write your answer. You might find it helpful to begin by discussing your overview of the passage as an example of crime or political and social protest writing. This can be helpful in rooting your answer firmly in what the extract is about, but make sure that you quickly begin to refer to the terms of the question, addressing in a logical order the sequence of points for discussion you've identified in your plan.

Significance

When used in AS and A-Level English Literature B questions, the term 'significance' has a very specific use and gives access to Assessment Objectives (AOs) 2, 3, 4 and 5. Its use here derives from semiotics and involves understanding the idea of signification. In this context, 'significance' involves weighing up all of the potential contributions to how a text can be analysed: for example, through the way the text is constructed and written; through text-specific contexts that can be relevantly applied; through connecting the text(s) to other texts; and then finding potential meanings and interpretations.

11.1.7 How should you approach an essay question on one set text?

The Section B questions in both of the AS Level papers, and in both of the A Level papers, will follow a similar format. A Level questions will ask to what extent you agree with a view. You will be reminded to include relevant comment or exploration of the writers' methods. AS Level will ask you to explore a view and analyse or comment on the writers' methods.

Tragedy: Practice question on *Richard II* – William Shakespeare

At AS Level: Explore the view that, despite his tragic flaws, Richard is 'ultimately magnificent'.

Remember to include in your answer relevant comment on Shakespeare's dramatic methods.

Comedy: Practice question on *Twelfth Night* – William Shakespeare

At A Level: '*Twelfth Night* delights in the folly of misrule.' To what extent do you agree with this view?

Remember to include in your answer relevant comment on Shakespeare's dramatic methods.

Crime Writing: Practice question on 'The Rime of the Ancient Mariner' – Samuel Taylor Coleridge

At A Level: To what extent do you agree with the view that the Mariner deserves his punishment for the crimes he commits?

Remember to include in your answer relevant detailed exploration of Coleridge's authorial methods.

Political and Social Protest Writing: Practice question on *Songs of Innocence and of Experience* – William Blake

At A Level: 'Opposition to anything that oppresses the human spirit is the element that dominates *The Songs of Innocence* and *The Songs of Experience*.' To what extent do you agree with this view?

Remember to include in your answer relevant detailed exploration of Blake's authorial methods.

You will need to show that you have read your set text with an awareness of the different meanings that are possible. You will also need to show your understanding of the methods used by the author in using aspects of the genre of tragedy or comedy, or elements of the genre of political and social protest writing or crime writing.

As this question asks you to explore a particular viewpoint, you will need to plan your response carefully.

You will need to draw on your detailed knowledge and understanding of the text, engage in debate and select appropriate references to support and illustrate your argument.

1 Begin by reading the question and making sure that you understand what it is asking. Annotating the question will help you to define what you need to do. Look at the example in Text 11C.

Text 11C

Suggests it's unproblematic – just designed to entertain. Is the play more complex? Darkness of ending; smugness of Orsino and Olivia; treatment of outsiders

Examples of elements of comedy

'*Twelfth Night* delights in the folly of misrule.'

To what extent do you agree with this view?

How does Shakespeare present the folly of misrule?

2 You could then extend these annotations to develop your ideas more fully. Remember to think about the specific pieces of evidence you will use to support your argument. You should aim to learn and use relevant quotations, but you will also be credited for close, detailed reference to the text.

3 Use these initial ideas to formulate your thesis. Think about how your argument will unfold and how you will organise your response. Then give yourself enough time to write your response.

Remember that you will need to:

- construct your argument clearly and express your ideas in a coherent, accurate manner
- explore the ways in which the author's use of particular methods shapes meanings in relation to the task
- show your understanding of the text in relation to the genre of tragedy, comedy, crime writing or political and social protest writing
- consider relevant aspects of the text's context, including when it was written and how it has been received at different times
- engage with different potential interpretations and show to what extent you agree with them.

11.1.8 How should you approach an essay question linking two texts?

The questions in Section C in A Level Papers 1 and 2 will ask to what extent do you agree with a statement about tragedy, comedy, crime writing or political and social protest writing with reference to the other two set texts you have studied, bearing in mind the ways in which the authors you have studied. You will be reminded to include in your answer relevant comment on the ways the writers have shaped meanings.

Practice questions

'Tragedies leave readers and audiences with a final sense of emptiness and disillusion.' To what extent do you agree with this view in relation to **two** texts you have studied?

Remember to include in your answer relevant comment on the ways the writers have shaped meanings.

'In comedic literature, humour is primarily provided by the uncultivated behaviour and speech of the lower social classes.' To what extent do you agree with this view in relation to **two** texts you have studied?

Remember to include in your answer relevant comment on the ways the writers have shaped meanings.

'In crime writing there are always victims.'

Explore the significance of the ways that victims are presented in **two** crime texts you have studied.

'Political and social protest writing often focuses on rebellion against those in power.'

Explore the significance of rebellion as it is presented in **two** political and social protest texts you have studied.

You should spend about an hour on this question. You will need to construct an argument about both of the texts you have studied, and should be prepared to write a substantial amount about both of them. However, you do not need to write the same amount about both texts. Also, although you will be *connecting* the two texts through writing about aspects of tragedy or comedy, or elements of crime or political writing, you do not need to *compare* them.

Tackling this type of question will require a considerable amount of thought, and you should be prepared to spend some time gathering your ideas and planning your response.

1 Begin by reading the question and identifying the key words and phrases. Annotating the question will help you to start to gather your ideas. Look at the example Text 11D.

Text 11D

Element of genre. What kinds of people/organisations/ideas are powerful?

Element of genre. What are the examples of rebellion?

'Political writing often focuses on <u>rebellion</u> against <u>those in power</u>.'

Explore the <u>significance</u> of rebellion as it is presented in two political texts you have studied.

What different meanings arise out of the rebellions? Do they succeed?

2 Once you have done this, think in detail about how you can connect the question to each of your texts. The texts will be very different, and these differences will offer ways of approaching the critical statement. You might want to write the critical statement in the centre of a page and build up your ideas as a spider diagram around it (see Text 11E).

Text 11E

Louisa's rebellion against her upbringing in *Hard Times* – personal rebellion

Rebellion of the workers – more overtly political form of rebellion

'Political writing <u>often</u> focuses on <u>rebellion</u> against <u>those in power</u>.'

Explore the <u>significance</u> of rebellion as it is presented in two political texts you have studied.

Harrison's rebellion against conventional language – 'Them &[uz]' – different kind of power being represented

Vandals' rebellion in 'v' – what are they rebelling against? Reactions to this – how significant is this kind of rebellion?

3 Use these initial ideas to formulate your thesis. Think about how your argument will unfold and how you will organise your response. You might be able to identify one idea that could act as a starting point for your essay. (If you were going to do the question in Text 11E, which feature of rebellion would you use as your starting point?)

4 Now write your answer.

Remember that you will need to:

- show your understanding of the texts as political and social protest writing
- construct your argument clearly and express your ideas in a coherent, accurate manner
- give substantial treatment to both texts
- explore the ways in which the authors' use of particular methods shapes meanings
- consider relevant aspects of the texts' context, including when they were written and how they have been received at different times
- engage with different potential interpretations and show to what extent you agree with them.

See 11.2.2 and 11.2.3 for more on planning critical essays

11.2 Writing critical essays

You will already have had plenty of experience of writing critical essays in your study of literature, but writing critical essays at A Level is more demanding. You will need to produce critical essays under examination conditions in response to set texts and unseen texts, as well as in more extended form as part of non-exam assessment. Some of the writing skills needed in these different contexts are easily transferrable, but others are not: an essay written under exam conditions must be approached differently from an extended non-exam assessment; a reflective commentary on re-creative writing or a response to an unseen text is different to a fully fledged critical essay on set texts. Some key things to think about in relation to the task are how to:

- write in more sustained ways
- formulate arguments
- deal with increasingly complex concepts
- work with quotation and other forms of textual reference
- work with criticism and theory
- use appropriate methods of referencing.

A useful way of understanding how effective critical essays are written is to read and analyse models of critical writing. As part of your studies you will receive a Critical Anthology, and critical writings about many of the texts you will study are readily available. Reading these will give you an insight into the ways in which critics write about literature and the qualities of such writing. It is also very useful to explore examples of A Level students' writing. Examples might be available from your peers, but exemplar work - often with helpful commentaries - is also made available by the exam board.

ACTIVITY 1

In practice

Read the extract in Text 11F from an essay about Kazuo Ishiguro's use of an unreliable first-person narrator in *The Remains of the Day*. Think about:

- how the response is constructed
- what it is aiming to achieve in response to the focus on unreliable narrative
- the kinds of textual evidence it uses (for example, quotation, reference, recount) and how it uses them
- the limitations of this response.

Text 11F

During the course of a journey to visit an ex-colleague, Miss Kenton (now Mrs Benn), Stevens, the narrator of Ishiguro's novel *The Remains of the Day*, reflects at length on his life of service as butler at Darlington Hall – first to Lord Darlington and latterly to Mr Farraday. This retrospective account, covering nearly thirty years of his life, at first appears to be a rather moving account of a loyal life of service, but it soon becomes apparent that Stevens' presentation of events is deeply unreliable, motivated by a desire to minimise the politically suspect behaviour of his employer, Lord Darlington, and to rewrite the actions of his past (including his own complicity) in a more favourable light.

It emerges from Stevens' narrative that, in the wake of World War I, Lord Darlington developed an increasingly pro-German stance, believing the Versailles settlement took ungentlemanly advantage of a defeated enemy. Throughout the 1930s Darlington actively attempts to build relationships between English politicians and royalty and the Nazis. So far from challenging the views and actions of his employer, Stevens becomes complicit in them, most notably in the anti-semitic sacking of two Jewish servants working on the household staff.

Stevens' account of his employer's actions and his own role in the household is an attempt to minimise his failure to challenge Lord Darlington's attitude towards Nazi Germany, Oswald Moseley and others. He seeks, for example, to belittle the significance of 'his lordship's attitude to Jewish persons'. On another occasion Mr Cardinal tries to point out the falseness of Stevens' position when Herr Ribbentrop, the Nazi Foreign Minister, visits Darlington Hall to try to persuade the Prime Minister to visit Hitler. Stevens stalwartly refuses to understand: 'I cannot see what there is to object to in that, sir. His lordship has always striven to aid better understanding between nations.'

Bear in mind that much can be learned from bad examples as well as from good ones! Where examples seem to be weaker, think about:

- what issues need to be developed
- rewriting and developing the material for yourself, or at least planning how you would do so.

11.2.1 Working with sources

As an A Level student of literature you will be expected not only to read your set texts, but also to explore a range of views *about* them. These views will come from a variety of sources, including your teachers, your family and your peers. In addition, many textbooks (like this one), critical works, study guides and online sources are available.

Why do we use sources?

Sources like these are very important to you. You will, quite rightly, have your own views about the texts you're studying. What would be the point of

Figure 11A

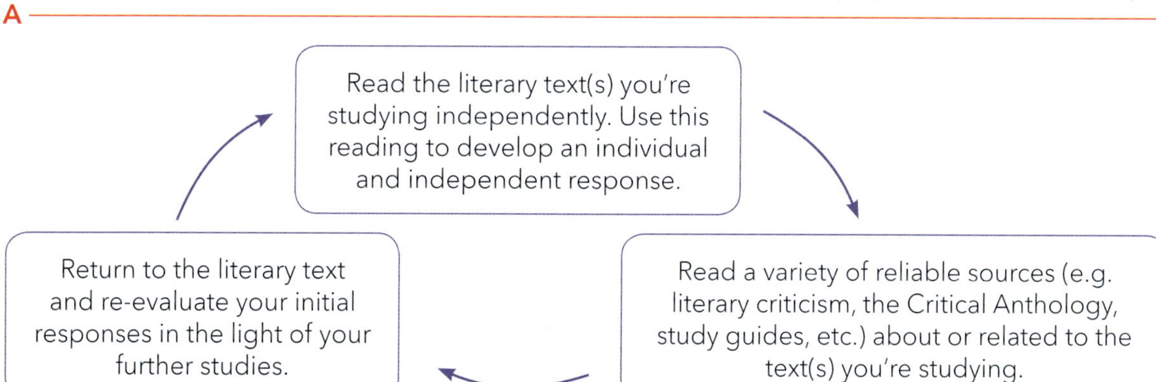

reading if you did not have the right to form your own views? But you do not have a unique right to establish meaning, and it is important to consider a variety of ways of looking at and understanding texts. Working with a range of sources is, therefore, very helpful in consolidating and clarifying your own ideas. The trouble is that it is all too easy to take the interpretations and views on offer and adopt them uncritically. Remember that, as part of your literary studies, you are required to demonstrate your abilities to debate ideas about literature; this implies a range of views. You are also expected to explore potential meanings using critical theories and concepts from literary theory. Use of the Critical Anthology will be central here.

So how can you use such materials to help you develop informed personal responses to literature and to particular texts? The ability to use others' interpretations is very important. To demonstrate that you have thought deeply about the issues involved in the texts you're studying, wider reading and discussion are key. Using others' interpretations as a stimulus to developing ideas of your own is central in this process. Referring to a range of critical interpretations and acknowledging that complex literary texts can be read and understood in different ways demonstrates that you have considered a number of alternative ways of interpreting texts, and have not simply taken one idea from one source and adopted it. The key issue here is to be critical; don't be afraid to challenge others' views (including critics' and your teachers'). A good model for working with the available resources in relation to your texts is as shown in Figure 11A.

You should not, of course, be reusing other people's ideas extensively in your own writing. The ideas should be mainly your own. They should be grounded in your set texts and your personal reading and understanding of them and others' ideas should be incorporated where they are relevant and helpful in developing your argument. We call this the 'assimilation' of ideas - where others' ideas become an organic part of your own. This is fine, as long as you acknowledge your sources.

Good and bad sources

Not all sources are good sources. Here are some guidelines.

- Textbooks and study guides are often reviewed by experts before they are published, but this is not true of all online sources. You need to be careful to ensure that you are working with high-quality materials.
- Don't rely on a single point of view. Check out your sources against a range of others. Is there broad agreement or general disagreement on the topic or text you're considering? This will help you understand how to deal with your sources. Highly individualistic and isolated views are especially unhelpful.
- Generally it's best to stick to sources that give the name of the author, ideally an established critic.
- Beware of views expressed in chat rooms and other online forums. These are not necessarily wrong or ill-informed, but it is always important to check them out with a reliable source. Certain texts (for example, *Frankenstein* and *Dracula*) tend to gather a vast array of ill-informed, dubious and sometimes just plain weird attention online.
- Websites are variable in terms of content. Some (for example, the Joseph Conrad Society or other literary societies) are of high quality, but others are much less so. Most websites contain writing that is not attributed to an individual. In such cases, naming the organisation the website represents is acceptable (for example, the Thomas Hardy Society).
- Wikipedia, Brainyquote and other similar sites are unauthored texts and the information contained on them is not always reliable. Teachers and examiners will always be suspicious of such references.
- We strongly recommend you not to consult websites of student essays. These are not considered good sources.

Don't simply reproduce what somebody else has written - it is essential that you show how you have engaged with your sources and how you see these in relation to the set text. Explicit reference to other people's work, either by quoting it directly or by using their ideas, must always be referenced.

Plagiarism

Academic honesty is very important. So much online material is available at the click of a mouse that **plagiarism** has become a serious problem.

Key terms

plagiarism: the deliberate and unacknowledged presentation of somebody else's work as your own

Using material from any text without acknowledgement is plagiarism. Using the odd word from a source may not matter, but using phrases and longer extracts - even if you change one or two words - is still plagiarism.

The important rule in your own writing is to acknowledge anything that you have found elsewhere. Whenever you quote someone else's words, or even if you paraphrase their ideas in your own words, you must provide reference details. This is particularly important in writing non-exam assessments, where you are more likely to be drawing on a range of outside sources.

When you submit your non-exam assessment, you will also have to sign a declaration that it is all your own work. This means that you may receive general guidance from your teacher, family and friends but that specific detailed advice must not be given. It is your responsibility to apply the advice you are given. You and you alone will be considered responsible for the written work you submit, so it is essential to make sure that you do not engage in unfair or dishonest practice.

In exams, and even when researching and discussing ideas and meanings in class or in presentations, you also need to be honest about referring to other people's work.

So as you study, make a note of all the sources you consult and especially any you might want to use directly. Then you will be in a position to give the details in your written work.

This is good preparation if you are planning to go on to higher education, but is also essential for any writing you'll do in the world of work. However, referencing your work according to academic practice is not a requirement of the AQA Literature B Non-exam Assessment (NEA).

Remember, teachers and examiners:

- have access to internet sources and online books too - they can (and do!) check for plagiarism by entering groups of words into search engines
- are highly experienced readers and usually quickly spot things from others' work or sense when writing does not 'sound' like yours - if they suspect that you've plagiarised, you will be investigated and, at worst, your work could be disqualified.

Quoting and referencing sources

When you are planning and drafting work, you should read around the topic you're focusing on. You should take your own ideas about the text(s) you're dealing with and develop them by seeing how a variety of other readers have responded to the same topic. Your essay should be followed by a bibliography in which you must acknowledge the sources of any ideas that have influenced your work. This includes books, websites, films, or any other medium. You especially need to include any works you have quoted from, or from which you have directly taken ideas.

See 11.2.6 for more on preparing a bibliography

If you quote from a critical text, you ought to indicate in your essay where the quotation is taken from. You should include the author's surname, the date of the publication and the page number on which the quotation appears. This information should all be put in brackets next to the quotation - for example, (Fernie 2003: 158) - the full name of the text by Fernie along with the date of its publication should then be listed alphabetically in your bibliography.

References are when you refer to, but do not quote from, an idea from a critical text. Because such ideas are not your own, you must acknowledge them. You do this by writing something like 'Eaglestone (2000) suggests that…' or 'Leavis (1932) is of the opinion that…'. As for quotations, the details of the text to which you've referred need to be included alphabetically in your bibliography.

11.2.2 Working with questions

Whether it is as part of a timed examination or as part of non-exam assessment, your central focus must always be the task that you have been set or that you have selected. Making good selections of questions is a skill in its own right that you need to develop. Written responses should never be simply an account of all that you know about the text(s) you're writing about. The most effective responses will always be well targeted and involve the use of well-selected materials. In order to make sure that your written responses are always as effectively targeted as possible and demonstrate your abilities to work with the text(s) you've studied, you must identify the key focuses of tasks. Even under the time pressure of an examination, you need to spend time reading through all the available options so that you can make an informed decision about the tasks that best allow you to demonstrate your abilities and understanding.

One of the major skills you need to learn is how to pinpoint key terms in a question and to use these in formulating your answer. Sometimes in an examination or when preparing for non-exam assessment, you will not be certain about which questions will serve you best. Under these circumstances, it is a good idea to draft out quick plans for each question, and one will normally emerge as the stronger contender. Texts 11G and 11H illustrate how one student defined the scope of their response to a question on *Wuthering Heights*.

Note: Texts 11G and 11H illustrate how to develop ideas for arguments in your A Level essays but are different from the written tasks you will need to do for your Non-exam Assessment (NEA).

Text 11G

Implies he's either one or the other: is it more complex than this?

Need to include a range of viewpoints

Object of terror, or object of pity? Discuss Emily Brontë's depiction of Heathcliff in *Wuthering Heights*.

Focus on authorial technique and the role that Heathcliff plays in the narrative.

Text 11H

Way Heathcliff is introduced: mysterious child from the Liverpool docks; an outsider; Mr Earnshaw's 'favourite'; Brontë's use of the gothic.

How Heathcliff is described by the inhabitants of Thrushcross Grange and Wuthering Heights: animalistic imagery; supernatural; excessive; violence; a man of contradictions; sometimes the object of sympathy.

How Heathcliff functions within the narrative: contrast to his foil, Edgar; potential obstacle to Catherine's marriage to Edgar; Heathcliff's revenge marriage to Isabella; we sympathise with Heathcliff in spite of his brutality; his deeply flawed but deeply passionate relationship with Catherine.

Heathcliff described from differing narrative perspectives of Mr Lockwood, Nelly Dean, Catherine and others: not allowed to tell his own story.

Heathcliff's uncertain ethnicity: stereotypes and prejudice attached.

Contrasts between Heathcliff and Lockwood/Heathcliff and Edgar – in what ways are they opposites and in what ways doubles?

The process of writing an essay

This is the first of a sequence of examples relating to a critical essay on the character of Heathcliff in *Wuthering Heights*. It demonstrates how the process of writing an essay can be broken down into stages so you can learn to plan, organise and develop your critical responses.

Initial planning such as this should be used to formulate a **thesis**, which is basically a short statement of your beliefs or point of view regarding the proposition(s) in a writing task. The thesis will, therefore, provide the focus for your introduction. Writing a short bullet-point list or a few short sentences in response to the task is a useful way of establishing what you think.

Key term

thesis: a short statement of beliefs or point of view regarding the proposition(s) in a writing task

ACTIVITY 2

Developing a thesis

Choose one or more of the following propositions with regard to studying literature and develop a set of ideas that could inform your thesis in response to each.

- All pupils, including those of very limited attainments, need the civilising experience of contact with great literature, and can respond to its universality. (Newsom Report, CACE 1963)
- Any belief that the study of literature is the study of a stable, well-definable entity, as entomology is the study of insects, can be abandoned as a chimera. Some kinds of fiction are literature and some are not; some literature is fictional and some is not; some literature is verbally self-regarding, while some highly wrought rhetoric is not literature. Literature, in the sense of a set of works

of assured and unalterable value, distinguished by certain shared inherent properties, does not exist. (Eagleton 1983)

- Because it is such a profound and universal experience, Literature must be taught to school pupils, whereupon it becomes an instrument within the whole apparatus of filtering whereby schools adjust young people to an unjust social order. (Sinfield 1985)
- Is Literature an ideological instrument: a set of stories that seduce readers into accepting the hierarchical arrangements of society? … Or is literature the place where ideology is exposed, revealed as something that can be questioned? Both claims are thoroughly plausible… (Culler 1997)

11.2.3 Structuring critical essays

You will have more time to spend on some critical essays than others and will be expected to go into appropriate amounts of detail to reflect this. Critical essays written for non-exam assessment, for instance, give space and time to develop your thinking in ways that essays written under exam conditions do not. Likewise, the ways you work with texts in closed-book exams is obviously in some ways different to the ways in which you work with texts in open-book exams. You will, therefore, need to adapt your writing techniques to reflect a variety of different contexts for writing. In general, however, whether they are written over a long or short period of time, in response to text extracts (seen or unseen), in closed-book or open-book format, on single texts or combinations of texts, critical essays generally consist of the same basic components:

- an introduction: where you set out initial ideas about the topic and the text (s) you're writing about - it is important that introductions are stimulating and engage at once with the terms of the question, allowing you to pick up marks from the outset
- a main body: this generally consists of a sequence of paragraphs in which you develop your thoughts about the topic and text(s) you are covering in more detail
- a conclusion: where you draw together your thinking on the task you've been writing about - note that your conclusion should not simply be a restatement of what you've already said in the main body of the essay; it should provide your readers with a stimulating final set of conclusions.

This structure will probably be familiar to you from your experiences of writing about literature to date. You will also probably have learned particular formulae - formulae don't only belong in Maths and Physics! - and constructions. Some common - and not necessarily helpful - examples are:

- PEE (Point, Evidence, Explanation)
- the paragraph 'burger'
- the five-paragraph essay
- the assignment map ('In this essay I will …. Next, I will… and then … and finally …').

All of these approaches have their virtues in helping you to develop effective arguments and good structures for writing about literary texts and will be a useful starting point for you when you begin to think about your writing at A Level. As you develop into your studies, however, it is important to realise that these approaches have their limitations and can lead to rather dry, repetitive writing. As you develop as a writer you need to adopt bold, confident and individual approaches towards writing about literary texts. In other words, you need to explore how you can play with these formulae to achieve a variety of effects. Why, for instance, does the point of the argument always need to come first? What would be the impact if you were to open with a quotation or some other form of reference to the text? Does your reader need the rather pedestrian kind of guidance embodied in the assignment map model? As you learn to accommodate the increasingly complex demands of A Level writing about literary texts, developing complex views and alternative perspectives on texts, multiple paragraphs may be needed to deal with individual ideas.

ACTIVITY 3

Thinking about critical writing

Think back over the ways you've been taught to write critical essays.

a Have you been taught to use formulae like PEE (Point Evidence Explanation) or PEEL (Point Evidence Explanation Link)?

b How have you been taught to connect ideas? How have you been taught to construct an argument?

c How have you been taught to use evidence? Does evidence always mean quotation?

There is nothing wrong with such ways of thinking about critical and analytical writing, but as you progress in your studies, it is important that you see writing less as a formula and more as a vibrant and creative means of personal expression. You need to become more critical in thinking about how and when the formulae and methods you've learned for writing are useful and when newer, more personal approaches will be more effective.

Talk to your classmates about writing at A Level. What do you think the new demands of writing at this level will be?

The introduction

Learning to frame your thesis succinctly and effectively is a key skill – especially under exam conditions. It is also essential to engage from the very first sentence with the question you are answering. When you learn to do this effectively, you will find that it offers both you and your readers with a clear insight into the specific focuses and concerns of your writing. In other words, the thesis defines the 'ground' of your response, and this may on occasion mean identifying what you are not going to cover (with reasons why) as well as what you are. It might also allude to critical background information to establish the context of your writing. You may or may not choose to include the thesis in your written response. In either case, however, the formulation of the thesis is a very important part of establishing your response to any task.

Text 11I is an example of a thesis on the previous question on *Wuthering Heights* and how it could be developed into an introduction.

Text 11I

Thesis: From the moment he is introduced in the narrative Heathcliff creates sensations of mystery and fear, intensified by Brontë's use of features from the Gothic tradition. However, at the same time he appears as a victim of circumstances and attracts our sympathy. The contrasts and parallels between Heathcliff, Lockwood and Edgar allow Brontë to explore the complexities of this brutal but passionate and misunderstood man.

Introduction: From the moment he enters the narrative of Wuthering Heights, Heathcliff evokes a variety of emotions in those around him. For some he is an object to be pitied (a poor waif rescued from the dark streets of Liverpool), while for others he is an unwanted intruder into the close-knit social circles of Thrushcross Grange and the Heights. He plays a central role in every aspect of the narrative, but particularly through his strange triangular relationship with Catherine and Edgar. He represents a powerful but strangely ambiguous force in the novel. Often dark, brooding and brutal, he is also capable of great emotional depth and frequently wins our sympathy and disgust in equal measure. Brontë's narrative draws deeply on the gothic and the idea of the Byronic hero to add to Heathcliff's dubious appeal.

ACTIVITY 4

Developing a thesis and introduction

To practice developing an effective thesis and introduction, it is a good idea to work with others – perhaps in pairs or small groups.

a Ask your teacher to give you a set of potential tasks on the texts or topics you're studying.

b Individually, write your thesis in response to each, remembering to be as concise and clear as possible.

c Share these with your partner or group and offer each other feedback, using this as an opportunity to debate the merits and disadvantages of the various theses.

d Adapt and develop your own thesis as appropriate.

e On the basis of these discussions, write the full introductory paragraph for the essay.

f Offer each other feedback again, including comment on expression, accuracy and use of appropriate terminology.

g You might even use the various examples on offer as an exercise in shared writing, talking in detail about how most effectively to express and introduce ideas at this point in an essay.

The body of the essay

Cohesion is essential when you are developing the main body of essay responses. Here are some key issues:

- developing clear and extended lines of thought
- organising ideas into logical and progressive sequences
- using effective supporting reference to texts
- building out of your thesis towards coherent and justifiable conclusions.

It is very important to spend time writing essay plans. For non-exam assessment responses, careful planning allows you to develop effective structures for writing, making sure you cover all the main topics you need to include and thinking carefully about how they most effectively fit together as a sequence leading towards the conclusions you wish to draw. Under examination conditions, time spent planning is even more important. This may seem counter-intuitive, as your first reaction may be to use all the available time for writing. Planning *is* writing, however. A few minutes spent thinking through what you want to say and the order in which you want to say it is invaluable. Planning makes it much more likely that your thoughts will be coherent and measured rather than random and haphazard. It will also maximise the likelihood of remaining clearly focused on the task you're responding to and drawing effective conclusions about it.

Planning can be converted into a sequence of concise and efficient topic sentences that can be used to introduce each paragraph and direct your developing argument. In order to create logical and coherent structures, regularly check your writing against your topic sentences and original thesis. This will ensure that your writing remains relevant at all times and moves effectively towards your conclusions. As you do this, it is important to make regular reference to your original ideas and to ensure that you are using well-selected examples from and references to the text(s) you're writing about. Making this process a part of your writing - both in non-exam assessment and under timed conditions - will minimise unhelpful detours and irrelevancies.

Text 11J shows how the thesis in our exemplar essay could be developed into an essay plan (note that this is just one approach). Topic sentences are underlined to show an effective sequence of ideas. Connecting ideas are in italics, demonstrating how key elements in each paragraph can be linked back to the question.

It is a useful exercise to learn to distil your ideas on topics into single paragraphs. The ability to express your ideas concisely using precise, clear vocabulary is an essential skill. The incorporation of short apposite examples from the text(s) you're writing about is also central. In non-exam assessment tasks, of course, you are expected to develop your ideas more fully, reflecting the greater complexity of thought that non-exam assessment allows.

Developing analytical skills

You will already be familiar with literary analysis, but as your A Level studies progress you will need to learn more sophisticated models of analysis. Like all genres, literary analysis has characteristic forms and features, and a good place to start is to spend time reading good examples.

The English and Media Centre publishes *e magazine* and Philip Allan produces *The English Review*. Both of these are written specifically for A Level students and provide excellent examples of literary analysis. Never mind if the articles don't specifically address the literary texts or topics you're studying; reading good writing about literature and understanding how it functions (the use of quotation, other means of referring to text, construction of argument and so on) can all be learned, and you will widen your literary knowledge and find all kinds of interesting and useful connections to your own studies in the process.

It is particularly important that you move beyond simply describing what is happening in the text(s) you're writing about. Using your topic sentences to develop strong sequential arguments will help with this, as will recognising that quotations and references - to both primary and critical texts - should not simply be illustrative, but need to serve an integral function in developing thought and argument.

ACTIVITY 5

Developing sequential arguments

Look at the four example writing tasks in Text 11K. There is one for each of the units covered by your course, and each has been selected from Section B or Section C of the relevant examination paper. For each task:

a develop an initial thesis, using Activity 4 as a guide
b develop a set of topic sentences that will offer a detailed exploration of your thesis
c experiment with placing these topic sentences in different orders.

Text 11J

Paragraph 1: From the very opening of the novel, when Lockwood arrives in Yorkshire, the reader is made aware of the force and ambiguity of Heathcliff's character, and he is surrounded by a sense of mystery. Brontë's use of Gothic tropes and imagery – the dark and threatening interior of the Heights; Heathcliff's profound and unexplained emotion after the visitation by Catherine's ghost; the deliberate contrast/parallel Brontë establishes between Heathcliff and Lockwood; the casual violence of life at the Heights as contrasted with Heathcliff's status as Victorian gentleman. *At this point, the reader is uncertain of how to understand the ambiguous nature of Heathcliff.*

Paragraph 2: Heathcliff often appears as a brutal and animalistic man. Animalistic imagery is often used to dehumanise him and create a sense of fear surrounding him – though we should note that the same is also true of many other characters in the novel. Brontë uses language and images of the supernatural to create a firm connection in her readers' minds between Heathcliff and malign forces (a further example of the gothic) – comparisons to sprites and vampires. Do these make him seem less or more than human? Give examples of how he is associated with casual brutality towards animals and humans alike. Introduce the shared brutality that characterises his relationship with Catherine. *Brontë's language encourages us to see Heathcliff as a creature to be afraid of rather than a human being.*

Paragraph 3: However, at other times Heathcliff appears as a victim of circumstances and attracts our sympathy. As we learn more of the story of Heathcliff's life in Yorkshire – from his arrival from Liverpool with Mr Earnshaw, through his rejection and mistreatment by the members of the household, his rejection in love by Catherine (who holds a deeply ambiguous view of him throughout), his disappearance and eventual return to Yorkshire as a gentleman, Nelly Dean's evident love for him in spite of his many weaknesses, etc. – we become aware that Heathcliff has in many ways been made into the hard and brutal man he is rather than being purely bad. *The unfolding events of the narrative win him some sympathy.*

Paragraph 4: The contrasts and parallels between Heathcliff, Lockwood and Edgar allow Brontë to explore the complexities of this brutal but passionate and misunderstood man. Brontë deliberately sets the character of Heathcliff – self-made gentleman and upstart (as many see him) – against the conventional gentleman figures of Lockwood and Edgar. This serves both to expose his limitations and to highlight his positives. His vitality and energy sets him apart from the other two men, who both appear as rather affected by comparison. His manners and behaviour, on the other hand, inevitably appear coarse and even delinquent. His close relation to the roguish, criminal and dashing Byronic hero makes him both attractive and repellent to modern readers and must have been profoundly shocking to Victorian audiences. The disdain with which he views Heathcliff demonstrates Edgar's engrained social views. *These contrasts encourage an ambiguous view of Heathcliff.*

Paragraph 5: This sense of ambiguity is most evident in Heathcliff's relationship with Catherine. She is in one sense utterly dependent on him – she compares him to the eternal rocks – and from their childhood they have been inseparable. At the same time, however, she rejects him and refuses to marry with him. Instead she marries the conventional and dull Edgar, provoking Heathcliff beyond his endurance. Their connection is in some ways violently physical, but is also deeply spiritual. Neither of them can endure the separation that Catherine's marriage to Edgar enforces and Heathcliff marries Isabella as an act of vengeance. While we sympathise with his pain at losing Catherine, we cannot condone his brutal mistreatment of Isabella and their son Linton towards the end of the novel. Brontë uses a powerful image of the edge of the graveyard and the three graves of Edgar (completely in holy ground), Catherine's (straddling the wall of the graveyard) and Heathcliff's (on the wild moor) to capture this powerful ambiguity.

Think about the following questions:

i What is the effect on your developing argument in each case?
ii How does your connection and flow of ideas vary from one to another?
iii Decide on the best order for your topic sentences.

Discuss this with your teachers or peers.

Text 11K

Example writing tasks:

Aspects of Tragedy

'Cordelia's death is the shocking climax of cruelty in Shakespeare's exploration of evil.' To what extent do you agree with this view? Remember to include in your answer relevant comment on Shakespeare's dramatic methods.

Aspects of Comedy

'In comedic literature, humour is primarily provided by the uncultivated behaviour and speech of the lower social classes.' To what extent do you agree with this view in relation to two texts you have studied? Remember to include in your answer relevant comment on the ways the writers have shaped meanings.

Elements of Crime Writing

'In *Oliver Twist* Dickens presents criminals as products of their society.' To what extent do you agree with this view? Remember to include in your answer relevant detailed exploration of Dickens' authorial methods.

Elements of Political Writing

'Political and social protest writing often focuses on rebellion against those in power.' Explore the significance of rebellion as it is presented in two political and social protest texts you have studied.

Expressing tentativeness

Learning how to handle uncertainty is also increasingly important at A Level. As you become a more sophisticated reader, you will become more and more aware that meaning in literary texts is tentative and open to interpretation - sometimes many interpretations. In order to express this tentativeness, you will often need to qualify what you say and to acknowledge that there are various ways in which texts may be read and understood.

ACTIVITY 6

Expressing tentativeness

Look at the following words and phrases. Rank them in terms of the certainty they express from 1 - the most certain - to 10 - the least certain:

- This may suggest …
- This means that …
- This seems to indicate that …
- Some readers may feel …
- We may infer …
- The writer implies …
- The word … indicates …
- One interpretation of this could be …
- Perhaps this might be seen as …
- Some critics, such as [critic's name], believe …

These sentence starters are all useful in conveying shades of meaning. They help to show you are thinking critically, but at the same time acknowledge that there other ways of seeing things.

Now try the following tasks.

a Discuss the sentence starters with your peers and teachers to explore how and when each might be used.
b Think about a text you know well from your previous studies or one you are working on at the moment. Write a sequence of sentences about it using these sentence starters to reflect your response to different elements of the text.
c Consider how definite a statement each represents.
d Develop other ways of your own in which tentativeness might be expressed.

Developing as an academic writer

As you progress through your A Level studies of literature, you need to develop your skills as an academic writer. Here are some key issues.

- Think carefully about the needs of your readers, including anyone assessing your work.
- Avoid unsubstantiated generalisations and instead substantiate your points by using academic sources.
- You need to develop increasingly precise and controlled use of language.
- Make sure that your ideas are always as clearly expressed as possible and that you focus on using appropriate vocabulary.
- High levels of accuracy in spelling, punctuation and grammar are required.

- Standard academic style tends to be formal and objective, but you also need to retain an element of personal style.
- In critical essays you will be exploring your personal views of literary texts, so there are times when the first person is appropriate, but do not overuse it. In some kinds of writing (for example, reflective commentaries on creative, re-creative or transformative writing tasks) the first person is more likely to be used.

The conclusion

You may think that the conclusion of an essay is simply a restatement of its thesis and/or a restatement of its major arguments. In reality, however, conclusions like this rarely satisfy. In fact, the best conclusions often look forward rather than backwards! Strong conclusions must, of course, relate closely to the topic of the essay, but also point readers to the wider implications of the topic they've covered. Experiment with a range of ways of drawing such conclusions and discuss these with your peers and teachers. Some possible ways of doing this are:

- using a rhetorical question
- using a quotation from the text
- using a quotation from a secondary source
- pointing out how readers might see the world or the text differently as a result of the essay.

Texts 11L and 11M are two alternative conclusions for the essay on *Wuthering Heights* that we've been considering.

Text 11L

In this essay, I have explored a range of ways of interpreting the character of Heathcliff. While he in some ways appears frightening, he can also evoke feelings of pity, living his lonely life at Wuthering Heights and rejected by society. Emily Brontë's portrayal of him therefore allows scope for readers to make up their own minds.

Text 11M

It may be that the most important question to ask about Heathcliff is not whether we pity him, but whether he is something other than simply a depraved and violent man. As the narrative progresses, we become aware that Heathcliff is not simply a figure of fear, but there are many ways in which he is himself a victim. Heathcliff is the towering figure of the novel who is capable of inspiring fear and disgust, but along with Catherine and Edgar, he forms part of a powerful trinity of characters that leads to the possibility of resolution. In exploring the role Heathcliff plays in <u>Wuthering Heights</u>, we move beyond questions of pity and fear and achieve a very different kind of understanding of him.

ACTIVITY 7

Conclusions

a Read again the two possible conclusions to the essay. Which of the two conclusions do you feel is the more sophisticated and effective. Why?

b Try rewriting one or both with the purpose of improving the quality of the writing.

c Discuss the effect of these changes with your peers.

11.2.4 Presentation of names and titles

You also need to think about how elements within essays at A Level should be presented. This is not simply being pedantic – learning how to present your work according to academic expectations is an important part of your understanding, especially if you are thinking of going on to higher education.

Names of characters, texts, authors, places and so on all require initial capital letters and should be written in full – so write *The Merchant of Venice*, not *TMOV*. Generally only the main words in titles are capitalised, not small words like 'of' and 'and'. The exception is when they come at the beginning of the title, for example, *Of Mice and Men* or *The Day of the Triffids*.

Never refer to an author by their first name only e.g. (Margaret or William), always use their surname (e.g. Atwood or Blake).

Titles of prose and drama texts should be in italics, if typed, or underlined, if hand written (*Macbeth*, or <u>Macbeth</u>) and not in inverted commas ('Macbeth'). Take care when the title of a text is the same as the name of one of the characters in it and make sure that you use the correct convention to distinguish between them (for example, in *Tom Jones*, Fielding presents Tom Jones as a lovable but immoral rogue).

Use inverted commas for titles of poems and short stories. This helps to differentiate them from the titles of the collections in which they appear. So:

- the poem 'Death of a Naturalist' is found in the book *Death of a Naturalist*
- 'The Dead' is the final story in *Dubliners*.

11.2.5 Presentation of quotations

If you are using a short quotation, it can flow naturally out of your own writing as shown in Text 11N.

Text 11N

In The Big Money, Dos Passos uses information in a different way; he takes us into the world of advertising and brand identity where people are encouraged to 'walk the streets and walk the streets inquiring of Coca Cola signs Lucky Strike ads'.

Sometimes the quotation will not flow naturally but sits slightly separate from your own writing, in which case you will need to introduce it using a colon as shown in Text 11O.

Text 11O

On another occasion, Mr Cardinal tries to point out the falseness of Stevens' position, when Herr Ribbentrop, the Nazi Foreign Minister, visits Darlington Hall to try to persuade the Prime Minister to visit Hitler. Stevens stalwartly refuses to understand: 'I cannot see what there is to object to in that, sir. His lordship has always striven to aid better understanding between nations.'

If you want to quote at greater length, you should break your own paragraph to insert the quotation by indenting and leaving space around it. Under exam conditions, where time and words are of the essence, you will probably want to use shorter quotations. However, if you do so, use a colon to introduce the quotation. Note that in this case you don't need to use quotation marks (see Text 11P).

Text 11P

In Storm of Steel the German writer Ernst Junger captures a sense of yearning for home and its influence on his commitment to Germany's war effort. This sense of belonging and the need to defend his land is just as strong as the English troops' beloved 'Blighty' or the Anzacs' Antipodes:

> At the sight of the Neckar slopes wreathed with flowering cherry trees, I had a strong sense of having come home. What a beautiful country it was, and eminently worth our blood and our lives.

When quoting poetry, use a forward slash (/) to indicate where line breaks occur if you are incorporating the quotation into your own writing as shown in Text 11Q.

Text 11Q

Eliot captures the provisional nature of personality and voice in 'Portrait of a Lady' as the central persona concludes: 'I must borrow every changing shape/To find expression'.

If using a longer quotation from poetry, the original layout of the poem should be retained (see Text 11R).

Text 11R

In his Choruses from 'The Rock', Eliot adds gravity to his tone by adopting and adapting an array of biblical voices:

> Sanballat the Horonite and Tobiah the Ammonite
> and Geshem the Arabian: were doubtless men
> of public spirit and zeal.
>
> Preserve me from the enemy who has something
> to gain: and from the friend who has something
> to lose.
>
> Remembering the words of Nehemiah the prophet:
> 'The trowel in hand, and the gun rather loose in
> the holster.'

If you wish to clarify an aspect of your quotation, use square brackets to demonstrate writing that isn't part of the text. In Text 11S the word 'Saturn' has been included to clarify the meaning of the pronoun 'his'.

Text 11S

Forest on forest hung about his [Saturn's] head/Like cloud on cloud.

If you need to omit words from a quotation in order to make it make sense, you should use ellipsis as shown in Text 11T.

Text 11T

It is a truth universally acknowledged that a single man … must be in want of a wife.

It is normal to use single rather than double inverted commas for quotations. If you are quoting dialogue, however, you will need to use speech marks within your quotation marks, as shown in Text 11U.

Text 11U

'"I don't know," said Peter. "I need to think about that."'

11.2.6 Bibliography

Non-examined assessment responses should be followed with a bibliography. This is the list of books you've consulted in researching and writing your work. This allows others to locate and read these materials if they want to. You should include literary texts to which you refer and secondary reading, and you need to provide certain key details:

- the author's name
- the date the material was published
- the full title of the work
- the name of the publisher
- the place where the work was published.

Text 11V is an example of this.

Text 11V

Books

McEvoy, S. (2009) *Tragedy: A Student Handbook*. London: English and Media Centre.

Shakespeare, W. (1993) *Hamlet*. Cambridge: Cambridge University Press.

Book chapters

Brooke, N. (2004) 'Language and Speaker in *Macbeth*', in P. Edwards, I. Ewbank & G.K. Hunter (eds.) *Shakespeare's Styles: Essays in Honour of Kenneth Muir*. Cambridge: Cambridge University Press, pp. 67–78.

Journal articles

Green, A. (2012) 'Moral Economies and Revolution: Marxism and Joseph Conrad's *The Secret Agent*'. *e magazine*, Issue 57, pp.32–35.

You also ought (but don't have) to provide details of web-based sources you've used, including the date on which you accessed the material as shown in Text 11W.

Text 11W

http://www.josephconradsociety.org/student_resources.htm Accessed: 5 August 2014.

11.3 Writing creative responses to literary texts

One of the ways you can respond to texts is through producing literary texts of your own. This might be through creative writing unrelated to the texts you are studying in which you explore the ways in which different types of text are constructed (for example, the haiku or sonnet form in poetry, the ways in which drama texts are presented, methods of creating character. Such creative opportunities to explore texts creatively need to be distinguished from re-creative writing, which is undertaken in direct response to a specific literary text. You are probably already used to this from your previous studies.

ACTIVITY 8

Your experience of creative and re-creative writing

Think about the occasions when you have produced creative literary texts of your own or have undertaken re-creative writing in your study of English up until now.

a What kinds of activities have you done? Which were purely creative tasks and which were re-creative?

b How do you feel about writing literary texts of your own and producing re-creative writing in response to base texts you've studied?

c What do you think creative writing and re-creative tasks add to your understanding of your literary studies?

It is important to think about the different ways in which creative and re-creative writing might be used throughout your A Level course. If you're studying for the full A Level, re-creative writing with an accompanying commentary is an option as part of your non-exam assessment. We will look at this in more detail later.

11.3.1 What is re-creative writing?

Re-creative writing is designed to make some kind of intervention in another text, and as such it does a number of major things with the original text:

- it interprets it
- it enters into 'dialogue' with it
- it evokes new potential meanings in it.

Re-creative writing tasks can come in many different shapes and sizes, but all allow you to play with the base text and to explore your understanding of what it is about (its themes, purposes, concepts) and the ways in which it functions (its structure, genre, audience, language, narrative method and so on). The process of re-creative writing and critically commenting on it engages you, in other words, in a detailed consideration of how literary texts are produced and received – how meanings are created and how they are received.

Some re-creative tasks are designed to build upon and cooperate with the original text. These types of task enhance understanding, as both are based on the principle of critical dialogue with the base text, which cannot be changed: anything you write must be consistent with the base text and so be able to either fit into, before or after it. See Figure 11B for possible ways of thinking about re-creative interventions.

Figure 11B

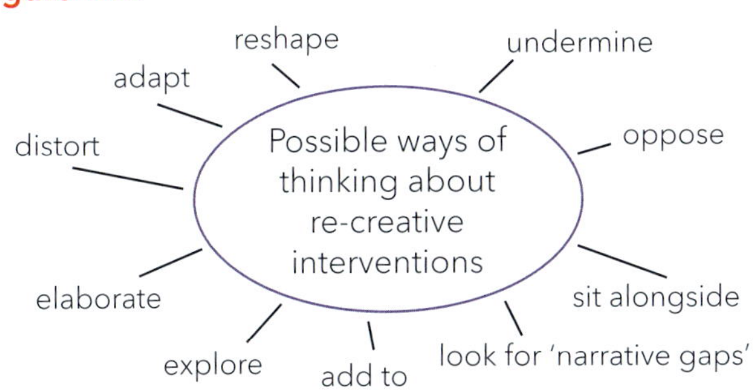

All provide useful and interesting alternative means of engaging with the texts you are studying and can provide all kinds of fascinating insight into the ways in which texts function. Here are some examples of the kinds of re-creative writing activities you might undertake in response to literary texts:

- adding scenes or stanzas to the original to explore theme, language and character
- imagining and constructing in writing certain key locations, settings, people, objects and so on
- writing empathic responses such as diaries or monologues to capture characters' responses to events
- rewriting a particular 'moment' from the point of view of a different character
- writing a prequel (what happens before) for a text.

These kinds of activity, where you write imaginatively 'into', 'out of' and 'parallel to' texts, help you explore the choices authors make and the positions readers and writers adopt as they work together to create meaning from text. This is obviously very useful as you focus on different aspects of texts (for example, language, form, structure and narrative voice) and how these affect potential textual meanings. These processes help you to develop critical understanding of how literary texts work, especially where accompanied by a critical analysis.

ACTIVITY 9

Thinking about re-creative tasks

Take a selection (or all) of these suggested re-creative writing activities. For each one, think about:

- what kind of re-creative intervention it is
- the different types of insight it would afford into any literary text you are studying.

11.3.2 Re-creative writing and set texts

While re-creative writing for the purposes of non-exam assessment has to be based on texts which are not named for study, re-creative tasks in response to set texts are also very beneficial (though not a requirement of the AQA Literature B Non-exam Assessment (NEA)). Even if your teacher does not set you such tasks, you could always develop them for yourself if you find this a useful way of working. The following are some example ideas.

Aspects of tragedy

In *Romeo and Juliet*, Shakespeare uses a sonnet as a prologue to the play, summarising its key events for the audience. Write such a sonnet by way of a prologue to either *Othello* or *King Lear*. Think about:

- how you set about constructing a summary in such a condensed form
- the likely impact of such a prologue on how audiences might respond to the play
- the experience of writing in verse.

Aspects of comedy

Read the opening scene of either *The Taming of the Shrew* or *Twelfth Night*. Imagine that Shakespeare had decided to write a novel instead of a play. Write the opening pages. Think about:

- how narrative in drama differs from narrative in prose fiction
- how you use Shakespeare's dialogue – what did you use, what did you cut?
- how you use dialogue and stage directions to help you construct narrative.

Elements of crime writing

Write a screenplay adaptation of the opening sequence of *Brighton Rock* by Graham Greene.

Think about:

- Greene's use of visual imagery
- how narrative methods in novel and film vary
- the role of dialogue and music in the text.

Elements of political writing

Write a pair of poems (or even a sequence of paired poems) for inclusion in a contemporary *Songs of Innocence and of Experience* by William Blake – one for the Innocence section and one for the Experience section – exploring issues of social and political significance in the 21st century. Issues to consider include:

- Blake's use of simple, nursery-rhyme-like forms and language
- presentation of political 'messages'
- connections and differences between the poems.

Writing an accompanying commentary or rationale, giving an analysis of your own writing process and how your re-creative text relates to the source text helps to clarify such insights.

See 11.3.3 for more on writing a critical commentary

11.3.3 Non-exam assessment

The purpose of this unit is to give you the opportunity to read and explore texts through the lens of different critical ideas. One option for doing this is to use re-creative writing as a means of exploring interpretations – this is an engaging way to consider various factors that affect the creation of meanings in literary texts. Re-creative pieces must be accompanied by a critical commentary which draws upon ideas from the Critical Anthology and explores how these help you in developing your interpretation of the base text. Together the re-creative piece and the commentary must be between 1250 and 1500 words in length. (Remember that re-creative writing, like the critical essay option for non-exam assessment, must not be based on a set text.)

The re-creative piece

Because the re-creative piece and commentary must make reference to the Critical Anthology, your re-creative writing task must allow you to address at least one of the following areas:

- ideas about narrative
- Marxist ways of reading
- feminist ways of reading
- post-colonial ways of reading
- eco-critical ways of reading
- literary value and the canon.

The re-creative piece will be an implicit exploration of the theoretical approach chosen, and the commentary will be explicit in this respect. As you have already seen, re-creative writing works in a variety of ways into 'narrative gaps' or 'absences' in the base text and seeks to shed light on its meaning or create new possible meanings. It is worth noting that there is no requirement beyond what AO1 allows for you to replicate the form and language of the base text – though you may if you wish. More important is that you engage with critical concepts through your writing.

If you select this option, therefore, you obviously need to think very carefully and work closely with your teachers to ensure that the task allows you to meet the requirements of the non-exam assessment. Because this unit is intended to allow you to develop your independence in research and study, you should be actively involved in establishing the writing task.

Note how the following example task focuses clearly on issues of critical perspective so that you can build transparent connections to the Critical Anthology.

Write a series of journal entries by Miss Kenton written at different points in the narrative of *The Remains of the Day* in which she reflects on her treatment by Stevens and others at Darlington Hall. Use ideas from the Critical Anthology to inform your work and include a commentary explaining how you have explored ideas from feminism and/or Marxism in your re-creative piece.

The critical commentary

The re-creative writing is the 'doing', and the critical commentary is the explanation of what you did and why, but both parts involve in-depth analysis and understanding of the text and its potential meanings. The commentary demonstrates how ideas from the Critical Anthology have informed both your creative reading of the base text and your re-creative writing into it.

Your commentary needs to:

- communicate what insights about the base text informed the re-creative strategies
- explain what interpretative effects were intended
- discuss the new meanings and interpretations evoked by those choices
- reflect on the structural relationships between genre, context, language and meaning in the base text and the new writing.

Example non-exam assessment

Text 11X is an extract from a re-creative writing task based on Henrik Ibsen's play *Hedda Gabler*. The task is to write a journal entry in character as Brack reflecting on Hedda's death. It illustrates very effectively the kinds of writing you might do and how these relate back to source texts, but remember that for non-exam assessment, re-creative writing may only be based on either poetry or prose texts.

Text 11X

Well, it came as a tremendous shock, indeed. Just think, to find the lady lying there, her eyes wide open and perfectly fixed, staring out of the window, with blood welling from the side of her head. Quite frightening it was to see her body so very still, the shell of the dark and curious woman she was. Hedda Gabler. How she could work a room.

Tesman seemed to think she was fooling around when he first heard the gunshot, but I'll admit it, I had a sort of feeling that those pistols were more than a game to her. I remember taking the back route through the house upon one of my visits, and being given quite a nasty start when I looked up and the lady was poised with a gun, aiming straight at me. There was a look of passion in her eyes, of a somewhat demonic nature: it suited her somehow. She fired, and the almighty sound rang about the house. I was really taken aback to see such a fine creature of a woman with such heavily masculine contraptions.

Oh, but I suppose a woman like her must have had to find the means to intensify her life, for she seemed most idle and dissatisfied. She spent most of her time fidgeting in that dim, empty house, searching for the world beyond. The life she wanted was on the wrong side of the Tesman walls. The way she would drum her fingertips on the glass panes made me want to throw open the doors and set her free. The lady needed stimulation, intrigue, mystery; I could see it in her eyes. I felt as though I was feeding a ravenous creature with scraps of succulent meat whenever I brought news to her. Such an untamed woman, so different from the docile Thea Elvsted – the two looked most peculiar side by side in those armchairs. The way poor Thea's pretty little bourgeois face would contort when Hedda leaned in close.

Text 11Y is an extract from the student commentary written to accompany this piece, illustrating the kinds of thinking such activities give access to.

Text 11Y

'Gabler' in English translates to 'freedom'. The essence of Ibsen's tragedy is that of a society whose binds destroy a woman in pursuit of autonomy. Hedda only releases herself through her own death – 'a fatal or disastrous conclusion' (definition of tragedy from 'The Oxford Companion to English Literature'). Brack's character is a catalyst for the tragedy: his independence gives Hedda enticing glimpses of freedom; and his eventual control over her tips the tragedy into irreversibility.

I gave Brack a stiff and proper tone ('rather taken aback'), to reflect the constraining nature of society. He only expresses his sadness at the end of the piece, illustrating the power of social conditioning in Ibsen's late nineteenth century world, and how it stifles individual sentiment. Brack notes Hedda 'fidgeting in that dim, empty house' suggesting that the house, for Hedda, embodies claustrophobia and restraint. I decided to have her, in death, 'staring out of the window' to illustrate the tragic ensnarement of her life. Between the darkened walls, Hedda must assume the role of Tesman's possession, and the thought of this consumes her. She is expected to raise a family for him and devote herself to domesticity; and yet she is bound to the idea of loosely-led, romantic existence. Hedda will not allow herself to be defined by her husband: her unrelenting restlessness on stage ('[she] moves irritably'; 'walks about the room … as though in a frenzy') creating distance between them. It also expresses her discomfort in the house; and, in the broader sense, her unease in society. Tesman, as a contemporary man, wants to cage and display 'the wonderful Hedda Gabler'; but his predictable, bourgeois world suffocates her, reflecting the plain conventionality of a society which does not suit her. Brack sees Hedda's 'drumming of fingertips' on the panes, and admits to wanting to 'set her free'. The drumming reveals her feelings of alienation from the secure, intimate family she has been invited into. As an upper class man, Brack can see the flaws of this set-up. It also suggests there is something on the other side of the window that she wants to get to: perhaps a world of beauty untainted by the disappointment of reality.

ACTIVITY 10

Writing critical commentaries

a Look closely at the re-creative writing and commentary in Text 11Y. Think carefully about the following questions.
- How does the student refer to their own re-creative writing?
- How does the student connect their re-creative writing to the base text?
- How do they use wider textual and contextual information in the commentary?
- How have they commented on their use of voice?
- What insights into the base text do you think the student has gained from the re-creative process?

b Think about a text you know well, either from your A Level studies or from your personal reading. Develop your own re-creative writing task and critical commentary on it, remembering to establish a clear critical focus.

Check your responses in the Ideas section on Cambridge Elevate

11.4 Bringing it all together

11.4.1 Assessment objectives

In relation to the assessment objectives, you have:

- thought in detail about how to develop increasingly sophisticated ways of articulating your ideas, about the importance of using your reading to develop informed, personal responses, about writing literary texts of your own and re-creative writing as ways of developing responses to literary texts, and about the importance of developing coherent ways of talking and writing about literary texts (AO1)
- considered how you can use both critical and imaginative writing to analyse a variety of ways in which meanings are shaped in literary texts (AO2)
- considered issues surrounding the contexts in which texts – not just literary texts – are produced and received; you have also considered the different conditions under which you are expected to write as an A Level student; you have thought about how writing your own literary texts and re-creative writing can engage you with both textual production and reception (AO3)
- considered how to write in connected ways about literary texts making use of materials from the Critical Anthology (AO4)
- considered why it is important to look at alternative ways of understanding literary texts; you have considered how and in what ways you can use such alternative perspectives in your own writing (AO5).

Summary

In this unit, you have learnt about:

- the variety of ways in which you might write during your AS or A Level studies, their differing functions and the relationship between them
- the close relationship between reading and writing and how you can learn to 'read like a writer and write like a reader'.
- the close relationship between critical responses and creative responses to literary texts
- how writing your own literary texts and re-creative writing can enhance your engagement with literature
- different techniques you can use as a basis for writing and for developing your skills and confidence as a writer
- how to use secondary sources and wider reading as a way of developing and communicating your understanding and ideas.

ENRICHING

12

Tragedy

12.1 Enrichment activities

12.1.1 Exploring tragic protagonists

In Unit 5, sections 5.1.2 and 5.3.1, you considered the nature of the tragic protagonist, from the genre's origins in ancient Greece. You learned that tragic protagonists are flawed in some way, and that their errors lead to great suffering, for themselves and others. You also learned that aspects of the tragic genre have been used by different authors in different ways, often reflecting the contexts in which they write.

ACTIVITY 1

Tragic protagonists in literature and popular culture

a Make a list of characters in literature and popular culture - television, film and computer games - who could be seen as tragic protagonists. (You could think, for instance, of Sirius Black and Severus Snape in the *Harry Potter* series, Anakin Skywalker in the *Star Wars* films, Harvey Dent in *The Dark Knight*, Tony Soprano in *The Sopranos*, Walter White in *Breaking Bad* and Dexter Morgan in *Dexter*). Using what you know about aspects of tragedy, make brief notes on why each of these characters could be considered as a tragic protagonist.

b The critic Raphael Falco has said that tragic protagonists possess a 'charismatic authority'. Is this true of the tragic protagonists you have identified? Explain your answer.

c Why do you think audiences are drawn to tragic protagonists?

d Can you think of any real people - politicians, sportspeople, musicians, celebrities - whose lives embody aspects of tragedy?

12.1.2 Tragedy on stage and screen

Tragedy began as a dramatic genre, and two of your set texts are plays. In Unit 3, you learned that different productions of plays are, in effect, different interpretations of the plays, emphasising particular themes and depicting characters in a variety of ways. Watching performances of your set plays is an excellent way of exploring the variety of ways in which they can be interpreted.

ACTIVITY 2

Tragedy in performance

If possible, go to a stage production of one of your set plays. Alternatively, find clips from stage productions and film adaptations of your set plays on YouTube. Drawing on what you know about aspects of tragedy, think about questions a–c.

a How are the tragic protagonist and other key characters portrayed?

b In what ways do staging, lighting and sound contribute to the effect of the tragedy?

c Focus on two or three key points within the action of the tragedy (for example, hamartia, peripeteia, anagnorisis) and consider the different ways in which these are depicted.

12.1.3 Two different views of Shakespeare's tragedies

One of the most famous books about Shakespeare's tragedies is *Shakespearean Tragedy*, written by A.C. Bradley in 1904. Bradley described tragedy as a struggle between eternal forces, a 'painful mystery'. He wrote about Shakespeare's tragedies as if they were psychological studies of real people. A very different view of Shakespeare's tragedies is advanced by the critic Fintan O'Toole in his book *Shakespeare is Hard, but so is Life* (2002). O'Toole argues that Bradley's interpretation of Shakespeare - with its focus on character and morality - said more about the context in which Bradley was writing than it did about the Elizabethan theatre.

ACTIVITY 3

Comparing Bradley and O'Toole

Read the introductory chapters of Bradley's *Shakespearean Tragedy* and O'Toole's *Shakespeare is Hard, but so is Life*. Then read the chapters in each book that focus on the major Shakespearean tragedy you are studying.

a What observations can you make about the different approaches taken by Bradley and O'Toole?
b What does each critic say about the protagonist of the Shakespearean tragedy you are studying?
c Whose approach do you think is more convincing? Explain your answer.

12.1.4 Tragic bystanders

We often tend to think of tragedy in terms of protagonists and antagonists - and the victims who suffer as a result of the protagonist's errors. Sections 5.3.2 and 5.3.3 explored three other types of character often found in tragedies - Machiavels, malcontents and fools. What about the bystanders - the characters who witness the action of the tragedy and often try to support and protect the tragic protagonist? In what ways are they affected by the actions of the protagonist, and the consequences that follow?

ACTIVITY 4

Creative rewriting: the witnesses of tragedy

Choose a 'bystander' character from one of the texts you are studying. For instance, you could think about:

a Kent in *King Lear*
b Lodovico in *Othello*
c Jordan Baker in *The Great Gatsby*
d Wagner in *Dr Faustus*
e Charley in *Death of a Salesman*
f Liza-Lu in *Tess of the D'Urbervilles*.

Write a monologue from the point of view of this character, to be spoken after the action has concluded. What would your chosen character say about what has happened?

12.1.5 Nietzsche on tragedy

The German philosopher Friedrich Nietzsche saw tragedy as the product of a struggle between two opposing forces, which he termed the Apollonian and the Dionysian. The Apollonian was characterised by balance, order and reason, while the Dionysian was characterised by disorder, revelry and an abandonment of oneself to instinct and desire. Nietzsche saw Ancient Greek tragedy as breaking through the calmness of the Apollonian and giving access to the turmoil of the Dionysian. He claimed that tragedy offered its audiences an intense emotional experience that contrasted with the mundane routines of everyday life.

ACTIVITY 5

Exploring Nietzsche

Listen to the Philosophy Bites podcast by Aaron Ridley on 'Nietzsche on Art and Truth'.
What connections can you make between Nietzsche's view of tragedy and the texts you have studied?

Listen to the Philosophy Bites podcast by Aaron Ridley on 'Nietzsche on Art and Truth' on Cambridge Elevate

12.2 Wider reading

12.2.1 Key texts on tragedy

There are many texts about tragedy that you could use to develop your understanding further. These include:

- Bradley, A. C. (1904) *Shakespearean Tragedy* (reissued by Penguin Classics) - Perhaps the most famous study of Shakespeare's major tragedies, although one that has been criticised for writing about characters as psychological case studies rather than dramatic constructs.
- McEvoy, S., with Coult, T. and Sandford, C. (2009) *Tragedy: A Student Handbook* (English and Media Centre) - Wide-ranging, readable and hugely informative: an excellent starting point for your further reading.
- O'Toole, F. (2002) *Shakespeare is Hard, But So is Life: A Radical Guide to Shakespearean Tragedy* (Granta) - A provocative exploration of Shakespeare's major tragedies that challenges Bradley's interpretation.
- Poole, A. (2005) *Tragedy: A Very Short Introduction* (Oxford) - As its subtitle indicates, this is an accessible overview of the genre of tragedy.
- Wallace, J. (2007) *The Cambridge Introduction to Tragedy* (Cambridge) - A wide-ranging exploration of tragedy that looks at tragedy in the novel, in the visual arts and on film as well as at tragic drama.

12.2.2 Further useful resources

In addition to the books listed in 12.2.1, there are a number of web-based resources that will enrich and extend your study of tragedy. Four of the most useful are as follows.

- BBC Radio 4: *In Our Time*
  Each episode of Melvyn Bragg's wide-ranging discussion series features a particular topic discussed by three experts. All past episodes (over 600 of them) are available online via the programme's homepage. There are episodes on Elizabethan Revenge, *King Lear* and Marlowe, as well as on the genre of tragedy.
- Oxford Podcasts: *Approaching Shakespeare*, with Emma Smith
  Emma Smith's contributions to the Oxford Podcasts series are both accessible and informative. The *Approaching Shakespeare* series, which draws on Smith's own research, includes lectures on *King Lear, Othello* and *Richard II*, as well as other Shakespearean tragedies.
- Royal Shakespeare Company: Online Resources
  The RSC's Online Resources include images from past productions that enable you to compare aspects of characterisation and staging. Education packs are also available for many plays.
- Shakespeare's Globe: Adopt an Actor
  The Globe Theatre website's Adopt an Actor resource contains blog entries and reflections from many of the Globe's actors on the process of bringing Shakespeare's characters to life.

12.3 Sean McEvoy on modern approaches to tragedy

Sean McEvoy teaches literature in Brighton and Cambridge, and writes books and articles on the theatre. He is currently writing *Tragedy: The Basics*, to be published in 2016. Here he introduces some theories of tragedy from the nineteenth and twentieth centuries.

Aristotle's ideas about tragedy don't take into account the fact that the world changes and that we live in changing societies. Shakespeare's England, for example, was in transition between the mediaeval and the modern world. Othello is an outsider in Venice who talks and behaves like a feudal warrior, or a hero out of knightly romance – as he says, these are the qualities that make Desdemona love him. But Venice is a very modern place, and its individualism, self-interest and ruthlessness are nowhere better embodied than in the figure of Iago. The German philosopher Hegel (1770–1831) locates tragedy where people are caught between two historical forces pulling in different directions. No matter how heroic or pitiable an individual might be, there is no escape because their world-view is out of joint with historical change – a force which Hegel thought was ultimately progressive. For him there is something positive in tragedy.

It's also possible to think of the heroine of *Tess of the D'Urbervilles* (1891) in a similar way. The dominant moral values of an 'unnatural' Victorian Christianity in the novel cannot be reconciled with Tess, who appears to be the embodiment of a ancient pagan morality rooted in nature. She is arrested in the pre-Christian 'temple' of Stonehenge, where she feels 'at home' as a 'heathen'.

Tess's tragedy is that she is a 'pure woman' in tune with the ancient demands of nature who lives in a time where to have a child out of marriage, even after rape, entails total social rejection. Yet Hardy's novel not only looks forward to, but actually helped to bring about a time when women would be relatively free from the tyranny of Victorian sexual morality. Tess might be seen as an early tragic victim in the larger movement for female emancipation in the coming twentieth century.

Tragedy can also expose the contradictions and injustices of ideas which are otherwise utterly dominant. In Miller's *Death of a Salesman* (1949), the salesman Willy Loman has inevitably ended up selling himself, as Raymond Williams wrote in 1979, and has become an economic commodity to be discarded like any other: 'he brings down tragedy on himself, not by opposing the lie, but by living it'. In living the false dream of American capitalism Willy unwittingly shows to at least one of his sons that the dreams of some are built on the nightmares of many.

But perhaps tragedy need not teach anything. *King Lear* (1606) depicts a whole society in meltdown, a world in which both feudal values (as represented by Kent, Albany and Lear) and modern individualism (Edmund, Cornwall, Goneril, Regan) do not so much conflict as both fail utterly. In 1964 Jan Kott wrote that the play showed life to be absurd, bleak and grotesque, devoid of hope, likening *King Lear* to Samuel Beckett's *Endgame* (1957). The German philosopher Nietzsche (1844–1900) had suggested that tragedy can offer a kind of thrill in contemplating death and destruction (and by implication our own), as if the shaping of suffering into art is what validates why we enjoy watching tragedy. Another German, the dramatist Brecht (1898–1956), condemned tragedy as a kind of smokescreen put up by those whose wealth and power depends on the suffering they cause, making it appear mysterious by calling it 'tragedy'. But British tragedy still refuses to find the world as irremediable. Edward Bond's reworking of Shakespeare in *Lear* (1971) shows how revolutions against tyranny produce tyranny, but endorses the continued resistance of the powerless. Even the bleakest of Bond's successors, Sarah Kane (1971–99), suggests the saving power of love in her work.

12.4 Video interview

Watch Dan Rebellato, Professor of Drama and Theatre at Royal Holloway, University of London, talk about tragedy on Cambridge Elevate

ENRICHING

13 Comedy

13.1 Enrichment activities

13.1.1 Exploring comic characters

In Unit 6, you explored a variety of different comic characters – heroes and heroines; villains, rivals and adversaries; clowns, fools and buffoons. You learned that a comic protagonist might display the characteristics both of a fool or clown and of a hero or heroine. You also learned that aspects of the comic genre have been used by different authors in different ways, often reflecting the contexts in which they write.

ACTIVITY 1

Comic characters in literature and popular culture

a Make a list of characters in literature and popular culture – television, film and computer games – who could be seen as comic characters. (You could think, for instance, of Professor Sprout in the *Harry Potter* series, R2D2 in the *Star Wars* films, Truman in *The Truman Show*, Mr Burns in *The Simpsons*, Mr Bean and Miranda in the TV sitcoms of those names, The Joker in *Batman*, Bridget Jones in *Bridget Jones's Diary*.) Using what you know about aspects of comedy, make brief notes on why each of these could be considered as a comic character.

b The critic Eric Weitz writes: 'Clown figures … allow a universal identification with uphill struggle. Despite unswerving determination and fantastic invention, clowns spend much of their times failing.' To what extent is this true of the comic characters you have identified? Explain your answer.

13.1.2 Comedy on stage and screen

Comedy began as a dramatic genre, and two of your set texts are plays. In Unit 3, you learned that different productions of plays are, in effect, different interpretations of them, emphasising particular themes and depicting characters in a variety of ways. Watching performances of your set plays is an excellent way of exploring the variety of ways in which they can be interpreted.

ACTIVITY 2

Comedy in performance

If possible, go to a stage production of one of your set plays. Alternatively, find clips from stage productions and film adaptations of your set plays on YouTube.

Drawing on what you know about aspects of comedy, think about questions a–c.

a How are the comic protagonist and other key characters portrayed?

b In what ways do staging, lighting and sound contribute to the effect of the comedy?

c Focus on two or three key points within the action of the comedy (for example, moments of confusion, disorder, disguise or deceit) and consider the different ways in which these are depicted.

Check your responses in the Ideas section on Cambridge Elevate

13.1.3 Views of Shakespeare's comedies

Both *Twelfth Night* and *The Taming of the Shrew* have been the subject of much critical discussion. Although the issues of interpretation are different for the two plays, critical readings of some significant critical works about Shakespearean comedy may help you develop your understanding of both plays. *Shakespeare's Festive Comedy* by C.L. Barber is a classic text written in 1959 that seeks to understand the comedies in the context of the holidays and festivities of Shakespeare's age. Catherine Bates' essay 'Love and Courtship' and Barbara Hodgdon's essay 'Sexual disguise and the theatre of gender' in the *Cambridge Companion to Shakespeare* (2002) look at the comedies from a different angle, that of ideas about gender.

ACTIVITY 3

Reading Barber, Bates and Hodgdon

Read the introductory chapters of Barber's *Shakespeare's Festive Comedy*, Bates' essay 'Love and Courtship' and Hodgdon's essay 'Sexual disguise and the theatre of gender'.

a How might Barber's ideas be applied to *Twelfth Night* or *The Taming of the Shrew*?

b What do Bates and Hodgdon have to say about the protagonists of the two plays in their essays?

c How does the approach of these three writers differ? Whose approach do you think is more convincing? Explain your answer.

d If you are studying *Twelfth Night*, you can also go on to read the chapter of Barber's book that is specifically about that play.

13.1.4 Comic bystanders

The main comic characters in a comedy - whether hero or buffoon, or a combination of both - are often observed, supported, protected or manipulated by characters who have a greater awareness of what is going on, or who are less involved in the main action. How are these 'bystander' characters affected by the actions of the protagonists, and the consequences that follow, and what is their perspective on the actions of the protagonists?

ACTIVITY 4

Creative rewriting: the witnesses of comedy

Choose a 'bystander' character from one of the texts you are studying. For instance, you could think about:

a Maria in *Twelfth Night*

b George Hastings in *She Stoops to Conquer*

c Mr Knightley in *Emma*

d Queenie in *Small Island*

e Kate in *Tam O'Shanter*.

Write a monologue from the point of view of this character, to be spoken after the action has concluded. What would your chosen character say about what has happened?

13.1.5 Adapting the comic novel

If you are studying one of the two set comic novels, *Emma* or *Small Island*, you can easily find screen adaptations of the novels to enrich your reading - a film of *Emma* from 1996, starring Gwyneth Paltrow, and a TV adaptation of *Small Island* from 2009.

ACTIVITY 5

Exploring screen adaptations of novels

Watch the adaptation of the novel you are studying.

a How faithful a representation of the novel do you think the adaptation is? What changes have been made, and why do you think they may have been made?

b To what extent do its interpretations of the characters, events and settings match those you have made in your reading of the novel?

c In transferring a novel to the screen, one of the major changes is usually the loss of the prose narrative in a specific narrative voice. To what extent does this loss change the experience of the story? What other losses happen in the transfer to the screen? What benefits might there be?

13.2 Wider reading

13.2.1 Key texts on comedy

There are many texts about comedy that you can use to develop your understanding further. These include the following titles.

- Bevis, M. (2012) *Comedy: A Very Short Introduction*. Oxford: Oxford University Press – A short and accessible introduction to comedy drawing on examples from drama, the novel, poetry, film, TV and many others. This is an excellent starting point for your further reading.
- Gay, P. (2008) *The Cambridge Introduction to Shakespeare's Comedies*. Cambridge: Cambridge University Press – A detailed introduction to all the major aspects of Shakespearean comedy with sections on each play; good support for your Shakespeare text.
- Leggatt, A. (2001) *The Cambridge Companion to Shakespearean Comedy*. Cambridge: Cambridge University Press – A series of authoritative essays by different critics on various aspects of Shakespeare's comedies.
- Stott, A. (2014) *Comedy*. Abingdon: Routledge – A longer, more theoretical examination of the idea of comedy than Bevis', with specific sections on race, gender, sexuality and politics.
- Weitz, E. (2009) *The Cambridge Introduction to Comedy*. Cambridge: Cambridge University Press – A wide-ranging exploration of the history and elements of dramatic comedy. This is an enjoyable, accessible and enlightening read.

13.2.2 Further useful resources

In addition to the books listed in 13.2.1, there are a number of web-based resources that can enrich and extend your study of comedy. Some of the most useful are as follows.

- BBC Radio 4: *In Our Time*
  Each episode of Melvyn Bragg's wide-ranging discussion series features a particular topic discussed by three experts. All past episodes (over 600 of them) are available online via the programme's homepage. There are episodes on Comedy in Ancient Greek theatre, Chaucer, pastoral literature and Shakespeare's life and work.
- Oxford Podcasts: *Approaching Shakespeare*, with Emma Smith
  Emma Smith's contributions to the Oxford Podcasts series are both accessible and informative. The *Approaching Shakespeare* series, which draws on Smith's own research, includes lectures on *Twelfth Night* and *The Taming of the Shrew*, as well as other Shakespearean comedies. The associated website *Great Writers Inspire* contains a range of other useful information on many writers, including Chaucer, Shakespeare, Austen and Wilde.
- Royal Shakespeare Company: Online Resources.
  The RSC's Online Resources include images from past productions that enable you to compare aspects of characterisation and staging. Education packs are also available for many plays.
- Shakespeare's Globe: Adopt an Actor
  The Globe Theatre website's Adopt an Actor resource contains blog entries and reflections from many of the Globe's actors on the process of bringing Shakespeare's characters to life.
- Victoria and Albert Museum: Theatre and Performance
  A wealth of information about the history of theatre, with material on Shakespeare and Wilde in particular.

13.3 Sean McEvoy on comedy and politics: the question of class

Sean McEvoy teaches literature in Brighton and Cambridge, and writes books and articles on the theatre. Here he looks at how attitudes to social class have been important in English theatrical comedy.

One theory which has been used to explain the pleasure we get from comedy suggests that laughter both includes and excludes. When an audience laughs at a character on stage their laughter unites them at the expense of the 'butt' of the joke. If this is true, in the English theatre social class division has been reinforced and asserted in comedy. In *Twelfth Night* (1601) Countess Olivia's steward Malvolio is duped into believing he will marry his mistress. His deluded pomposity can produce the play's loudest laughs in performance. An audience's shared derision might be seen as a common feeling that class boundaries should not be crossed, and that servants should know their place.

Classical comedies also often feature aristocrats in disguise amongst their social inferiors, like Kate Hardcastle in *She Stoops to Conquer* (1773). The humour resides in the dramatic irony: Charles Marlow cannot see Kate's innate superiority, but the audience can, and underlying the fantasy that the nobility are just like the rest of us is the final realisation that virtue does reside in our betters. Again, we are laughing at those who realise that class boundaries are immutable, and enjoying the idea that we are happily united in knowing our place. This kind of conventional comedy – with mistaken identity, lost babies found, and a blocked path to happiness for young love – is tested to destruction in *The Importance of Being Earnest* (1895). Wilde exposes the absurdity of these comic conventions with such brilliant wit that the genre was finally killed off, but he also revels in the sparkingly witty, amoral triviality of his idle upper-class characters. Earnest middle-class 'respectability' is wonderfully beneath these people, and as Lady Bracknell remarks, 'If the lower orders don't set us a good example, what on earth is the use of them?'

From the late eighteenth century onwards the theatre became more and more a middle-class institution. 'Respectability' became the quality that differentiated this increasingly powerful class from their loose-living aristocratic superiors and their foul-mouthed and coarse-humoured inferiors. Laughing out loud became regarded as unrespectable, and English comedy came to rely on the wry chuckle at those who behave above themselves or the righteous giggle at the stupid behaviour of the working classes. Even when it later became acceptable to guffaw, the same source of humour was important even in television comedy, for example in the jumped-up bank manger Captain Mainwaring in *Dad's Army* (1968-77), the fawning Basil in *Fawlty Towers* (1975 and 1979), or the nasty stereotyping of working-class girls and old women in *Little Britain* (2003-06) or *The Catherine Tate Show* (2004-06).

But comedy does not always include and exclude. In Trevor Griffiths' ground-breaking play *Comedians* (1975), a group of working-class would-be stand-up comics are challenged to tell jokes that aren't based on exclusion, or, actually, hate, and to tell jokes that make the audience see the world in its absurdity and injustice more clearly, and come to see their common humanity. The play's central figure, Gethin Price, performs a comedy act full of hatred for his ruling-class enemies, but it just isn't funny. And perhaps the greatest stage comedy creation of the twentieth-century so far, Johnny Byron in Jez Butterworth's *Jerusalem* (2009) is a drug-dealing, con-artist caravan-dwelling gypsy, at war with every notion of 'respectability'. And yet Byron's outrageous story-telling, his verbal brilliance and love of life make him, despite everything, provoke laughter that delights in challenging the numbing nature of life for everyone in class-divided modern Britain, as he stages one last fight to defend the wood where he lives from the bailiffs and bulldozers.

13.4 Video interview

Watch Dan Rebellato, Professor of Drama and Theatre at Royal Holloway, University of London, talk about comedy on Cambridge Elevate

ENRICHING

14 Crime writing

14.1 Enrichment activities

14.1.1 Investigating detectives

In Unit 7, section 7.2.8, you considered the rise of detective police forces in Europe and the United States, and the relationship of these emerging forces to popular views of the detective. Kate Summerscale's book *The Suspicions of Mr Whicher* presents a fascinating picture of the emergence of the first modern detective force in Victorian England, tracing the bizarre case of a murder committed at Road Hill House. She sets the development of the figure of the real-life detective alongside fictional counterparts in the works of Charles Dickens, Wilkie Collins and Mary Elizabeth Braddon and in doing so provides a very interesting picture of how the contemporary figure of the detective emerged in the popular imagination.

ACTIVITY 1

Fiction or reality?

a Read Summerscale's account of a genuine Victorian mystery, *The Suspicions of Mr Whicher*. What do you note about the ways in which she claims that real detectives were shaped almost in tandem with their fictional counterparts?

b Sir Arthur Conan Doyle openly acknowledged his debt to Professor Joseph Bell as the inspiration for the character of Sherlock Holmes. Explore the connection between real-world detection and the fictional world of Holmes at the *sherlockian-sherlock* website.

c In what ways do you think the detectives of Victorian fiction, including Sherlock Holmes, have had an influence on more recent detectives and investigators in the crime writing you've read?

d Explore what is called the CSI effect – the inflated public perception of the possibilities of crime detection based upon television portrayals of detection. Think about this in relation to your reading of crime fiction and your viewing of contemporary crime drama. How do you think it affects your views of writing about crime?

e Read David Hare's play *Murmuring Judges*. How far does his portrayal of the British legal system seem to reflect contemporary perceptions?

14.1.2 Crime and guilt

In Unit 7, section 7.3.3, you looked at the idea of guilt and its relationship to writing about crime. Franz Kafka's *The Trial* offers a very interesting exploration of guilt. K is on trial for an unspecified crime. His guilt is presented as a certainty, but neither he nor the reader knows what crime he has allegedly committed. The novel takes the biblical stance that we are all somehow guilty – inverting the assumed legal supposition that defendants are innocent until proven guilty. Text 14A shows a brief exchange with the judge.

Text 14A

'But I'm not guilty,' said K. 'There's been a mistake. How is it even possible for someone to be guilty? We're all human beings here, one like the other.'
'That is true,' said the priest, 'but that is how the guilty speak.'

Source: Franz Kafka, *The Trial*

A revolution in digital technology has given a voice to many of society's constituents who might, in the past, have been disenfranchised and therefore silent. Criminals in the form of hacktivists, hackers, hoaxers, Internet trolls, pranksters, terrorists, embezzlers and con artists can now interact freely and form unlikely alliances and organisations broadcasting messages sometimes explicitly, but often under assumed or stolen identities. Due to the anonymity that is so easily provided by the Internet, it is often impossible to be certain of the identity of the person or persons to whom one is communicating at any given time, providing the criminally-minded with rich pickings.

News stories abound of people who might never have considered undertaking an illegal activity becoming emboldened by apparent anonymity on social media to behave in what is now considered to be a criminal manner. So it is understandable that genuinely criminal elements in society have been quick to explore the boundless opportunities of this wild new frontier. Cyber crime is on the rise all over the world and our legal guardians are fighting a losing battle to keep up with the perpetrators' ever more ingenious methods.

All of this provides writers of crime fiction with plenty of raw material from which they can imagine new patterns of criminal behaviour. It also creates paranoia and uncertainty, literary moods which are the lifeblood of an effective crime story. How many of us while using our computers or smart phones have looked at the tiny eye-like camera lens above the screen and wondered if we are being watched, or if our every move on the Internet is being logged? The American whistleblower, Edward Snowden, has provided us with revelations that only serve to fuel our paranoia as we realise that all of us are subject to covert surveillance to greater or lesser degrees.

No criminal constituency has embraced the Internet with more relish than terrorist organisations. Utilising the instant distribution of images and messages that are often extremely brutal in nature – and the more brutal and horrific ones often serve their purposes most effectively – we can see the terrorist networks employing new media while utilising the philosophy and tactics of old media. To coin a newsroom adage, 'if it bleeds, it leads'. The use of new media to perpetrate – or assist in – terrorist acts features heavily in my novels *Baptism* and *Sacrifice*. In both books, terrorists – of very different stripes – utilise the Internet to spread their respective messages. By exploring new areas of criminality in the world at large, I am continuing traditions employed by crime writers throughout the ages. The criminal and the crime writer share a similar mindset. They are both constantly contemplating ever more ingenious, profitable and undetectable criminal enterprises.

Digital surveillance – both by the establishment and targeted at the establishment – has led to a blurring of the lines between good and evil. The lives of the great and the good and their claims to moral standing have increasingly come under media attention and are available for our scrutiny. Surveillance is now possible on an unprecedented scale. While this might be potentially unsettling in our everyday lives, it bodes well for the evolution of crime writing in the 21st century. For what is crime writing for, ultimately, if not the cathartic exploration of humanity's ever-present propensity for criminal behaviour?

ACTIVITY 6

Elements of crime writing

Think back over the content of Unit 7. What elements of crime writing does Max Kinnings pick up on here?

ACTIVITY 7

Changes and continuity

In what ways does Max Kinnings identify that crime writing in the 21st century has changed? And in what ways does he identify continuity with the crime writing of the past?

ACTIVITY 8

New contexts for crime

Read *Baptism* and/or *Sacrifice*. How does Kinnings use virtual space and the cyberworld as new contexts for crime and thinking about crime?

ACTIVITY 9

Relationship between crime and writing about crime

Think about high-profile news events involving the virtual world and crime. How do you see the developing relationship between 'real world' crime and writing about crime?

14.4 Video interview

Watch novelist Nicola Monaghan, aka Niki Valentine, Lecturer in Creative and Professional Writing at the University of Nottingham, talk about her writing on Cambridge Elevate

ENRICHING

15

Political and social protest writing

15.1 Enrichment activities

15.1.1 Writers and political protest

As we have seen, writing can be considered in and of itself as a political act, and authors frequently attract fierce condemnation for their work. Lists of banned books and book burnings are a regular feature of literary history and demonstrate the perceived threat that literary works can represent to societies and ideologies.

Text 15A shows what Aristotle has to say about the role of the author in *Poetics* (II.9).

Text 15A

The poet's function is to describe, not the thing that has happened, but a kind of thing that might happen, i.e. what is possible as being probable or necessary ... And if he should come to take a subject from actual history, he is none the less a poet for that.

Aristotle, *Poetics*

Writing, Aristotle is suggesting, is always an act of representation and as such, even if it uses the real world and real-world events as its starting point, it always projects these out of the world of the 'actual' and into the world of the 'visionary' or the 'possible'. That is an act of political significance as it explicitly changes readers' potential ways of seeing. The psychologist and educationist Jerome Bruner in *Actual Minds, Possible Worlds* argues that it is for this very reason that 'tyrants so hate and fear poets and novelists and, yes, historians'.

ACTIVITY 1

Tyrants and literature

Look at the quotations shown in Texts 15B–15D about book-burning from well-known political figures of World War II. How do they capture the 'danger' and 'fear' that tyrants perceive in literary texts?

Text 15B

Any book which acts subversively on our future or strikes at the roots of German thought will be destroyed ... These flames not only illuminate the end of an old era, they also light up a new.

Joseph Goebbels at a book burning on the Unter den Linden in Berlin, 10 May 1933

Text 15C

You see these dictators on their pedestals, surrounded by the bayonets of their soldiers and the truncheons of their police. Yet in their hearts there is unspoken – unspeakable! – fear. They are afraid of words and thoughts! Words spoken abroad, thoughts stirring at home, all the more powerful because they are forbidden. These terrify them. A little mouse – a little tiny mouse! – of thought appears in the room, and even the mightiest potentates are thrown into panic.

Winston Churchill

Text 15D

Books cannot be killed by fire. People die, but books never die. No man and no force can abolish memory... In this war, we know, books are weapons. And it is a part of your dedication always to make them weapons for man's freedom.

Franklin D. Roosevelt

15.1.2 Victorian radical poetry

Although almost certain never to find their way on to A Level specifications, there exists a body of explicitly political verse by a group of radical Victorian working-class poets such as J.B. Leno, Ebenezer Elliott and Thomas Cooper. It is interesting to think, of course, why these poets have not been and are not studied. The exclusion of them and their work from conventional canons of literature and courses of literary study is in itself an interesting political act.

ACTIVITY 2

Victorian radical poetry

Read 'The Song of the Spade', a poem by the radical working-class poet J.B. Leno. You can find it in the Wikipedia article 'John Bedford Leno'. How does it present political and social concepts? Why do you think that such works are relatively unknown, rarely read and even more rarely studied as part of literature courses?

15.1.3 Crime and politics

The relationship between crime and politics is a very interesting one. A range of writers have chosen to explore the connections between these two domains:

- William Godwin: *Things As They Are*: or the *Adventures of Caleb Williams*
- Joseph Conrad: *Heart of Darkness*, *Under Western Eyes* and *The Secret Agent*
- John Buchan: The 39 Steps, Greenmantle and The Three Hostages
- George Orwell: *Animal Farm* and *1984*
- Graham Greene: *The Heart of the Matter*, *The Power and the Glory*, *The Honorary Consul* and *The Quiet American*
- Ian Fleming: *Goldfinger* and *The Man with the Golden Gun*
- John le Carré: *Tinker Tailor Soldier Spy* and *The Russia House*
- Frederick Forsyth: *The Day of the Jackal* and *The Odessa Files.*

ACTIVITY 3

The relationship between crime and politics

Try reading some of the texts listed in 15.1.3.

a In what ways do crime and politics relate to one another?
b How do these texts explore political crime?
c What is the relationship between politics, espionage and the law?

15.1.4 Politics in film

Film has made a major contribution to political drama over the last century, and it is worth thinking about the way a range of political issues have been represented in film.

ACTIVITY 4

Politics in film

a Think about films you have seen that include coverage of political issues and struggles. What different types of film can you think of? What kind of political issues are dealt with?
b The film director Ken Loach is perhaps the most important contemporary political dramatist in Britain. Do some research into his films *Land and Freedom* (1995), *Bread and Roses* (2000), *The Wind that Shakes the Barley* (2006), and *Jimmy's Hall* (2014), and think about the political issues they raise.
c The following is a list of some other well-known political films: *Dr Strangelove* (1964), *All The President's Men* (1976), *Gandhi* (1982), *Good Morning Vietnam* (1987), *The Hunt for Red October* (1990), *JFK* (1991), *Malcolm X* (1992), *Hotel Rwanda* (2004), *Babel* (2006), *The Queen* (2006), *Frost/Nixon* (2008), *Green Zone* (2010), *Lincoln* (2012), *Zero Dark Thirty* (2012), *The Long Walk to Freedom* (2013). Research these films and consider what political issues they raise.

15.2 Wider reading

There are many texts you could read to develop your understanding of political and social protest writing further. These include the following examples.

- Kelleher, J. (2009) *Theatre and Politics*. Palgrave Macmillan - A short, wide-ranging introduction to the various ways in which theatre can be, and has been, political. Other books in the same series (*Theatre and…*) also discuss political issues (education, nation, human rights, ethics, etc.)
- Billington, M. (2007) *State of the Nation*. Faber - A fascinating overview of political theatre in Britain since 1945.
- Childs, P. (1998) *The Twentieth Century in Poetry* - An accessible overview of the way politics has featured in poetry over the last century.
- Hulse, M. and Rae, S. (2011) *The 20th Century in Poetry* - An anthology of 20th-century verse reflecting the history, politics and culture of the century.
- Sinfield, A. (2007) *Literature, Politics and Culture in Postwar Britain*. Bloomsbury - An accessible overview of the relationship between literature and politics in Britain since 1945.
- Fielding, S. (2014) *A State of Play: British Politics on Screen, Stage and Page, from Anthony Trollope to The Thick of It*. Bloomsbury - A complex but interesting reflection on the relationship between literature and politics.

You might also want to look at introductions to specific literary authors, periods and genres, which often discuss political background in detail - especially Shakespeare's histories, the Romantic poets and the rise of the novel.

Other resources include:

- The Great Writers Inspire website, which has an overview of political literature from Shakespeare to the present, with articles and podcast lectures by Oxford University lecturers.
- Olive Senior's speech on politics and literature at the Edinburgh World Writers' Conference in Trinidad, 2013.
- *The Guardian*, which has a webpage devoted to articles on the relationship between politics and theatre.

Visit the Great Writers Inspire website via Cambridge Elevate

Read Olive Senior's speech on politics and literature via Cambridge Elevate

Visit the *Guardian* website via Cambridge Elevate for articles on the relationship between politics and theatre

15.3 John Gardner on political writing and political action: challenging power, changing minds

John Gardner is Professor of English Literature at Anglia Ruskin University. In the piece shown here, he reflects on the ways in which literature can both reflect and affect politics.

All writing is, to some extent, political. Texts either uphold the dominant ideologies of their time, or challenge them. Texts might criticise explicitly, as in William Godwin's *Political Justice*, where he writes that 'government even in its best state, is an evil'; or implicitly, like George Orwell's allegory *Animal Farm*. Political writing therefore engages with systems of thought that can be conservative or revolutionary, public or personal, as in William Blake's *Jerusalem*, where he writes 'I must create a system or be enslaved by another man's.'

Accessibility is the key to political writing. A speech from the pulpit or soapbox will only reach a few, whereas literature can create a consensus that can change society. Literature, responding to specific events, can represent political issues within stories that then become vehicles to carry ideas as well as being artistic works. For example, Swift's satire 'A Modest Proposal' deals with starvation in Ireland; Blake's *Songs of Innocence and of Experience* responds to the French Revolution; Shelley's poem 'England in 1819' was written in response to the Peterloo Massacre in Manchester; Dickens' *Hard Times* deals with Victorian industrial life.

Since literature is produced in a political moment, it can be used to try to create change. In his two 'Chimney Sweeper' poems, Blake highlights the plight of child chimney-sweeps. This is a political intervention because in 1793 it was legal for children to clean chimneys – even over a burning fire. The slave trade was legal when the freed black slave Olaudah Equiano intervened in slavery debates in 1789, exposing the conditions that he lived in after being kidnapped from Nigeria and sent on the middle passage to the West Indies. William Cowper did the same in his poem 'The Negro's Complaint' (1788) when he wrote about slavery from the perspective of a slave. These writers were part of a movement that alerted individuals to the horrors of slavery, and changed public opinion – and eventually the law when the slave trade was abolished in Britain in 1807.

Writing is always directed at an audience; nonetheless it can also have a broad, cross-class appeal. Dickens wrote for poor people who could only afford to buy his works in weekly magazines, as well as the wealthy who could buy the same works as expensive bound volumes. Dickens' literature always has the poor and vulnerable in its sights and importantly gives a voice to people who did not have one before. The plight of poor, abused, uneducated children is always there, particularly in *Great Expectations* and *David Copperfield*; the unfairness of the Law in *Bleak House*; and the need to empathize with others in *A Christmas Carol*. Literature, with its ability to awaken sensibilities and create empathy could become a way of making people think about others. Poetry about the plight of animals by Clare, Cowper and Shelley preceded the first animal rights legislation. Henrik Ibsen's play *A Doll's House* shows a woman, who has been dominated by men, shockingly leave her children so that she can find her own character, decades before women could even vote.

Political writing is always interventionary if it challenges established power. It can give a voice to those who have been denied it: children, women, slaves, the poor, minorities, radicals, revolutionaries and criminals. Literature can create empathy for others, and in turn can radicalize people. Political power can be achieved through physical force, or through cultural power in the form of arguments, persuasion and propaganda delivered through various media – including literature. However it is this latter force, cultural power, that is most influential as it, unlike violence, can alter minds and perhaps even the world.

ACTIVITY 5

Writing and action

How does John Gardner's text help you to reflect on the political nature of the texts you have read and studied during the course? For instance, which texts are *explicitly* political and which only *implicitly* political? To what extent are the texts aimed at the powerful or the powerless (or both)? To what extent do you think the texts have changed or have the potential to change society?

15.4 Video interview

Watch Benjamin Zephaniah, poet, novelist and Professor of Creative Writing at Brunel University, talk about how political and social issues affect his writing on Cambridge Elevate

ENRICHING

16

Literary theory

16.1 Enrichment activities

16.1.1 'The composition of a man'? Reactions to *Jane Eyre*

Do readers expect men and women to write differently, to focus on different topics and use different styles? In the 19th century, women writers were subject to various judgements as to what they should and should not write about, and the way they should express themselves. One very famous example is the way readers reacted to the novel *Jane Eyre* by Charlotte Brontë. When it was first published in 1847, it was under the pseudonym 'Currer Bell'. Like her sisters, Brontë chose a pseudonym to conceal her identity and deliberately leave her gender ambiguous. When *Jane Eyre* was published, it was an instant success, and there was much debate as to whether it had been written by a man or a woman. Texts 16A–16C show a few responses and reviews that give a flavour of this debate.

Text 16A

I wish you had not sent me *Jane Eyre*. It interested me so much that I have lost … a whole day in reading it at the busiest period … Who the author can be I can't guess – if a woman she knows her language better than most ladies do, or has had a 'classical' education. It is a fine book though … the style very generous and upright so to speak … Some of the love passages made me cry … there are parts excellent I don't know why I tell you this but that I have been exceedingly moved & pleased by *Jane Eyre*. It is a woman writing but who? Give my respects and thanks to the author – whose novel is the first English one … that I've been able to read for many a day.

Novelist William Makepeace Thackeray, writing to Charlotte Brontë's publisher, 1847

Text 16B

We, for our part, cannot doubt that the book is written by a female, and, as certain provincialisms indicate, by one from the North of England … Yet we cannot wonder that the hypothesis of a male author should have been started, or that ladies especially should still be rather determined to uphold it. For a book more unfeminine, both in its excellencies and defects, it would be hard to find in the annals of female authorship. Throughout there is masculine power, breadth and shrewdness, combined with masculine hardness, coarseness, and freedom of expression.

Anne Mozley, review in the *Christian Remembrancer*, April 1848

Text 16C

From the masculine tone of *Jane Eyre*, it might pass altogether as the composition of a man, were it not for some unconscious feminine peculiarities, which the strongest-minded woman that ever aspired after manhood cannot suppress. These peculiarities refer not only to elaborate descriptions of dress, and the minutiae of the sick-chamber, but to various superficial refinements of feeling in regard to the external relations of the sex. It is true that the noblest and best representations of female character have been produced by men; but there are niceties of thought and emotion in a woman's mind which no man can delineate, but which often escape unawares from a female writer. There are numerous examples of these in

Jane Eyre. The leading characteristic of the novel, however, and the secret of its charm, is the clear, distinct, decisive style of its representation of character, manners, and scenery; and this continually suggests a male mind. In the earlier chapters, there is little, perhaps, to break the impression that we are reading the autobiography of a powerful and peculiar female intellect; but when the admirable Mr. Rochester appears, and the profanity, brutality, and slang of the misanthropic profligate give their torpedo shocks to the nervous system, — and especially when we are favored with more than one scene given to the exhibition of mere animal appetite, and to courtship after the manner of kangaroos … we are gallant enough to detect the hand of a gentleman in the composition.

Edwin Percy Whipple, review in the *North American Review*, October 1848

ACTIVITY 1

Exploring reactions to *Jane Eyre*

a Read the responses to Jane Eyre in Texts 16A–16C. What evidence do the different readers use to support their judgements as to whether 'Currer Bell' was male or female?

b What impression do you get from these responses as to the different judgements that were made of male and female writers?

c Do you think people still expect male and female writers to write in different ways and about different subjects? Find examples to support your argument.

16.1.2 'Rise like lions after slumber': Percy Bysshe Shelley's 'The Masque of Anarchy'

Unit 9, section 9.6.2 introduced you to Marxist criticism's analysis of oppression and control. Shelley's poem 'The Masque of Anarchy' was written in 1819, in response to the Peterloo Massacre in Manchester, and represented, for many, an extreme example of the abuse of political power. It involved the violent suppression of a demonstration in favour of parliamentary reform. A peaceful gathering of men, women and children was charged by the armed local yeomanry: 15 people were killed, and around 700 injured. Shelley's poem was suppressed during his lifetime, and was not published until 1832. However, it quickly became popular with left-wing thinkers, and verses from it were recited by protesters in the Tiananmen Square demonstrations in Beijing in 1989 and in Tahrir Square in Cairo in 2011.

ACTIVITY 2

Exploring the background to 'The Masque of Anarchy'

a Read the poem, which is widely available online. Pay particular attention to Shelley's use of abstract figures such as Murder, Fraud and Hypocrisy. What effects are created by this use of abstractions? What observations can you make about Shelley's use of rhyme, rhythm and verse-form?

b The British Library website has a fantastic range of resources on 'The Masque of Anarchy'. Read the essay by John Mullan, *An introduction to 'The Masque of Anarchy'* and use the links on the British Library website to explore the poem's historical background.

c In his essay, Mullan describes 'The Masque of Anarchy' as 'a poem devised to be accessible to a wide readership'. In the light of what you know about it, and about Marxist approaches to literature, why do you think it was important that Shelley's poem was accessible to a range of readers?

d For some further thoughts on literature and social protest in the 19th century, read Chapter 5 of Gary Day's *Class*, in the Routledge *New Critical Idiom* series (2001).

16.2 Wider reading

16.2.1 Key texts on literary theory

Literary theory is a fascinating field to explore, but its central texts can often seem difficult and confusing. Fortunately, there are a number of very accessible introductions to literary theory, aimed specifically at A Level students and undergraduates.

- Barry, P. (2009) *Beginning Theory: An Introduction to Literary and Cultural Theory*, third edition (Manchester) – A comprehensive survey of a wide range of critical approaches.
- Culler, J. (2011) *Literary Theory: A Very Short Introduction* (Oxford) – A clear, concise overview of some of the key questions asked by literary theory.
- Eaglestone, R. (2009) *Doing English: A Guide for Literature Students*, third edition (Routledge) – The best starting point for anyone wanting to learn more about the discipline of English literature.

- Eagleton, T. (2008) *Literary Theory: An Introduction*, anniversary edition (Wiley-Blackwell) – Terry Eagleton's provocative introduction to literary theory was first published in 1983, and has been a staple of student reading lists ever since. It is a lively, thought-provoking read.
- Jacobs, R. (2001) *A Beginner's Guide to Critical Reading: An Anthology of Literary Texts: Readings for Students* (Routledge) – Aimed at A-Level students, Jacobs' book looks at a range of literary texts through the lens of different theoretical approaches.
- Tyson, L. (2006) *Critical Theory Today: A User-Friendly Guide* (Routledge) – Tyson's innovative handbook demonstrates different theoretical approaches by applying them all to F. Scott Fitzgerald's *The Great Gatsby*.

16.2.2 Further useful resources

The following resources will help to broaden your understanding of literary theory, introducing you to a range of different arguments and perspectives.

- BBC Radio 4: *In Our Time*
  Melvyn Bragg's discussion series features a number of topics relevant to literary theory, including episodes on cultural imperialism, epistolary literature, modernism, the pastoral, reading, Marx and feminism. All past episodes (over 600 of them) are available online via the programme's home page.
- Oxford Podcasts: Challenging the Canon
  A provocative series of lectures, aimed at potential undergraduates, exploring some of the debates surrounding the literary canon.
- Purdue University's Online Writing Lab
  A useful online guide to the key questions raised by different critical and theoretical approaches.

16.3 Sophie Breese on 'Good Literature'

Sophie Breese, teacher, writer and traveller, describes her journey in search of the truth about 'Good Literature'.

Sometimes my students come to me with a dilemma: they know they ought to be reading *Great Expectations* by Charles Dickens but they are reading *The Hunger Games* instead and loving it. The former is on their reading list and often studied at school; the latter is a best-seller and they can't put it down. Is *The Hunger Games*, they ask me, a bad novel because it's popular and easy to read?

The answer is no.

I happen to think that *The Hunger Games* is not well-written. While I was engaged, fascinated, horrified throughout, I don't think the language is interesting or that it makes profound observations about society. Flora, one of my students disagrees: for her, *The Hunger Games* is a good novel.

Who is right?

Both of us. Neither of us.

There is no such thing as Good Literature. There was, for a long time. For all sorts of reasons that Literary Theory has uncovered, various texts were chosen, identified as Good and put on syllabi at universities and schools. My course at university in the 1980s explored what came to be known as the Canon – a series of texts that could 'propagate the best that was known and thought in the world'[1]. During one term we chose a writer to study for the 'Special Authors' Paper from a list that included only male English poets, beginning with Chaucer and ending with T. S. Eliot. My study of Eliot established a life-long passion for his writing, but I would like to have been able to consider the writers that the 2014 version of the course provides: Irish, Saint Lucian, female; novelists, playwrights, poets.

Literary Theory has challenged the idea that the Canon appeared magically, already complete and perfectly formed[2]. Sometimes I would like there to be a universal truth about literature, to be able to say, 'Yes, that is a great book,' and for everyone to know exactly what I mean. But the Canon, like our personal taste, is a cultural, linguistic, social, political, and economic construction. How could it be possible, for instance, for a woman to be a Good

Writer if the default gender until recently when referring to a writer, any writer, was 'he'? Female writers were out of the equation the minute that personal pronoun was used.

My own critical position (because it's important to declare my bias) is a fusion of feminist theory and Marxist theory. Through my reading I have come to understand that until relatively recently women were not in a position to write until they found a room and economic support of their own. Then the next hurdle was to convince a publisher to take a financial risk on the second sex; for a (male) reviewer to admire the work in a paper; for bookshops to stock the novel; and for a reader, already told that women were lesser mortals, to choose to buy it. It is not surprising that there are fewer novels written by women before the twentieth century than there are by men, and even fewer included in the Canon.

I would still hold that Dickens' novel is better than Collins' and I will continue to argue the point with Flora, but I accept that I am 44 and she is 16, that we have had different educations in different moments of time, and that what I want from a novel is different to what she wants. Literary Theory got me to that point of acceptance.

References

1 Matthew Arnold, 'The Function of Criticism at the Present Time' (1864). This short essay by the Victorian writer suggests some of the criteria required for Good Literature; it was highly influential in the selection of texts for the Canon.

2 Chris Baldick's *The Social Mission of English Criticism, 1848–1932* (1983) had an enormous influence on me: he considers the historical, political and social reasons for the creation of the idea of Good Literature.

16.4 Video interview

Watch Robert Eaglestone, Professor of Contemporary Literature and Thought at Royal Holloway, University of London, talk about the value of literary theory to the study of literature on Cambridge Elevate

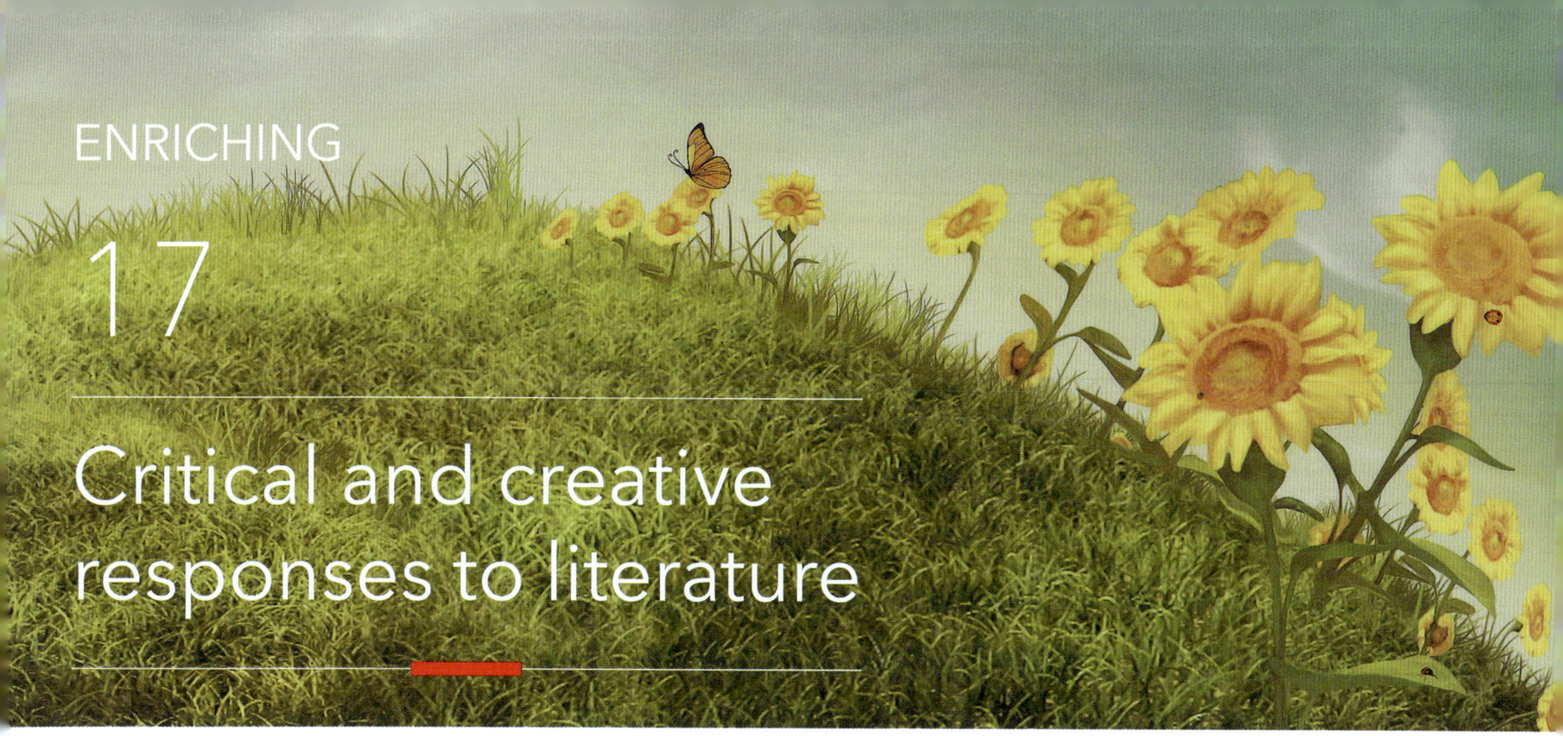

ENRICHING

17 Critical and creative responses to literature

17.1 Enrichment activities

17.1.1 Developing critical thought

In 10.2 you considered some ideas to do with dialogue derived from the writings of Roland Barthes. In *S/Z*, Barthes imagines the 'ideal text' (see Text 17A).

Text 17A

... the networks are many and interact, without any one of them being able to surpass the rest; this text is a galaxy of **signifiers**, not a structure of **signifieds**; it has no beginning; it is reversible; we gain access to it by several entrances, none of which can be authoritatively declared to be the main one; the codes it mobilizes extend as far as the eye can reach, they are indeterminable ... ; the systems of meaning can take over this absolutely plural text, but their number is never closed, based as it is on the infinity of language.

Roland Barthes

Key terms

signifier: any material thing that signifies, for example, words on a page, a facial expression, an image

signified: the concept that a signifier refers to

ACTIVITY 1

Working with Barthes

Read the passage from Barthes' essay in Text 17A.

a What does he seem to be saying about the nature of the 'ideal text'?
b Barthes does not explicitly refer to writers and readers in this passage, but what does he seem to imply is the relationship between the writer and the reader?
c How does Barthes' emphasis on plurality develop your thinking about meaning and interpretation in relation to your study of literature?
d In what ways does this change your thinking about your roles as writer and reader in your literary studies?
e How will you change your thinking about critical and/or creative writing as a result?

17.1.2 Writers on writing

In 10.4 you thought a little about your views of writing. Text 17B shows a number of writers reflecting on the processes and outcomes of writing.

Text 17B

There's nothing to writing. All you do is sit down at a typewriter and open a vein.

Walter Wellesley 'Red' Smith

A word is not the same with one writer as with another. One tears it from his guts. The other pulls it out of his overcoat pocket.

Charles Peguy

Writing became such a process of discovery that I couldn't wait to get to work in the morning: I wanted to know what I was going to say.

Sharon O'Brien

I'm not a very good writer, but I'm an excellent rewriter.

James Michener

Easy reading is damn hard writing.

Nathaniel Hawthorne

The difference between the right word and the almost right word is the difference between lightning and a lightning bug.

Mark Twain

Write down the thoughts of the moment. Those that come unsought for are commonly the most valuable.

Francis Bacon

Write your first draft with your heart. Re-write with your head.

From the movie *Finding Forrester*

ACTIVITY 2

Your views of writing

Consider each of the quotations about writing shown in Text 17B.

a How do you respond to or relate to each of these views about writing?
b Do they apply in the same way to critical writing and to creative writing?
c Which comes nearest to your own views of writing?
d In view of these quotations and the passage from Text 17A, what do you see as the relationship between reading and writing?

17.1.3 Famous recreative writing

In 11.3 you looked at recreative writing. There are many famous examples of literary recreative writing. Jean Rhys' novel *Wide Sargasso Sea* is developed from Charlotte Brontë's novel *Jane Eyre*, telling events from the perspective of Bertha Mason, Mr Rochester's first wife - the mad woman in the attic. In *Rosencrantz And Guildenstern Are Dead*, Tom Stoppard wryly explores what happens to those characters both on and off stage in Shakespeare's *Hamlet*. Daphne du Maurier's classic tale *Rebecca* has spawned two sequels - Susan Hill's *Mrs de Winter* and Sally Beauman's *Rebecca's Tale*. *The Hours* by Michael Cunningham emerges from *Mrs Dalloway* by Virginia Woolf, and Dickens has spawned a varied set of literary recreations: *Jack Maggs* (Peter Carey), *Havisham* (Ronald Frame) and 'Havisham' (Carol Ann Duffy) from *Great Expectations*, and *Dodger* (Terry Pratchett) from *Oliver Twist*.

ACTIVITY 3

Reading recreations

Read a selection of the literary recreations in section 17.1.3 and the originals on which they draw. Then think about the following questions.

How do writers of literary recreations:

a make use of plot-lines from the base text?
b make use of characters from the base text?
c work with the language of the base text?
d work with the form of the base text?
e work with the style of the base text?

17.1.4 Other literary adaptations

Adaptations of literary works for the screen, both large and small, are a staple of our culture. This is a form of literary recreation in which a base text is transformed for a different medium. Many literary texts are also adapted for performance on the radio or on stage (as either plays or musicals), and it is also increasingly common for books to become the basis for video games.

ACTIVITY 4

Other literary adaptations

a Explore a selection of the literary recreations in section 17.1.3 and the originals on which they draw. Then in relation to these, revisit the questions in Activity 3. In addition, how do writers of these various forms experiment with the base text and its possibilities in the new medium?

b Now have a go at adapting a section of a base text you have particularly enjoyed into two or three different media. How are the demands of each recreation different? What different effects can you achieve? Which do you prefer and why?

17.1.5 An example from poetry

In order to explore a relatively brief example, Text 17C is a very well-known poem – 'The Daffodils' by William Wordsworth. Look online to find a recreated version of it by the contemporary poet Adrian Henri.

Text 17C

The Daffodils

I wander'd lonely as a cloud
That floats on high o'er vales and hills,
When all at once I saw a crowd,
A host of golden daffodils,
Beside the lake, beneath the trees,
Fluttering and dancing in the breeze.

Continuous as the stars that shine
And twinkle on the Milky Way,
They stretch'd in never-ending line
Along the margin of a bay:
Ten thousand saw I at a glance,
Tossing their heads in sprightly dance.

The waves beside them danced, but they
Outdid the sparkling waves in glee:—
A poet could not but be gay
In such a jocund company!
I gazed, and gazed, but little thought
What wealth the show to me had brought:

For oft, when on my couch I lie
In vacant or in pensive mood,
They flash upon that inward eye
Which is the bliss of solitude;
And then my heart with pleasure fills,
And dances with the daffodils.

William Wordsworth, 'The Daffodils'

ACTIVITY 5

Flowers as you've never seen them before

a Read both the Wordsworth and the Henri poems several times. Originally, Henri used a cut-up of Wordsworth's poem plus a Dutch motor-car leaflet in order to create his poem.

- How do you feel about this as a method of literary composition?
- How does such a method place the author?
- How do the 'voices' of Wordsworth and Henri interact in the second poem?
- Is there a dominant 'voice' in the second poem? If so, which?

b Try developing a similar poem of your own using Adrian Henri's method, using a well-known base poem and another unlikely source – perhaps the back of a cereal box or the listings from the TV pages. What kinds of effects can you achieve? What insights does this give you into the recreative writing process?

17.2 Wider reading

17.2.1 Selected reading on key areas

- Mikhail Bakhtin (1992) *The Dialogic Imagination: Four Essays*. Austin: University of Texas Press – For the adventurous, Bakhtin's fascinating book is a hard read, but explores many very stimulating ideas about the functions of language and how writers and readers interact.
- Roland Barthes (1974) *S/Z*. Oxford: Blackwell – This is a classic of literary theory, but provides a reasonably accessible read in which Barthes explores the central relationship between readers and writers and the texts they share.
- Andrew Green (2009) 'Adapting Austen – an interview with Fay Weldon', *e magazine*, Issue 44, pp. 56–59.
- Philip Larkin (1983) 'The Pleasure Principle' in *Required Writing: Miscellaneous Pieces 1955–1982*. London: Faber and Faber, pp. 80–2 – In this short and very readable essay the poet, novelist and jazz critic Philip Larkin explores the processes of writing poetry.

17.2.2 Further useful resources

For anyone interested in creative writing, a plethora of creative writing opportunities – some very informal, some very formal – now exist. These vary from informal local writing groups (often with specific focuses such as drama or poetry), college courses (an A Level in Creative Writing is now on offer) and writers' workshops right up to degree level qualifications and beyond, as now taught in many universities.

A number of interesting books on creative writing exist:

- Stephen Earnshaw (2014) *The Handbook of Creative Writing*, 2nd Edition. Edinburgh: Edinburgh University Press – This book provides an accessible and interesting way into thinking about creative writing in a wide variety of forms.
- Graeme Harper (2012) *Inside Creative Writing*. London: Palgrave MacMillan – In this book, Harper interviews a selection of well-known contemporary authors such as Robert Pinsky, Iain Banks and Philip Pullman and explores their processes and thoughts as writers.
- David Lodge (1992) *The Art of Fiction*. London: Penguin – As its title suggests, this book focuses on issues surrounding the writing of fiction. Drawing on a wide range of texts, this is a very good read for stimulating thinking about both writing and reading.
- For those interested in the adaptation of literary works for the screen, acclaimed screen writer Andrew Davies – most famous for his adaptation of Pride and Prejudice – writes for *The Telegraph* about his processes as an adaptor.

Read Andrew Davies' *Telegraph* article 'Andrew Davies on how to adapt literary classics for TV' via Cambridge Elevate

17.3 Robert Eaglestone on using critical and creative ideas

Robert Eaglestone is Professor of Contemporary Literature and Thought at Royal Holloway, University of London. Here he explains one reason why criticism is as creative as 'creative writing'.

How do we 'apply theory' or 'use critical ideas'? This sensible question has somehow got off on the wrong foot. Although we often talk about critical or theoretical ideas as 'tools' that we 'use' on a novel or a poem that's not really how it works. It's more a question of looking at things from different points of view. And that's where creative and critical responses work in the same sort of way. Of course, there's some technical language: we say 'a protagonist', not a 'hero' (because protagonists are not always heroic). But central to reading literature is not this technical language but an imaginative moment where criticism and creativity are the same. How does this happen?

First, you have your own response to a text. You might really like it or you might, perhaps, be bored. (Oddly being bored is an interesting response. What is the text *not* doing for you? *Why* is it *not* doing it?) It's always worthwhile stopping to reflect on your own response. Then, it's important to listen to what your friends and people in your class or seminar think. Texts are not just designed to be read but to be talked about and argued over. Other people will have had different reactions, responded to different things.

Next think about what the text looks like from another point of view. A common and interesting creative exercise is called 'creative critical rewriting'. This takes part of the text and rewrites it, often from a different point of view. What, for example, does *Hamlet* look like from the point of view of some of the minor characters? Or imagine a Jane Austen novel told by one of the servants. All sorts of strange things might appear or disappear from the narrative. A similar exercise is to imagine a text in a different form: I've found rewriting a poem as a short film script very useful. It helps focus on 'what is going on' in a visual way, and this in turn leads to a better, more concrete understanding.

Although it looks different, a critical approach works in a similar way. Different sorts of critics ask different questions: feminist critics might ask how women are represented; critics interested in the mind (in psychoanalysis) might ask how ideas about the self or sexuality are woven into the text. Just as a creative response might take the view point of someone in a novel, so a critical one might take the view of a particular critical perspective. Find out what sort of questions critics ask and so what points of view they might take.Sometimes this might be a quick sound bite – the sort of thing you might get from a newspaper. But often, more rewardingly, other views come from longer and more thoughtful critical essays or books on literature. Just as you might imagine what another character in a novel would say, so you can begin to learn or imagine what different sorts of critics might say. This is 'thinking as a critic', the core of the creative act of literary criticism.

Finally, you can let these critical or imaginative 'points of view' expand. Tom Stoppard wrote *Rosencrantz and Guildenstern are Dead*, the story of two minor characters from *Hamlet*. The novelist Sarah Waters reuses recognisable characters from Dickens in her page turner *Fingersmith*. Critics' ideas flourish and grow too, pointing out aspects of literature that you might not have noticed, bringing different ideas and thoughts to reading. The more you learn creatively to 'think as a critic', the richer and stranger literature becomes.

17.4 Video interview

Watch Rob Pope, Emeritus Professor of English at Oxford Brookes University, talk about textual intervention on Cambridge Elevate

Index

Note: Key Terms, and the page with their definition, are shown in **bold**. Glossary terms are in red.

Acknowledgements

The authors and publishers acknowledge the following sources of copyright material and are grateful for the permissions granted. While every effort has been made, it has not always been possible to identify the sources of all the material used, or to trace all copyright holders. If any omissions are brought to our notice, we will be happy to include the appropriate acknowledgements on reprinting.

AQA examination questions are reproduced by permission of AQA

Text 1E, page 17: From *Truckers: The First Book of the Nomes*, by Terry Pratchett. Reprinted by permission of The Random House Group; Text 1J, page 22: 'Faber & Faber; "Wind" from *Collected Poems*, by Ted Hughes. Copyright © 2003 by The Estate of Ted Hughes. Reprinted by permission of Farrar, Straus and Giroux, LLC; Text 2A, page 27: With permission from Curtis Brown on behalf of the Estate of WH Auden; Text 2B, page 31: Faber & Faber; "Lineage" from *Collected Poems*, by Ted Hughes. Copyright © 2003 by The Estate of Ted Hughes. Reprinted by permission of Farrar, Straus and Giroux, LLC; Text 3A, page 41: Reproduced courtesy of David Fulton Publishers; Quotation from Jean E. Howard, 1984, pp178-9, page 42: Reproduced courtesy of University of Illinois Press; Text 3B, page 44: 'Death of a Salesman', by Arthur Miller, published by Penguin, The Wylie Agency (UK) Ltd, copyright (c) 2000 by Arthur Miller. Used by permission of Penguin Group (USA) LLC; Text 3E, page 52: Reproduced by permission of Curtis Brown on behalf of the Estate of WH Auden; Six words from *Animal Farm* by George Orwell (Penguin Books, 2000), page 57: Copyright 1945 by Eric Blair. This edition copyright © the Estate of the late Sonia Brownwell Orwell, 1987; Text 4A, page 62: Guardian News and Media Ltd 2005; Text 4B, page 63: Rose Tremain writing about her novel *The Road Home*. The Random House Group with permission; Text 4C, page 63: In an article by Margaret Wappler for Goodreads; Text 4D, page 65: 57 words from *Regeneration* by Pat Barker (Penguin Books Ltd, 1992). Copyright © Pat Barker, 1991; Text 4E and Text 4F, page 65: From *Nice Work* by David Lodge. Published by Vintage. Reprinted by permission of The Random House Group; Text 4G, page 66: *If on a Winter's Night a Traveller* by Italo Calvilo, Vintage Classics 1992, The Random House Group; *If on a Winter's Night a Traveller* by Italo Calvilo, Vintage Classics 1992 ,The Wylie Agency (UK) Ltd; Text 4H, page 66: Pan Macmillan; *Waterland* by Graham Swift published by Picador, United Agents with permission; Text 4I, page 66: Faber & Faber; Text 4J, page 67: From *Changing Places* by David Lodge. Published by Vintage. Reprinted by permission of The Random House Group; Penguin Inc; Quotation from Simon Goldhill, *Love, Sex and Tragedy: Why Classics Matter Publisher*: John Murray (7 Feb. 2005), page 73: John Murray; Quotation from Robert N. Watson's essay 'Tragedy', in *The Cambridge Companion to English Renaissance Drama*, edited by A.R. Braunmuller and Michael Hattaway (Cambridge University Press, 1990). The essay is on pages 301-351 and the quotation is on page 302, page 73: A.R. Braunmuller and Michael Hattaway, *The Cambridge Companion to English Renaissance Drama*, 1990 Cambridge University Press; Quotation from Barbara A. Mowat and Paul Werstline, Folger Shakespeare Library edition of King Lear, Introduction Simon & Schuster; 1 edition (0100) ASIN: B00E31EEC2, page 79: Reprinted with the permission of Washington Square Press, a Division of Simon & Schuster, Inc. from *King Lear* by William Shakespeare, edited by Barbara A. Mowat and Paul Werstine. Copyright © 1993 The Folger Shakespeare Library; Extracts from *Tragedy: A Student Handbook*, by Sean McEvoy with Tony Coult and Chris Sandford (English and Media Centre, 2009), page 83: Reproduced by kind permission of the English and Media Centre; Excerpt from Martin Earl's poem guide on John Keats' 'La Belle Dame Sans Merci,' published on the Poetry Foundation's Learning Lab website, www.poetryfoundation.org/learning, page 88: Copyright 2011 by Martin Earl; Quotation from Philip V. Allingham, *Aristotle's Dramatic Unities of Time, Place, and Action and Hardy's Use of the Ballad Tradition*, page 91: *Aristotle's Dramatic Unities of Time, Place, and Action and Hardy's Use of the Ballad Tradition* by Philip V. Allingham, Contributing Editor, Victorian Web http://www.victorianweb.org/authors/hardy/pva187.html; Quotation from Matthew C. Roudané, *The Cambridge Companion to Arthur Miller* (2010), page 98: Christopher Bigsby, *The Cambridge Companion to Arthur Miller*, 2010 Cambridge University Press; Text 5R, page 106: Curtis Brown on behalf of the Estate of WH Auden; Opening directions from Arthur Miller, *All My Sons*, page 103: From *All My Sons* by Arthur Miller. Copyright (c) 2009 by Arthur Miller; From *Death of a Salesman* by Arthur Miller. Copyright (c) 2000 by Arthur Miller. Used by permission of Penguin Group (USA) LLC; Penguin Ltd; Text 6O, page 140: R V Bailey with permission; Quotation by W.H. Auden from The Guilty Vicarage Notes on the detective story, by an addict From the May 1948 issue Harper's Magazine, page 164: Curtis Brown on behalf of the Esate of WH Auden; Text 7K, page 178: David Higham Ltd with permission on behalf of Graham Greene. Published by The Random House Group; Text 7L, page 179: From *When Will There Be Good News?* by Kate Atkinson. Published by Black Swan. Reprinted by permission of The Random House Group; Text 7M, page 179: From *Atonement* by Ian McEwan. Published by Vintage. Reprinted by permission of The Random House Group; Quotation by T.S. Eliot from Selected Essays Faber & Faber. New ed of 3 Revised ed edition (7 Jun. 1999), page 184: Faber and Faber; Text 7N, page 184: From *The Seville Communion* by Arturo Pérez-Reverte. Translated by Sonia Soto. Published by The Harvill Press and reproduced by permission of The Random House Group Ltd; Text 7S, page 189: 56 words from *The Big Sleep* by Raymond Chandler (Penguin Books, 2011). Copyright 1939 by Raymond Chandler; Text 7T, pages 189-90: From *Brighton Rock* by Graham Greene. Reprinted by permission of The Random House Group; Text 7U, page 191: From *When Will There Be Good News?* by Kate Atkinson. Published by Black Swan. Reprinted by permission of The Random House Group; Quotation by Shami Chakrabarti taken from http://www.telegraph.co.uk/news/1495572/Reaction-to-anti-terror-plans.html Reaction to anti-terror plans 05 Aug 2005, page 199: *The Telegraph* 2005; Text 8F, 8G Text 8H and Text 8P, pages 218-220: From *The Kite Runner* by Khaled Hosseini. Copyright (c) 2003 by Khaled Hosseini. Used by permission of Riverhead, an imprint of Penguin Publishing Group, a division of Penguin Random House LLC.; Bloomsbury Publishing Plc; Text 8L and Text 8M, page 225: From *The Handmaid's Tale* by Margaret Atwood. Published by Vintage. Reprinted by permission of The Random House Group; Curtis Brown; Text 8N and Text 8O, page 227: Pan Macmillan; Quotation from W.K. Wimsatt and Monroe C. Beardsley essay 'The Intentional Fallacy' (1946) published in The verbal icon: studies in the meaning of poetry, page 232: By permission of University Press of Kentucky; Text 9C, page 236: *The Telegraph* 2011; Text 9D, page 236: *The Sunday Times* 2014; Text 9E, page 238: From 'How should one read a book?' (1926) from The Common Reader, Second Series by Leonard & Virginia Woolf. Reprinted by permission of The Random House Group; Quotation from Oxford English Dictionary OUP Oxford; 7 edition (10 May 2012), page 237: By permission of Oxford University Press; Text 9J, page 252: *The Idea of Perfection* (2000) by Kate Grenville, Picador; Text 9K, page 253: Orion Publishing Group; Quotation from Hanif Kureishi, *The Buddha of Suburbia*, Faber & Faber (8 Jan. 2009), page 257: Faber & Faber; Quotation from Daljit Nagra, *Look We Have Coming to Dover!*, Faber & Faber; First Edition edition (1 Feb. 2007), page 258: Faber & Faber;

Text 10A, page 262: Faber & Faber; Extract from poem, 'Not My Best Side', U.A. Fanthorpe, page 274: R V Bailey with permission; Quotations from Kazuo Ishiguro, *The Remains of the Day*, Faber & Faber (1 April 2010), made in Text 11F, page 281: Faber & Faber; Quotation from the Newsom Report, CACE 1963, page 284: London: Her Majesty's Stationery Office 1963 © Crown copyright material is reproduced with the permission of the Controller of HMSO and the Queen's Printer for Scotland; Quotation from Eagleton, *Literary Theory: An Introduction Wiley-Blackwell*; 2nd Edition edition (26 Oct. 1996), page 284: By permission of Wiley-Blackwell; Quotation from *Political Shakespeare* 2nd edition: Essays in cultural materialism, Sinfield 1985, page 285: By permission of Manchester University Press; Quotation from *Literary Theory: A Very Short Introduction*, 2nd Edition by Cueller (2011) 41w from p.39, page 285: By permission of Oxford University Press; Quotation from Ernst Junger, Storm of Steel Penguin Classics; New Ed edition (3 Jun. 2004), made in Text 11P, page 291: 36 words from *Storm of Steel* by Ernst Jünger. First published in German as *In Stahlgewittern* 1920, final revised version first published 1961. Copyright © 1920, 1961 J.G. Cotta'sche Buchhandlung Nachfolger GmbH, Stuttgart. This translation first published by Allen Lane, 2003. Introduction and translation © Michael Hoffmann, 2003; Quotation from T.S. Eliot, 'Portrait of a Lady' from Prufrock and Other Observations Faber & Faber (19 Feb. 2001), made in Text 11Q, page 291: The Estate of T.S. Eliot represented by The Society of Authors; Quotation from T.S. Eliot, The Rock. A pageant play ... Book of words, Faber & Faber, made in Text 11R, page 291: The Estate of T.S. Eliot represented by The Society of Authors; Text 11X and Text 11Y, page 295: Georgia Gildea with permission; Text 14A, page 305: 164 words from *The Trial* by Franz Kafka, translated by Idris Parry (Penguin Books 1994, Penguin Classics 2000). Translation copyright © Idris Parry, 1994; Text 14B, page 306: By permission of Cornell University Press; Quotation from Jerome Bruner, *Actual Minds, Possible Worlds*, (1986), p.54 Harvard University Press; New edition (1 July 1986), page 309: By permission of Harvard University Press; Text 15C, page 309: Winston Churchill/ Curtis Brown Group Ltd; Text 17A, page 317: Blackwell Publishing; Quotation by Sharon O'Brien in Text 17B, page 318: Reprinted by permission of Professor Sharon J. O'Brien.

Photo acknowledgements

Splash image on front cover: Copyright 2013 Fabian Oefner www.fabianoefner.com

p. 4 (T): fotohunter/Thinkstock; p. 4 (C): Sixdun/Thinkstock; p. 4 (B): Alexei Novikov/Thinkstock; p. 8: vasabii/Thinkstock; p. 13: LuminaStock/Thinkstock; p. 15: Matt_Gibson/Thinkstock; p. 22: rosalind morgan/Thinkstock; p. 25: fotohunter/Thinkstock; p. 26: Stacey Newman/Thinkstock; p. 29: zhudifeng/Thinkstock; p. 30: Pukkasott/Thinkstock; p. 36: Claudio Divizia/Thinkstock; p. 40: cosmin4000/Thinkstock; p. 42: lofilolo/Thinkstock; p. 45: KateJoanna/Thinkstock; p. 47: AF Archive/Alamy; p. 49: Tracy Whiteside/Thinkstock; p. 50: sergio_kumer/Thinkstock; p. 53: Digital Vision/Thinkstock; p. 56: Studio-Annika/Thinkstock; p. 58: Photos.com/Hemera Technologies/Thinkstock; p. 63: vofpalabra/ Thinkstock; p. 62: Geraint Lewis/Alamy; p. 67: Stephen Rees/ Thinkstock; p. 69: Sixdun/Thinkstock; p. 71: Alastair Muir/Rex features; p. 73: Yoemi/Thinkstock; p. 87: Artepics/Alamy; p. 90: Wafue/Thinkstock; p. 95: Purestock/Thinkstock; p. 101: Mary Evans Picture Library/Mary Evans Picture Library; p. 104: Warner Br/Everett/ Rex features; p. 110: Donald Cooper/Photostage; p. 114: Image Source Pink/Thinkstock; p. 115: Studio-Annika/Thinkstock; p. 117: PanosKarapanagiotis/Thinkstock; p. 120: Ivan Bastien/Thinkstock; p. 125: Donald Cooper/Photostage; p. 129: AF Archive/Alamy; p. 131: Jasmin Awad/Thinkstock; p. 136: AF Archive/Alamy; p. 140: Adrian Hancu/Thinkstock; p. 144: dpapicture alliance archive/Alamy; p. 150: Geraint Lewis/Alamy; p. 152: Roksana Bashyrova/Thinkstock; p. 157: Donald Cooper/Photostage; p. 160: Aleramo/Thinkstock; p. 161: Meinzahn/Thinkstock; p. 162: Biletskiy_Evgeniy/Thinkstock; p. 167: AF Archive/Alamy; p. 174: Hulton-Deutsch Collection/ Corbis; p. 178: BBC Films/Kudos/Optimum/The Kobal Collection; p. 182: Wolfi Poelzer/Alamy; p. 186: Studio-Annika/Thinkstock; p. 189: AF Archive/Alamy; p. 191: Brian Jackson/Thinkstock; p. 197: jon11/Thinkstock; p. 199: graphicsdunia4you/Thinkstock; p. 204: Antonio Gravante/Thinkstock; p. 206: Geraint Lewis/Alamy; p. 208: AF Archive/Alamy; p. 210: sugar0607/Thinkstock; p. 214: Pictoral Press Ltd/Alamy; p. 219: mustafabilgesatkin/Thinkstock; p. 225: Geraint Lewis/Alamy; p. 228: Wavebreakmedia/Thinkstock; p. 231: lamiquela/Thinkstock; p. 233: creighton359/Thinkstock; p. 237: demachi/Thinkstock; p. 241: sosobuzuk/Thinkstock; p. 243: AF Archive/Alamy; p. 249: Donald Cooper/Photostage; p. 250: iSock/ Heiko Küverling/Thinkstock; p. 252: Andrew_Mayovskyy/Thinkstock; p. 256: pxhidalgo/Thinkstock; p. 261: MarianVejcik/Thinkstock; p. 266: dorian2013/Thinkstock; p. 268: kiddy0265/Thinkstock; p. 297: Digital Vision/Siri Stafford/Thinkstock; p. 301: Sadeugra/ Getty; p. 305: Alexei Novikov/Thinkstock; p. 309: BrightViewPhoto/ Thinkstock; p. 313: ramzihachicho/Thinkstock; p. 317: maroznc/ Thinkstock.